Praise for *Jenkins 2: Up and Running*

"This is now both my new go-to book for reference as well as the one I recommend to those new to Jenkins. It's quite a feat to write a book that can serve both audiences and Brent has pulled it off in spades."

—Chaim "Tinjaw" Krause

"Brent Laster does a fantastic job at distilling the power of Jenkins down to its essential components while still providing the comprehensive guide to getting the most out of Jenkins 2. Valuable examples of the pipeline as code provide building blocks for implementing continuous delivery. This belongs in the toolbox of new and experienced Jenkins users alike."

—Brian Dawson, DevOps Evangelist, CloudBees

Jenkins 2: Up and Running

Evolve Your Deployment Pipeline for Next-Generation Automation

Brent Laster

Beijing • Boston • Farnham • Sebastopol • Tokyo

Jenkins 2: Up and Running
by Brent Laster

Published by O'Reilly Media, Inc., 1005 Gravenstein Highway North, Sebastopol, CA 95472.

O'Reilly books may be purchased for educational, business, or sales promotional use. Online editions are also available for most titles (*http://oreilly.com/safari*). For more information, contact our corporate/institutional sales department: 800-998-9938 or *corporate@oreilly.com*.

Acquisitions Editor: Brian Foster
Development Editor: Angela Rufino
Production Editor: Justin Billing
Copyeditors: Dwight Ramsey and Rachel Head
Proofreader: Jasmine Kwityn
Indexer: Judith McConville
Interior Designer: David Futato
Cover Designer: Karen Montgomery
Illustrator: Rebecca Demarest

May 2018: First Edition

Revision History for the First Edition
2018-05-02: First Release

See *http://oreilly.com/catalog/errata.csp?isbn=9781491979594* for release details.

978-1-491-97959-4

[LSI]

To my best friend and wife, Anne-Marie,
who brings beauty and happiness to each day.
And to my sons Walker, Chase, and Tanner,
who have taught me more than I could ever teach them.

Table of Contents

Foreword

The software development industry is going through a slow but real transformation. Software is increasingly a part of everything, and we, the software developers, are trying to cope with this exploding demand through more automation. I'd imagine you are reading this book because you are a part of that transformation.

To serve you better in this transformation, Jenkins is itself going through a major transformation of its own as well—from the world of "classic" Jenkins, where you configure Jenkins through a series of jobs from server-rendered GUI, to the world of "modern" Jenkins, where you configure Jenkins through Jenkinsfiles in Git repositories and look at results through a pleasant single-page application.

As we develop the modern Jenkins in the community and roll out these new features, I keep running into this challenge. Most users are simply unaware of this transformation that's going on in Jenkins. People keep using Jenkins like they have been doing for years!

And to be fair, it made complete sense. On the one hand is people's inertia and this massive body of information and knowledge accumulated in Google, Stack Overflow, our mailing lists, issue trackers, and so on that tells people how to effectively use Jenkins the "classic" way. On the other hand, we have the community that is, generally speaking, too busy building the "modern" Jenkins; and collectively not enough effort has been spent on telling people how to effectively use Jenkins the modern way.

So I was very happy to hear about this book, which really takes this challenge head on. In this book, Brent steps back and forgets everything we've known about Jenkins from the past decade. Then he goes on to reconstruct how Jenkins should be used today. Unlike Google, Stack Overflow, and so on, where knowledge is captured piecemeal, this book gives you a systematic path to explore the whole landscape, which makes it really valuable.

It's an ideal book for those who are new to CI/CD, as well as those who have been using Jenkins for many years. This book will help you discover and rediscover Jenkins.

— Kohsuke Kawaguchi
Creator of Jenkins
CTO, CloudBees, Inc.
February 2018

Preface

How to Use This Book

This book is big—bigger than I ever thought it would be. I've worried about this at some level, but decided that there were two ways to go when writing it: I could either limit the content to only what was needed to do a basic tutorial, or I could spend some time explaining concepts, creating code examples, and diving into what terminology, functions, and programming with pipelines-as-code really mean. If you've scanned the book, you can probably figure out that I opted to do the latter.

My reasoning for that was due to my experiences over many years of training people on using Jenkins. In a short class or workshop, we could only cover a small number of topics. And people were always hungry for more—more detail and more examples that they could apply. At the end of conference presentations, I would invariably get lines of people asking for more information sources, examples, and where to find info about such and such. Oftentimes, it would come down to "Google this" or "See this question on Stack Overflow." Nothing wrong with that, but also not the most convenient approach.

This book is intended to help you find answers on how to use this powerful technology. Granted, it's more mechanics than DevOps, but chances are if you are reading this, you already have some grasp of continuous integration (CI), continuous deployment (CD), DevOps, and Jenkins, and are looking for how to make the most out of the new Jenkins features.

So here are a few guidelines (feel free to use them or ignore them as fits your situation):

- Don't try to read the entire book through—unless you need to get a lot of sleep.
- Scan the sections listed in the Table of Contents. A chapter's title only hints at its full contents. Also, don't forget about consulting the index to find topics you might be interested in.

- If you want to understand the basic ideas and get going quickly, read the first two chapters and then start playing with some basic pipelines. As you run into questions or problems, consult the appropriate chapters in the book for the particular areas.
- If you already know the basics of Jenkins and want to convert to pipelines-as-code, take a look at Chapter 10 to get some ideas on conversions and then consult other chapters as needed.
- If you're looking to create a larger pipeline, take a look at the chapter on conversions and the various chapters on integration with the OS and other technologies (Chapters 10–14). And don't forget about security—there's a chapter on that, too (Chapter 5).
- If you're looking to automate Jenkins, take a look at Chapter 15.
- If you run into problems, each chapter contains some details that may help. Look at the notes, warnings, and sidebars for information on unusual situations or functionality that may trip you up (or provide an advantage you hadn't thought about). There's also a chapter on more general troubleshooting at the end of the book.

I freely acknowledge the problem with any technical book these days: that the technology is rapidly evolving. Over the course of writing the chapters for the book, I've gone back and tried to keep up with the latest changes and innovations and revised as appropriate. It is my firm belief that the material in the book will provide you with a good foundation and reference for working with Jenkins 2. But, of course, you should always consult the latest community documentation for updates and new innovations.

Finally, a request—even if you don't need to read most of the book, if you find the parts you read useful, please take a moment and post a review. The main way people find out about useful books is by word of mouth and online reviews. Your review can have a tremendous impact.

Thank you, and I hope to see you in a future training or conference!

Conventions Used in This Book

The following typographical conventions are used in this book:

Italic
: Indicates new terms, URLs, email addresses, filenames, and file extensions.

`Constant width`
: Used for program listings, as well as within paragraphs to refer to program elements such as variable or function names, databases, data types, environment variables, statements, and keywords.

`Constant width bold`
: Shows commands or other text that should be typed literally by the user.

`<Constant width in angle brackets>`
: Shows text that should be replaced with user-supplied values or by values determined by context.

This element signifies a tip or suggestion.

This element signifies a general note.

This element indicates a warning or caution.

Using Code Examples

Supplemental material (code examples, exercises, etc.) is available for download at *https://resources.oreilly.com/examples/0636920064602*.

This book is here to help you get your job done. In general, if example code is offered with this book, you may use it in your programs and documentation. You do not need to contact us for permission unless you're reproducing a significant portion of the code. For example, writing a program that uses several chunks of code from this book does not require permission. Selling or distributing a CD-ROM of examples from O'Reilly books does require permission. Answering a question by citing this book and quoting example code does not require permission. Incorporating a significant amount of example code from this book into your product's documentation does require permission.

We appreciate, but do not require, attribution. An attribution usually includes the title, author, publisher, and ISBN. For example: "*Jenkins 2: Up and Running* by Brent Laster (O'Reilly). Copyright 2018 Brent Laster, 978-1-491-97959-4."

If you feel your use of code examples falls outside fair use or the permission given above, feel free to contact us at *permissions@oreilly.com*.

Important Note About Code Examples in This Book

In many cases where code listings occur in the book, individual lines of the code are too long to fit in the printed space. In those cases, the code is wrapped around and continued on the next line(s). There are generally not line continuation characters on these lines. However, you can usually tell where code has been continued from the line above by the semantics of the command or by the indentation.

A Note About the Figures in This Book

Many screenshots and figures have been used throughout this book to help clarify information for the reader. The quality and scaling of some visual elements may vary depending on the methods used to capture them. As well, since the Jenkins community frequently releases updated versions of the application and its plugins, visual representations shown in the book are subject to change.

O'Reilly Safari

Safari (formerly Safari Books Online) is a membership-based training and reference platform for enterprise, government, educators, and individuals.

Members have access to thousands of books, training videos, Learning Paths, interactive tutorials, and curated playlists from over 250 publishers, including O'Reilly Media, Harvard Business Review, Prentice Hall Professional, Addison-Wesley Professional, Microsoft Press, Sams, Que, Peachpit Press, Adobe, Focal Press, Cisco Press, John Wiley & Sons, Syngress, Morgan Kaufmann, IBM Redbooks, Packt, Adobe Press, FT Press, Apress, Manning, New Riders, McGraw-Hill, Jones & Bartlett, and Course Technology, among others.

For more information, please visit *http://oreilly.com/safari*.

How to Contact Us

Please address comments and questions concerning this book to the publisher:

O'Reilly Media, Inc.
1005 Gravenstein Highway North
Sebastopol, CA 95472
800-998-9938 (in the United States or Canada)
707-829-0515 (international or local)
707-829-0104 (fax)

We have a web page for this book, where we list errata, examples, and any additional information. You can access this page at *http://bit.ly/jenkins-2-ur*.

To comment or ask technical questions about this book, send email to *bookquestions@oreilly.com*.

For more information about our books, courses, conferences, and news, see our website at *http://www.oreilly.com*.

Find us on Facebook: *http://facebook.com/oreilly*

Follow us on Twitter: *http://twitter.com/oreillymedia*

Watch us on YouTube: *http://www.youtube.com/oreillymedia*

Acknowledgments

The biggest thanks of all for this book has to go to the Jenkins community. Jenkins is proof that community-developed and community-supported software can be of incredible utility, versatility, and quality. To all those who have contributed to Jenkins or played a role in developing plugins or training materials, answering questions, or getting releases of Jenkins out, thank you.

On the individual side, there are many people to thank. The only way I can think to do this is via some broad categories.

Thank you to Kohsuke Kawaguchi for creating Hudson—and then Jenkins—and agreeing to write the foreword for this book. The technical drive and leadership you bring to Jenkins through the community and CloudBees has made a huge and positive difference in how we create and deliver software.

Thanks to the technical editors, Patrick Wolfe, Brian Dawson, and Chaim Krause. Their investment of time in agreeing to review this book was significant—and appreciated. The content is immeasurably better because of their feedback.

Patrick Wolfe has been instrumental in providing technical updates and additional information since the book's early stages. This has helped to ensure that the book is, hopefully, up to date with the current state of Jenkins in most cases (at least at its release date). His input has been invaluable and I appreciate the time and openness that he has given to this project.

Brian Dawson has also been extremely helpful in noting changes and places where the book could be improved for Jenkins users. Though Brian and Patrick both work at CloudBees, they exemplify the focus of the company on freely giving back to the Jenkins community.

Chaim Krause is among the most dedicated people I know. Having worked with him on two books now, I always appreciate his effort and attention to detail. He takes the time to try things out and point out where wording or examples need updates or don't make sense initially. There are a number of details in the book that owe their correctness to him.

A huge thanks to the staff at O'Reilly. First, thanks to Brian Foster, the editor who was willing to take a chance on this book and supported it all along the way. Thanks to Angela Rufino, who has helped keep the book on course, answered all of my questions, and provided the oversight to see the book through to completion. Thanks also to Nan Barber for her early work on the book editing.

Shoutouts as well to Dwight Ramsey and Rachel Head, the copyeditors, for making my writing readable and clear, and to Justin Billing, the production editor, and Jasmine Kwityn, the proofreader, for bringing everything together to create a final, polished product.

Much of the material in this book was first shared and honed in the live training classes I do for O'Reilly's Safari platform and at conference workshops. Thanks to Susan Conant (along with Brian Foster again) for listening to my ideas for Jenkins 2 live trainings and helping develop them. Also, thanks to Virginia Wilson for the additional writing opportunities around CI and CD and to conference organizers Rachel Roumeliotis and Audra Carter for shepherding the conference sessions.

Finally at O'Reilly, I want to thank the training staff who have supported the many live training sessions I've done around Git and Jenkins. Thank you to Yasmina Greco, Lindsay Ventimiglia, Nurul Ishak, and Shannon Cutt for overseeing all of the trainings and keeping everything on track in such a professional manner.

I would be remiss if I did not also mention Jay Zimmerman on the conference side. Jay is the founder and organizer of the No Fluff Just Stuff conference series and first provided me an opportunity to speak at events all across the country on Jenkins.

Thanks to the management at SAS for supporting my initiatives to create and present corporate training courses over the years to employees across the company and around the world. I especially thank Glenn Musial, Cyndi Schnupper, and Andy Diggelmann for their encouragement and support of my endeavors.

To everyone who's attended one of my trainings or workshops on Jenkins, thanks—especially to those who have asked a question and/or provided feedback to cause me to think more about topics and ways to improve content.

To those at CloudBees, acting on behalf of the Jenkins community to evolve Jenkins, answer questions, and provide documentation for all of us as users, your efforts are appreciated. There are too many to list them all, but several names have come up repeatedly as I researched material for the book, including Patrick Wolfe, Jessie Glick, Andrew Bayer, James Dumay, Liam Newman, and James Brown. If you see content by these guys, read it and you will likely learn something useful. Also thanks to Max Arbuckle for his coordination of the Jenkins World conferences, where much of the information about Jenkins 2 was first presented.

The deepest gratitude of all must go to my wife, Anne-Marie, and to my children. This book was written over a long period of time, mostly nights and weekends, which took time away from them while I wrote about something that seemed very foreign to them. Nevertheless, they never failed in their words of encouragement. Anne-Marie, you have been my greatest support and source of strength and encouragement, as you are in everything. Thank you for that and for helping me keep a sense of order and balance between life, dreams, and work. You bring me kindness, love, and inspiration each and every day of our lives together, and for that I am truly grateful.

Finally, thanks to the readers of this book. It is my sincere hope that you will get value out of it and it will help you make progress in your use of Jenkins and all the related pieces.

CHAPTER 1

Introducing Jenkins 2

Welcome to *Jenkins 2: Up and Running*. Whether you're a build administrator, developer, tester, or any other role, you've come to the right place to learn about this evolution in Jenkins. With this book, you're on your way to leveraging the features of Jenkins 2 to design, implement, and execute your pipelines with a level of flexibility, control, and ease of maintenance that hasn't been possible with Jenkins before. And, no matter what your role, you'll quickly see the benefits.

If you're a developer, writing your pipeline-as-code will feel more comfortable and natural. If you're a DevOps professional, maintaining your pipeline will be easier because you can treat it like any other set of code that drives key processes. If you're a tester, you'll be able to take advantage of increased support for features such as parallelism to gain more leverage for your efforts. If you're a manager, you'll be able to ensure the quality of your pipeline as you do for your source code. If you're a Jenkins user, you're going to grow your skill base substantially and be ready for this new evolution of "pipelines-as-code."

Getting to these goals requires understanding and mapping out the transition from your existing implementations. Jenkins 2 represents a significant shift from the older, more traditional, form-based versions of Jenkins. And with such a shift, there's a lot to learn. But it's all manageable. As the first step, we need to lay a solid foundation of Jenkins 2 fundamentals (What is it? What are the big-ticket items?), including its new features, the changes in the working environment, and an understanding of the new concepts that it is based on. That's what this chapter and the next are all about. Some of this you may already be familiar with. And if so, that's great. But I suggest at least scanning those sections that look familiar. There may be something in there that's new or has changed enough to be worth noting.

In this chapter, we'll explore at a high level what makes Jenkins 2 different and how that will fit in with what you're accustomed to. We'll look at three key areas:

- What is Jenkins 2, in terms of the significant new features and functionality it introduces?
- What are the reasons (motivations and drivers) for the shift in Jenkins?
- How compatible is Jenkins 2 with previous versions? What are the compatibility considerations?

Let's get started by taking a look at what makes Jenkins 2 different from the traditional Jenkins versions.

What Is Jenkins 2?

In this book, the term "Jenkins 2" is used a bit loosely. In our specific context, this is a way to refer to the newer versions of Jenkins that directly incorporate support for pipelines-as-code and other new features such as *Jenkinsfiles* that we will talk about throughout the book.

Some of these features have been available for Jenkins 1.x versions for some time via plugins. (And, to be clear, Jenkins 2 gains much of its new functionality from major updates of existing plugins as well as entirely new plugins.) But Jenkins 2 represents more. It represents a shift to focusing on these features as the preferred, core way to interact with Jenkins. Instead of filling in web forms to define jobs for Jenkins, users can now write programs using the Jenkins DSL and Groovy to define their pipelines and do other tasks.

DSL here refers to *Domain-Specific Language*, the "programming language" for Jenkins. The DSL is Groovy-based and it includes terms and constructs that encapsulate Jenkins-specific functionality. An example is the `node` keyword that tells Jenkins that you will be programmatically selecting a node (formerly "master" or "slave") that you want to execute this part of your program on.

Jenkins and Groovy

Jenkins has included a Groovy engine for a long time. This was used to allow advanced scripting operations and to provide access/functionality not available through the web interface.

The DSL is a core piece of Jenkins 2. It serves as a building block that makes other key user-facing features possible. Let's look at a few of these features to see how they differentiate Jenkins 2 from "legacy" Jenkins. We'll quickly survey a new way to separate your code from Jenkins in a Jenkinsfile, a more structured approach to creating workflows with Declarative Pipelines, and an exciting new visual interface called Blue Ocean.

The Jenkinsfile

In Jenkins 2, your pipeline definition can now be separate from Jenkins itself. In past versions of Jenkins, your job definitions were stored in configuration files in the Jenkins home directory. This meant they required Jenkins itself to be able to see, understand, and modify the definitions (unless you wanted to work with the XML directly, which was challenging). In Jenkins 2, you can write your pipeline definition as a DSL script within a text area in the web interface. However, you can also take the DSL code and save it externally as a text file with your source code. This allows you to manage your Jenkins jobs using a file containing code like any other source code, including tracking history, seeing differences, etc.

The JobConfigHistory Plugin

For completeness, I should mention that there is a JobConfigHistory plugin available for Jenkins that tracks the history of the XML configuration changes over time and allows you to look at what was changed each time. It is available on the Jenkins wiki (*http://bit.ly/2J5fmyb*).

The filename that Jenkins 2 expects your job definitions/pipelines to be stored as is *Jenkinsfile*. You can have many Jenkinsfiles, each differentiated from the others by the project and branch it is stored with. You can have all of your code in the Jenkinsfile, or you can call out/pull in other external code via shared libraries. Also available are DSL statements that allow you to load external code into your script (more about these in Chapter 6).

The Jenkinsfile can also serve as a marker file, meaning that if Jenkins sees a Jenkinsfile as part of your project's source code, it understands that this is a project/branch that Jenkins can run. It also understands implicitly which source control management (SCM) project and branch it needs to work with. It can then load and execute the code in the Jenkinsfile. If you are familiar with the build tool Gradle, this is similar to the idea of the *build.gradle* file used by that application. I'll have more to say about Jenkinsfiles throughout the book.

Figure 1-1 shows an example of a Jenkinsfile in source control.

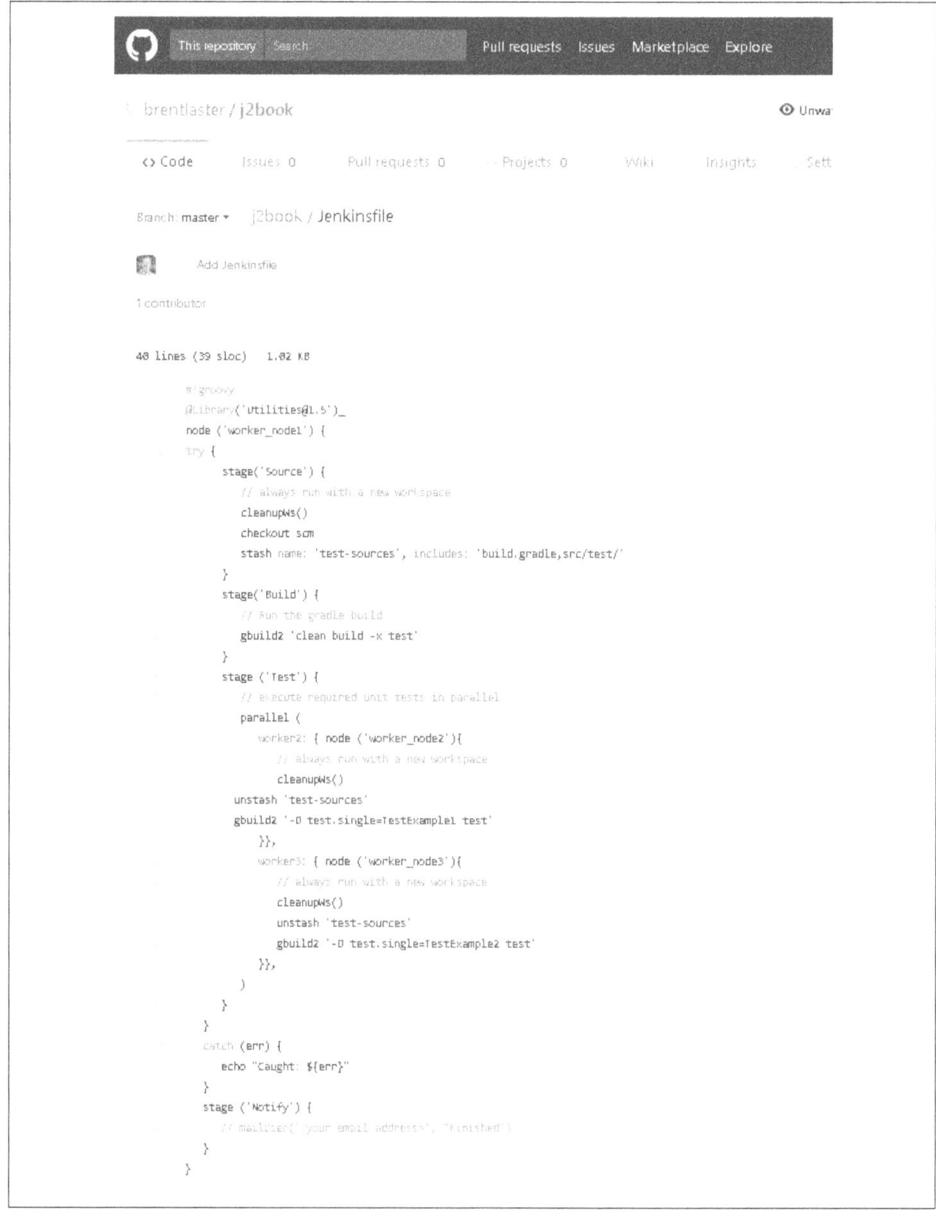

Figure 1-1. An example Jenkinsfile in source control

Declarative Pipelines

In the previous incarnations of pipelines-as-code in Jenkins, the code was primarily a Groovy script with Jenkins-specific DSL steps inserted. There was very little imposed structure, and the program flow was managed by Groovy constructs. Error reporting and checking were based on the Groovy program execution rather than what you were attempting to do with Jenkins.

This model is what we now refer to as *Scripted Pipelines*. However, the DSL for the pipeline has continued to evolve.

In Scripted Pipelines, the DSL supported a large number of different steps to do tasks, but was missing some of the key metafeatures of Jenkins-oriented tasks, such as post-build processing, error checking for pipeline structures, and the ability to easily send notifications based on different states. Much of this could be emulated via Groovy programming mechanisms such as `try-catch-finally` blocks. But that required more Groovy programming skills in addition to the Jenkins-oriented programming. The Jenkinsfile shown in Figure 1-1 is an example of a Scripted Pipeline with `try-catch` notification handling.

In 2016 and 2017, CloudBees, the enterprise company that is the majority contributor to the Jenkins project, introduced an enhanced programming syntax for pipelines-as-code called *Declarative Pipelines*. This syntax adds a clear, expected structure to pipelines as well as enhanced DSL elements and constructs. The result more closely resembles the workflow of constructing a pipeline in the web interface (with Freestyle projects).

An example here is post-build processing, with notifications based on build statuses, which can now be easily defined via a built-in DSL mechanism. This reduces the need to supplement a pipeline definition with Groovy code to emulate traditional features of Jenkins.

The more formal structure of Declarative Pipelines allows for cleaner error checking. So, instead of having to scan through Groovy tracebacks when an error occurs, the user is presented with a succinct, directed error message—in most cases pointing directly to the problem. Figure 1-2 shows a snippet of the output produced by the following Declarative Pipeline with the enhanced error checking:

```
pipeline {
   agent any
   stages {
      stae('Source') {
         git branch: 'test', url: 'git@diyvb:repos/gradle-greetings'
         stash name: 'test-sources', includes: 'build.gradle,/src/test'
      }
      stage('Build') {

      }
   }
}
```

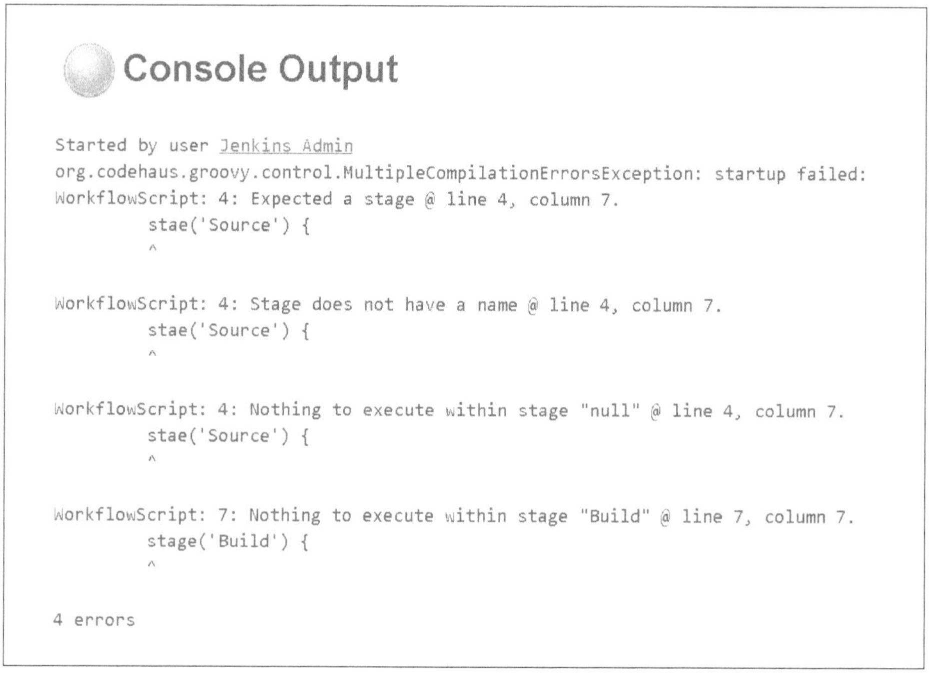

```
Console Output

Started by user Jenkins Admin
org.codehaus.groovy.control.MultipleCompilationErrorsException: startup failed:
WorkflowScript: 4: Expected a stage @ line 4, column 7.
          stae('Source') {
          ^

WorkflowScript: 4: Stage does not have a name @ line 4, column 7.
          stae('Source') {
          ^

WorkflowScript: 4: Nothing to execute within stage "null" @ line 4, column 7.
          stae('Source') {
          ^

WorkflowScript: 7: Nothing to execute within stage "Build" @ line 7, column 7.
          stage('Build') {
          ^

4 errors
```

Figure 1-2. Declarative Pipeline with enhanced error checking

Blue Ocean Interface

The structure that comes with Declarative Pipelines also serves as the foundation for another innovation in Jenkins 2—Blue Ocean, the new Jenkins visual interface. Blue Ocean adds a graphical representation for each stage of a pipeline showing indicators of success/failure and progress, and allowing point-and-click access to logs for each individual piece. Blue Ocean also provides a basic visual editor. Figure 1-3 shows an example of a successful pipeline run with logs as displayed in Blue Ocean. Chapter 9 is devoted entirely to the new interface.

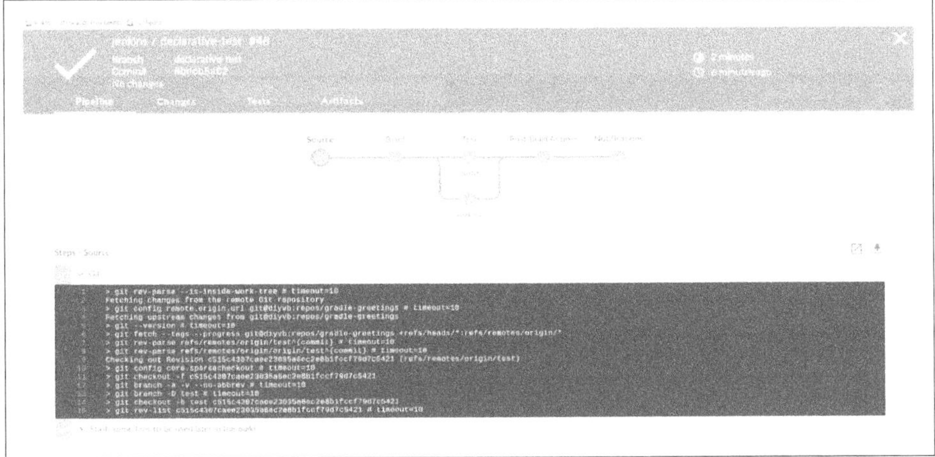

Figure 1-3. Displaying a successful run and examining logs via the Blue Ocean interface

New Job Types in Jenkins 2

Jenkins 2 comes with a number of new job types, mostly designed around taking advantage of key functionalities such as pipelines-as-code and Jenkinsfiles. These types make it easier than ever to automate job and pipeline creation and organize your projects. Creation of each new job/item/project starts the same way.

New Job Types and Plugins

To be clear, having these new job types available is dependent on having the requisite plugins installed. If you accept the recommended plugins during the install process, you will get the job types discussed here.

Once Jenkins 2 is installed and you have logged in, you can create new jobs just as before. As Figure 1-4 shows, the blurb under the "Welcome to Jenkins!" banner suggests users "create new jobs," but the menu item for this is actually labeled "New Item." Most of these items are ultimately a kind of project as well. For our purposes, I'll use the terms "job," "item," and "project" interchangeably throughout the book.

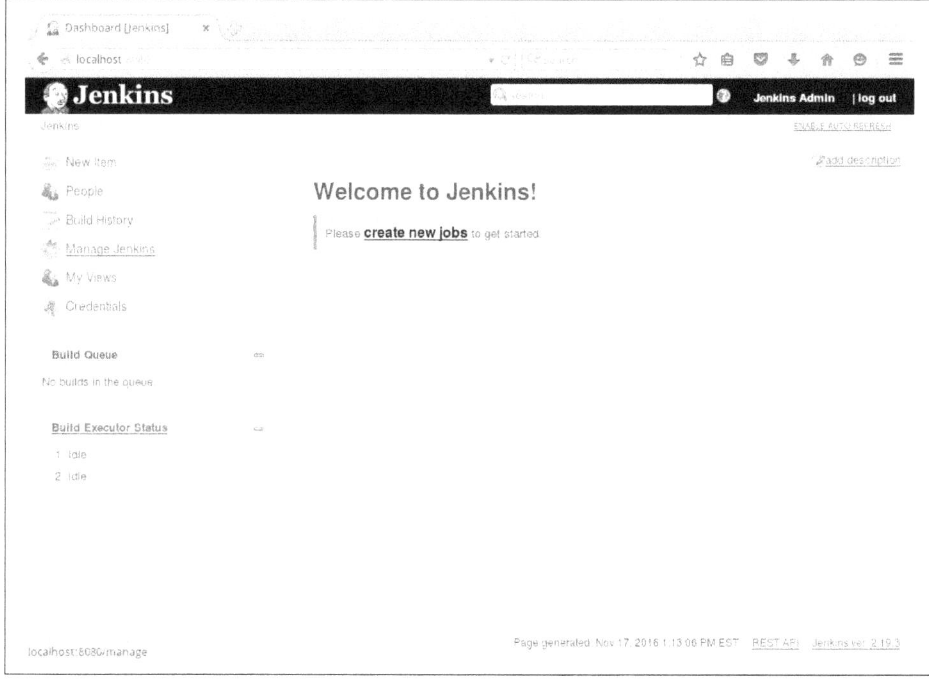

Figure 1-4. The Jenkins welcome screen: the launching point for creating new jobs, items, and projects

When you choose to create a new item in Jenkins 2, you're presented with the screen to select the type of new job (Figure 1-5). You'll notice some familiar types, such as the Freestyle project, but also some that you may not have seen before. I'll briefly summarize the new job types here and then explain each of them in more detail in Chapter 8.

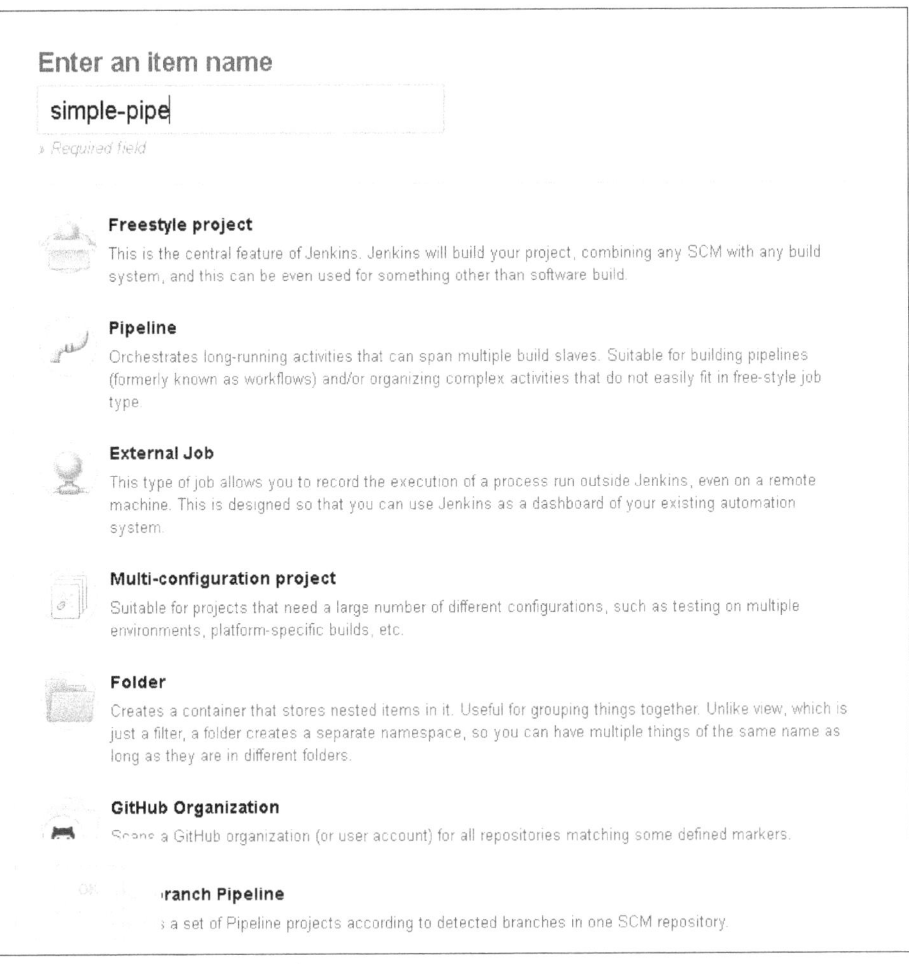

Enter an item name
simple-pipe
» Required field
Freestyle project
This is the central feature of Jenkins. Jenkins will build your project, combining any SCM with any build system, and this can be even used for something other than software build.
Pipeline
Orchestrates long-running activities that can span multiple build slaves. Suitable for building pipelines (formerly known as workflows) and/or organizing complex activities that do not easily fit in free-style job type.
External Job
This type of job allows you to record the execution of a process run outside Jenkins, even on a remote machine. This is designed so that you can use Jenkins as a dashboard of your existing automation system.
Multi-configuration project
Suitable for projects that need a large number of different configurations, such as testing on multiple environments, platform-specific builds, etc.
Folder
Creates a container that stores nested items in it. Useful for grouping things together. Unlike view, which is just a filter, a folder creates a separate namespace, so you can have multiple things of the same name as long as they are in different folders.
GitHub Organization
a GitHub organization (or user account) for all repositories matching some defined markers.
ranch Pipeline
a set of Pipeline projects according to detected branches in one SCM repository.

Figure 1-5. Jenkins 2 project choices

Pipeline

As the name implies, the Pipeline type of project is intended for creating pipelines. This is done by writing the code in the Jenkins DSL. This is the main type of project we'll be talking about throughout the book.

As already noted, pipelines can either be written in a "scripted" syntax style or a "declarative" syntax style. Pipelines created in this type of project can also be made easily into Jenkinsfiles.

Folder

This is a way to group projects together rather than a type of project itself. Note that this is not like the traditional "View" tabs on the Jenkins dashboard that allow you to filter the list of projects. Rather, it is like a directory folder in an operating system. The folder name becomes part of the path of the project.

Organization

Certain source control platforms provide a mechanism for grouping repositories into "organizations." Jenkins integrations allow you to store Jenkins pipeline scripts as Jenkinsfiles in the repositories within an organization and execute based on those. Currently GitHub and Bitbucket organizations are supported, with others planned for the future. For simplicity in this book, we'll talk mainly about GitHub Organization projects as our example.

Assuming sufficient access, Jenkins can automatically set up an organization *webhook* (a notification from the website) on the hosting side that will notify your Jenkins instance when any changes are made in the repository. When Jenkins is notified, it detects the Jenkinsfile as a marker in the repository and executes the commands in the Jenkinsfile to run the pipeline.

Multibranch Pipeline

In this type of project, Jenkins again uses the Jenkinsfile as a marker. If a new branch is created in the project with a Jenkinsfile in it, Jenkins will automatically create a new project in Jenkins just for that branch. This project can be applied to any Git or Subversion repository.

We'll be taking a closer look at each of these new project types in Chapter 8 of the book. However, it is also worth noting that Jenkins still supports the traditional workhorse of jobs—Freestyle projects. You can still create jobs using web-based forms there and execute them as you have before. But certainly the emphasis in Jenkins 2 is on Pipeline jobs.

It's easy to see that Jenkins 2 represents a major shift from the traditional Jenkins model. As such, it's worth spending a few minutes to discuss the reasons for the change.

Reasons for the Shift

Arguably, Jenkins has been the most prolific workflow and pipeline management tool for many years. So what drove the need to make the shift in Jenkins 2? Let's look at a few potential causes, both external and internal to Jenkins.

DevOps Movement

The ideas behind continuous integration, continuous delivery, and continuous deployment have been around for a number of years. But early on, they were more of an end goal rather than a starting point. With the increased focus on DevOps in recent years, users and enterprises have come to expect that tooling will support them in implementing DevOps and continuous practices out of the box (or at least not make it more difficult).

Given its place in the workflow automation space, it was somewhat expected (and perhaps required) that Jenkins would evolve in its capabilities to support these industry drivers.

Assembling Pipelines

Creating any one job in the Jenkins Freestyle interface wasn't necessarily problematic. But trying to assemble multiple jobs into a continuous software delivery pipeline, that could take code from commit to deployment, could frequently be a challenge. Jenkins' core functionality allowed for kicking off a specific job after another one finished, but sharing data between jobs, such as workspaces, parameters, etc., was often problematic or required special plugins or tricks to accomplish.

Resumability

A key part of Jenkins 2 functionality hinges on the ability of pipelines to be durable—meaning jobs continue to run on agents or pick up where they left off if the master node restarts. In fact, one of the requirements for a plugin to be compatible with Jenkins 2 is the ability to serialize states so that those can be recovered in the event of a master restart. That was not the case with prior versions of Jenkins; users and processes were often left in a place where they needed to either wade through logs to figure out where things were left or just opt to start the process again from the beginning.

Configurability

Since users were largely limited to the web-based interface, working with legacy Jenkins usually required finding the right place on the screen, figuring out the buttons and fields, and trying not to make typos when entering data. Workflow changes (such as reordering steps in a job or changing the order in which jobs executed) could require multiple interactions of clicking and dragging and typing, as opposed to simpler updates available in a text editor interface. In some cases where GUI elements were provided to interface with tooling, ways to send particular commands to the tooling through the Jenkins interface weren't available. The web-based forms prevalent in Jenkins lent themselves well to simple, structured choices, but not as well to iterative or decision-based flow control.

Sharing Workspaces

Traditionally in Jenkins, each job had its own workspace to pull down the source code, do builds in, or do whatever other processing was needed. This worked well for distinct jobs, isolating their environments and preventing writing over data. However, when chaining jobs together, this could result in an ineffective process that was challenging to overcome. For example, if multiple jobs in a pipeline needed to perform processing on built artifacts, having to rebuild the artifacts each time was highly inefficient. Storing and retrieving the artifacts in a repository between execution of the jobs required adding multiple steps and configuration to each job. A more efficient strategy would be to share the workspace between the jobs—but doing this in legacy Jenkins was not easily supported. Rather, the user was required to define custom workspaces and employ parameters that pointed to the workspace, or use a specialized plugin to make it work.

Specialized Knowledge

As the previous shared workspaces discussion illustrates, users often needed to know the "right tricks" to implement something in the legacy Jenkins system that they could easily do in a typical program or script (data transfer, flow control, external calls, etc.).

Access to Logic

Legacy Jenkins typically relied on web forms to input data and stored it in XML configuration files in its home directory. With this implementation, there was no easy way to view at a glance the logic involved in executing multiple jobs. For users not familiar with it, understanding a Jenkins setup and job definitions could require quite a bit of scrolling through screens, looking at values in forms, flipping back and forth between global configurations, and so on. This made wider support, collaboration among multiple users, and understanding of multijob pipelines challenging, especially if there were substantial changes, reviews, or debugging that needed to be done.

Pipeline Source Management

As highlighted in the previous section, the "source" for a legacy Jenkins job was an XML file. This was not only difficult to read, but difficult to change and get correct without going through the web interface. The configuration was not designed to exist in the same place as the source code. Configuration and source code were two separate entities, managed in two different ways.

A corollary was lack of auditability. While there were plugins to help track changes over time, this was not as convenient as tracking simple source file changes and still required the Jenkins application itself to be able to track changes in jobs.

Competition

One additional factor that undoubtedly has come into play here is that other applications have sprung up around setting up pipelines-as-code. There are various examples, such as Pivotal's Concourse, which uses containerization to do jobs and allows pipelines to be described in YAML files.

Meeting the Challenges

So how does Jenkins 2 meet these challenges? I've already alluded to some of the ways, but there are a few points that are worth highlighting in this space:

- Pipelines are treated as first-class citizens. That means that there is design and support for working with pipelines as an entity in the application, rather than pipelines being something produced from connecting together jobs in Jenkins.
- Pipelines can be programmed through coding, rather than just expressed through a configuration interface. This allows for additional logic and workflows to be used, as well as programming constructs that were not available or not surfaced in legacy Jenkins.
- There is a structured DSL specifically to program pipelines.
- A pipeline can be created directly as a script in a job without requiring any substantial web form interaction. Additionally, they can be created completely separately in Jenkinsfiles.
- Pipelines stored as Jenkinsfiles can now be stored with the source code separate from Jenkins.
- The DSL includes functions to easily share files across workspaces.
- There is more advanced, built-in support for working with Docker containers.

All of this leads to easier maintainability and testing as well as more resiliency. We can handle exception cases with typical constructs and better survive events like restarts.

Before we go further into the Jenkins 2 features, it's worth taking a moment to talk about compatibility between the old and new.

Compatibility

For the vast majority of items, there are corresponding ways to get the same functionality through pipelines as through the traditional web interface and Freestyle jobs. In fact, there may be multiple ways, some built-in and some more contrived. This can best be described with a brief discussion about the two different syntax styles that Jenkins supports for creating pipelines.

Pipeline Compatibility

As noted, Jenkins 2 now supports two styles of pipelines—scripted and declarative—each with their own syntax and structure. We will delve more into both types in the next few chapters, but for now let's look at one specific example: post-build notification in a traditional Freestyle structure and corresponding functionality in Scripted and Declarative Pipelines.

Figure 1-6 shows a traditional Freestyle project's post-build configuration for a typical operation, sending email notifications. In a Freestyle project, there's a specific web page element for this with fields to fill in to do the configuration.

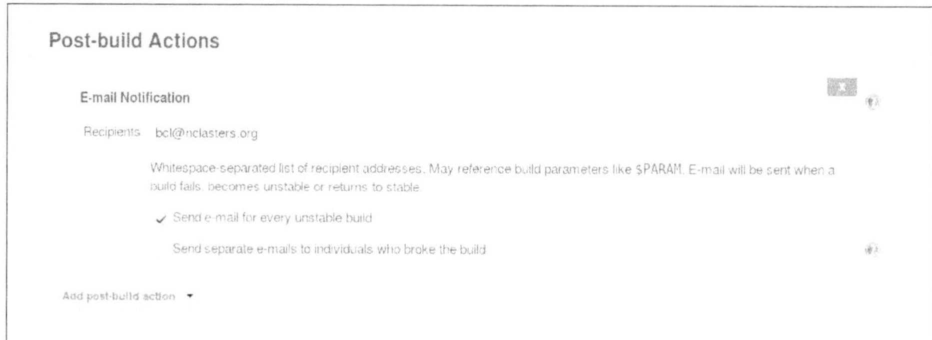

Figure 1-6. Post-build actions in a Freestyle project

In the syntax for a Scripted Pipeline, we don't have a built-in way to do such post-build actions. We are limited to the DSL steps plus whatever can be done with Groovy coding. So, to always send an email after a build, we need to resort to coding as shown here:

```
node {
        try {
            // do some work
        }
        catch(e) {
            currentBuild.result = "FAILED"
            throw e
        }
        finally {
            mail to:"buildAdmin@mycompany.com",
              subject:"STATUS FOR PROJECT: ${currentBuild.fullDisplayName}",
              body: "RESULT: ${currentBuild.result}"
        }
}
```

Assuming we have our email setup already configured globally in Jenkins, we can use the DSL `mail` statement to send an email. Because we don't have a pipeline statement/

feature in the scripted syntax to always do something as a post-build operation, we fall back to the Groovy `try-catch-finally` syntax.

This highlights compatibility exceptions in the case of some Jenkins functions such as post-build processing. DSL constructs can be missing for cases like this. In those instances, you may have to resort to using Groovy constructs that can mimic the processing that Jenkins would do. (This approach is covered in more detail in Chapter 3.)

If you choose to use the Declarative Pipeline structure, then chances are good that you will have constructs available to handle most of the common Jenkins functions. For example, in the Declarative Pipeline syntax, there is a `post` section that can be defined to handle post-processing steps along the lines of the traditional post-build processing and notifications (we cover this more in Chapter 7):

```
pipeline {
    agent any
    stages {
        stage ("dowork") {
           steps {
              // do some work
           }
        }
    }
    post {
       always {
          mail to:"buildAdmin@mycompany.com",
            subject:"STATUS FOR PROJECT: ${currentBuild.fullDisplayName}",
            body: "RESULT: ${currentBuild.result}"
       }
    }
}
```

Compatibility doesn't just come into play in the actual coding. An additional area that's worth mentioning is plugin compatibility.

Plugin Compatibility

As with legacy Jenkins, the majority of functionality for Jenkins 2 is provided through integration with plugins. With the advent of Jenkins 2, new requirements were created for plugins to be compatible. We can broadly categorize the requirements into two categories: they must survive restarts and provide advanced APIs that can be used in pipeline scripts.

Surviving restarts

One of the features/requirements of Jenkins 2 pipelines is that they must be able to survive restarts of a node. In order to support this, the main criterion is that stateful objects in plugins be *serializable*—that is, able to have their state recorded. This is not a given for many of the constructs in Java and Groovy, so plugins may have to be substantially changed to meet this requirement.

Having Restartable Pipeline Scripts

If there is a certain piece of code that is not serializable, there are ways to work around its use in some cases. See Chapter 16 for some suggestions on how to work around this type of issue.

Providing scriptable APIs

To be compatible with writing pipeline scripts, steps that were formerly done by filling in the Jenkins web forms now have to be expressible as pipeline steps with compatible Groovy syntax. In many cases, the terms and concepts may be close to what was used in the forms. Where `Foo` was a label for a text entry box in the form-based version of the plugin, there may now be a DSL call with `Foo` as a named parameter with a value passed in.

As an example, we'll use configuration and operations for Artifactory, a binary artifact manager. Figure 1-7 shows how we might configure the build environment for a Freestyle Jenkins job to be able to access Artifactory repositories.

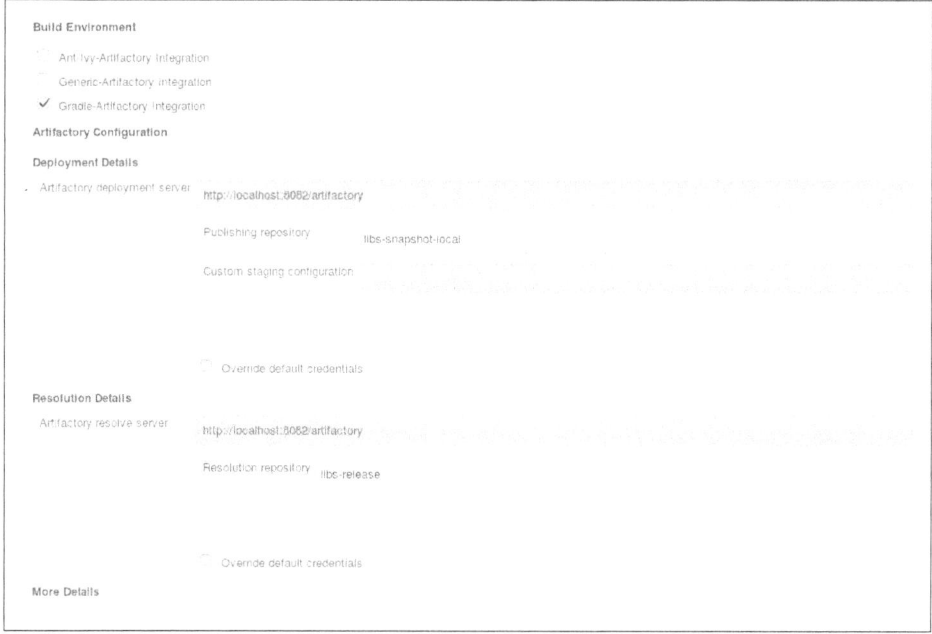

Figure 1-7. Configuring Artifactory servers in a Freestyle job

And here's how we could do the similar configuration in a pipeline script:

```
// Define new Artifactory server based on our configuration
def server = Artifactory.server "LocalArtifactory"
// Create a new Artifactory for Gradle object
def artifactoryGradle = Artifactory.newGradleBuild()
    artifactoryGradle.tool = "gradle4" // Tool name from Jenkins configuration
    artifactoryGradle.deployer repo:'libs-snapshot-local', server:server
    artifactoryGradle.resolver repo:'remote-repos', server:server
```

Beyond configuration, we have the actual operations that need to be done. In the Freestyle jobs, we have checkboxes and web forms again to tell Jenkins what to do. (See Figure 1-8.)

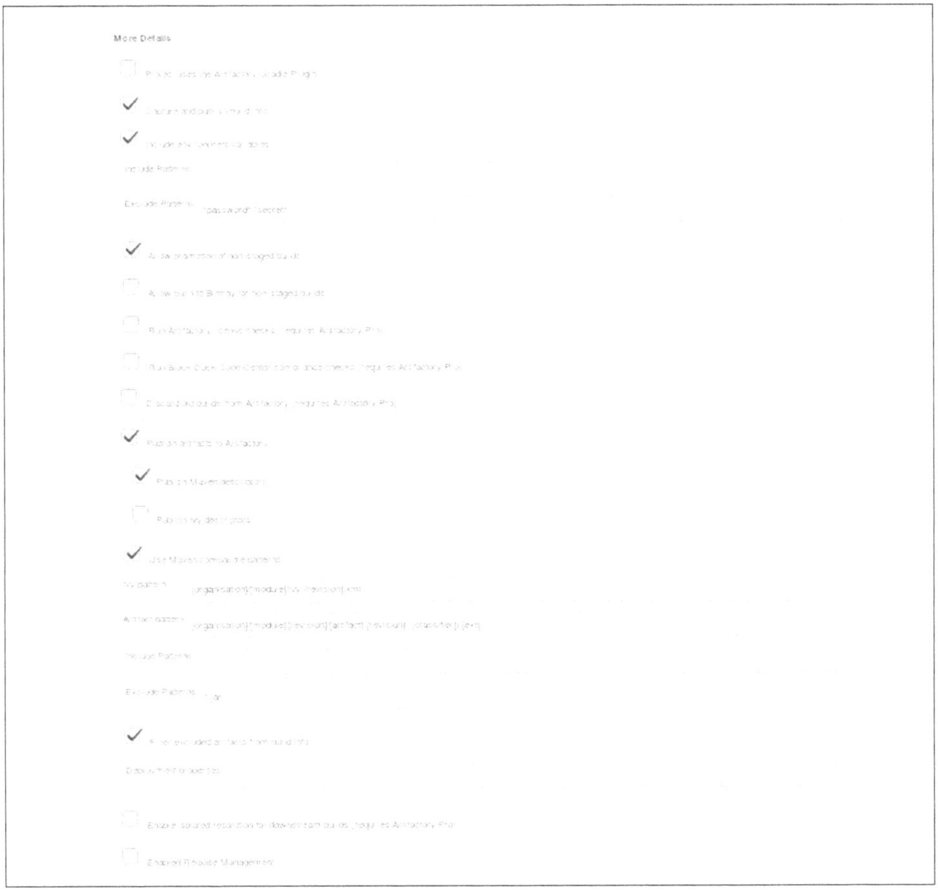

Figure 1-8. Specifying Artifactory operations in a Freestyle job

And, again, in the context of a pipeline script, if the plugin is pipeline-compatible we will likely have similar DSL statements to make the API calls to provide the same functionality. The following shows a corresponding pipeline script example for the preceding Artifactory Freestyle example:

```
// buildinfo configuration

def buildInfo = Artifactory.newBuildInfo()

buildInfo.env.capture = true

// Deploy Maven descriptors to Artifactory

artifactoryGradle.deployer.deployMavenDescriptors = true

// extra gradle configurations
artifactoryGradle.deployer.artifactDeploymentPatterns.addExclude("*.jar")

artifactoryGradle.usesPlugin = false

// run the Gradle piece to deploy

artifactoryGradle.run buildFile: 'build.gradle'
                      tasks: 'cleanartifactoryPublish'
                      buildInfo: buildInfo

// publish build info

server.publishBuildInfo buildInfo
```

In some cases, pipeline scripts may also take advantage of items already configured in the traditional Jenkins interface, such as global tools. An example with the use of Gradle is shown next.

In the first figure (Figure 1-9), we see the global tool setup for our Gradle instance. Then we see it used in a Freestyle project (Figure 1-10), and finally we see it used in a pipeline project via a special DSL step called `tool` that allows us to refer back to the global configuration based on the supplied `name` argument.

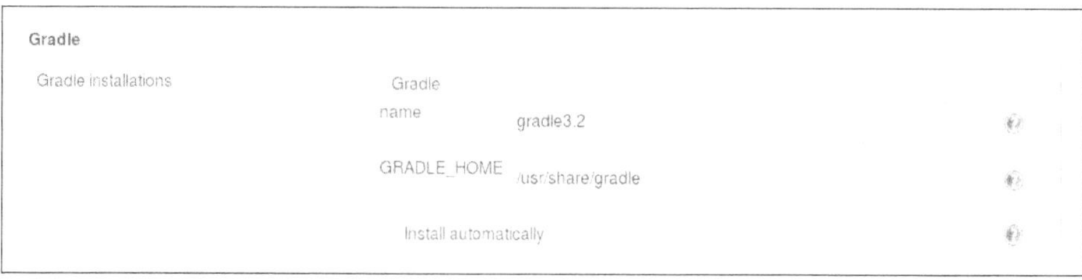

Figure 1-9. Global tool configuration for Gradle

Figure 1-10. Using the global tool Gradle version in a Freestyle project

```
stage('Compile') { // Compile and do unit testing
    // Run gradle to execute compile
    sh "${tool 'gradle3.2'}/bin/gradle clean build"
}
```

Declarative Pipelines also have a `tool` directive that allows for the same functionality in that type of pipeline. (Chapter 7 discusses Declarative Pipelines in detail.)

Global Configuration

In older versions of Jenkins, most of the global configuration was set up via the Configure System page accessible from the Manage Jenkins screen. In the current versions of Jenkins, global configuration is split between Configure System and Global Tool Configuration pages.

It can be confusing at first to remember which section you should go to for which kinds of configuration. One trick I use is to think of "systems" as being similar to "servers" (easy to remember because they both start with "s"). In general, any kind of server setup or similar task is done on the Configure System screen.

Also, if you think of tools as frequently being standalone executable applications (Git, Gradle, etc.), then those belong in the Global Tool Configuration section. Obviously these aren't exact classifications, but they may serve you as a handy memory device when you are first getting familiar with this arrangement.

As we have seen, providing APIs (and thus plugin pipeline compatibility) is central to being able to execute traditional functionality in pipelines. Eventually all plugins will need to be Pipeline-compatible, but at this point, there are still plugins that are not compatible, or not completely compatible. There are places a user can go to check for compatibility, though.

Checking Compatibility

To help users know whether or not existing plugins are compatible with using pipelines in Jenkins 2, there are a couple of websites available. Note that information here is not guaranteed to be up to date, but these sites offer probably the best summary information available.

One site is on GitHub (*http://bit.ly/2qQ3gT5*), as shown. An example of the page from it is shown in Figure 1-11.

Figure 1-11. GitHub page for Jenkins plugin pipeline compatibility

The other is the Pipeline Steps Reference on the Jenkins.io site (*https://jenkins.io/doc/pipeline/steps/*), which lists the pipeline-compatible plug-ins.

Some of these specific plugins and their steps will be discussed in later chapters of this book.

Summary

This chapter has provided a quick survey of what makes Jenkins 2 different from traditional Jenkins. There is core support for pipelines both as jobs themselves and also separate from Jenkins, as Jenkinsfiles. In writing your code for a pipeline, you can choose from the traditional, more flexible Scripted Pipeline or the more structured Declarative Pipeline syntax.

Jenkins 2 also provides several new project types. The Folder type allows for grouping projects together under a shared namespace and shared environment. The Multibranch Pipeline type provides easy automated job creation per branch and continuous integration, all triggered by Jenkinsfiles residing in the branches. And the organization project type extends the multibranch functionality across all projects in an organization structure on GitHub or Bitbucket.

We also looked at some of the drivers for the evolution from the traditional Jenkins model to the pipeline-centric model. These included the growth of pipelines as an entity, as well as the challenges of making multiple jobs work together across Jenkins. Another factor was the traditional tight coupling of the pipeline configuration to the Jenkins application.

Finally, we discussed some of the compatibility factors to be aware of when moving from classic Jenkins to Jenkins 2. We will discuss specifics for various applications throughout the book, but familiarity with the general ideas laid out here will give you a good foundation to understand this, and begin thinking about what it may take to convert your existing pipelines.

Speaking of foundations, in Chapter 2 we'll cover more of the foundational aspects of working with pipelines in Jenkins 2. This will help to fill out the basic knowledge you need to begin making use of pipelines.

CHAPTER 2

The Foundations

Now that you understand the big ideas around which Jenkins 2 is built, we can move on to how Jenkins 2 supports pipelines-as-code. A key first step is understanding the development environment that Jenkins provides specifically for working with pipelines. This includes the systems we run our pipelines on as well as the interfaces for creating, executing, and monitoring pipelines. Additionally, you need to know about some of the basic structures that make up a pipeline, and how they fit together. Together, these elements will provide a solid foundation to build on for the rest of the book.

We'll approach this task by concentrating on four basic areas:

- The two styles of *syntax* that can be used for creating pipelines
- The *systems* used to run the pipeline processes
- The basic *structure* of a pipeline
- The *support* environment (and tooling) that Jenkins provides for pipeline development and execution

We'll start by defining and disambiguating some key concepts and terminology used with pipelines. Then we'll survey the required DSL structures. Along the way, we'll look at how to use the built-in editor and how to use a new tool in Jenkins to help figure out pipeline syntax.

Once you know how to input your pipeline code, we'll move on to executing a pipeline and understanding the new views that Jenkins provides. We'll also look at how to access logs from a run. Finally, we'll explore new functionality in Jenkins that allows us to try out changes to pipelines, without overwriting our existing versions.

Let's get started by learning more about the different pipeline syntax styles supported in Jenkins 2.

Syntax: Scripted Pipelines Versus Declarative Pipelines

In Chapter 1, we discussed some of the motivations that led to the shift to pipelines-as-code and making that support central to Jenkins 2. As we author our pipelines in Jenkins, we now have two different styles we can use to code them: scripted syntax and declarative syntax.

Scripted syntax refers to the initial way that pipelines-as-code have been done in Jenkins. It is an imperative style, meaning it is based on defining the logic and the program flow in the pipeline script itself. It is also more dependent on the Groovy language and Groovy constructs—especially for things like error checking and dealing with exceptions.

Declarative syntax is a newer option in Jenkins. Pipelines coded in the declarative style are arranged in clear sections that describe (or "declare") the states and outcomes we want in the major areas of the pipeline, rather than focusing on the logic to accomplish it. The following code example shows a pipeline written in scripted syntax on top and a similar one written in declarative syntax underneath:

```
// Scripted Pipeline
node('worker_node1') {
    stage('Source') { // Get code
        // get code from our Git repository
        git 'git@diyvb2:/home/git/repositories/workshop.git'
    }
    stage('Compile') { // Compile and do unit testing
       // run Gradle to execute compile and unit testing
       sh "gradle clean compileJava test"
    }
}

// Declarative Pipeline
pipeline {
    agent {label 'worker_node1'}
    stages {
        stage('Source') { // Get code
            steps {
                // get code from our Git repository
                git 'git@diyvb2:/home/git/repositories/workshop.git'
            }
        }
        stage('Compile') { // Compile and do unit testing
            steps {
                // run Gradle to execute compile and unit testing
                sh "gradle clean compileJava test"
            }
```

```
        }
    }
}
```

You can think of it this way: Scripted Pipelines are more like scripts or programs written in any imperative language to execute the program flow and logic, while Declarative Pipelines are more like what was traditionally done in Jenkins if you were using the web forms—filling in key information in predefined sections that have a predefined purpose and expected behavior. Like with the traditional web forms, when you run a Declarative Pipeline the type of each section defines what happens and how, based on the data you entered.

Choosing Between Scripted and Declarative Syntax

So what are the factors that come into play in choosing between scripted and declarative? As with most things, it's not an exact science; in any particular situation, one model may work better than the other based on the need, the structures and flows to be implemented, and the skill and background of the person(s) implementing the pipeline.

We can best derive guidance here by looking at the advantages and disadvantages of each model and then making some general observations.

Briefly, a Scripted Pipeline has the following advantages:

- Generally fewer sections and less specification needed
- Capability to use more procedural code
- More like creating a program
- Traditional pipeline-as-code model, so more familiar and backward compatible
- More flexibility to do custom operations if needed
- Able to model more complex workflows and pipelines

A Scripted Pipeline has the following disadvantages:

- More programming required in general
- Syntax checking limited to the Groovy language and environment
- Further away from the traditional Jenkins model
- Potentially more complex for the same workflow if it can be comparably done in a Declarative Pipeline

A Declarative Pipeline has the following advantages:

- More structured—closer to the traditional sections of Jenkins web forms

- More capability to declare what is needed, so arguably more readable
- Can be generated through the Blue Ocean graphical interface
- Contains sections that map to familiar Jenkins concepts, such as notifications
- Better syntax checking and error identification
- Increased consistency across pipelines

A Declarative Pipeline has the following disadvantages:

- Less support for iterative logic (less like a program)
- Still evolving (may not support or have constructs for things you would do in traditional Jenkins)
- More rigid structure (harder to handle custom pipeline code)
- Currently not well suited for more complex pipelines or workflows

In short, the declarative model should be easier to learn and maintain for new pipeline users or those wanting more ready-made functionality like the traditional Jenkins model. This comes at the price of less flexibility to do anything not supported by the structure.

The scripted model offers more flexibility. It provides the "power-user" option, allowing users to do more things with less imposed structure.

But, ultimately, either model can be made to work in most cases.

We'll talk more about declarative syntax and pipelines in Chapter 7, which is devoted to helping you understand that model. In this book, which only aims to provide small examples of specific concepts, we won't worry about the distinctions or differences in syntax. Where I need to explain larger constructs, I'll include examples of both, where it would make a difference.

For now, let's move on to exploring the *systems* that Jenkins can make use of to run these pipelines.

Systems: Masters, Nodes, Agents, and Executors

Regardless of whether we are using scripted or declarative syntax, every Jenkins pipeline has to have one or more systems to execute code on. The term *system* is used here as a generic way to describe all of the items we're talking about. Keep in mind, though, that there can be multiple instances of Jenkins on any given system or machine.

In traditional Jenkins, there were only two categories: masters and slaves. Those are probably familiar to you. Here's a brief description of similar terms, highlighting some of the main points for comparison.

Master

A Jenkins *master* is the primary controlling system for a Jenkins instance. It has complete access to all Jenkins configuration and options and the full list of jobs. It is the default location for executing jobs if another system is not specified.

However, it is not intended for running any heavyweight tasks. Jobs requiring any substantial processing should be run on a system other than the master.

Another reason for this is that a job running on the master has the master's access to all data, configuration, and operations, which can pose a security risk. It is also important to note that a master system should not have potentially blocking operations executed on it, since it needs to be able to respond and manage operations continuously.

Node

Node is the generic term that is used in Jenkins 2 to mean any system that can run Jenkins jobs. This covers both masters and agents, and is sometimes used in place of those terms. Furthermore, a node might be a container, such as one for Docker.

A master node is always present in any Jenkins installation, but for the reasons already cited, it is not recommended to run jobs on the master node. We'll talk more about how to define nodes in an upcoming section of this chapter.

Agent

An *agent* is the same as what earlier versions of Jenkins referred to as a *slave*. Traditionally in Jenkins, this refers to any nonmaster system. The idea is that these systems are managed by the master system and allocated as needed, or as specified, to handle processing the individual jobs. For example, we might allocate different agents to do different builds for different OS flavors, or we might allocate multiple agents to run in parallel for testing.

In order to simplify the load on these systems and reduce security concerns, typically only a lightweight Jenkins client application with limited access to resources is installed to handle running jobs.

As far as the relationship between agents and nodes goes, agents run on nodes. In a Scripted Pipeline, "node" is used as the term for a system with an agent. In a Declarative Pipeline, specifying a particular agent to use allocates a node.

Directives Versus Steps

There is a high-level distinction we can make between a node and an agent in terms of how they are used in the respective declarative versus scripted syntax.

`node` is associated with a Scripted Pipeline. It is technically a step, meaning something that can be used to cause an action to occur in a pipeline. It allocates an executor on a node with an agent and further runs code that is in its definition block. The following code excerpt shows a simple example of specifying a `node` step:

```
// Scripted Pipeline
node('worker') {
    stage('Source') { // Get code
        // Get code from our Git repository
```

`agent`, on the other hand, is a directive in a Declarative Pipeline. Unless you use the special case `agent none`, it causes a node to be allocated. A simple `agent` declaration is shown here:

```
// Declarative Pipeline
pipeline {
    agent {label:'worker'}
    stages {
        stage('Source') { // Get code
```

Outside of the syntax for the two different pipeline specifications, this distinction is not significant and you can think of them as the same. Just use `node` for Scripted Pipelines and `agent` for Declarative Pipelines.

Executor

Related to all the previous systems are executors. Let's clarify here what Jenkins means with this term.

Basically, an *executor* is just a slot in which to run a job on a node/agent. A node can have zero or more executors. The number of executors defines how many concurrent jobs can be run on that node. When the master funnels jobs to a particular node, there must be an available executor slot in order for the job to be processed immediately. Otherwise, it will wait until an executor becomes available.

The number of executors and other parameters can be configured when creating nodes, the subject of our next section.

Figure 2-1 shows a representation comparing the different kinds of systems we just talked about.

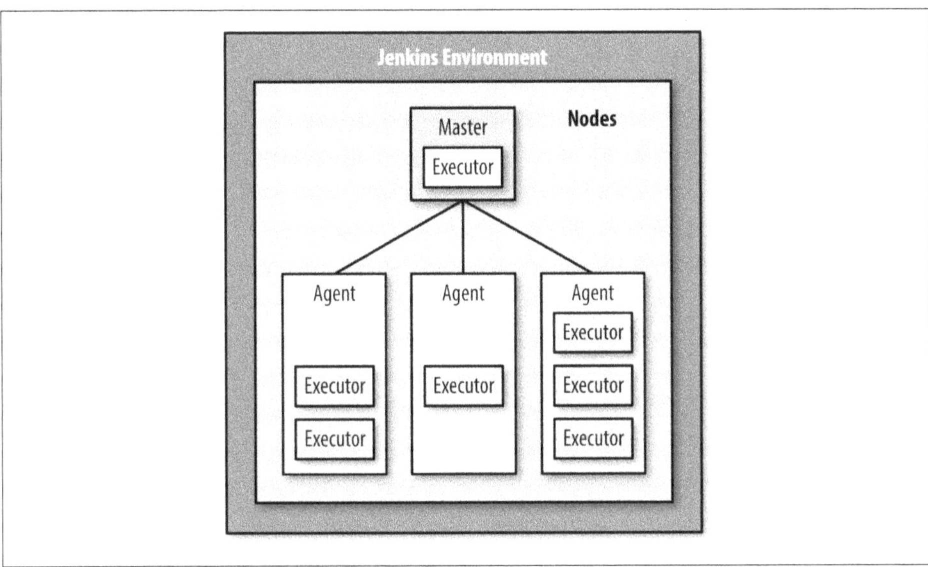

Figure 2-1. Types of systems involved in doing work in Jenkins

Creating Nodes

In traditional versions of Jenkins, jobs would run either on the master instance or on slave instances. As noted previously, in Jenkins 2 terminology these kinds of instances are both referred to by the generic term "node." We can set up new nodes just as we would have set up slaves on legacy Jenkins instances. A quick example follows.

To start with, after logging into Jenkins, go to the Manage Jenkins page and select the Manage Nodes link (Figure 2-2).

Figure 2-2. The Manage Nodes option on the Manage Jenkins page

On the Manage Nodes screen, select New Node and fill in the forms, including the number of executors (see Figures 2-3 and 2-4).

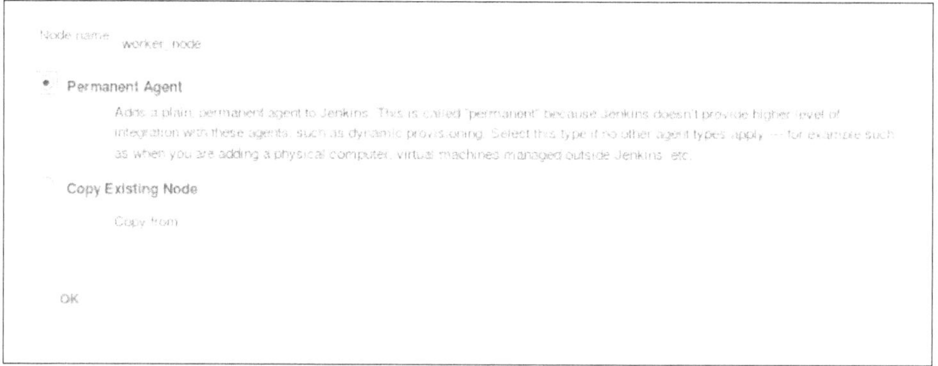

Figure 2-3. Node basics: choosing the node's name and type

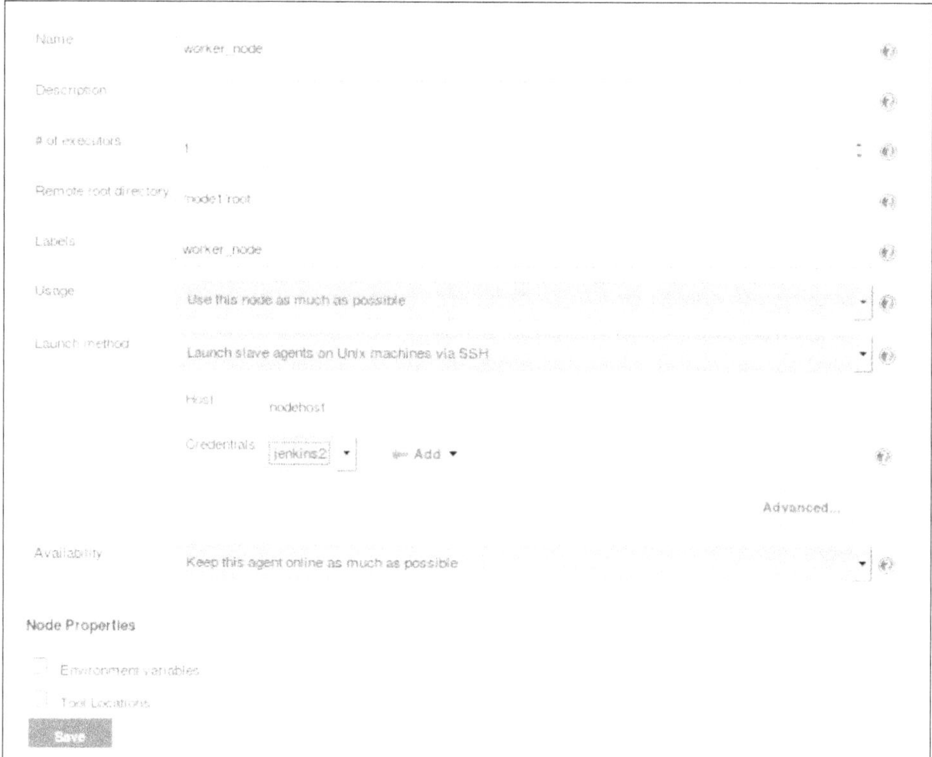

Figure 2-4. Entering parameters to define how the node should be used

If you need to first set up credentials, you can find more information about that in Chapter 5. Notice that you also have checkboxes near the bottom of the page for

"Environment variables" and "Tool Locations." Checking these will allow you to specify particular variables and tools for use on this node. This is only necessary if you need or want to use ones other than those set up on the master.

In the Labels section of the configuration, you can supply multiple labels. Spaces can be included in a label name with quotes around the label.

A quick note about node labels

Labels can be used for both system and user purposes. For example, labels can be used to:

- Identify a specific node (via a unique label).
- Group classes of nodes together (by giving them the same label).
- Identify some characteristic of a node that is useful to know for processing (via a meaningful label, such as "Windows" or "West Coast").

The last bullet is a recommended practice.

These labels can be referenced directly in the pipeline to define where to run code. An example is discussed in "node" on page 32.

For information on the different launch methods and other settings for nodes, consult the online Jenkins documentation.

Once nodes are available to execute code, we can start focusing on creating pipelines. We do this with a structured program using the Jenkins DSL.

Structure: Working with the Jenkins DSL

As previously mentioned, DSL stands for *Domain-Specific Language*, a type of programming language for a particular context. The context in Jenkins is creating pipelines.

The Jenkins DSL, like many others, is written using the Groovy programming language. This is done because of some of the nice features that Groovy provides that make creating DSLs easier than in other languages. However, that also comes with a caution against relying on Groovy aspects too heavily (see the sidebar on the Jenkins DSL and Groovy to follow).

In this section, we'll cover some basic terms and the structure and functionality of a Jenkins DSL pipeline. We'll be talking about this in terms of a Scripted Pipeline (meaning without the enhancements that the declarative functionality adds). In

Chapter 7, we'll explain the differences and look at the changes that creating a Declarative Pipeline entails.

The Jenkins DSL and Groovy

The DSL for Jenkins pipelines is based on the Groovy language (*http://www.groovy-lang.org*).

This means we can use Groovy constructs and idioms in our pipeline code if needed.

Normally, however, we want to avoid using any strictly Groovy code that is too complex, or at least separate it from the main script. The reason is that too much Groovy code makes the script less readable and maintainable by someone who doesn't know Groovy.

Declarative Pipelines prevent the use of nearly all Groovy code outside of their defined structure. They also provide more capabilities that resemble traditional Jenkins features, so you have to resort less to using custom Groovy code.

Leveraging Other Languages

If you need to access/use functions written in Groovy or another language, or ones that involve a more iterative workflow, you can make them part of a shared library, as we'll talk about in Chapter 6. That way they will be abstracted out from your main pipeline code base.

Here's a very simple pipeline expressed in the Jenkins DSL:

```
node ('worker1') {

     stage('Source') { // for display purposes

      // Get some code from our Git repository

      git 'https://github.com/brentlaster/gradle-greetings.git'

      }
}
```

Let's break this down and explain what each part is doing.

node

First, we have the keyword `node`. As mentioned in "Node" on page 27, we can think of this as the new term for a master or agent. Nodes are defined through the Manage Jenkins → Manage Nodes interface and can be set up just like slaves. Each node then has a Jenkins agent installed on it to execute jobs. (Note that in this case we are assuming we have a node already set up on the Jenkins instance labeled `worker1`.)

Nodes and Agents

We previously talked about the difference between nodes and agents in Jenkins terminology. In the context here, we're using *agent* to mean the Jenkins code running on the "nonmaster" nodes.

This line tells Jenkins on which node it should run this part of the pipeline. It binds the code to the particular Jenkins agent program running on that node. A particular one is specified by passing a defined name as a parameter (label). This must be a node or system that has already been defined and that your Jenkins system is aware of. You can omit supplying a label here, but if you omit a label, then you need to be aware of how this will be handled:

- If `master` has been configured as the default node for execution, Jenkins will run the job on `master`. (`master` can be configured to not run any jobs.)
- Otherwise, an empty node label (or `agent any` in declarative syntax) will tell Jenkins to run on the first executor that becomes available on any node.

On the other hand, using multiple names here (with logic operators) is perfectly valid and can make a lot of sense when you need to select nodes based on multiple dimensions (such as location, type, etc.). The following sidebar explains how to take advantage of this functionality.

Leveraging Multiple Labels on a Node

In the configuration for a node, you can assign multiple labels in the Labels entry box. To do this, separate them by spaces. Then, when specifying a node to execute part of your pipeline, you can specify multiple labels using standard logic operands such as `||` for "or" and `&&` for "and."

Why would you do this? Suppose that you had two sets of Linux systems on different coasts of the United States. Depending on the particular processing, you might want some Jenkins jobs sent to one set, and some sent to the other set.

So, in this case, you could add the label `Linux` to all of the nodes and an additional label to indicate where each is located—i.e., `east` or `west`. Once that's done, you could specify which nodes to use by using combinations of operands and labels. For example, to direct a job to run on a Linux node on the East Coast, you could use:

```
node("linux && east") {
```

There are more sophisticated operands available as well, which you'll find if you look in the help for the `node` step.

The braces construct ({}) here is known as a Groovy *closure* and essentially marks the start and end of the block of code associated with this node for this part of the pipeline. Closures also act like entities that can be passed around in a program, with the last statement being the return value. (See the Groovy documentation (*http://groovy-lang.org/closures.html*) for more information about closures.)

When this part of the pipeline is executed, it connects to the node, creates a workspace (working directory) for the code to execute in, and schedules the code to run when an executor is available.

Nodes and Mappings

In addition to defining nodes to run particular stages, nodes can also be associated with mappings to designate where to run other sections of code, such as in the `parallel` structure shown here:

```
parallel (
                win: { node ('win64'){
                  ...
                 }},
                linux: { node ('ubuntu') {
                  ...
                 }},
          )
```

stage

Within a node definition, a `stage` closure allows us to group together individual settings, DSL commands, and logic. A stage is required to have a `name`, which provides a mechanism for describing what the stage does. As of the time of this writing, it doesn't actually do anything in the script but does show up in the output to identify the stage when running a pipeline.

How much of the pipeline's logic goes into a particular stage is up to the developer. However, a general practice is to create stages that mimic the separate pieces of a traditional pipeline. For example, you might have a stage that handles retrieving the source code, one that handles compiling the source code, one that handles running unit tests, one that handles integration tests, and so on. We'll use this sort of structure when we work with example pipelines in the book.

steps

Inside the stage, we have the actual Jenkins DSL commands. These are referred to as *steps* in Jenkins terminology. A step is the lowest level of functionality defined by the DSL. These are not Groovy commands, but can be used with Groovy commands. In the case of our example, we have this initial step to get our source:

```
git 'https://github.com/brentlaster/gradle-greetings.git'
```

This is pretty straightforward to figure out. It calls Git and passes a parameter—the location from which to pull the code (using the secure HTTP protocol). This is using a shorthand format for the full step syntax.

You will be encountering both the shorthand and full step syntax when working with the DSL in scripts, so it's worth taking a moment to better understand the syntax model in more detail.

Understanding step syntax

Steps in the Jenkins DSL always expect mapped (named) parameters. To illustrate this, here's another version of the `git` step definition:

```
git branch: 'test',
    url: 'https://github.com/brentlaster/gradle-greetings.git'
```

Notice that we have two named parameters here, mapped to their intended values: `branch` to `'test'` and `url` to `'http://github.com/brentlaster/gradle-greetings.git'`.

This syntax itself is actually a shorthand notation for a mapping syntax used by Groovy. The *[named parameter: value, named parameter: value]* form equates to the Groovy mapping syntax of *[key: value, key: value]*. The named parameters function as the keys of the map.

Groovy also allows skipping the parentheses for parameters. Without these shortcuts, the longer version of our step would be:

```
git([branch: 'test',
   url: 'http://github.com/brentlaster/gradle-greetings.git'])
```

Another trick is this: if there is a single required parameter, and only one value is passed, the parameter name can be omitted. This is how we arrive at our short version of the step as:

```
git 'https://github.com/brentlaster/gradle-greetings.git'
```

The required `url` parameter here is the only one we needed to provide in this case.

If a named parameter is not required, then the default parameter is the `script` object. An example here is with the `bat` step, which is used to run batch or shell processing on Windows system. Writing this with the full syntax would look like this:

```
bat([script: 'echo hi'])
```

Taking into account the shortcuts that are offered, this can simply be written as:

```
bat 'echo hi'
```

Figure 2-5 shows a graphical representation of the relationship between nodes, stages, and steps.

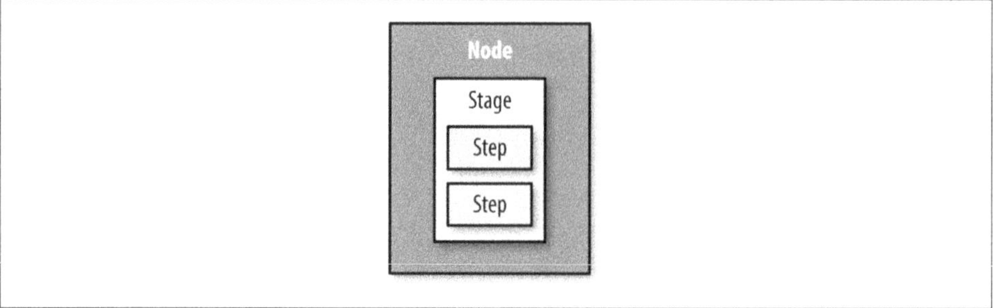

Figure 2-5. Relationship between nodes, stages, and steps

Now that we understand the basic structure of a Scripted Pipeline, let's examine the process of creating a pipeline job in Jenkins and using the associated tools to create a script.

Supporting Environment: Developing a Pipeline Script

In all versions of Jenkins, you begin a new project by creating a new item of a particular type. Jenkins 2 supports an integrated project type of "Pipeline." This type of project creates an environment to develop code to define a pipeline. As you start to work with this type of project, it will be beneficial to understand how to set it up and how to use the environment to create, edit, run, and monitor your pipelines.

A pipeline script in Jenkins can either be created within a Jenkins job of type *Pipeline* or as an external file named *Jenkinsfile*. If created as a Jenkinsfile, then it can be stored with the source. While learning about creating DSL scripts here, we'll use the approach of creating a script in a pipeline job. Creating a Jenkinsfile can be done in any editor, or it can even be copied from the pipeline job. However, there may need to be adjustments made for actions such as calling external routines. We'll look at those considerations more when we discuss Jenkinsfiles in detail in Chapter 10.

Starting a Pipeline Project

When you select Pipeline as the type of project to create, you're presented with a familiar web-based form for a new Jenkins project. Each major section of the form has a tab associated with it. You start out on the General tab (Figure 2-6).

Tabs and Navigation

The tabs for sections make it easier to jump between the major sections of the page. However, you can still scroll to the individual sections as well.

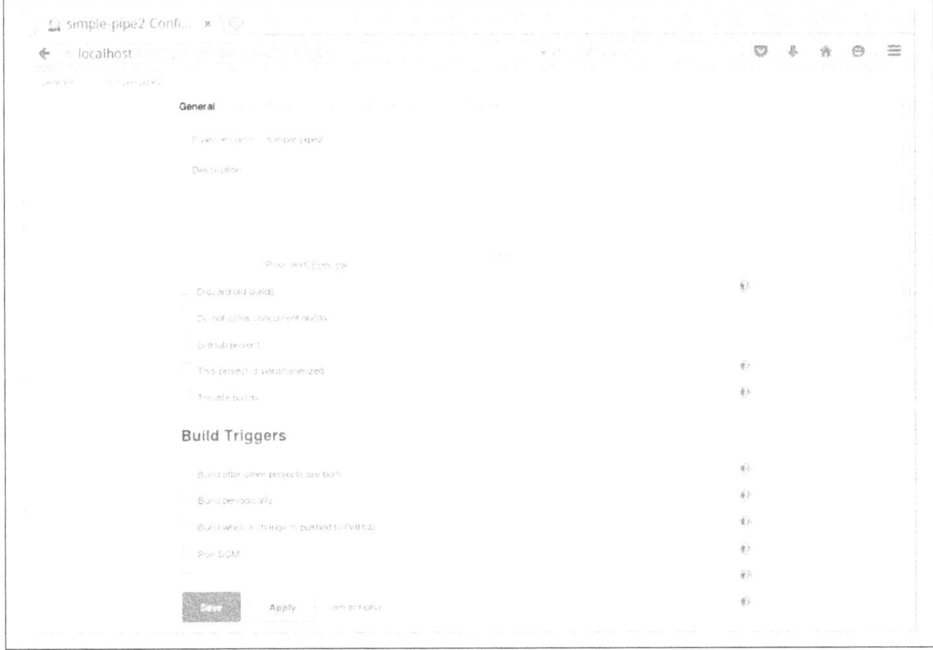

Figure 2-6. The General tab of a new Pipeline project

This tab should look familiar if you've used Jenkins before. You can configure any of these sections as needed or not. The main tab we are interested in for our new Pipeline project is the Pipeline tab. Switching to that presents a text entry screen where we can enter the code for our pipeline script. Figure 2-7 shows an example of the tab with a simple pipeline script typed in.

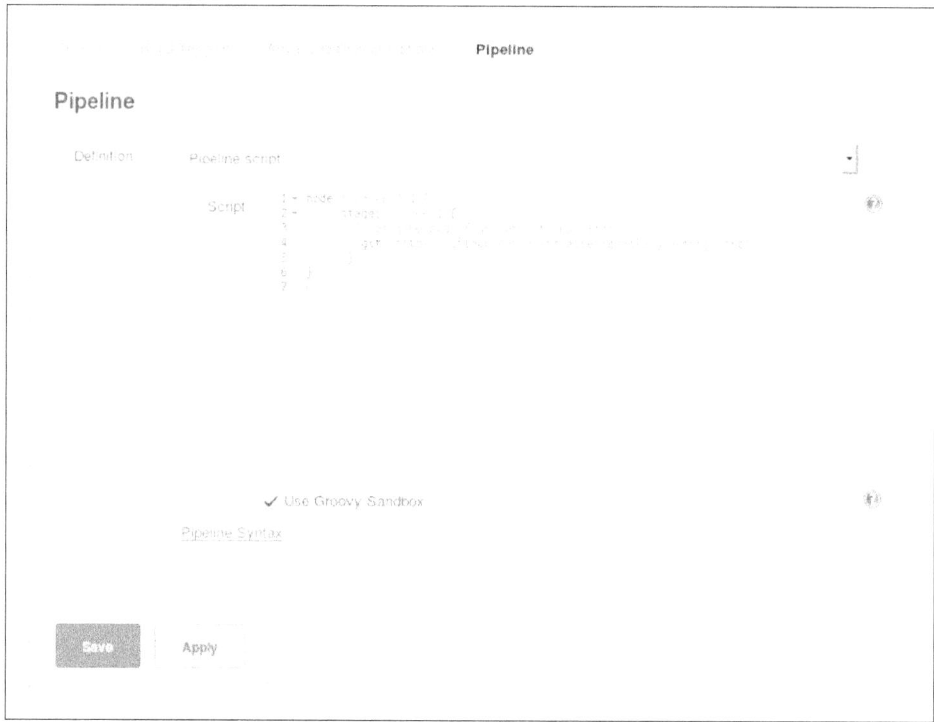

Figure 2-7. Pipeline tab with a simple script example

The code for our pipeline is entered through the built-in Jenkins editor.

Visual Editor

With the advent of the new Blue Ocean interface and Declarative Pipelines, a visual pipeline editor is available in Jenkins. The Blue Ocean interface and editor are discussed in Chapter 9.

The Editor

As you begin to work with the editor, there a couple of features that are helpful to be aware of:

Syntax checking
: Where possible, the editor will make an attempt to check for valid Groovy syntax and references. As Figure 2-8 shows, it will mark any problems it finds with a red square with an "X" in it beside the offending line.

Figure 2-8. Error indications in the pipeline script window

However, it is possible that not all the errors flagged are actual errors—in some cases the script may not have been able to yet resolve a dependency or an import that was recently created, although this is the exception rather than the rule.

Extended error information
: While the "X" indicator provides a quick visual way to identify lines with problems, it is not very informative beyond that. You can see more information by hovering over the "X." When you do this, a pop-up is displayed with the full text of the error (Figure 2-9).

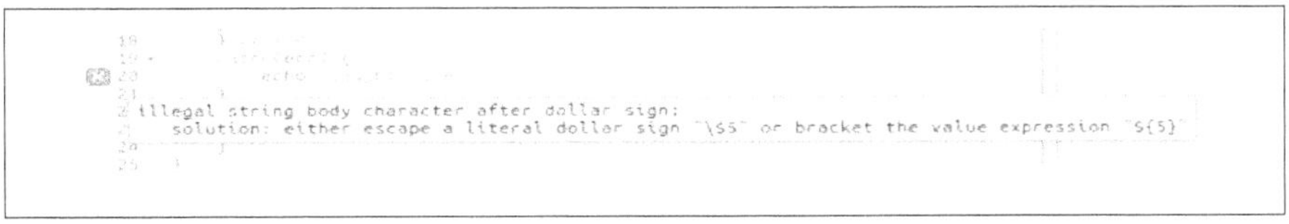

Figure 2-9. Hovering displays the full text of the error message

Autocomplete
: The editor also includes autocomplete functionality for items like brackets. That is, if you type an opening bracket, {, the editor will automatically insert (after a space) a corresponding closing bracket, } (Figure 2-10). This is a convenient feature, but can also trip you up until you get accustomed to it. The reason is that if you're in the habit of always typing a closing bracket and one is inserted for you, you'll end up with an extra bracket in your program that won't compile.

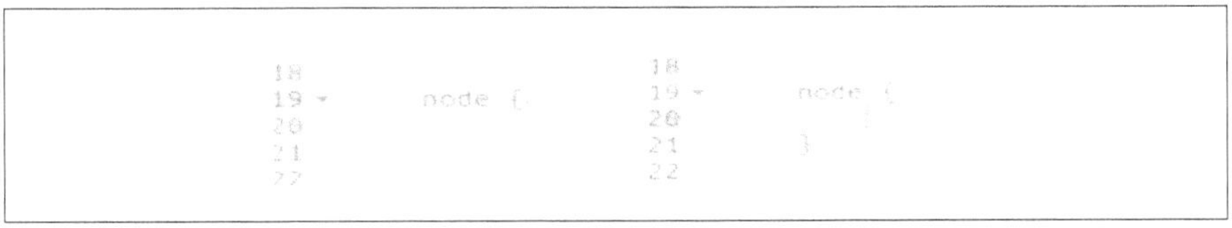

Figure 2-10. Autocompletion of brackets

Outside of the editor, we have an additional tool to help us get the syntax correct. It's called the Snippet Generator.

Working with the Snippet Generator

Switching from a form-based web interface for configuring jobs and pipelines to using a DSL script has many advantages—but having to know the right step and syntax to use for each task is not one of those. For some cases, such as our simple `git` step from earlier, the syntax and parameters may be fairly intuitive, but for others, not so much. To simplify finding the correct semantics and syntax for steps, Jenkins 2 includes a pipeline syntax help wizard, also known as the *Snippet Generator*.

Snippet Generator Content

The Snippet Generator content is seeded and updated based on definitions of pipeline steps added by plugins. If a plugin provides a pipeline-compatible step, that is included in the Snippet Generator. This also means the content of the Snippet Generator on any particular Jenkins instance is a function of what plugins are installed on that instance.

The Snippet Generator provides a way to search through the available DSL steps and find out the syntax and semantics of ones you are interested in. Additionally, it provides online help to explain what the step is intended to do. But perhaps the most useful option it provides is a web form with areas to enter values for the parameters you want to use. You can then, with the push of a button, generate the needed Groovy DSL code to call the step. Once you have that, it's a simple cut and paste to get it into your program. This greatly simplifies trying to figure out how to use a particular step.

Let's work through a simple example to see how this works. Suppose we want to create the earlier step to retrieve our Git code. Figure 2-11 shows our starting point.

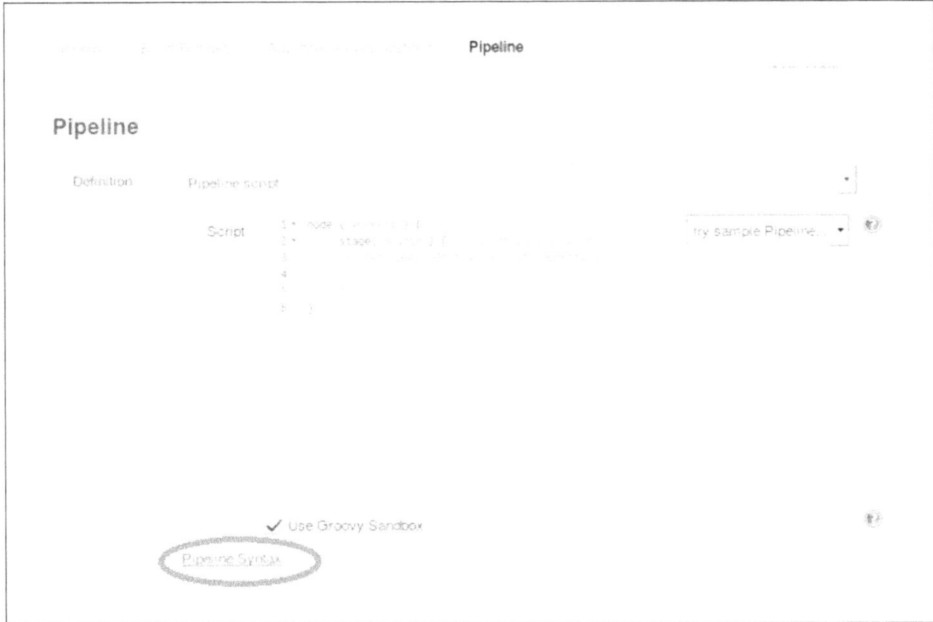

Figure 2-11. Code block for source pull

We know we want to use Git, but we're not sure of the syntax, so we click the Pipeline Syntax link at the bottom of the Pipeline tab's window, as shown in Figure 2-12. This takes us to the opening screen for the Snippet Generator.

Figure 2-12. The Snippet Generator

From here, we can select the "git" step from the Sample Step drop-down, as seen in Figure 2-13. This brings up additional fields for the named parameters that we can supply to the step. We can then accept the defaults for those parameters or set them to specific values as needed. Finally, we click the button to generate the pipeline script. As the figure shows, this results in the simple `git` step we saw earlier.

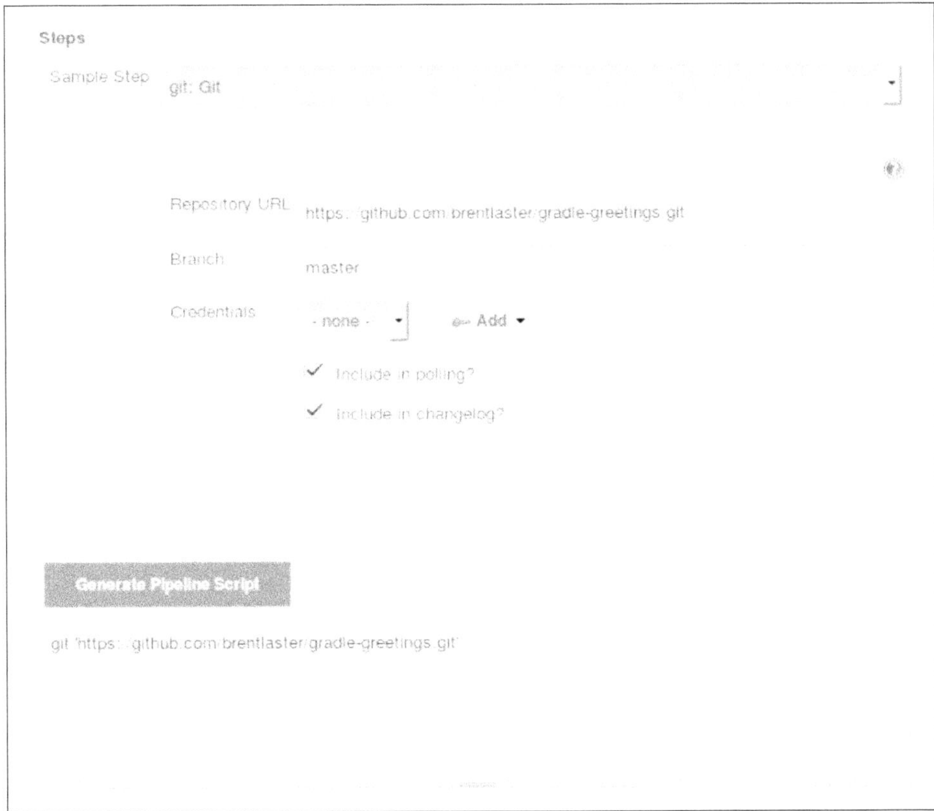

Figure 2-13. Generating pipeline code for the git step with defaults

Putting this into our `stage` closure, we end up with this:

```
stage('Source') {
 // Get some code from our Git repository
     git 'https://github.com/brentlaster/gradle-greetings.git'
}
```

If, on the other hand, we choose to override the defaults, our step changes to reflect passing those overrides (Figure 2-14). Notice that, in this case, overriding those values requires unchecking the checkboxes.

Steps

Sample Step git: Git

Repository URL https://github.com/brentlaster/gradle-greetings.git

Branch test

Credentials jenkins2 Add

Include in polling?

Include in changelog?

Generate Pipeline Script

git branch: 'test', changelog: false, credentialsId: 'jenkins2-ssh', poll: false, url: 'https://github.com/brentlaster/gradle-greetings.git'

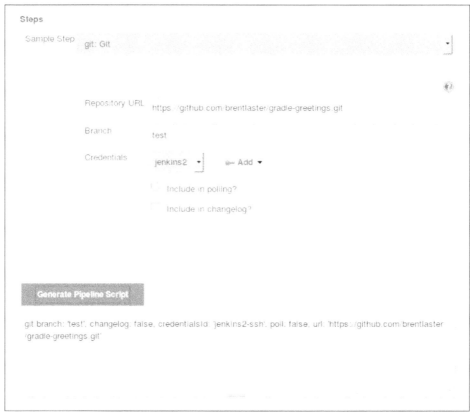

Figure 2-14. Overriding default values for the git step

Any time multiple parameters are specified, they must all be named. As with the previous example, this code could be directly copied and pasted into a script to use.

Polling and Changelog Options

In case you are wondering, setting `poll` to `false` means that changes in the source management repository will not be automatically detected and rebuilt. Without this set to `false`, after an initial run, *and* if polling is configured for the job, changes in the source management repository will be detected and cause another run of the job.

Setting the `changelog` option to `false` means that Jenkins will not compute the changes that initiated a new run (and thus they will not show up in the `Changes` section of the job output). The only benefit of doing this is that it reduces some load on the SCM.

Running a Pipeline

With code entered, we're ready to run our pipeline. Pipelines are made up of several stages, such as compilation, integration testing, analysis, etc. It was typical in past versions of Jenkins to set up the different parts as separate Freestyle jobs and chain them together by having one job kick off another job when it finished.

Over the years, plugins were created to help visualize the flow of these jobs representing the stages. One of the common ones used was the *Build Pipeline* plugin. This plugin allowed for setting up special views that displayed a series of jobs in a pipeline as a connected set of boxes. The boxes were color-coded depending on the current activity happening in them: blue for the job not having been run yet, yellow for the job in progress, green for a successful run, and red for a failed run. Figure 2-15 shows what this looked like.

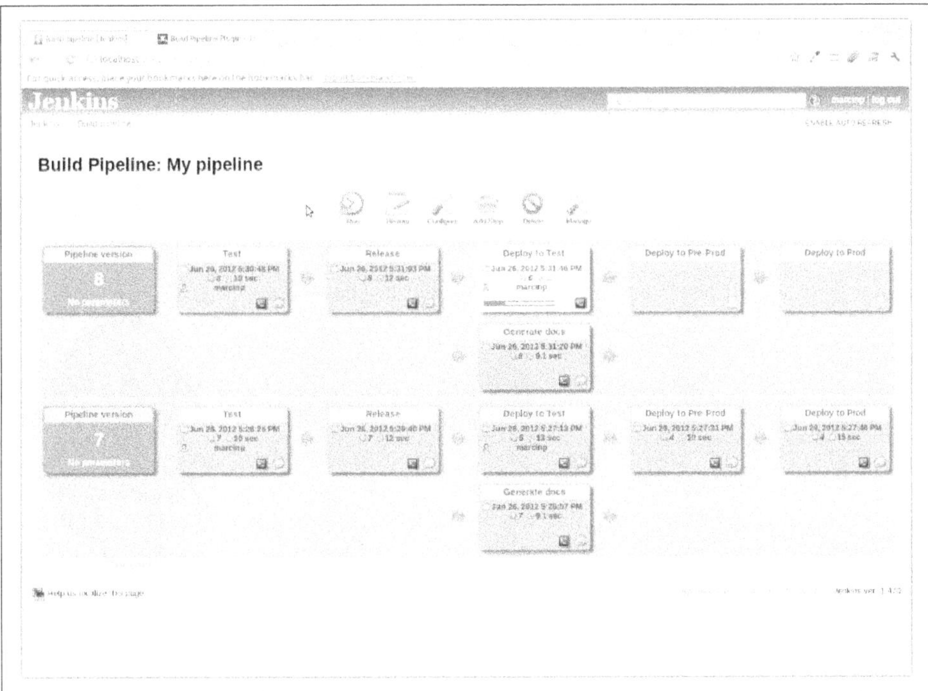

Figure 2-15. The original Build Pipeline plug-in

In Jenkins 2, we have the Pipeline project type for scripting an entire pipeline. We can represent the larger pieces of the pipeline via `stage{}` blocks, as we did for the `git` command previously. To illustrate this, let's add another stage to our pipeline. To keep things simple for now (since we haven't covered using globally configured tools in pipelines yet), we'll just add a placeholder for the build step.

To do this, we add another stage definition and insert a call to the `sh` step to echo out a message ("sh" stands for "shell," and this allows us to make calls to the OS on *nix systems; the corresponding command for Windows systems is `bat`):

```
node ('worker1') {
     stage('Source') {
      // Get some code from our Git repository
         git 'https://github.com/brentlaster/gradle-greetings.git'
     }
     stage('Build') {
      // TO-DO: Execute the gradle build associated with this project
         sh 'echo gradle build will go here'
     }
}
```

Figure 2-16 shows the script in the Pipeline tab.

Figure 2-16. Script in the Pipeline tab

When we first save this pipeline, the UI reminds us that we haven't run it yet with a message (Figure 2-17): "No data available. This Pipeline has not yet run." Note the heading above it that reads "Stage View"—this is the new default pipeline output view in Jenkins 2.

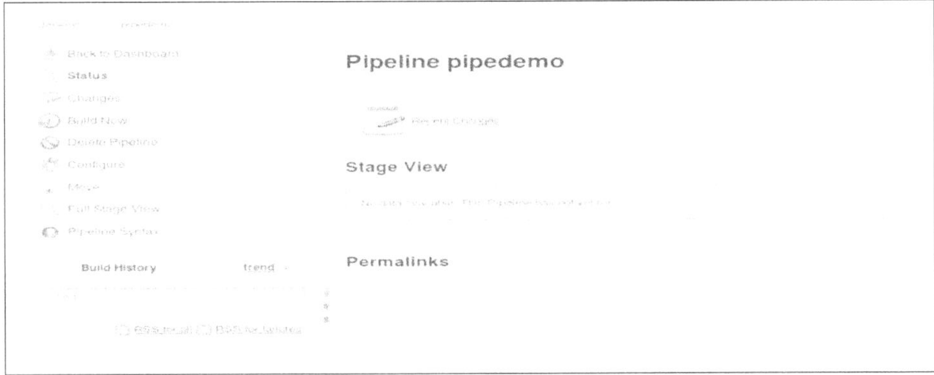

Figure 2-17. Before the first run

If we click Build Now in the menu on the left, Jenkins executes the pipeline build. In our case, everything is successful. Notice the representation of the job execution as tiles in the Stage View output in Figure 2-18. The tiles are green, indicating success. More explanation of how to interpret this view follows.

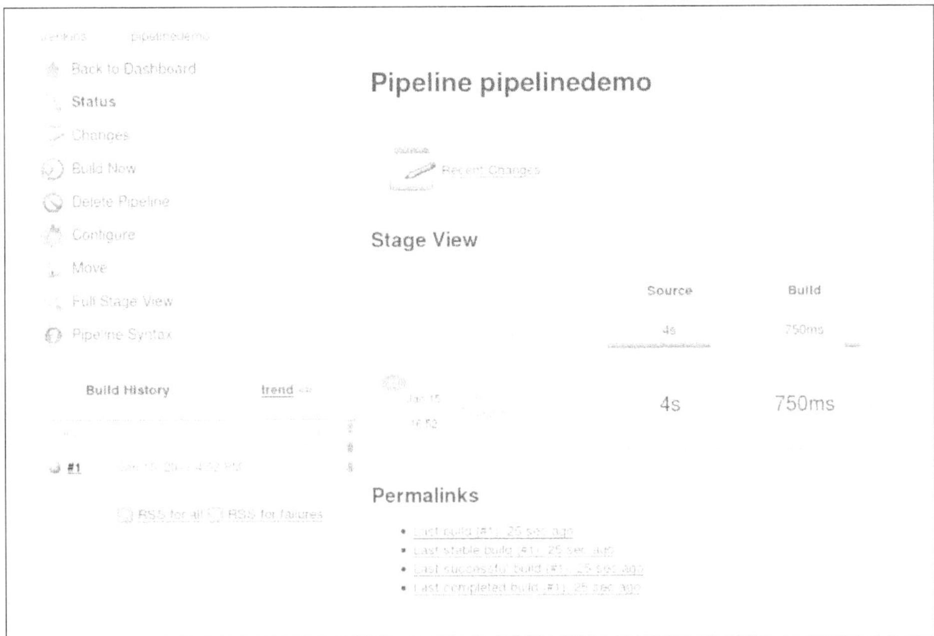

Figure 2-18. Successful first run

In each build, for each stage in the pipeline, Jenkins creates a new tile. Each row represents a build of the project and each column represents a stage in the pipeline, so each tile represents one run of a particular stage. Note that the text that was passed as the parameter (`name`) to the `stage` step in our code is listed at the top of each column. The amount of time the processing in the stage took to execute is shown inside the tile.

As we alluded to, the color of the tiles is significant as well. The general meanings for the color codes are shown in Table 2-1.

Table 2-1. Color processing legend

Color	Meaning
Blue stripes	Processing in progress
White	Stage has not been run yet
Rose stripes	Stage failed
Green	Stage succeeded
Rose	Stage succeeded but some other stage failed downstream

Color Changes When Processing

Even though a tile may be green at one point, it can still change to the rose color later if a downstream stage fails.

Viewing logs

As with traditional Jenkins, you can view the console output by clicking on either the Console Output link or the colored ball next to the build in the Build History window.

The Stage View also provides a shortcut for seeing the logs related to any particular stage for a particular run of a build. Simply hover over the tile representing the build and stage that you're interested in and click the Logs button in the block that appears, and you'll get a pop-up showing the stage logs. Figures 2-19 and 2-20 illustrate the steps in the process.

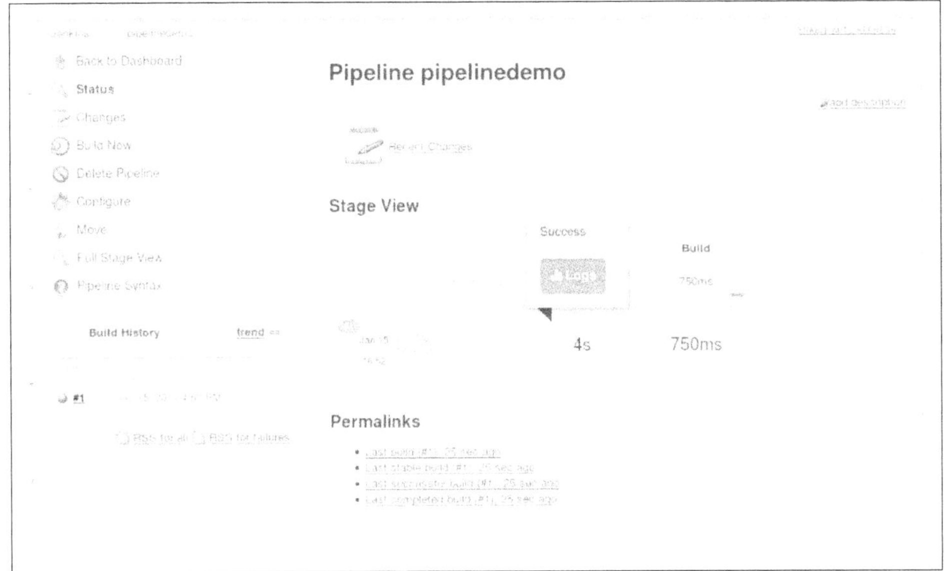

Figure 2-19. Hover over a tile to get the pop-up with the Logs button

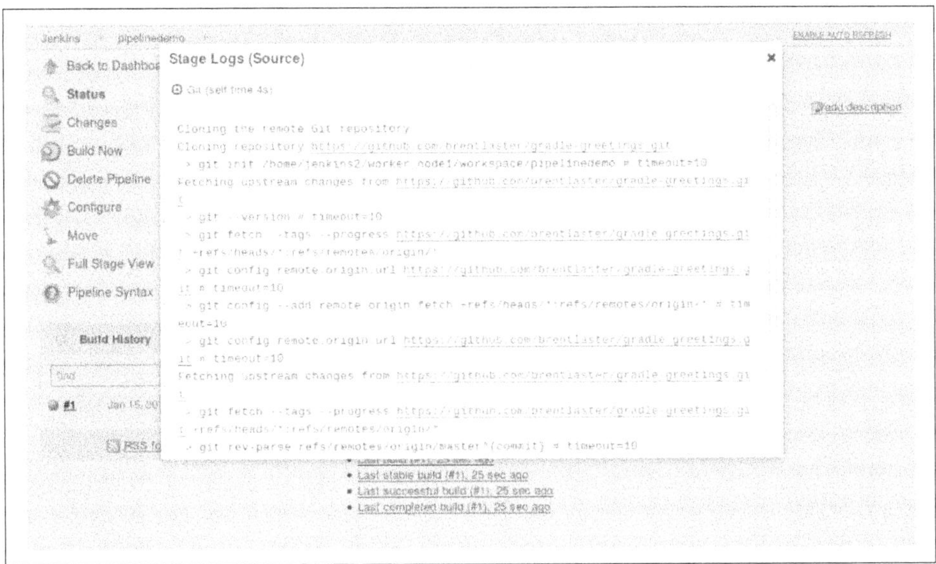

Figure 2-20. Click on the Logs button to get the pop-up with the actual logs for the stage

Jenkins Pop-ups and Autorefresh

Since the log window is a pop-up window, you may want to disable the autorefresh feature, if it is turned on, so that it doesn't automatically dismiss the pop-up window with the log in it. (This is done by clicking DISABLE AUTO REFRESH in the upper-right corner.)

Stage View with errors

Now let's see what the Stage View looks like when we have errors. Assume that our code was running on a Windows system instead of Linux. There would have been only one small change in our pipeline; instead of:

```
sh 'echo gradle build will go here'
```

the line would be:

```
bat  'echo gradle build will go here'
```

Now suppose that we had copied over the code with the `bat` command exactly to a Linux system. When we tried to build it, we would get a Stage View that looked something like Figure 2-21.

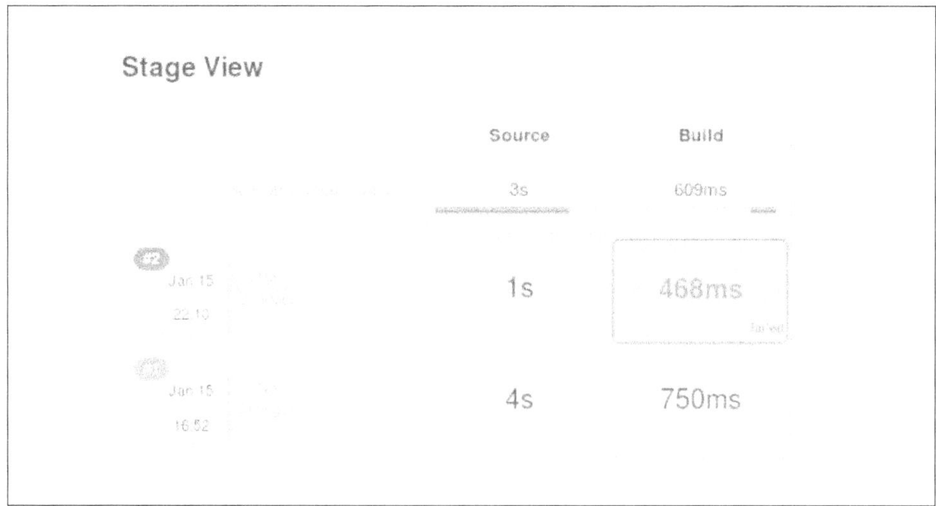

Figure 2-21. Stage View with errors

Notice that the second run added another row to our matrix. The row at the top represents the stages in the latest run. The striped color of the Build tile in the top row indicates that that stage failed (and thus our run failed). The lighter solid rose color of the Source stage indicates that it succeeded but another stage downstream failed.

When an Earlier Stage Fails

If the Source stage had failed, the Build stage would not have been attempted. In that case, the Source stage would have been striped and the Build stage would have been white.

To see the error, we can apply the same steps as before. When we hover over the failed tile, we again get a pop-up displaying the link to the logs—but notice that it also has information about what failed. At the top of the pop-up is the text "Failed with the following error(s) Windows Batch Script Batch scripts can only be run on Windows nodes." Figure 2-22 displays this condition.

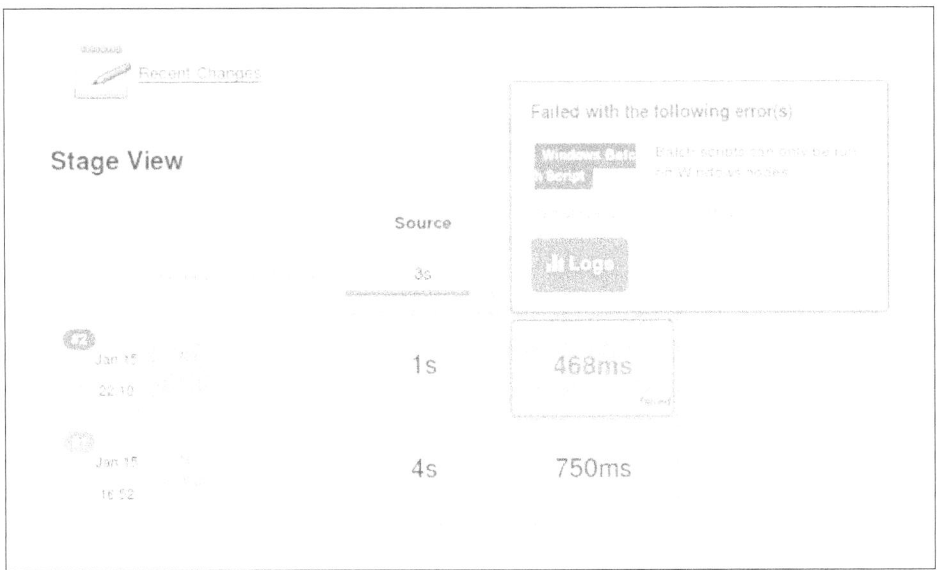

Figure 2-22. Viewing the failures in one stage

Jenkins attempts to display meaningful information about the failure in the pop-up. We could click on the Logs button and open up the log, but in this case, we wouldn't get more information. The first executable statement in this stage is the one that is failing, so there's no further execution information to log.

This essentially completes our quick tour of Jenkins 2 and the basic features you need to be aware of when coding pipelines. But there is one more feature that Jenkins provides to allow you to experiment and try things out without having to change your saved pipeline code. That feature is called *Replay*.

Replay

Coding pipelines is more involved than web form interaction with Jenkins. There may be times where something fails and you want to retry it in a temporary way without modifying your code. Or you may want to prototype a change and try it out before committing to it. Jenkins 2 includes functionality called Replay for such cases. Replay allows you to modify your code after a run, and then run it again with the modifications. A new build record of that run is kept, but the original code remains unchanged.

We can see how that works using our current failure. Suppose we think the right step to use is `sh`, but we want to try it out before changing our code. First we switch to the Console Output for the job, and then we select Replay in the lefthand menu as shown in Figure 2-23.

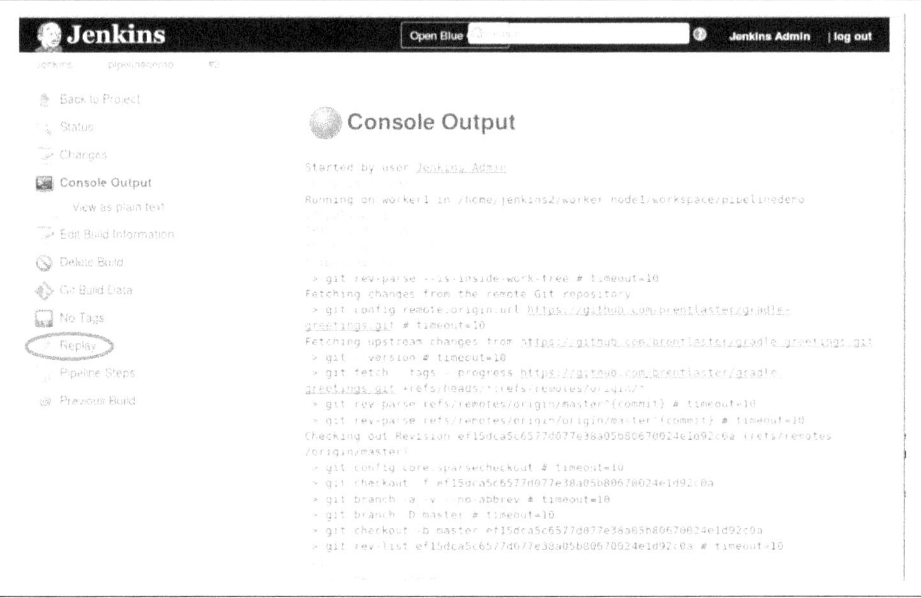

Figure 2-23. Location of the Replay menu item

Now Jenkins presents us with an edit window just like the one for the Pipeline tab of a Pipeline project (Figure 2-24). In this window, we can make any changes to our program that we want and then select Run to try out the changes. (Here, we're changing `bat` back to `sh`.)

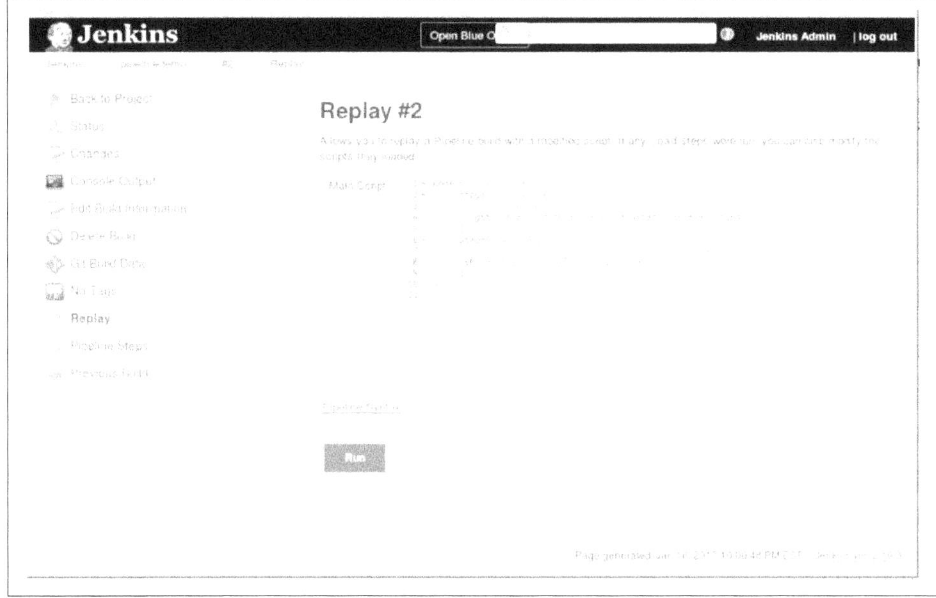

Figure 2-24. Instituting a replay for a failed run

Jenkins will attempt to run the edited code in the Replay window. In this case it will succeed, creating run #3 (Figure 2-25).

Replay and Source Code Versions

Be aware that, at least at the time of this writing, if you use a direct SCM step (such as `git`) in your pipeline code, replays will always pull the latest code from the SCM repository, even if you are replaying an earlier run. If the code is using the more generic `checkout scm` step in a Jenkinsfile (discussed in Chapter 10), then a replay will pull the code that was current at the time of the run.

Pipeline Testing Framework

A question that frequently comes up for both new and experienced pipeline users is whether there are frameworks available to test pipelines. In early 2017, work was begun on an independent unit testing framework for pipelines called Jenkins Pipeline Unit. As of fall 2017, that framework has been incorporated officially into the Jenkins Project. You can find the latest code and documentation on GitHub (*http://bit.ly/2HCTCg3*).

What does it do? From the project description: "This testing framework lets you write unit tests on the configuration and conditional logic of the pipeline code, by providing a mock execution of the pipeline. You can mock built-in Jenkins commands, job configurations, see the stacktrace of the whole execution and even track regressions."

Examples on the documentation page show ways to test functions used in pipelines, including shared libraries. The basic execution mechanism is to import the pipeline unit classes into your Gradle or Maven projects and execute them in a way similar to JUnit tests. The basic testing functionality allows producing tracebacks that can be programmatically searched and compared for regressions.

The project has a good working premise and is promising. It is currently not intuitive to use, however, as it requires wrapping pipeline code in a job or structure that emulates an external routine that can be loaded and executed. It's also important to note that most pipeline steps will need to be mocked via special mapping code.

In its current state, while a valid option, this framework is challenging for the typical user to make use of and looks poised for refining, so we do not cover it in more detail here. Going forward, since it has been transferred to Jenkins community ownership, we expect this project to grow in ease of use and utility and provide even more value for pipeline authors.

Summary

In this chapter, we walked through the foundational concepts needed to start working with Jenkins 2. From a high level, we explored the differences between two syntactical models (Scripted Pipelines and Declarative Pipelines), disambiguated the different types of systems that pipelines can be executed on, examined the core structure expected in Scripted Pipelines, and walked through the supporting environment and tools that Jenkins provides for developing our pipelines.

This information should provide a solid basis for you to use in your work and to explore the remaining content of the book. We'll be diving into more details in the following chapters, with the assumption that you have the knowledge from this chapter. Feel free to refer back to it as many times as needed as you begin using Jenkins 2 and creating your pipelines-as-code.

In the next chapter, we'll move from exploring the structure of pipelines to understanding the flow of execution through the pipeline, and the different ways we can control and direct that.

CHAPTER 3

Pipeline Execution Flow

Working with the legacy Jenkins web interface and items such as Freestyle jobs, our ability to control the flow of processing was limited. Typically, this would take the form of *job chaining*—having jobs kick off other jobs when they completed. Or we might include post-build processing to always do things like send notifications no matter whether the job finished successfully or not.

Beyond that basic functionality, we could also add the Conditional BuildStep plugin (*http://bit.ly/2Hc46zp*) to define more complex flows of build steps based on single or multiple conditions. But even that was limited, compared to the ways we can direct the execution flow when writing programs.

In this chapter, we'll explore the different constructs provided by the Jenkins pipeline DSL for controlling the execution flow in pipelines. We'll start with specifying properties to trigger jobs and how to accept input.

Then we'll look at how to keep things moving through constructs including timeouts, retries, and running tasks in parallel. We'll also look at the constructs available to map the Conditional BuildStep functionality into pipelines.

Finally, we'll see how to use pipeline methods to emulate the post-build processing functionality of traditional Jenkins jobs. Along the way, we'll see how things differ for Scripted and Declarative Pipelines.

Let's get started with defining the properties for triggering jobs.

Triggering Jobs

To specify triggering events for pipeline code, there are three different approaches:

- If working in the Jenkins application itself in a pipeline job, the trigger(s) can be specified in the traditional way within the project's General configuration section in the web interface.
- If creating a Scripted Pipeline, a `properties` block can be specified (usually before the start of the pipeline) that defines the triggers in code. (Note that this properties section will be merged with any properties defined in the web interface, with the web properties taking precedence.)
- If creating a Declarative Pipeline, there is a special `triggers` directive that can be used to define the types of things that should trigger the pipeline.

We'll briefly look at each of the trigger options available in the traditional Jenkins interface, along with the corresponding scripted syntax and declarative syntax (if there is one).

Other Types of Triggering for Special Projects

Note that the triggers discussed here do not apply to Multibranch Pipeline, GitHub organization, or Bitbucket team/project jobs. These types of jobs are identified by having Jenkinsfiles and are triggered otherwise, such as by a webhook that notifies Jenkins when a change is made.

These project types are discussed in more detail in Chapter 8.

Sections on each of the available options for build triggers follow.

Build After Other Projects Are Built

As the name implies, selecting this option allows you to start your project building after one or more other projects. You can choose the ending status you want the builds of the other projects to have (stable, unstable, or failed).

For a Scripted Pipeline, the syntax for building your pipeline after another job, `Job1`, is successful would be like the following:

```
properties([
  pipelineTriggers([
    upstream(
      threshold: hudson.model.Result.SUCCESS,
      upstreamProjects: 'Job1'
    )
```

```
    ])
])
```

If you need to list multiple jobs, separate them with commas. If you need to specify a branch for a job (as for a multibranch job), add a slash after the job name and then the branch name (as in `'Job1/master'`).

Build Periodically

This option provides a *cron* type of functionality to start jobs at certain time intervals. While this is an option for builds, this is not optimal for continuous integration, where the builds are based on detecting updates in source management. But it may have use in other types of applications for Jenkins, such as starting jobs at particular intervals to avoid collisions for resources. (Related: See the discussion on the `H` symbol in the "Cron syntax" section.)

Here's an example of the syntax in a Scripted Pipeline. In this case, the job runs at 9 a.m., Monday–Friday:

```
properties([pipelineTriggers([cron('0 9 * * 1-5')])])
```

And here's an example of the syntax in a Declarative Pipeline:

```
triggers { cron(0 9 * * 1-5)
```

This trigger (and the polling one) both make use of the Jenkins cron syntax, which is described next (with examples in the declarative format).

Cron syntax

The cron syntax used in Jenkins is a specification of when (how often) to do something based on five fields, separated by spaces. Each of the fields represents a different unit of time. The five fields are:

MINUTES
: Desired minutes value within the hour (`0-59`).

HOURS
: Desired hours value within the day (`0-23`).

DAYMONTH
: Desired day of the month (`1-31`).

MONTH
: Desired month of the year (`1-12`).

DAYWEEK
: Desired day of the week (`0-7`). Here, `0` and `7` both represent Sunday.

Also, the `*/<value>` syntax can be used in a field to mean "every `<value>`" (as in `*/5` meaning "every 5 minutes").

Additionally, the symbol `H` can be used in any of the fields. This symbol has a special meaning to Jenkins. It tells Jenkins to, within a range, use the hash of the project name to come up with a unique offset value. This value is then added to the lowest value of the range to define when the activity actually starts within the range of values.

The idea with using the symbol is to not have all projects with the same cron values starting at the same time. The offset from the hash serves to stagger the execution of projects that have the same cron timing.

Use of the `H` symbol is encouraged to avoid having projects starting execution at the same time. Note that since the value is a hash of the project name, each value will be different from all others, but will remain the same for that project over time.

The `H` symbol can also have a range attached to it to specify limits on the interval it can pick. See the following note on Advanced cron syntax for more details.

To solidify this a bit more, let's look at some examples:

```
// Start a pipeline execution at 15 minutes past the hour
triggers { cron(15 * * * *) }

// Scan for SCM changes at 20-minute intervals
triggers { pollSCM(*/20 * * * *) }

// Start a pipeline session at some point between
// 0 and 30 minutes after the hour
triggers { cron(H(0,30) * * * *) }

// Start a pipeline execution at 9 a.m. Monday through Friday
triggers { cron(0 9 * * 1-5) }
```

Advanced cron Syntax

The help for building periodically in Jenkins contains some advanced cron syntax examples, excerpted below.

The `H` symbol can be used with a range. For example, `H H(0-7) * * *` means some time between 12:00 AM (midnight) to 7:59 AM. You can also use step intervals with `H`, with or without ranges.

The `H` symbol can be thought of as a random value over a range, but it actually is a hash of the job name, not a random function, so that the value remains stable for any given project.

Beware that for the day of month field, short cycles such as `*/3` or `H/3` will not work consistently near the end of most months, due to variable month lengths. For example, `*/3` will run on the 1st, 4th, ...31st days of a long month, then again the next day of the next month. Hashes are always chosen in the 1–28 range, so `H/3` will produce a gap between runs lasting from 3 to 6 days at the end of a month. (Longer cycles will also have inconsistent lengths but the effect may be relatively less noticeable.)

Empty lines and lines that start with # will be ignored as comments.

In addition, `@yearly`, `@annually`, `@monthly`, `@weekly`, `@daily`, `@midnight`, and `@hourly` are supported as convenient aliases. These use the hash system for automatic balancing. For example, `@hourly` is the same as `H * * * *` and could mean at any time during the hour. `@midnight` actually means some time between 12:00 AM and 2:59 AM.

Examples:

```
# every fifteen minutes (perhaps at :07, :22, :37, :52)
H/15 * * * *

# every ten minutes in the first half of every hour
# (three times, perhaps at :04, :14, :24)
H(0-29)/10 * * * *

# once every two hours at 45 minutes past the hour
# starting at 9:45 AM and finishing at 3:45 PM every
# weekday
45 9-16/2 * * 1-5

# once in every two hours slot between 9 AM and 5 PM
# every weekday (perhaps at 10:38 AM, 12:38 PM,
# 2:38 PM, 4:38 PM)
H H(9-16)/2 * * 1-5

# once a day on the 1st and 15th of every month except
# December
H H 1,15 1-11 *
```

GitHub Hook Trigger for GitSCM Polling

A GitHub project configured as the source location in a Jenkins project can have a push hook (on the GitHub side) to trigger a build for the Jenkins project. When this is in place, a push to the repository causes the hook to fire and trigger Jenkins, which then invokes the Jenkins SCM polling functionality. So the SCM polling functionality has to be configured for this to work as well.

Most of the initial work for this is in the setup for the hook side and in the source setup in the Jenkins project. More information is available on the Jenkins wiki (*http://bit.ly/2HM7a6z*).

The syntax for setting the property in a Scripted Pipeline is as follows:

```
properties([pipelineTriggers([githubPush()])])
```

There currently isn't a specific syntax for Declarative Pipelines.

Poll SCM

This is the standard polling functionality that periodically scans the source control system for updates. If any updates are found, then the job processes the changes. This can be a very expensive operation (in terms of system resources) depending on the SCM, how much content is scanned, and how often.

Specifying the values for this uses the same Jenkins cron syntax as is used for the "build periodically" option.

The syntax for Scripted Pipelines is as follows (polling every 30 minutes):

```
properties([pipelineTriggers([pollSCM('*/30 * * * *')])])
```

The corresponding syntax for Declarative Pipelines would be this:

```
triggers { pollSCM(*/30 * * * *) }
```

Quiet Period

The value specified here serves as a "wait time" or offset between when the build is triggered (an update is detected) and when Jenkins acts on it. This can be useful for staggering jobs that frequently have changes at the same time, for example. If a value is not provided here, the value from the global configuration is used.

While the pipeline `build` step has a `quietPeriod` option, as of this writing, there isn't a direct pipeline option or step to do this. You may be able to achieve a similar effect by using the `throttle()` step from the Throttle Concurrent Builds plugin (*http://bit.ly/2Hf0pJs*).

Trigger Builds Remotely

This allows for triggering builds by accessing a specific URL for the given job on the Jenkins system. This is useful for triggering builds via a hook or a script. An authorization token is required. For an example, see the note on "URLs and Crumbs" later in this chapter.

In the pipeline-as-code semantics, Multibranch Pipelines can be triggered via changes in a Jenkinsfile. See Chapter 8 for more details on those.

After being triggered, certain stages of a pipeline may request or require input from a user for purposes such as verification, or to direct processing down one of multiple paths. We'll look next at how to handle collecting that input in our pipelines.

User Input

A key aspect of some Jenkins jobs is the ability to change their behavior based on user input. Jenkins offers a wide variety of parameters for gathering specific kinds of input. Jenkins pipelines provide constructs for this as well.

The DSL step `input` is the way we get user input through a pipeline. The step accepts the same kinds of parameters as a regular Jenkins job for a Scripted Pipeline. For a Declarative Pipeline, there is a special `parameters` directive that supports a subset of those parameters.

We describe this step and the parameters, as they can be used in the pipeline, next.

input

As the name suggests, the `input` step allows your pipeline to stop and wait for a user response. Here's a simple example:

```
input 'Continue to next stage?'
```

This step can also optionally take parameters to gather additional information. Within the Jenkins application, the default form is to print a message and offer the user a choice of "Proceed" or "Abort." In the GUI Stage View, this will be a dialog box that looks like Figure 3-1. In the console output, this will be a line of output with links to click on to continue or stop (Figure 3-2).

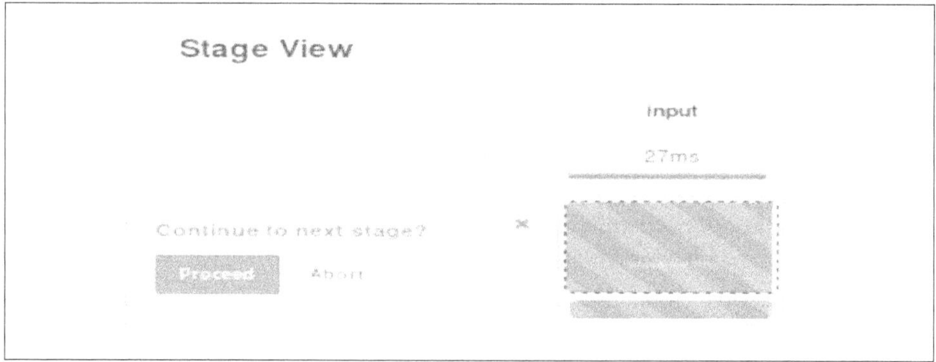

Figure 3-1. GUI prompt for input

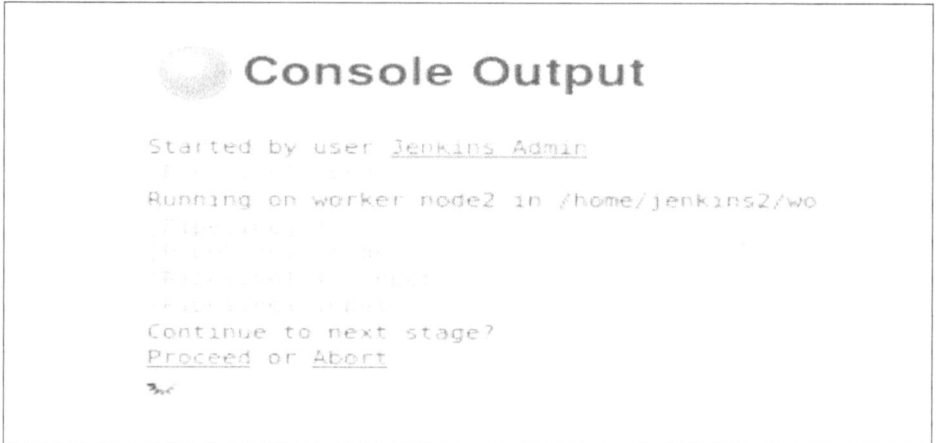

Figure 3-2. Console prompt for input

Choosing Proceed allows the pipeline to continue. Choosing Abort causes the pipeline to stop at that point with a status of "aborted."

It is important to note that when the system executes an `input` step, the processing is paused on that node. This can lead to monopolizing system resources, as explained in the following warning.

The input Step and Executors

As defined earlier in the book, an *executor* is a slot on a node for processing code. Using the `input` step in a `node` block ties up the executor for the node until the `input` step is done.

The `input` step can have several parameters. These include:

Message (`message`)
: The message to be displayed to the user, as demonstrated in the previous example. Can also be empty, as indicated by `input ''`.

Custom ID (`id`)
: An ID that can be used to identify your `input` step to automated or external processing, such as when you want to respond via a REST API call. A unique identifier will be generated if you don't supply one.

  As an example, you could add the custom ID, `ctns-prompt` (for "Continue to next stage" prompt) to our `input` step definition. The `input` step would then look as follows:

```
input id: 'ctns-prompt', message: 'Continue to the next stage?'
```

  Given this step, when you run the job, a `POST` to this URL could be used to respond. The URL format would be:

```
http://[jenkins-base-url]/job/[job_name]/[build_id]/input/Ctns-prompt/
proceedEmpty
```

  to tell Jenkins to proceed without any input, or:

```
http://[jenkins-base-url]/job/[job_name]/[build_id]/input/Ctns-prompt/
abort
```

  to tell Jenkins to abort. (Notice that the parameter name is capitalized in the URL.)

URLs and Crumbs

If your Jenkins is configured to prevent Cross-Site Request Forgery (CSRF) exploits via the Security settings (strongly recommended), then any URL used to POST will need to also include a CSRF protection token.

One way to do this is to first define an environment variable to get the token:

```
CSRF_TOKEN=
 $(curl -s 'http://<username>:<password
 or token>@<jenkins base
 url>/crumbIssuer/api/xml?xpath=
concat(//crumbRequestField,":",//crumb)')
```

If you look at the environment variable with the token afterwards, you'll see something like this:

```
$ echo $CSRF_TOKEN
Jenkins-Crumb:0cd0babef95a70d0836c3f3e5bc4eea8
```

Then you can include the token in your POST call. Here's an example using curl:

```
$ curl --user <userid>:<password or token>
 -H "$CSRF_TOKEN" -X POST
 -s <jenkins base url>/job/<job name>/<build number>/
input/
 <input parameter with 1st letter capped>/proceedEmpty
```

If you don't include the token, you'll end up with a 403 error.

OK button caption (ok)
: A different label you can use instead of "Proceed." For example:

```
input message: '<message text>', ok: 'Yes'
```

Allowed submitter (submitter)
: A comma-separated list of user IDs or group names for people authorized to respond. For example:

```
input message: '<message text>', submitter: 'user1,user2'
```

Submitter Caveats

There are two points to be aware of when working with the submitter option:

- Do not use spaces (only commas) within the list of users/groups.
- At least in some cases, users not in the list may still be able to abort the `input` step.

Parameter to store the approving submitter (`submitterParameter`)
: A variable to store the user that approves proceeding. To use this, you define a variable to hold the response(s) from the `input` step. If there are no other parameters (see below) specified, then the name given to the `submitterParameter` argument doesn't matter—the return value is dereferenced simply by accessing the name of the variable.

```
def resp = input id: 'ctns-prompt', message:
   'Continue to the next stage?', submitterParameter: 'approver'
   echo "Answered by ${resp}"
```

If you have any other parameters, then you must supply the submitterParameter's name to access it:

```
def resp = input id: 'ctns-prompt', message:
 'Continue to the next stage?',
 parameters: [string(defaultValue: '', description: '',
 name: 'para1')], submitterParameter: 'approver'
 echo "Answered by " + resp['approver']
```

Traditional Jenkins parameter types
: These are explained more in the next section.

Parameters

With the `input` statement, you have the option to add any of the standard Jenkins parameter types. If you've done any work with Jenkins before, you're probably already familiar with most of these. The following sections briefly introduce each one and offer an example of what it looks like when used in a script.

For each parameter type, the different "subparameters" (arguments) that it can take are also listed. If the purpose of the subparameter is self-evident from its name (e.g., name, default value, description), the argument name will be listed without additional explanation.

Boolean

This is the basic true/false parameter. The subparameters for a Boolean are Name, Default Value, and Description.

An example of the syntax would be:

```
def answer = input message: '<message>',
 parameters: [booleanParam(defaultValue: true,
 description: 'Prerelease setting', name: 'prerelease')]
```

Note that this returns a `java.lang.boolean`.

Figure 3-3 shows what this looks like in the Stage View when run.

Figure 3-3. Boolean parameter console input

In the console output, you will simply get an "Input requested" link that, when clicked, takes you to a screen like Figure 3-4.

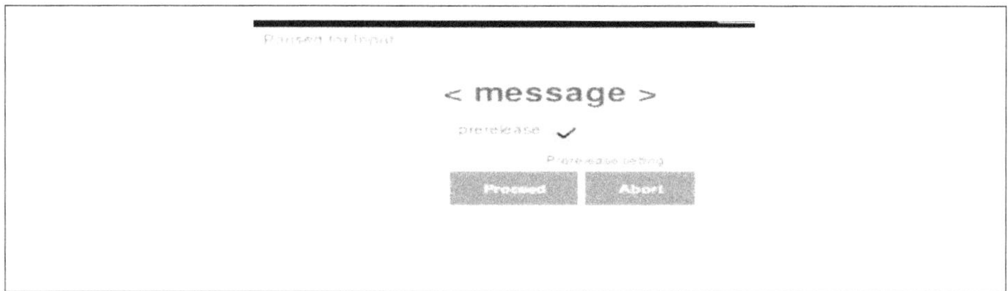

Figure 3-4. Redirect screen for parameter input from console

Choice

This parameter allows the user to select from a list of choices. The subparameters for a Choice are Name, Choices, and Description. Here, Choices refers to a list of choices you enter to present to the user. The first one in the list will be the default.

An example of the syntax would be:

```
def choice = input message: '<message>',
 parameters: [choice(choices: "choice1\nchoice2\nchoice3\nchoice4\n",
 description: 'Choose an option', name: 'Options')]
```

Notice the syntax here for the list of choices—a single string with each choice separated by a newline character. There are other ways to instantiate a set of choices, but this is the simplest.

Snippet Generator Generated Incorrect Code for choice Parameter

In versions of Jenkins prior to 2.112, the Snippet Generator generated incorrect code for a Choice parameter. The syntax looks like this:

```
input message: '<message>',
    parameters: [choice(choices: ['choice1', 'choice2',
    'choice3', 'choice4'],
    description: 'Choose an option', name: 'Options')]
```

This resulted in a `java.lang.IllegalArgumentException`. If you encounter this, upgrade to a more recent version of Jenkins or you can just follow the suggested syntax previously noted.

Running a pipeline and having it prompt you with this parameter type is similar to the Boolean example. In the Stage View, there is a graphical dialog with a drop-down list to select the choice in place of the checkbox.

In the console output, you again have the "Input requested" link, which takes you to a screen with graphical elements where you can select your choice.

Credentials

This parameter allows the user to select a type and set of credentials to use. The available subparameters include Name, Credential Type, Required, Default Value, and Description.

The options for Credential Type include Any, Username with password, Docker Host Certificate Authentication, SSH Username with private key, Secret file, Secret text, and Certificate.

If Required is specified, then a credential must be specified when the user is asked for this field. (It can't be empty.) This doesn't imply that a build will be able to use the credentials or that they will be valid, but just specifies that a selection is required.

The Default Value is the default credentials (selected from the set of ones already defined in Jenkins).

An example of the syntax follows for an SSH key:

```
def creds = input message: '<message>',
 parameters: [[$class: 'CredentialsParameterDefinition', credentialType:
 'com.cloudbees.jenkins.plugins.sshcredentials.impl.BasicSSHUserPrivateKey',
 defaultValue: 'jenkins2-ssh', description: 'SSH key for access',
 name: 'SSH', required: true]]
 echo creds
```

This will print out the ID of the selected credentials.

And here is an example for username and password:

```
def creds = input message: '', parameters: [[$class:
   'CredentialsParameterDefinition', credentialType:
   'com.cloudbees.plugins.credentials.impl.UsernamePasswordCredentialsImpl',
   defaultValue: '', description: 'Enter username and password',
   name: 'User And Pass', required: true]]
```

Note that this will not prompt with fields to enter a username and password. Rather, it presents the interface to select an existing credential or add a new one. In the Stage View, it looks like Figure 3-5.

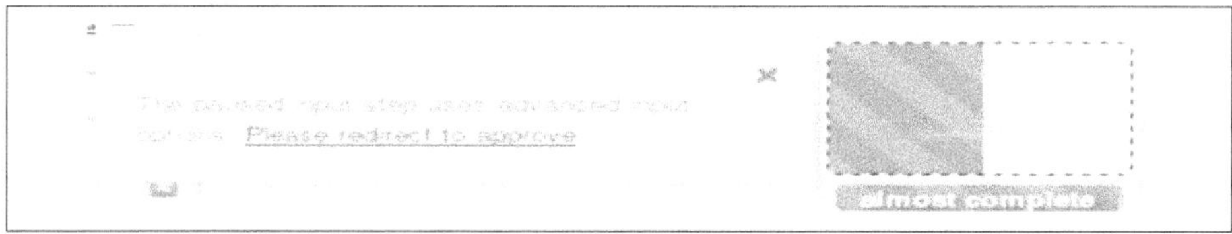

Figure 3-5. Credentials input prompt in Stage View

Once you click the "Please redirect to approve" link, you are taken to the prompts for selecting credentials (Figure 3-6). The prompt from the console is the same as in the previous cases.

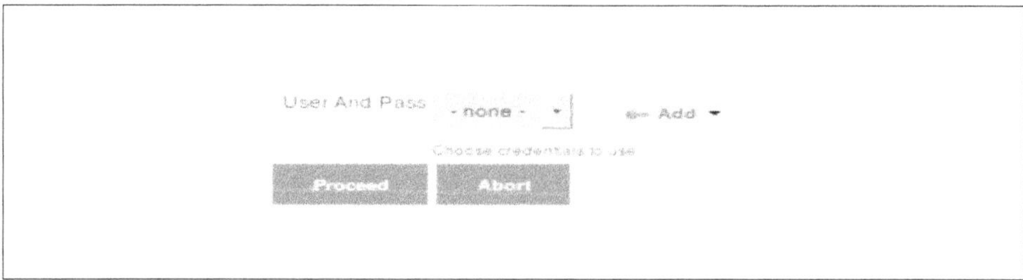

Figure 3-6. Credentials prompt

File

This parameter allows for choosing a file to use with the pipeline. The subparameters include File Location and Description. The syntax is:

```
def selectedFile = input message: '<message>',
 parameters: [file(description: 'Choose file to upload', name: 'local')]
```

Note that the item returned for this type of parameter is a `hudson.FilePath` object. Some of the methods associated with `FilePath` are not permitted to be used by default by Jenkins scripts, and may require approval by an administrator through the process outlined in Chapter 5.

Processing for This Parameter Is Currently Broken

The File Location is intended to specify where to put the file that will be selected and uploaded, relative to the workspace. However, as of the time of this writing, while you can select a file via a File parameter, the file is not uploaded or placed anywhere. Check the latest Jenkins documentation for your version to see if this has been corrected.

The interface is the same as the advanced ones previously described, except that you have a Browse button to select a file.

List Subversion tags

This parameter allows you to specify a set of tags in Subversion to select from when running a build. The subparameters include Name, Repository URL, Credentials, Tag Filter, Default Value, the Maximum tags to display, and sorting options for newest first and/or alphabetical sorting.

For the Repository URL subparameter, Jenkins expects you to specify the URL of the Subversion repository that contains the tags you want to display. If this does not contain the tags and there are subfolders, then the subfolders will be displayed to enable drilling down.

Jenkins will check whether it can access this repository or not and prompt for credentials if needed.

The Credentials subparameter contains the credentials to access the repository, if required. (See Chapter 5 for an explanation of credentials.)

The Tag Filter refers to a regular expression to filter the list of tags presented.

The Default Value is used only if required for SVN polling or similar features.

Here's some example syntax:

```
def tag = input message: '<message>',
 parameters: [[$class: 'ListSubversionTagsParameterDefinition',
 credentialsId: 'jenkins2-ssh', defaultValue: '', maxTags: '',
 name: 'LocalSVN', reverseByDate: false, reverseByName: false,
 tagsDir: 'file:///svnrepos/gradle-demo', tagsFilter: 'rel_*']]
```

The interfaces act like the ones for the File and Credentials parameters, except that there is a drop-down with the matching list of tags to choose from instead of a file or credential selection widget.

Multiline String

This parameter allows the user to input multiple lines of text. The subparameters include Name, Default Value, and Description.

Here's some example syntax:

```
def lines = input message: '<message>',
 parameters: [text(defaultValue: '''line 1
 line 2
 line 3''', description: '', name: 'Input Lines')]
```

Notice the entries in the commands are on different lines. This is because they have newlines entered with the default values. Also notice the triple quotes before and after the multiline message. The triple quotes are a standard notation used with Groovy for things that span multiple lines.

As you might expect, when executing, this will pop up (or link to) an entry box where you can type multiple lines of text.

Password

This parameter allows the user to enter a password. For passwords, the text the user enters is hidden while they type it. The available subparameters are Name, Default Value, and Description.

Here's an example:

```
def pw = input message: '<message>',
 parameters: [password(defaultValue: '',
 description: 'Enter your password.', name: 'passwd')]
```

When run, the user is presented with a field to enter the password, with the text being hidden as they type.

Run

This parameter allows the user to select a particular run (executed build) from a job. This might be used, for example, in a testing environment. The subparameters available include Name, Project, Description, and Filter.

The Project subparameter is the job that you want to allow the user to select a run from. The default run will be the most recent one.

The Filter subparameter allows you to filter the type of runs to offer based on the overall build status. Choices include:

- All Builds (including "in-progress" ones)
- Completed Builds
- Successful Builds (this includes stable and unstable ones)
- Stable Builds Only

Here's an example of code for this one:

```
def selection = input message: '<message>',
 parameters: [run(description: 'Choose a run of the project',
 filter: 'ALL', name: 'RUN', projectName: 'pipe1')]
 echo "selection is ${selection}"
```

This will output a response like:

```
selection is <project name> #<run number>
```

String

This parameter allows the user to enter a string. (This value is not hidden, like with a Password parameter.) The subparameters include Name, Default Value, and Description.

Here's an example:

```
def resp = input message: '<message>', parameters: [string(defaultValue: '',
   description: 'Enter response', name: 'Response')]
```

When run, the user is presented with a field to enter in the desired string.

Return Values from Multiple Input Parameters

In all of the examples just shown, we included only a single parameter. This syntax provides a simple return value that directly contains the value input by the user. If there were instead no parameters, such as having only a Proceed or Abort option, then the return value would be `null`. And when you have multiple parameters, a map is returned where you can extract each parameter's return value via the parameter's name. An example follows.

Suppose we wanted to add a traditional login screen to our pipeline. We would use two parameters—one String parameter for the login name and one Password parameter for the password. We can do that in the same `input` statement and then extract the return values for each from the returned map.

The following example code shows how to define the `input` statement along with some print statements that show different ways to access the individual return values (don't forget that you can use the Snippet Generator for generating the `input` statement as well):

```
def loginInfo = input message: 'Login',
     parameters: [string(defaultValue: '', description:
       'Enter Userid:', name: 'userid'),
        password(defaultValue: '',
        description: 'Enter Password:', name: 'passwd')]
      echo "Username = " + loginInfo['userid']
      echo "Password = ${loginInfo['passwd']}"
      echo loginInfo.userid + " " + loginInfo.passwd
```

Parameters and Declarative Pipelines

Since creating new local variables to hold the return values from `input` statements doesn't fit the declarative model, you may be wondering how we can use the `input` statement in Declarative Pipelines. There are several approaches here, including one that leverages the declarative structure and one that works around it.

Using the parameters section

Within the Declarative Pipeline structure, there is a section/directive for declaring parameters. This is within the `agent` block of the main `pipeline` closure. Figure 3-7 shows where this fits overall.

Use of the `parameters` directive is covered in detail with Declarative Pipelines in Chapter 7, but here's a simple example of the syntax (see "parameters" on page 236 for more details):

```
pipeline {
    agent any
    parameters {
        string(name: 'USERID', defaultValue: '',
         description: 'Enter your userid')
    }
    stages {
        stage('Login') {
            steps {
                echo "Active user is now ${params.USERID}"
            }
        }
```

```
        }
    }
```

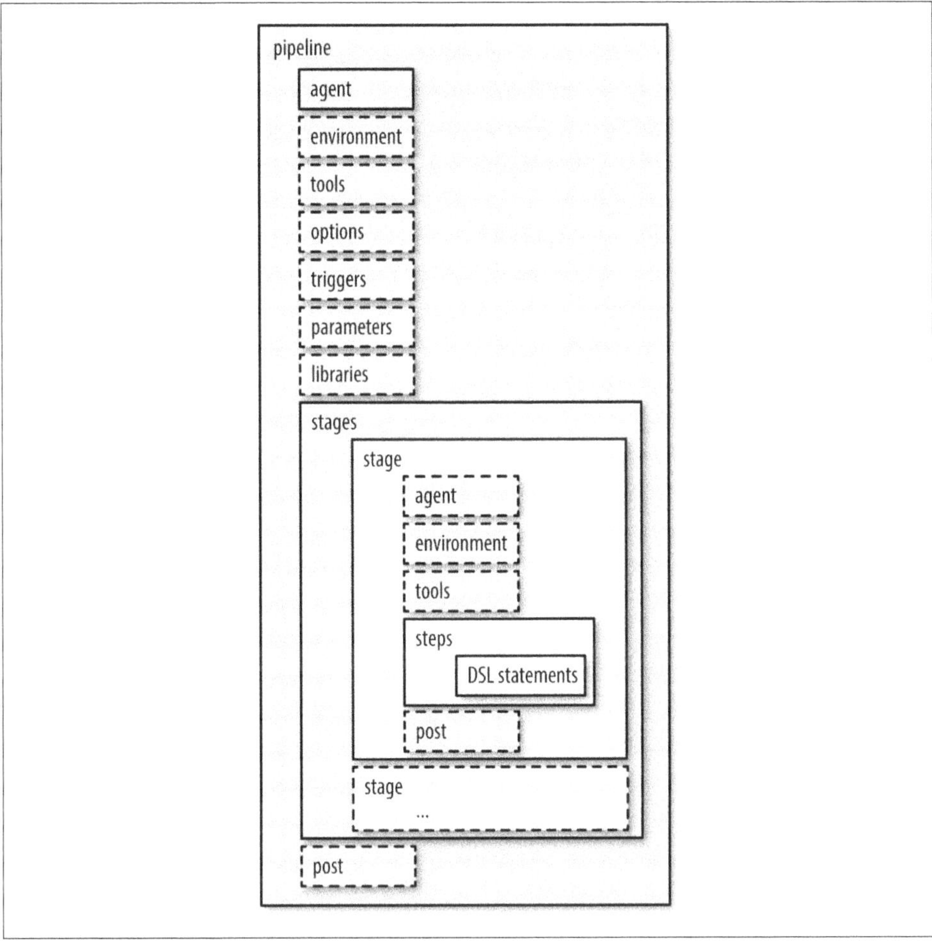

Figure 3-7. Declarative Pipeline structure

If you are working in the Jenkins application itself, creating parameters like this in the code will also instantiate the "This build is parameterized" part of the job.

This approach is the recommended approach for Declarative Pipelines.

Using the Jenkins application to parameterize the build

If you have created a job in the Jenkins application (rather than using a Jenkinsfile automatically), a second approach for adding parameters is to simply use the traditional method for parameterizing a job. That is, in the General configuration section, select the checkbox for "This project is parameterized" and then define your parameters as normal in the job's web interface (Figure 3-8).

Figure 3-8. Corresponding generation of parameters in Jenkins job

You can then simply reference the job parameters via `params.<name of parameter>` without having the input line in the code, as shown here:

```
pipeline {
    agent any
    stages {
        stage('Login') {
            steps {
                echo "Active user is now ${params.USERID}"
            }
        }
    }
}
```

A variant of this approach is to define the parameters as properties before the pipeline. This can actually be done either for Scripted or Declarative Pipelines. Here's how it might look in the code:

```
properties ([
    parameters ([
        string(defaultValue: '', description: '', name : 'USERID')
    ])
])
pipeline {
    agent any
    stages {
        stage('Login') {
            steps {
                echo "Active user is now ${params.USERID}"
            }
        }
    }
}
```

However, since this works only within the scope of the Jenkins application and the particular job within it, this is not recommended for production use. It also will overwrite any existing properties defined in Jenkins for the job.

With that said, it can be a useful way to prototype parameter usage in a pipeline for certain cases.

Using a script block

While Declarative Pipelines are continuing to evolve and add more functionality, there may still be instances where you need to do something in one that the declarative style doesn't support or renders very difficult to implement. For those cases, the declarative syntax supports a `script` block.

A `script` block allows you to use nondeclarative syntax within the bounds of the block. This includes defining variables, which is not something you can do in a Declarative Pipeline outside of a `script` block. This also means that you cannot reference variables that are defined inside a `script` block outside of that block. Jenkins flags those with a "no such property" error.

As an example of all of this, consider the following section of code:

```
stage ('Input') {
          steps {
             script {
                def resp = input message: '<message>',
                 parameters: [string(defaultValue: '',
                 description: 'Enter response 1',
                 name: 'RESPONSE1'), string(defaultValue: '',
                 description: 'Enter response 2', name: 'RESPONSE2')]
                echo "${resp.RESPONSE1}"
             }
             echo "${resp.RESPONSE2}"
          }
}
```

Here we have two parameters defined as part of an `input` step inside of a stage in a Declarative Pipeline. Since the first `echo` is in the `script` block where the variable `resp` is also defined, it will print out the response that is entered for that parameter as expected.

Notice, though, that the second `echo` is outside of the scope where the `resp` variable is defined. Groovy/Jenkins will throw an error when it gets to this one.

Because of this, it is advisable to try to limit accessing input to a small section of your code if you have to use a `script` block. However, there is one other workaround if you need to use the value outside the scope of the `script` block. You can put the return value into an environment variable and then access the environment variable wherever you need the value.

Updating our code to use this method could look like the following:

```
stage ('Input') {
        steps {
               script {
                  env.RESP1 = input message: '<message>', parameters: [
                     string(defaultValue: '', description: 'Enter response 1',
                     name: 'RESPONSE1')]
                  env.RESP2 = input message: '<message>', parameters: [
                     string(defaultValue: '', description: 'Enter response 2',
                     name: 'RESPONSE2')]
                  echo "${env.RESP1}"
               }
               echo "${env.RESP2}"
            }
        }
```

We are putting the results of the `input` steps into the environment variable namespace (`env`). Because these are environment variables, the values are set in the environment and therefore available for the pipeline to use wherever it needs.

Note that we've broken the single `input` statement down into two separate `input` statements. This results in the two environment variables `RESP1` and `RESP2` each having just the contents of their respective `input` lines. You can instead use multiple parameters in an `input` statement and set an environment variable with the results. The environment variable will have the form:

```
<parameter_name>=<input_value>, <parameter_name>=<input_value>, ...
```

You will then need to write code to parse out the unique values you are interested in.

Using external code

One other option available to you is putting scripted statements (like the calls to input) in an external shared library or an external Groovy file that you load and execute. For example, we could code our input processing in a file named *vars/getUser.groovy* in a shared library structure, like this:

```
#!/usr/bin/env groovy

def call(String prompt1 = 'Please enter your data', String prompt2 = 'Please
enter your data') {
   def resp = input message: '<message>', parameters: [string(defaultValue: '',
description: prompt1, name: 'RESPONSE1'), string(defaultValue: '', description:
prompt2, name: 'RESPONSE2')]
   echo "${resp.RESPONSE1}"
   echo "${resp.RESPONSE2}"
   // do something with the input
}
```

If our library were named `Utilities`, then we could import it and call the `getUser` function as shown here:

```
@Library('Utilities')_
pipeline {
    agent any
    stages {
        stage ('Input') {
           steps {
              getUser 'Enter response 1','Enter response 2'
           }
        }
    }
}
```

Chapter 6 discusses creating and using shared pipeline libraries in detail.

Nondeclarative Code and Blue Ocean

If you plan to use your pipeline with Blue Ocean, be aware that the built-in editor is designed to work primarily with declarative syntax. Any nondeclarative syntax may be ignored or may not work as expected in the Blue Ocean editor.

One of the challenges with using an `input` statement is what happens if you don't get input in an expected amount of time. While waiting for input, the node is effectively stopped, waiting on a response. To prevent this from going on too long, you should consider wrapping the input call with another type of flow control construct: the `timeout` statement. We'll discuss that in the next section.

Flow Control Options

One of the benefits of writing your pipeline-as-code in Jenkins (versus using the traditional web forms) is that you have more options for controlling the flow through the pipeline. This includes handling cases that might otherwise cause your pipeline to stop or fail. The options available include ways to accomplish waiting, retries, etc. We'll walk through each of them now.

timeout

The `timeout` step allows you to limit the amount of time your script spends waiting for an action to happen. The syntax is fairly simple. Here's an example:

```
timeout(time:60, unit: 'SECONDS') {
  // processing to be timed out inside this block
}
```

The default unit for time is minutes. If you only specify a time value, it will be assumed to be in minutes. If the timeout is hit, then the step will throw an exception. This will cause the processing to abort if the exception isn't handled some other way.

A best practice is to wrap any step that can pause the pipeline (such as an `input` step) with a `timeout`. This is so that your pipeline continues to execute (if desired) even if something goes wrong and the expected input doesn't occur within the time limit. Here's an example:

```
node {
    def response
    stage('input') {
       timeout(time:10, unit:'SECONDS') {
          response = input message: 'User',
           parameters: [string(defaultValue: 'user1',
           description: 'Enter Userid:', name: 'userid')]
       }
       echo "Username = " + response
    }
}
```

In this case, Jenkins will wait for 10 seconds for the user to enter a response. If that time passes, Jenkins will throw an exception causing the pipeline to abort. You can see the sequence in the output captured in Figure 3-9.

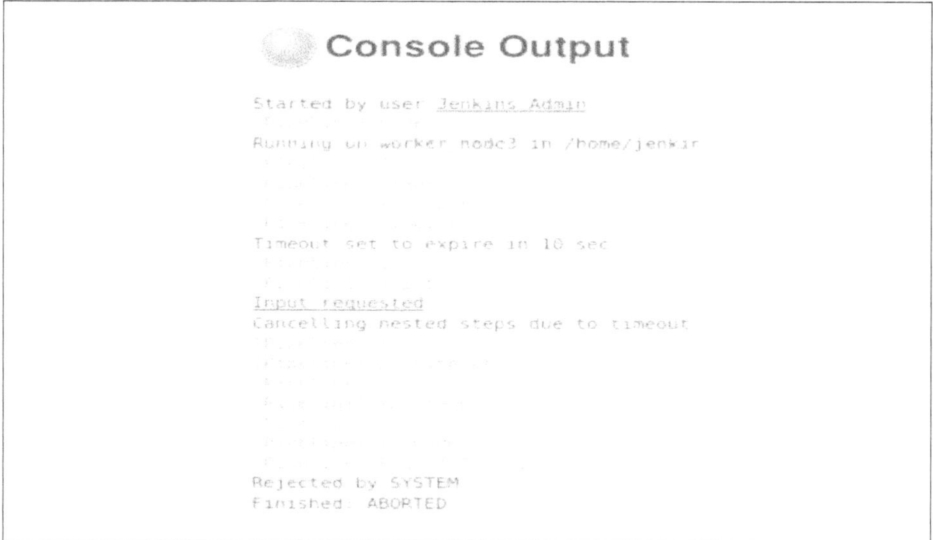

Figure 3-9. Console output from a timeout

As shown by the console output, the timeout does stop the pause in processing while waiting on input. However, when it does this, it throws an exception, causing our pipeline to abort. In order to not abort the pipeline, we can wrap the `timeout` in a traditional `try-catch` block, as shown in the following code. Notice that we set the response to the desired default when we handle the exception:

```
node {
    def response
    stage('input') {
       try {
         timeout(time:10, unit:'SECONDS') {
            response = input message: 'User',
             parameters: [string(defaultValue: 'user1',
             description: 'Enter Userid:', name: 'userid')]
         }
       }
       catch (err) {
          response = 'user1'
       }
    }
}
```

retry

The `retry` closure wraps code in a step that retries the process *n* times if an exception occurs in the code. *n* here refers to a value you pass in to the `retry` step. The syntax is just:

```
retry(<n>) { // processing }
```

If the retry limit is reached and an exception occurs, then the processing is aborted (unless that exception is handled, such as with a `try-catch` block).

sleep

This is the basic delay step. It accepts a value and delays that amount of time before continuing processing. The default time unit is seconds, so `sleep 5` waits for 5 seconds before continuing processing. If you want to specify a different unit, you just add the unit name parameter, as in:

```
sleep time: 5, unit: 'MINUTES'
```

waitUntil

As you might guess, this step causes processing to wait until something happens. The "something" in this case is the closure returning `true`.

If the processing in the block returns `false`, then this step waits a bit longer and tries again. Any exceptions thrown in the processing cause the step to exit immediately and throw an error.

The syntax for `waitUntil` is simply:

```
waitUntil { // processing that returns true or false }
```

How Long Does It Wait?

I mentioned that if the processing in the block returns `false`, then the `waitUntil` step waits a bit longer and tries again. You may be wondering what is meant by "a bit longer" here. Currently, the system starts out with a 0.25 second wait time. If it needs to loop again, it multiplies that by a factor of 1.2 to get 0.3 seconds for the next wait cycle. On each succeeding cycle, the last wait time is multiplied again by 1.2 to get the time to wait. So, the sequence goes as 0.25, 0.3, 0.36, 0.43, 0.51...

Figure 3-10 shows an example of what this looks like.

```
[pipe2] Running shell script
+ test -e /home/jenkins2/marker.txt

Will try again after 0.25 sec

[pipe2] Running shell script
+ test -e /home/jenkins2/marker.txt

Will try again after 0.3 sec

[pipe2] Running shell script
+ test -e /home/jenkins2/marker.txt

Will try again after 0.36 sec

[pipe2] Running shell script
+ test -e /home/jenkins2/marker.txt

Will try again after 0.43 sec
```

Figure 3-10. Example retry run

Because this step could end up waiting indefinitely if the processing never returns `true` (whether by intention or not), it is recommended to wrap this step with a `timeout` step so that eventually processing will.

Here is an example of using a `waitUntil` block to wait until we have a marker file in place. Notice that we have a `timeout` around the `waitUntil` to avoid staying in the `waitUntil` indefinitely. Also, we are setting the `returnStatus` parameter to `true` for the shell call, so that we get the return code back from the operation to check for success:

```
timeout(time:15, unit:'SECONDS') {
   waitUntil {
```

```
        def ret = sh returnStatus: true,
          script: 'test -e /home/jenkins2/marker.txt'
        return (ret == 0)
    }

}
```

As another example, suppose we are waiting for a Docker container to start up so that we can get some data via a REST API call as part of our pipeline testing. In this case we get an exception if the URL isn't available yet. To ensure that we don't exit right away when the exception is thrown, we can use a `try-catch` structure to catch the exception and return `false` in that case. We also wrap it in a `timeout` as a guard against it not being available at all for some reason and holding up our pipeline:

```
timeout(time: 120, unit: 'SECONDS') {
   waitUntil {
      try {
         sh "docker exec ${webContainer.id} curl
            --silent http://127.0.0.1:8080/roar/api/v1/registry
            1>test/output/entries.txt"
         return true
      }
      catch (exception) {
         return false
      }
   }
}
```

Note that if we were doing this inside of a Declarative Pipeline, we would have to use a method such as a `script` block or shared library to handle this code.

Now that we understand how to process individual flow control sections within a pipeline, the next step up is dealing with multiple simultaneous lines of pipeline execution and concurrency.

Dealing with Concurrency

For the most part, having concurrency in your pipeline builds is a good thing. Typically, concurrency refers to parallelism—being able to run similar parts of your jobs concurrently on different nodes. This can be especially useful in cases such as running tests, as long as you limit duplicate access to resources appropriately.

Another form of concurrency in Jenkins is when multiple builds of the same job try to run at the same time or use the same resources. In the case of very active repositories, branches, or pull requests, this may be an expected, common situation.

But there may also be cases where this is not expected and not desirable. Let's look briefly at two mechanisms that Jenkins pipelines have to address that situation.

Locking Resources with the lock Step

If you have the Lockable Resources plugin (*http://bit.ly/2vtAOej*) installed, there is a DSL `lock` step available to restrict multiple builds from trying to use the same resource at the same time. (There will also be a Lockable Resources section on the Configure System page where you can globally define and reserve resources if necessary—for example, if you temporarily need to take a set of resources offline for a system.)

"Resource" here is a loose word. It could mean a node, an agent, a set of them, or just a name to use for the locking. If the specified resource isn't defined in the global configuration, it will be added automatically.

The DSL `lock` step is a blocking step. It locks the specified resource until the steps within its closure are completed. In its simplest case, you just supply the resource name as the default argument. For example:

```
lock('worker_node1') {
  // steps to do on worker_node1
}
```

Alternatively, you can supply a label name to select a set of resources that have a certain label and a quantity to specify the number of resources that match that label to lock (reserve):

```
lock(label: 'docker-node', quantity: 3) {
    // steps
}
```

You can think of this as, "How many of this resource do I have to have available to proceed?" If you specify a label but no quantity, then all resources with that label are locked.

Finally, there is an `inversePrecedence` optional parameter. If this parameter is set to `true`, then the most recent build will get the resource when it becomes available. Otherwise, builds are awarded the resource in the same order that they requested it.

As a quick example, consider a Declarative Pipeline where we want to use a certain agent to do the build on, no matter how many instances of the pipeline we are running. (Perhaps it is the only agent with the specific tools or setup we want at the moment.) Our code might look like this with the `lock` step:

```
stage('Build') {
   // Run the gradle build
   steps {
      lock('worker_node1') {
         sh 'gradle clean build -x test'
      }
   }
```

```
}
```

If we start multiple builds running of the same project or if we have multiple projects with this same lock code for the resource, then one build/project will get the resource first and other builds/projects will have to wait.

For the first build or project that gets the resource, the console log might show something like this:

```
[Pipeline] stage
[Pipeline] { (Build)
[Pipeline] lock
00:00:02.858 Trying to acquire lock on [worker_node1]
00:00:02.864 Resource [worker_node1] did not exist. Created.
00:00:02.864 Lock acquired on [worker_node1]
[Pipeline] {
[Pipeline] tool
[Pipeline] sh
00:00:02.925 [gradle-demo-simple-pipe] Running shell script
00:00:03.213 + /usr/share/gradle/bin/gradle clean build -x test
00:00:06.671 Starting a Gradle Daemon
...
00:00:16.887
00:00:16.887 BUILD SUCCESSFUL
00:00:16.887
00:00:16.887 Total time: 13.16 secs
[Pipeline] }
00:00:17.187 Lock released on resource [worker_node1]
[Pipeline] // lock
```

And for the other builds/jobs trying to acquire the same lock, console output might look like this:

```
[Pipeline] // stage
[Pipeline] stage
[Pipeline] { (Build)
[Pipeline] lock
00:00:03.262 Trying to acquire lock on [worker_node1]
00:00:03.262 Found 0 available resource(s). Waiting for correct
 amount: 1.
00:00:03.262 [worker_node1] is locked, waiting...
```

Locks allow us to control access to resources that eventually should become available. Another method of controlling concurrency is preventing other builds from continuing past a point once a build has already gotten there. These points can be established with *milestones*.

Controlling Concurrent Builds with Milestones

One of the scenarios that you might have to deal with at some point in Jenkins is builds of the same pipeline running concurrently that can have contention for resources. The runs could be reaching key points at different times and stepping on each other, or one run could be modifying required resources that leave things in a bad state when the other run makes it to that point. In short, there's no guarantee that after one run has modified a resource, another run won't come along and modify it while the earlier run is still in progress.

To prevent the case where builds could run out of order (in terms of the order they were started) and step on each other, Jenkins pipelines can use the `milestone` step. When a `milestone` step is put in the pipeline, it prevents an older build from moving past the milestone, if the newer build has already gotten there.

The following example shows a `milestone` step placed in a script after a Gradle build:

```
        sh "'${gradleLoc}/bin/gradle' clean build"
    }
    milestone label: 'After build', ordinal: 1
    stage("NotifyOnFailure") {
```

Suppose we have two runs of this build happening concurrently, as shown in Figure 3-11.

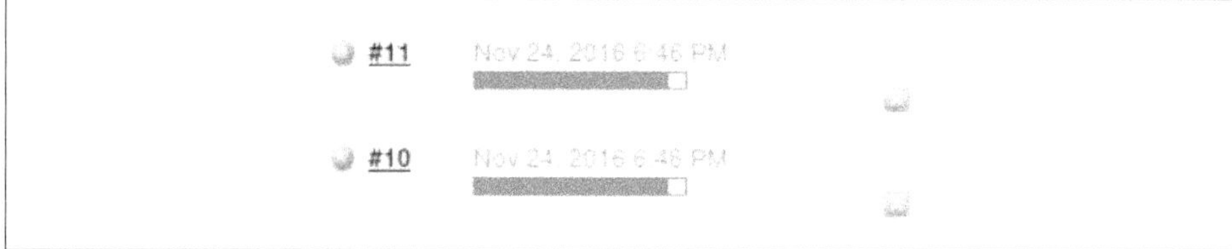

Figure 3-11. Two ordered builds of the same job running concurrently

If build #11 gets to the `milestone` step first during its processing, then when build #10 arrives, it will be canceled. This prevents build #10 from overwriting or modifying any resources already in use or modified by build #11. The console log for build #10 for this part of the process is shown in Figure 3-12.

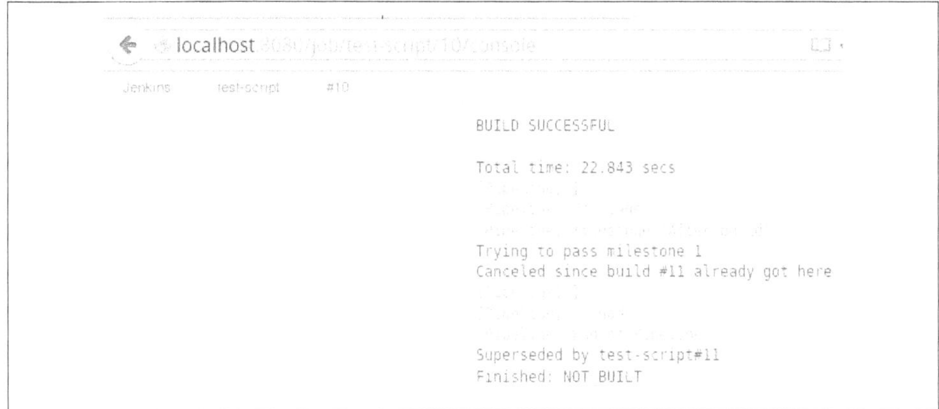

Figure 3-12. Console log for build #10

The rules for milestone processing can be summed up as:

- Builds pass the milestones in order by build number.
- Older builds abort if a newer build has already passed the milestone.
- When a build passes a milestone, Jenkins aborts older builds that have passed the previous milestone, but not this milestone.
- If an older build passes a milestone, newer builds that haven't passed the milestone won't abort it.

To be clear, if concurrent builds reach the milestone in the order they were started, they can all pass the milestone.

The `milestone` step can take a couple of parameters. The first is a label, which is to identify the milestone. It will be shown in the build log. The second is an ordinal number. This is autogenerated if not set specifically. You only need to do this if you're going to be adding/deleting milestones during the builds. There is also a way to restrict concurrent builds running for multiple branches in a Multibranch Pipeline project. That's covered in the next section.

Restricting Concurrency in Multibranch Pipelines

The pipeline DSL includes a way to restrict Multibranch Pipelines to only building one branch at a time. This is done with a property for either a Scripted or Declarative Pipeline. When this is in place (in the Jenkinsfiles of the branches), requested builds for branches other than the one currently building will be queued.

In a scripted syntax, the property can be set this way:

```
properties([disableConcurrentBuilds()])
```

In declarative syntax, it would look like this:

```
options {
    disableConcurrentBuilds()
}
```

Next, we'll look at one of the main ways to benefit from concurrency—running tasks in parallel.

Running Tasks in Parallel

In addition to the other constructs for controlling the logic flow of a pipeline, steps can also be run in parallel. In fact, the pipeline DSL has special constructs for doing this—a traditional one that fits both Scripted and Declarative Pipelines, and a newer one just for Declarative Pipelines. To illustrate the main points, we'll talk about the more general one first and then the newer declarative syntax.

Traditional parallel syntax

The traditional `parallel` pipeline step takes a map as an argument. For this construct, the values of the map are generally closures consisting themselves of `pipeline` steps. Wrapping those steps in different nodes allows for the best parallelism. If specific nodes aren't indicated, Jenkins will run the `parallel` steps on unused nodes.

Map Is Required

For this `parallel` step, if you don't supply a map as the argument, then your jobs will not be run in parallel. Also note that stages cannot be used inside of this `parallel` block (unlike the newer syntax for Declarative Pipelines).

The following is a simple script that constructs a set of parallel operations. In this example, `stepsToRun = [:]` is the Groovy syntax for declaring a map. The loop then iterates, setting the key to `"Step<loop counter>"` and the value for each to a `node` block that echos `start`, sleeps, and then echos `done`. Finally, the `parallel` step executes, taking the map as an argument:

```
node ('worker_node1') {
   stage("Parallel Demo") {
   // Run steps in parallel

      // The map we'll store the steps in
      def stepsToRun = [:]

      for (int i = 1; i < 5; i++) {
         stepsToRun["Step${i}"] = { node {
            echo "start"
            sleep 5
```

```
                echo "done"
            }}
        }
        // Actually run the steps in parallel
        //  parallel takes a map as an argument,
        parallel stepsToRun
    }
}
```

Figure 3-13 shows the console output of this section of code running. Note that since we didn't specify any specific nodes, each step is allowed to run on any available node. If you look carefully at the output, you can see the interleaving of the steps as the parallel jobs run.

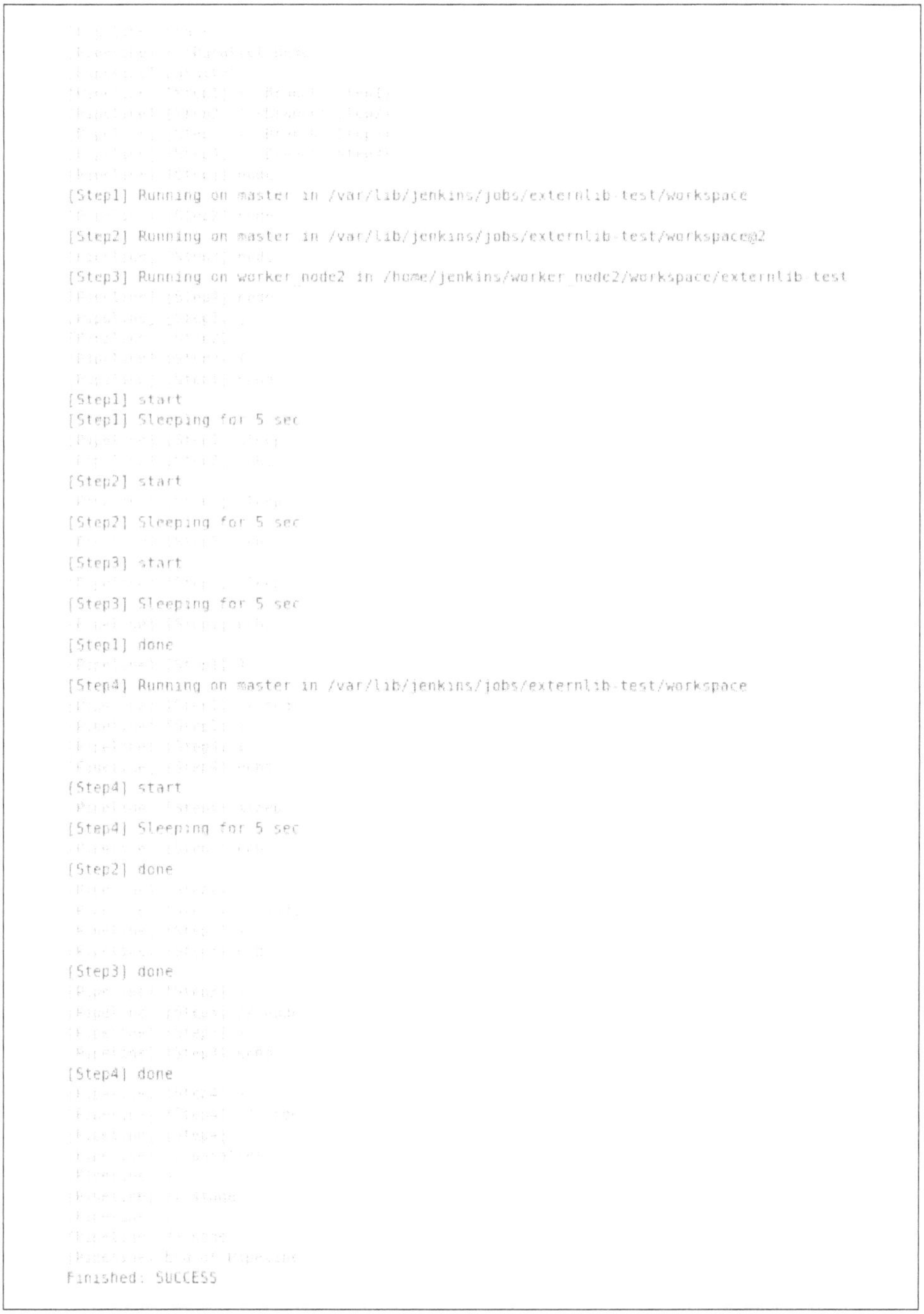

```
[Step1] Running on master in /var/lib/jenkins/jobs/externlib-test/workspace
[Step2] Running on master in /var/lib/jenkins/jobs/externlib-test/workspace@2
[Step3] Running on worker_node2 in /home/jenkins/worker_node2/workspace/externlib-test
[Step1] start
[Step1] Sleeping for 5 sec
[Step2] start
[Step2] Sleeping for 5 sec
[Step3] start
[Step3] Sleeping for 5 sec
[Step1] done
[Step4] Running on master in /var/lib/jenkins/jobs/externlib-test/workspace
[Step4] start
[Step4] Sleeping for 5 sec
[Step2] done
[Step3] done
[Step4] done
Finished: SUCCESS
```

Figure 3-13. Parallel execution of dynamic steps

It is also possible to just define the mapping directly in the invocation of the `parallel` step. The following is an implementation done this way. Notice again that we are passing in a mapping with closures and nodes. In this implementation, the first occurrences of `master` and `worker2` are the *keys* to the maps. The sections after the colons are the closures that make up the *value* portions of the map. In each of the closures for the map values, we allocate a block of code to run on specific nodes. In this case, the code block is a shell step (`sh`) that invokes Gradle to run a single test—a different one on each node.

```
stage ('Test') {
// execute required unit tests in parallel

   parallel (
      master: { node ('master'){
         sh '/opt/gradle-2.7/bin/gradle -D test.single=TestExample1 test'
      }},
      worker2: { node ('worker_node2'){
         sh '/opt/gradle-2.7/bin/gradle -D test.single=TestExample2 test'
      }},
   )
}
```

However, trying to run this particular piece of code in most instances will run into a problem, as shown in Figure 3-14.

```
[master]
[master] FAILURE: Build failed with an exception.
[master]
[master] * What went wrong:
[master] Task 'test' not found in root project 'workspace@2'.
[master]
[master] * Try:
[master] Run gradle tasks to get a list of available tasks. Run with
option to get more log output.
[master]
[master] BUILD FAILED
[master]
[master] Total time: 22.374 secs
```

Figure 3-14. Error trying to run parallel jobs without a workspace

The challenge here is that the original build happened in a workspace on a different node and the new node (`master`, in this case) does not have access to that workspace.

We could archive artifacts here or try to copy them over ourselves, but Jenkins includes special steps to help with such a case. This is a good place to cover those.

stash and unstash

In the Jenkins DSL, the `stash` and `unstash` functions allow for saving and retrieving (respectively) files between nodes and/or stages in a pipeline. Their format is:

```
stash name: "<name>" [includes: "<pattern>" excludes: "<pattern>"]
```

```
unstash "<name>"
```

The basic idea here is that we designate a set of included or excluded files via names and/or patterns. This stash of files is given a name to refer to it by.

Then, when we need to retrieve the set of files, we can simply pass the name of the stash to the `unstash` command. This can be done on a different stage or node.

Git stash Versus Jenkins stash

To be clear, these functions are different from the Git `stash` function. The Git `stash` function allows for stashing the contents of a working directory and cache that haven't yet been committed to the local repository. The Jenkins `stash` function allows for stashing files to share between nodes.

The `stash` and `unstash` functions are not intended for formal management of large groups of files such as where you need to keep track of version numbers. For that type of requirement, it is better to use an artifact repository designed for managing binary artifacts such as Artifactory or Nexus. (Artifactory and integration with Jenkins is discussed in Chapter 13.)

An example of the use of the `stash` and `unstash` commands across nodes is shown next. In this case, after we get the source, we are stashing the *build.gradle* file and the entire *src/test* tree. This stash is given the name `test-sources`. Then, in the parallel section that runs on the other node (`worker_node2` in this case), the `unstash` command creates a copy of the stashed files and tree on that node. This allows the files to be present so the testing can take place on that node as well and we can achieve the parallelism:

```
stages {

   stage('Source') {
      git branch: 'test', url: 'git@diyv:repos/gradle-greetings'
      stash name: 'test-source', includes: 'build.gradle,src/test/'
   }
   ...
   stage ('Test') {
   // execute required unit tests in parallel

      parallel (
         master: { node ('master') {
            unstash 'test-sources'
            sh '/opt/gradle-2.7/bin/gradle -D test.single=TestExample1 test'
         }},
         worker2: { node ('worker_node2') {
```

```
                unstash 'test-sources'
                sh '/opt/gradle-2.7/bin/gradle -D test.single=TestExample2 test'
            }},
        )
    }
}
```

The log of running this sequence can be seen in Figure 3-15. Again, note the interleaving of execution between the nodes. (In this case there is a test that is supposed to fail, so this run is successful.)

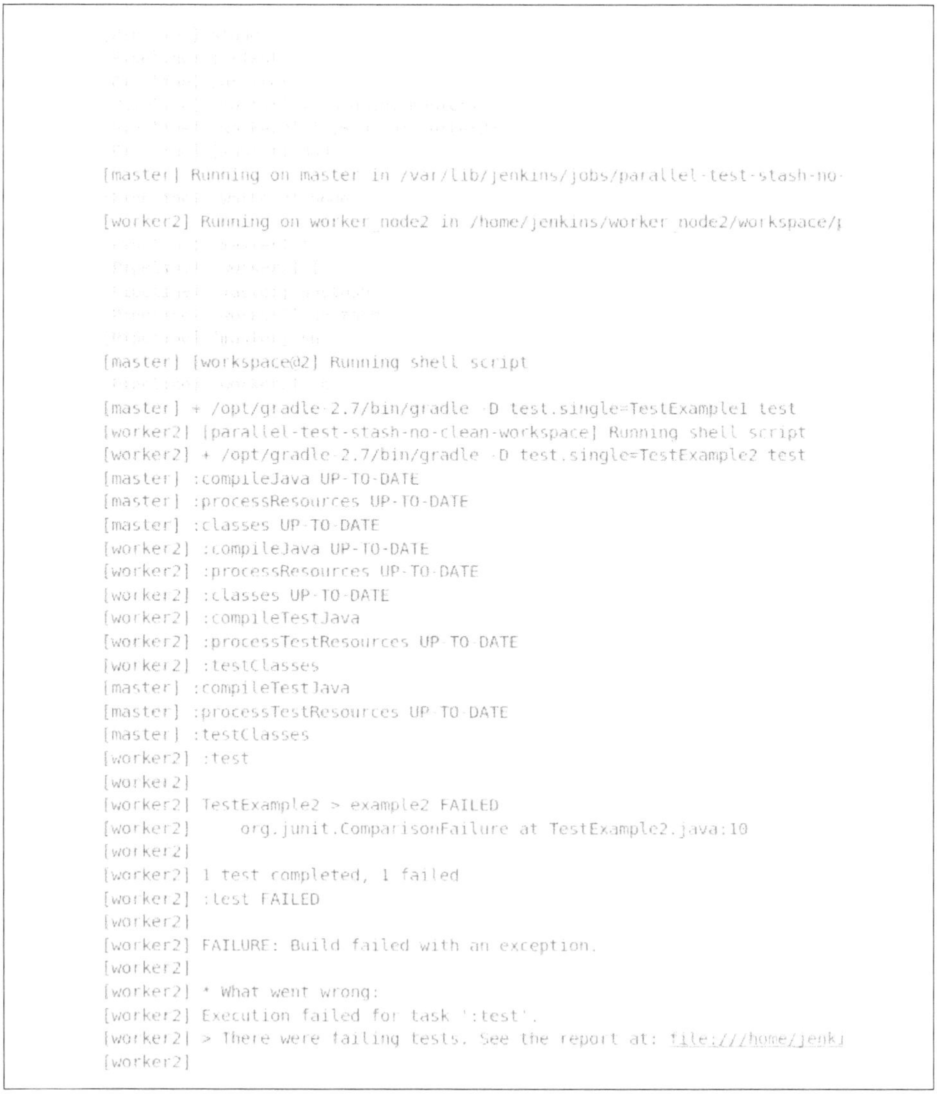

```
[master] Running on master in /var/lib/jenkins/jobs/parallel-test-stash-no-
[worker2] Running on worker_node2 in /home/jenkins/worker_node2/workspace/
[master] [workspace@2] Running shell script
[master] + /opt/gradle-2.7/bin/gradle -D test.single=TestExample1 test
[worker2] [parallel-test-stash-no-clean-workspace] Running shell script
[worker2] + /opt/gradle-2.7/bin/gradle -D test.single=TestExample2 test
[master] :compileJava UP-TO-DATE
[master] :processResources UP-TO-DATE
[master] :classes UP-TO-DATE
[worker2] :compileJava UP-TO-DATE
[worker2] :processResources UP-TO-DATE
[worker2] :classes UP-TO-DATE
[worker2] :compileTestJava
[worker2] :processTestResources UP-TO-DATE
[worker2] :testClasses
[master] :compileTestJava
[master] :processTestResources UP-TO-DATE
[master] :testClasses
[worker2] :test
[worker2]
[worker2] TestExample2 > example2 FAILED
[worker2]     org.junit.ComparisonFailure at TestExample2.java:10
[worker2]
[worker2] 1 test completed, 1 failed
[worker2] :test FAILED
[worker2]
[worker2] FAILURE: Build failed with an exception.
[worker2]
[worker2] * What went wrong:
[worker2] Execution failed for task ':test'.
[worker2] > There were failing tests. See the report at: file:///home/jenki
[worker2]
```

Figure 3-15. Parallel run with stash and unstash used to share files across nodes

Parallel Test Executor Plugin

A separate plugin is available that can help with parallelizing sets of tests if they are taking up significant time in your pipeline. The Parallel Test Executor plugin (*http://bit.ly/2HCEJdw*) looks at a run of your tests with the execution times and attempts to split the tests up into groups of roughly equal size. (This is done with a `splitTests` DSL step that is added by the plugin.) The groups are put into lists that you can then map into the `parallel` step in your pipeline. Optimally, each group would be mapped to run on a separate node.

Using this plugin requires that your test environment/setup:

- Create JUnit-compatible XML files.
- Use a tool that can accept a test-exclusion list in a file.

Alternative parallel syntax for Declarative Pipelines

With the release of Declarative Pipeline 1.2 in September 2017, a new, alternative syntax was introduced for use in Declarative Pipelines. The new syntax more closely matches the structured form of Declarative Pipelines. It also doesn't require the setup of a map or use of `node`, and produces output separated by each branch of the parallel operation.

The new syntax elevates the `parallel` step to a separate construct within a stage. It can have stages defined within itself for each branch to run in parallel. Within each branch you can define an agent to run on and steps to execute just as you can for other Declarative Pipeline sections.

An excerpt of a stage from a Declarative Pipeline that uses this syntax is shown here:

```
stage('Unit Test') {
          parallel{
              stage ('Util unit tests') {
                 agent { label 'worker_node2' }
                 steps {
                    cleanWs()
                    unstash 'ws-src'
                    gbuild4 ':util:test'
                 }

              }
              stage ('API unit tests set 1') {
                 agent { label 'worker_node3'}
                 steps {
                    // always run with a new workspace
                    cleanWs()
                    unstash 'ws-src'
```

```
                    gbuild4 '-D test.single=TestExample1* :api:test'
                }
            }
            stage ('API unit tests set 2') {
                agent { label 'worker_node2' }
                steps {
                    // always run with a new workspace
                    cleanWs()
                    unstash 'ws-src'
                    gbuild4 '-D test.single=TestExample2* :api:test'
                }
            }
        }
    }
```

As you can see, this syntax is somewhat "cleaner" than the map syntax and more consistent with the declarative syntax. When run, due to the individual stage definitions, it will also produce stage output for each "substage" (Figure 3-16) as opposed to the single set of output of the traditional parallel syntax (Figure 3-17).

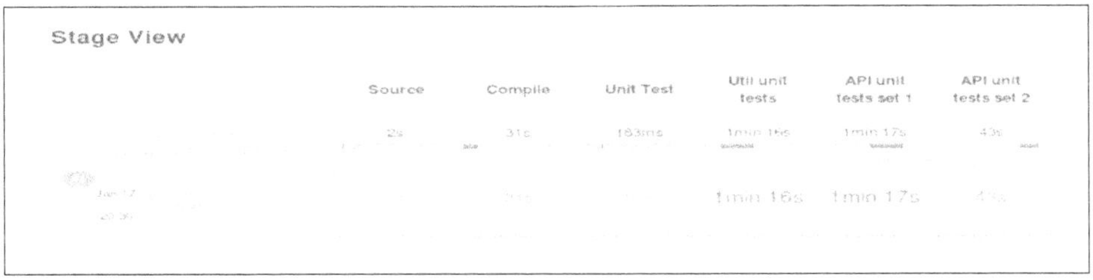

Figure 3-16. Stage output for new parallel syntax

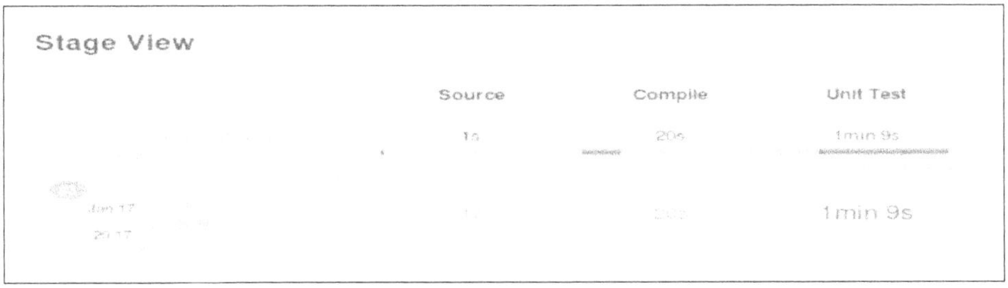

Figure 3-17. Stage output for traditional parallel syntax

parallel and failFast

Sometimes when doing multiple processing steps in a `parallel` block, you may want to quit processing all steps if one branch fails. For example, if you are doing deployment in one parallel section and testing in another section, you may want to abort the deployment if testing fails and abort the testing if deployment fails. To facilitate this, Jenkins pipelines can use the `failFast` option when invoking the `parallel` step.

To use this option, you add `failFast:true` to the `parallel` step options. When this option is present and one of the branches in the `parallel` step fails, Jenkins will terminate all running branches.

As an example, consider the following code. This is a simple Declarative Pipeline with one stage to demonstrate the parallel `failFast` usage. In the `parallel` step, we have the `group1` branch that simply sleeps for 10 seconds and then echos out a message. The `group2` branch sleeps for 5 seconds before throwing an error (via the `error` step) that will cause the `failFast` (the last argument to the `parallel` step) to fire. We have wrapped the `group1` branch in `catchError` and `timestamps` steps so that we can detect when the branch is interrupted/terminated by the `failFast` operation:

```
pipeline {
    agent any
    stages {
       stage ('Parallel') {
          steps {
             parallel (
                'group1': {
                    timestamps {
                       catchError {
                          sleep 10
                          echo 'Completed group1 processing'
                       }
                    }
                },
                'group2': {
                    sleep 5
                    error 'Error in group2 processing'
                },
                failFast: true
             )
          }
       }
    }
}
```

When we run this pipeline, we will get output like that shown in Figure 3-18.

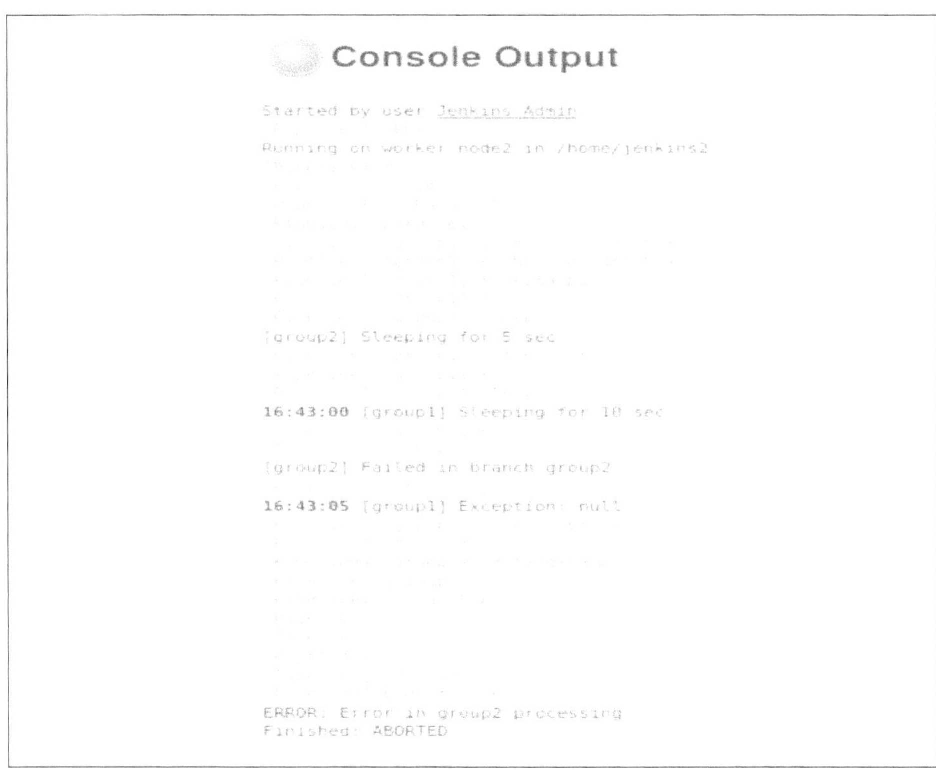

Figure 3-18. Running with the failFast option enabled

Looking at this output, you can see that 5 seconds into the `group1` branch processing, the branch was terminated (note the "Exception" in the log). This was because after the 5-second sleep, the `group2` branch threw the error. Then the `failFast` option terminated `group1`.

If we were to take the `failFast` option out or set it to *false*, then we would still see the `group2` branch terminate with the error, but the `group1` branch would run to completion after the 10-second sleep, as shown in the alternate output in Figure 3-19.

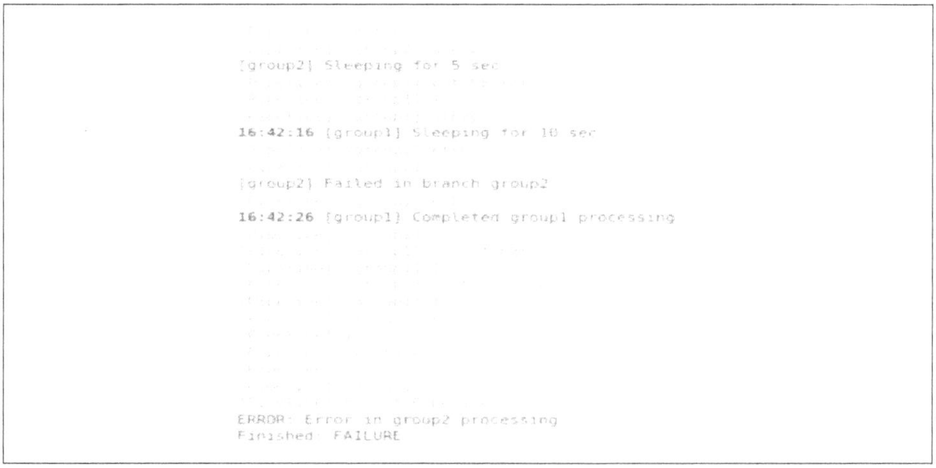

```
[group2] Sleeping for 5 sec

16:42:16 [group1] Sleeping for 10 sec

[group2] Failed in branch group2

16:42:26 [group1] Completed group1 processing

ERROR: Error in group2 processing
Finished: FAILURE
```

Figure 3-19. Running without the failFast option

We move on now from dealing with running multiple operations in parallel to executing operations based on (potentially multiple) conditions.

Conditional Execution

Historically, the Conditional BuildStep plugin let users add conditional execution functionality to Freestyle jobs in Jenkins. It allowed a way to test certain conditions, and, based on the outcome, execute single or multiple build steps.

Jenkins pipelines can provide similar functionality. In the case of a Scripted Pipeline, it's as simple as using the Groovy/Java language conditionals in your pipeline code. An example is included here using an `if` statement with conditions that must be true for multiple parameters:

```
node ('worker_node1') {
    def responses = null
    stage('selection') {
        responses = input message: 'Enter branch and select build type',
         parameters:[string(defaultValue: '', description: '',
         name: 'BRANCH_NAME'),choice(choices: 'DEBUG\nRELEASE\nTEST',
          description: '', name: 'BUILD_TYPE')]
    }
    stage('process') {
        if ((responses.BRANCH_NAME == 'master') &&
            (responses.BUILD_TYPE == 'RELEASE')) {
            echo "Kicking off production build\n"
        }
    }
}
```

Since these kinds of Groovy/Java-specific language features don't fit in a declarative model, Declarative Pipelines in Jenkins provide their own implementation for executing code based on conditionals. In general, it takes the form of a `when` that tests one or more `expression` blocks to see whether they are `true`. If so, then the remaining code in a stage is executed. If not, then the code is not executed.

Here's an example of a Declarative Pipeline that corresponds to the Scripted Pipeline just shown:

```
pipeline {
   agent any
      parameters {
         string(defaultValue: '',
               description: '',
               name : 'BRANCH_NAME')
        choice (
            choices: 'DEBUG\nRELEASE\nTEST',
            description: '',
            name : 'BUILD_TYPE')
      }
   stages {
      stage('process') {
         when {
            allOf {
               expression {params.BRANCH_NAME == "master"}
               expression {params.BUILD_TYPE == 'RELEASE'}
            }
         }
         steps {
            echo "Kicking off production build\n"
         }
      }
   }
}
```

Notice the use of the `parameters` section to formally define the parameters in use in the Declarative Pipeline. Also, you can see how the `when` and `allOf` blocks combine like the `if-&&` construct in the Scripted Pipeline.

Using these kinds of conditional constructs in Declarative Pipelines is covered in more detail in "Conditional execution of a stage" on page 241.

Post-Processing

Traditional (web-based) Jenkins Freestyle jobs include a Post-build Actions section where users can add actions that always occur after a build is finished, regardless of whether it completed successfully, failed, or was aborted.

We can replicate this functionality in both Scripted and Declarative Pipelines. The Scripted Pipeline relies on programming constructs to emulate this, while Declarative Pipelines have built-in functionality for it. We'll look at both of these implementations next.

Scripted Pipelines Post-Processing

Scripted Pipelines do not have built-in support for post-build processing. In Scripted Pipelines, when we don't have built-in functionality, we traditionally rely on Groovy programming constructs to provide it. This applies in this case as well, if we use the `try-catch-finally` mechanism.

However, the Jenkins DSL includes another step that acts as a shortcut for the `try-catch-finally` functionality: `catchError`. The `catchError` step can be useful in multiple instances, but fits well for our post-build use case here.

More details on these scripted choices follow.

try-catch-finally

What we want to have is a way to always do certain actions regardless of the final state of the build. We can accomplish that by catching any exceptions with a `try-catch` and using the `finally` clause to then do our processing based on the build's state. Most commonly, the processing we do in the `finally` clause would be sending mail or other notifications about the build's state. Here's an example of the structure with `try-catch-finally`:

```
def err = null
try {
   // pipeline code
   node ('node-name') {
      stage ('first stage') {
         ...
      } // end of last stage
   }
}
catch (err) {
   currentBuild.result = "FAILURE"
}
finally {
   (currentBuild.result != "ABORTED"){
       // Send email notifications for builds that failed
       //  or are unstable
   }
}
```

Notice that we are setting the value of `currentBuild.result` if there is an error, to ensure the build status is consistent with what we expect from Jenkins. Also, we don't send mail if the build was aborted. (For examples of how to send mail and other notifications, see Chapter 4.)

The `try-catch` could also be within the `node` block if we preferred. That would, however, not catch issues thrown while trying to get the node, which might also not be able to send the notification. Finally, if we wanted to propagate the error, we could throw it again in our `finally` block.

catchError

The Jenkins pipeline syntax also provides a more advanced way of handling exceptions. The `catchError` block provides a way to detect the exception and change the overall build status, but still continue the processing.

With the `catchError` construct, if an exception is thrown by a block of code, the build is marked as a failure. But the code in the pipeline continues to be executed from the statement following the `catchError` block.

The advantage of this processing is that you can still do things like send notifications after processing has failed. This simulates the post-build processing that we're accustomed to in the more traditional Jenkins model and also provides a shortcut over the `try-catch` block.

An example of using this is shown here:

```
node ('node-name') {
   catchError {
      stage ('first stage') {
         ...
      } // end of last stage
   }
   // step to send email notifications
}
```

This is essentially equivalent to the following code:

```
node ('node-name') {
    try {
       stage ('first stage') {
         ...
       } // end of last stage
    } catch (err) {
       echo "Caught: ${err}"
       currentBuild.result = 'FAILURE'
    }
    // step to send email notifications
}
```

The advantages are the simpler syntax and the build result automatically being marked as failed if an exception occurs.

Declarative Pipelines and Post-Processing

Declarative Pipelines have a dedicated section for post-build processing. Not surprisingly, the section is called `post`. A `post` section can be at the end of a stage or at the end of a pipeline—or both.

The most common use for this is to mimic the post-build operations, especially notifications, that are available for Freestyle jobs. The declarative syntax provides several predefined "build conditions" that can be checked and, if `true`, then initiate further action. Their names and uses are explained in tTable 3-1.

Table 3-1. Declarative build conditions for post-processing

Condition	Description
`always`	Always executes the steps in the block
`changed`	Executes the steps in the block if the current build's status is different from the previous build's status
`success`	Executes the steps in the block if the current build was successful
`failure`	Executes the steps in the block if the current build failed
`unstable`	Executes the steps in the block if the current build's status is unstable

So, for example, we can declare that if the `failure` condition is `true`, we want to send an email about the failure.

The syntax here is fairly simple. Here's an outline for a simple `post` structure at the end of a build:

```
      }
    } // end stages
    post {
       always {
          echo "Build stage complete"
       }
       failure {
          echo "Build failed"
          mail body: 'build failed', subject: 'Build failed!',
             to: 'devops@company.com'
        }
        success {
          echo "Build succeeded"
          mail body: 'build succeeded', subject: 'Build Succeeded',
             to: 'devops@company.com'
        }
    }
} // end pipeline
```

Notice that the `post` section for the entire build comes after all of the stages in the pipeline. Also, we could do other things when checking these conditions, such as archiving artifacts.

Summary

In this chapter, we've looked at pipeline constructs and steps that affect the overall execution flow of your pipeline.

We started with seeing how to specify the kinds of events that you want to trigger your pipeline. And once triggered, we saw how to accept different kinds of input to direct the behavior of the pipeline.

We looked at ways to have the pipeline try again when there's a failure or move on after a certain time period. And we saw ways to deal with concurrency—both to prevent it for multiple runs of the same pipeline, and to leverage it for running tasks in parallel. And we noted how to provide conditional build execution.

Finally, we looked at ways to accomplish post-build processing in pipelines similar to the functionality provided in Freestyle projects.

All of this should give you a good start on controlling the flow of execution through your Scripted or Declarative Pipeline. In the next chapter, we'll look at ways that Jenkins can send messages and notifications through some of the more popular communication tools.

CHAPTER 4

Notifications and Reports

One of the core uses of Jenkins is implementing automation. In addition to repeatable processing that is triggered by some event, we also rely on being automatically notified when processes have completed, and of their overall status. Additionally, many plugins and steps produce useful reports as part of their processing.

The pipeline DSL contains steps that help with notifications. In this chapter, we'll look at what it takes to configure Jenkins and implement code to leverage some common notification methods and services.

Starting out, we'll look at some of the types of notifications that Jenkins can send—from basic and extended email to using services such as Slack and HipChat.

Then we'll move on to how to surface reports that are generated by pipeline processing to a more convenient location.

With these tools, you should be equipped to get the information you need from Jenkins and share it with other users.

Notifications

In this section, we'll look at notifications—that is, informing users of some status, event, or piece of information that we want them to be aware of. For most cases, this will happen in the "post-processing" parts of a pipeline. In a Scripted Pipeline, this usually entails using a `try-catch-finally` construct if you want to always do post-processing (as described in Chapter 3). For Declarative Pipelines, we have the more straightforward `post` section that we can use.

Regardless of where you employ notifications, users today have a lot more options with Jenkins than just the traditional email route. Many of the options fall into the area of instant messaging, and even allow the user to do things like specify coloring for messages. We'll look at several of these in this chapter.

Email

Traditionally in Jenkins, email was the primary means of notification. As such, there is significant support (and significant options) for configuring email notifications in Jenkins. The options are managed on the Configure System page of the Manage Jenkins area. We'll break these down for simplicity.

Jenkins Location

In addition to the "nice" URL that you can set in this section (see the following note), this is where you can set the system administrator's email address. This is intended to be the "from" address that users will see in emails from Jenkins to the project owners. As described in the help screen shown in Figure 4-1, this can be a simple email address or a fuller one with a name for your Jenkins instance. Regardless, it is a required field.

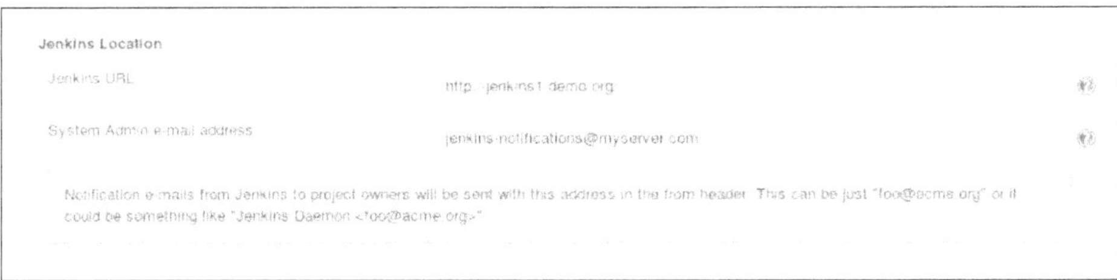

Figure 4-1. Jenkins Location settings

Jenkins URL

The Jenkins URL field in this section provides a place to put in the more user-friendly name of your Jenkins system. Jenkins can't detect the URL itself. Note that this is optional, and you could leave it as something like "localhost:8080". However, this is the Jenkins URL that will appear in the links in emails sent from Jenkins. So you will need to reference a clickable URL.

In reality, for most purposes, the email address for the user (configured later) will be the one surfaced in the emails. In most cases, you likely won't see the admin address unless you dig into the headers for the email. An example of deep-diving into those is shown next. Here, you can see the value of the "System Admin e-mail address" field in the `X-Google-Original-From` header:

```
X-Received: by 10.55.93.197 with SMTP id r188mr35950021qkb.277.1502803051345;
 Tue, 15 Aug 2017 06:17:31 -0700 (PDT)
Received: from diyvb2 (sas08001.nat.sas.com. [149.173.8.1])
```

```
        by smtp.gmail.com with ESMTPSA id 131sm6301940qki.23.2017.08.15.06.17.30
        for <bcl@nclasters.org (https://emailmg.webhost4life.com/sqmail/src/
compose.php?send_to=bl1%40nclasters.org) >
        (version=TLS1 cipher=ECDHE-RSA-AES128-SHA bits=128/128);
        Tue, 15 Aug 2017 06:17:30 -0700 (PDT)
From: jenkins-demo@gmail.com (https://emailmg.webhost4life.com/sqmail/src/
compose.php?send_to=nfjsuser1%40gmail.com)
X-Google-Original-From: jenkins-notification (https://emailmg.webhost4life.com/
sqmail/src/compose.php?send_to=jenkins-notifications
%40myserver.com)s@myserver.com (https://emailmg.webhost4life.com/sqmail/src/
compose.php?send_to=jenkins-notifications%40myserver.com)
Date: Tue, 15 Aug 2017 09:17:30 -0400 (EDT)
Reply-To: no-reply@jenkins.foo (https://emailmg.webhost4life.com/sqmail/src/
compose.php?send_to=no-reply%40jenkins.foo)
To: bcl@nclasters.org (https://emailmg.webhost4life.com/sqmail/src/compose.php?
send_to=bl1%40nclasters.org)
Message-ID: <2007092803.5.1502803050373.JavaMail.jenkins@diyvb2>
Subject: Test email #6
MIME-Version: 1.0
Content-Type: text/plain; charset=UTF-8
Content-Transfer-Encoding: 7bit
```

Next, we'll look at the traditional settings for email notifications in Jenkins.

E-mail Notification

Still on the global configuration page, there is an E-mail Notification section that you fill in to set up the basic email functionality. These fields should be pretty much self-explanatory in terms of setup, as long as you can gather the details for your email configuration. Note that there is an Advanced button to the right that you need to click to get access to some fields.

Figure 4-2 shows this section of the page.

Figure 4-2. E-mail Notification settings

A couple of notes:

- The SMTP server will default to the one on localhost if this field is left empty.
- If using SSL, the port will default to 465; otherwise, it defaults to 25.
- The Reply-To Address field here is optional, but can be convenient if you need to set one.
- Arguably the most important part of this section is the ability to test your email configuration by sending a test email (the last fields at the bottom). Doing this is highly recommended. If this test fails, you will commonly see a Java error traceback, as shown in Figure 4-3. This is typically due to a bad username or password, or a bad address for the email recipient.

Figure 4-3. *Traceback for failure sending test email*

With this background, let's see how we might use this in a pipeline script.

Sending email in pipelines

The following code listing shows an example of using the basic `mail` step in a Scripted Pipeline. As explained in other chapters of the book, the `try-catch-finally` block is the primary way with a Scripted Pipeline to ensure that post-processing is always done regardless of success or failure:

```
node ('worker_node1') {
  try {
      ...
    }
    currentBuild.result = 'SUCCESS'
  }
  catch (err) {
    currentBuild.result = 'FAILURE'
  }
  finally {
    mail to: 'bcl@nclasters.org',
      subject: "Status of pipeline: ${currentBuild.fullDisplayName}",
      body: "${env.BUILD_URL} has result ${currentBuild.result}"
  }
}
```

Setting Build Results

You may have noticed that we specifically set the `currentBuild.result` value in this listing. The reason for this is that you can't depend on pipeline steps to explicitly set the build result, and if the build result is not set the emails will show a status of `null`.

In a similar way, the pipeline `mail` step can be used in a Declarative Pipeline. Here's a simple example:

```
pipeline {
  agent any
  stages {
   ...
  }
  post {
    always {
       mail to: 'bcl@nclasters.org',
          subject: "Status of pipeline: ${currentBuild.fullDisplayName}",
          body: "${env.BUILD_URL} has result ${currentBuild.result}"
    }
  }
}
```

post Section of a Declarative Pipeline

Note that, as described in Chapter 7, the `post` section supports separate processing for build statuses such as success, failure, etc. In this case, we are simply using the `always` clause for a generic demonstration.

These pipelines will produce an email like the following if there is a failure:

```
---------------------------- Original Message ----------------------------
Subject: Status of pipeline: pipeline2 #1
From:    jenkins-demo@gmail.com
Date:    Tue, August 15, 2017 9:33 pm
To:      bcl@nclasters.org
--------------------------------------------------------------------------

http://jenkins1.demo.org/job/pipeline2/1/ has result FAILURE
```

If there is a successful build, this will look the same except `FAILURE` will be replaced with `SUCCESS`.

While the built-in functionality covers the basic email needs, there may be times when you need or want to further customize and control the emails that Jenkins sends. The Email Extension plugin (*https://plugins.jenkins.io/email-ext*) provides many additional options for expanding how emails are handled, but it also comes with trade-offs when using it in a pipeline environment. We'll dive into it next.

Extended email notifications

In addition to the basic email functionality, there is also an Extended Email (email-ext) plugin that adds numerous additional options and levels of control for sending email through Jenkins. It contains a similar general mail configuration section similar to the mail plugin, but also adds functionality in three areas:

Content
: It's possible to dynamically modify the contents of an email notification's subject and body.

Recipients
: You can define which user roles should receive an email notification.

Triggers
: You can specify what conditions should initiate sending an email notification. (Note that these do not currently apply to pipelines.)

We'll look at each of these areas in more detail next and see how to incorporate them where applicable.

Global configuration. The email-ext plugin requires some global configuration before being used in Pipeline jobs. Most of this is the same as the configuration we did for the basic email functionality (see Figure 4-4).

Figure 4-4. General configuration for extended emails

A few new fields deserve further explanation. They include:

Use List-ID Email Header

Selecting this option allows you to apply a list-id header to all emails. As the help suggests, this can be useful with filtering and also avoiding autoresponders. The help contains example formats.

Add 'Precedence: bulk' Email Header

This option adds a header to emails from Jenkins. Based on a standard used by mail systems, this option should eliminate or cut down on autoresponses being sent back to Jenkins.

Reply To List

This isn't a new one, but note that we can provide a comma-separated list of users/addresses.

Emergency reroute

If this field is filled in, all Jenkins emails will be sent to just that or those recipients. This could be useful for temporarily not allowing Jenkins to send out wider emails if there is an issue that warrants that.

Excluded Recipients

As the name implies, this can exclude (filter out) any email addresses from the list generated by other functionality in this plugin.

Next, we'll look at the functionality in the plugin that allows us to set the default elements of emails.

Content. Still in the global configuration, we have a set of fields that are intended to allow us to dynamically generate/modify the contents of the email notices sent out from Jenkins. Figure 4-5 shows these fields.

Figure 4-5. Default global content settings for extended email

The emailext Step and Default Fields

Currently, these fields are of no value in Pipeline scripts as there doesn't seem to be a way to tell the `emailext` step to use the defaults from here. However, we're including them in our discussion in case that functionality becomes available later.

The first three fields (Default Subject, Maximum Attachment Size, and Default Content) are pretty self-explanatory. Note that the attachment size should be expressed in terms of megabytes and this is cumulative for all attachments.

The Default Pre-send Script and Default Post-send Script areas offer places to enter a Groovy script to run before the email is sent (and potentially modify it) and after the email is sent, respectively. If you're interested in these, there are a number of "recipes" available on the web. A good place to start is the plugins page (*https://plugins.jenkins.io*).

You can also use a number of tokens in constructing the contents of the Default Subject and Default Content fields. "Tokens" here refers to what we might call build or environment variables filled in by Jenkins in other contexts. `$BUILD_NUMBER` contains the number of the build and `$PROJECT_NAME` contains the name of the project, for example. If defined, the default pre-send and post-send scripts can be referenced in other jobs as `${DEFAULT_PRESEND_SCRIPT}` and `${DEFAULT_POSTSEND_SCRIPT}`, respectively.

As well as providing more options for the content of emails, the extended email functionality also provides more options for choosing the types of recipients to send emails to. That's next.

Recipients. The Email Extension plugin provides several categories of recipients through the `emailext` pipeline step. These are in addition to any designated individual recipients.

Figure 4-6 shows the selectable categories in the drop-down for the step.

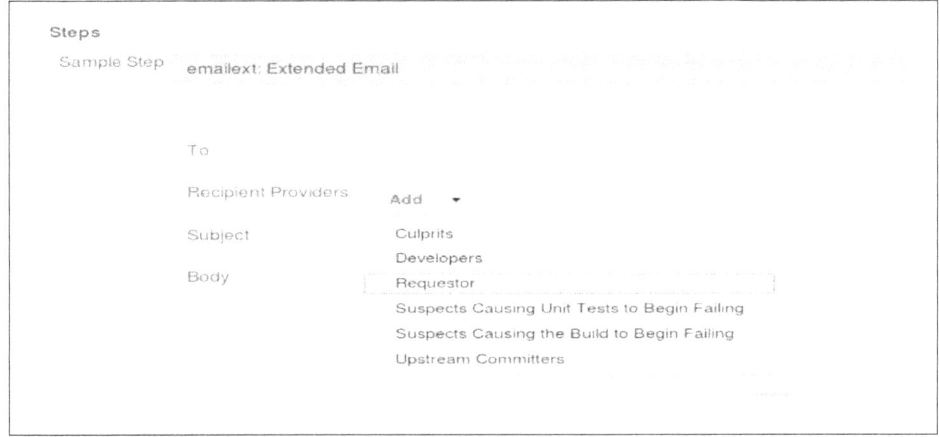

Figure 4-6. Adding extended email recipients

Table 4-1 lists the categories along with their definitions, drawing on the wording from the plugin documentation.

Table 4-1. Extended email recipients categories

Name	Description (from plugin documentation)
Culprits	Sends email to the list of users who committed a change between the last nonbroken build and now. This list at least always includes people who made changes in this build, but if the previous build was a failure it also includes the culprit list from that.
Developers	Sends email to all the people who caused a change in the changeset.
Requestor	Sends email to the user who initiated the build (assuming it was manually initiated).
Suspects Causing Unit Tests to Begin Failing	Sends email to the list of users suspected of causing a unit test to begin failing. This list includes committers and requestors of the build where the test began to fail, and of any consecutive failed builds prior to the build in which the test began to fail.
Suspects Causing the Build to Begin Failing	Sends email to the list of users suspected of causing the build to begin failing.
Upstream Committers	Sends email to the list of users who committed changes in upstream builds that triggered this build.

When using these in the `emailext` pipeline step, we need to use the `$class` notation to reference the names (at least as of the time of this writing). For example:

```
emailext body: 'body goes here',
 recipientProviders: [[$class: 'CulpritsRecipientProvider'],
 [$class: 'DevelopersRecipientProvider'],
 [$class: 'RequesterRecipientProvider'],
 [$class: 'FailingTestSuspectsRecipientProvider'],
 [$class: 'FirstFailingBuildSuspectsRecipientProvider'],
 [$class: 'UpstreamComitterRecipientProvider']],
 subject: 'subject goes here'
```

Triggers. The global configuration for the email-ext plugin also allows you to select a set of default triggers for events to send email on. However, this adds those automatic emails only when you are using Freestyle jobs and add "Editable Email Notifications" to the "Post-build Actions" part of the job. As such, they are not useful in the Pipeline context.

A similar approach can be constructed in a pipeline by doing things like checking the build status in a `finally` block in a Scripted Pipeline, or in a `post` block with conditionals in a Declarative Pipeline, and sending email off of that. See Chapter 3 (on Pipeline flow) and Chapter 7 (on Declarative Pipelines) for examples of post-build processing like this.

Including logs. One of the other useful built-in functions for the email-ext plugin is that it can also include (and compress) logs. To use this setting in the `pipeline` step, you can simply enable the options shown here:

```
attachLog: true, compressLog:true
```

Ultimately, the plugin provides a mixed bag for Pipeline developers. On the good side, it allows adding the extended classes of recipients and doing things like attaching logs. On the downside, `emailext` is one of those steps that was targeted to do a lot by default based on global configuration and adding a post-build action to a Freestyle job. That doesn't translate well into a Pipeline environment unless (until) there is some way to set a similar post-processing property, so the default functionality can be activated. Perhaps that will be added in the future, past this writing.

One other note is that using pre-send or post-send scripts in the `emailext` pipeline step seems to currently be broken. Objects that those scripts should have access to, such as the `build` object, are not accessible. Hopefully, this too will be fixed in the not-too-distant future.

With all that in mind, here's a final example of using the `emailext` pipeline step with many of the useful components:

```
emailext attachLog: true, body:
   """<p>EXECUTED: Job <b>\'${env.JOB_NAME}:${env.BUILD_NUMBER})\'
   </b></p><p>View console output at "<a href="${env.BUILD_URL}">
   ${env.JOB_NAME}:${env.BUILD_NUMBER}</a>"</p>
     <p><i>(Build log is attached.)</i></p>""",
    compressLog: true,
    recipientProviders: [[$class: 'DevelopersRecipientProvider'],
     [$class: 'RequesterRecipientProvider']],
    replyTo: 'do-not-reply@company.com',
    subject: "Status: ${currentBuild.result?:'SUCCESS'} -
    Job \'${env.JOB_NAME}:${env.BUILD_NUMBER}\'",
    to: 'bcl@nclasters.org Brent.Laster@domain.com'
```

There are several items worth noting about this step:

- The step is formatted to fit the space available on the page.
- A better approach when you're writing a Scripted Pipeline would be to define variables to hold some of the longer values and then use the variables in the step.
- Note the use of the triple double quotes around the text of the body. This is a Groovy-ism, where triple quotes are used to encapsulate multiline messages.
- We are using HTML tags in the body of the email. In order for this to be rendered as HTML, the default content type needs to be set to HTML (not text) in the global configuration for the email-ext plugin.
- Note the use of double quotes around strings that have variables to interpolate—another Groovy-ism.
- The syntax `${currentBuild.result?:'SUCCESS'}` checks whether `currentBuild.result` is `NULL` and, if so, assigns it the `'SUCCESS'` value. This is necessary because a `NULL` value in Jenkins for the build result indicates success.
- We have used the `replyTo` field to set an address for replies.
- Note that multiple names can be used in the `to` string, separated by spaces.

Figure 4-7 shows an example of an email generated by the previous command.

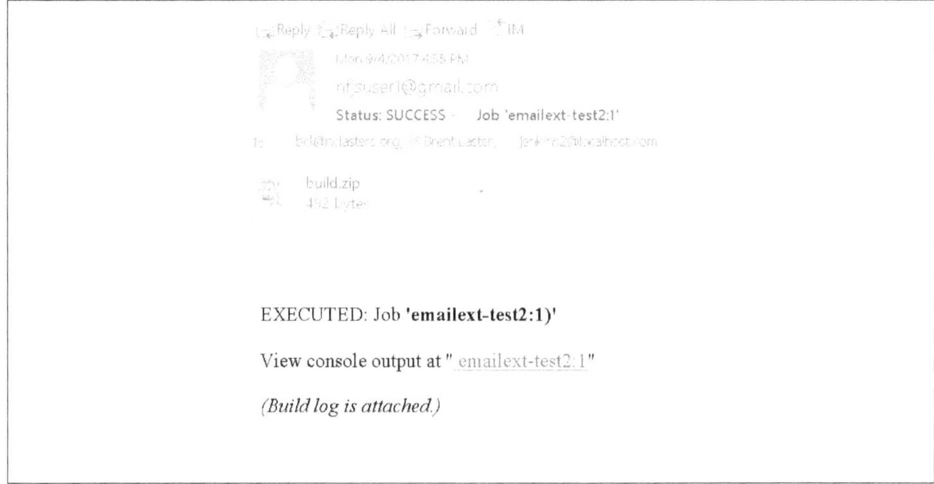

Figure 4-7. Example email from sample command

While emails still provide the most ubiquitous means of notifying Jenkins users of events and sharing information, more and more teams are using instant messaging services for collaboration and notifications. Two of the most popular are Slack and HipChat. Let's look at how Jenkins can work with each of them.

Collaboration Services

For several of the popular messaging/communications services, there are plugins to provide notifications to the services from Jenkins. In this section, we'll look at two of these—for Slack and HipChat.

Slack notifications

To send notifications to Slack, you first need to install the Slack Notification plugin (*https://plugins.jenkins.io/slack*). After installing and configuring the global parts of this plugin, your pipeline will be able to send notifications to a Slack channel via a `slackSend` step. But first, you'll need to enable the integration through Slack.

Setup in Slack. Enabling the Jenkins integration with Slack assumes you have a Slack account, a team, and a channel defined first. (We won't cover that here, but there is plenty of documentation for this available on the web.) For our purposes here, I've created an `explore-jenkins` team and a `#jenkins2` channel on Slack.

Next, you'll want to configure the Jenkins integration (*http://bit.ly/2vuSVjV*). This will guide you through creating a Slack API integration token to allow Jenkins to connect to Slack.

Figure 4-8 shows an example of the first screen of the configuration. Here, we are logged into the explore-jenkins team and are going to enable Jenkins CI integration for the #jenkins2 channel within that team.

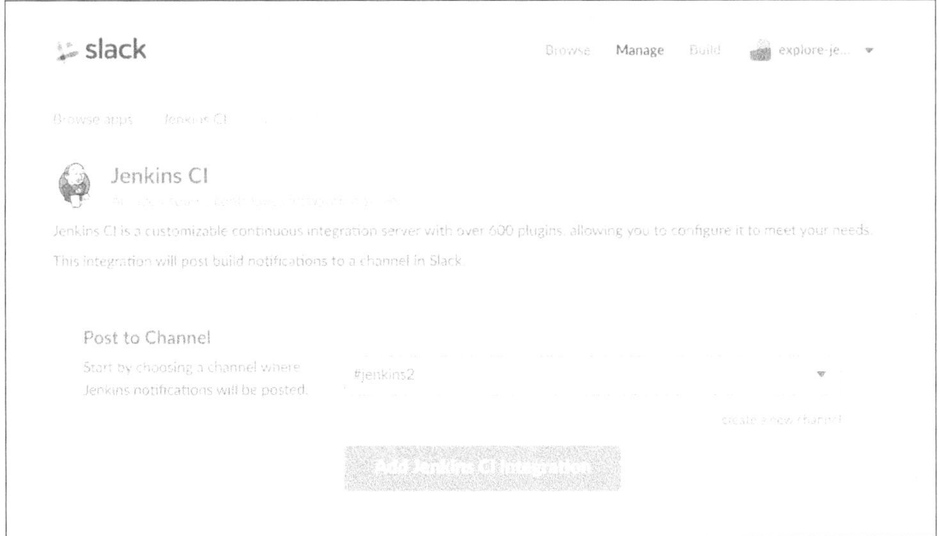

Figure 4-8. Enabling the Jenkins Slack integration on a channel

After clicking the "Add Jenkins CI integration" button, you'll be taken to the next screen, which will have directions for what to do in Jenkins to use the integration. Further down on the page will be the integration settings to use in Jenkins.

The main things you need from this are the base URL and the token. Both of these currently can be found in the output for Step 3 on the page (Figure 4-9). Modify any other settings you want and then click the Save Settings button at the bottom of the page. This will save the options but will return you to the same page.

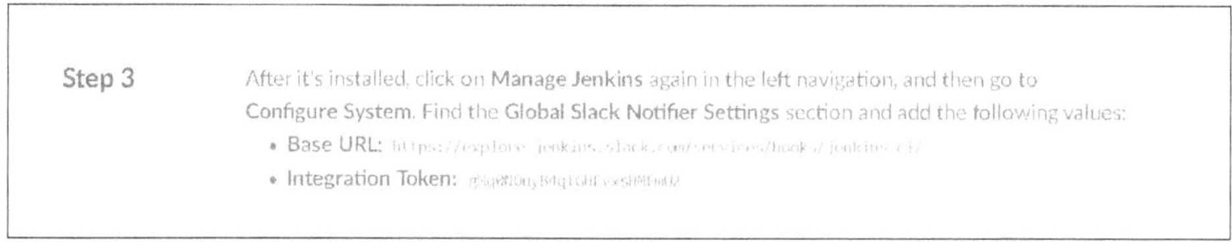

Figure 4-9. Information from Slack integration page with info needed for Jenkins config

This is a good time to take care of a security issue. While you could use the token directly in the Jenkins global configuration, this is considered a security risk. You are better off creating a "Secret text" credential to hold this. More information on creating credentials is in Chapter 5, but Figure 4-10 shows the main step of filling in the dialog for a new credential.

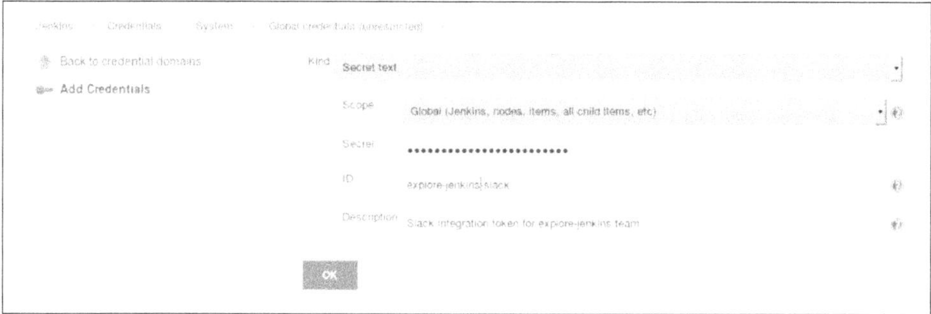

Figure 4-10. Creating a new "Secret text" credential for Slack

The next section assumes that you've created such a credential to use in the global configuration.

Global configuration in Jenkins. The global setup for the Slack notifications involves just a few basic pieces of information, as shown in Figure 4-11.

Figure 4-11. Global configuration for the Jenkins/Slack notifications

First is the base URL. This can be obtained from the Slack integration output as described in the previous section.

Next is the team subdomain, which is the team you will be using in Slack (the same one you configured the token for). Likewise, you can fill in the last argument with the channel that you configured the token for.

As we discussed in the previous section, it's better to create a new credential to use for the Slack integration token than to directly expose the token itself. The Integration Token Credential ID field is where you select the credential you previously set up that contains the token. When using this option, you can leave the "Integration Token" field blank.

Finally, there's the "IsBot User?" checkbox. Enabling (checking) this option allows notifications to be sent from a bot user. For this to work, credentials for the bot user (integration token credentials) need to be provided.

Once you have these fields filled in, you can test the connection by clicking the Test Connection button. If all went well, you should see a Success message. And then, in Slack itself, you'll be able to see the notifications regarding the integration setup (Figure 4-12).

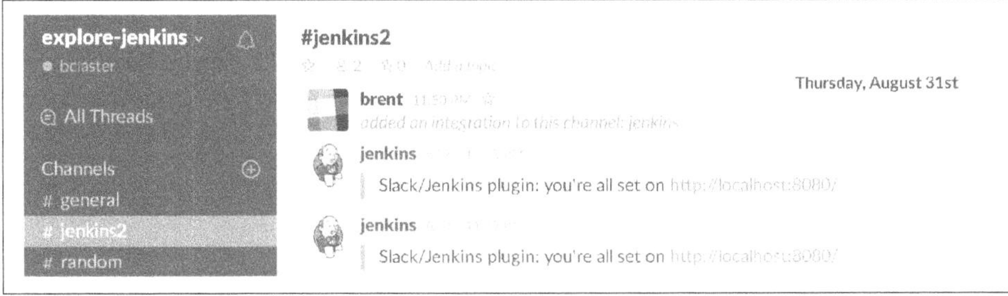

Figure 4-12. Notifications of Slack integration setup

Webhooks in Slack. While API tokens are fairly easy to set up for integration, there is another approach that can be used—webhooks. This is the newer approach for integration between Jenkins and Slack, allowing Slack to send a payload to a public endpoint defined in Jenkins when it has something to share. This is also the approach for Slack-compatible applications. We won't go into all the details here, but I'll provide some pointers on getting this set up just in case you need to at some point.

As with the Jenkins CI integration previously outlined, you first need to enable the webhook integration for your subdomain/team from within Slack. Note that you want to set up an outgoing webhook (information sent from Slack) as opposed to an incoming webhook. Figure 4-13 shows the screen in Slack to enable the outgoing webhook integration.

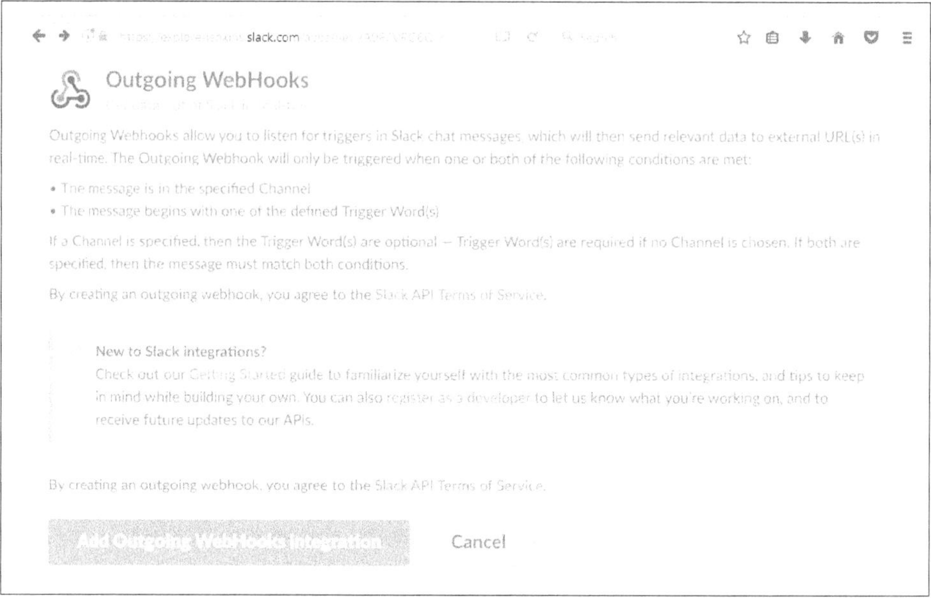

Figure 4-13. Enabling the outgoing webhook integration in Slack

After you click the "Add Outgoing WebHooks Integration" button, you'll be taken to a screen where you'll find additional information about your new integration, including the token (Figure 4-14).

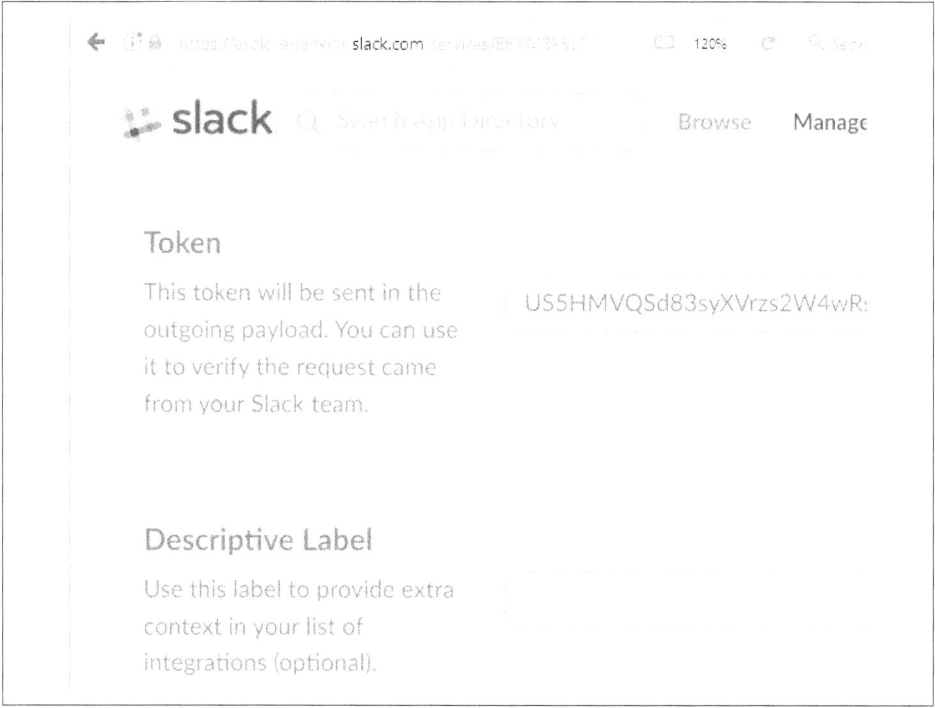

Figure 4-14. Outgoing webhook integration details—including token

You can then configure the global setup for Slack webhooks with the token and your endpoint (Figure 4-15).

Figure 4-15. Setting global configuration in Jenkins for Slack webhooks

Sending Slack notifications in a job. The `slackSend` pipeline step allows for actually sending the message via Slack. The only required (default) parameter is the message string to send. While you can send any message string, if you are using this for notifications from Jenkins then you probably want to include Jenkins environment variables or global variables, such as `env.JOB_NAME`, `env.BUILD_NUM`, etc. When using these, remember to enclose them in the `${}` syntax in a string that is enclosed itself in double quotes so that the Groovy interpolation will work correctly. Here's a simple example with only the default parameter:

```
slackSend  "Build ${env.BUILD_NUMBER} completed for ${env.JOB_NAME}."
```

Adding Links in the Message

Links can be added using standard HTML code (assuming the "Text format" option is not set)—simply code the item as `(<link | text>)`. For example, to add a link to the URL you send out, you could modify the previous step this way:

```
slackSend "Build ${env.BUILD_NUMBER} completed for
${env.JOB_NAME}.  Details: (<${env.BUILD_URL} | here >)"
```

The other likely parameter that you'll use will be `color`. This setting is used to color the border along the left side of the message attachment.

Colors can be specified via a couple of predefined labels or a hex string (explained more in the upcoming note). The predefined labels are `good` (dark green), `warning` (orange-yellow), and `danger` (dark red).

Adding in a color and a link, the example step might look like this:

```
slackSend color: 'good', message: "Build ${env.BUILD_NUMBER}
 completed for  ${env.JOB_NAME}.  Details: (<${env.BUILD_URL} |
 here >)"
```

Note that the part of the message with the variables must be enclosed in double quotes to allow for the interpolation of the values.

Colors and Color Codes

The `slackSend` step can use a color code represented by a string of hexadecimal (base-16) characters. The `hipchatSend` step (discussed shortly) uses a name for the color. Let's take a moment and see how these map.

The hex representation for a color consists of six characters, which can be numbers from 0–9 or characters from A–F. Each character position represents a certain part/tone of the color, and the combination of values for the six characters makes up a unique color.

Within this combination, the first two characters represent the red elements, the next two colors represent the green elements, and the final two characters represent the blue elements.

Using combinations of the hex digits in the different positions allows us to create any unique color with different combinations of the red, green, and blue elements. Here are some examples:

- `#000000` means that all color parts are off, so this equates to black.
- `#FFFFFF` means that all color parts are on, so this equates to white.
- `#FF0000` means that all of the red elements are on, so this is red.
- `#00FF00` means that all of the green elements are on, so this is green.
- `#FFFF00` means that all of the red and green elements are on, which makes yellow (red mixed with green).

So, if you wanted to have the color be purple, you could turn on the red components (two left hex digits) and the blue components (two right hex digits) and turn off the green components (middle two digits), as in `#FF00FF`.

There are additional parameters that the `slackSend` step can take. Most of these have the same names and types of settings as the values in the global configuration for Slack integration. They are designed to allow the step to override the default settings if desired. You can find out more about these by going to the Pipeline Syntax screen, selecting the `slackSend` step, and clicking the Advanced button.

Finally, one other parameter that is available is `failOnError`. Setting this to `true` causes the run to abort if there is a problem sending the notification.

HipChat notifications

Similar to the Slack Notification plugin, there is also a HipChat Notification plugin. It adds a `hipchatSend` step to the Pipeline DSL. Like the Slack plugin, the HipChat plugin requires some configuration in the application itself first. Unlike with Slack, you have a choice (currently) of using either HipChat's version 1 API or the new version 2 API. Although version 2 is recommended going forward, as of the time of this writing version 1 is still supported, so we'll cover setup for both.

For these examples, I assume that you have an account already with at least one room set up. For the example here, I have a room set up named *explore-jenkins*.

Setup in HipChat for version 1 API use. From your room's menu, you can select Integrations and then browse to find the Jenkins tile (Figure 4-16).

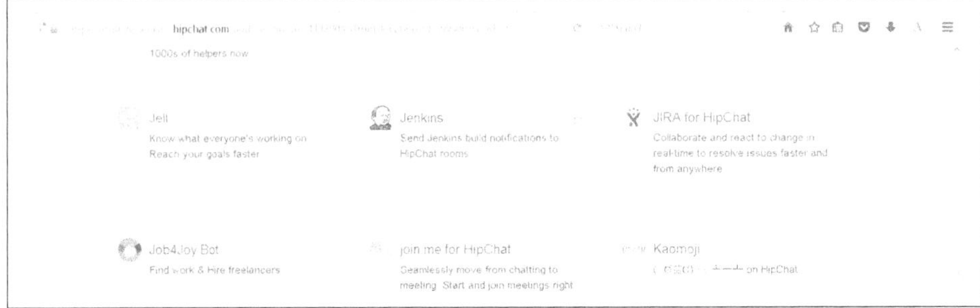

Figure 4-16. The Jenkins integration tile in HipChat

Select this tile and you'll be presented with a screen that has the version 1 token on it (Figure 4-17).

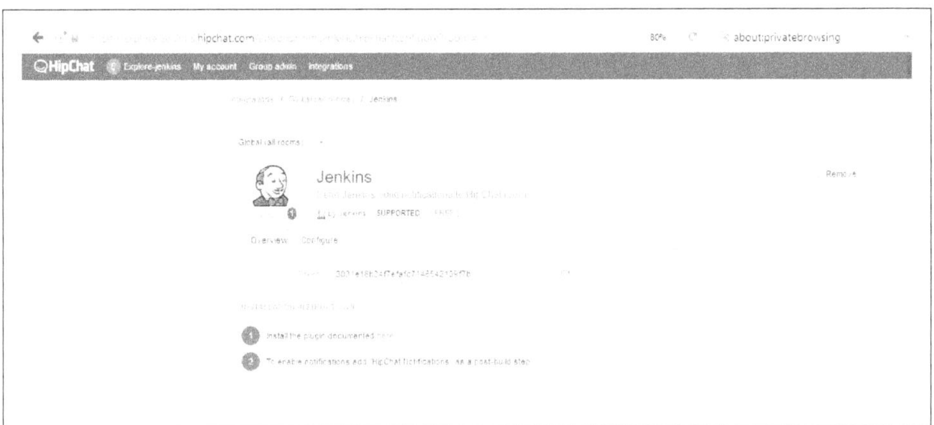

Figure 4-17. v1 token screen

To use this token in the Jenkins global configuration, you must create a new Jenkins "Secret text" credential. The process is shown in "Setup in Slack" on page 119. Note that you do not have the option to use the token in plain text in the Jenkins global configuration, as you do with the Slack setup.

Setup in HipChat for version 2 API use. If you want to (or are required to) use the HipChat version 2 API, the easiest way to get a token is to go to *http://<your room>.hipchat.com/account/api*. (Note that this is for a personal token.) Once there, in the "Create new token" section, provide a label for the token and select the type. (The examples here use the label "jenkins" and the Send Notification scope). Click the Create button and you'll see a v2 token that you can use (Figure 4-18).

Figure 4-18. Getting a HipChat v2 token

To use this token in the Jenkins global configuration, you must create a new Jenkins "Secret text" credential. The process is shown in "Setup in Slack" on page 119.

Global configuration in Jenkins. For the HipChat global configuration, you need to first fill in the location of the HipChat server. Unless you have a dedicated server with its own name for this, you can just leave it as the default *api.hipchat.com*.

Next is the checkbox to indicate whether or not you are using the v2 API. If you are using the v1 API, leave it unchecked.

Under that, enter the room name you want to send notifications to. This can be either the room name (case-sensitive) or the HipChat ID number. Multiple names can be provided as long as they are comma-separated.

Next, if you are using v1, you can specify a different ID from which to send the notifications. The default is "Jenkins".

The Card Provider field has to do with notification cards in HipChat. A discussion of notification cards is outside the scope of this book; unless you have a specific reason to do otherwise, you can just leave this as "Default cards".

Figure 4-19 shows an example of the global configuration for HipChat in Jenkins.

Figure 4-19. HipChat global configuration

Once you have this information filled in, it is a good time to test out the communication between Jenkins and HipChat. You can do that by pressing the "Test configuration" button. If all is set up correctly, you should see a Test Notification Sent message like that in Figure 4-20.

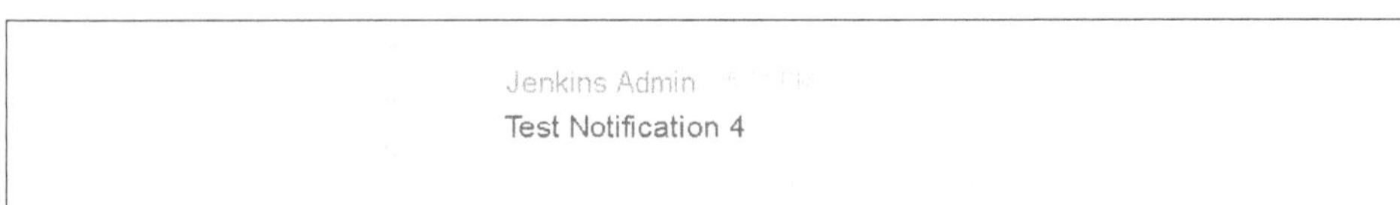

Figure 4-20. Test notification from Jenkins

Default notifications. There is one more piece of global configuration for the HipChat plugin—default notifications. This is the last section of the globally configured options. The boldfaced headers in that section are columns that you can configure when you add a default notification. To add a default notification, you simply click the Add button and fill in the fields.

As the name implies, the intent is to allow setting up default notifications for a job. However, these notifications are only sent if specific notifications aren't configured in a job *and* if the HipChat Notifications option is added as a post-build action. Since those conditions can only be met with a Freestyle project, and since Pipeline projects using the HipChat integration will have a specific notification step by definition, these don't apply for Pipeline projects.

Sending HipChat notifications in a job. The HipChat Notification plugin provides the previously mentioned `hipchatSend` step that you can use in your pipeline. The only required (default) parameter is a message. While you can send any message string, if you are using this for notifications from Jenkins then you probably want to include Jenkins environment variables or global variables, such as `env.JOB_NAME`, `env.BUILD_NUM`, etc. When using these, remember to enclose them in the `${}` syntax in a string that is enclosed itself in double quotes so that the Groovy interpolation will work correctly. Here's a simple example with only the default parameter:

```
hipchatSend "Build Started: ${env.JOB_NAME} ${env.BUILD_NUMBER}"
```

The other common option to use sets the color for the background of the message in the interface. Unlike the Slack color options, the color value can only be one of `GREEN`, `YELLOW`, `RED`, `PURPLE`, `GRAY`, or `RANDOM`. The default is `GRAY`.

Additional options control other aspects of the message. The `notify` option can be set to `true` or `false`; it indicates whether the message should trigger a user notification with sounds for notifying mobile devices and so on. And the `textFormat` option indicates whether the message should be sent in text format (if set to `true`). The default is `false` (HTML).

Adding Links in the Message

Assuming the `textFormat` option is not set to `true`, links can be added in `hipchatSend` messages by just using standard HTML. For example:

```
hipchatSend "Build ${env.BUILD_NUMBER} completed for
   ${env.JOB_NAME}. Details: <a href=${env.BUILD_URL}>
   here</a>"
```

An example of a more elaborate command with the `color` option and notifications for the room would look like this:

```
hipchatSend color: 'GREEN',
     notify: true,
     message: "Build ${env.BUILD_NUMBER} completed for
     ${env.JOB_NAME}.  Details: <a href=${env.BUILD_URL}>here</a>"
```

The notification in HipChat would look like Figure 4-21.

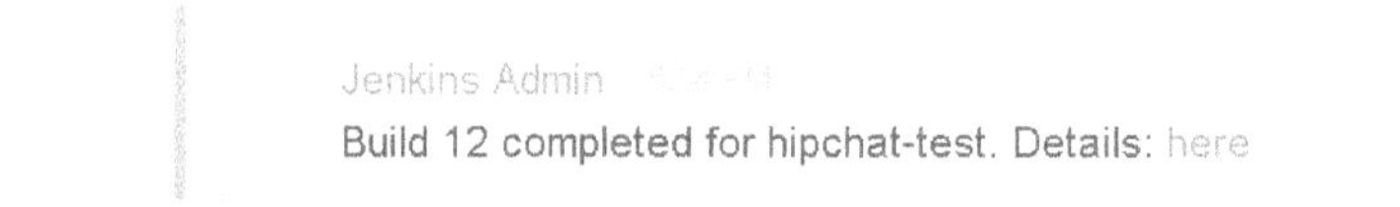
Jenkins Admin
Build 12 completed for hipchat-test. Details: here

Figure 4-21. HipChat notification from Jenkins

There are additional parameters that the `hipchatSend` step can take. These have the same names and types of settings as the values in the global configuration for HipChat. They are designed to allow the step to override the default settings if desired. You can find out more about these by going to the Pipeline Syntax screen, selecting the `hipChat` step, and clicking the Advanced button.

Unlike the underlying email functionality, the integration points for the collaboration services continue to evolve. HipChat is moving from the v1 API to the v2 API. Slack is adding more support for webhooks. And compatible services may also use slightly different approaches. Always check the Plugins index (*https://plugins.jenkins.io*) for the latest information.

There are certainly other types of notifications that Jenkins can provide with appropriate plugin integration, but hopefully this section has given you enough to get going with meaningful communication.

Another means that Jenkins uses to convey information is producing reports—or rather, the applications that Jenkins integrates with produce reports. Getting these exposed for easier access is the subject of our next section.

Reports

Many plugins or tools used with Jenkins generate HTML reports for various tasks. Example tasks include code analysis, code coverage, and unit test reports. Some of these, such as those for SonarQube and JaCoCo, provide custom integrations with Jenkins job output. These usually take the form of visual elements such as badges or graphs or simple links that the user can click to get to the application itself and view the reports.

However, some tooling doesn't supply that level of integration with Jenkins. It simply creates the reports in a location relative to the workspace and leaves it up to the user to determine the location, browse to it, and view the content there. This is less convenient than having a link to the report on the job output page, especially if you are trying to locate the report within one of Jenkins's workspaces and/or need to access this information over multiple runs of a job.

Fortunately, the HTML Publisher plugin (*https://plugins.jenkins.io/htmlpublisher*) is available. This plugin allows you to add a step in your pipeline code to point to an

HTML report. It also allows you to have a custom link created on the job's output page, and it provides options such as ensuring that reports are preserved over time (archived).

Publishing HTML Reports

To see how the HTML Publisher plugin works, let's look at an example. Assume we have a Gradle build for a project with multiple subprojects, including one named *api* and one named *util*. Our pipeline runs the Gradle *test* task against these subprojects, exercising a set of unit tests that we have created for each.

By convention, Gradle creates a report named *index.html* for any unit testing it does, and places it in a *<component>/build/reports/test* directory. For our pipeline, we want to add links to the HTML test reports produced by Gradle for the *api* and *util* subprojects.

This provides us with the basic information we need to pass to the DSL step, which is named `publishHTML`. An invocation of this step for the *api* report might look like this:

```
publishHTML (target: [
      allowMissing: false,
      alwaysLinkToLastBuild: false,
      keepAll: true,
      reportDir: 'api/build/reports/test',
      reportFiles: 'index.html',
      reportName: "API Unit Testing Results"
    ])
```

The purpose of most of the fields specified for the step are obvious from their names, and with the HTML Publisher plugin installed the syntax is available via the Snippet Generator. We'll cover the fields here anyway, but as usual, it may be easier to generate the actual code through the generator.

To start with, notice that we have the `target` block as the main parameter. Within that we have a number of subparameters:

`allowMissing`
: This setting has to do with whether or not the build should fail if the report is missing. If set to `false`, a missing report will fail the build.

`alwaysLinkToLastBuild`
: If this setting is `true`, then Jenkins will always show a link to the report from the last successful build—even if the current build failed.

`keepAll`
: If this is set to `true`, then Jenkins archives the reports for all successful builds. Otherwise Jenkins only archives the report for the most recent successful build.

`reportDir`
: This is the path to the HTML file, relative to the Jenkins workspace.

`reportFiles`
: This is the name of the HTML file(s) to display (if multiple, they should be separated by commas).

`reportName`
: This is the name you want the link to the report to have on the job output page.

Typically, like a notification, we may want this step to run at the end of the build. And we may want it to run regardless of whether the build succeeded (especially if we have it set up to link to the last successful build). We can add it to a notifications stage in a `try-catch-finally` section for a Scripted Pipeline or a `post` stage for a Declarative Pipeline. An example `finally` section of a pipeline script with this step is shown next. Note that here we are unstashing content because it was produced on separate nodes running in a `parallel` step:

```
finally {

   unstash 'api-reports'

   publishHTML (target: [
      allowMissing: false,
      alwaysLinkToLastBuild: false,
      keepAll: true,
      reportDir: 'api/build/reports/test',
      reportFiles: 'index.html',
      reportName: "API Unit Testing Results"
  ])

   unstash 'util-reports'

   publishHTML (target: [
      allowMissing: false,
      alwaysLinkToLastBuild: false,
      keepAll: true,
      reportDir: 'util/build/reports/test',
      reportFiles: 'index.html',
      reportName: "Util Unit Testing Results"
  ])
 }
```

A corresponding `post` section could be used in a Declarative Pipeline.

Figure 4-22 shows the output page from our job with the custom report name links that we created on the left side.

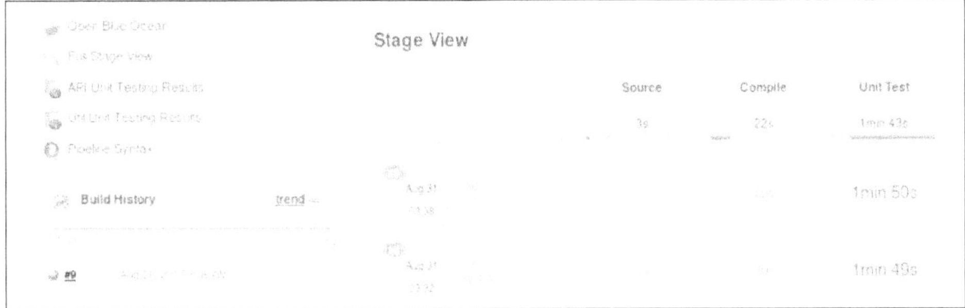

Figure 4-22. Job output showing the custom report links in the left menu

Summary

In this chapter, we've covered some of the basic ways to facilitate Jenkins-to-user communication when working with pipelines. We've looked at the built-in and extended email functionality and how we can leverage those, and we've seen how to use collaboration services like Slack and HipChat to send dynamic status information back to wherever you use those apps.

We also looked at how to better integrate the HTML reports produced by many applications with the job's output page for easier access.

It's important to realize that the information presented here is the most basic implementation for several of the steps, particularly the ones on notifications. Other pipeline constructs could certainly be used to render these in a more elegant way in the code.

For example, for the sake of space, long strings were included in some of the steps that, in a Scripted Pipeline, would be better defined as variables and passed in to the step.

As another point, shared library routines could be used to encapsulate functions with any of the steps to make them easier to call and more generic. (Shared libraries are discussed in Chapter 6.)

However, hopefully this chapter has given you the information you need to get started. I encourage you to explore and build on these examples to make your pipeline the best fit for the notification mechanisms that you and your team need.

In the next chapter, we'll explore how to set up and use Jenkins credentials and some key items around securing your pipelines.

CHAPTER 5

Access and Security

Being able to create pipelines-as-code offers enormous potential and flexibility. In Scripted Pipelines, calls to any Groovy construct or Jenkins functionality or external method can be keyed into the pipeline script. However, that also significantly increases the ability to accidentally or intentionally do something within the code for a pipeline that shouldn't be done. So, security has to be a first-class concern—and a first-class feature—for both pipelines and the Jenkins environment they are created and run in.

In this chapter, we'll survey the different ways that Jenkins has for controlling access and security. We'll first look at the overall security options, then we'll survey the traditional credentials mechanisms that Jenkins offers and how to use those in pipelines.

After that, we'll do a deeper dive into the advanced functionality available via the Role-Based Access Control (RBAC) plugin (*http://bit.ly/2uEfJNP*). We'll then explore how Jenkins can integrate with Vault, a modern approach to storing credentials with a limited lifetime.

Finally, we'll see what new features Jenkins 2 provides for ensuring that the steps in a pipeline have only the appropriate access and are executed in an approved context.

Let's start off by looking at the most basic options for securing Jenkins once it's installed.

Securing Jenkins

Prior to Jenkins 2.0, the default configuration for Jenkins was to have security disabled—not doing any security checking. This meant that Jenkins was wide open by default. Since Jenkins 2.0, the default has changed to have security enabled. Initially this means that when you use Jenkins, you need to supply a user ID and password. In fact, when you install Jenkins 2.0, you must enter a generated initial password—provided in an obscure file—as part of the installation. You also need to create an initial user with a user ID and password.

Beyond the basic logins, a number of security mechanisms are available through the Configure Global Security link on the Manage Jenkins page. This should be your starting point for a secure instance. (See Figure 5-1.)

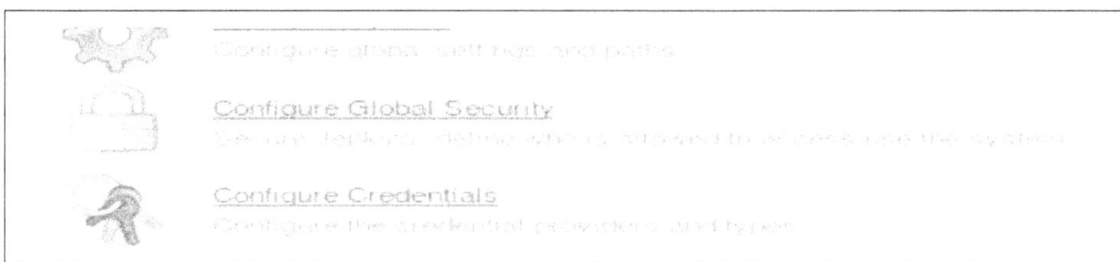

Figure 5-1. Accessing the configuration for the Global Security options

We'll briefly look at each of the security options configurable from this page next.

Enabling Security

The top option on the global security configuration page is also the most high-level one—meaning that it encompasses the most related functionality. Without the "Enable security" option checked, security-checking operations are not enabled. With this option turned on, security can be configured along two dimensions—authentication and authorization.

Authentication here refers to how users can identify themselves to the system, such as by user ID and password. This is now called "Security Realm" in Jenkins. *Authorization* refers to what permissions authorized users have. These two orthogonal dimensions can, together, implement nearly any desired security policy.

Setting Permissions Too Loosely

It is possible to implement policies using authentication and authorization that actually make your Jenkins instance very insecure. For example, Jenkins provides an option to allow users to sign up for access—less secure authentication. If you also use very open authorization policies, such as allowing logged-in users to do most/all operations, then you are effectively leaving your system wide open to anyone who wants to use it in whatever way they want.

The username/password login info is required for any operation unless anonymous users are specifically allowed to do the operation. In Jenkins 2, by default, logged-in users have full control and anonymous users have no access.

Under the checkbox to enable security, we have the "Disable remember me" checkbox. Checking this option to enable it removes the "Remember me on this computer" option from the login screen.

Next, we have the Access Control section. This section provides the options to configure the two dimensions we talked about earlier (authentication and authorization).

Access Control—Security Realm

This section allows us to specify which entity will be responsible for authenticating users to Jenkins. There are several choices.

Delegate to servlet container. The servlet container being referenced here is the one running the Jenkins instance. These days, this is usually Jetty, but it might also be Tomcat or some other servlet if the installation has been customized. With this option, you are allowing authentication via whatever mechanism the servlet container uses.

The specifics of how to set this up depend on how authentication is configured for the particular servlet container being used. The best approach is to consult the documentation for the servlet container. Up until v1.163 this was the default security realm. It is not as likely to be used these days given the other options, but can still be worthwhile for backward compatibility, or if you have invested significant setup for authentication in the servlet container's configuration.

Jenkins' own user database. This option delegates authentication to the list of people maintained by/known to Jenkins. This is not a typical use case, but can be suitable for smaller, basic setups. Note that this includes not only all the users that Jenkins specifically knows about, but also users mentioned in commit messages.

A suboption allows enabling users to "sign up"—meaning they can create their own accounts at the time they first need to log in to Jenkins. This suboption is disabled by default to more tightly control access.

LDAP. The Lightweight Directory Access Protocol (LDAP) is a software protocol for locating people, organizations, devices, and other resources on a network. If your company uses LDAP, this is where you can configure it for Jenkins. You can add more than one LDAP server (each having a different configuration if needed).

Unix user/group database. This option delegates authentication to the host Unix system's user database. If this is used, users can log into Jenkins using their Unix username and password. Unix groups can also be used for authentication. If a user and a group have the same name, prepending an "@" onto the name differentiates it as a group. Note that there may be extra configuration required to make this all work, such as making Jenkins a member of the shadow group for access on operating systems that use that.

Access Control—Authorization

Once authenticated, Jenkins needs to know what kind of operations users should be allowed to do. Like in the Security Realm section, there are several options here.

Anyone can do anything. No real authentication is done with this option. Basically, everyone is considered as "trusted"—including anonymous users (even if they haven't logged in yet). This is not recommended, but can be suitable in rare cases for completely trusted environments to allow unrestricted access for simplicity and efficiency.

Legacy mode. This mode emulates Jenkins behavior prior to v1.164: anyone who has the "admin" role has full control, and everyone else has read-only access.

Logged-in users can do anything. As the name implies, users must first log in, but then have full access. This is useful if you don't mind allowing everyone full access, but want to keep track of who is doing what (via them being logged in).

A suboption here enables anonymous users to have read-only access.

Matrix-based security. This option allows you to specify very specific permissions for individual users or groups via checkboxes in a matrix arrangement. The columns in the matrix are divided into categories (groupings) such as "Overall," "Job," "Run," etc. Then underneath each of those items are further specific permissions related to that category.

The rows of the matrix each represent a user or group. There are two default groups that are automatically added: "Anonymous Users" (users who have not logged in) and "Authenticated Users" (users who have logged in). A text box under the matrix allows you to add new users.

Granting a particular permission to a user or group is just a matter of clicking in the box that corresponds to the appropriate row for the user/group and the column for the specific permission. Removing a permission involves just clicking again to clear the checkbox.

At the end of each row are boxes you can click on to grant all permissions or remove all permissions for that user/group.

Figure 5-2 shows an example matrix.

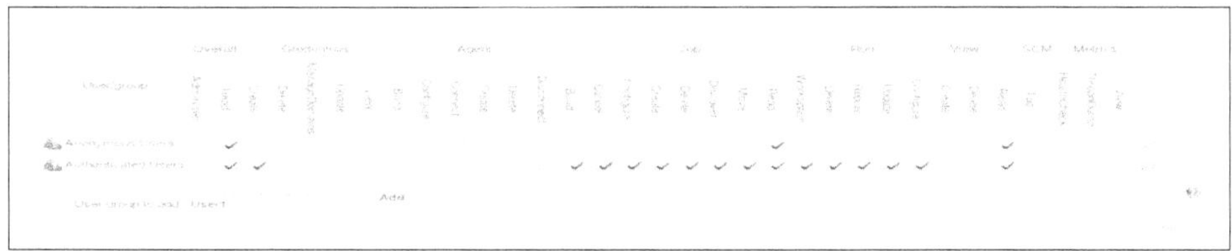

Figure 5-2. Example of matrix-based authentication

Project-based matrix authorization strategy. This option is an extension to the "Matrix-based security" model described in the preceding section. When selected, this adds a similar matrix to each project's configuration page. This allows for configuration by user/group per project, so you can restrict access to some projects while allowing it for others.

More specifically, when this option is set in the global security page, each project's configuration page will have an "Enable project-based security" option in the General configuration section. Selecting this option will then present an authorization matrix for that project that can be configured like the global matrix to provide project-specific access. An additional option allows you to select whether to inherit permissions from a parent access control list, the globally defined permissions, or not at all.

Figure 5-3 shows an example of one such matrix in a project.

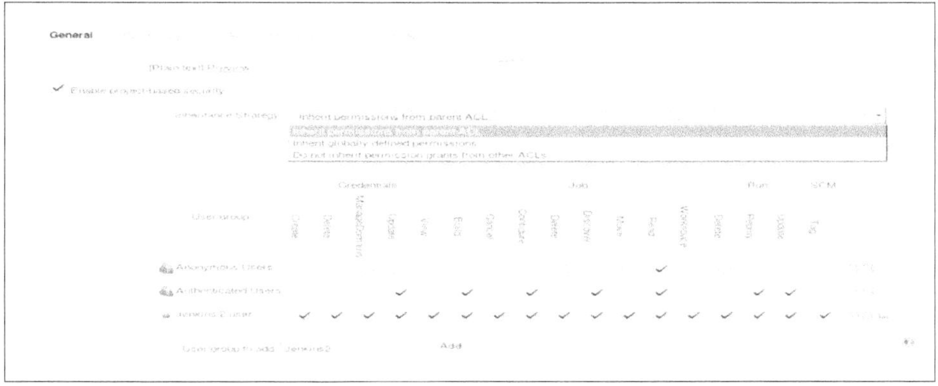

Figure 5-3. Per-project authorization matrix

Other Global Security Settings

Beyond the authentication and authorization settings, there are a number of other options on the global security configuration page that can be set. This is a miscellaneous collection centered around keeping Jenkins implicitly safe (locking down security holes) rather than explicitly defining access.

Markup formatter

Jenkins allows users to put in free-form text in various fields, such as job descriptions, build descriptions, etc. You can choose to format those as plain text or HTML. If you want to use HTML, set this option to Safe HTML. "Safe" here refers to allowing only HTML constructs that don't pose a security risk of being hacked (i.e., modified in a way that would execute operations that would put the system at risk). Examples of safe HTML constructs include the basic ones such as bold, italics, hyperlinks, etc.

Agents

Despite the generic name, this section is about configuring the TCP port for agents launched through the JNLP process. (JNLP refers to the Java Network Launch Protocol—a way that an application can be launched on a client's desktop using resources hosted on a remote server.)

Normally, a random port is used for this. However, you can specify a fixed port instead to make it more secure (only having to open the firewall for the fixed port). If you are not making use of the JNLP functionality, you can use the Disable option here to make your system even more secure.

A suboption allows you to choose a particular version of the JNLP protocol if needed.

Prevent Cross-Site Request Forgery exploits

Cross-Site Request Forgery (CSRF) is a type of attack that can force a user to execute unwanted actions on a web application that they are authenticated to. Part of the prevention of this has to do with verifying that a crumb trail (navigation history) exists for the user in Jenkins.

A suboption allows specifying proxy compatibility to help prevent the proxy from filtering out information about the crumb trail.

CLI

A legacy option for using the command-line interface allowed what was called "remoting" as a mode. This mode is considered insecure, as opposed to other modes such as HTTP or SSH. This has to do with its use of certain programming styles, such as Java serialization, that open up security holes and concerns. The legacy protocol was also viewed as slow and challenging to understand, and so newer, safer options were implemented starting in Jenkins 2.54.

The "Enable CLI over Remoting" option is off by default, but can be turned back on here if you understand the risk and need it for backward compatibility.

(You can learn more about the command-line interfaces available in Jenkins in Chapter 15.)

Plugin manager

The option here is "Use browser for metadata download," and it is normally unchecked (off). Turning this option on tells Jenkins to let the browser download metadata around plugins instead of Jenkins doing it itself. Unless you have a specific reason to activate this, it is best to just leave it turned off and allow Jenkins to do the downloads.

Access Control for Builds

If you choose to install the Authorize Project plugin (*https://plugins.jenkins.io/authorize-project*), you may have additional entries here. This plugin allows additional per-project options for running builds with specific authorization.

The global configuration part that would appear here allows you to select which types of authorized users appear as choices in projects. The list is shown in Figure 5-4 and is fairly self-explanatory.

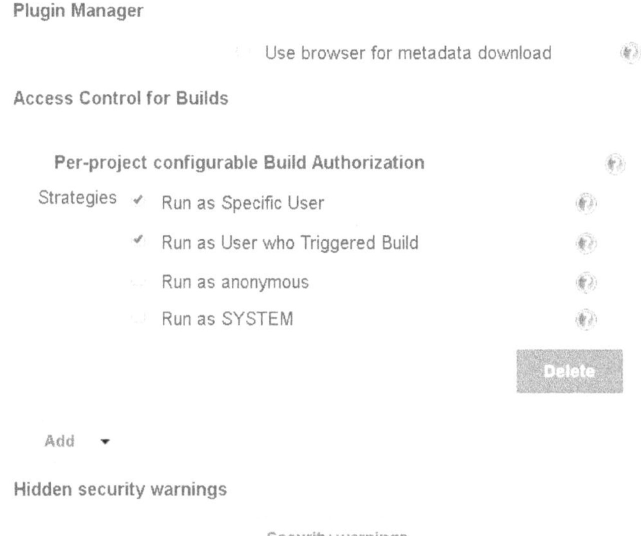

Figure 5-4. List of choices to present in project authorization if Authorize Project plugin is installed

The plugin adds a new Authorization item on the page for each job (Figure 5-5).

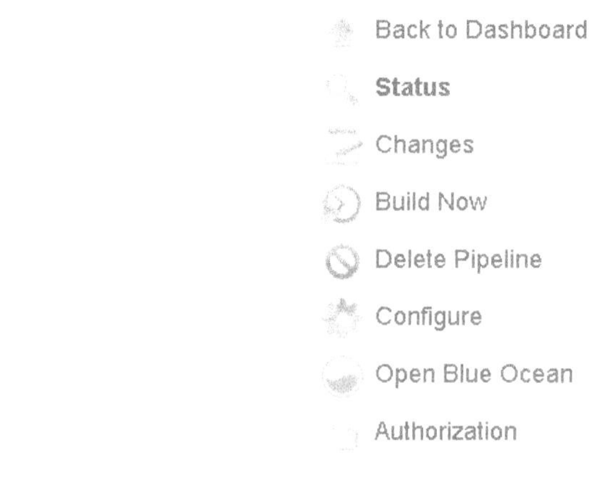

Figure 5-5. Job Authorization link

Clicking on that link brings up a simple configuration screen that allows you to select from the choices configured globally for the plugin, to control who can run the job (Figure 5-6).

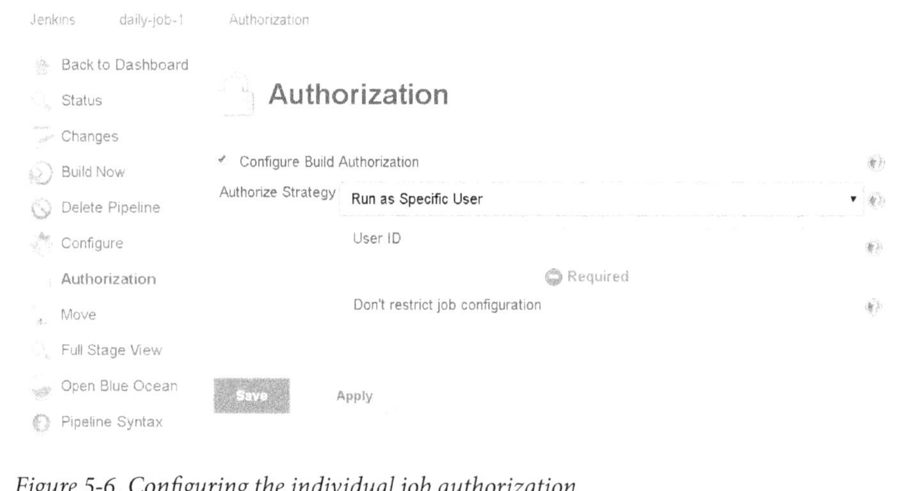

Figure 5-6. Configuring the individual job authorization

Hidden security warnings

The options here have to do with surfacing security warnings from update sites for installed components. (In older versions of Jenkins, these weren't shared directly in Jenkins but rather in emails, blogs, etc. Starting with v2.40, they can now be shown directly in Jenkins.) If you have a list of warnings present, then checked warnings are shown, and unchecked ones aren't.

Figure 5-7 shows an example of configuring these warnings if they exist. Note that there are two warnings—one is unchecked here and one is checked.

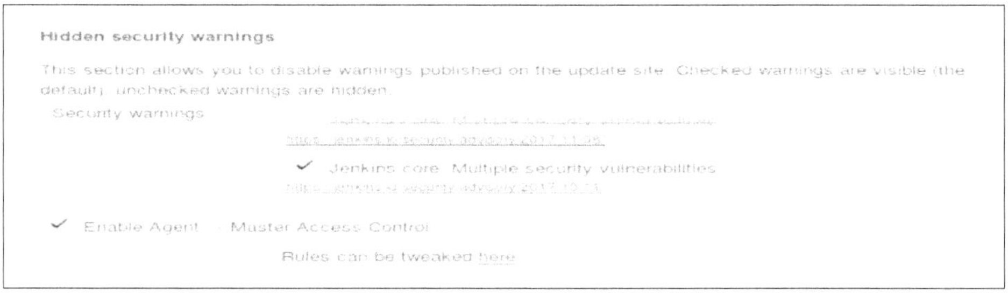

Figure 5-7. Configuring the hidden security warnings

Figure 5-8 shows what the warnings look like with this configuration. Notice that only the one that is checked is shown.

Figure 5-8. Shown security warnings

Another option here is to enable "agent to master" access control. This has to do with what commands agents can send to the master to make those interactions safer. If you need to tweak those rules to work with a specific instance or plugin, there is a link here to do that as well.

SSH server

For executing a subset of command-line commands over SSH, Jenkins can function as an SSH server. Some plugins may also use this functionality. If this is needed, a fixed port can be set up here to simplify security. A random port can also be chosen each time to avoid conflicts. If this functionality is not needed, it is best to use the Disable option to disable having an open port exposed.

See Chapter 15 for more on command-line usage and options in Jenkins. Now that we've covered the general security options, let's talk about how we can use credentials to secure access to more specific items.

Credentials in Jenkins

In addition to globally securing different aspects of Jenkins, using specific, secure credentials forms a key part of having a secure Jenkins environment. The Credentials plugin (included with installations of Jenkins) provides mechanisms for users to create and manage credentials, as well as an API for plugins to use to store and access credentials.

It's worth saying a word here about what we mean by the general term "credentials." Often you will hear this also described as a "secret." In general, we mean any value or values that provide access to a restricted resource. A list of the credential types includes:

- Usernames with passwords—may be conjoined when used (treated as one item) or separated
- Docker certificates directories (now deprecated)
- Docker host certificate authentications
- SSH usernames with private keys
- Secret ZIP files—ZIP files with the credentials
- Secret files—flat files with the credentials
- Secret texts—tokens or other chains
- Certificates—Java KeyStores with the certificates/certificate chain

Specific examples might include:

- A username and password combination to gain access to a source control repository
- A digital key and certificate to sign an entity
- A secret text string that can be matched to identify that content is from a specific source
- An SSH key set to deploy to a server

Other types of credentials could include less formalized items, such as binary data, or more formalized ones, such as OAuth credentials.

Once created, credentials have to be stored somewhere. The Credentials API allows for accessing an external credential store (an application capable of storing and retrieving credentials). However, Jenkins has an internal encrypted credential store that is used by default.

Securing Access to the Internal Credential Store

The internal credential store in Jenkins is stored in the *JENKINS_HOME* directory. It is also encrypted with a key that is stored in the *JENKINS_HOME* directory. If a malicious user can get access to this, and in particular to the *JENKINS_HOME/secrets* directory, they can gain access to the secrets. For this reason, it is important to secure the filesystem access to *JENKINS_HOME* if you want to be truly secure. Furthermore, you should follow the recommended settings described in "Securing Jenkins" on page 135.

One other fundamental point about credentials is that they are associated with a *context*. Contexts represent a way of thinking about the different entities that make up Jenkins as a hierarchy. The root context is Jenkins itself. Other contexts include jobs, users, build agents, and folders. Additionally, plugins can define new contexts.

With this background, we can delve more into the characteristics and properties associated with managing credentials in Jenkins. The first one we'll look at is the credential's *scope*.

Credential Scopes

Credentials have a scope associated with them. This is a way to say how they can be exposed. There are three main scopes that Jenkins uses:

System
: As the name implies, this scope is associated with the root context, the Jenkins system. Credentials in this scope are only exposed to system and background tasks and may be used to do things such as connect to build nodes/agents.

Global
: The global scope is the default scope and the one to use generally to ensure that credentials are available to jobs in Jenkins. Credentials in this scope are exposed to their context and all child contexts of that context. (Recall that credentials are associated with a context and that contexts represent a hierarchical structure of the main parts of Jenkins.)

User
: As the name implies, this scope is per-user. This means that the credentials are only available when threads in Jenkins are authenticating as that user.

Credential Domains

Credential domains provide a way to group together, under a common domain name, sets of credentials. Typically, the common domain name will imply some functionality or application type that the credentials are expected to work with.

When you define a credential domain, you provide a domain name and a "specification" such as a hostname or URL pattern.

Jenkins always has at least one credential domain—the global domain. The global credential domain has no specification, so it is available for anything in Jenkins to use.

Credential Providers

A credential provider is a place where credentials can be stored and retrieved. This can be an internal credential store or an external credential vault.

There are several standard credential providers. These are:

System credentials provider (Jenkins credentials provider)
: This exposes credentials at the root context (Jenkins itself). Two credential scopes are available: system and global. To look at this, you can go to Jenkins → Credentials → System.

User credentials provider
: This exposes a per-user credential store for a user. Only the user scope is available, and a user cannot see the per-user credentials of another user. To see these credentials, you can either go to Jenkins → *<username>* → Credentials → User or Jenkins → People → *<username>* → Credentials → User.

Folder credentials provider
: This is provided by the Folders plugin. It exposes a per-folder credential store and supports the global scope for the folder and any children. To see these credentials, go to Jenkins → *<folder name>* → Credentials → Folder.

BlueOcean credentials provider
: This scopes credentials to the Blue Ocean interface and items created/accessed directly through it.

All of these can be used with credential domains.

Credential Stores

Credential stores allow credential providers to expose credentials to Jenkins. Stores are associated with a specific context and are either tied to the global domain or can use a custom domain. They can support a set of credential domains.

Internal stores store the actual credentials. External stores will typically be either a simple flat reference of credentials or a service with metadata and more advanced features like querying. Later in this chapter we'll look at one such external store, called Vault.

Administering Credentials

Administration for credentials can be done through the Configure Credentials interface, accessible under the Manage Jenkins menu. The options on this screen allow a Jenkins user to:

- Select which credential providers will be available to Jenkins to resolve credentials.
- Select the types of credentials that can be resolved and configured.
- Specify the types of credentials that can be included or excluded for a specific provider.

Selecting Credential Providers

At the top of the Configure Credentials screen is a drop-down list to tell Jenkins which credential providers it can use. The default choice is to use "All available" providers. However, if you need to subset the list by including or excluding certain providers, there are options to do that. (See Figure 5-9.)

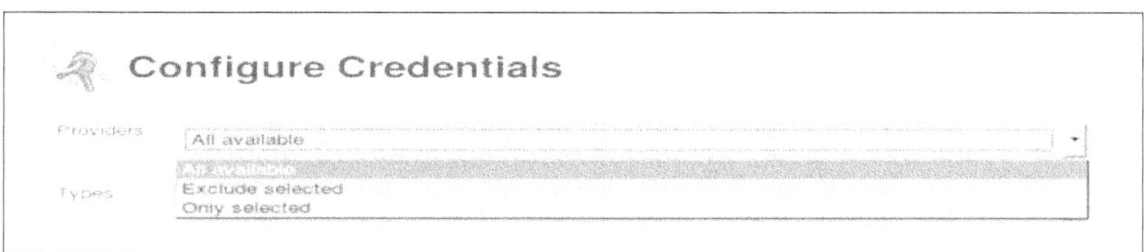

Figure 5-9. Options for selecting credential providers

If either the "Exclude selected" (exclude providers) or "Only selected" (include providers) option is chosen, a list of providers with checkboxes is displayed. Depending on the option, the checkboxes next to the appropriate providers can be checked to either exclude them from the set of available providers or include them in the set of available providers (see Figure 5-10).

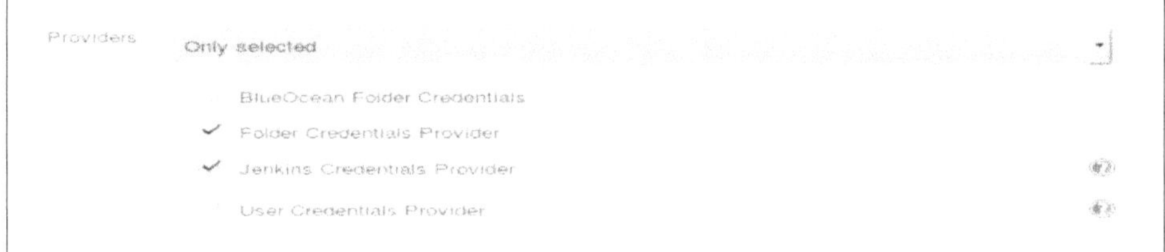

Figure 5-10. Selecting specific providers to include as available

Selecting Credential Types

Just as the subset of credential providers can be chosen, the next section on the screen allows you to select the set of credential types that Jenkins can use. The default choice is to use "All available" types. However, if you need to subset the list by including or excluding certain types, there are options to do that. (See Figure 5-11.)

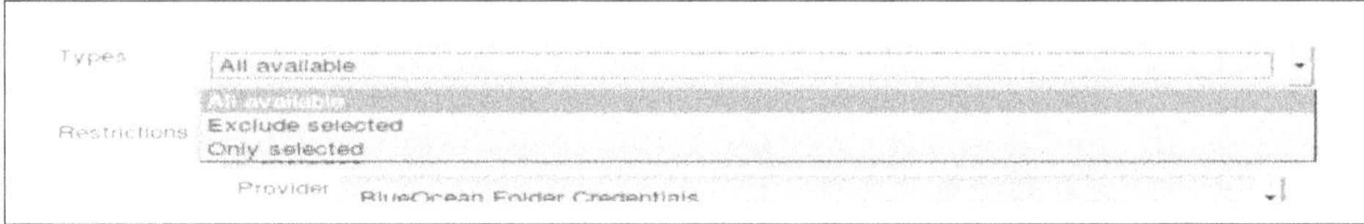

Figure 5-11. Selecting which types of credentials are available in Jenkins

If either the "Exclude selected" (exclude types) or "Only selected" (include types) option is chosen, a list of types is provided with checkboxes. Depending on the option, the checkboxes next to the appropriate types can be checked to either exclude them from the set of available types (see Figure 5-12) or include them in the set of available types.

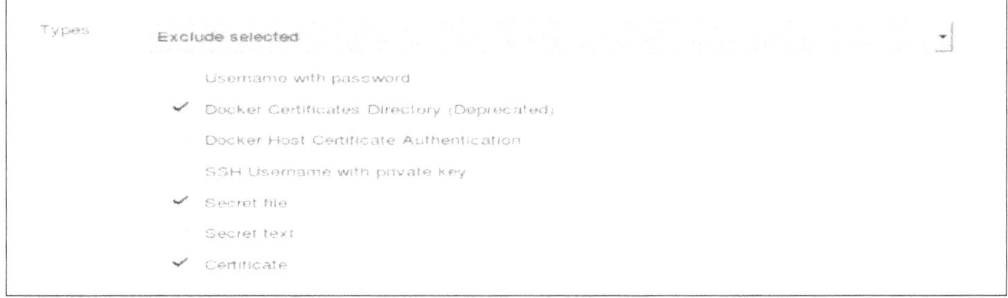

Figure 5-12. Selecting which specific types of credentials to exclude

Specifying Credential Types by Provider

The last part of the Configure Credentials screen is the Restrictions section. This allows you to specify the types of credentials Jenkins will allow or exclude from a specific provider (see Figure 5-13). This is a way to fine-tune what Jenkins can use from a provider. Note that doing this is optional and not required.

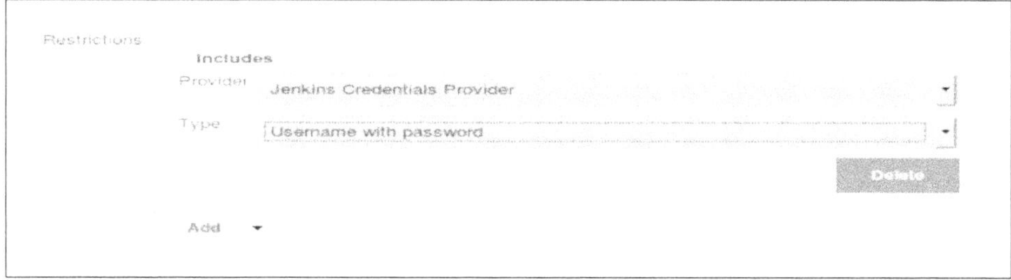

Figure 5-13. Refining/restricting the credential types allowed from a credential provider

The Add button in this section has two options ("include" and "exclude"). Selecting either will create a new page element allowing you to select a provider and then a type. If you have selected "include," this type of credential will be included for that provider, and vice versa for "exclude."

If you need to set up restrictions for multiple types and/or multiple providers, adding all of the elements can take some time. However, as noted earlier, using this is optional, not required.

Limiting Access for Build Jobs

As discussed in "Credential Scopes" on page 145, most internal operations and connections between systems in Jenkins run at the "system" level—meaning they have full permissions to the system.

For build jobs, this high level of access is not always advisable or desirable. To allow build jobs to run at lower levels of authorization, the Authorize Project plugin (*https://plugins.jenkins.io/authorize-project*) has been developed.

With this plugin installed, new controls are added to the global security configuration page and to each individual build job that allow users to specify the "authorizations" (types of credentials) to use for the job. See "Access Control for Builds" on page 141 for more on how this works.

Creating and Managing Credentials

Suggested Reading

If you haven't already read the previous sections on credential domains, stores, providers, etc., it is recommended to read over those to have a foundation for this section.

Earlier, we discussed the notion of "contexts" in Jenkins. Each context in Jenkins that has an associated credential store will also have a credential "operation" added to it by the Credentials plugin. That means that, by default, you will have Credentials menu items specific to the system, user, and folder contexts.

Management for system-level credentials can be accessed simply by selecting Credentials from the top level of Jenkins (Figure 5-14).

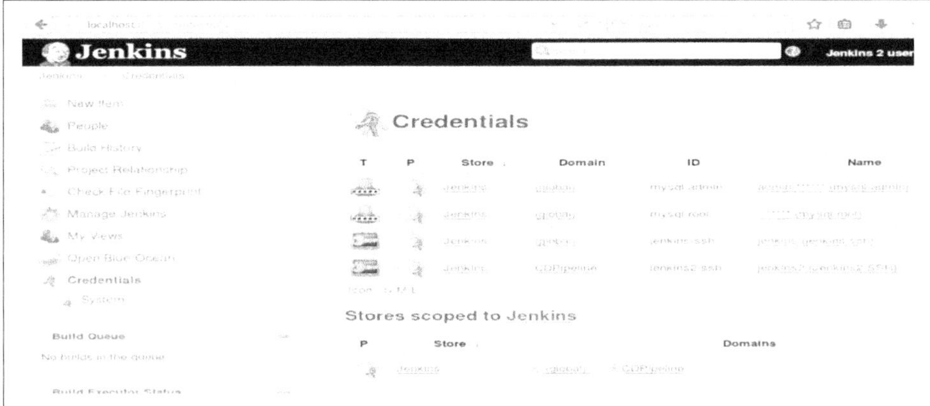

Figure 5-14. Accessing system credentials

Management for user-level credentials can be accessed by selecting the People menu, and then the desired user, and then Credentials (Figure 5-15).

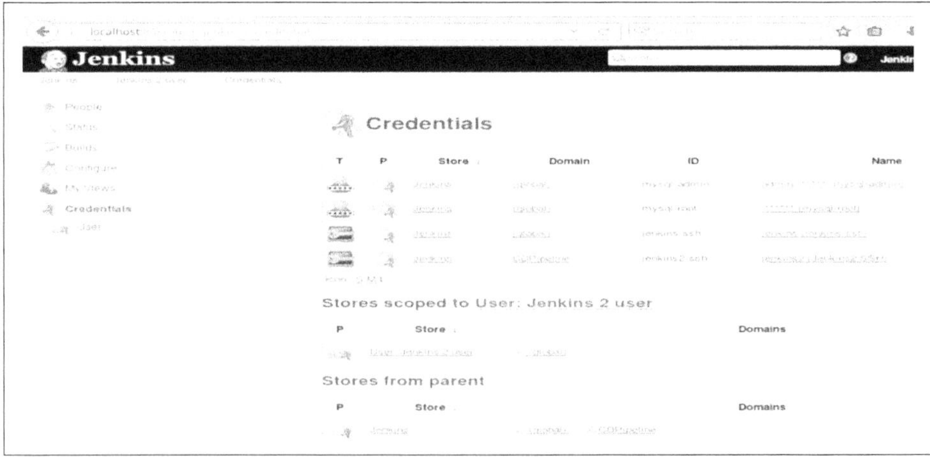

Figure 5-15. Accessing user credentials

Management for folder-level credentials can be accessed by selecting a particular folder item and then Credentials (Figure 5-16).

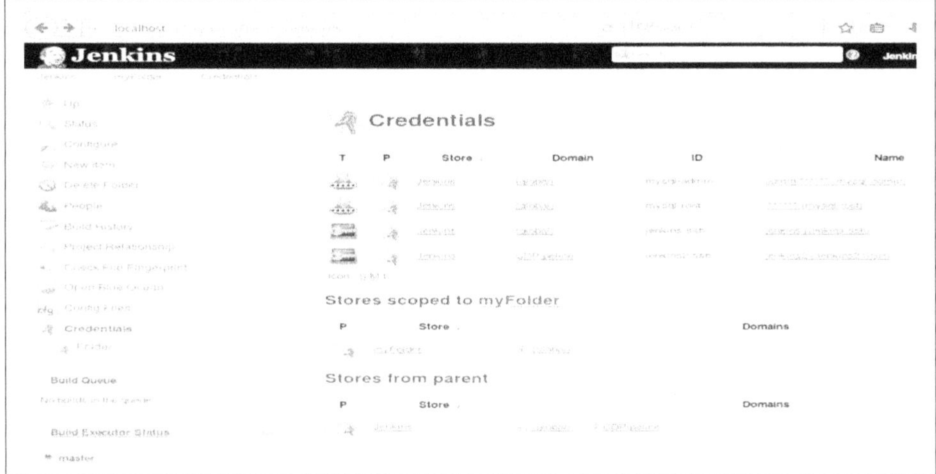

Figure 5-16. Accessing folder credentials

On each credentials screen, the top table lists the available credentials in this context and any parent contexts. This table has six columns:

- Type(T)
- Provider(P)
- Store
- Domain
- ID
- Name

Grayed-out Credentials

If you happen to have a credential in this table that has the same ID as a credential in the parent context, it will be grayed out in this table to indicate that.

The next table (in the middle) lists the credential stores available in the current context. The columns here are:

- Provider
- Store
- Domains

The bottom block lists the credential stores available in the parent context. It has the same three columns as the preceding table.

Context Links

On any of these credentials pages, the links in the tables are "context links"—meaning that if you hover over them, a small downward-pointing arrowhead will appear to the right of the link. Clicking on that will then display a small pop-up menu that will provide shortcuts to certain actions or quick navigation links.

The basic rules for what shows up in the pop-ups when you click on one of these context links follows from the hierarchy of *store, domain, credentials.*

If you click on the link itself:

- For a store link, it will take you to a page that shows information about the domains in the store.
- For a domain link, it will take you to a page that shows information about the credentials defined in that domain.
- For a credentials link, it will take you to a page that shows usage information for that credential (whether or not that credential has been recorded as used).

If you click on the drop-down arrow next to the link:

- For a store link, it will give you a menu option to create a new domain.
- For a built-in domain, it will give you a menu option to create a new credential.
- For a custom domain (one that has been created by a user), it will give you a menu with options to create a new credential, configure the domain, or delete the domain.
- For a credential, you will get an option to update, move, or delete a credential.

Moving Credentials

Note that it is currently only possible to move credentials between domains that are in the same store, not across stores.

With this background, let's look at an example of how to add a new domain, add new credentials, and use them in Jenkins.

Adding a New Domain and Credential

From several of the context links on the credentials screens or by drilling down from the Credentials menu item, you can get to the screen to add a new domain.

Figure 5-17 shows an example of filling in that screen. In this example, we're adding a new credential domain for a set of nodes geographically located on the East Coast. (Perhaps we want to shift processing to those at a certain time of day.)

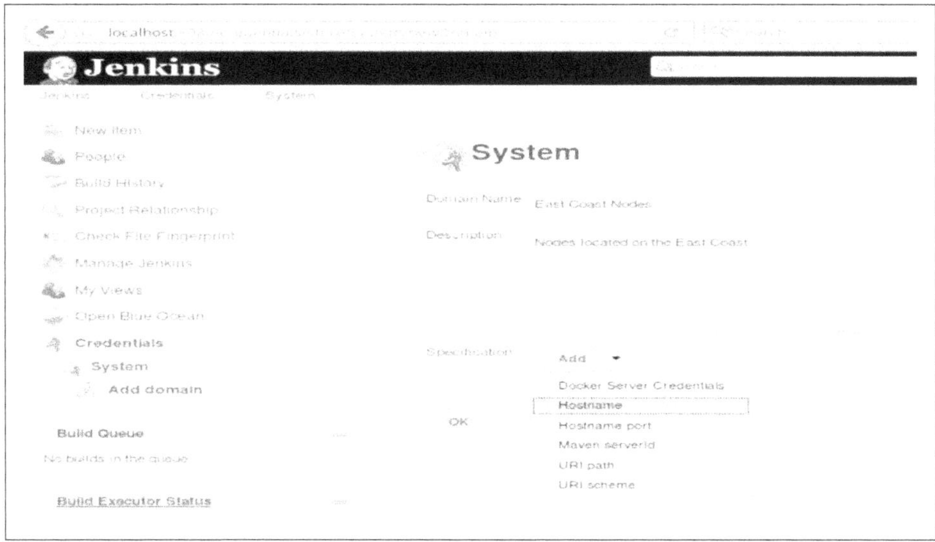

Figure 5-17. Adding a new credential domain and selecting the specification

The Domain Name and Description are simply text fields. The Specification field allows us to differentiate this domain. This field lets you specify a type of filtering via patterns. After the specification is created, when you are choosing a credential for use in Jenkins and enter a related value that matches the pattern, credentials from this domain will be presented as options. (We'll see an example of this shortly.) Note that if you don't provide a specification for a new domain, that domain will be effectively equal to the global domain.

For the example we're working with here, we'll choose the simplest kind of specification: Hostname. Then we can add a pattern to match the naming convention of our nodes, as shown in Figure 5-18.

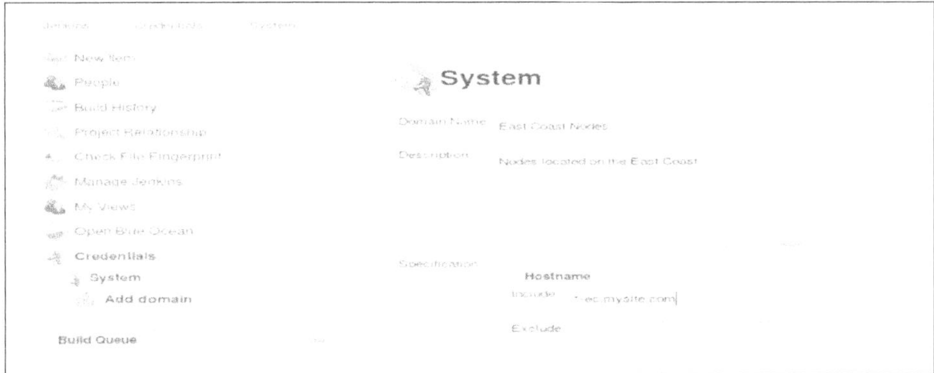

Figure 5-18. Filling in a Hostname specification

Once the domain is created, it is ready to have credentials created for it (Figure 5-19).

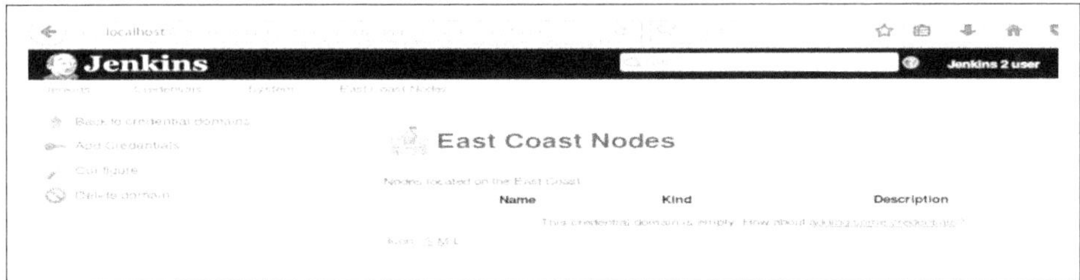

Figure 5-19. Domain created and ready for credentials

On the screen to create a credential, we can select a kind (such as username and password, SSH key, secret file, etc.). We can then fill in the actual values needed for access and supply an ID and a description. If you don't provide an ID, a rather long random ID will be supplied. Because of the length and format, this ID can be difficult to specify manually, so it is recommended to provide a simpler, more easily handled ID that has meaning to you.

In our example, we'll add an SSH key credential (Figure 5-20) associated with our new domain.

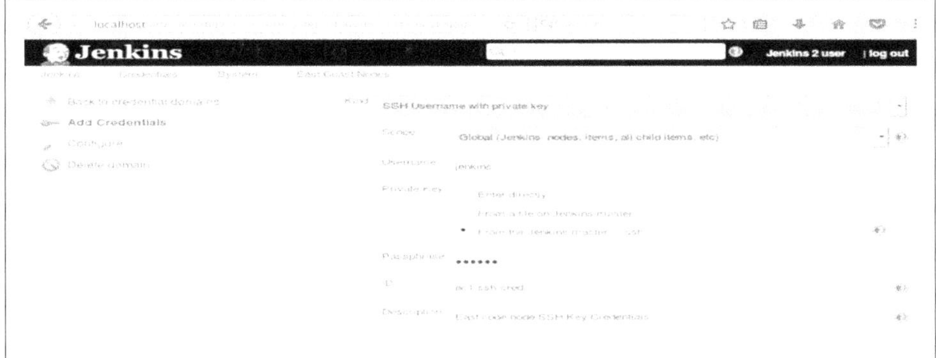

Figure 5-20. Adding an SSH credential to our new domain

After the credential is added, a summary screen is shown (Figure 5-21).

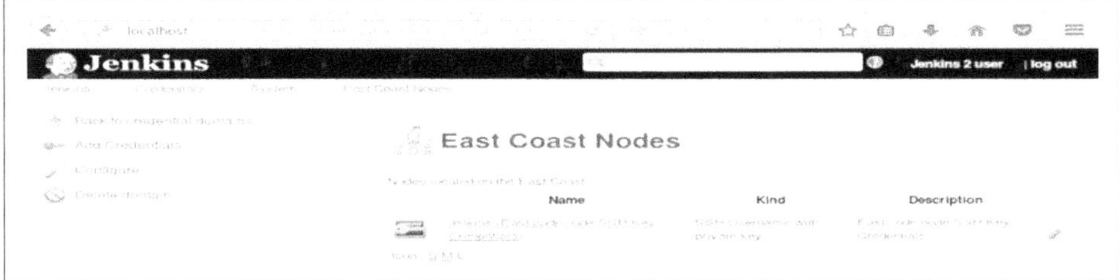

Figure 5-21. Summary screen after credential is added

Now that we have the new domain and credential set up, let's see how we might use them in practice.

Using the New Domain and Credential

Suppose that we want to now set up some new worker nodes for our Jenkins master based on the East Coast systems. After going through the Manage Jenkins → Manage Nodes → New Node menus, we arrive at the configuration page for the new node.

For the launch method we want to use SSH, so we select that and then type in the name of our host. Notice that in Figure 5-22, the pattern we type in ("primary-ec1.mysite.com") matches the hostname specification ("*-ec1.mysite.com") we used in setting up our domain. Because of this, when we go to choose a credential, our SSH credential from the East Coast Nodes domain shows up in the drop-down list (the third item from the top).

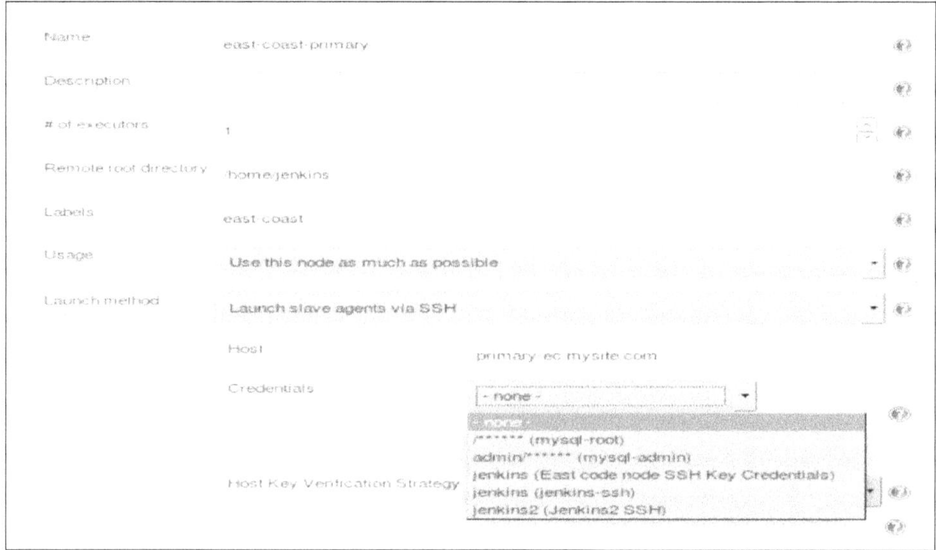

Figure 5-22. Host pattern matches domain's hostname specification, allowing credentials from domain to be included

If the hostname we entered did not match the specification, then the credential entry from the domain would not be listed, as shown in Figure 5-23.

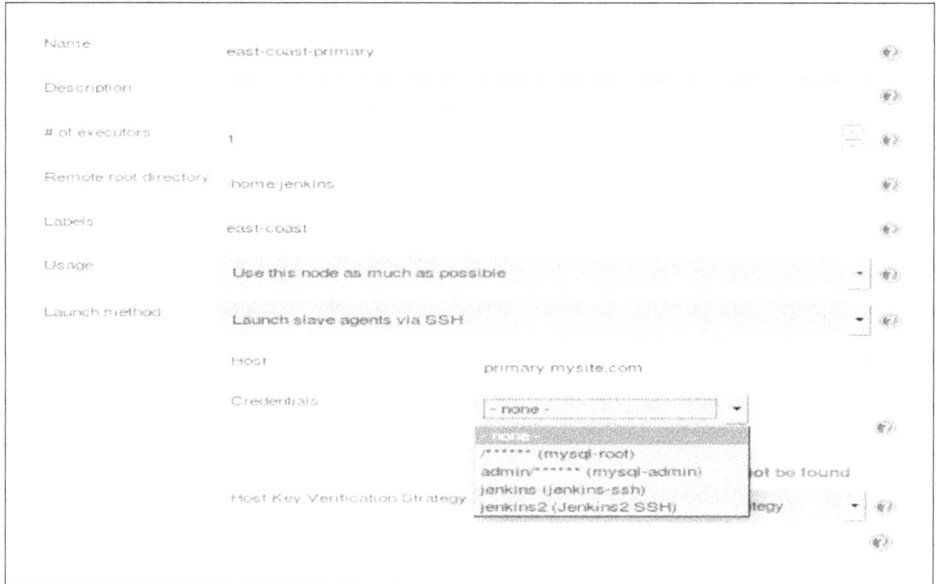

Figure 5-23. Host pattern does not match hostname specification from East Coast nodes domain, so corresponding credential from that domain is not listed

Note that in both cases (matching and nonmatching), credentials from the global domain are available by default.

Beyond the basic credential setup we've described here (for access to resources via simple credentials), there is a plugin that provides a way to define roles with certain levels of access that users can be added to. We'll look at this more advanced functionality next.

Advanced Credentials: Role-Based Access

While the common credentials options will handle many use cases, there may be times where you want to use a more granular approach to security and authorization. An example use case would be creating new roles with a set of specific permissions assigning roles to individual users. The Role-based Authorization Strategy plugin (*https://plugins.jenkins.io/role-strategy*) is designed to provide this kind of functionality.

More specifically, the plugin allows for the definition of three types of roles:

Global roles
: Roles that span across projects with permissions such as Job, Run, and SCM

Project roles
: Roles particular to a project from the Job or Run category

Slave roles
: Roles with permissions to administer nodes

The plugin also provides a macro facility so that macros can be used as criteria for what roles apply to.

Basic Use

Installation of the plugin is the same as for any other Jenkins plugin. Once installed, if security is enabled in Jenkins, there will be a new option named Role-Based Strategy under Authorization in the Access Control section of the global security configuration page (Figure 5-24).

Figure 5-24. Selection enabled for the Role-Based Strategy Authorization setting

If this option is selected and saved, there will then be a new selection on the Manage Jenkins page named "Manage and Assign Roles" (Figure 5-25). This is the gateway to the plugin's functionality.

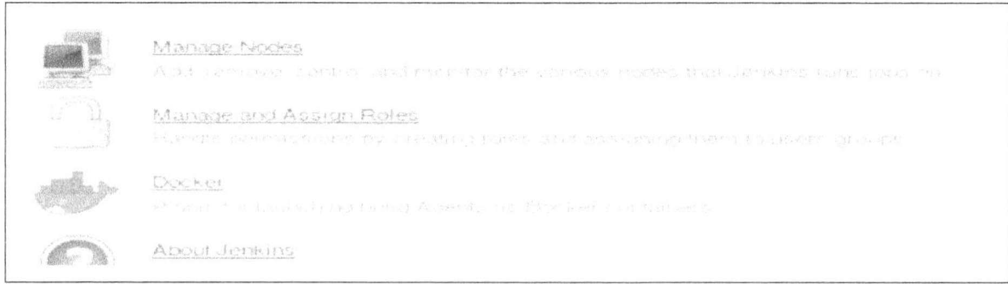

Figure 5-25. "Manage and Assign Roles" option on Manage Jenkins page

On the Manage and Assign Roles screen are three selections for the main functions: Manage Roles, Assign Roles, and Role Strategy Macros (Figure 5-26). We'll look at each of those in more detail in the next sections.

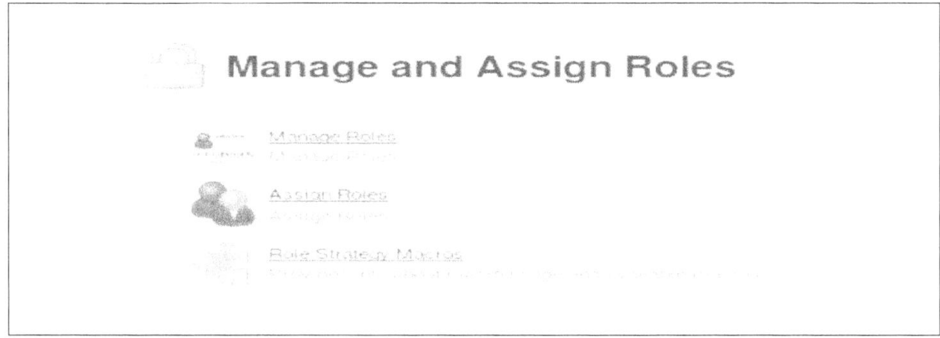

Figure 5-26. Manage and Assign Roles selections

Manage Roles

As the name implies, this screen allows you to create or delete roles and assign permissions to them. There are three sections here for each of the three kinds of roles mentioned earlier: global, project, and slave.

The mechanics of using each section are similar to the Jenkins matrix–based authorization model. There is a matrix where each row contains a defined role and each column is a specific permission within a category of Jenkins object (Overall, Credentials, Agent, etc.). To grant a permission to a role, you simply click on the checkbox for the column of the desired permission in the row for the role. If a checkbox is blank, that indicates the role does not have that permission. To remove an existing permission for a role, simply uncheck the box in the appropriate column.

You can create a new role by entering the desired role name in the "Role to add" box. The Project and Slave sections also expect a pattern. These patterns are used to associate the project or slave role to matching project names or node names, respectively. The Global section does not require a pattern, since we assign specific users to those roles rather than relying on matching user IDs. The following note details more about the syntax of the patterns.

Defining Role Patterns

Role patterns are regular expressions designed to match based on the names of objects—either projects or nodes depending on the type of role. The name of a project includes any Jenkins folder name in the path.

You can use these like any other regular expression—for example, if you have projects that start with *Daily*, you could use a pattern here of *Daily-**. The patterns are case-sensitive unless you use something like *(?i)Daily-** to indicate that it should be a case-insensitive match.

Let's take a look at an example of how to set up each type of role.

Global role example

By default, we have an *admin* role that has all permissions. To add a new role, we simply type in the desired role name in the "Role to add" box and click Add. In this case, let's suppose we want to create a new *job-admin* role. The idea is that this role can administer things around jobs. It does not need (and should not have) all the permissions of the traditional admin role. Figure 5-27 shows the initial step to add this role.

Figure 5-27. Setting up a global role

Extended Descriptions

Figure 5-27 also demonstrates another aspect of the controls on this page. If you want to know more about what a permission in a particular category does, you can hover over the permission name in the column. A pop-up window will appear with a brief explanation of what that particular permission does.

After adding the role, we can check the appropriate boxes to give the role the desired permissions, as shown in Figure 5-28.

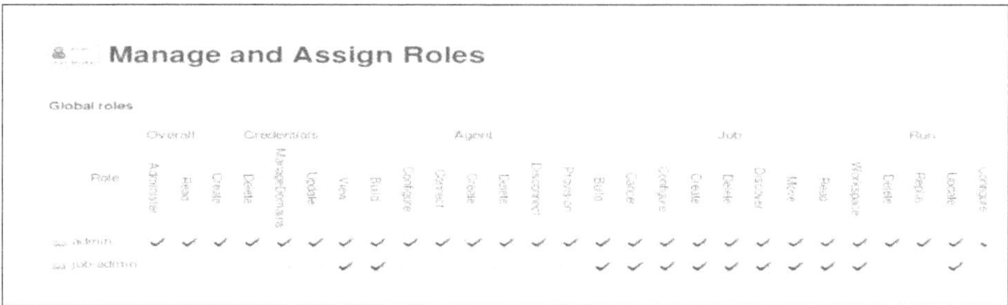

Figure 5-28. Selecting permissions for the global role

One additional role that you should consider adding here is a global role specifying the permissions that you want available to authenticated users. There is a built-in *authenticated* group that you can assign to a role, but you first need a role available that represents what authenticated users can do. For simplicity, you can just create an *authenticated* role with Overall/Read access (Figure 5-29).

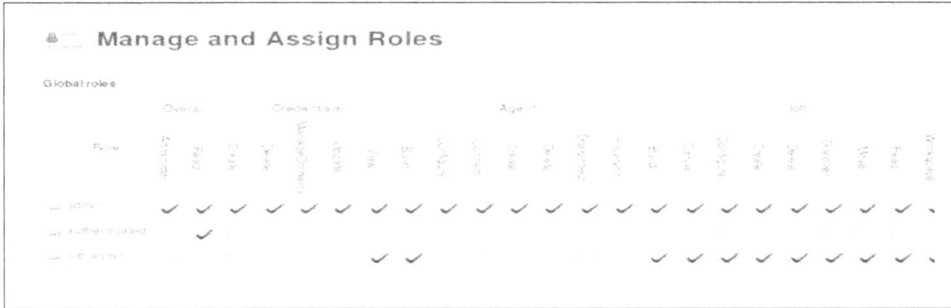

Figure 5-29. Creating an authenticated role

Project example

Carrying our example further, let's suppose that we have two main types of jobs that we run on our Jenkins instance—daily and weekly. We want to define a role of *daily-job-admin* to allow a subset of people to administer the daily jobs but not the weekly jobs. Our daily jobs all have names or folder paths that start with *daily*, so we can use that for a pattern. Figure 5-30 shows the initial steps to set this up.

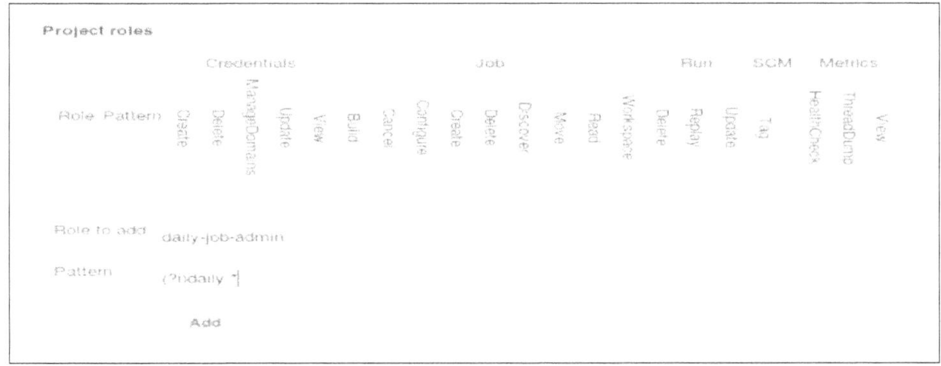

Figure 5-30. Defining a new daily project role

Once we add the new project role based on the project pattern, we can select permissions for the role just as we did for the global one (Figure 5-31). However, because we've supplied the pattern, users with this role will only have the selected permissions for jobs matching that pattern.

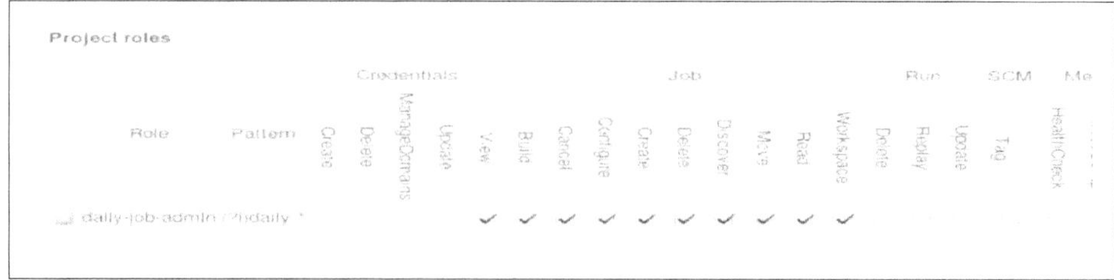

Figure 5-31. Assigning permissions to the project role

To round out our example, we would also add a *weekly-job-admins* role and roles for the daily and weekly users (nonadmins). An example of the completed list is shown in Figure 5-32.

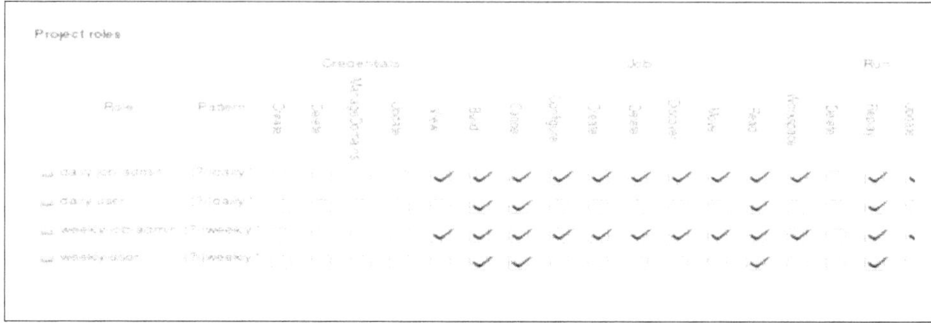

Figure 5-32. Daily and weekly roles added in for projects

Order of Precedence

Permissions in a global role override permissions in a project role, so if a user has both a global role with a given permission and a local role without that permission, they will have access via the global specification.

If you plan for project-specific roles to be additive to a global role (global + project = full set), then you'll want to only set the smallest base subset of common permissions in the global role and add less common ones in the project roles. If, on the other hand, you intend for the global role to be a separate superset of permissions (global or project), you can define the wider set of permissions in the global role.

Slave role example

In addition to defining global and per-project roles, we can also define roles around the administration of nodes. This is done via the last section on this screen. Figure 5-33 shows an example of adding a new role to administer nodes with names starting with *node-day*. (This pattern identifies nodes that we are using to run our daily jobs.)

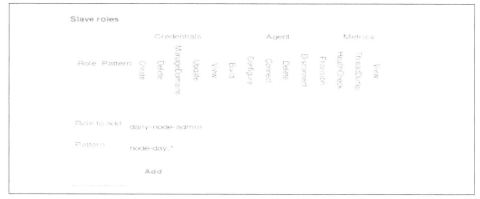

Figure 5-33. Defining a new node (slave) role

Once added, we can assign permissions to the role just as with the previous sections for global and project roles (Figure 5-34).

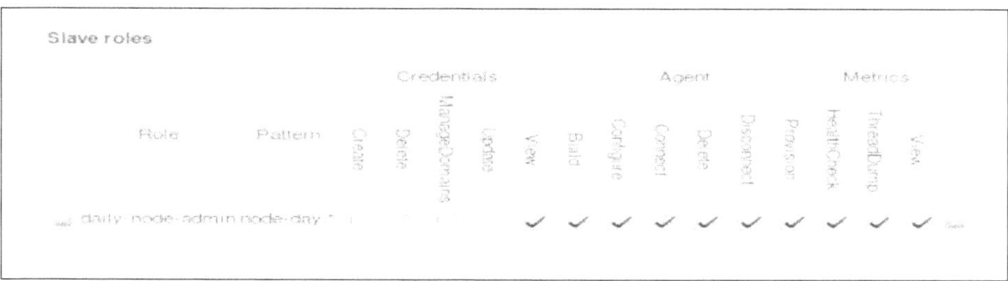

Figure 5-34. Adding permissions to the node role

To finish out our example model, we can add a project role for the jobs that run weekly, and a slave role for users who can administer the nodes that run the weekly jobs (see Figure 5-35).

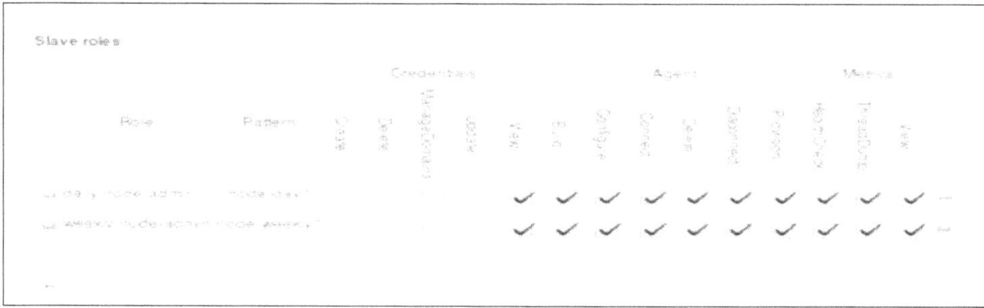

Figure 5-35. Adding the weekly node role

Assign Roles

Once we have our desired roles set up, we can assign users or groups to particular roles. We do this using the Assign Roles screen, accessible from the "Manage and Assign Roles" page). For each category of role on the Manage Roles page, we have a corresponding section on the Assign Roles page. However, corresponding sections on the latter have the more "modern" names—"Item roles" and "Node roles." To be clear, "Item roles" here corresponds to "Project roles" and "Node roles" corresponds to "Slave roles." Figure 5-36 shows an example of a starting page for assigning roles.

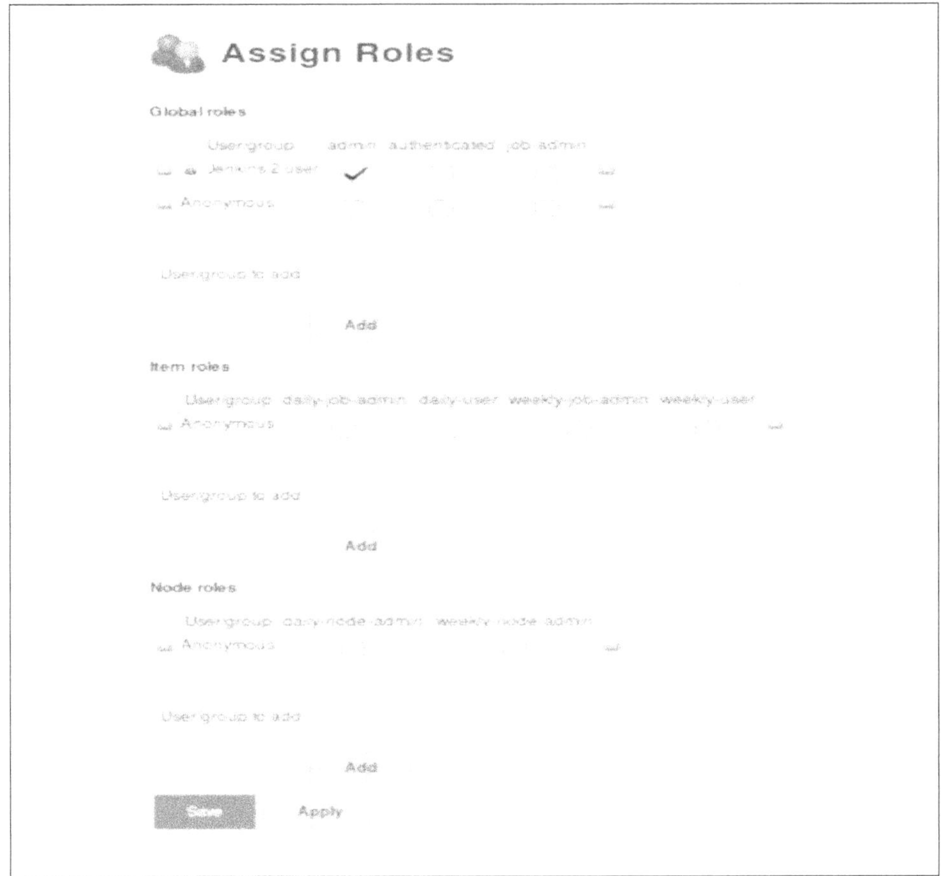

Figure 5-36. Assign Roles screen

Usage here is straightforward. Within each section (Global, Item, and Node), the rows represent users or groups, and the columns represent the roles that have been defined for that category. Note that there is a default entry for the *Anonymous* user. Any other users/groups already defined will have rows as well.

To allow a user/group to have the permissions associated with a role, you simply enter the user/group name into the "User/group to add" text box, click the Add button, and then check the boxes in the columns corresponding to the roles you want them to have.

For example, suppose that we have the following user IDs: *all-jobs-admin*, *day-admin-user*, *day-user*, *weekly-admin-user*, *weekly-user*, *sysadmin-daily*, and *sysadmin-weekly*. The "admin" user IDs are intended to be the administrators for their respective categories. Once we fill in the particular users to match up to the intended categories, we will have a configuration like the one in Figure 5-37.

Figure 5-37. Finished configuration for assigning roles

Adding the "authenticated" Group

The *authenticated* group (meaning anyone who can log in) is a built-in group in Jenkins. We can simply type in "authenticated" and add it to the *authenticated* role we defined previously.

Dealing with invalid users

The forms for assigning users will allow you to type in and add any user/group name initially. Once you save your changes, validation will be done to make sure the user/group is valid. If it is not, then when you go back into the Assign Roles page, you will see the user/group name with a line through it—indicating the user/group doesn't exist or isn't valid (Figure 5-38). At that point, you can delete the user/group by clicking on one of the small, red "X" symbols on either end of the row.

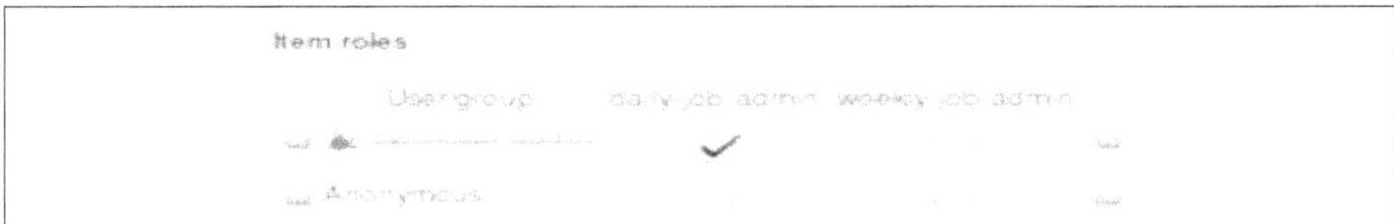

Figure 5-38. Identifying an invalid user

Verifying the roles setup

Now, we can verify that our roles setup works. First, if we log in as the *all-jobs-admin* user, we can see the list of all of our jobs (Figure 5-39).

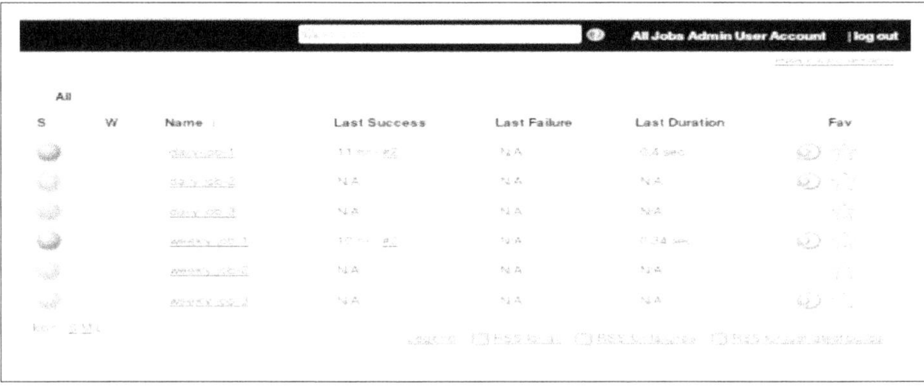

Figure 5-39. Verifying that the role allows seeing all jobs

If we log in as *day-admin-user*, we can see only the set of daily jobs, and we have the ability to configure them (as one example of the admin permissions). Figures 5-40 and 5-41 show this.

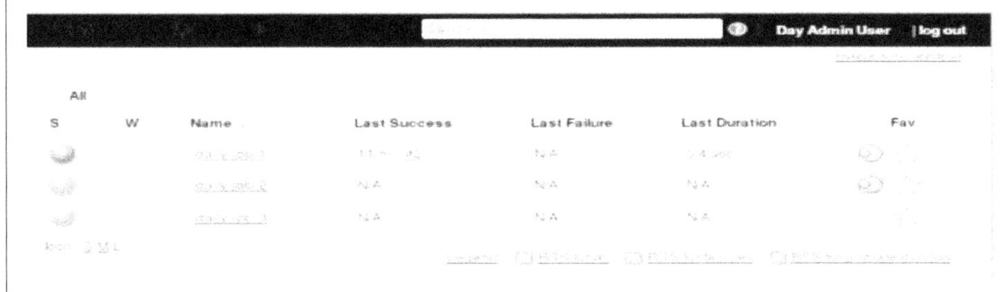

Figure 5-40. The restricted view of the day-admin-user

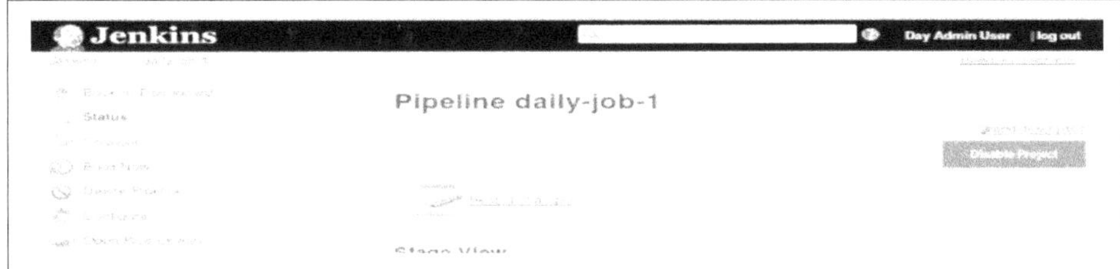

Figure 5-41. The day-admin- user has the Configure option

If we log in as *day-user* (a nonadmin user), note that we can again see only the daily jobs but that we do not have the Configure permission (Figures 5-42 and 5-43).

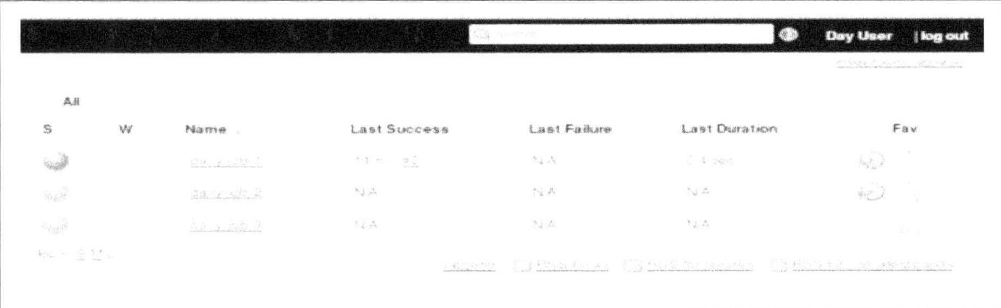

Figure 5-42. The view of the day-user (nonadmin)

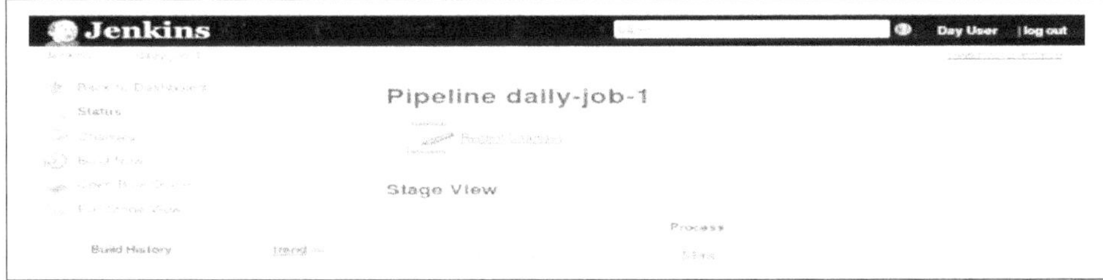

Figure 5-43. The day-user does not have permission to configure jobs

Role Strategy Macros

The third piece of functionality provided by the Role-based Authorization Strategy plugin is the ability to use *Role Strategy Macros*. The idea behind this is to be able to have macros that define access permissions based on some characteristic of an item. As of the time of this writing, there is only one available example—the *BuildableJob* macro. This macro is designed to filter the list of jobs to only ones that are "buildable." There are several reasons why an item in Jenkins might not be buildable, but at the level of an individual job, it would typically be because the job has been disabled. A quick indicator that a job is not buildable is the absence of a Build Now icon and menu option.

If you go to the Role Strategy Macro screen, there is general information about how macros are intended to work. One of the key phrases here is "Listed macros should be used in the 'Role' field of the 'Manage Roles' page." After that, you can see information about the *BuildableJob* macro (Figure 5-44).

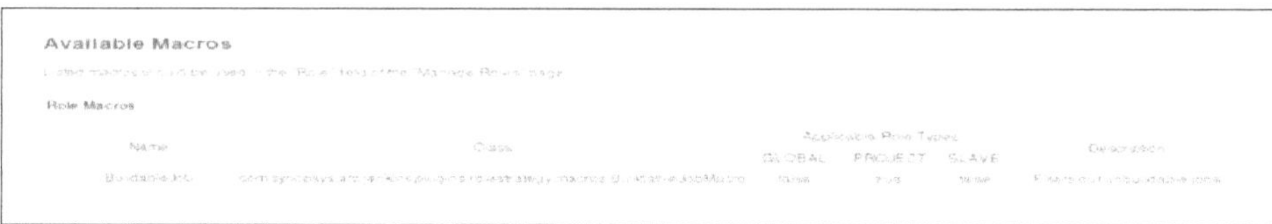

Figure 5-44. Listing macros available for use in roles

From this table, apart from the name and description, the Applicable Role Types column is the most useful. It notes which of the role types that this macro applies to. In this case, the listed macro is intended for the Project role type.

To add a macro to a role, we use the @ sign in front of the macro name. Figure 5-45 shows adding the macro as a role in our set of Project roles. We're giving it the same permissions as the *weekly-user* role.

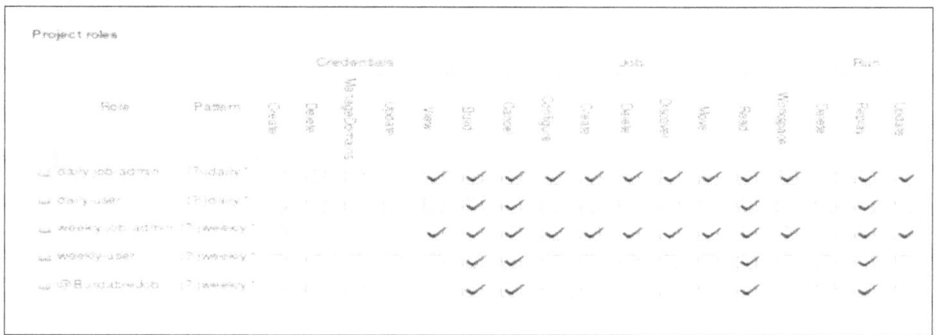

Figure 5-45. Using a macro in defining a role

Assume we have created a new user called *Weekly User 2*. After adding the *@BuildableJob* role, on the Assign Roles page we can assign the new user to the *@BuildableJob* role (Figure 5-46).

Figure 5-46. Adding a user to a role defined by a macro

Let's now look at the macro use in practice. If we first log in as the user *Weekly User*, which has the *weekly-user* role, we can see the list of all weekly jobs—including *weekly-job-2*, which is not currently buildable (note the absence of the Build Now icon). This is shown in Figure 5-47.

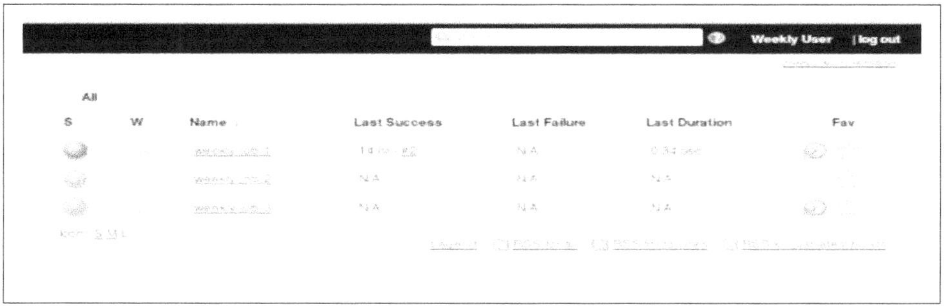

Figure 5-47. User view not filtered by @BuildableJob role

If we then log in as the user *Weekly User 2*, which is attached to our *@BuildableJob* role, we only see the weekly jobs that are actually buildable (Figure 5-48).

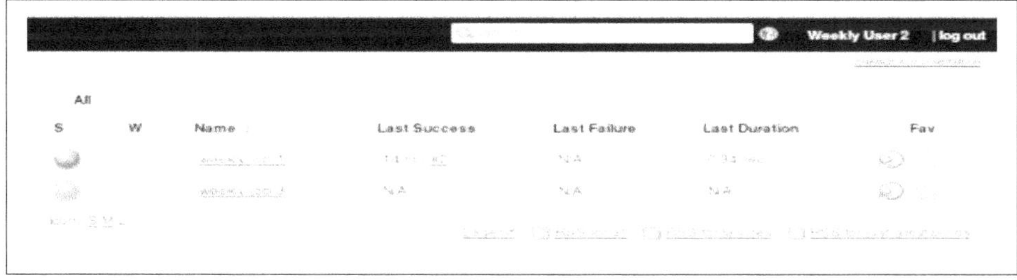

Figure 5-48. User view filtered by @BuildableJob role

As you can see, the advanced credentials functionality allows for much more flexibility in defining roles around specific criteria.

Next, we'll look at the basics of using credentials in the pipeline.

Working with Credentials in the Pipeline

There will be times you'll need to supply credentials in your pipeline for your pipeline steps. In this section, we explore some Pipeline constructs for working with the basic types of credentials.

Username and Password

First, we want to make sure we have the Credentials Binding plugin (*https://plugins.jenkins.io/credentials-binding*) installed. Then we'll define a set of credentials with a username and password in Jenkins (Figure 5-49).

Figure 5-49. Username/password credentials in Jenkins

We can now use the `withCredentials` block in our pipeline to work with the designated credentials. The syntax for this block starts with the following:

```
withCredentials([usernamePassword(credentialsId: '<ID>',
 passwordVariable: '<variable to hold password>',
 usernameVariable: '<variable to hold username>')])
```

The idea here is that whatever variables are used for *usernameVariable* and *passwordVariable* will be filled in the username and password from the credentials specified by *credentialsId*.

SSH Keys

To use SSH credentials in our pipeline, we can use the `withCredentials` block again, as shown here:

```
withCredentials([sshUserPrivateKey(credentialsId: '<credentials-id>',
  keyFileVariable: 'MYKEYFILE',
  passphraseVariable: 'PASSPHRASE',
  usernameVariable: 'USERNAME')])
   {
     // some block
   }
```

As an alternative, we can use an *sshagent* block. For this, we first need to make sure we have the SSH Agent plugin (*https://plugins.jenkins.io/ssh-agent*) installed.

Now, we can use the *sshagent* block to do our access, passing in the credentials ID:

```
sshagent([<credentials id>]) { }
```

Figure 5-50 shows an example of using this in a pipeline script.

Figure 5-50. Using the SSH credentials in a pipeline script

Token Credentials

When working with other types of credentials, the same general idea (using the `withCredentials` block) applies. The following is an example of using a token credential modeled on an example in the Jenkins documentation:

```
node {
  withCredentials([string(credentialsId: '<token>', variable: 'TOKEN')])
  {
    sh '''
      set +x
      curl -H "Token: $TOKEN" https://some.api/
    '''
  }
}
```

A couple of points are worth mentioning about this:

- The shell script uses the triple quotes to handle a multiline script inline. (You can discover more about using the *sh* step in Chapter 11.)
- The `set +x` prevents echoing out the credential as the script executes.

For other types of credentials, you can use the Snippet Generator for the `withCredentials` step and fill in the desired binding.

As we introduce credentials into the pipeline, it's important to understand more about what we can and can't do in scripts, and how Jenkins handles it when something we try to do isn't approved.

Controlling Script Security

The pipeline functionality introduces the ability to run any arbitrary script. With this increased flexibility to execute commands and do processing comes an increased importance of being able to control script security. In Jenkins 2, this security is provided by the Script Security plugin (*https://plugins.jenkins.io/script-security*).

Scripts Written as Declarative Pipelines

To some degree, Declarative Pipelines lessen the likelihood of scripts violating security concerns. Their required structure and syntax limit the programming you can do with Groovy and so make the pipeline conform better to best practices.

By default, users with the Overall/Administer permission can write or run whatever scripts they want. This level of permissions is equivalent to admin permissions on the Jenkins instance, and so is not appropriate for all users. So, Jenkins 2 includes two mechanisms to help with script security: script approval and Groovy sandboxing.

Deprecated Permissions

In previous versions of the role-based access/matrix plugin, there were additional permissions that could be set:

- Overall/Run Scripts
- Overall/Upload Plugins
- Overall/Configure Update Center

This was deemed a security risk because these permissions were as powerful in some cases as the Overall/Administer permissions, so now you need to have the Overall/Administer permission to automatically be able to run scripts without approval.

If you do need to go back to the old insecure permissions for some reason, the `org.jenkinsci.plugins.rolestrategy.permissions.DangerousPermissionHandlingMode.enableDangerousPermissions` system property can be set to `true`.

Script Checking

When a Jenkins administrator creates a script or includes a script in a configuration and saves it, the script is automatically approved and added to an approved list. Those scripts in the approved list can be run by anyone. If a nonadministrator tries to run a script and it is not one in the approved list, then it is prohibited from running until/unless approved by an administrator.

The reason for this is that, unlike filling in web forms, scripts can (attempt to) do any arbitrary operations, including referencing internal objects in Jenkins. This could be a security risk as well as a technical risk, depending on what the script is trying to do.

An example of a script that needs to be approved is shown in Figure 5-51. This one is flagged because it is trying to use the internal `rawBuild` object to get information. The figure also shows the output from trying to run the script—note the error message.

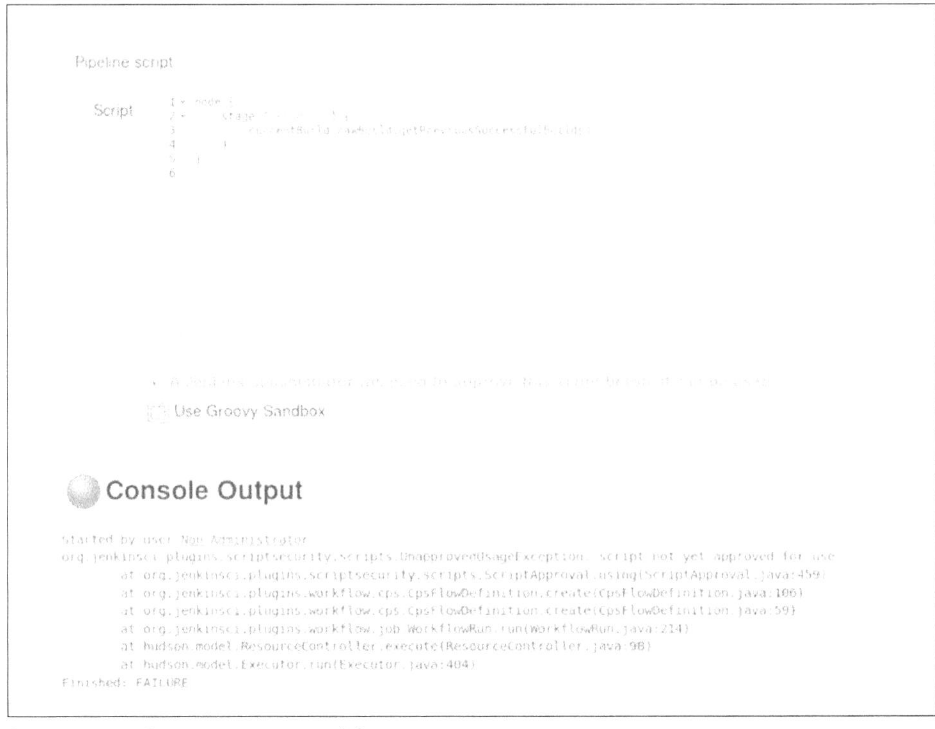

Figure 5-51. Script not approved for use

Script Approval

If a nonadministrator tries to run a script that needs approval, Jenkins will prohibit running it. It will also add a notice about the need for approval to a queue, for an administrator to review. An administrator can then log in to Jenkins and go to Manage Jenkins → "In-process Script Approval." An alert of the form "1 scripts pending approval" will be waiting for the administrator (Figure 5-52).

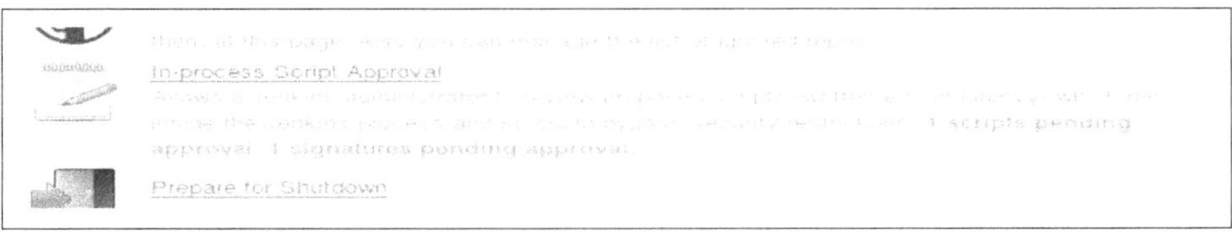

Figure 5-52. Script pending approval

Once the administrator goes to the script approval area, they will have an option to approve or deny executing the script. The upper part of Figure 5-53 shows this part of the form.

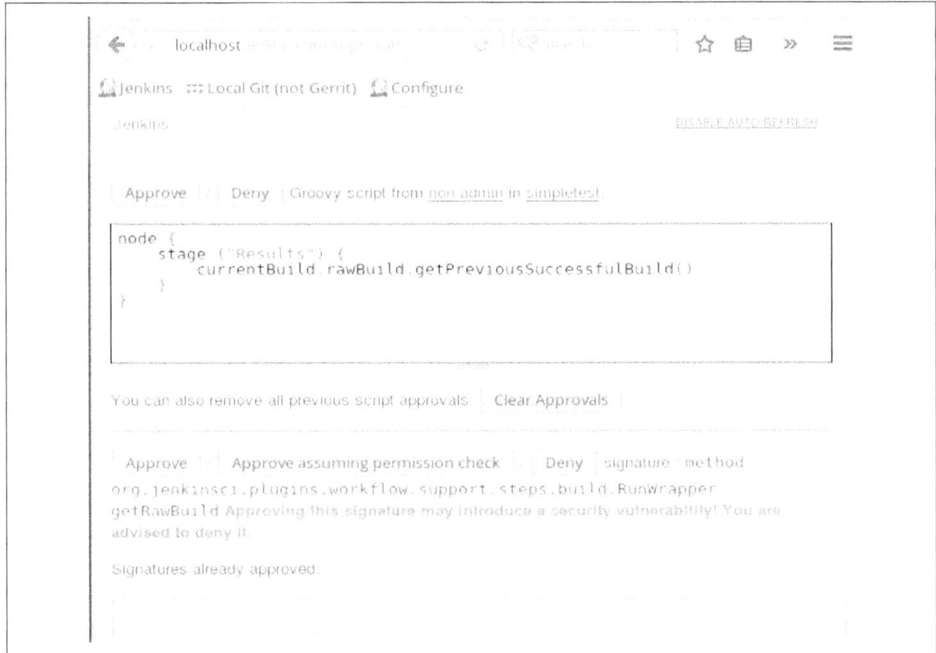

Figure 5-53. Script approval interface for administrators

Groovy Sandboxing

While the script approval mechanism provides a good signoff mechanism to validate scripts, approving every new script from a nonadministrator can become laborious and unmanageable over time. To help with simplifying that burden, Jenkins 2 also supports the ability to run scripts in a Groovy Sandbox. This is enabled by checking the Use Groovy Sandbox option at the bottom of the pipeline script text window (Figure 5-54).

Figure 5-54. Running in the Groovy Sandbox

The basic idea here is that there are a set of "whitelisted" methods maintained by Jenkins. This means that these methods are deemed to be safe to use in any script. If the option to use the Groovy Sandbox is selected and the script only makes use of methods in the whitelist that are known as safe, the script is allowed to run without approval. This saves the extra overhead of requiring an administrator to approve it.

However, if any of the methods in the script are not in the whitelist, then the script is not allowed to run and an error is flagged (Figure 5-55). In that case, the method is queued for approval by the administrator—just as the scripts are in the regular script approval process.

```
Running on master in /var/lib/jenkins/jobs/simpletest/workspace
org.jenkinsci.plugins.scriptsecurity.sandbox.RejectedAccessException: Scripts not permitted to
use method org.jenkinsci.plugins.workflow.support.steps.build.RunWrapper getRawBuild
        at
org.jenkinsci.plugins.scriptsecurity.sandbox.whitelists.StaticWhitelist.rejectMethod(StaticWhiteli
st.java:176)
        at
org.jenkinsci.plugins.scriptsecurity.sandbox.groovy.SandboxInterceptor$6.reject(SandboxInterceptor
.java:243)
        at
org.jenkinsci.plugins.scriptsecurity.sandbox.groovy.SandboxInterceptor.onGetProperty(SandboxInterc
eptor.java:363)
        at org.kohsuke.groovy.sandbox.impl.Checker$4.call(Checker.java:241)
```

Figure 5-55. Method flagged as not allowed in the Sandbox

Here again, when the administrator logs in and goes to Manage Jenkins, they will see the alert that there is a method signature waiting for their approval (Figure 5-56).

Figure 5-56. Method signature pending approval

On the "In-process Script Approval" page, the administrator will be presented with a choice to Approve, Approve assuming permission check, or Deny the method (Figure 5-57). The Approve and Deny options are self-explanatory. The "Approve assuming permission check" option permits running this method if an actual user is doing it (not a system call) and assuming the user has appropriate Jenkins permissions to allow doing the operation. If approved, the method will be added to the internal whitelist.

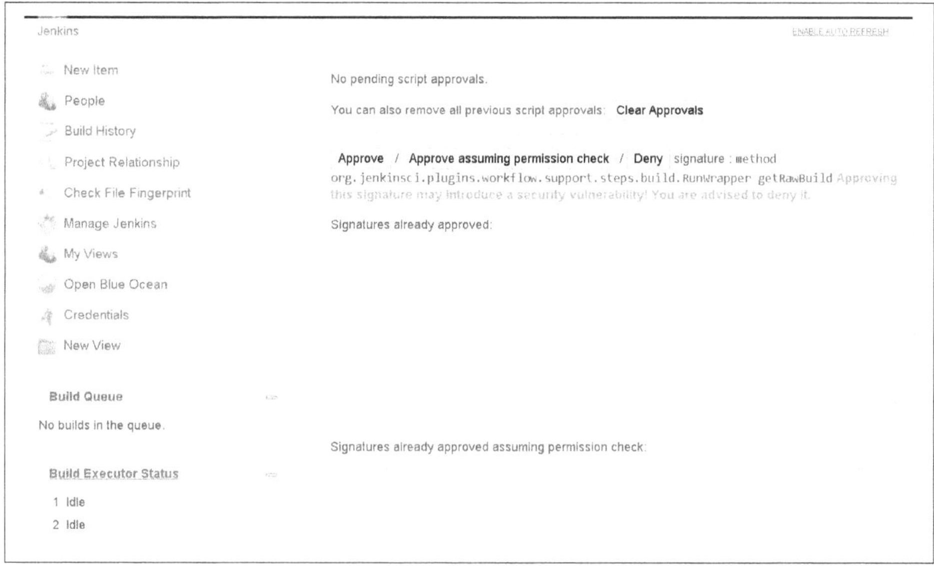

Figure 5-57. Administrator option to approve use of a method

Using Jenkins Credentials with Vault

HashiCorp's Vault application (*https://www.hashicorp.com/products/vault?*) bills itself as a tool for managing secrets. At its core that's what it is, but it also handles far more —including providing leasing, key revocation, token generation, and auditing services. It also provides external "auth backends" for different kinds of user and system authentication and access to stored credentials.

For Jenkins, Vault can be used as an external credential store that Jenkins authenticates to (through one of Vault's auth backends); it gets a temporary token and then is able to pull in the credentials in the pipeline. We'll look at a simplistic example of how to make Jenkins work with Vault in this section as a final example of working with credentials.

Approach

Vault includes a number of interfaces for working with it. These include a command-line interface as well as a REST API. As you might expect, there is also a Jenkins plugin for working with Vault (*https://plugins.jenkins.io/hashicorp-vault-plugin*).

In this section, we'll show how to spin up Vault and do initial setup via its command-line interface. We'll also leverage the "dev" mode that Vault comes with to further simplify things. Within Jenkins, we'll use the Jenkins plugin for Vault, but be aware that there are other approaches (such as the REST API and shell commands) that could be used to do these things, and that you would not want to use the dev mode in a production setting.

Setup

To start the Vault server running in dev mode, you simply do:

```
vault server -dev
```

Vault and Dev Mode

One of the reasons we start with dev mode is because that starts Vault in an unsealed state, meaning that it already knows how to decrypt information in it. The default mode starts Vault in a sealed state where it knows how to access information but not decrypt it. In that scenario, a longer process must be used to reconstruct the master key to use for decryption purposes.

With our Vault server running, we simply need to export the URL as a `VAULT_ADDR` environment variable to complete the basic setup:

```
export VAULT_ADDR='http://127.0.0.1:8200'
```

Creating a Policy

From the standpoint of how to use Vault, you can think of it as similar to a filesystem with the top level being the root path *secret*. We can define subpaths under this to hold our various "secrets" and write data into the subpaths of the form *key* = *value*.

Policies describe what capabilities are provided once someone or something gets access to a path. Capabilities here might include such operations as "list", "read", etc. for the secrets stored in this path. You can think of these as being like the read, write, and other permissions that are attached to files in a directory path. We'll start out by creating a simple policy for Jenkins to use. To create the policy, we specify the path and the capabilities in Vault and use the Vault `policy-write` command to store the new policy. We can write this into a file or just take a shortcut and echo it out:

```
echo 'path "secret/example" {
   capabilities = ["read", "list"]
}' | vault policy-write jenkins-example -
```

Vault should then respond with a message like:

```
Policy 'jenkins-example' written.
```

With this in place, once Jenkins has access to this area it can read and list the secrets stored under this path, supplying a key and getting the secret value back.

Authentication

To be precise, Jenkins itself won't have direct access to this area—rather, it will receive a token assigned to this policy, and that token will have the specified capabilities. You can think of the token in a similar way to having a session available after you log on to a system. While the session is active, you can execute the specified capabilities (permissions) against the objects stored in the system.

To continue our analogy, to get a session, you must be able to log on, or "authenticate," to the system. That is, you must be able to supply credentials up front to a login process to authenticate and get a session to do your work.

Vault supports various types of authentication. Each authentication type is implemented via an interface that Vault refers to as an *auth backend*.

Authentication (auth) backends are Vault components that do two things:

- Handle the different types of authentication.
- Assign a set of policies and identities to users.

There are a number of auth backends for many of the most popular services and applications that may make use of Vault. These include GitHub, Google Cloud, Kubernetes, AWS, LDAP, etc. One that you may not recognize is called AppRole. This is the one we would typically use in Jenkins. We'll look at it in more detail next.

AppRole

The idea with the AppRole backend is that services and systems can communicate with Vault through a defined set of roles (thus, "App" for services plus "Role"). These can be used at multiple scopes, including an individual system, a service that exists on multiple systems, or even a particular user on a particular system.

To use an auth backend like AppRole, we first need to enable it using Vault's `auth-enable` functionality, as shown here (again from a command-line perspective):

```
vault auth-enable approle
```

And Vault should respond with something like:

```
Successfully enabled 'approle' at 'approle'!
```

To make this work, we need two pieces of information to pass to Vault: a `role-id` to identify a role to use and a `secret-id` to identify a secret. A `secret-id` in this case is a temporary access "token" to a secret stored in Vault. Typically, the `secret-id` exists for only a short time after creation.

To create the `role-id`, we can just use Vault's `write` command and write a new role that maps to the policy we set up earlier. This definition also includes various "time-to-live"(`ttl`) settings for the generated info. An example syntax for this is shown here:

```
vault write auth/approle/role/jenkins-example
 secret_id_ttl=200m token_ttl=20m token_max_tll=40m
 policies=jenkins-example
```

And Vault should respond with:

```
Success! Data written to: auth/approle/role/jenkins-example
```

Once we've completed this operation, we can get our `role-id` token:

```
vault read auth/approle/role/jenkins-example/role-id
```

Vault will then display the information:

```
Key     Value
---     -----
role_id 5e50c99a-1b96-e747-f310-81451b78977c
```

Now we need to create another policy that allows us to use the `role-id` to generate `secret-id`s. This is similar to the way we created the earlier policy example. The following command shows how to do this:

```
echo 'path "auth/approle/role/jenkins-example" {
  capabilities = ["read", "create", "update"]
}' | vault policy-write jenkins -
```

And here's Vault's output:

```
Policy 'jenkins' written.
```

We can now ask Vault for a `secret-id` to use to access our data and retrieve it as shown next. When we set up the `secret-id`, we also specify a number of lease timeouts via the `ttl` (time-to-live) values:

```
vault write auth/approle/role/jenkins-example
  secret_id_ttl=100m
  token_ttl=200m token_max_ttl=300m
  policies=jenkins-example

vault write -f auth/approle/role/jenkins-example/secret-id
```

Vault will display the following:

```
Key                     Value
---                     -----
secret_id               eba9887f-afa7-5e0a-9b55-5cfbf1668a6d
secret_id_accessor      2323f05f-5312-895a-3902-46250cbed6a4
```

secret_id_accessor

The `secret_id_accessor` value can be used to find the properties of the `secret_id` without having to share the `secret_id` itself. It can also be used to delete the `secret_id` from the AppRole.

With the basic setup and authentication ready from the Vault side, we are ready to configure Jenkins for Vault use and include it in our pipeline.

Using Vault in Jenkins

We can move on now to using Vault in Jenkins. The first prerequisite is to make sure you have the Vault plugin installed (Figure 5-58).

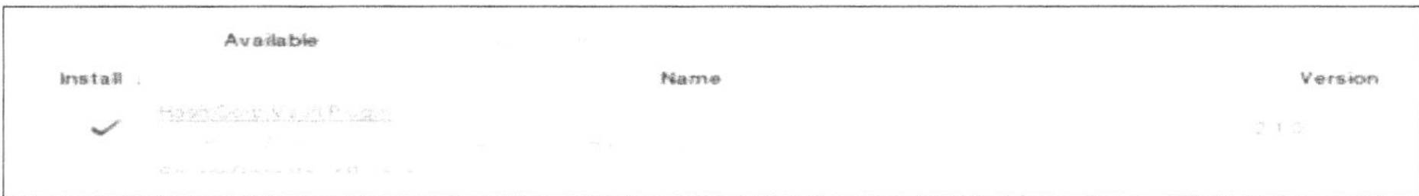

Figure 5-58. Installing the Vault plugin

Once that is done, you can move on to defining credentials for use with Vault.

Jenkins credentials for Vault

The Vault plugin allows us to select from a number of different types of credentials:

Vault AppRole credential
: For supplying a `role-id` and `secret-id` as we've been discussing

Vault GitHub Token credential
: Allows for authentication to GitHub via a personal access token (Vault does not use OAuth with GitHub and so requires a personal access token, as of the time of this writing)

Vault Token credential
: For basic authentication using a user-supplied token.

Vault Token File credential
: The same as the Vault Token credential, but the token is read from a file on your Jenkins system

Since we've been talking about AppRole and it is generally recommended for systems to use when accessing Vault, we'll use that one. Primarily, what we need to do is just plug in our `role-id` and `secret-id` (Figure 5-59).

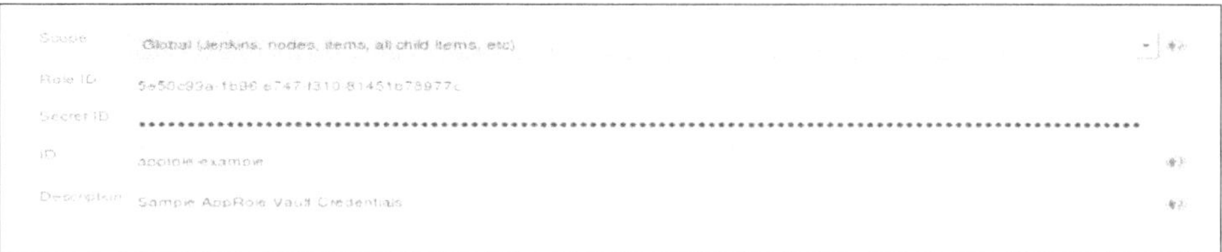

Figure 5-59. Setting up an AppRole credential

Credential Lifetimes

Note that since credentials here have a limited lifetime, using a static `secret-id` in an AppRole credential may not be the best choice unless the `secret-id` is set up to be long-lived.

In such a case, you may want to instead use the Vault Token File credential, where Jenkins reads the credential from a file. Arguably, having the credential exposed in a file is not as secure—but doing it this way, another process could monitor when the token is about to expire, get another one from Vault, and then update the file to make the process of token expiration/renewal a nonevent for Jenkins.

With our credential set up, we can then do the system configuration for the plugin. This is done on the Manage Jenkins → Configure System page and is straightforward; just put in the Vault URL and select the credential you have set up (Figure 5-60).

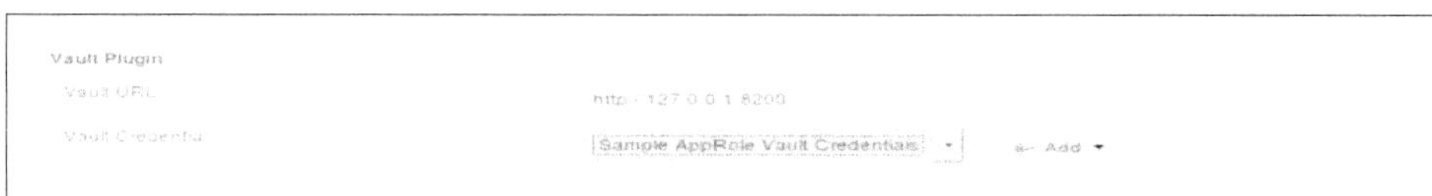

Figure 5-60. Vault global configuration in Jenkins

Folders and Vault

It's worth noting that Vault settings can also be configured at the folder level. Look for the Vault Plugin section in the folder configuration.

With the basic Jenkins configuration out of the way, we can move on to using Vault in our pipeline.

Using Vault in a Pipeline

To use Vault in a pipeline, there are a couple of steps.

First, we want to define an object that can identify which secret(s) and value(s) we want to access, as well as the environment variables we want to put them in for using in the pipeline. An example in Scripted Pipeline syntax is shown here (at the time of this writing, the Vault integration doesn't seem to be supported for Declarative Pipelines):

```
// define the secrets we want to access and the env variables
// we want to put the retrieved values in
def secrets = [
  [$class: 'VaultSecret', path: 'secret/example', secretValues:
    [[$class: 'VaultSecretValue', envVar: 'msg', vaultKey: 'value']]
]]
```

Here, `secret/example` is the path, `'value'` is the key to the keypair stored in Vault, and `'msg'` is the environment variable we will access in our script.

Once we have that set up, we can use the pipeline DSL step/construct "`wrap`" to access the credentials, as shown here:

```
// inside this block our credentials will be accessible as env variables
wrap([$class: 'VaultBuildWrapper', vaultSecrets: secrets]) {
  def myMsg = "The message is $msg"
  ...
}
```

About the wrap Step

The `wrap` step is a special step that allows a pipeline to call "build wrappers" (aka "environment configuration" in Freestyle jobs). This is a block step/construct, meaning that it defines an environment or setup that is in effect for all statements inside the block.

As far as using this for Vault integration, be aware that in the future, the plugin might migrate to an actual DSL build step of its own just for Vault.

There is one other configuration/pipeline item that is worth being aware of here. It is also possible to define your own local configuration for Vault within your pipeline. Code similar to the following could be used (plugging in our previous configuration values):

```
def configuration = [$class: 'VaultConfiguration',
                     vaultUrl: 'http://127.0.0.1:8200',
                     vaultCredentialId: 'approle-example']
```

To use this configuration locally, we would include it in our `wrap` step as shown here:

```
// inside this block our credentials will be accessible as env variables
wrap([$class: 'VaultBuildWrapper', configuration: configuration,
vaultSecrets: secrets]) {
  def myMsg = "The message is $msg"
  ...
}
```

We have only scratched the surface of working with Vault and how it can be used with Jenkins here. There are many more things it can do for you that can be useful in a pipeline, such as helping to automatically instantiate database credentials. For more details and use cases, you're encouraged to explore the documentation and various examples on the Vault website (*https://www.vaultproject.io/intro/index.html*).

Summary

In this chapter, we've covered some key elements of securing and accessing Jenkins. We dove into setting up user permissions and extended functionality that allows for defining role-based permissions not only for global tasks, but also for projects and nodes. We then spent some time looking at how to work with credentials in Jenkins and the various entities associated with them, such as providers, stores, and scopes.

Then we looked at some common problems authors and users of pipelines may encounter when invoking scripts, operations, and methods that need additional approval.

Finally, we took a look at how to use Jenkins with one of the newer secret-management applications, Vault, and saw how to make use of it.

Security and access control are constantly evolving topics in any application such as Jenkins. Securing Jenkins and controlling access is not only a good practice, but also a requirement for safety for any public multiuser instances. To ensure that your Jenkins instance is kept as secure as possible, pay attention to security notices on plugins and Jenkins itself, and update as frequently as your use cases and policies will allow.

In the next chapter, we'll look at how to extend our pipelines and Jenkins by using shared libraries and other methods to bring in external code.

CHAPTER 6

Extending Your Pipeline

Like in any programming environment, in Jenkins pipelines, centralizing functions, sharing common code, and code reuse are all essential techniques for quickly and effectively doing development. These practices encourage standard ways to invoke functionality, create building blocks for more complex operations, and mask complexity. They can also be used to provide uniformity and encourage convention over configuration to simplify tasks.

One key way that Jenkins allows users to do all of this is through the use of shared pipeline libraries. Shared pipeline libraries are composed of code stored in a source code repository that is automatically downloaded by Jenkins and made available to pipelines.

In this chapter, we'll explore the structure, implementation, and use of pipeline libraries, as well as seeing how to create our own global functions and even incorporate code that's not written in Groovy or Java. To start building our understanding, let's look at the different classifications of shared libraries that are available in Jenkins.

Trusted Versus Untrusted Libraries

Shared libraries in Jenkins can be in one of two forms: trusted or untrusted.

Trusted libraries are ones that can call/use any methods in Java, the Jenkins API, Jenkins plugins, the Groovy language, etc. Because trusted libraries have such wide latitude in what they can call and use, it's important that access to add or change code in them is managed. Making updates to trusted libraries should require an appropriate level of source control access and verification. For these same reasons, code that can potentially do any damage should always be contained in a trusted library where there is oversight.

Untrusted code is code that is restricted in what it can invoke and use. It is not allowed the same level of freedom to call the previously listed kinds of methods, and it cannot access the larger set of internal objects that trusted code can.

Untrusted code is run in the Groovy Sandbox, which has a list of methods that are "safe" to call. When running in the Sandbox, Jenkins monitors to see whether the library code attempts to call any methods not in the safe list. If so, the code is stopped and approval must be granted by an administrator. (See Chapter 5 for a discussion of the Groovy Sandbox and the related method approval process.)

Scope of Trust

As we will talk about later in this chapter, shared libraries can have a "scope" associated with them. Those at the "root" level of Jenkins are global (available to all jobs). By virtue of being at the root level, they are trusted. Those that are specified for use for specific sets of jobs (in folders, for example) are untrusted. (See Chapter 8 for more on Folder projects.)

Internal Versus External Libraries

Another distinction for shared libraries refers to where the source management repository is hosted—whether internally within the Jenkins instance or in an external source management system. Internal is viewed as more of a legacy option in most cases, but a description of it is included here for completeness.

Internal Libraries

This is an older method for managing libraries, but still an option. Jenkins 2 includes an internal Git repository that can be leveraged to store internal libraries or for testing purposes. Any content put in this library is trusted for all scripts, but anyone pushing to it has to have the appropriate administrative permissions.

Internal Library Use in CloudBees Jenkins

The internal Git repository is leveraged more in the internal CloudBees Jenkins system to provide a way to do code review checking before changes are added in to the system.

The internal Git repository has a specific name: *workflowLibs.git*. Note the mixed case in the name. It can be used with Git either through SSH access or through HTTP access. Details of how to use each protocol for this are next.

SSH access

To use this functionality you need to do a couple of things first:

1. Specify the SSHD port in Jenkins via Manage Jenkins → Configure Global Security. Use a high number here to avoid needing to use a privileged port. (See Figure 6-1.)

Figure 6-1. Setting up the SSHD port for internal library usage

2. Add the user's public SSH key in the SSH Public Keys field on *http://<jenkins-url>/user/<userid>/configure* page. (See Figure 6-2.)

Figure 6-2. Adding in the public SSH key

Once this is set up, then you should be able to clone down the internal Git repository, *workflowLibs.git*. The clone command would be:

```
git clone ssh://<userid>@<system-name>:<port>/workflowLibs.git
```

In our example, this would translate into:

```
git clone ssh://jenkins2@localhost:22222/workflowLibs.git
```

HTTP access

The HTTP access is fairly straightforward. Assuming your local Jenkins system is running on localhost on port 8080, you can clone the repository with the command:

```
git clone http://localhost:8080/workflowLibs.git
```

Potential Issue During HTTP Access of Internal Git Repository

The one "gotcha" you can sometimes run into with this is an error message like the following:

```
Error: RPC failed; HTTP 403 curl 22 The requested URL
returned error: 403 No valid crumb was included in the
 request
fatal: The remote end hung up unexpectedly
```

If this happens, it may be due in part to being logged out of Jenkins. So try logging back in. If the problem persists or you were logged in when the problem occurred, you may need to disable the option to prevent CSRF attacks in the Jenkins security settings (temporarily at least). The setting to disable is shown in Figure 6-3.

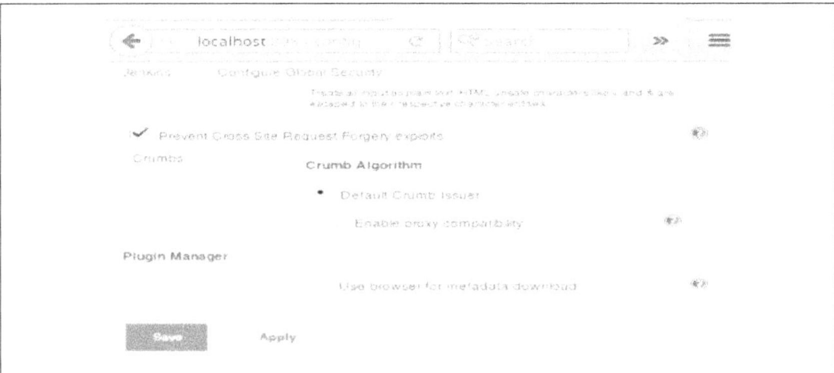

Figure 6-3. Try temporarily disabling the "Prevent Cross Site Request Forgery exploits" option if you run into problems cloning the internal Git repo via HTTP

Once you've cloned the internal repository down, it will be empty initially. To begin working with it, you'll need to change into the working directory and create a new master branch:

```
cd workflowLibs
git checkout -b master
```

External Libraries

To define an external library (one stored in a source repository separate from Jenkins) you need to provide a couple of pieces of information:

- A name for the library (this will be used in your scripts to access it)
- A way to get it from the source repository
- A version (optional)

Figure 6-4 shows an example.

Figure 6-4. Defining an external library

The "Default version" can be a branch or a tag. Note the information underneath the completed field that describes what that value currently maps to for the Git reference. This information is available after saving the library specifications since Jenkins needs to check the revision in the repository.

The "Load implicitly" option is intended to allow users to have the external library loaded automatically.

If the "Allow default version to be overridden" option is checked, then scripts can override the default version selected here. This can be done by specifying `@version` in the `@Library` annotation. That looks like this:

```
@Library('libname@version')_
```

The "Include @Library changes in recent job changes" option has to do with whether or not library code changes are included in the changesets of a build. If this is checked, they will be. This setting can be overridden by adding the `changelog=<boolean>` parameter in the actual annotation, as in:

```
@Library(value="libname[@version]", changelog=true|false)
```

More detail on how to include libraries in your pipeline scripts is found in "Using Libraries in Your Pipeline Script" on page 191.

After completing this part of the library configuration, we need to specify how to retrieve the library from source control.

Getting a Library from the Source Repository

There are two options to select from for Jenkins to be able to get the library code out of source control: *Modern SCM* and *Legacy SCM*.

Modern SCM

Most Jenkins SCM plugins have been updated with a new API to handle pulling a named version. Currently, nearly all of these should fall into this category. Figure 6-5 shows an example of the configuration section for this. At the top, you can see the name and version followed by the choice of Modern SCM for the retrieval method.

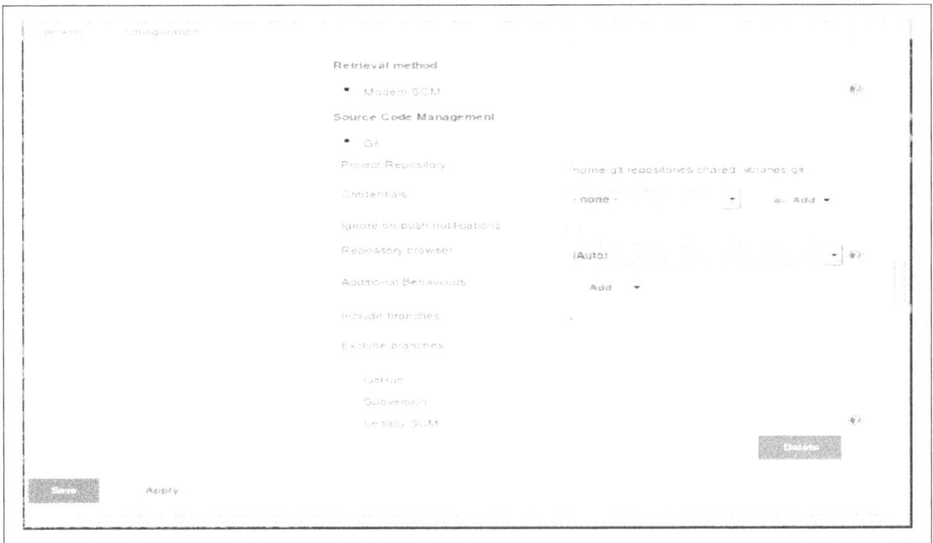

Figure 6-5. Using the Modern SCM retrieval method

Legacy SCM

If your particular SCM plugin for Jenkins isn't in the Modern SCM list, you can fall back to using the Legacy SCM option, shown in Figure 6-6. When using this option, the Jenkins documentation recommends including the string `${library.<your library name>.version}` in the specification somewhere. Here, `<your library name>` should actually be replaced with the name of your library. The other parts are literals in the string.

Figure 6-6. Using the Legacy SCM retrieval method

The idea here is that this string will get expanded to allow Jenkins to pick up the specific version of your content that is needed. In the Git example in the figure, I've put it in the refspec area. For SVN, you might include it at the end of the URL. In general, if you just always want to get the latest from a particular branch, you may be able to omit it altogether.

For the Branch Specifier field, you can enter any branch or tag. If you want to include a specific version of the library (and don't overwrite that version in the script), you can tag the code, and include the tag in this field. If you do include a tag for Git, a good practice is to include the fully qualified tag, as in *refs/tags/<tag>*. Notice that you can also specify multiple branches by clicking the Add Branch button to add new ones. If you select multiple branches, they will all be brought down. The "default version" setting can be used to specify which one is the default.

Modern Preferred

In some instances, a particular source control tool may show up in both the Legacy and Modern options. In such cases, the Modern SCM option is recommended.

Using Libraries in Your Pipeline Script

Now that we know how to define and configure libraries for availability in Jenkins, we need to understand how to load them into our pipelines. The first thing to understand is how Jenkins actually handles making libraries available for pipelines.

Automatic Downloading of Libraries from Source Control

When we either have content in the internal library or have declared external libraries that we want Jenkins to make available, Jenkins takes care of getting the correct content at the start of the run for each job.

Suppose for our example setup we have added content to the internal *workflowLibs.git* repository and configured a repository external to Jenkins at */home/git/repositories/shared-libraries*. Figure 6-7 shows what happens when we run a job with this setup. You can see both the external library and the internal one being downloaded so they are available in that run's workspace.

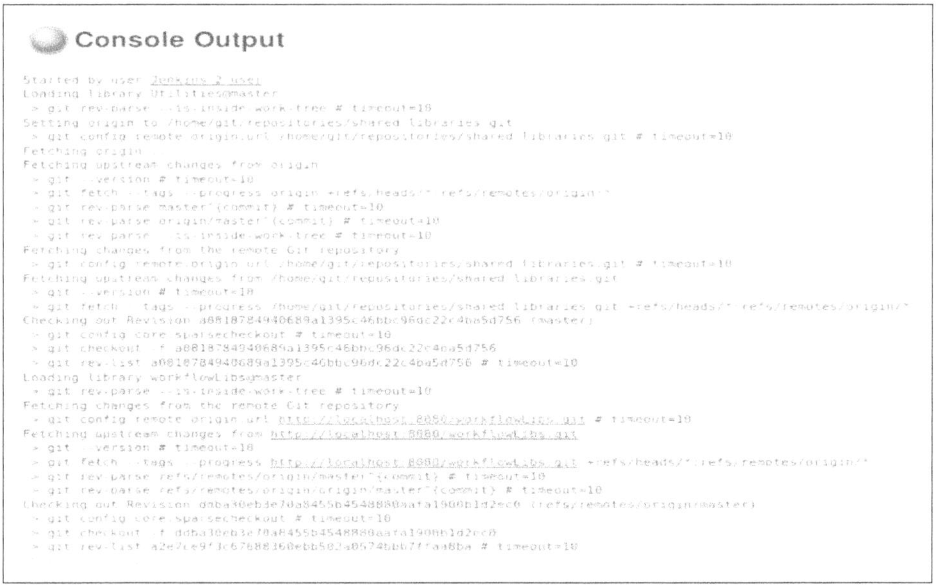

Figure 6-7. Shared global libraries being downloaded at the start of a job

Loading Libraries into Your Script

If there is content, the `workflowLibs` global internal library will be loaded automatically. You can specify that external libraries should be loaded automatically for your pipeline using the "Load implicitly" option.

If you choose to load the library implicitly, you can still specify a set of methods by using an `import` statement of the following form:

```
// importing a collection of methods
import static org.demo.Utilities.*
```

If you do not use an option that loads the library automatically, then you must use a statement in your pipeline script to explicitly load the library and make it available. There are a couple of different ways to do this, detailed next.

The @Library annotation

In Java-based languages, an annotation is metadata that can be put in the code to augment (or "annotate") other code. In the case of Jenkins pipeline syntax, the annotation construct is used less as an annotation and more as another syntax construct.

Specifically, you can use the `@Library` annotation in your pipeline script to load a library. The name of the library to load, and optionally a version, are specified as arguments. Here's the basic syntax:

```
@Library('<libname>[@<version>]')_ [<import statement>]
```

A couple of points about the syntax:

- The library name is required.
- The version should be preceded by the @ sign.
- The version can be a tag, branch name, or other specification of a revision in the source code repository.
- Specific subsets of methods can be imported by including an `import` statement at the end of the annotation or on the next line.
- An `import` statement is not required. If one is not specified, all methods will be imported.
- If no `import` statement is specified, then an underscore (_) *must* be placed at the end of the annotation, directly after the closing parenthesis. (This is required since an annotation needs something to annotate by definition. In this case, the _ is simply serving as a placeholder.)
- Multiple library names (with respective versions if desired) can be specified in the same annotation. Just separate them with commas.

Here are some simple examples:

```
// Load the default version of a library
@Library('myLib')_

// Override the default version and load a specific version of a library
@Library('yourLib@2.0')_

// Accessing multiple libraries with one statement
@Library(['myLib', 'yourLib@master'])_

// Annotation with import
@Library('myLib@1.0') import static org.demo.Utilities.*
```

The annotation would be placed at the beginning of your script, above the node line for a Scripted Pipeline, or above the pipeline line for a Declarative Pipeline.

Using @Library with Declarative Pipelines

While you can use the @Library annotation with a Declarative Pipeline, you have to put it outside of the pipeline closure. Putting code outside of the main closure is not recommended as it may cause confusion. A better approach for loading libraries in declarative syntax is to use one of the other methods we discuss.

The library step

Starting in Jenkins 2.7, an actual library step is available to use in pipelines. The syntax is similar to that of the annotation:

```
library "<libname>[@<version>]"
```

Since this is an actual pipeline step, it can be placed anywhere in the pipeline. It also allows using variables in place of the arguments. For example, you could define it to pick up the shared library from whatever version is currently represented by the built-in BRANCH_NAME variable.

```
library "<libname>@$<BRANCH_NAME>"
```

Or, in a Scripted Pipeline, you could create your own variable to use here. Another option would be to pass a version in as a parameter, and use that in the step.

The libraries directive

Within a Declarative Pipeline, we have one other option for pulling in libraries. We can use the libraries directive to specify a library to load. Within the directive, we can specify libraries using a lib statement. The syntax for each lib statement is similar to the syntax we've already seen in the other approaches: <libname>@<version>. Given the previous sections, a simple example should suffice:

```
pipeline {
     agent any
     libraries {
        lib("mylib@master")
        lib("alib")
    }
    stages {
       ...
```

Declarative Pipelines are covered in detail in Chapter 7.

Library Scope Within Jenkins Items

So far, we have only talked about pipeline libraries in a global context—usable for all projects. However, Jenkins 2 has many different types of items that can be created. And, for a subset of those types, shared libraries can be defined that only apply to items in a particular scope.

Specifically, the Folder, Multibranch Pipelines, GitHub Organizations, and Bitbucket Team/Project types can each have their own "local" shared pipeline libraries that they use. Limiting the scope allows for more dedicated, related functions to be available at that granularity.

For example, if you specify "Load implicitly" at the global/root level in Jenkins, all jobs will have the library automatically downloaded and available. But if you are configuring a folder and specify a shared library to load implicitly, only the jobs in that folder will have the library automatically downloaded and accessible.

One other note about shared libraries at these local scopes: they are considered untrusted and run in the Groovy Sandbox.

Figure 6-8 illustrates the different granularities of shared libraries available in Jenkins. While not specifically shown, any pipeline job has access to the global libraries.

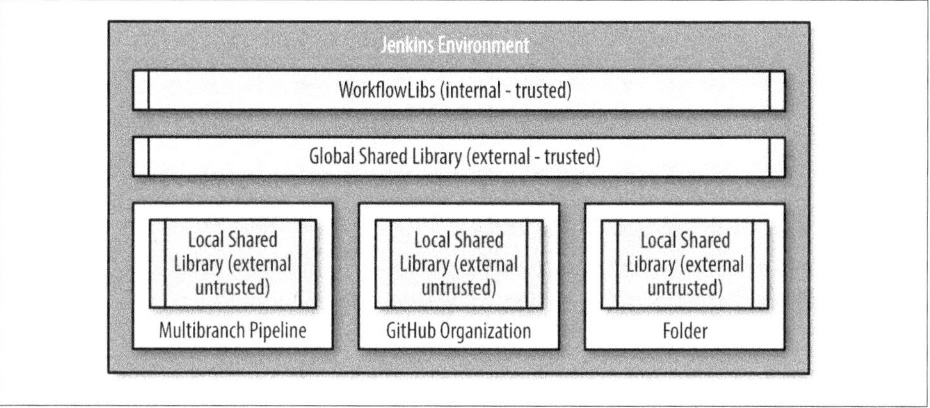

Figure 6-8. Shared library scope in Jenkins items

Library Structure

Now that we've covered the configuration of shared libraries, we can move on to looking at how to write and create them, and the structure that Jenkins provides for that. To start, we'll outline a sample routine that we'll use in many of the examples.

Sample Library Routine

To give us something to work with as we explore using pipeline libraries, we'll create a simple routine that invokes a Gradle build for us and adds timestamps to it.

In its simplest form, our routine will look something like this:

```
timestamps {
      <path-to-gradle-home>/bin/gradle <tasks>
}
```

`timestamps` is a Jenkins pipeline DSL step. The `timestamps` closure here simply tells Jenkins to add timestamps to the console output for this part of our pipeline (the Gradle build step).

We don't want to have to supply the `<path-to-gradle-home>` value every time we call this, and we don't want to hardcode it in. If we have Gradle configured globally in Jenkins, we can have this routine automatically use the global version of Gradle. Let's assume for the cases here, we have version 3.2 of Gradle installed in */usr/share/gradle* and configured in our Global Tool Configuration under the name "gradle3.2," as shown in Figure 6-9.

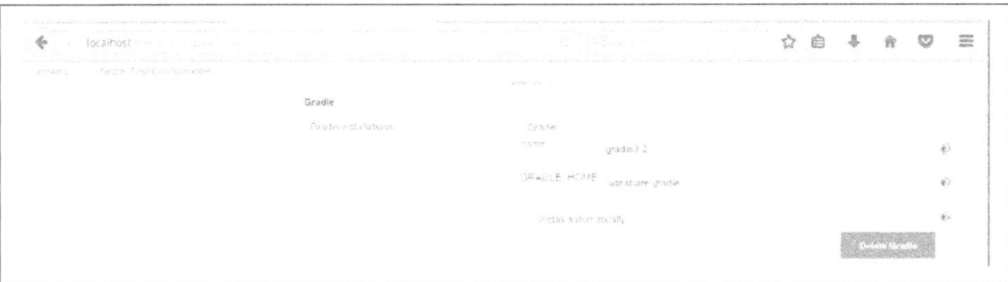

Figure 6-9. Our local installation of Gradle

With this in place, we'll be able to then reference our global tool location for Gradle in the library routines.

Our second set of code, for example use in the shared libraries, will run a shell command and print out the result with timestamps:

```
def commandOutput
timestamps {
   commandOutput = sh(script: "${<command-to-run>}",
   returnStdout: true).trim()
}
echo commandOutput
```

Here, we intend `<command-to-run>` to be the shell command we pass in—the one that we want to be executed. In the third line, we are invoking the pipeline DSL's `sh` command. As we have discussed previously, when we have more than one argument to a

DSL command, we pass them as a map. Here, our first argument is the "script" that we want to execute (i.e., our command), and the second argument is telling it to return the output of `stdout` (which our statement will print). The `trim()` command on the end is simply making the output cleaner.

We will tweak and wrap other code around these basic forms as we explore the different ways to create and use pipeline libraries. Now let's talk about the expected structure for a pipeline library.

Structure of Shared Library Code

The shared libraries feature has a predefined structure it expects. At the highest level, a shared library tree has three subtrees: *src*, *vars*, and *resources*. We describe each section in detail here.

src

This area is intended to be set up with Groovy files in the standard Java directory structure (i.e., *src/org/foo/bar.groovy*). It is added to the classpath when pipelines are executed.

Any Groovy code is valid to use here. However, in most cases, you'll probably want to invoke some kind of pipeline processing, using actual pipeline steps. There are several options for how to implement the step calls within the library, and correspondingly, how to invoke them from the script.

Here are some examples of things you could have in the *src* area:

- You can create a simple method, not enclosed by a class. Fitting our example code into this model could look like this:

  ```
  // org.demo.buildUtils

  package org.demo

  def timedGradleBuild(tasks) {
     timestamps {
        sh "${tool 'gradle3.2'}/bin/gradle ${tasks}"
     }
  }
  ```

  This can be invoked within a pipeline by:

  ```
  def myUtils = new org.demo.buildUtils()
  git "<gradle project to clone>"
  myUtils.timedGradleBuild("clean build")
  ```

- You can create an enclosing class (to facilitate things like defining a superclass). You can then get access to all of the DSL steps by passing the `steps` object to a method, in a constructor or in a method of the class:

```
// org.demo.buildUtils
package org.demo

class buildUtils implements Serializable {
    def steps
    buildUtils(steps) { this.steps = steps}
       def timedGradleBuild(tasks) {
       def gradleHome = steps.tool 'gradle3.2'
       steps.timestamps {
            steps.sh "${gradleHome}/bin/gradle ${tasks}"
       }
    }
}
```

Here, the `tool` step in *steps.tool* again references the installed version of Gradle that we have configured in the Global Tool Configuration. It returns the path associated with the tool of that name. This is a cleaner way to do it than the way we did it in the preceding example.

Since we are enclosing this in a class, the class must implement `Serializable` to support saving the state if the pipeline is stopped or restarted.

Once loaded, libraries defined in this way can be invoked from the main script via calls like the following:

```
@Library('bldtools') import org.conf.buildUtils.*
def bldtools = new buildUtils(steps)

node {
      git "<gradle project to clone>"
      bldtools.timedGradleBuild 'clean build'
}
```

Other items, like environment variables, can be passed in in the same way as the steps. In the following code we pass in the `env` object and utilize it in our code:

```
// org.demo.buildUtils
package org.demo

class buildUtils implements Serializable {
    def env
    def steps
    buildUtils(env,steps) {
       this.env = env
       this.steps = steps
    }
    def timedGradleBuild(tasks) {
```

```
            def gradleHome = steps.tool 'gradle3.2'
            steps.sh "echo Building for ${env.BUILD_TAG}"
            steps.timestamps {
               steps.sh "${gradleHome}/bin/gradle ${tasks}"
            }
        }
    }
```

- For a simpler case, you can just pass in the `script` object, which already has access to everything. In this case, we are passing it into a static method:

```
// org.demo.buildUtils
package org.demo

class buildUtils {
   static def timedGradleBuild(script,tasks) {
      def gradleHome = script.tool 'gradle3.2'
      script.sh "echo Building for ${script.env.BUILD_TAG}"
      script.timestamps {
         script.sh "${gradleHome}/bin/gradle ${tasks}"
      }
   }
}
```

  This version uses the `sh` step from the script as well as the `env` value from the script to do the same things as the previous version.

  This can then be invoked as:

```
@Library('<library-name>') import static org.demo.buildUtils.*
node {
    git "<gradle project to clone>"
    timedGradleBuild this, 'clean build'
}
```

vars

This area is for hosting scripts that define variables and associated methods that you want to access in the pipeline. The basename of a script should be a valid Groovy identifier. You can have a *<basename>.txt* file that contains help or other documentation for the variable. This documentation file can be HTML or Markdown.

You can define whatever methods you may want to use for variables in your pipeline in a Groovy file in the *vars* area. As an example, let's use the timed command example from the beginning of this section. Recall that this code is intended to take a command, call the DSL function `sh` on it to execute it as a shell script, capture the output, and print out timestamps during the operation. Let's first create a *timedCommand.groovy* file in the *vars* area for this with a few basic methods:

```
// vars/timedCommand.groovy
def setCommand(commandToRun) {
    cmd = commandToRun
}

def getCommand() {
    cmd
}

def runCommand() {
   timestamps {
      cmdOut = sh (script:"${cmd}", returnStdout:true).trim()
   }
}

def getOutput() {
   cmdOut
}
```

`cmd` and `cmdOut` here are not fields. These are objects created on demand. Now, we can use the `timedCommand` object as follows in our pipeline script:

```
node {
      timedCommand.cmd = 'ls -la'
      echo timedCommand.cmd
      timedCommand.runCommand()
      echo timedCommand.getOutput()
}
```

Using a Class with vars

As was done with the code in *src*, you could create a class to encapsulate the *vars* commands. However, doing so is problematic and not particularly beneficial.

Automatic documentation references for global variables. As mentioned previously, one of the types of files that can be in the *vars* section is a *.txt* file with the same name as the *.groovy* file containing code. This *.txt* file can be used for documentation on the operation and can be written in either Markdown or HTML. Figure 6-10 shows an example *timedCommand.txt* file. This file has corresponding user-facing documentation about the functions defined in our *timedCommand.groovy* file. The file is optional, but if created, it should be committed and pushed in the *vars* directory of the same shared library structure as the corresponding *.groovy* file.

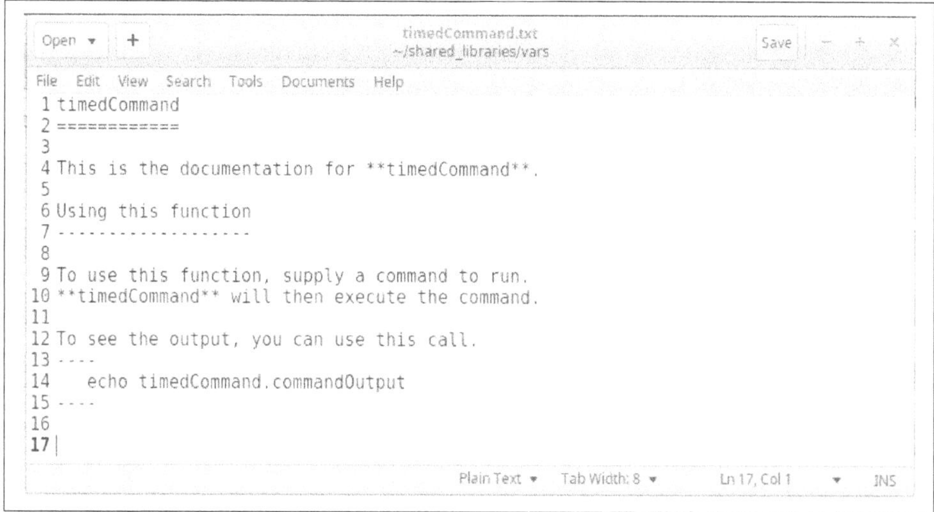

Figure 6-10. Creating a timedCommand.txt file to correspond to our implementation file

After the variable code has been loaded and executed in a successful run of a pipeline script, an entry for the variable will be added to the list of global variables in the pipeline syntax section (accessible via the Pipeline Syntax screen). Figure 6-11 shows how to get to that area through the interface.

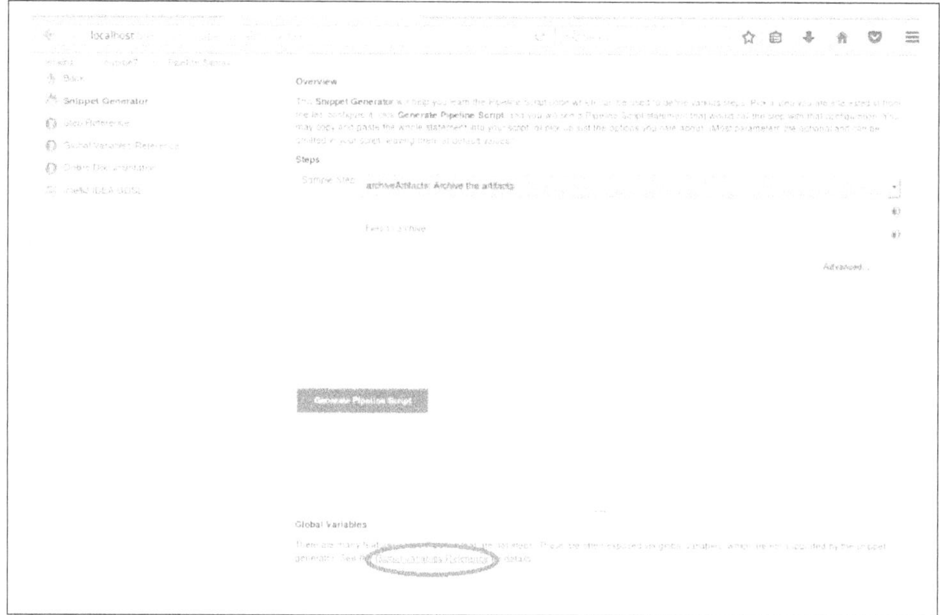

Figure 6-11. Accessing the Global Variable Reference

If you're not familiar with the Global Variable Reference page, its purpose is to provide documentation on variables and their associated methods (see Figure 6-12).

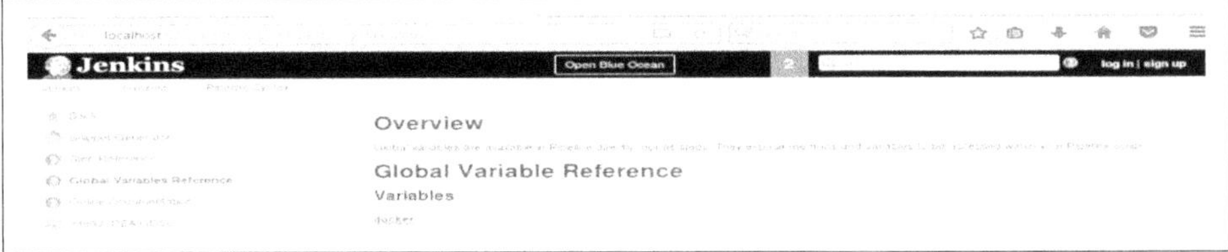

Figure 6-12. The Global Variable Reference

After we have a successful run of a job with our `timedCommand` variable, the contents of our *timedCommand.txt* file will be included in this page (Figure 6-13). This provides a convenient way of documenting any variables we add in the application.

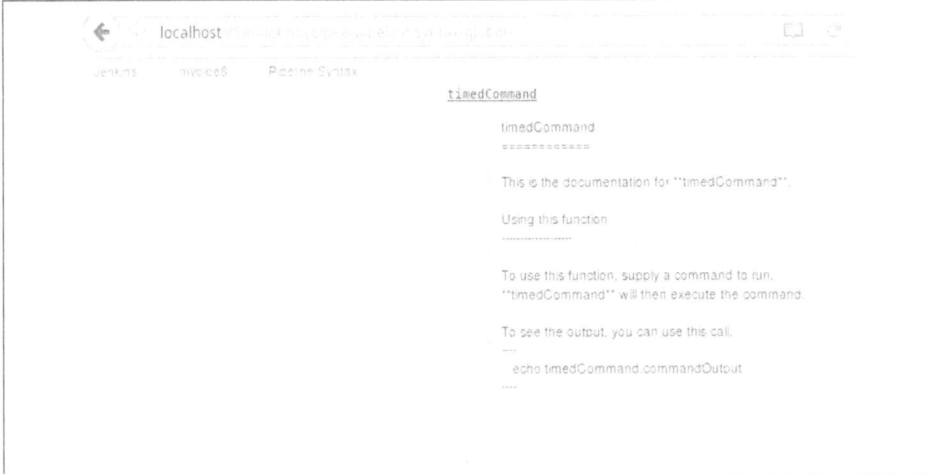

Figure 6-13. Our timedCommand variable is included now in the Global Variable Reference

Using global variables like steps. You can create global variable definitions that act like steps in pipeline scripts. That is, they can be called like regular pipeline steps. The trick to this is to define the `call` method in the global variable's definition. Let's see what it would look like to do this for our `timedCommand` code. Since this is a slightly different version, we'll refer to it as `timedCommand2`:

```
// vars/timedCommand2

def call (String cmd) {
   timestamps {
      cmdOutput = echo sh (script:"${cmd}", returnStdout:true).trim()
   }
```

```
    echo cmdOutput
    writeFile
}
```

We can use any valid pipeline DSL code in the body of the call. Let's suppose that we decide we want to add code to write our output to a log file as well as printing it out. For this, we will need the `writeFile` sDSL statement. If we're not clear on the syntax, we can use the pipeline syntax generator (aka Snippet Generator) to help us with that. Figure 6-14 shows using the Snippet Generator to determine the right format of the command for our purposes. (Notice that we just supply the variable names we intend to use in the individual fields.)

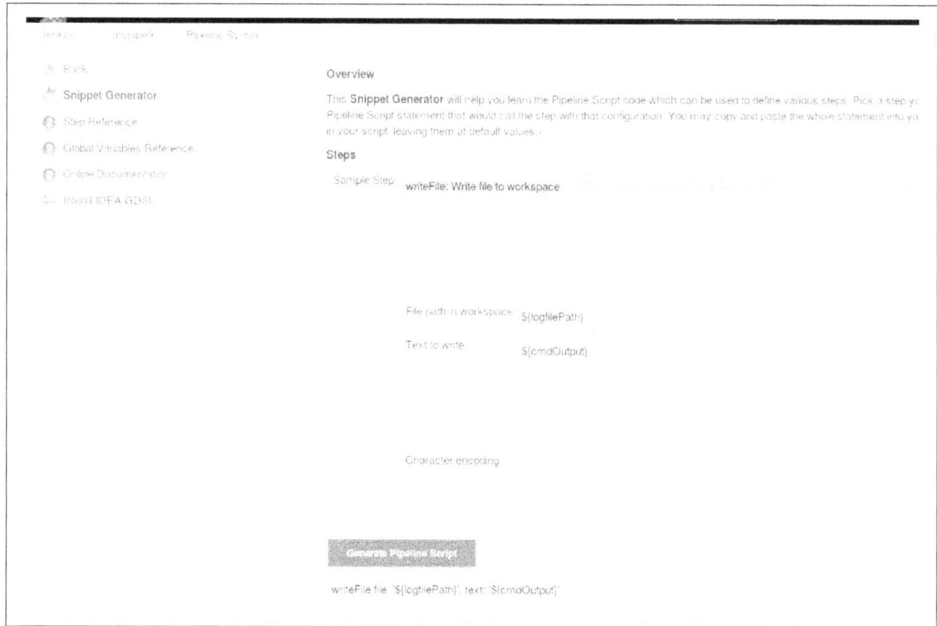

Figure 6-14. Using the Snippet Generator to get the correct syntax for the writeFile DSL call

Now we can add the `writeFile` command to our function and pass in a value for the location:

```
// vars/timedCommand2

def call (String cmd, String logFilePath) {
   timestamps {
      cmdOutput = sh (script:"${cmd}", returnStdout:true).trim()
   }
   echo cmdOutput
   writeFile file: "${logFilePath}", text: "${cmdOutput}"
}
```

Here's an example of using the command this way. Notice the invocation resembles a pipeline step:

```
timedCommand2 'ls -la', 'listing.log'
```

Suppose that we want to pass a block of code to a library "step". When that happens, our library step will receive a Groovy closure. To handle this case, we define our step to accept the closure and then execute it:

```
// vars/timedCommand3

def call(Closure commands) {
   timestamps {
      commands()
   }
}
```

Or suppose we want to time how long it takes to read a file, do some kind of transformation on it, and then write the transformed data back out to another location. An example of how this could be called from a script is:

```
timedCommand3 {
       def content = readFile file: '<path to huge datafile>'
       sh "<some processing on content>"
       writeFile file: '<path to transformed file>', text: content
       echo "Done"
}
```

This becomes even more useful if we want to do something like restrict the routine to a particular environment, such as a particular node. For example, we could set up two nodes, one running Windows and one running Linux, and then define two separate routines in *vars*, one to run our timing of commands on Windows and one to run the timing on Linux. Our code in *vars* might look like this:

```
// vars/timedCommandWindows.groovy

def call(Closure commands) {
   node('windows') {
       timestamps {
          commands()
       }
   }
}

// vars/timedCommandLinux.groovy

def call(Closure commands) {
   node('linux') {
       timestamps {
          commands()
       }
   }
}
```

Finally, in this category, we can extend the call mechanism to create a simple framework that makes using the "step" in our scripts very simple and more like standard DSL calls with multiple values.

This is done by delegating the values passed in to a mapping and then using the mapping in additional processing in the step. This is easiest to understand with an example:

```
// vars/timedCommand4.groovy

def call(body) {
    // collect assignments passed in into our mapping
    def settings = [:]
    body.resolveStrategy = Closure.DELEGATE_FIRST
    body.delegate = settings
    body()

    // now, time the commands
   timestamps {
      cmdOutput = echo sh (script:"${settings.cmd}", returnStdout:true).trim()
   }
   echo cmdOutput
   writeFile file: '${settings.logFilePath}', text: '${cmdOutput}'
}
```

In this form, we declare a Groovy map via the `def settings = [:]` syntax. Then the values we pass in get mapped and we can execute whatever other steps we need to. The references to `delegate` here have to do with Groovy functionality. A complete discussion of delegation behavior in Groovy is beyond the scope of this section, but you can essentially think of it as telling Groovy to allow us to reference any values passed in utilizing the mapping we're doing in this function.

Note that here, as in other *vars* steps, you should only use valid pipeline steps. Non-step Groovy code may not work or may have uncertain behavior.

With this form, we can invoke the code from our pipeline script very simply, as shown here:

```
node {
    timedCommand4 {
        cmd = 'sleep 5'
        logfilePath = 'log.out'
    }
}
```

What this really buys us is the ability to invoke our function with named parameters, passed in whatever order we choose. This can make our code in the pipeline script simpler and easier to understand and maintain.

resources

Non-Groovy files can be stored in this directory. They can be loaded via the `libraryResource` step in an external library.

This is intended for allowing your external libraries to load up any additional non-Groovy files they may need. An example could be a datafile of some kind, such as an XML or JSON file, or any other file that the library needs to use. The file is loaded as a string.

The syntax is straightforward. In your library code, you would have something like the following:

```
def datafile = libraryResource 'org/conf/data/lib/datafile.ext'
```

Another Use of libraryResource

While typically used for loading resources from external files for use in shared libraries, the `libraryResource` feature can be used to load up any resource you need to use in your script. Here's an example:

```
def myExternalScript =
  libraryResource 'externalCommands.sh'
sh myLatestScript
```

Of course, this should be used carefully and not in a way that could lead to masking potentially dangerous code. But it can be useful in certain cases, such as if you want to separate out nonpipeline code or need to programmatically specify different files to load based on conditions.

Mapping library Step Calls to src and vars

The form of the `library` step that we saw earlier in the chapter works for global variables (items made available from the *vars* structure). This means that any global variables from the library will be available in the script.

However, if you want to reference classes from the *src* area using the `library` step, the process is not as straightforward. The `@Library` annotation updates a script's classpath before compiling, but since `library` is a step, compilation has already occurred. This means you can't import items from the library.

You can, though, still get to individual classes by referencing their fully qualified paths based on the return value from the `library` step. For example:

```
library('<libname>').com.mypipe.demo.Utilities.myStaticMethod
```

Here's a simple script using this type of syntax:

```
node ('worker_node1') {
    stage('Source') { // Get code
       // Get code from the source repository
       git url: 'http://github.com/brentlaster/greetings.git',
          branch: 'demo'
    }
    stage('Compile') { // Compile and do unit testing
       // Run Gradle
       library('Utilities').org.demo.BuildUtils3.timedGradleBuild
          this, 'clean build'
    }
}
```

Using Third-Party Libraries

Shared libraries can also make use of third-party libraries using the `@Grab` annotation. The `@Grab` annotation is provided through the *Grape* dependency manager that is built into Groovy. It allows you to pull in any dependency from a Maven repository, such as Maven Central. This can be done from trusted libraries, but does not work in the Groovy Sandbox.

Here's an example function using `@Grab` to pull in an Apache Commons dependency. In a similar vein to our other examples, we're using a "stopwatch" function here to time how long execution of a command takes. The routine is written entirely with Groovy code (as noted earlier, libraries have access to all Groovy constructs):

```
// vars/timedCommand5

@Grab('org.apache.commons:commons-lang3:3.4+')
import org.apache.commons.lang.time.StopWatch

def call(String cmdToRun) {
      def sw = new StopWatch()
      def proc = "$cmdToRun".execute()
      sw.start()
      proc.waitFor()
      sw.stop()
      println("The process took ${(sw.getTime()/1000).toString()} seconds.\n")
}
```

Assuming this code has been pushed into the shared library area that is being implicitly loaded, the code could be invoked like this from a pipeline script:

```
node {
         timedCommand5("sleep 10")
}
```

Other than the downloads for the libraries, the output would look something like this:

```
[Pipeline] node
Running on worker in /home/jenkins2/worker_node1/workspace/mypipe11
[Pipeline] {
[Pipeline] echo
The process took 10.009 seconds.

[Pipeline] }
[Pipeline] // node
[Pipeline] End of Pipeline
Finished: SUCCESS
```

Loading Code Directly

You can also load code directly via the `load` operation. This is similar to the shared library code in terms of the syntax. It is different in that it is not pulling it from source control. In order to use this, you just need to have your function stored in a location that is accessible. Here's an example using one of our `timedCommand` implementations:

```
def call(String cmd, String logFilePath) {
   timestamps {
      cmdOutput = sh (script:"${cmd}", returnStdout:true).trim()
   }
   echo cmdOutput
   writeFile file: "${logFilePath}", text: "${cmdOutput}"
}
return this;
```

The `def` here could also be `public`. Notice that we have made one change to the function: we added a `return this` line at the end of the definition. This line is necessary to make sure the correct scope is returned so the `load` function works correctly.

Once this is in place, we can load it and invoke it from our pipeline script through the following:

```
node {
   def myProc = load '/home/diyuser2/timedCommand2.groovy'
   myProc 'ls -la', 'command.log'
}
```

We can utilize the direct `myProc(...)` syntax here because the function was defined with `call`. If we used a formal name instead of `call`, then we would invoke the function in the pipeline with `myProc.<name>(...)` instead. For example, if the first line of our function definition was:

```
def timedCommmand(String cmd, String logFilePath) {
```

then we would need to invoke it in the pipeline script via:

```
myProc.timedCommand("sleep 5","command.log")
```

Loading Code from an External SCM

We have seen how to both define an external shared library and load code directly from a location in our filesystem. There is another process that allows for a sort of hybrid approach: it allows us to directly load code from an external SCM, without having to include it as part of a shared library.

To make this work, we first need to install the Pipeline Remote Loader plugin, if it is not already installed. Figure 6-15 is a screenshot showing how to locate this plugin.

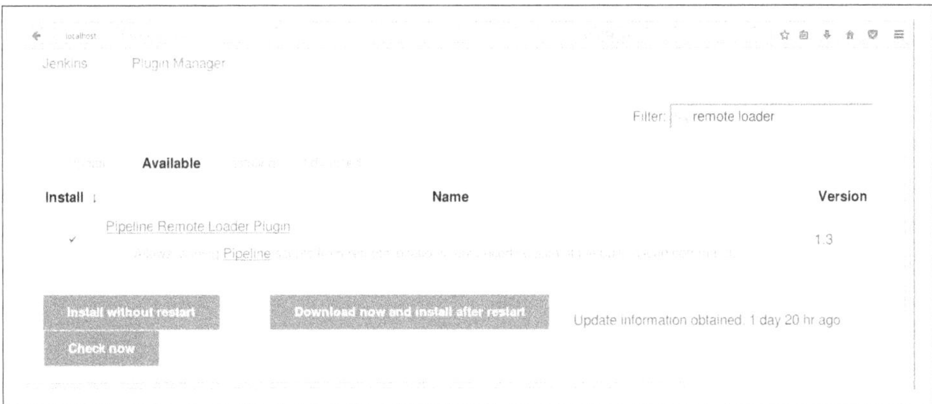

Figure 6-15. Installing the Remote Loader plugin

This plugin provides a `fileLoader` DSL function to load code from Git, GitHub, or SVN repositories (assuming you have the appropriate plugins installed for Git or SVN). After installation, you'll have a Global Variable Reference entry for it that you can look at for more details. This is shown in Figure 6-16.

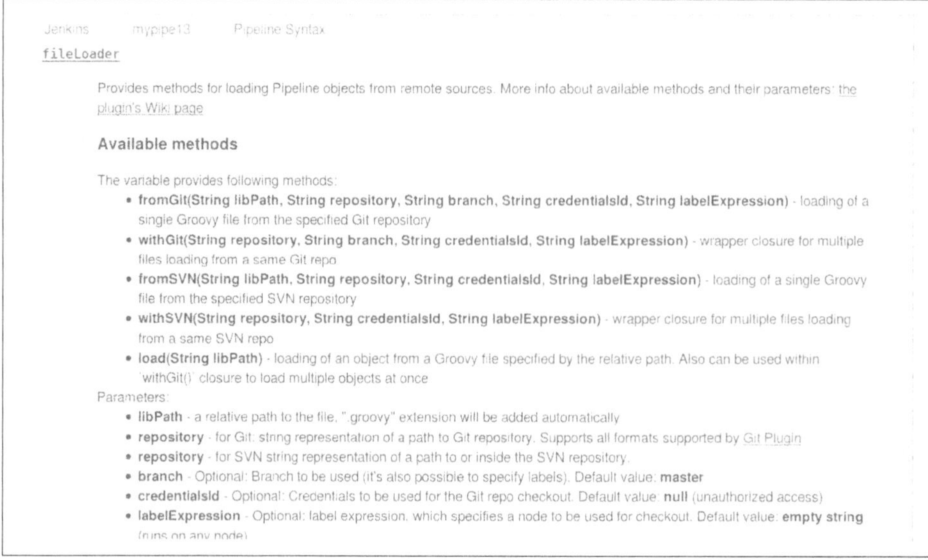

Figure 6-16. The global variable pipeline syntax reference for the fileLoader command

Let's look at a quick example of this. On one of my GitHub sites (*http://bit.ly/2vz147g*), I have the same `timedCommand` code as used in the preceding section.

An example of running this from a pipeline script is shown here:

```
def timestampProc = fileLoader.fromGit('jenkins/pipeline/timedCommand',
        'https://github.com/brentlaster/utilities.git', 'master', null, '')

timestampProc.timedCommand("ls -la","command.log")
```

Support for the Remote Loader Plugin

Be aware that while this functionality is still available, it is no longer being supported and updated. It served a more substantial purpose prior to the development of shared pipeline libraries.

Replaying External Code and Libraries

In Chapter 2, we introduced the Jenkins pipeline *Replay* functionality. After a successful run of a pipeline item, you can select a run and edit it from the job screen to try out changes. These changes cause another run to happen, but do not update the original job. This provides a powerful way to try out fixes or other changes to your code without having to go back and change the configuration every time.

In addition to providing the replay capability for basic jobs, Jenkins also provides it for code brought in via the `load` and `fileLoader` statements discussed in the preceding sections, and for untrusted libraries.

Untrusted Libraries

Recall from our earlier definition in this chapter that an *untrusted* library is one that has to run in the Sandbox and doesn't have unlimited access to Groovy constructs, Jenkins objects, etc. This includes libraries that are shared across a Folder, Multibranch Pipeline, GitHub Organization, Bitbucket Team/Project.

To see how Replay looks for these cases, let's take a quick look at a couple of examples. First, in Figure 6-17, we can see a Replay screen for our direct loading of the code from GitHub via the `fileLoader` DSL function that we looked at in the last section. In this case, we have had a successful run of the job, then gone to the job output screen for the run and selected Replay.

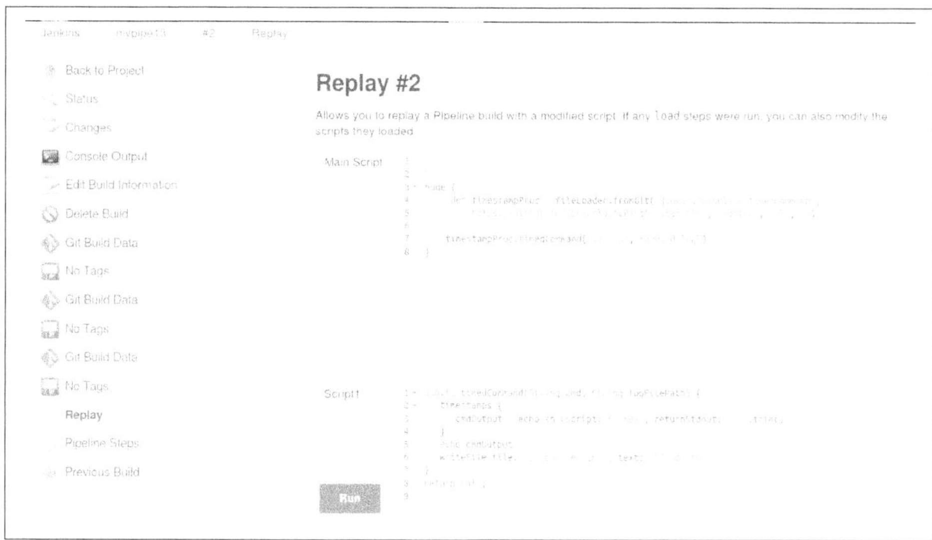

Figure 6-17. Replay of a pipeline script and script loaded from a GitHub site

This looks similar to the Replay screen for other jobs, except that we have two Replay areas: one for the main pipeline script and one for the script we loaded from GitHub. We can modify either or both and then click the `Run` button to see the results. Again, this doesn't modify the original saved script (either the main one or the one loaded from GitHub). What it does do is provide a significant time and cost savings, by not having to modify the scripts in their stored locations just to test changes.

As another example, consider a case where we have created a Folder project and set up a shared pipeline library for it (Figure 6-18).

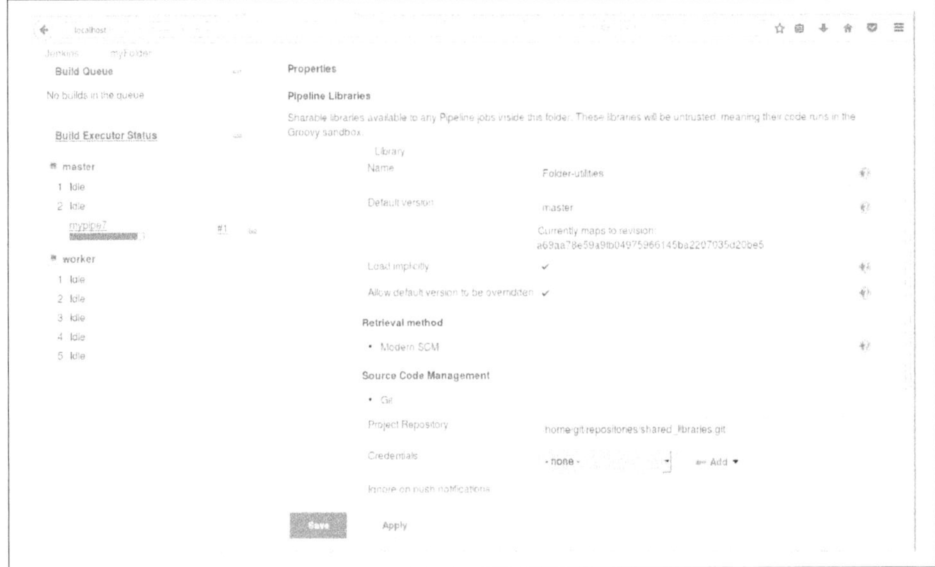

Figure 6-18. Setting up a shared pipeline library for a folder

Since this is a shared pipeline library for a Folder, it is considered untrusted. Untrusted libraries that are loaded are included in Replay operations, so after we create an item in the folder and successfully run it, we can use the Replay operation. When we invoke the Replay command, Jenkins presents sections for all of the pieces of the shared library (Figure 6-19). This way, we have an opportunity to modify any of the library functions.

Figure 6-19. Replay for untrusted library components

A Closer Look at Trusted Versus Untrusted Code

We previously discussed the distinction between trusted and untrusted code. We can demonstrate the difference here simply by trying to reference a restricted Jenkins object. In keeping with our time theme, we'll attempt to use a Jenkins internal object that allows us to get the elapsed time since the build started—the `getTimestampString` method of the `rawBuild` object of the `currentBuild`. Putting this into a `println`, it might look like this:

```
println "ELAPSED TIME: ${currentBuild.rawBuild.getTimestampString()}"
```

First, we'll try adding the line to our current pipeline script, as seen in Figure 6-20.

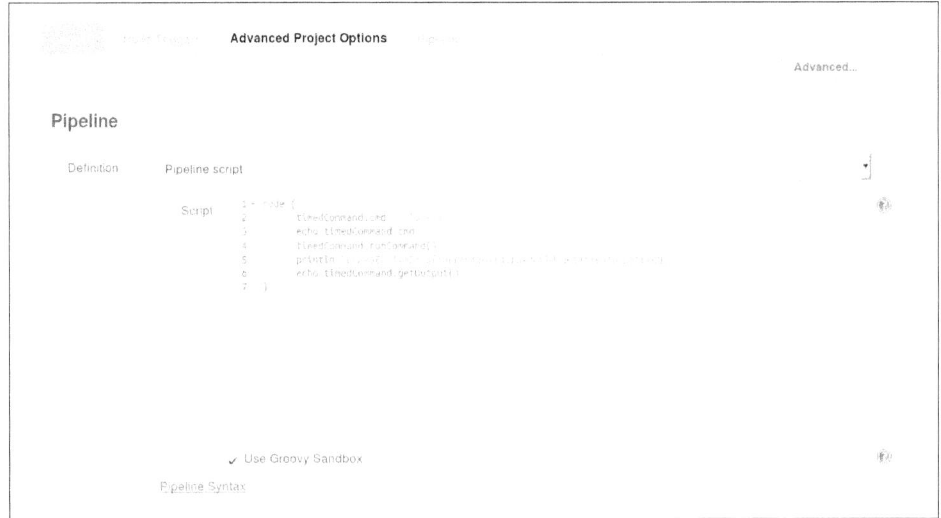

Figure 6-20. Adding the getTimestampString call to the main script

Notice that we're running this in the Groovy Sandbox. If we try to execute this script we'll get a `RejectedAccessException` error, as seen in Figure 6-21. Since untrusted libraries run in the Sandbox, they get the same exception as if they were specifically limited to an untrusted type, such as a Folder, GitHub Organization, Bitbucket Team/Project, or Multibranch Pipeline project.

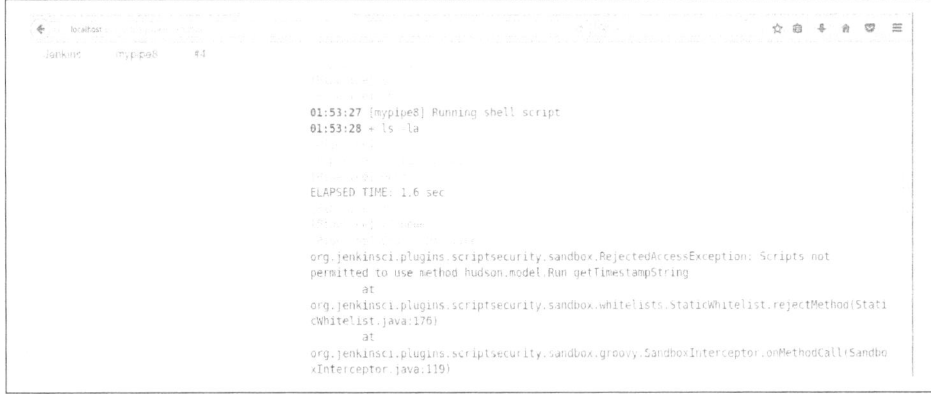

Figure 6-21. Access failure trying to use internal method in script

However, if we add the method to a trusted library, such as our global shared library, *and* remove it from our pipeline script, it should work. Figure 6-22 shows the edit to add this to the appropriate `runCommand` library routine.

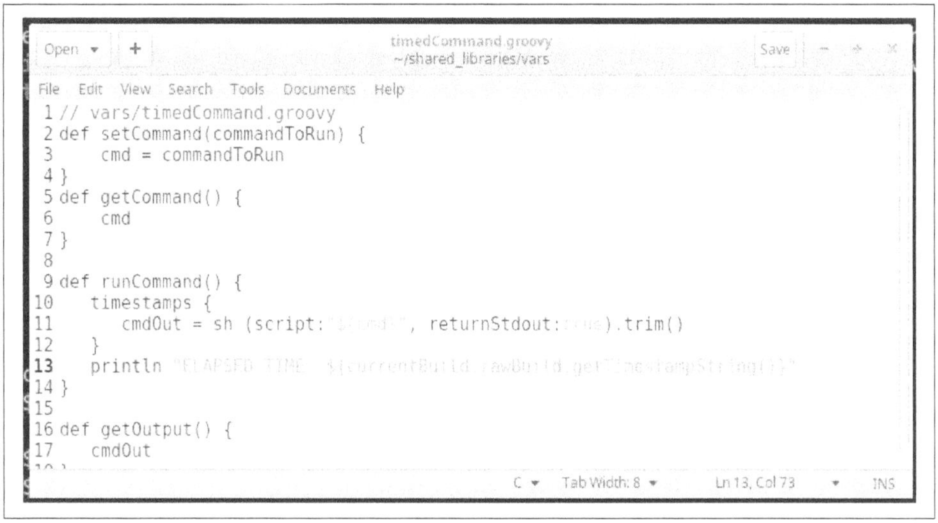

Figure 6-22. Adding the getTimestampString command to our trusted pipeline library

And, in fact, when we run the original script now (without the call in it), we can see that the call gets executed successfully in the trusted library code (Figure 6-23) even though our main script is still running in the Sandbox.

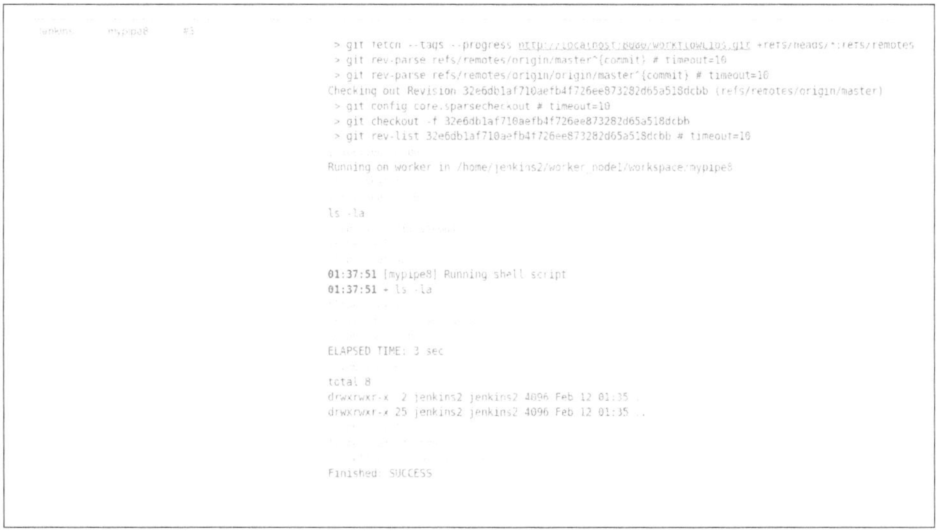

Figure 6-23. Successfully executing the command through the trusted library instead of the restricted pipeline script

Summary

In this chapter, we explored the many ways you can utilize external library routines in your Jenkins pipelines. We looked at the different classifications that shared pipeline libraries can have (trusted, untrusted, internal, external), and we saw how to tell Jenkins to load code from its own internal library or from an external library. We also examined the structure that an external library is expected to have, and what kind of content is in each section.

We spent time in the *vars* section to understand how we can create global variables and functions that can be used in pipelines. We also noted how you can create code that can be called like a DSL step or with named parameters to make using it simple in pipelines. We also talked about how to create and automatically get integrated documentation for global variables that you create.

We noted the newer types of projects that Jenkins supports now and how shared libraries fit into their structure. These include the Multibranch Pipeline, GitHub Organization, and Bitbucket Team/Project types.

Finally, we got a feeling for how the Replay functionality can be used for untrusted libraries, and walked through an example demonstrating trusted versus untrusted calls.

This information provides examples of how you can create and leverage common library code for pipelines and how to store and reference that code in external source management systems, including GitHub projects.

In the next chapter, we'll explore Declarative Pipelines in more detail.

CHAPTER 7

Declarative Pipelines

In this part of the book, we're going to be talking about another evolution in Jenkins pipelines—Declarative Pipelines. Declarative Pipelines allow users to define a pipeline in a way similar to how they would define jobs in the traditional Jenkins web forms. By this we mean:

- There is a well-defined, enforced structure. (You can think of this like the sections on the pages of a Jenkins web form.)
- Defining a pipeline section is more about declaring the high-level steps/goals than defining the logic to accomplish it. (This is similar to filling in the fields in a Jenkins web form.)
- Familiar Jenkins processing constructs are provided and don't have to be emulated with programming. (For example, you have a way to do post-build processing and send notifications, as opposed to having to use `try-catch-finally` Groovy programming to handle this.)
- All of the above enable better validation and error checking. (Errors are identified and presented in the context of the expected structure and keywords, not just Groovy tracebacks.)

These features distinguish Declarative Pipelines from the alternative way of creating a pipeline that ties DSL steps and sections together with programming constructs (assignments, conditionals, etc.)—essentially writing a program. That style of freeform coding for a pipeline is what we call a "Scripted Pipeline."

Both types of pipelines have their place, with advantages and disadvantages to each. Broadly speaking, Declarative Pipelines are easiest for someone new to using the pipeline functionality. This is because they more closely resemble what was done and available in the web forms, and they have clearer, more contextual validation and error checking.

Scripted Pipelines provide more flexibility and the ability to mix in programming constructs to execute logical flows, decision handling, assignments, etc. that are not available in Declarative Pipelines. For more experienced users or advanced applications, Scripted Pipelines can be the best option.

It is also worth noting that not all plugins that support Scripted Pipelines have interfaces and flows that support Declarative Pipelines directly.

One last general note about Declarative Pipelines: you may be wondering how support for them is integrated with Jenkins. Like nearly every piece of additional functionality in Jenkins, they're supported via plugins. The set of plugins that support Declarative Pipelines and the new Blue Ocean interface (described in Chapter 9) are largely tied together.

Now, let's start diving into the world of Declarative Pipelines by taking a look at the motivation behind them.

Motivation

To understand why we can benefit from another way to structure pipelines in Jenkins, it's helpful to understand some of the shortcomings specifically associated with the traditional Scripted Pipeline creation and model.

Not Intuitive

As we've discussed, moving from a web interface (with specific forms, help buttons, and UI elements that guide you in setting up jobs) to creating scripts, is not intuitive. One key part of the original UI job pages was the separation into sections, such as post-build processing, that guided users through the various phases. When moving to scripts, the elements for the different phases are available, but it's not clear how to structure or order them out of the box. Worse, some familiar processes don't have corresponding constructs in the nondeclarative DSL.

Getting Groovy

While it's not a requirement to be able to program in Groovy to create DSL scripts, sometimes it can feel that way to users. For missing functionality, Groovy constructs may be the only alternative. Verification such as syntax checking is done at the Groovy level. Also, errors are surfaced as Groovy errors (tracebacks) and not as DSL-specific ones.

Additional Assembly Required

Building on a point raised earlier, additional code can be required to get the familiar Jenkins constructs we had in the web forms version. For example, the simple task of sending email after a failed build has to be handled with something like a `try-catch-finally` construct, instead of the familiar built-in post-build functionality.

The following code highlights the contrast between sending emails after a failure in a Scripted Pipeline versus the way this was typically handled in traditional Jenkins, as shown in Figure 7-1.

```
node {
  try {
    sendEmailStarted()
    stage('Source') {...}
    stage('Build')  {...}
    ...
    sendEmailSuccess()
  } catch (err) {
    currentBuild.result = "FAILED"
    sendEmailFail()
    throw err
  }
}
```

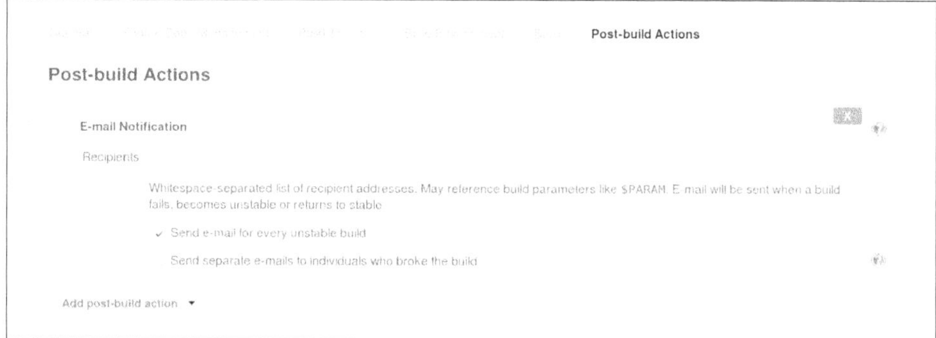

Figure 7-1. Post-build action in a Freestyle project in Jenkins

For these and other reasons, the CloudBees staff, as part of the Jenkins community, created an expanded DSL and simpler environment for programming pipelines. Note that Declarative Pipelines are still pipelines-as-code. We are still using the same environment to code our pipelines; we enter the Declarative Pipeline syntax in the Pipeline tab script window or in Jenkinsfiles, just as we would for any other pipeline code. However, as we've noted, the Declarative Pipeline syntax is more structured and the environment provides improved DSL-specific validation and error checking. We'll explore that structure next and discuss script checking and error reporting later in this chapter.

The Structure

A declarative is made up of an outer block that contains *directives* and *sections*. Each section in turn can contain other *sections, directives,* and *steps*, and in some cases *conditionals*. The distinction between blocks, sections, and directives is somewhat arbitrary, but since they're used in the formal documentation, we'll define those and the other terms more clearly.

Block

A block here is really just any set of code that has a beginning and end. In Groovy, this translates to a *closure* (a section of code where the beginning and end are bracketed with { and }).

While many parts of the pipeline are technically blocks, that term is used primarily to describe the overall `pipeline` block, which contains all of the code associated with a Declarative Pipeline.

It looks like this:

```
pipeline {
 // code in declarative syntax
}
```

Section

Sections in a Declarative Pipeline are a way to collect items that need to be executed at particular points during the overall flow of the pipeline. The grouped items may include directives, steps, and conditionals (defined in the following sections). As the pipeline is executed, it looks for sections to define the various groupings and phases.

Currently, there are three areas we refer to as sections:

`stages`
: This section wraps all of the individual stage definitions (directives) that define the main body and logic for the pipeline.

`steps`
: This section wraps a set of DSL steps within a stage definition. It serves to separate the collection of steps from other items within a stage, such as environment definitions.

`posts`
: This section wraps around steps and conditions to be done or checked at the end of a pipeline run or at the end of a stage.

An example layout with sections identified in bold font is shown here:

```
pipeline {
  agent any
  stages {
     stage('name1') {
       steps {
          ...
       }
       post {
         ...
       }
     }
     stage('name2') {
       steps {
          ...
       }
     }
  }
  post {
    ...
  }
}
```

Directives

A directive can be thought of as a statement or block of code that does any of the following in a pipeline:

Defines values
: An example of this is the `agent` directive, which allows us to specify a node or container to run an entire pipeline or a stage in. If we wanted to run our pipeline on a node named `worker`, we could use `agent ('worker')`.

Configures behavior
: An example of this is the `triggers` directive that lets us configure how often Jenkins checks for source updates or triggers our pipeline. If we wanted it to retrigger our pipeline at 7 a.m. every weekday, we could use `triggers { cron ('0 7 0 0 1-5') }`.

Specifies actions to be done
: An example of this is the `stage` directive, which is expected to have a `steps` section containing DSL steps to be executed.

Steps

The label `steps` itself is a section title with in a stage of the pipeline. However, within the `steps` section, we can have any valid DSL statement, such as `git`, `sh`, `echo`, etc. You can think of a step here as corresponding to one of these statements.

Conditionals

Conditionals supply a condition or criteria under which an action should occur. These are optional. There are two cases you may encounter/use:

- *When*: Strictly speaking, this is a directive. It resides within a `stage` definition and defines criteria for whether or not a stage should be executed. For example:

```
stage ('build') {
  when {
    branch 'foo'
  }
  <steps>
}
```

- *Conditions* blocks in the `post` section that define the criteria for doing post-processing. The criteria (conditions) here refer to the status of the build, such as `success` or `failure`.

Now that we have a basis for the terminology, let's look at the different building blocks in more detail.

The Building Blocks

In this section we'll cover specifics on each of the sections and directives available to you to use in a Declarative Pipeline, including syntax, parameters, and example usage.

At a high level, the blocks stack up as shown in Figure 7-2. Here, each box represents the specific section or directive indicated by its text, and their placement indicates where they can be in the Declarative Pipeline structure. For example, `pipeline` is the outermost block, and all of your other sections and directives must be inside of it.

Those with dotted lines around them are optional in that part of the structure. Those with solid lines are required in that part of the structure. Note that there are some directives that can occur at both the pipeline and stage level. They may be required in one area and optional in another.

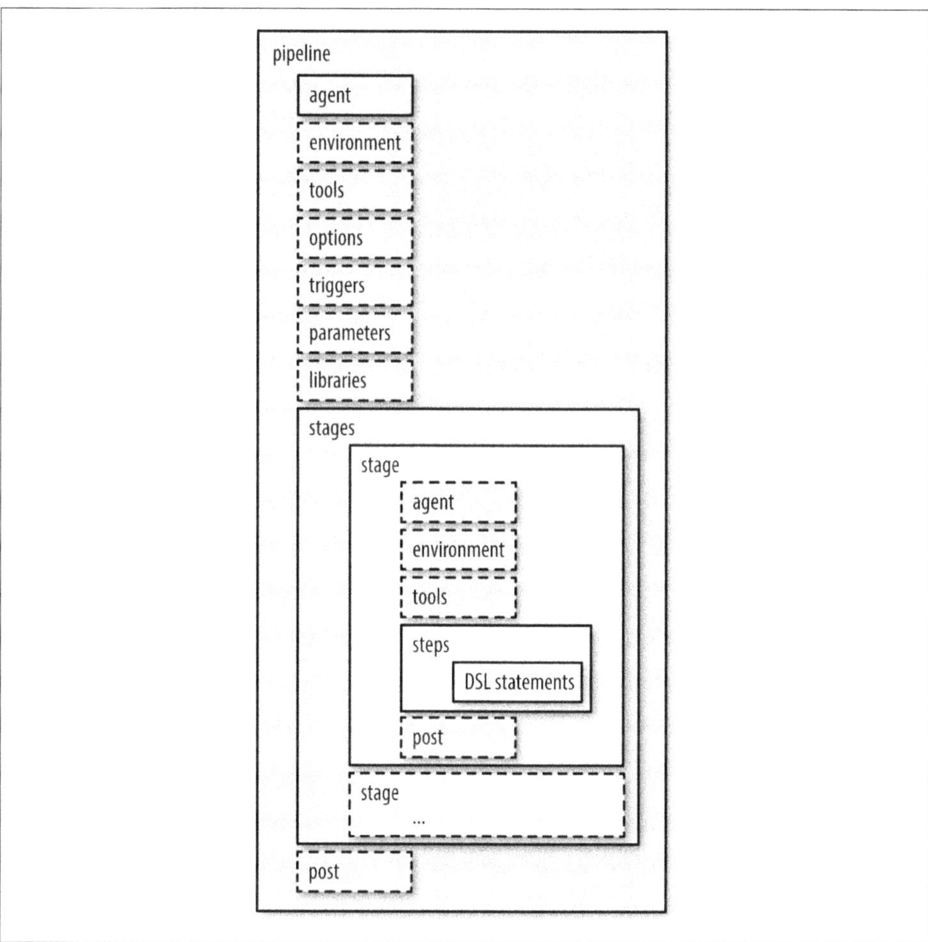

Figure 7-2. Overview of Declarative Pipeline structure

Obviously, there are directives here that we haven't talked about yet. So, let's dive in deeper to learn about each of the areas in the structure.

pipeline

The `pipeline` block is required in a Jenkins Declarative Pipeline. It is the outermost section and signals that this is a Pipeline project. The syntax is simply `pipeline {}` with the rest of the code within the closure:

```
pipeline {
   // pipeline code
}
```

agent

The `agent` directive specifies where the entire pipeline or a specific stage runs. This is similar to how the node directive is used in Scripted Pipelines. In fact, you can reasonably think of an agent as a node, except that the master node is not an agent.

An `agent` directive near the top of the `pipeline` block is required as a "default" place for execution. However, individual `agent` directives can optionally be specified at the beginning of individual stages to indicate where the code in those stages should be run.

Label Refresher

As a reminder, a label is an identifier attached to a node. You can have as many labels as you like, and the same label can be used across multiple nodes to identify a "class" of nodes. Configuring labels is done in the node setup under Manage Nodes. An example is shown in Figure 7-3.

Figure 7-3. Specifying labels for a node

What the `agent` directive actually does is indicate which (if any) nodes to use in the execution of the pipeline or stage. It does this by mapping the argument supplied to it to the label(s) specified for the nodes in your Jenkins system. The format of the argument can be a single predefined type, an indicator with a specific label, or a label block with additional characteristics, such as for Docker containers. The possible options are summarized in the following sections.

agent any
: This syntax tells Jenkins that the pipeline or stage can run on *any* agent that is defined, without regard to what label it has.

agent none
: When used at the top level, this indicates that we are not specifying an agent globally for the pipeline. The implication is that an agent will be specified, if needed, for individual stages.

agent { label "<label>"}
: This indicates that the pipeline or stage can run on any agent that has the label <label>.

More About Labels

Note that `<label>` here cannot be a regular expression or use wildcard characters. However, multiple nodes/agents can have the same label specified. In this way, `<label>` may match a label specified on multiple systems, thus allowing multiple options to choose from.

Labels and custom workspaces

A recent addition to the label syntax for agents allows us to specify a custom workspace for a pipeline or stage. Given an agent definition, we can include the `customWorkspace` directive to specify where the workspace that the agent uses should live. The syntax looks like this:

```
agent {
   label {
      label "<labelname>"
      customWorkspace "<desired directory>"
   }
}
```

node and label

It's worth mentioning that you can use `node` in place of the `label` closure here. This is to help disambiguate the way `label` is used for the Docker agent, as described in the next section. The alternative syntax is:

```
agent {
   node {
      label "<labelname>"
       ...
```

Agents and Docker

The final agent options we'll look at are Docker containers. There are two shorthand ways to get a Docker image—specifying an existing image or creating an image from a Dockerfile—in the `agent` declaration. Alternatively, the longer version of the declaration can be used to specify additional elements, such as a node to use for the container, and arguments for the container.

First, we'll look at the formats for using an existing Docker image:

`agent { docker '<image>' }`
: This short syntax tells Jenkins to pull the given image from Docker Hub and run the pipeline or stage in a container based on the image, on a dynamically provisioned node.

`agent { docker { <elements> } }`
: This long syntax allows for defining more specifics about the Docker agent. There are three additional elements that you can add in the declaration (within the { } block):

  `image '<image>'`
  : Like the short form, this tells Jenkins to pull the given image and use it to run the pipeline code.

  `label '<label>'`
  : If this element is present in the declaration, it tells Jenkins to instantiate the container and "host" it on a node matching `<label>`.

  `args '<string>'.`
  : If this element is present in the declaration, it tells Jenkins to pass these arguments to the Docker container; the syntax here should be the same as you would normally pass to a Docker container.

Here's an example declaration using the long form:

```
agent {
   docker {
      image "image-name"
      label "worker-node"
      args "-v /dir:dir"
   }
}
```

The syntax for using a Dockerfile as the basis for the container is similar. Again, there are short and long forms:

`agent { dockerfile true }`
: This short syntax is intended to be used when you have a source code repository, that you retrieve, that has a Dockerfile in its root (note that `dockerfile` here is a literal). In that case, this will tell Jenkins to build a Docker image using that Dockerfile, instantiate a container, and then run the pipeline (or the stage's code if run in a stage) in that container.

`agent { dockerfile { <elements> } }`
: This long syntax allows for defining more specifics about the Docker agent you are trying to create from a Dockerfile. There are three additional elements that you can add in the declaration (within the { } block):

  `filename '<path to dockerfile>'`
  : This allows for specifying an alternate path to a Dockerfile, including a different name. Jenkins will try to build an image from the Dockerfile, instantiate a container, and use it to run the pipeline code.

`label '<label>'`
: If this element is present in the declaration, it tells Jenkins to instantiate the container and "host" it on a node matching `<label>`.

`args '<string>'`
: If this element is present in the agent Dockerfile declaration, it tells Jenkins to pass these arguments to the Docker container; the syntax here should be the same as you would normally pass to a Docker container.

An example of specifying a Docker agent via a Dockerfile using the long form is shown here:

```
agent {
   dockerfile {
      filename "<subdir/dockerfile name>"
      label "<agent label>"
      args "-v /dir:dir"
   }
}
```

Using the same node for Docker and non-Docker stages. There is one other aspect associated with using Docker agents. Suppose you define a particular non-Docker agent at the top of your pipeline:

```
pipeline {
    agent {label 'linux'}
```

Later, in a particular stage, you want to run the code in a Docker container—but you also want to use the same node and workspace that you defined for the pipeline. To enable this, the pipeline has a directive you can use with the Docker specification: `reuseNode`. It would look something like the following in practice:

```
stage 'abc' {
   agent {
      docker {
         image 'ubuntu:16.6'
         reuseNode true
```

This tells Jenkins to reuse the same node and workspace that were defined for the original pipeline agent to "host" the resulting Docker container.

Next, we'll look at how to configure environment values for a pipeline.

environment

This is an optional directive for your Declarative Pipeline. As the name implies, this directive allows you to specify names and values for environment variables that are then accessible within the scope of your pipeline. Like `agent`, you can have an instance of `environment` in the main pipeline definition and/or in individual stages.

An environment definition in the top-level pipeline block will make the variable accessible to all steps in the pipeline. An environment definition within a stage will make the variable accessible to only the scope of the stage.

Here is an example of defining an environment variable in this way:

```
environment {
              TIMEZONE = "eastern"
}
```

Environment variable definitions can also incorporate variables that are already defined. The syntax for this is just to include the existing variable in the definition string in `${<variable>}`:

```
environment {
              TIMEZONE = "eastern"
              TIMEZONE_DS = "${TIMEZONE}_daylight_savings"
}
```

Credentials and environment variables

We talked in Chapter 5 about the different kinds of credentials that can be used with pipelines. Each of those methods required the identifier of a set of credentials that had been defined in Jenkins. In the `environment` block, you can assign a global variable to a particular credentials ID. Then you can use that variable throughout your pipeline in place of the ID. This can simplify things if you need to specify the ID in multiple places. The syntax is to assign the variable name to the string `credentials('<credentials-id>')`. For example:

```
environment {
              ADMIN_USER = credentials('admin-user')
}
```

In this case, we would have `admin-user` previously defined as the specified ID for some set of credentials. If you hadn't explicitly specified a named string (`admin-user`) as the ID, you would use the identifying string that Jenkins automatically generates during the creation of the credentials.

While we can define environment variables for anything we want, Jenkins provides a specific directive to access globally defined tools: the `tools` directive.

tools

Jenkins users are familiar with using the Global Tool Configuration screen to configure versions, paths, and installers for tools. Once configured there, the `tools` directive allows us to specify which of these we want to have autoinstalled and made available in the path on the agent we've chosen.

tools Without an Agent

If an agent is not specified, such as when only `agent none` is used at the top of the pipeline, the `tools` directive does not have any effect. This is because there is no node/agent to make the tool available on.

For example, suppose we had the configuration shown in Figure 7-4.

Figure 7-4. Global configuration for a Gradle version

Then, in our `tools` block, we could refer to Gradle via:

```
tools {
   gradle "gradle3.2"
}
```

The lefthand part of this declaration is a specific string defined in the pipeline model. As of this writing, the valid tool types you can specify in declarative syntax are:

- `ant`
- `git`
- `gradle`
- `jdk`
- `jgit`
- `jgitapache` (JGit with Apache HTTP client)
- `maven`

Attempts to use other types that are not yet valid will result in an "Invalid tool type" error when running your pipeline.

Extended Tool Types for Scripted Pipelines

The `tool` DSL step (not the declarative section) can take an additional parameter of `type`. Some of the supported types correspond to the types you can specify in the declarative `tools` section, but some are only specifiable as class names currently and don't fit in the `tools` section.

Jenkins currently lists the full range of supported types as:

- `ant, hudson.tasks.Ant$AntInstallation`
- `org.jenkinsci.plugins.docker.commons.tools.DockerTool`
- `git`
- `hudson.plugins.git.GitTool`
- `gradle`
- `hudson.plugins.gradle.GradleInstallation`
- `hudson.plugins.groovy.GroovyInstallation`
- `jdk`
- `hudson.model.JDK`
- `jgit`
- `org.jenkinsci.plugins.gitclient.JGitTool`
- `jgitapache`
- `org.jenkinsci.plugins.gitclient.JGitApacheTool`
- `maven`
- `hudson.tasks.Maven$MavenInstallation`
- `hudson.plugins.mercurial.MercurialInstallation`
- `hudson.plugins.sonar.SonarRunnerInstallation`
- `hudson.plugins.sonar.MsBuildSQRunnerInstallation`

If you use the Snippet Generator, you'll see the more user-friendly versions of the names listed in the drop-down for the Tool Type parameter. Then, if needed, the class name is inserted when you select the type. For example, if you select SonarQube Scanner for the Tool Type and you have a scanner named `sq-scanner` configured in the global configuration, the generated step is:

```
tool name: 'sq-scanner',
   type: 'hudson.plugins.sonar.SonarRunnerInstallation'
```

In most cases, you don't need to specify the type when using the `tool` step. The current exception would be if you had two different types of tools configured with the same name in the global configuration. Then the `type` value could be used as a differentiator.

The righthand part should map to the Name field in the Global Tool Configuration.

Once this is set up, the tool is autoinstalled and put on the path. We can then simply use the string `gradle` in place of the `GRADLE_HOME` path in our pipeline steps and Jenkins will map it back to this Gradle installation on our system. For example:

```
steps {
   sh 'gradle clean compile'
}
```

Also, it's worth noting that the `tools` directive can use the value of a parameter if you need to input a particular version to use. Here's an example:

```
pipeline {
    agent any
    parameters {
       string(name: 'gradleTool', defaultValue: 'gradle3',
              description: 'Gradle Version')
    }
    tools {
       gradle  "${params.gradleTool}"
    }
```

Just keep in mind that there is currently a limitation with the declarative syntax such that Jenkins doesn't recognize that a build requires a parameter the first time the pipeline is run.

`tools` is another directive that can be used either in the `pipeline` block or separately in a stage.

Docker and the tools Directive

The `tools` directive does not work on Docker or Dockerfile agents. The recommended practice is to use an image with the tools already installed.

In addition to the `tools` directive to allow us to access the globally defined tools, we also have the `options` directive to allow us to set project-level options.

options

This directive can be used to specify properties and values for predefined options that should apply across the pipeline. These would be the type of things that we would set on the General tab of a project in the Jenkins web forms (other than parameters, which have their own section). You can think of it as a place to set Jenkins-defined job options.

A simple example is the option to discard builds. Assume we had the setup in Figure 7-5 in our Jenkins job.

Figure 7-5. Example job build discarder configuration

We could use the following code to achieve the same behavior in our Declarative Pipeline:

```
options {
   buildDiscarder(logRotator(numToKeepStr:'3'))
}
```

As well, there can be specific options for the declarative structure. Here's an example of one:

```
options {
               skipDefaultCheckout()
}
```

> ### About skipDefaultCheckout()
>
> Since we use this option as an example, it's worth saying a word about what it does. If you specify an agent in a Declarative Pipeline, Jenkins allocates a node for it, and then, if in a Jenkinsfile, it does a global `checkout scm`. The `checkout scm` syntax is a shorthand way to pull down a set of source code. It can work with this shorthand notation because the Jenkinsfile should be stored with the source and so it can use the location and branch from the repository.
>
> However, there might be instances where you don't want this global source checkout to happen. In such cases, you can use this option to prevent that. Note that if you do use this option, you are responsible for doing the `checkout scm` later in your script if needed.

Options summary

The following list below enumerates the available options and, briefly, their meaning and usage:

`buildDiscarder`
: Keep the console output and artifacts for the specified number of executions of the pipeline.

logRotator

If you're wondering what the `logRotator` element does here, it doesn't imply any particular functionality. It's there mainly for historical reasons.

```
options { buildDiscarder(logRotator(numToKeepStr: '10')) }
```

`disableConcurrentBuilds`
: Prevent Jenkins from starting concurrent executions of the same pipeline. The use case could be for preventing simultaneous access to shared resources or preventing a faster concurrent execution from overtaking a slower one. (This option is also discussed in Chapter 3.)

```
options { disableConcurrentBuilds() }
```

`retry`
: If the pipeline execution fails, retry the entire pipeline the specified number of times.

```
options { retry(2) }
```

`skipDefaultCheckout`
: As just explained in the ""About skipDefaultCheckout()" on page 232" sidebar, this removes an implied `checkout scm` statement, thus skipping the automatic source code checkout from a pipeline defined in a `Jenkinsfile`.

`skipStagesAfterUnstable`
: If a stage of the pipeline renders the pipeline unstable, don't process the remaining stages.

```
options { skipStagesAfterUnstable()}
```

`timeout`
: Sets a timeout value for an execution of the pipeline. If this timeout value is passed, Jenkins will abort the pipeline.

```
options { timeout(time: 15, unit: 'MINUTES') }
```

Scripted Versus Declarative Example

The `timeout` option here highlights another useful difference of declarative syntax versus scripted syntax. In a Scripted Pipeline (where we don't have a global options area), to get this same functionality we would have to wrap all of our code in a `timeout` block:

```
timeout(time: 2, unit: 'MINUTES') {
  // pipeline processing
}
```

`timestamps`
: Add timestamps to the console output. This option requires the *Timestamper* plugin. Note that this option applies globally to the whole pipeline execution.

```
options { timestamps() }
```

triggers

This directive allows you to specify what kinds of triggers should initiate builds in your pipeline. Note that these do not apply to Multibranch Pipeline or GitHub organization or Bitbucket team/project jobs that are marked by Jenkinsfiles and triggered otherwise—such as by a webhook that notifies Jenkins when a change is made.

There are four different (SCM-neutral) triggers currently available: `cron`, `pollSCM`, `upstream`, and `githubPush`.

`cron`
: Refers to executing the pipeline at a specified regular interval, and `pollSCM` is for checking for source code updates (polling the source control management system) at a specified regular interval. If a source change is detected, the pipeline will be executed.

`upstream`
: Takes a comma-separated string of Jenkins jobs and a condition to check. When a job in the string finishes and the result matches the treshold, the current pipeline will be retriggered. For example:

```
triggers {
    upstream(upstreamProjects: 'jobA,jobB', threshold:
        hudson.model.Result.SUCCESS)
}
```

`githubPush`
: Refers to the same kind of behavior as the "GitHub hook trigger for GitSCM polling" setting in the Build Triggers section of a project in the Jenkins application. That is, if a webhook is set up on the GitHub side for events related to the GitHub

repository, then when the payload is sent to Jenkins, it will trigger SCM polling for that repo from the Jenkins job to pick up any changes. The syntax should be simply:

```
triggers { githubPush() }
```

Bitbucket Project Triggers

According to some sources, there should also be a `bitbucketPush` trigger type available that should behave like the `githubPush` trigger. However, this doesn't seem to show up as a valid option with the versions of the plugins at the time of this writing. If you need this functionality, check the plugin pages and try adding it to your pipeline to see if it is available.

Both `pollSCM` and `cron` can use the cron syntax, a summary of which was given in an earlier chapter and which is repeated here for convenience.

Cron syntax

The cron syntax used in Jenkins is a specification of when and/or how often to do something based on five fields, separated by spaces. Each of the fields represents a different unit of time. The five fields are:

MINUTES
: The desired minutes value within the hour (`0-59`).

HOURS
: The desired hours value within the day (`0-23`).

DAYMONTH
: The desired day of the month (`1-31`).

MONTH
: The desired month of the year (`1-12`).

DAYWEEK
: The desired day of the week (`0-7`). Here, `0` and `7` both represent Sunday.

Also, the `*/<value>` syntax can be used in a field to mean "every `<value>`" (as in `*/5` meaning "every 5 minutes").

Additionally, the symbol `H` can be used in any of the fields. This symbol has a special meaning to Jenkins. It tells Jenkins to, within a range, use the hash of the project name to come up with a unique offset value. This value is then added to the lowest value of the range to define when the activity actually starts, within the range of values.

The idea here is not to have all projects that have the same cron values specified, starting at the same time. The offset from the hash serves to "stagger" the execution of projects that have the same cron timing.

Use of the `H` symbol is encouraged to avoid having projects start executing at the same time. Note that since the value is a hash of the project name, each value will be different from all others, but will remain the same for that project over time.

The `H` symbol can also have a range attached to it to specify limits on the interval it can pick. The syntax is `H(<start range>, <end range>)`.

To solidify this a bit more, let's look at some examples:

```
// Start a pipeline execution at 10 minutes past the hour
triggers { cron(10 * * * *) }

// Scan for SCM changes at 10-minute intervals
triggers { pollSCM(*/10 * * * *) }

// Start a pipeline session at some point between 0 and 30 minutes after
// the hour
triggers { cron(H(0,30) * * * *) }

// Start a pipeline execution at 8 a.m. Monday through Friday
triggers { cron(0 8 * * * 1-5) }
```

Next, we'll take a look at how we can supply input to a Declarative Pipeline via the `parameters` directive.

parameters

This directive allows us to specify project parameters for a Declarative Pipeline. The input values for these parameters can come from a user or an API call. You can think of these parameters as being the same sort that you would specify in the web form with the "This build is parameterized" option.

You can get an idea of the syntax for these from the Snippet Generator by selecting the `input` step and then selecting the parameters and values you want to use.

The valid parameter types, with a description and example of each, are listed here (these are the same kinds of parameters we discussed in conjunction with the `input` step in Chapter 3):

`booleanParam`
: This is the basic `true/false` parameter. The subparameters for a `booleanParam` are name, `defaultValue`, and `description`.

```
parameters { booleanParam(defaultValue: false,
 description: 'test run?', name: 'testRun')}
```

`choice`
: This parameter allows selection from a list of choices. The subparameters for a `choice` are `name`, `choices`, and `description`. Here, `choices` refers to a list of choices you enter, separated by newlines, to present to the user. The first one in the list will be the default.

```
parameters{ choice(choices: 'Windows-1\nLinux-2', description:
 'Which platform?', name: 'platform')}
```

`file`
: This parameter allows for choosing a file to use with the pipeline. The subparameters include `fileLocation` and `description`.

The selected file location specifies where to put the file that is selected and uploaded. The location will be relative to the workspace.

```
parameters{ file(fileLocation: '', description: 'Select the file to
 upload')}
```

`text`
: This parameter allows the user to input multiple lines of text. The subparameters include `name`, `defaultValue`, and `description`.

```
parameters{ text(defaultValue: 'No message', description:
 'Enter your message', name: 'userMsg')
```

`password`
: This parameter allows the user to enter a password. For passwords, the text entered is hidden. The available subparameters are `name`, `defaultValue`, and `description`.

```
parameters{ password(defaultValue: "userpass1", description:
'User password?', name: 'userPW')}
```

`run`
: This parameter allows the user to select a particular run from a job. This might be used, for example, in a testing environment. The subparameters available include `name`, `project`, `description`, and `filter`.

The `project` subparameter is the job that you want to allow the user to select a run from. The default run will be the last one. You also have access to certain environment variables in the script from whichever project you select. These include:

- `PARAMETER_NAME=<jenkins_url>/job/<job_name>/<run_number>/`
- `PARAMETER_NAME_JOBNAME=<job_name>`

- `PARAMETER_NAME_NUMBER=<run_number>`
- `PARAMETER_NAME_NAME=<display_name>`
- `PARAMETER_NAME_RESULT=<run_result>`

The `filter` subparameter allows you to filter the type of runs to offer based on the overall build status. Choices include:

- `All Builds`—including "in-progress" ones
- `Completed Builds`
- `Successful Builds`—this includes stable and unstable ones
- `Stable Builds Only`

```
parameters{ run(name: "Last success", description:
 'Last successful project', project: 'project1',
 filter: 'Successful Builds')}
```

`string`

This parameter allows for entering a string. (This is not hidden like a `password` parameter is.) The subparameters include `description`, `defaultValue`, and `name`.

```
parameters{ string(defaultValue: "Linux",
 description: 'What platform?', name: 'platform')}
```

Using parameters in a pipeline

Once you define a parameter in the `parameters` block, you can reference it in your pipeline via the `params` namespace, as in `params.<parameter_name>`. Here's a simple example using a `string` parameter in a Declarative Pipeline:

```
pipeline {
   agent any
   parameters{
      string(defaultValue: "maintainer",
             description: 'Enter user role:', name: 'userRole')
   }
   stages {
      stage('listVals') {
          steps {
            echo "User's role = ${params.userRole}"
          }
      }
   }
 }
```

Issues with Parameters on First Execution

As of this writing, the first time that you run a pipeline script, you won't be prompted for the parameter values. From the second time on, you will.

This is due to a type of catch-22. The parameters are defined in the pipeline script, so they are not known by Jenkins until the script is run. But it's when the script is first run that you would expect to have the parameters available. As of this writing, there isn't a workaround, although it is being considered by the Jenkins project.

As a suggested best practice, use the `params.<parameter_name>` syntax. Then you can at least get the default values (assuming they are set) for the parameters on the first run.

libraries

One of the newer directives introduced in Jenkins for Declarative Pipelines is the `libraries` directive. This directive allows Declarative Pipelines to import *shared libraries* so that code contained in them can then be called and used. As discussed in Chapter 6, a shared library is just a collection of code built to work with Jenkins pipelines, and stored and accessed from a source control system outside of your pipeline.

In addition to providing a way to share and include common code, shared libraries can also be valuable for Declarative Pipeline use by encapsulating code that is not declarative, and couldn't normally be directly used in a pipeline. (This is discussed more near the end of the chapter.)

The syntax here is pretty straightforward, as shown in the following example. Note that the `@` sign here provides a way of specifying (after it) which version of a shared library we want. In the first `lib` statement here, we are asking for the latest version from the master branch for this library:

```
pipeline {
     agent any
     libraries {
        lib("mylib@master")
        lib("alib")
    }
    stages {
       ...
```

Shared libraries are covered in much more detail in Chapter 6.

Now that we've covered the directives available for us to use in Declarative Pipelines, it's time to look at how to structure the code that will use those directives and DSL statements to do our pipeline actions. We start with the `stages` section.

stages

Whether in a Scripted Pipeline or a Declarative Pipeline, Jenkins wants our code steps to be contained in one or more stages. In a Declarative Pipeline, the collection of individual stages is wrapped by the `stages` section. This makes our Declarative Pipeline more structured and tells Jenkins where the stages begin and end, as opposed to the pipeline-level directives that we've been looking at. `stages` is a required section, and you must have at least one stage within it. A section of a pipeline demonstrating this syntax is shown here:

```
pipeline {
  agent any
  stages {
     stage('name1') {
       steps {
          ...
       }
```

stage

Within the `stages` section are the individual stages. Each stage has at least a name and one or more DSL steps. Within a stage, you may also have local `environment`, `tools`, and `agent` directives. If there are also corresponding global directives that define values with the same names, then the value defined in the directive in the stage will override the global one.

An example of this situation could be having the same environment variable defined in both an `environment` directive at the pipeline level and an `environment` directive in a stage.

If additional values (with different names) are defined in a directive at the `pipeline` level and the same directive in a stage, the additional settings in the stage are just added to the set already defined globally for the pipeline.

Other than the `stage` closure itself, the only required element in a stage (for a Declarative Pipeline) is the `steps` section.

steps

The `steps` block is required and indicates the actual work that will happen in the stage. It has the form:

```
steps {
    <individual steps - i.e., DSL statements>
}
```

The individual steps can be any valid DSL statements, such as `echo`, `archiveArtifacts`, `git`, `mail`, etc. The syntax at this level is the same for Scripted or Declarative

Pipelines in terms of using DSL statements. You cannot, however, use Groovy non-DSL statements or constructs, such as `if-then` or assignments.

Snippet Generator

Remember that if you need more information about the syntax for a particular DSL statement, you can look that up in the Jenkins *Snippet Generator*, available through the Pipeline Syntax links in Jenkins.

Execution of the `steps` section can also be done conditionally in a pipeline, based on a set of conditions defined at the start of the stage. Let's take a look at how that works.

Conditional execution of a stage. In any stage, you can have conditional execution. That is, you can have Jenkins decide whether or not to execute the steps in the stage based on one or more conditions evaluating to `true`. This is an optional construct that is not available at the top level of the script.

There are several different conditions that you can work with. The choices are:

`branch "<name>"`
: Only proceed if the branch name is `<name>` or matches the (Ant-style) pattern.

```
stage('debug_build') {
   when {
      branch 'test'
   }
   ...
}
```

`environment name: <name>, value: <value>`
: Only proceed if the specified environment variable `<name>` has the specified environment variable `<value>`.

```
stage('debug_build') {
   when {
      environment name: "BUILD_CONFIG", value: "DEBUG"
   }
   ...
}
```

expression <valid Groovy expression>
: Only proceed if the specified Groovy expression evaluates to `true` (meaning not `false` and not `null`).

```
stage('debug_build') {
   when {
      expression {
```

```
            echo "Checking for debug build parameter..."
            expression { return params.DEBUG_BUILD }
        }
        ...
    }
```

Conditional execution with and, or, not. In addition to using these conditions one at a time only when they are `true`, we can also use logical operators to check multiple conditions, or the inverse of one. The Declarative Pipeline syntax provides keywords that allow us to use the equivalent of "and," "or," and "not" logical operations with the three types of conditions we just discussed. The keywords for the three logical operators are:

`allOf`
: When used in a `when` statement for conditional stage execution, the `allOf` keyword functions like an "and." In order for the stage to proceed with its processing, "all of" the conditions included must be `true`.

```
when {
   allOf {
      environment name: "BUILD_CONFIG", value: "DEBUG"
      branch 'test'
   }
}
```

`anyOf`
: When used in a `when` statement for conditional stage execution, the `anyOf` keyword functions like an "or." In order for the stage to proceed with its processing, "any of" the conditions included must be `true`.

```
when {
   anyOf {
      environment name: "BUILD_CONFIG", value: "DEBUG"
      branch 'test'
   }
}
```

`not`
: When used in a `when` statement for conditional stage execution, the `not` keyword functions just as the name implies. In order for the stage to proceed with its processing, the specified conditions must not be `true`.

```
when {
   not {
      branch 'prod'
   }
}
```

There is one additional part of a stage that can also execute based on conditionals: `post`, for processing at the end of a stage. This is a powerful way to emulate the traditional post-build processing type of behavior within a stage.

post Subsection

Stages can also have a subsection called `post` defined in them. For more information, see the following section. We share the detail there since this is most commonly used at the pipeline level.

post

`post` is another section available for use in the pipeline or in a stage. It is optional in both places. If present, it gets executed at the end of a pipeline or stage if the conditions are met. You can think of it like post-build actions for a traditional Jenkins Freestyle job or set of jobs.

The conditions in the `post` block are based on the build status. The syntax is as follows:

```
post {
   <condition name> {
      <valid DSL statements>
   }
   <condition name> {
      <valid DSL statements
   }
...
```

The available conditions are:

`always`
: Always execute the steps in the block.

`changed`
: If the current build's status is different from the previous build's status, then execute the steps in the block.

`success`
: If the current build was successful, then execute the steps in the block.

`failure`
: If the current build failed, then execute the steps in the block.

`unstable`
: If the current build's status was unstable, then execute the steps in the block.

The Weird Status

There is also an "aborted" build status, but that one is described as "weird" (by a certain CloudBees employee) and not recommended to be used.

Here's an example of using these notifications in a stage:

```
stage('Build') {
   steps {
      gradle 'clean build'
      ...
   }
   post {
        always {
          echo "Build stage complete"
        }
       failure{
          echo "Build failed"
          mail body: <some text>, subject: 'Build failed!',
to: 'devops@mycompany.com'
        }
        success {
          echo "Build succeeded"
          archiveArtifacts '**/*'
        }
      }
 }
```

Dealing with Nondeclarative Code

The Declarative Pipeline syntax is great for simplifying the way we define pipelines. However, if you need to do something that can't be expressed declaratively, it can be challenging to figure out how to accomplish that within the declarative structure.

Let's take, for example, cases where you may need to do a simple assignment operation, or multiple ones. Here are some sample assignments needed to use Artifactory with Gradle in Scripted Pipeline code:

```
def server = Artifactory.server 'my-server-id'
def rtGradle = Artifactory.newGradleBuild()
rtGradle.tool = 'gradle tool name'
```

Attempting to put these in a `steps` section in a stage and run them yields a failed build with error messages like these:

```
org.codehaus.groovy.control.MultipleCompilationErrorsException:
startup failed:
WorkflowScript: 15: Expected a step @ line 15, column 16.
                  def server = Artifactory.server 'my-server-id'
                  ^
```

```
WorkflowScript: 17: Expected a step @ line 17, column 1.
   def rtGradle = Artifactory.newGradleBuild()
   ^
WorkflowScript: 19: Expected a step @ line 19, column 1.
   rtGradle.tool = 'gradle3'
   ^
3 errors
```

The problem here is that these assignment statements are trying to directly modify values via the DSL and are not declarative. While these statements are legal to use in Scripted Pipelines, they are not in Declarative Pipelines.

So how do we handle such cases? There are a couple of options, each with their advantages and disadvantages, as we discuss next.

Check Your Plugins

If you are trying to port scripted code that works with a plugin, check to see if there is an updated version of the plugin that supports the declarative syntax. There may not be currently, but it may be in the works, so it's worth checking periodically for updates.

Create a Shared Library

Earlier in this chapter, we discussed the `libraries` directive for importing shared libraries into Declarative Pipelines. Rather than having to try to embed the code directly in the pipeline, you can put it in a shared library, then load the shared library and call the function declaratively through that. This requires some knowledge of how to create a shared library—and how to create it such that its methods will be callable with declarative syntax—but this is the preferred way to make this work. Chapter 6 discusses shared libraries and using them to extend your pipeline in detail.

Place Code Outside of the Pipeline Block

Another alternative is to put your code outside of the entire `pipeline` block. For example, you could place it above the `pipeline {` statement. Any code that works in a Scripted Pipeline can be placed in the same file/script area as a Declarative Pipeline, as long as it is not within the pipeline block.

Problems with Putting Code Outside the Pipeline Block

While this is a valid alternative currently, it is not ideal. This can make the pipeline code difficult to read and manage since you're mixing the two styles, and it may also confuse the parser in certain cases. Worse, if you ever want to use the Blue Ocean pipeline editor (discussed in Chapter 10) with this code, it will get rid of the code outside of the `pipeline` block. The editor only understands things within the `pipeline` block.

The script Statement

The `script` DSL statement is a special statement intended just for use in Declarative Pipelines; it allows you to define a block/closure that can house any nondeclarative code. As you may have guessed, the name is a reference to "Scripted" Pipelines.

The statement is put inside your Declarative Pipeline wherever you have to have non-declarative code. This method is likely the best way to handle this sort of situation, if you must use nondeclarative code and don't want to create a shared library.

Turning back to our example assignment statements, wrapping them in a `script` statement would look like this:

```
stage('stage1') {
  <declarative code>
  script {
    def server = Artifactory.server 'my-server-id'
    def rtGradle = Artifactory.newGradleBuild()
    rtGradle.tool = 'gradle tool name'
  }
  <declarative code>
```

This will execute fine (assuming we have the requisite Artifactory integration set up).

Using parallel in a Stage

We covered the parallel syntax for declarative syntax in Chapter 3. With regard to using `parallel` in Declarative Pipelines, you can use it in a stage if it's the only step in that stage. Note that the `parallel` definition itself can be of the traditional style (using a mapping to define the different parallel "branches") or a newer style (as of Declarative Pipelines 1.2) that allows for the branches to be defined by stages. Code snippets of both are shown here (refer to Chapter 3 for more details and complete examples):

```
stage ('Unit Test') {
   steps  {
      parallel(
         set1 : {
```

```
            ...

    stage('Unit Test') {
            parallel{
                stage ('set1') {
                   agent { label 'worker_node2' }
                   steps {
```

Script Checking and Error Reporting

As mentioned at the beginning of the chapter, one of the other nice features of Declarative Pipelines is that the formal structure allows for better script checking and more precise error reporting. That is, the checking and reporting are expressed in terms of the DSL and not just Groovy code with stacktraces.

The verification is done at the start, in the editor, and errors are clearly identified, including line numbers. Argument types are also validated, and the environment is checked to make sure the necessary tools are available. If a required tool or tool version isn't installed, the script will stop with an error.

The following code shows a Scripted Pipeline listing with a syntax error (`stae` instead of `stage`). Figure 7-6 shows the resulting Groovy stacktrace that serves as error identification.

```
@Library('Utilities') import static org.foo.Utilities.*
node ('worker_node1') {
     stae('Source') { // for display purposes
       // Get some code from our Git repository
       git 'git@diyvb:repos/gradle-greetings.git'
    }
    stage('Build') {
...
```

```
First time build. Skipping changelog.
[Pipeline] node
Running on worker_node1 in /home/jenkins/worker_node1/workspace/simple
[Pipeline] {
[Pipeline] }
[Pipeline] // node
[Pipeline] End of Pipeline
java.lang.NoSuchMethodError: No such DSL method 'stae' found among ste
artifactoryUpload, bat, build, catchError, checkout, collectEnv, delet
fileExists, findFiles, getArtifactoryServer, git, input, isUnix, libra
properties, publishBuildInfo, pwd, readFile, readManifest, readMavenPo
unarchive, unstash, unzip, waitUntil, withDockerContainer, withDockerR
architecture, archiveArtifacts, artifactManager, batchFile, booleanPar
choiceParam, clock, cloud, command, commentAdded, commentAddedContains
draftPublished, dumb, envVars, file, fileParam, filePath, fingerprint,
jnlp, jobName, lastDuration, lastFailure, lastGrantedAuthorities, last
maven3Mojos, mavenErrors, mavenMojos, mavenWarnings, myView, nodePrope
pipelineTriggers, plainText, plugin, pollSCM, projectNamingStrategy, p
slave, stackTrace, standard, status, string, stringParam, swapSpace, t
currentBuild, docker, env, mailStatus, mailUser, manager, params, pipe
        at org.jenkinsci.plugins.workflow.cps.DSL.invokeMethod(DSL.jav
        at org.jenkinsci.plugins.workflow.cps.CpsScript.invokeMethod(C
        at groovy.lang.MetaClassImpl.invokeMethodOnGroovyObject(MetaCl
        at groovy.lang.MetaClassImpl.invokeMethod(MetaClassImpl.java:1
        at groovy.lang.MetaClassImpl.invokeMethod(MetaClassImpl.java:1
        at org.codehaus.groovy.runtime.callsite.PogoMetaClassSite.call
        at org.codehaus.groovy.runtime.callsite.CallSiteArray.defaultC
        at org.codehaus.groovy.runtime.callsite.AbstractCallSite.call(
        at com.cloudbees.groovy.cps.sandbox.DefaultInvoker.methodCall(
        at WorkflowScript.run(WorkflowScript:3)
        at ___cps.transform___(Native Method)
        at com.cloudbees.groovy.cps.impl.ContinuationGroup.methodCall(
        at com.cloudbees.groovy.cps.impl.FunctionCallBlock$Continuatio
        at com.cloudbees.groovy.cps.impl.FunctionCallBlock$Continuatio
        at sun.reflect.GeneratedMethodAccessor721.invoke(Unknown Sourc
```

Figure 7-6. Error reporting for Scripted Pipeline syntax error

The following code shows a corresponding Declarative Pipeline listing. Figure 7-7 shows the clearer error checking that surfaces from using it.

```
pipeline {
   // ensure we have the needed tools

   // run on worker node 1
   agent label:''

   stages {

      stae('Source') {
         git branch: 'test', url: 'git@diyvb:repos/gradle-greetings.git'
         stash name: 'test-sources', includes: 'build.gradle,src/test/'
      }
      stage('Build')
      ...
```

```
Checking out Revision bdcb5a023d11c812c6b6f533e48632edfa316bee (origin/master)
 > git config core.sparsecheckout # timeout=10
 > git checkout -f bdcb5a023d11c812c6b6f533e48632edfa316bee
 > git rev-list bdcb5a023d11c812c6b6f533e48632edfa316bee # timeout=10
org.codehaus.groovy.control.MultipleCompilationErrorsException: startup failed:
WorkflowScript: 9: Expected a stage @ line 9, column 7.
         stae('Source') {
         ^

WorkflowScript: 9: Stage does not have a name @ line 9, column 7.
         stae('Source') {
         ^

WorkflowScript: 9: Nothing to execute within stage 'null' @ line 9, column 7.
         stae('Source') {
         ^

3 errors

        at org.codehaus.groovy.control.ErrorCollector.failIfErrors(ErrorCollectc
        at org.codehaus.groovy.control.CompilationUnit.applyToPrimaryClassNodes(
        at org.codehaus.groovy.control.CompilationUnit.doPhaseOperation(Compilat
        at org.codehaus.groovy.control.CompilationUnit.processPhaseOperations(Cc
        at org.codehaus.groovy.control.CompilationUnit.compile(CompilationUnit.j
        at groovy.lang.GroovyClassLoader.doParseClass(GroovyClassLoader.java:29ε
        at groovy.lang.GroovyClassLoader.parseClass(GroovyClassLoader.java:268)
        at groovy.lang.GroovyShell.parseClass(GroovyShell.java:688)
        at groovy.lang.GroovyShell.parse(GroovyShell.java:700)
        at org.jenkinsci.plugins.workflow.cps.CpsGroovyShell.reparse(CpsGroovySh
        at org.jenkinsci.plugins.workflow.cps.CpsFlowExecution.parseScript(CpsFl
        at org.jenkinsci.plugins.workflow.cps.CpsFlowExecution.start(CpsFlowExec
        at org.jenkinsci.plugins.workflow.job.WorkflowRun.run(WorkflowRun.java:2
        at hudson.model.ResourceController.execute(ResourceController.java:98)
        at hudson.model.Executor.run(Executor.java:404)
Finished: FAILURE
```

Figure 7-7. Error reporting for declarative syntax error

Notice how much clearer and more precise the error message is, in terms of the Jenkins pipeline DSL, in the second example.

You may also recall the error messages we saw in the section "Dealing with Nondeclarative Code" on page 244 when we looked at trying to put nondeclarative code into a Declarative Pipeline:

```
org.codehaus.groovy.control.MultipleCompilationErrorsException:
startup failed:
WorkflowScript: 15: Expected a step @ line 15, column 16.
                  def server = Artifactory.server 'my-server-id'
                  ^
WorkflowScript: 17: Expected a step @ line 17, column 1.
   def rtGradle = Artifactory.newGradleBuild()
   ^
WorkflowScript: 19: Expected a step @ line 19, column 1.
   rtGradle.tool = 'gradle3'
```

```
    ^
3 errors
```

Notice again the DSL-oriented error message ("Expected a step") with the exact line number and column references.

Declarative Pipelines and the Blue Ocean Interface

Before we leave our detailed discussion of Declarative Pipelines, we should note one other aspect of them—they are uniquely suited for working with the new Jenkins Blue Ocean interface and the associated visual pipeline editor that it provides. This visual interface is regularly being enhanced and updated by CloudBees and the Jenkins community, and it presents an interesting new way to work with and create pipelines.

Blue Ocean plugins and Declarative Pipeline plugins go hand in hand. The well-defined structure of a Declarative Pipeline lends itself well to being parsed for presentation in a visual form. The limited structure also makes it easier to do the reverse: create a simple visual interface with specific selections that can be transformed into a pipeline.

That's not to say that Scripted Pipelines can't be used with the Blue Ocean interface—they will have a visual representation of separate stages, and point-and-click interfaces to view logs and errors. However, trying to dive deeper into the code in the visual interface will result in an error message, because Scripted Pipelines do not have "step" sections that contain the DSL statements. Likewise, Scripted Pipelines cannot be created or edited through the editor, since it expects to have a `pipeline` block (closure) encompassing all of the pipeline code.

Chapter 9 is devoted to the Blue Ocean interface, and the interactive features such as the editor.

Summary

In this chapter, we've looked at an alternative syntax and structure for creating a pipeline-as-code in Jenkins. We call this new type "Declarative" because it is more oriented around declaring what we want to instantiate and have occur.

In the other kind of pipelines we typically do more "programming," using Groovy constructs such as assignments, decision statements, exception handling, etc. Frequently, this is to compensate for some of the built-in Jenkins constructs we traditionally had available in Freestyle jobs. That kind of pipeline (which more closely resembles a Groovy program) is called "Scripted."

Declarative Pipelines have a well-defined structure, with code blocks, sections, and directives that are similar to the sections traditionally found on the page for a Freestyle job in the web interface. They also more clearly identify errors in the expected pipeline syntax, in comparison to the Groovy tracebacks that happen with errors in Scripted Pipelines.

Because of factors like the well-defined structure, similar "feel" to the traditional setup of a Freestyle job, and better error checking, Declarative Pipelines offer a simpler and clearer path for moving from Freestyle jobs and the web interface to crafting pipelines-as-code.

However, certain types of operations, such as assignments, do not fit in the declarative model, and so can present challenges when they are needed in a Declarative Pipeline. Ways to work around some of these issues are discussed in Chapter 16. If none of these are viable, or if they present significant challenges, that may be an indicator that a Scripted Pipeline would be a better option.

In the next chapter, we'll look at the different types of projects available in Jenkins, including several that are new with Jenkins 2.

CHAPTER 8

Understanding Project Types

In the Jenkins 2 environment, several new project types have been added to provide extended functionality. Many of them leverage Jenkinsfiles, as markers, to automatically create jobs for the user. In this chapter, we'll look at the most common project types in Jenkins, including these newer ones as well as traditional ones (like Freestyle and Maven projects).

For most of the project types, there are certain common options present on the configuration page. These are in sections such as General, Build, Source Code Management, etc. In the first part of this chapter, we'll cover those common options. Also, since we are focused on getting up and running with Jenkins 2, we'll cover the corresponding pipeline functionality where we have an equivalent.

Common Project Options

A number of the project types in Jenkins have configuration pages that are divided into specific sections. These sections can be scrolled to, or selected via tabs at the top of the page. We'll look at each of the major sections, explain what the options mean, and also look at ways to implement corresponding functionality in pipelines. We'll break these down based on the tab positions in a Freestyle project. Other types of projects may have some options on different tabs.

General

The General section is where we configure the unique identifying information about the project, such as the description. (The project name will have already been set when the type of project was selected from the project selection dialog.) Figure 8-1 shows this section.

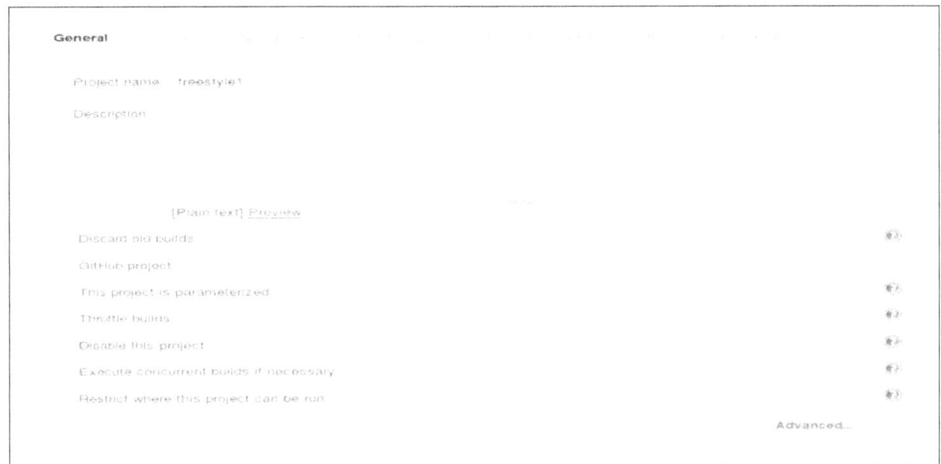

Figure 8-1. General configuration section for a Freestyle project

This is also where we can set some global options for the project, including ones that control job-level aspects. A survey of these follows.

Discard old builds

This option allows you to set up a strategy for Jenkins to follow in discarding previous builds of your project. While not required, it is helpful for aspects such as managing disk space (since each run of a project allocates a workspace area).

As shown in Figure 8-2, once you check the box, you can select the strategy to use for how many builds to keep. Although there is a Strategy drop-down, Log Rotation is currently the only choice; it is really the options underneath that dictate the strategy. Essentially, you can choose to keep each run's work items and artifacts for a particular number of days or a particular number of builds.

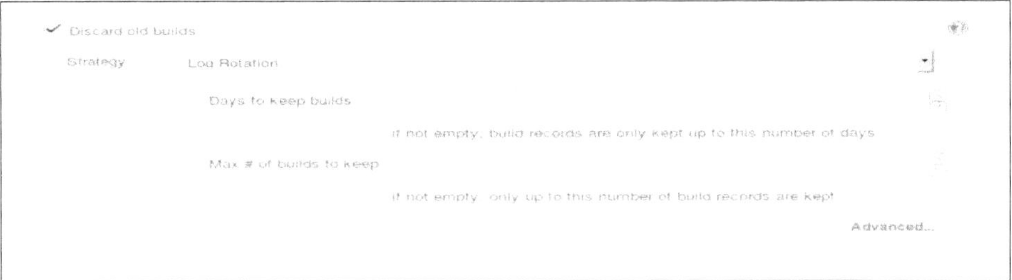

Figure 8-2. Options for deleting old builds

Clicking the Advanced button provides you with the further option to limit the delete operation to just artifacts (Figure 8-3).

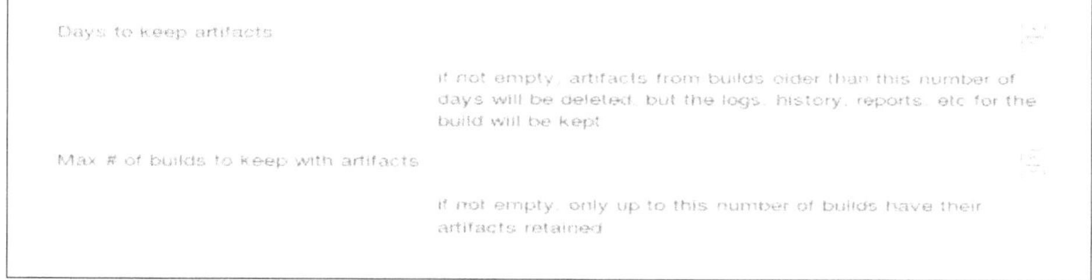

Figure 8-3. Advanced options for deleting just artifacts

Discarding builds in pipeline projects. For pipeline projects, there is a `buildDiscarder` option that can be configured. In a Scripted Pipeline, this is done via the `properties` step. Here's an example constructed from the Snippet Generator:

```
properties([buildDiscarder(logRotator(artifactDaysToKeepStr: '',
   artifactNumToKeepStr: '', daysToKeepStr: '3', numToKeepStr: '5')),
   pipelineTriggers([])])
```

In a Declarative Pipeline, a similar entry can be made in the `options` section:

```
options {
    buildDiscarder(logRotator(numToKeepStr:'5'))
}
```

GitHub project

If you have the GitHub plugin installed, this option allows you to specify a GitHub URL for integration. With this integration, you can have links to your GitHub project in Jenkins (such as on the Changes page), and you can do integration builds based on changes to GitHub repositories. (Note that to be notified of changes from GitHub, there is additional setup required. See "GitHub hook trigger for Git polling" on page 263.)

The project URL is the main parameter to set here. There is also an Advanced button, but it simply allows you to specify a simple name for information sent back to GitHub.

Note that using this functionality requires having a Jenkins URL reachable from the internet and some specific setup. See the GitHub plugin page (*https://plugins.jenkins.io/github*) for more information.

Specifying the GitHub project property in pipeline projects. For Scripted Pipelines, you can set the `GithubProjectProperty` values in the `properties` step. For example:

```
properties([[$class: 'GithubProjectProperty',
   displayName: '',
   projectUrlStr: 'http://github.com/brentlaster/sampleproject/'],
   pipelineTriggers([])]
```

This project is parameterized

This option allows you to add various kinds of input parameters to your job. Clicking the Add Parameter button brings up additional fields that you can fill in for the name of your parameter, default values, etc.

The different types of parameters and how to use them in pipeline projects are covered extensively in Chapter 3.

Throttle builds

This option allows you to specify the number of builds to be allowed within a given time period. One field is for the number of builds and one is for the time period (hour, day, etc.).

Throttling builds in pipelines. The `properties` step does have a way to call the throttle builds functionality, but as of this writing, that functionality seems to be broken. It is also currently missing for the Declarative Pipeline `options` section. Here is an example of what the Snippet Generator creates for this:

```
properties([[$class: 'JobPropertyImpl',
   throttle: [count: 1, durationName: 'hour']], pipelineTriggers([])])
```

Disable this project

As the name implies, clicking this box will disable the project (keep it from being executed). When this is unset, it will reenable the project.

Disabling Pipeline projects. For Pipeline projects within the Jenkins interface, there is an option in the Build Triggers tab to disable projects. See Figure 8-4.

Figure 8-4. Disabling Pipeline projects

Execute concurrent builds if necessary

By default, concurrent builds for the same project are not allowed. If this option is checked, and enough executors are available, then parallel builds are allowed. This can be useful for large or long-running project builds, and also for ones that are parameterized and can benefit from running with different parameters (such as for testing scenarios).

When concurrent builds happen, workspace names are appended with @# (where # is a number) to separate the workspaces. However, if a custom workspace is used, all of the concurrent builds run there.

Concurrent builds in pipelines. In the context of pipelines, the sense of this option is reversed. That is, we set an option to disable concurrent builds if desired. The syntax (*http://bit.ly/2HXNZH5*) looks like this:

```
properties([disableConcurrentBuilds()])
```

or:

```
options { disableConcurrentBuilds() }
```

Restrict where this project can be run

This option allows you to enter one or more "labels" identifying which nodes can be used to run the project. Labels are identifiers you put on nodes to make them selectable.

Selecting this option displays an additional entry box to enter the label(s).

Pipelines and nodes. The `node` block and `agent` step (in Scripted and Declarative Pipelines, respectively) allow for deciding where all or part of a pipeline should run. This and related steps are covered in Chapter 2 for Scripted Pipelines and Chapter 7 for Declarative Pipelines.

A set of additional options can also be set on the General tab by clicking on the Advanced button below the "Restrict where this project can be run" option. We cover those next.

Quiet period

Clicking on this option gives you a field where you can enter a number of seconds for Jenkins to wait before starting a build of this project. If builds are triggered, they will be added to the queue, waiting for this time period. If this is not set, the system will default to the global quiet period if one is configured in the Configure System settings (shown in Figure 8-5).

Figure 8-5. Global options including the default quiet period

This option is mainly a vestige from the early days of using systems like CVS where you might need to wait until all files were committed before initiating builds, rather than acting when the system saw the first one. It can still have similar applications today.

Pipelines and the quiet period. Pipelines have a `build` step where you can initiate the build of another project. From within that step, you can specify a quiet period for the intended job. The syntax is as follows:

```
build job: 'myJob', quietPeriod: 5
```

Retry count

This setting is for retrying SCM checkouts. Clicking on the option pops up a field where you can enter the number of attempts to make to check code out. There is a 10-second delay between attempts. If this value is not set, then the system will default to the global retry value, if set, in the Configure System settings (the "SCM checkout retry count" setting in Figure 8-5). Note that it is up to each SCM plugin provider to define what constitutes a failure that warrants a retry.

Pipelines and retry count. Currently, pipelines should honor the global (Configure System) retry count, if set. Pipelines also include a general `retry` step that can be used to retry any operation. This is discussed in detail in Chapter 3.

Block build when upstream project is building

When this option is checked, the project won't be allowed to build if one of its dependencies (direct or transitive) is building or in the queue.

Block build when downstream project is building

When this option is checked, the project won't be allowed to build if one of its children (direct or transitive) is building or in the queue.

Waiting for downstream in pipelines. For pipelines, the `build` step has an option that defaults to `true` to wait for downstream builds. If you do not want to wait, then you need to explicitly set that value to `false` as shown here:

```
build job: 'declar2', wait: false
```

Note that if you use the default value of `true`, then the return value from the step is an object that you can examine for the build result and other attributes. More details can be found in the Snippet Generator help.

Use custom workspace

As the name implies, selecting this option allows you to specify a particular directory as your workspace. (The location is entered in a separate field that opens up when this option is checked.) The location can be an absolute path or a relative path. If it is a relative path, it is relative to the node's root directory.

Normally, it's best (and easiest) to just let Jenkins manage the workspace. However, if the job requires builds or source downloads to be done in a specific location, this is a way you can accommodate that need.

Custom workspaces and pipelines. For Declarative Pipelines, there is a `customWorkspace` option to the label definition for an agent that can be used (see Chapter 7). Pipelines also include `dir` and `ws` steps to set custom areas. These steps are discussed in detail in Chapter 11.

Display name

The value put in this field is displayed in the Jenkins web interface as the name of the project. Duplicate names are allowed since this is just for display purposes. You could use this, for example, to display additional information about the project that is worth being easily seen.

Display name and pipelines. To set a display name and description in a pipeline, you can use code like the following:

```
currentBuild.displayName = <project name>
currentBuild.description = <project description>
```

Keep the build logs of dependencies

This option overrides log rotation policies for dependencies connected to your project. It is useful for ensuring those logs are still available to coincide with your project's logs.

Next is the Source Code Management section.

Source Code Management

Depending on which source code management plugins you have installed, you'll have options here to select one and configure it appropriately. The specific options will vary depending on the system selected, but there are certain common features.

Repository URL

This setting specifies the location of the repository you want to access for the project. Note that different protocols can be used, such as HTTPS or SSH.

Credentials

These are simply the credentials you've defined in Jenkins to access the SCM.

Revision

Specifying a revision is a way to specify a particular version of the code that you want to use (typically this might be a branch, but it could also be something like a tag or whatever the SCM uses to indicate a specific version).

Figure 8-6 shows a setup for accessing a Git repository.

Figure 8-6. Typical Git configuration

Source code management in a pipeline

The pipeline includes a corresponding `checkout` step that you can use in place of the source code management forms in this section. The easiest way to fill this in is via the Pipeline Syntax/Snippet Generator form. Figure 8-7 shows an example of using the Snippet Generator to duplicate the setup in the previous section.

Figure 8-7. Configuring the checkout pipeline step for a GitSCM operation

This in turn would generate the following code:

```
checkout([$class: 'GitSCM', branches: [[name: '*/master']],
 doGenerateSubmoduleConfigurations: false, extensions: [],
 submoduleCfg: [], userRemoteConfigs: [[credentialsId:
'localUser',
 url:'git@diyvb2:/home/git/repositories/shared_libraries']]])
```

Depending on the SCM, the pipeline may also have a dedicated step to use for that SCM. For example, for Git, there is a `git` step. The syntax for that is:

```
git credentialsId: 'localUser', url:
 'git@diyvb2:/home/git/repositories/shared_libraries'
```

Notice that the syntax for the dedicated step is somewhat simpler (although not all options are shown). For this reason, it is usually preferable to use a dedicated step if one exists for the SCM. However, if there is no dedicated step, then the `checkout` step is a fallback.

With the source management aspects defined, we can move on to what events or processes will cause the build to run. These are referred to as `Build Triggers`.

Build Triggers

In this section of the project configuration, we define the events and/or processes that will start a build of our project running. The basic options are described in the following sections.

Trigger builds remotely

If you select this option, then Jenkins will provide you with a special URL that you can use to trigger a build (see Figure 8-8). Jenkins also asks you to provide a string that can be used as an authorization token in the URL. This is an additional security step since anyone or anything trying to trigger the build needs to also know the token.

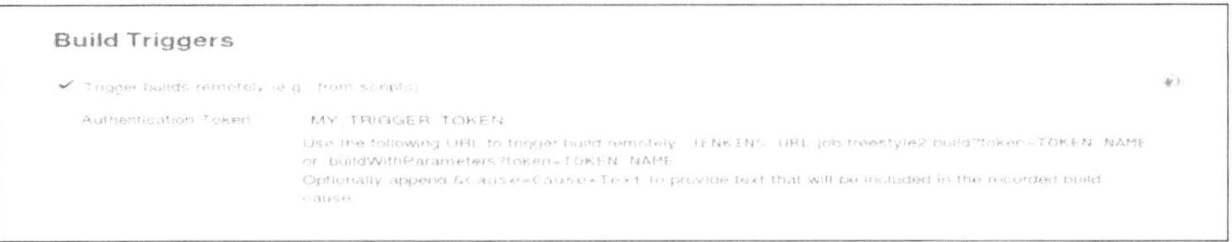

Figure 8-8. Setting up remote trigger

With this URL, you can then use tools like `wget` or `curl` or a custom web page to trigger the build. For example:

```
curl http://localhost:8080/job/freestyle2/build?token
 =MY_TRIGGER_TOKEN
```

The `localhost:8080` in this case is the Jenkins URL.

When you execute this, the target job will start doing a build. In the log it will say "Started by remote host..."

Tokens and Access

Assuming that you have Jenkins secured such that anonymous users lack read permissions, then you will need some kind of authentication to be able to trigger the build—especially since Jenkins checks the URL hierarchically down the path. If you do not have other access set up, then there is a Build Token Root plugin that offers an alternate URL that is accessible to anonymous users to trigger such builds.

Remotely triggering pipeline builds. You can use an `sh` call to `curl`, `wget`, etc. in your pipeline. to remotely trigger a build if it is set up as described. Or, if the build is on the same Jenkins instance, you can just use the `build` pipeline step and tell it which project to build.

Building after other projects are built

This option allows you to trigger a build of the current project based on completion of another project's build. There are options for building only if the build of the other project is stable (successful), is unstable, or failed.

Build after other projects in a pipeline. Getting this same functionality through the pipeline is a function of the `properties` step. The parameter for the upstream project to trigger from is `upstreamProjects`, and the result we look for is set by the `threshold` parameter. Here is a code sample:

```
properties([pipelineTriggers([upstream
 (threshold: 'SUCCESS',
 upstreamProjects: 'upstream-project')])])
```

Build periodically

When you click this option, it brings up a Schedule text box where you can specify how often to build using standard cron syntax (five space-separated fields in which you indicate values for the minute, hour, day of the month, month, and day of the week). For more details on cron syntax, see "Build Periodically" on page 61, or the online help for this option.

Building periodically in a pipeline. As with the previous option, the `properties` step can be used to set a periodic build schedule for a Pipeline project. The syntax follows the same format as discussed for other uses of the cron syntax.

For example, to build every 15 minutes, the step would look like this:

```
properties([pipelineTriggers([cron('H/15 * * * *')])])
```

GitHub hook trigger for Git polling

This method of triggering builds allows you to set up a GitHub service to send notifications to Jenkins when an event happens in your repository on GitHub. So, rather than polling for changes in the repository, Jenkins is notified of updates by GitHub.

To use this, first you'll need to have the GitHub Integration plugin installed. Then you need to do some global configuration for GitHub access.

On the Configure System screen, you will have a GitHub setup area (Figure 8-9). Initially there are two fields that need setup: the URL and credentials. If you just need to use the public GitHub, you can leave the API URL field as the default: *https://api.github.com*. If you had an enterprise GitHub system, you would put the URL for that in here instead. Likewise, the Name field can be left blank unless you have multiple GitHub enterprise systems, and need to easily differentiate one from the others.

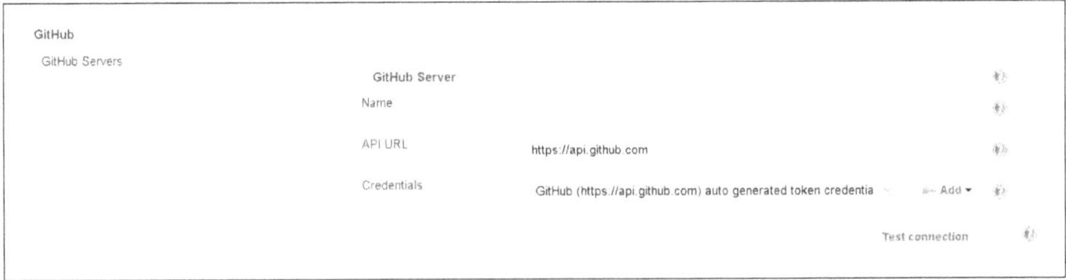

Figure 8-9. Basic GitHub setup in Configure System

For credentials, you need some kind of token to use with GitHub. One common choice is a personal access token. This can be set up in your personal settings area on GitHub, then added as a credential in Jenkins and selected here.

Alternatively, if you have a user ID and password that you use already with GitHub, you can let Jenkins automatically create a token for you. To do this, look for an the Advanced button further down in the GitHub section on this screen. Click that, then click Manage Additional GitHub Actions and "Convert login and password to token." From here, you can convert an existing user ID and password credential to a token (if you already have that set up in Jenkins) or just a standard user ID and password. See Figure 8-10.

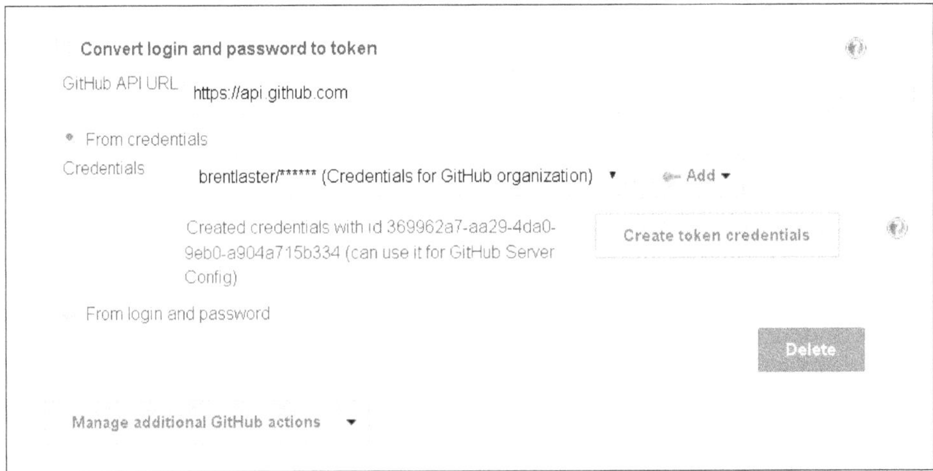

Figure 8-10. Creating a GitHub token from existing credentials

This will then show up in your list of credentials in Jenkins and can be selected to use with GitHub (Figure 8-11).

Figure 8-11. Credential token for GitHub

Now you want to tell Jenkins how to manage the notifications from GitHub. The notifications are sent as webhooks. There are two modes, referred to as "automatic" and "manual."

With the automatic mode, Jenkins automatically creates and sets up the webhook on the GitHub side. To use this mode, you need to have created an access token on the GitHub side that has (at least) the *admin:repo_hook* scope. If you don't already have such a token, log in to GitHub, go to your personal settings, and create it. Figure 8-12 shows a screenshot of a token with the appropriate scope.

Personal settings
Profile
Account
Emails
Notifications
Billing
SSH and GPG keys
Security
Blocked users
Repositories
Organizations
Saved replies
Authorized OAuth Apps
Authorized GitHub Apps
Installed GitHub Apps
Developer settings
OAuth Apps
GitHub Apps
Personal access tokens

Edit personal access token

If you've lost or forgotten this token, you can regenerate it, but be aware that any scripts or applications using this token will need to be updated.
Regenerate token

Token description
Jenkins GitHub Plugin token
What's this token for?

Select scopes
Scopes define the access for personal tokens. Read more about OAuth scopes.

[x] repo	Full control of private repositories
[x] repo:status	Access commit status
[x] repo_deployment	Access deployment status
[x] public_repo	Access public repositories
[x] repo:invite	Access repository invitations
[ ] admin:org	Full control of orgs and teams
[ ] write:org	Read and write org and team membership
[ ] read:org	Read org and team membership
[ ] admin:public_key	Full control of user public keys
[ ] write:public_key	Write user public keys
[ ] read:public_key	Read user public keys
[x] admin:repo_hook	Full control of repository hooks
[x] write:repo_hook	Write repository hooks
[x] read:repo_hook	Read repository hooks

Figure 8-12. Scopes for access token on GitHub to allow Jenkins to do automatic set up of webhook

Create a credential in Jenkins with this token, then, in the GitHub section of the Configure System screen, click the "Manage hooks" checkbox and supply the token as a credential (Figure 8-13).

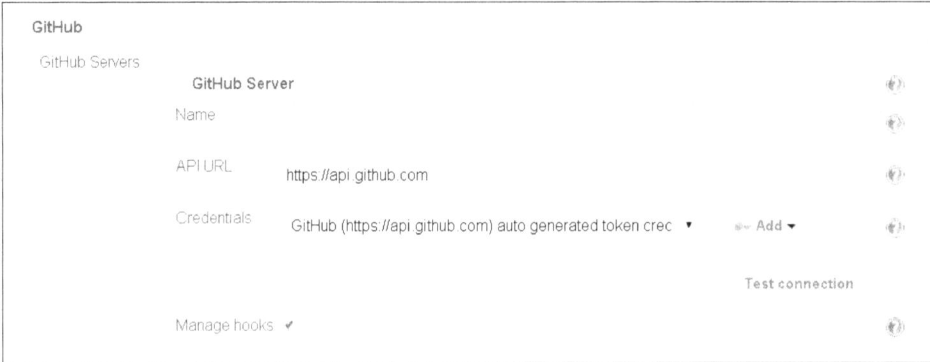

Figure 8-13. Configuration for GitHub token and managing hooks

As previously mentioned, using webhooks in this way assumes that your Jenkins instance is accessible to the outside world—at least on the particular URL used by the webhook. Jenkins can tell you what this URL is, but it does it in an indirect way.

To find the URL that the webhook will use, click the blue question mark help icon next to the "Test connection" button, to the right of the "Manage hooks" checkbox item. A new help text box will open up. This help box will have within it a URL on the local Jenkins system. This is the URL that the webhook will send information to. Figure 8-14 shows this part of the screen, with the help button to click and the webhook URL in the resulting dialog highlighted.

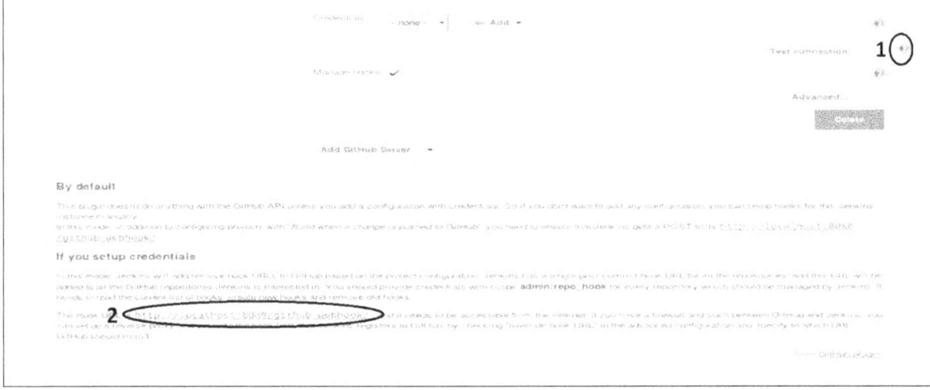

Figure 8-14. Locating the URL for the webhook

With all of this done, you then just need to update some settings in the project itself:

- Select the option to indicate that this is a GitHub project, and specify the GitHub URL in the Project URL field in the General section.
- In the Build Triggers section, select the "GitHub hook trigger for GitSCM polling" option.

Then when you save your changes, if everything is set up correctly, Jenkins will talk to your GitHub project and create a new webhook there. When a change is made to the project, that will send the webhook notification. Jenkins will respond accordingly. Most commonly, this would be a push to the project on GitHub that then causes a build of the project to start up (Figure 8-15).

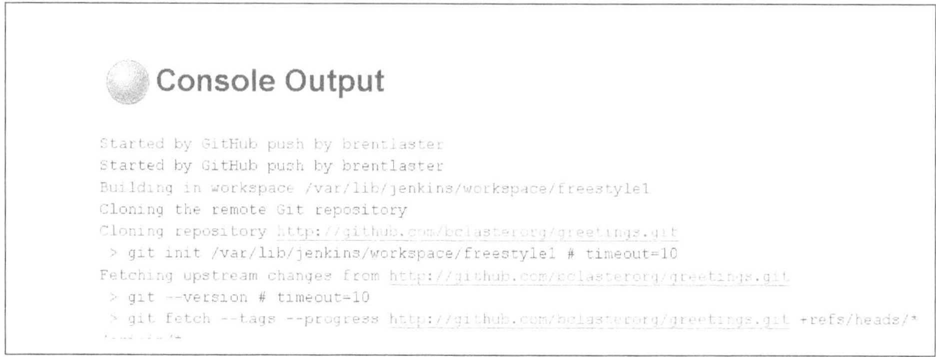

Figure 8-15. Build started by push to GitHub project and subsequent webhook from GitHub to Jenkins

For the manual mode, the main change is that you need to go to GitHub, then to the project, and then to "Integrations and Services" and create a webhook manually. This isn't hard. Figure 8-16 shows the setup screen.

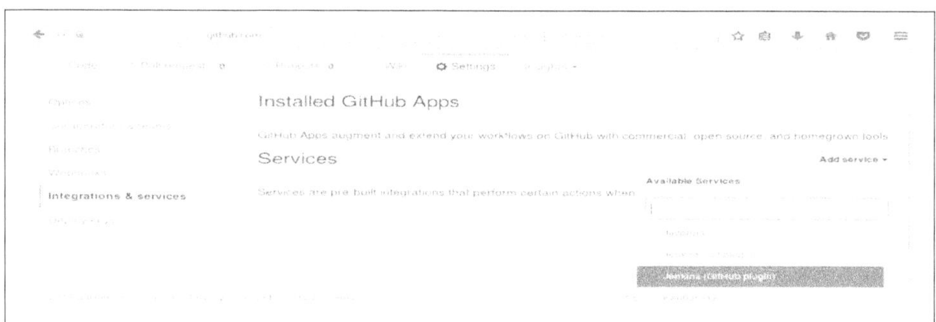

Figure 8-16. Manually adding a service on GitHub to create the webhook and send notifications

Once the webhook is set up, you'll see it listed on the GitHub page for your project (Figure 8-17).

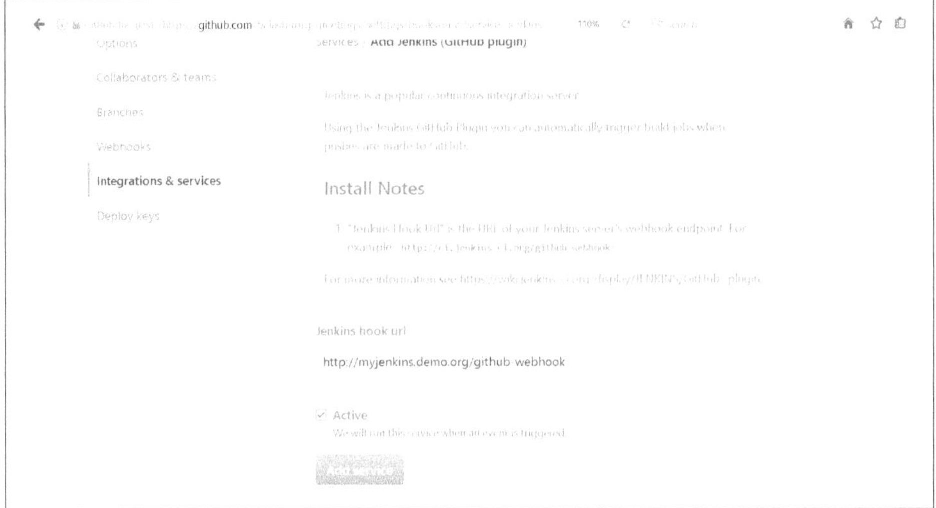

Figure 8-17. After manual webhook setup

Now, you just configure the GitHub section of the Configure System screen as described before, selecting the "Manage hooks" checkbox and using a credential that Jenkins knows about, and that supplies the appropriate accesses.

Then, again as noted in the automatic mode discussion, you just need to configure the project in the same way. That is, you select "GitHub project" in the General section of the project setup and put in the URL (Figure 8-18), and then select the "GitHub hook trigger for GitSCM polling" option in the Build Triggers section. Afterwards, a push made to the project on GitHub should trigger a new build of the project.

Figure 8-18. Configuring the project's general setup area for GitHub

GitHub triggering in a pipeline. Like the other build triggers, the `properties` step is used here again for specifying this option:

```
properties([pipelineTriggers([githubPush()])])
```

Here's an example set of code. This assumes we have set up the global configuration (via the Configure System screen) and also set up a webhook in GitHub for this project:

```
properties([[$class: 'GithubProjectProperty',
    displayName: '',
    projectUrlStr:
       'http://github.com/bclasterorg/greetings.git/'],
    pipelineTriggers([githubPush()])])
git url: 'https://github.com/bclasterorg/greetings.git',
    branch: 'master'
```

Note that you may need to manually run this once before the automatic notices take effect.

Bitbucket Project Triggers

According to some sources, there should also be a `bitbucketPush` trigger that behaves similarly to the `githubPush` trigger. However, at the time of this writing, this doesn't seem to be supported. If you need this functionality, you may want to try it in your pipeline to see if it is valid, and/or consult the latest documentation for the Bitbucket Source plugin.

Poll SCM

This option is like the "Build periodically" option discussed earlier. In fact, it uses the same cron-like syntax as that option. The difference is that instead of telling Jenkins when to start a build, we are telling it when to check the repository for changes. See "Cron syntax" on page 235 for details on the syntax.

This choice has an additional option to "Ignore post-commit hooks." Basically, this tells Jenkins to not start activities based on signals from hooks after changes are made, but only to respond to changes in the SCM. This prevents double-triggering operations.

Polling in the pipeline. Once more, we use the `properties` step and cron specification for this option. Here's the syntax for telling the pipeline to check every 15 minutes for changes in the repository, along with the option to ignore the post-commit hooks:

```
properties([pipelineTriggers
([pollSCM(ignorePostCommitHooks: true, scmpoll_spec:
 'H/15 * * * *')])])
```

Up next is the Build Environment section.

Build Environment

This section allows you to specify certain global actions and integration settings for the project. There can be many of these, depending on which plugins you have installed. (For example, if you have the Artifactory plugin installed, you'll have Artifactory integration items.) We'll cover some common ones here.

Delete workspace before build starts

This one is pretty self-explanatory. The workspace is removed before the build begins.

Deleting workspaces in a pipeline. The Jenkins pipeline DSL provides the `deleteDir` step to clean a directory out of the workspace and also the `cleanWs` (clean workspace) step to delete a workspace. These steps are covered in more detail in Chapter 11.

Provide configuration files

This option allows you to select files of a certain type and copy them to all your nodes, as well as providing a way to edit them through the Jenkins UI. Some global setup is required first.

Web Examples

For whatever reasons, at least at the time of this writing, many of the examples and some of the documentation provided online for the Config File Provider plugin (for use in both Freestyle and Pipeline jobs) is incorrect and/or out of date. Be aware that you may not be able to completely rely on these resources.

Under Manage Jenkins, there is a "Managed files" menu item to select to start the process (Figure 8-19).

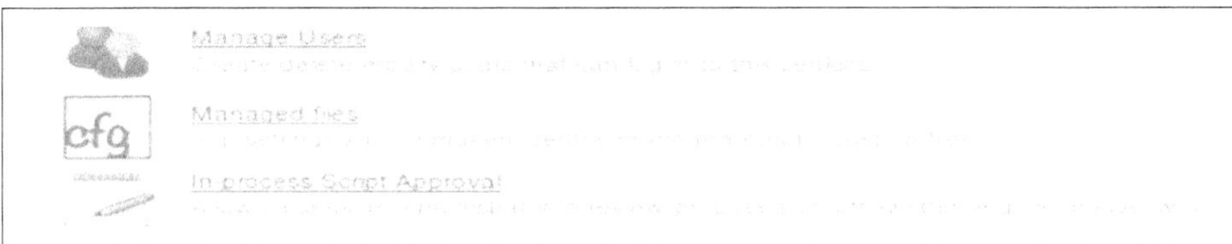

Figure 8-19. The global "Managed files" item

From there, you can select the type of file you want to include and also get an ID to work with it (Figure 8-20).

Config File IDs

Jenkins will automatically generate a default ID for your config file when you create it. However, it is a long hexadecimal string. If you prefer to have a more user-friendly ID, you can edit it when you are setting up your file on the Type screen and type in whatever name you want. You cannot edit it later.

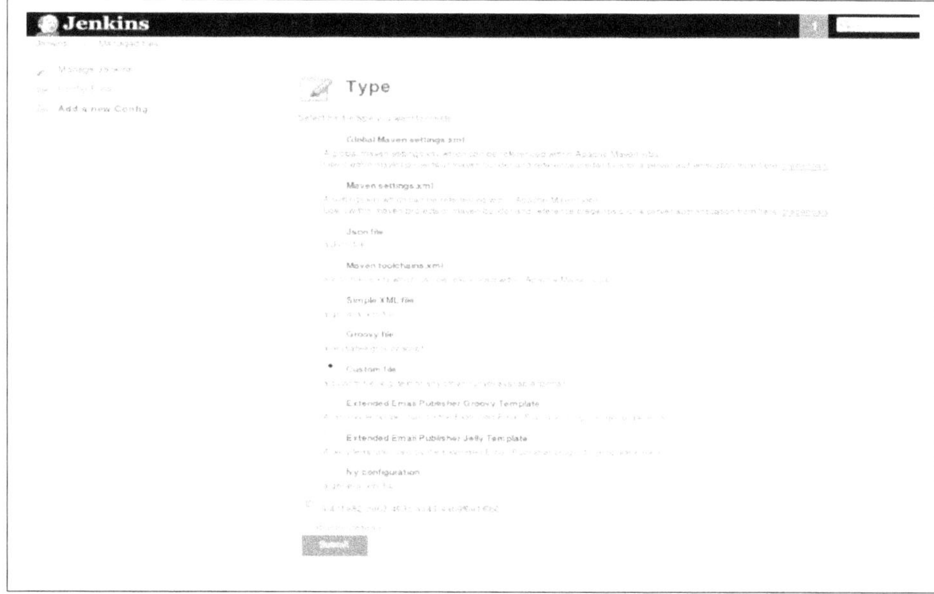

Figure 8-20. Choosing the managed file type (note that the ID is automatically filled in at the bottom)

After you click Submit here, you move on to filling in the file's actual content (Figure 8-21).

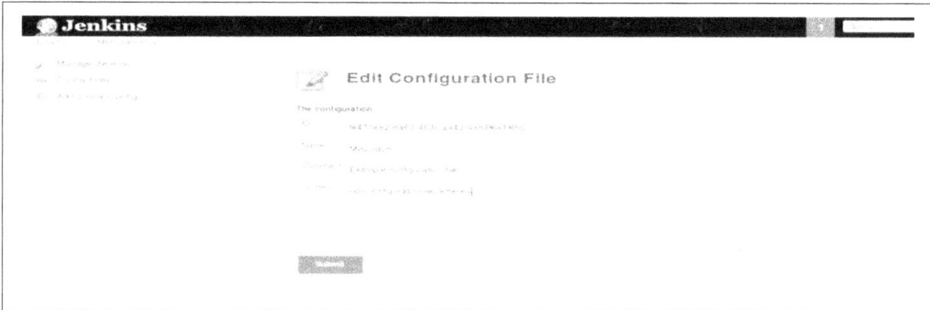

Figure 8-21. Supplying content for the managed file

Once you are done with that, you'll have a screen where you can edit or delete your new file (Figure 8-22). Note that there is also a menu item to add additional config files in the menu on the left.

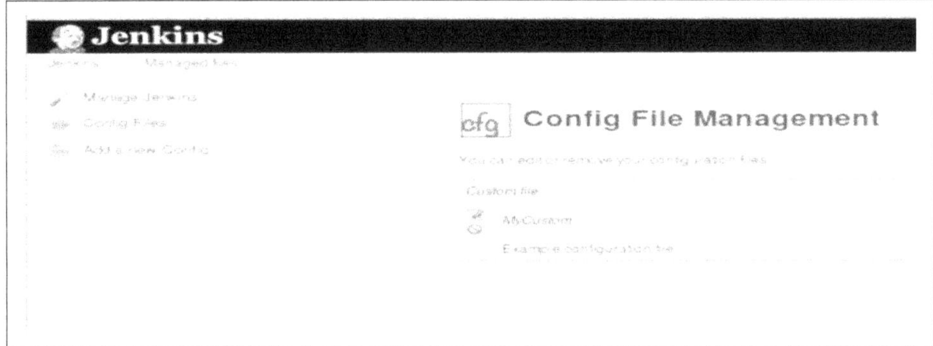

Figure 8-22. Options for working with the config file

Now that you've completed the global setup for this, you can use the file in your project. After selecting the "Provide Configuration files" option in the project, you're presented with a dialog like the one in Figure 8-23.

Figure 8-23. Selecting config files in the project

The File field allows you to select a file that you have previously configured globally as we just described.

The Target field allows you to specify where the file should be created on a node. If this is left blank, then the file will be created in a temporary location.

The Variable field allows you to define an environment variable name to reference the file in job steps. This also gives you a handle to get to the file in the temporary location if the Target field was left blank.

Finally, the Replace Tokens option replaces environment variables set by Jenkins and specified in your configuration file with their values. (This relies on the Token Macro plugin.) The syntax to use in your config files for token replacement is:

```
${ENV, var="<variable-name>"}
```

where `<variable-name>` is replaced with the name of the variable you want to get the value of (such as `JOB_NAME`).

Config Files and Credentials

Using some types of config files, such as ones associated with Maven, may require additional credential setup. See the Config File Provider plugin page (*https://plugins.jenkins.io/config-file-provider*) for more details.

Managing configuration files in a pipeline. There is a `configFileProvider` step that you can use in your pipeline code. This is another block step, meaning that you invoke the step with some context, and it provides a closure in which you execute other code. So, for example, if you were using this functionality to access a properties file or custom XML file, you would first configure the file globally (as described previously). Then, in your pipeline code, you would invoke the step, passing in the file ID and related information. Then, within the step block, you could invoke other pipeline commands that use the properties file, the XML file, or their data.

For example, suppose we have a config file set up as shown in Figure 8-24.

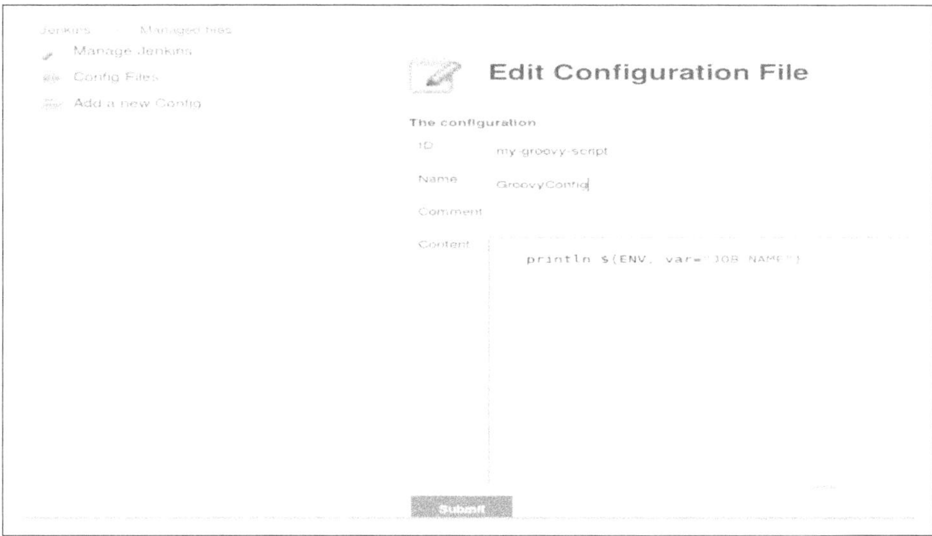

Figure 8-24. Example Groovy config file

We could then add a step in our pipeline like the following to use it:

```
configFileProvider(
      [configFile(fileId: 'my-groovy-script',
      variable: 'MY_GROOVY_SCRIPT',
      replaceTokens:true)]) {
          sh "cat ${MY_GROOVY_SCRIPT}"
      }
```

Notice the syntax here. We first have the `configFile` parameter, which takes arguments that correspond to our Freestyle ones:

`fileId`
: This is the file ID that was set up when you globally configured the file.

Meaningful File Identifiers

As mentioned previously, you can change the default hex string ID that Jenkins generates for your config file at the time you create it (on the Type screen). It is recommended that you do this for files that will be used in pipeline projects, since the `configFileProvider` step requires the file's ID string be passed in to the `fileId` parameter to identify the file.

`variable`
: This is a variable you can use to access the file itself on the node.

`replaceTokens`
: If set to `true`, this tells Jenkins to replace known environment variables with their actual values in the configuration file. (See the preceding section on Freestyle usage for syntax.)

Running this step in the pipeline would yield results like the following:

```
[Pipeline] node
Running on worker_node2 in
  /home/jenkins2/worker_node2/workspace/config-file1
[Pipeline] {
[Pipeline] configFileProvider
provisioning config files...
copy managed file [GroovyConfig] to
file:/home/jenkins2/worker_node2/workspace/
config-file1@tmp/config2453863098810806031tmp
[Pipeline] {
[Pipeline] sh
[config-file1] Running shell script
+ cat /home/jenkins2/worker_node2/workspace/
config-file1@tmp/config2453863098810806031tmp
println config-file1
[Pipeline] }
Deleting 1 temporary files
[Pipeline] // configFileProvider
[Pipeline] }
[Pipeline] // node
[Pipeline] End of Pipeline
Finished: SUCCESS
```

Note that when we ran the shell `cat` command in the block, we used the variable we defined in the step's invocation. And when the contents of the file were printed out, because we have the `replaceTokens` value set to `true`, the environment variable string inside the configuration file was replaced with the value of the environment variable in the output—in this case, the job name.

One other point about this step is that multiple config files can be specified in the step using an array syntax, as shown in the following example:

```
configFileProvider(
       [configFile(fileId: 'my-custom-file',
       variable: 'MY_CUSTOM_FILE',
       replaceTokens:true),
       configFile(fileId: 'my-groovy-script',
       variable: 'MY_GROOVY_SCRIPT',
       replaceTokens:true)]) {
            sh "cat ${MY_GROOVY_SCRIPT}"
       }
```

Abort the build if it's stuck

This setting allows you to specify a timeout strategy and related values to stop the build if it appears to be taking too long. The main parameters are a timeout value in minutes and the choice of strategy to use for determining when a build is stuck.

As defined in the help for the setting, the following strategies are available:

Absolute
: Abort the build based on a fixed timeout.

Deadline
: Abort the build based on a deadline time specified in HH:MM:SS or HH:MM (24-hour time) format.

Elastic
: Define the time to wait before killing the build as a percentage of the mean of the duration of the last *n* successful builds.

Likely stuck
: Abort the build when the job has taken many times longer than previous runs.

No Activity
: Trigger a timeout when the specified number of seconds have passed since the last log output.

Additionally, we can define an environment variable that is automatically filled in with the timeout value (in milliseconds) and can be referenced in our jobs. And finally, we can define what actions Jenkins should take when the timeout is hit. Options include failing the build, aborting the build, and writing information to the run's description. For the information that goes in the description, the special value "{0}" will be filled in with the timeout in minutes.

As an example, suppose we have a job where the properties are configured like in Figure 8-25.

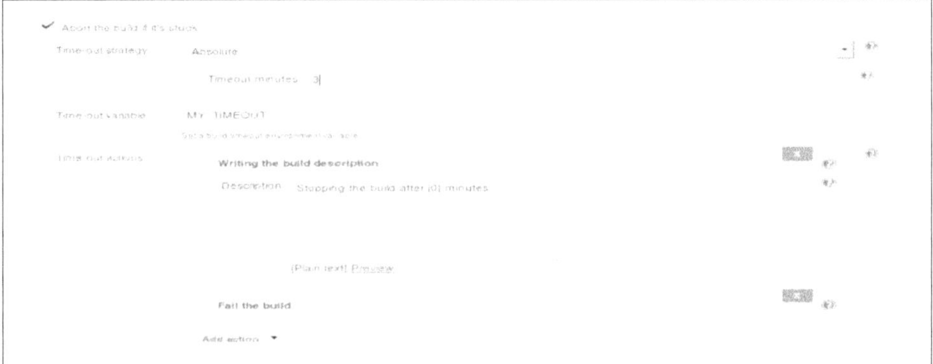

Figure 8-25. Configuring timeout information for a job

Here we are telling Jenkins to do an absolute timeout after the job has been running for three minutes. We've defined an environment variable named `MY_TIMEOUT` that we can reference in our job, and we've added some actions to happen after the timeout occurs. We will be writing the string "Stopping the build after {0} minutes" (using the special variable) and then failing the build.

An extremely simple job to test this could be a shell command that executes something like:

```
echo $MY_TIMEOUT
sleep 4m
```

When this runs, and the timeout occurs, the last part of the console log will be:

```
+ echo 180000
180000
+ sleep 4m
Build timed out (after 3 minutes). Marking the build as failed.
Build was aborted
Finished: FAILURE
```

And the latest run will have the description we set in it (Figure 8-26).

Figure 8-26. Custom timeout message written to description

Timing out builds in a pipeline. The pipeline DSL has a simple `timeout` step that provides similar functionality. This step is a block step, meaning it wraps around a set of code. It takes a default parameter of a number of minutes to wait for the code in the block to time out. If you want to use a different unit than minutes, you need to specify that as an additional parameter. A simple example is shown here (see Chapter 3 for more explanation and related examples):

```
timeout(time: 1, unit: 'HOURS') {
    // block of code
}
```

Add timestamps to console output

As the name implies, this setting will print timestamps in the console log as parts of your job are executed. An example of the default output is shown in Figure 8-27.

Figure 8-27. Console output with timestamps

Note that this option also adds a dialog on the console log screen with controls that allow you to modify the timestamps to show elapsed time (instead of clock time) or even turn off displaying the timestamps.

Adding timestamps to a pipeline. The `timestamps` step in the pipeline provides similar functionality. This is another block step that wraps around a block of code and generes timestamps in the console output for that block. The syntax is straightforward:

```
timestamps {
  // block of code
}
```

Use secret text(s) or files(s)

This option will be present if you have installed the Credentials Binding plugin (*https://jenkins.io/doc/pipeline/steps/credentials-binding/*). Activating this option allows you to add bindings in your Jenkins jobs between credentials defined in Jenkins and environment variables. Basically, you select the credential (one that is already defined in Jenkins) and then specify an environment variable name for it. Then you can use that environment variable in your job in place of the sensitive information from the credentials. When you execute the build, the environment variable(s) will be instantiated with the actual values of the credentials.

Checking the box brings up another control that allows you to select the type of credential to add, the actual credential to use, and the environment variable that will be used in the job in place of it. See Figure 8-28 for an example.

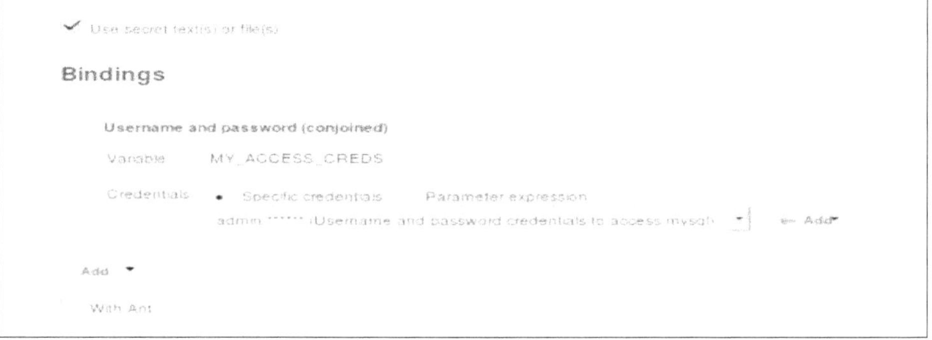

Figure 8-28. Setting up credential bindings

The With Ant option is for working with Apache Ant (doing setup, annotating Ant output, etc.).

Using credentials in a pipeline. A corresponding `withCredentials` block step exists for pipeline use. The matching step for the preceding setup in a pipeline would be:

```
withCredentials([usernameColonPassword(credentialsId:
     'mysql-access', variable: 'MY_ACCESS_CREDS')]) {
    // block of code in which you can use the variable
}
```

There is also a `withAnt` block step that corresponds to that option. See Chapter 5 for more details on using credentials in Jenkins and in pipelines.

Other build environment options

Depending on what other plugins you have installed in Jenkins and what other applications you are running on your system, you may have more environment options here. For example, if you are using the Artifactory plugin, you may have an option here to configure Artifactory integration with Ant, Gradle, or Maven.

Because of the number of possibilities we won't try to cover all of them here, but you can generally find out the details you need by clicking on the help buttons next to the options and/or going to the plugin's web page.

As far as corresponding pipeline steps, many are covered in related chapters of this book.

Build

The Build section of the configuration is where the main logic for your job goes. For many of the traditional job types that Jenkins supports, this is where the projects most extensively differentiate from one another—from the wide-open Freestyle project to the more specialized ones like Maven and Ivy. Depending on the type of project and the set of plugins and other applications you are using, you may have many different choices on this page; rather than attempting to detail all of them here, we will cover the most significant parts of each respective project type in later sections. For remaining items not covered in the project-specific sections in the chapter, refer to the help associated with each step (available via the blue help buttons as well as the plugins' web pages).

For corresponding pipeline functionality, see the other chapters of this book.

Post-Build Actions

The final configuration section allows us to select specific post-build actions for a job. These are actions that are always run after the build finishes—in some cases whether successfully or not.

Again, there are too many options based on plugins and integrations to cover here. See the help for a particular option or the plugin's web page to find out more about a particular available action.

Post-build actions in a pipeline

Post-build actions are not built in for Scripted Pipelines. Chapter 3 describes how you can use the `try-catch` Java/Groovy construct to create a workflow with similar actions.

For Declarative Pipelines, there is a specific `post` section that can be put in the pipeline to provide this functionality. See Chapter 7 for more information.

Types of Projects

Now that we have a basic understanding of the sections and options that are common to many of the Jenkins projects, we'll look at how those projects differ from one another.

The differentiation between project types can be based on one or multiple criteria, including:

- Open configuration to do any task: Freestyle, Pipeline projects
- Specialization for an application: Maven, Ivy projects
- Specialization for an advanced or challenging use case: Multiconfiguration, External Job projects
- Organizational purposes: Folder, Multibranch Pipeline, GitHub Organization, Bitbucket Team/Project projects
- Automated configuration and building: Multibranch Pipeline, GitHub Organization, Bitbucket Team/Project projects

In the following sections, we'll briefly cover the intent and main points for each of the basic set of Jenkins project types. Keep in mind that there are more aspects and details than we can cover here. Also, for many, the previous discussion of common options accounts for a substantial amount of the project's configuration.

Freestyle Projects

Freestyle projects are the traditional working base for most Jenkins jobs. The name "Freestyle" refers to the relatively open way that these projects can be constructed to do many different tasks. Prior to Pipeline projects, Freestyle projects were considered the most flexible. They were also considered the easiest to set up, at least for individual projects.

As pointed out at the start of the chapter, for the traditional Jenkins project types, what differentiated them mostly was the Build section. For Freestyle projects, probably the most common item in the Build section is a call to the shell. The Build section provides options to execute a shell call as well as a Windows batch command.

These steps are pretty straightforward; just type the command into the dialog box after selecting the type of shell step you want.

Pipeline Steps Like Freestyle

The pipeline DSL provides similar steps—one for Unix-style shells (`sh`) and one for Windows-style shells (`bat`). The `sh` and `bat` steps are described in detail in Chapter 11.

The Maven Project Type

In addition to the Freestyle project type, Jenkins also offers some project types customized for different applications. Probably the best-known legacy one is the Maven project type.

The Maven project type is intended to simplify some common tasks, such as triggering downstream dependency jobs, deploying artifacts to a Maven repo, optionally rebuilding only changed modules, and breaking out test results by module.

This type of project has a few additional options, such as a build trigger that you can set up to have the project build if dependencies are built on the same system (Figure 8-29).

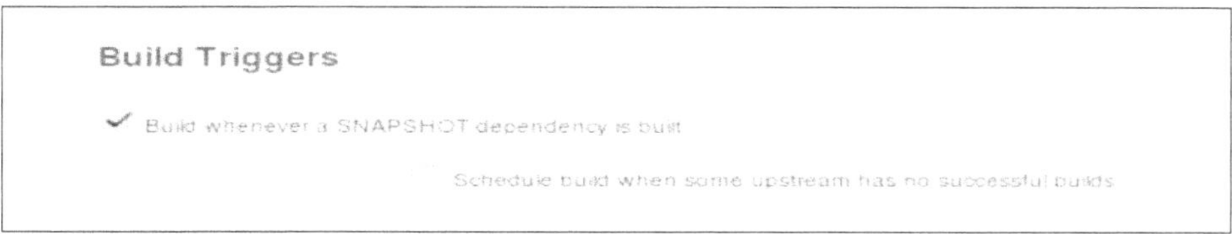

Figure 8-29. Maven project build trigger based on dependencies

Some traditional non-Maven build steps are moved to sections named Pre Steps (Figure 8-30) and Post Steps. (The same set of steps appears in both.)

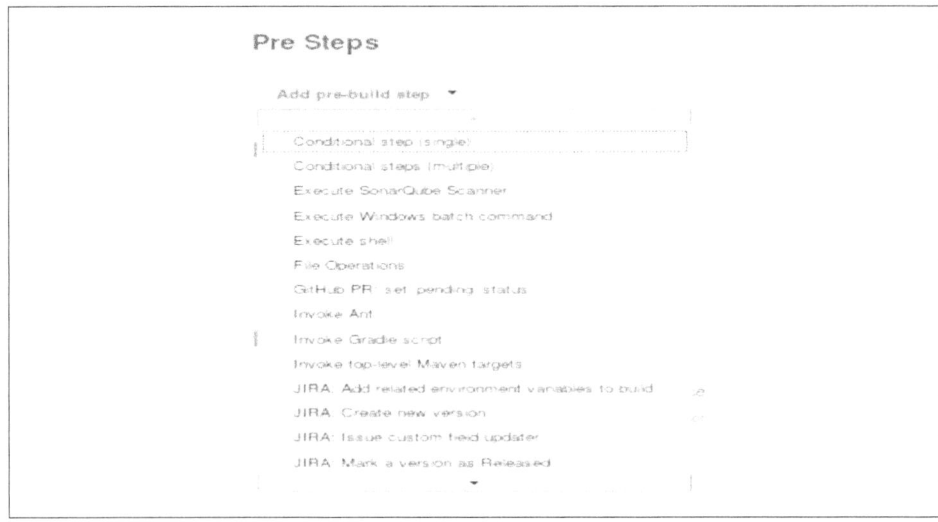

Figure 8-30. Pre-build steps defined for a Maven project

As seen in Figure 8-31, these Pre and Post Steps sections "sandwich" the main build area, where you can enter the root POM filename (if different from "pom.xml"), the Maven goals to build, and any Maven options (via the Advanced button).

Figure 8-31. Maven project primary options

Clicking the Advanced button reveals a number of other options you can set for your build (Figure 8-32).

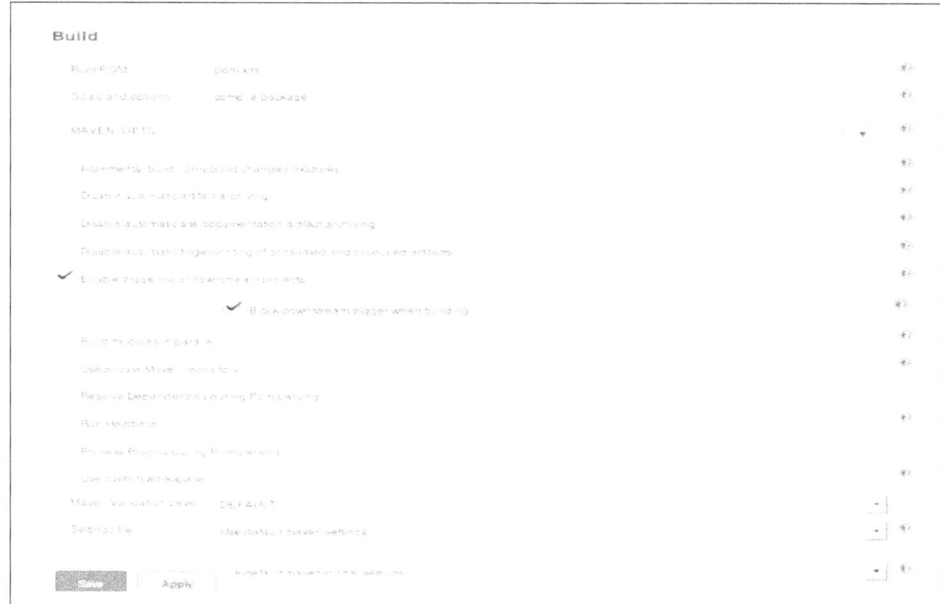

Figure 8-32. Maven project advanced options

After a successful build, Jenkins can do the archiving of your Maven artifacts for you (Figure 8-33).

```
[INFO] Downloaded: https://repo.maven.apache.org/maven2/org/codehaus/plexus/plexus-archiver
/2.8.1/plexus-archiver-2.8.1.jar (140 KB at 139.5 KB/sec)
[INFO] Downloaded: https://repo.maven.apache.org/maven2/com/google/guava/guava/18.0/guava-
18.0.jar (2204 KB at 2057.3 KB/sec)
[INFO]
[INFO] --- maven-source-plugin:3.0.1:jar-no-fork (default) @ MavenTestApp ---
[INFO] Building jar: /home/jenkins2/worker_node2/workspace/maven1/target/MavenTestApp-
sources.jar
[INFO] ------------------------------------------------------------------------
[INFO] BUILD SUCCESS
[INFO] ------------------------------------------------------------------------
[INFO] Total time: 27.346 s
[INFO] Finished at: 2017-09-25T19:34:53-05:00
[INFO] Final Memory: 43M/177M
[INFO] ------------------------------------------------------------------------
[JENKINS] Archiving /home/jenkins2/worker_node2/workspace/maven1/pom.xml to
org.demo.mavenapp/MavenTestApp/1.0-SNAPSHOT/MavenTestApp-1.0-SNAPSHOT.pom
[JENKINS] Archiving /home/jenkins2/worker_node2/workspace/maven1/target/MavenTestApp.jar to
org.demo.mavenapp/MavenTestApp/1.0-SNAPSHOT/MavenTestApp-1.0-SNAPSHOT.jar
[JENKINS] Archiving /home/jenkins2/worker_node2/workspace/maven1/target/MavenTestApp-sources.jar
to org.demo.mavenapp/MavenTestApp/1.0-SNAPSHOT/MavenTestApp-1.0-SNAPSHOT-sources.jar
channel stopped
Finished: SUCCESS
```

Figure 8-33. Automatically archiving artifacts from a Maven build

And within the job output, you can easily get to the artifacts and even redeploy them if needed: simply click on the "modules" item in the lefthand menu on the build status page and drill down to get to the various artifacts/modules (Figure 8-34).

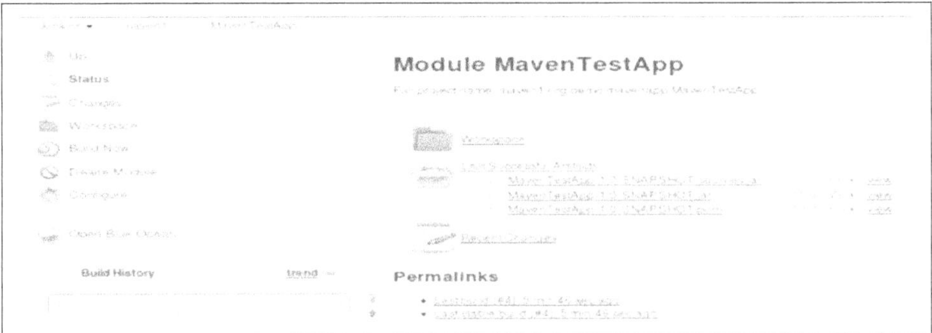

Figure 8-34. Looking at modules after a build

The Pipeline Project Type

Pipeline projects are the main focus of this book, so we won't go into too much detail on them here. The simple way to define a Pipeline project is as a Jenkins project type where the steps and logic are specified in a structured Groovy script instead of in a web form. That script can be structured in a declarative or scripted form. It can also be entered as part of a Jenkins Pipeline project or stored externally in a file named *Jenkinsfile*.

Since our focus here is on the configuration aspects of the various project types, it is worth briefly calling out some of the ways that the Pipeline project configuration overlaps with the actual pipeline scripts themselves.

On the Pipeline project configuration page, the area where you can type in the pipeline script is located in a dedicated tab/section named Pipeline (just like the General, Build Triggers, and other tabs/sections).

At the top of this section, there is a configurable option—the Definition field. The choices here are either "Pipeline script" or "Pipeline script from SCM" (Figure 8-35).

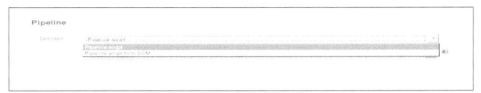

Figure 8-35. Pipeline definition option

The "Pipeline script" option represents the default: defining the script in the text entry box below the Definition field. The option that appears underneath the text entry box—"Use Groovy Sandbox"—is explained in Chapter 3.

If you instead choose the "Pipeline script from SCM" option, this will allow you to specify the location in a source management system of a Jenkinsfile to use with this job instead of entering the script in the text entry area.

Once you have selected the "Pipeline script from SCM" option, you'll be presented with additional fields to indicate where to get the script from. These fields are the typical SCM type of fields for a location, revision, etc. (see Figure 8-36).

Figure 8-36. Completing the specification to use a pipeline script from an SCM instead of entering it directly

While the Script Path field is editable here, unless you have a particular reason to use something else, the recommended approach is to stay with the Jenkinsfile in the root of the project.

The "Lightweight checkout" option refers to telling the SCM plugin to try to check out only the Jenkinsfile initially instead of the entire project. This is an efficiency to avoid checking out the entire project twice—once to get the Jenkinsfile and once when the Jenkinsfile executes the `checkout scm` statement. Note that this option may not be supported by all SCM plugins and so may not appear in all cases.

Read-Only Pipeline Definition Options

There is at least one other value you may see in the Definition field: "Pipeline from multibranch configuration" (Figure 8-37). This selection applies for the Multibranch Pipeline, GitHub Organization, and Bitbucket Team/Project types of projects, discussed later in this chapter.

While this field appears to be selectable when drilling into the configuration for those types of projects, it is automatically set and there is, by design, no way to save changes to it.

Figure 8-37. Pipeline definition field for element in a multibranch type of project

One other interaction to be aware of between the Jenkins Pipeline project configuration page and the script that defines your Jenkins pipeline has to do with setting options on the Jenkins configuration screen. In many cases, the options can be set in the configuration web interface and will define behavior for your script even though there are no lines explicitly defining or setting those options in your script.

As an example, you can select the "This project is parameterized" option on the configuration web page and define parameters through that interface. Those parameters will then be accessible in the pipeline script you define in the Pipeline section.

This behavior is both convenient and inconvenient. It is convenient while you are running your script within the context of a Pipeline project in the Jenkins application itself; you don't have to add the code in your pipeline to define those parameters. It is inconvenient if you want to use your pipeline script as a Jenkinsfile, separate from the Jenkins application itself. Then you need to go back and update the code in the script to explicitly define the parameters.

Chapter 3 discusses this particular interaction with parameters in more detail, but it is good to be aware of the interdependence between options defined only in the Jenkins application for a Pipeline project's configuration, and how those options are referenced in the pipeline script itself. A best-practice approach is to define all such options and functionality in the script.

The External Job Project Type

This type of job is intended to allow you to easily monitor an external job run via a Jenkins process. Unfortunately, the way to go about this is not clearly documented and certainly not obvious. We'll walk through the basic steps here.

When you create an External Job project, you're presented with a very simple job configuration—basically all it needs is a name (Figure 8-38).

Figure 8-38. External Job config

The idea here is that the name will map to an external job run in a process outside of the Jenkins GUI. Of course, this assumes that you have an external job you want to monitor. For an extremely simple example, suppose we have a small file called *list.sh* that just does a directory listing (with the `ls -latr` command).

To use Jenkins to monitor this, you'll need a set of JARs in place to support the external monitoring process.

On some Debian systems, you may be able to issue standard commands like:

```
sudo apt-get install jenkins-external-tool-monitor
```

But if that doesn't work, then you'll need to extract out individual JARs from the Jenkins WAR file. To do this, go to the system where you want to run the external job, get the *jenkins.war* file, and extract the following JARs from the *WEB-INF\Lib* folder into a directory:

- *jenkins-core-*.jar*
- *remoting-*.jar*
- *ant-*.jar*
- *commons-io-*.jar*
- *commons-lang-*.jar*
- *jna-posix-*.jar*
- *xstream-*.jar*

With this part of the setup done, you can create a simple wrapper file to run your command. Basically, you just need two lines. The first is to set the location of your `JENKINS_HOME` variable (if not already set in the environment).

The second line is the line that calls `java` using the WAR to run your command. It has the following syntax:

```
java -jar jenkins-core-<version-#>.jar <jenkins project name>\
 <shell executable> <command or file to monitor>
```

So, our command to run the external job and sync the results back to Jenkins could look like this:

```
export JENKINS_HOME=http://localhost:8080
java -jar jenkins-core-2.46.2.jar extern1 sh list.sh
```

Here, `extern1` is the job name we created in Jenkins and `list.sh` is our command to run. The setting of `JENKINS_HOME` and the matching job name are what make the connection with Jenkins. `sh` is just our system shell executable. You could use `cmd` and a *.bat* file on Windows.

Assume we put these lines into an executable file named *demo.sh*. If we then execute *demo.sh*, it will run `list.sh` and send the results back to the Jenkins external job. The job runs then show up in the output of our external monitoring job (as shown in Figures 8-39 and 8-40).

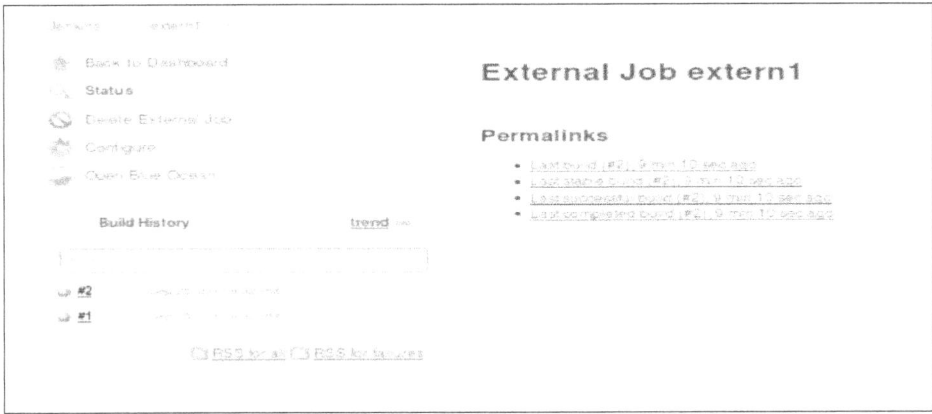

Figure 8-39. External monitoring job output

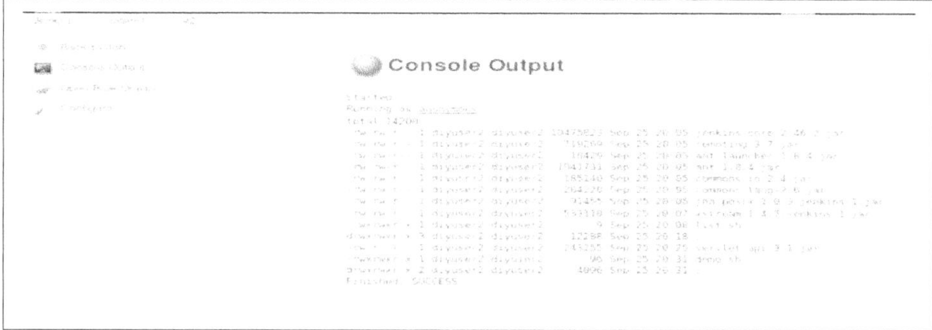

Figure 8-40. External monitor console output

Java Issues Running External Jobs

With recent versions of the external job functionality, you may get an error like this when you try to invoke `java` to run your external job:

```
Exception in thread "main"
java.lang.NoClassDefFoundError:
 javax/servlet/ServletContextListener
    at java.lang.ClassLoader.defineClass1(Native Method)
    at java.lang.ClassLoader.defineClass
       (ClassLoader.java:763)
    at java.security.SecureClassLoader.defineClass
       (SecureClassLoader.java:142)
```

If you hit this, there is a kludge you can use to get around it: find the *javax.servlet-api-<version number>.jar* file, and copy it into your JRE's *lib/ext* subdirectory. This is not elegant, but it seems to work.

The Multiconfiguration Project Type

This type of project is designed to simplify running a set of project builds that only differ in terms of parameters. For example, suppose you needed to run a test build against a set of five different browsers (IE, Firefox, Safari, etc.) and across a set of five different operating systems (Debian, Centos, Windows, etc.).

Without the Multiconfiguration project type, you would need 25 jobs (5 browsers tested against each of 5 operating systems) to accomplish this. With the Multiconfiguration type, you only need one job that does the work of executing the various possible combinations for you.

The way this works is that you define your base job to do whatever you need to do based on parameters that represent each of the different "axes" you are using. For the example just mentioned, one axis would be the set of browsers and the second would be the set of operating systems.

Like the other project types we've discussed, the Multiconfiguration project has the common setup, environment, build, post-processing, and other configuration. sections. But it also includes a separate new Configuration Matrix section. This is where you define the axes that you want to include in the job. There are three types of axes that you can create. Each one takes a name that will become an environment variable (which you can use in the build step) and a definition. The types of axes that can be added to the Configuration Matrix are:

Slaves
: This type of axis definition allows you to specify either a node's name or a label on a node to include in the set of nodes to iterate over. (As discussed elsewhere in the book, a label is simply a tag or identifying name that we can attach to one or more nodes. Then we can select one or multiple nodes by specifying a label that they have.)

Label expression
: This type of axis definition allows you to use advanced syntax to choose which set of nodes to include. For example, you can combine node labels and operators, as in `label1&&label2`, to indicate that only a node having both labels is eligible to be included.

User-defined axis
: This type allows you to specify a set of items as values to iterate over in building the set of jobs.

Multiconfiguration example

Let's consider a use case for this type of project. We have some jobs to build to create web pages for a set of company job families in each of several different regions (where each region has a dedicated node).

In our setup, we have three worker nodes available, with various labels, defined like as in Table 8-1.

Table 8-1. Available worker nodes

Name	Labels
`worker_node1`	`northwest open region1`
`worker_node2`	`northeast open region2`
`worker_node3`	`southwest restricted region3`

The regions (and thus the one-to-one mapping to the nodes) make up one of the axes our job will use. For the other, we will use a set of company job families defined as `development`, `infrastructure`, `management`, and `testing`. We can now define the two axes in our Multiconfiguration project's configuration as shown in Figure 8-41.

Figure 8-41. Defining the axes in the project's configuration

Note that within the Slaves list, we can select systems based on Labels or Individual Nodes. The latter term just means selecting them by their name (e.g., `worker_node1`).

With our axes configured, we can set up our build step to use them. The name supplied when configuring each axis becomes an environment variable we can reference in our build step. For example, if we wanted to print out a message for each combination when the build ran, we could use a simple `echo` statement like the one in Figure 8-42 in our build step.

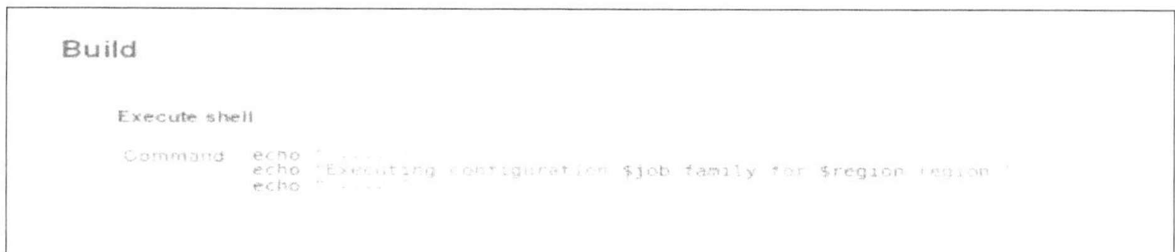

Figure 8-42. Build step using names of axes via environment variables

We can then run our build and Jenkins will automatically create the appropriate matrix of jobs to run based on the allowed combinations of our axes (Figure 8-43).

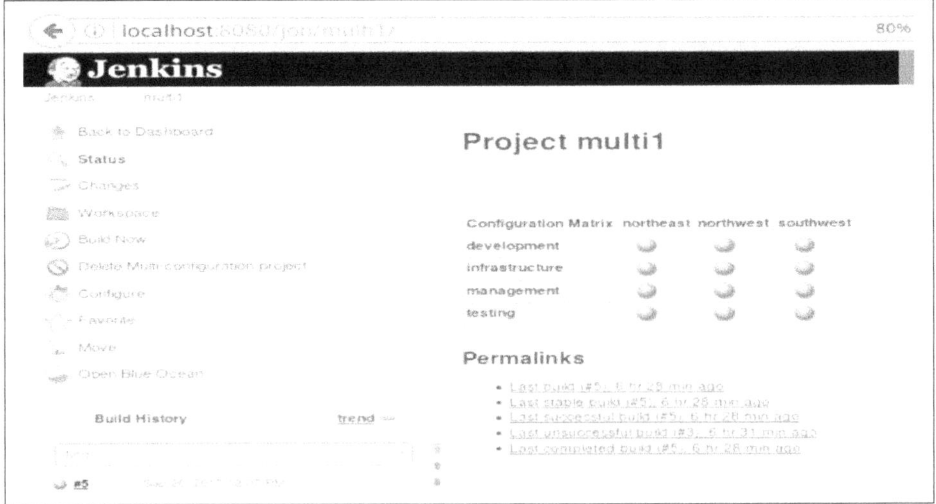

Figure 8-43. Job matrix based on axes

We can drill into any of the combinations by clicking on the blue ball in the matrix for the appropriate row and column. Figure 8-44 shows one example.

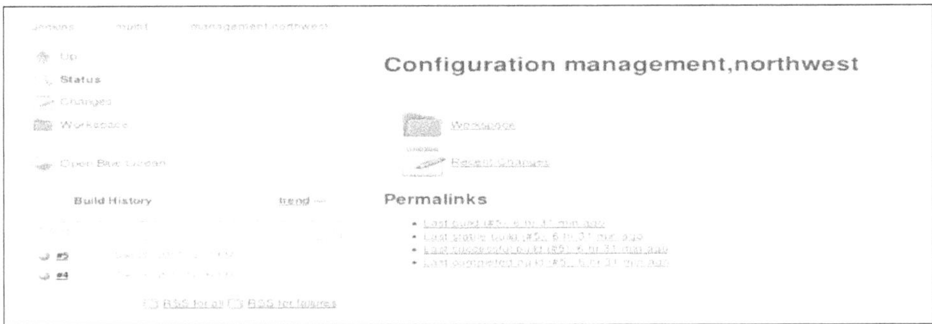

Figure 8-44. Drilling into results for a particular job

From there, we can also drill into the console output for a particular run of a job in the matrix, as shown in Figure 8-45.

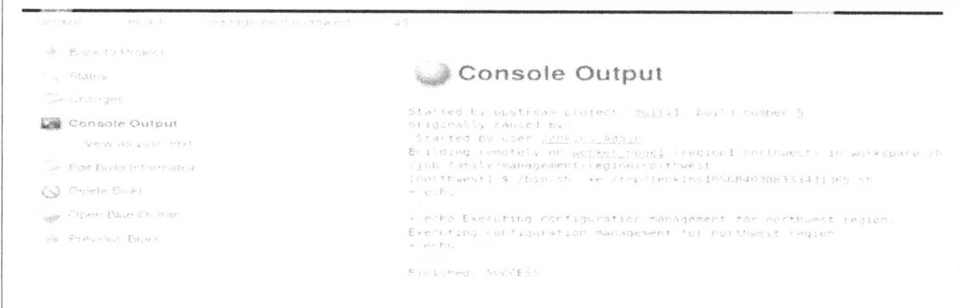

Figure 8-45. Console output for a particular job in the multiconfiguration matrix

Note that you can have more than two axes, though at some point, having more axes may get prohibitive in terms of trying to navigate through the output.

The Matrix Configuration section also includes a few additional options that may be helpful:

Combination filter
: The default for a Multiconfiguration project is for Jenkins to build all combinations of values in the defined axes. If this is too many, or you need to limit which ones it builds, you can use this area to define filters to limit which combinations are built. An example might be:

```
!(job_family=="management" && region=="northwest")
```

to prevent running the job for management in the Northwest region. Note the use of the double equals sign here to check for equality. See the help for the step for more examples.

Run each configuration sequentially
: This option tells Jenkins to build each possible combination one at a time (not in parallel). This might be needed to limit multiple jobs stepping on each other if using a shared resource, for example.

Execute touchstone builds first
: This option allows you to specify a set of builds to run first as a sort of "sanity check." Enabling this option brings up two additional fields. The first is for a combination filter (as discussed previously) to define which builds to run first. The second is to select the condition that those builds must match in order for the rest of the processing to continue (see Figure 8-46). Your choices for the second field are Stable or Unstable.

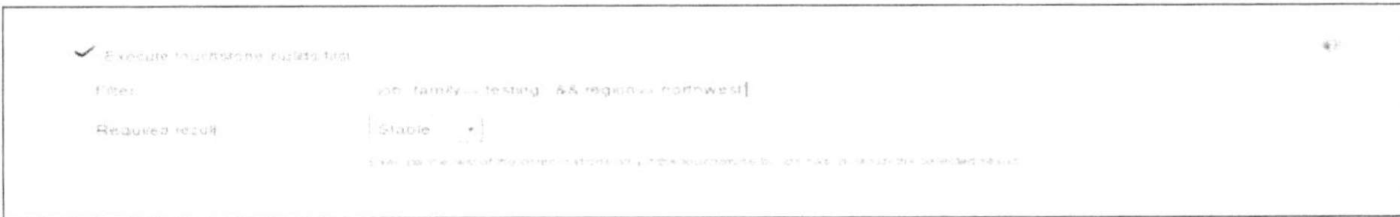

Figure 8-46. Configuring touchstone builds

With the touchstone builds in place, the overall console output for the job would look something like Figure 8-47.

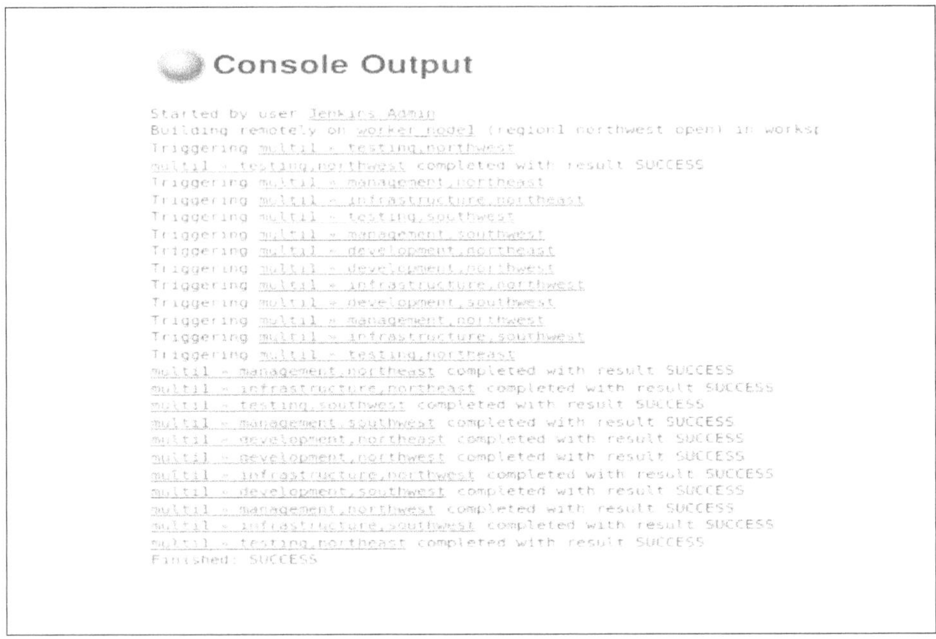

Figure 8-47. Overall console output for a Multiconfiguration job (with touchstone builds)

Notice the various links in the console output that allow you to drill down to the output for various combination builds.

Pipeline compatibility

There is no direct correlation to the Multiconfiguration project encapsulated into a single pipeline step. However, if you are working in a Scripted Pipeline, you can use Groovy looping constructs to iterate across defined "axes" and create tasks that can then be executed in parallel. Based on of a CloudBees example, here's corresponding pipeline code for the example in the previous section:

```
def axisRegions = ["northwest","northeast","southwest"]
def axisJobFamilies = ["developers","infrastructure",
```

```
 "management","testing"]
def myTasks = [:]

for(int i=0; i< axisRegions.size(); i++) {
    def axisRegionSetting = axisRegions[i]
    for(int j=0; j< axisJobFamilies.size(); j++) {
        def axisJobFamilySetting = axisJobFamilies[j]
        myTasks["${axisRegionSetting}/${axisJobFamilySetting}"] = {
            node(axisRegionSetting) {
                println "Running task on job family ${axisJobFamilySetting}
                  for region ${axisRegionSetting}"

            }
        }
    }
}

stage ("BuildMatrix") {
    parallel myTasks
}
```

For more detail on how the `parallel` step works, see Chapter 3.

Ivy Projects

In an Ivy project, Jenkins uses Ivy-related files to provide simplified build operations and additional functionality. If you're familiar with Ivy, the setup is pretty straightforward. You have the usual common options and sections we covered at the start of the chapter, and then you have an "Ivy Module Configuration" section where you can base your Ivy build off of the *ivy.xml*, *build.xml*, and other files (Figure 8-48).

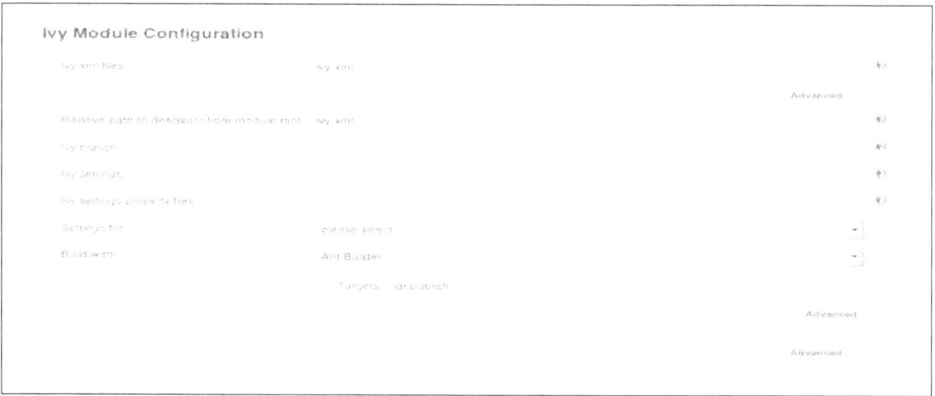

Figure 8-48. Basic configuration options

For fields that need locations, these are relative to the workspace you're using. For most of these fields, if you have a standard structure and straightforward build, you can just take the defaults. Of course, you'll need to fill in the actual targets.

Note that there are two Advanced buttons right below the Targets field. The first (top) one expands to advanced options for the "Build with" section, such as a place to specify an alternatively named build file.

The second (bottom) Advanced button expands into more options for the Ivy Module Configuration section in general, including one to build modules as separate jobs. Figure 8-49 shows both sets of expanded options.

Figure 8-49. Advanced configuration options

When you run a build, Jenkins will execute the targets and produce the appropriate artifacts, as shown by the console output in Figure 8-50.

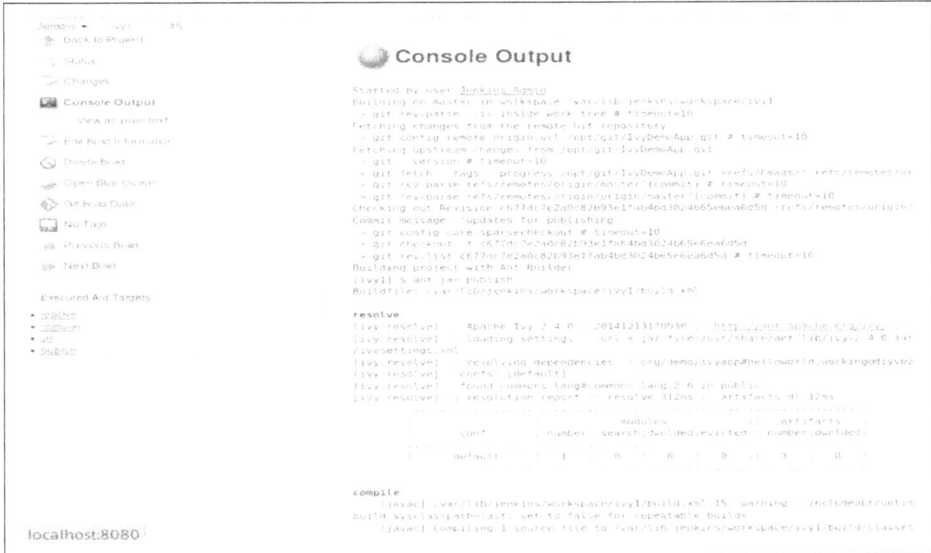

Figure 8-50. Ivy build console output

Note the list and links to executed Ant targets on the left side.

When building modules as separate jobs, you can use the Modules menu item on the left of the Ivy job's output page to go to the build information for each module. An example is shown in Figure 8-51.

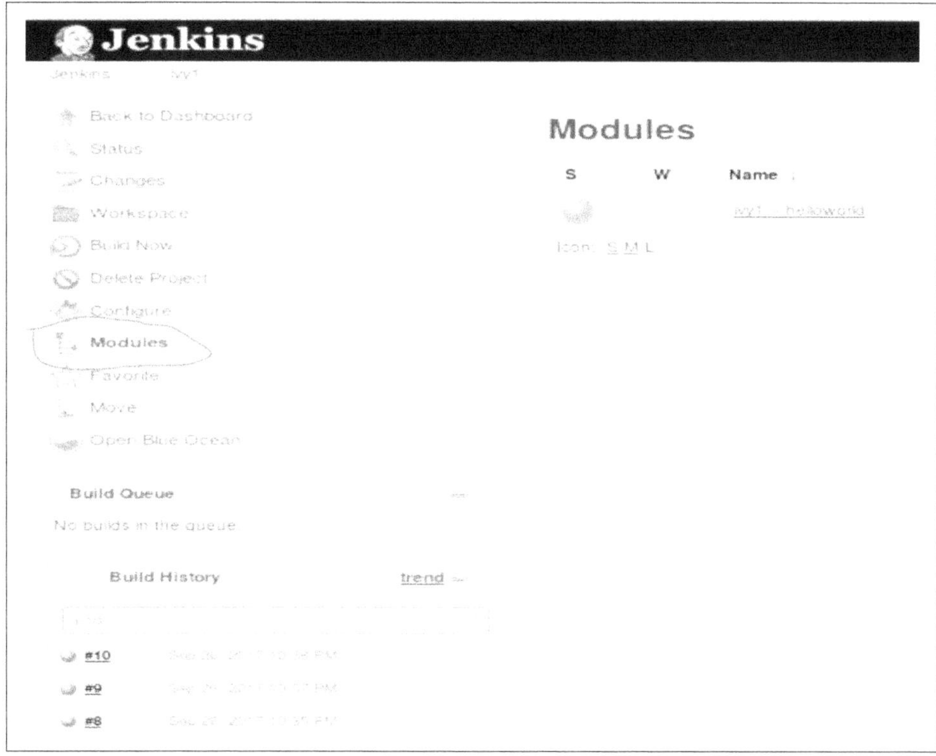

Figure 8-51. Accessing builds of individual modules in an Ivy project

Folders

One of the newer types of items you can create in Jenkins 2 is a *folder*. As the name implies, this is an organizing structure rather than a job or project. Traditionally, *views* have been used in Jenkins to filter lists of items on the dashboard. Views offered the ability to create limited lists of jobs via configuration (by clicking on the "+" tab at the top of the main project list). Figure 8-52 shows the configuration screen for a typical list view.

Figure 8-52. Configuring a typical Jenkins list view

Unlike views, folders actually add the ability to group items together into a common namespace, structure, and environment. Specifically, a folder allows a set of jobs to share:

A container
: Creating a folder creates a container to hold a set of jobs. As noted previously, this is different from a traditional Jenkins view, which only allowed filtering a list of jobs to restrict which jobs were visible.

A namespace
: This namespace also becomes part of the path to the job.

Shared libraries
: A folder can have its own set of shared libraries just for the projects in the folder.

Separate permissions
: These are available provided the Role-Based Authorization Strategy plugin is installed and role-based permissions are configured. More details on this are included later in this section.

All of these elements allow for new ways in Jenkins to organize jobs and restrict the environment in which they run. This could be used, for example, to separate or group the projects for a department or larger effort.

We'll explore some of the properties and uses of a Jenkins folder in the next section.

Creating a folder

To create a folder, select the folder item from the Jenkins dashboard (Figure 8-53) and enter a name for the folder.

Folder
Creates a container that stores nested items in it. Useful for grouping things together. Unlike view, which is just a filter, a folder creates a separate namespace, so you can have multiple things of the same name as long as they are in different folders.

Figure 8-53. Folder item

This will take you to the configuration page for the folder, an example of which is shown in Figure 8-54.

Health metrics
Child item with worst health
Add metric
Properties
JIRA
Add
Pipeline Libraries
Add
Pipeline Model Definition
Add
Apply

Figure 8-54. Folder configuration page

At the top, you can enter user-facing details such as a separate display name to show for the folder and a description.

Below that is a section for adding "health metrics"—that is, identifying properties of items in the folder that should contribute to an overall health indication (how successful or not builds for items in the folder have been). As of the time of this writing, the only available health metric is "Child item with worst health." There is also a Recursive option to indicate whether items in subfolders should contribute to this metric.

Next is a Properties section. You may or may not have anything in this section, depending on what plugins you have installed. The idea is to provide a place to define tools or setups specific to items in this folder or its subfolders (if it has any). An example here might be a JIRA project configuration for items in the folder.

Further down on the page is the section where you can configure a shared library to be available to all jobs in the folder structure (this folder and any subfolders). The same configuration fields and settings are available as for global shared libraries (see Chapter 6 for details and examples); the only differences are that these libraries are not trusted (so they cannot make unapproved calls or method invocations, as global shared libraries can), and they are only available to the items in the folder structure.

Finally, we have the Pipeline Model Definitions section. This one requires some additional explanation. (Like for shared libraries, there is also a section for this in the global Jenkins Configure System screen, so this can be configured at different granularities.)

By default, Jenkins pipelines make the assumption that all agents are able to run Docker pipelines. (See Chapter 14 for information on using Docker and Docker-based agents in your pipelines.) However, in some cases, such as if you're running on Windows, where you traditionally can't run the Docker daemon directly, this assumption can be incorrect. So, if you don't explicitly specify an agent that can run Docker in your pipeline, and you get one of the agents that can't, your pipeline won't work.

Assuming you have a label that identifies one or more of your agents as being capable of running Docker, you can specify that label here. This tells Jenkins to use one of those agents for any folder items that need Docker, but don't directly specify an agent that can run it.

Likewise, you can specify a Docker registry to use here that is scoped to just the items in the folder.

Creating items in a folder

Once you've created a new folder in Jenkins 2, you can create new items in it just like you've always done. When you switch to a Folder project, you have a link in the center of the page to "create new jobs" as well as the New Item link in the lefthand menu (Figure 8-55). (Note that there is also a Delete Folder item in the lefthand menu.)

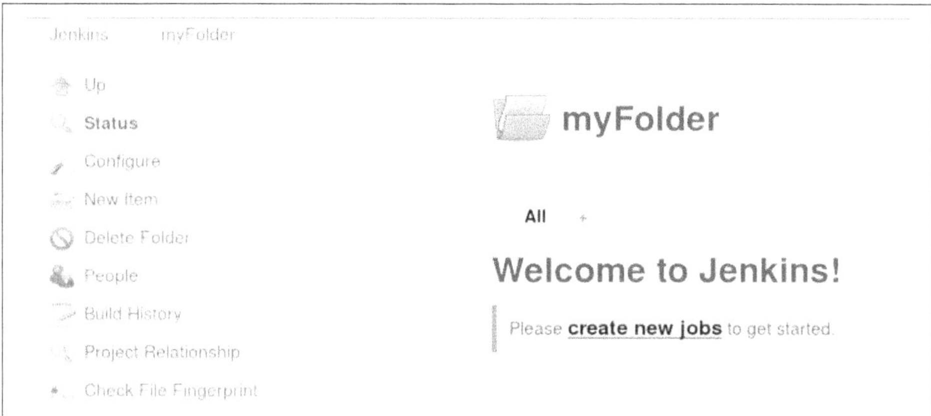

Figure 8-55. Folder links

Views Within Folders

On the main folder page, you'll also see two small tabs—one that says All and one that has a + sign in it. These are tabs for working with view of jobs in this folder. Just like in the dashboard view, the All tab shows all jobs in the folder. The + tab takes you to a screen where you can configure custom list views of the jobs in the folder.

Clicking on either of these item creation options takes you to the same screen you always use for this. The only difference is that any items you create at this point are organized under the folder's namespace, and the full name of the new item will include that namespace.

This is just like creating a file within a directory on the operating system, and just as you can create directories within directories, you can also create folders within folders in Jenkins.

Moving existing items into a folder

In addition to being able to create new items in a folder, you can also move existing items into a folder. The key is the "move" icon in the lefthand menu of the main page of an item. This is the icon that looks like a hand truck. (You can also just add "move" at the end of the URL for a job.) Once you select that icon, you will have a drop-down list to select the folder to move the item to (Figure 8-56). You simply select the destination and then click the Move button.

Figure 8-56. Moving an item to a folder

You can also move an item from a folder back up to the top level in Jenkins by selecting "Jenkins" in the list of destinations.

Managing permissions for folders

If you need to manage permissions separately for items in a folder, take a look at the Role-based Authorization Strategy plugin. This plugin allows you to define roles and groups around items in Jenkins. This is especially useful if you have multiple teams sharing a Jenkins instance.

An administrator can create groups in a folder around each defined role that a user can have. A team leader can then be authorized to manage group membership for the groups in a folder.

The Role-based Authorization Strategy plugin is covered in more detail in Chapter 5.

Multibranch Pipeline Projects

One of the other new project types in Jenkins 2 is the Multibranch Pipeline project. The primary feature of this type of project is that Jenkins can automatically manage and build branches of projects managed in a source control management system if it recognizes them as Jenkins projects. It can also create new Pipeline projects for each branch it detects in the source control repository.

You can effectively think of this type of project as a Folder project with different jobs in the folder for each branch of a source project. Creating and automatically building these jobs is possible by using the presence of a Jenkinsfile as a marker and utilizing a scanning process known as *branch indexing*.

Configuration

When you create a new Multibranch Pipeline project, you will typically point the job to an SCM repository instead of to a specific branch of a project. Figure 8-57 shows an example of the configuration screen for this type of project.

Figure 8-57. Example Multibranch Pipeline project config screen

The first few settings here are pretty standard. However, notice that in the Behaviors section under Branch Sources, there is a default behavior of "Discover branches." This is one of the key elements of a Multibranch Pipeline project: the ability to look into the SCM repository, figure out what branches are there, and set up jobs for them. Other typical behaviors (as provided by the particular SCM plugin) can be added with the Add button. For Git, these might include, for example, ignoring branches based on patterns, specifying options when cloning, and cleaning out workspaces.

Underneath that is the "Property strategy" section. For Multibranch Pipeline projects, this is either "All branches get the same properties" or "Named branches get different properties." Selecting the latter allows you to specify one or more named branches (in a "Branch name" field) and choose a property to apply. Currently the only available property is "Suppress SCM triggering," which suppresses the normal commit trigger for Jenkins in that branch.

In the Build Configuration section, we have only one option currently: "by Jenkinsfile." This is the functionality we've already talked about where Jenkins will look for a file named *Jenkinsfile* in the root of the checked-out project to see if it can automatically build the branch of a project. While you could change the path for the Jenkinsfile in the Script Path field underneath, it's best to just leave it as the default for standardization.

Next on that page is a Scan Multibranch Pipeline Triggers setting. This can be set to "Periodically if not otherwise run" if desired. Basically, if set, this is a fallback in case one of the standard notification mechanisms (commit trigger, etc.) doesn't work. The idea is that you can set a time interval here that specifies the longest period you're willing to wait to check for changes if an event doesn't automatically trigger Jenkins.

The remaining sections on the configuration page are the same as the standard ones for a Folder project, such as "Health metrics," Pipeline Libraries, and Pipeline Model Definition. These are discussed in "Folders" on page 297.

Branch indexing

After initial configuration, Jenkins will run a "branch indexing" function to look for the presence of a Jenkinsfile in the branches of the project. If it finds a Jenkinsfile in any of the branches, it will automatically create a job for those branches and build them. Figure 8-58 shows what this looks like in the console output for the overall job. Notice the places in the log where Jenkins is checking to see if the branch meets the criterion of having a Jenkinsfile and, if so, kicking off a build for it. You can see the builds running in the lower-left build section.

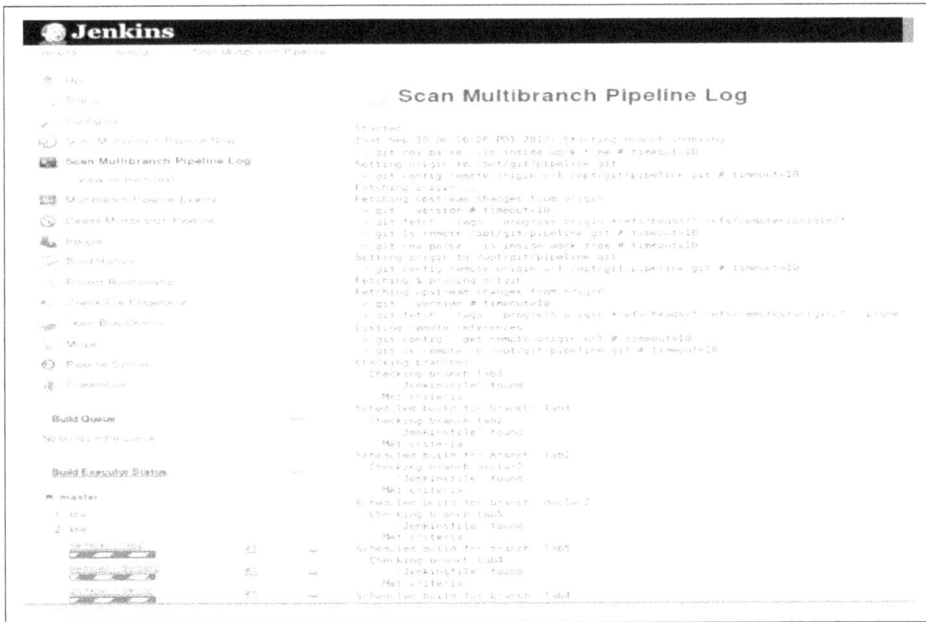

Figure 8-58. Automatic branch scanning after initial configuration

After the branch indexing completes, you'll have individual jobs for each of the matching branches within your Multibranch Pipeline project (Figure 8-59).

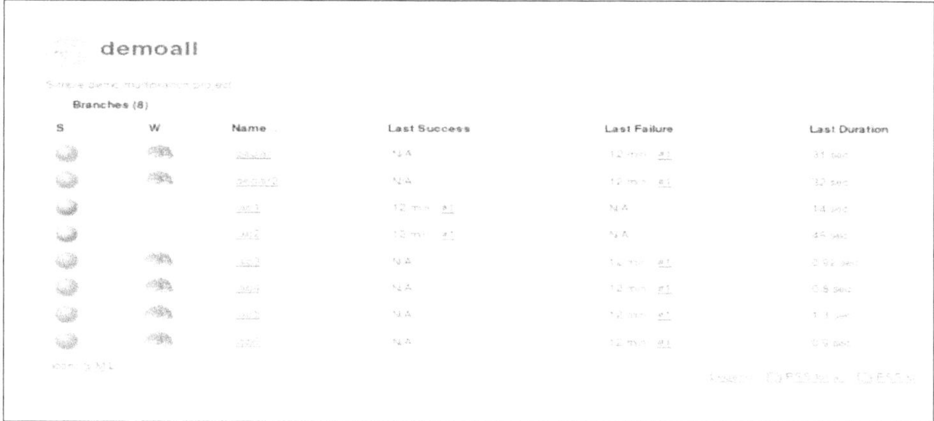

Figure 8-59. Multibranch Pipeline jobs corresponding to branches with Jenkinsfiles

Individual job output and configuration

You can drill into each of the individual jobs created automatically for the project and see the output/build results page in the Stage View form.

There is also a View Configuration link on that page. If you click that link, it will take you to a configuration page for the individual job. On that page you will see some of the common sections we have talked about previously, such as General and Build Triggers. You can check boxes in these sections, type things in, etc. However, this is a bit misleading as there is no Save or Apply button at the bottom of the page. As the menu item implies, you can view the configuration (which isn't particularly useful in this case), but you can't modify it. It is generated by the branch indexing functionality of the higher-level Multibranch Pipeline project.

Not being able to configure the individual jobs here might seem like a disadvantage, but remember that you can manage your pipeline through the Jenkinsfile instead of through the job's configuration.

Incorporating new branches

Once you have a Multibranch Pipeline project set up, Jenkins can automatically detect new branches and create corresponding jobs for them as well. Let's look at an example.

Suppose that you have a Multibranch Pipeline project set up in Jenkins for a local Git location. In your repository, you have a `master` branch that does not have a Jenkinsfile, and a branch named `test` that has a Jenkinsfile in it. Since you have set up a Multibranch Pipeline project, you have a job for `test` in Jenkins that was created automatically. There isn't a job for `master`, because it did not have a Jenkinsfile.

Now suppose you clone that repository down and create a new branch called `newbranch` from `test`. `newbranch` inherits all of the files from `test`, including the Jenkinsfile.

Next, you push the changes back to the remote Git repository. At this point, if you go back into Jenkins and tell it to run the branch indexing, it will go out to the repository and check each branch. Figure 8-60 shows the branch indexing running.

Figure 8-60. Branch indexing after newbranch is created

Jenkins identifies that the new branch "Met criteria." This means that it has a Jenkinsfile. So, Jenkins creates a new job for it (Figure 8-61) and starts up a build for it (Figure 8-62).

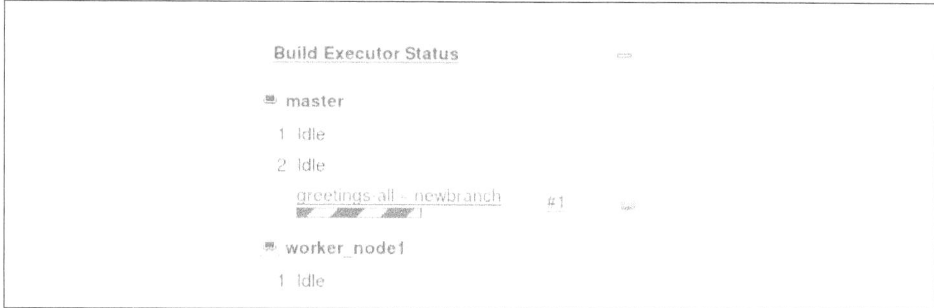

Figure 8-61. Kicking off a build for newbranch

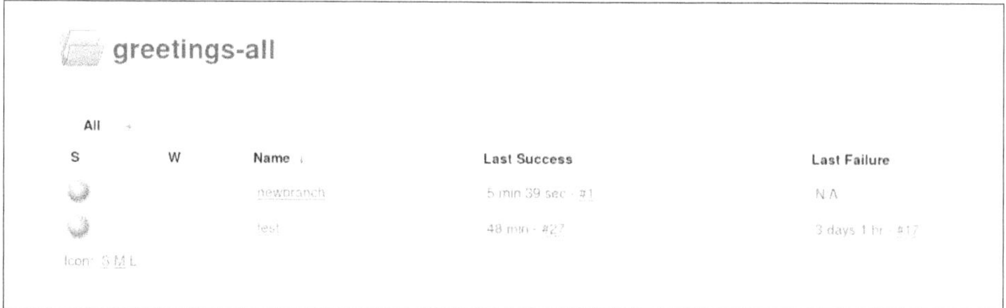

Figure 8-62. The new job for newbranch in the Multibranch Pipeline project

The nice thing about this setup is that it allows you to create branches in Git as you need them (for experimentation, for example) and automatically have corresponding Jenkins jobs created to execute the pipeline on those branches.

Branch Indexing Versus Build Now

One final note here regarding branch indexing and jobs in a Multibranch Pipeline project. You have two ways to manually kick off builds for the jobs. First, you can initiate the branch indexing functionality by clicking the Scan Multibranch Pipeline Now entry in the lefthand menu.

Second, for each individual job, you can go to the job's page and tell it to Build Now, just as for any other job. However, be aware that even if you have already built the new changes via Build Now, when you run branch indexing again it will still rebuild the project a second time for the same changes.

GitHub Organization Projects

GitHub is a popular hosting site for open-source projects developed with Git. A GitHub Organization is a collection of such projects, with infrastructure that provides for setting up groups (called *teams*), that can have different access to sets of projects. A typical use for a GitHub Organization would be to group together, under a single umbrella, a company's collection of projects. To make it easy for an entire GitHub organization to work with Jenkins, Jenkins provides the GitHub Organization project type.

Types of Organization Projects

While we are using GitHub here as our detailed example of an organization project, it should be noted that Bitbucket repositories can also have "organization" projects (and other types may be added later). We'll cover accessing a Bitbucket Team/Project project as far as setting it up. From there, the general ideas and overall mechanics we outline here for GitHub Organization projects should apply to the other types as well.

In terms of structure, it is probably easiest to think of a GitHub Organization project as a collection of Multibranch Pipeline projects, with each multibranch area corresponding to one repository in the GitHub organization.

And, like in a Multibranch Pipeline project, Jenkins relies on there being a Jenkinsfile in each branch of each repository in the GitHub organization that you want to work with. For each repository in the organization, Jenkins will create a corresponding Multibranch Pipeline project with corresponding jobs for each branch (assuming they have Jenkinsfiles).

Creating a GitHub Organization project

Before creating a GitHub Organization project, you'll need to make sure that you have the GitHub plugin installed and a GitHub server configured in the Configure System settings. The setup for that is pretty straightforward (see "GitHub project" on page 255).

Assuming that is in place, to create a GitHub Organization project, you simply supply a project name and select the entry for it from the new item screen, as shown in Figure 8-63.

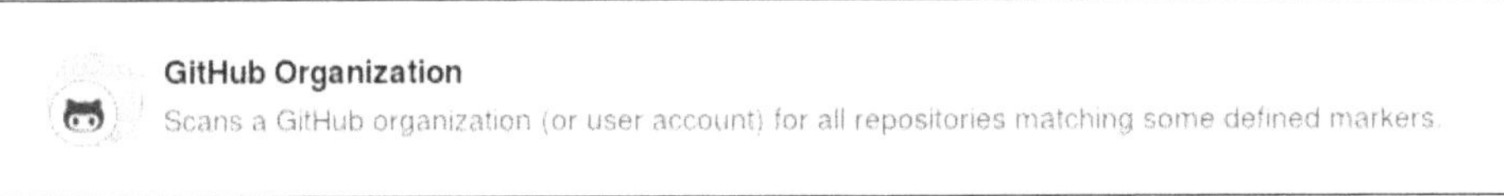
GitHub Organization
Scans a GitHub organization (or user account) for all repositories matching some defined markers.

Figure 8-63. Item to create a GitHub Organization project

In order for Jenkins to be able to locate and work with the GitHub organization, you first have to tell it the name of the organization and supply any needed credentials to access it (Figure 8-64).

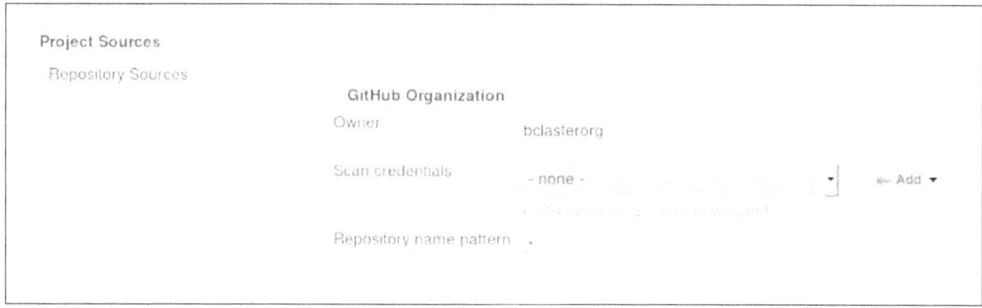

Figure 8-64. Pointing Jenkins to the GitHub organization

Credentials for GitHub

Note that Jenkins can generate a token type of credential based on your GitHub username and password. We discussed this in more detail in "GitHub hook trigger for Git polling" on page 263.

In addition to the basic source configuration, you can also add additional advanced behaviors. Many of these are geared around automatic discovery or inclusion/exclusion of branches, projects, and pull requests. There are help buttons available for most of these next to the fields themselves. If your intent is just to have Jenkins work with every project and branch that has a Jenkinsfile, then you probably don't need to change these.

The rest of the options for a GitHub Organization project are the same ones we've already covered in earlier sections of this chapter; they include configuring shared libraries local to the project, health metrics, and a pipeline model definition (for Docker agents). See the other sections for relevant details.

The last option on the configuration page deserves a little bit of explanation. Under the heading "Automatic branch project triggering" is a field for "Branch names to build automatically." This field takes a regular expression specifying which branches to actually build when triggered. This doesn't keep Jenkins from creating jobs automatically, just from building if changes are indicated. By default, the regular expression is set to have all branches build.

Webhooks

The other significant aspect of a GitHub organization project is that it can leverage webhooks sent by the GitHub organization. Webhooks allow applications to "subscribe" to events that happen on GitHub. When one of those events happens, an

HTTP POST is made to a specified external URL to notify it of the event. GitHub also sends any additional configured information as the webhook's payload.

With appropriate permissions, Jenkins can even set up the webhook automatically. Note that in order for all of this to work, Jenkins must have access to the GitHub organization to set up the webhook, and Jenkins must be accessible for GitHub to complete the POST. This means, for example, that the Jenkins URL can't be behind a firewall.

An example of the GitHub setup is shown in Figure 8-65, and an example of a webhook payload is shown in Figure 8-66.

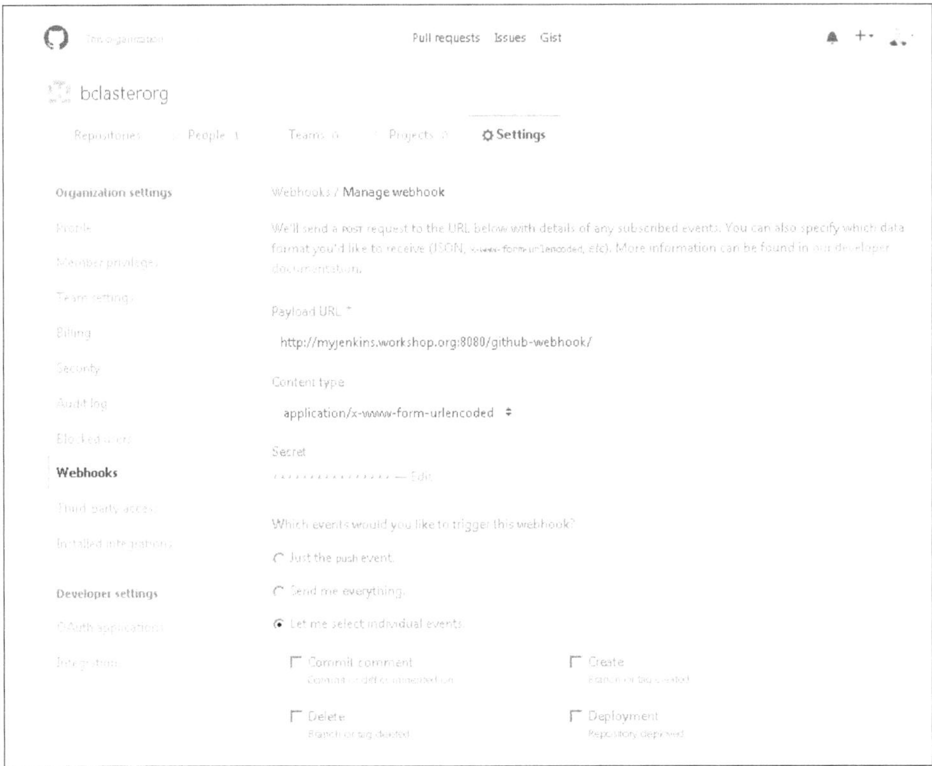

Figure 8-65. Example GitHub webhook setup

Payload


```
{
  "ref": "refs/heads/master",
  "before": "cce532c6b3813eea37707d6a600dabc5c403959b",
  "after": "923f56aee10e5e0941c913fb7ae989f6fc60b4b7",
  "created": false,
  "deleted": false,
  "forced": false,
  "base_ref": null,
  "compare": "https://github.com/bclasterorg/greetings/compare/cce532c6b381...923f56aee10e",
  "commits": [
    {
      "id": "923f56aee10e5e0941c913fb7ae989f6fc60b4b7",
      "tree_id": "35d8462f385fdb599ed5f10c3d71f2ba32eac862",
      "distinct": true,
      "message": "update for testing",
      "timestamp": "2017-10-01T08:47:17-04:00",
      "url": "https://github.com/bclasterorg/greetings/commit/923f56aee10e5e0941c913fb7ae989f6fc60b4
      "author": {
        "name": "Brent Laster",
        "email": "bcl@nclasters.org"
      },
      "committer": {
        "name": "Brent Laster",
        "email": "bcl@nclasters.org"
      },
      "added": [

      ],
      "removed": [

      ],
      "modified": [
        "helloWorkshop.java"
      ]
    }
  ],
  "head_commit": {
    "id": "923f56aee10e5e0941c913fb7ae989f6fc60b4b7",
    "tree_id": "35d8462f385fdb599ed5f10c3d71f2ba32eac862",
    "distinct": true,
    "message": "update for testing",
    "timestamp": "2017-10-01T08:47:17-04:00",
    "url": "https://github.com/bclasterorg/greetings/commit/923f56aee10e5e0941c913fb7ae989f6fc60b4b7
    "author": {
      "name": "Brent Laster",
```


Figure 8-66. Part of an example webhook payload

In addition to the webhook push technology, the GitHub Organization project includes a way to "scan" the organization to check for any pull requests or updates. This is done by selecting the "Scan Organization" menu item in the upper-left menu. You can think of this as rerunning branch indexing for each project in the organization. Figure 8-67 shows an example of running this.

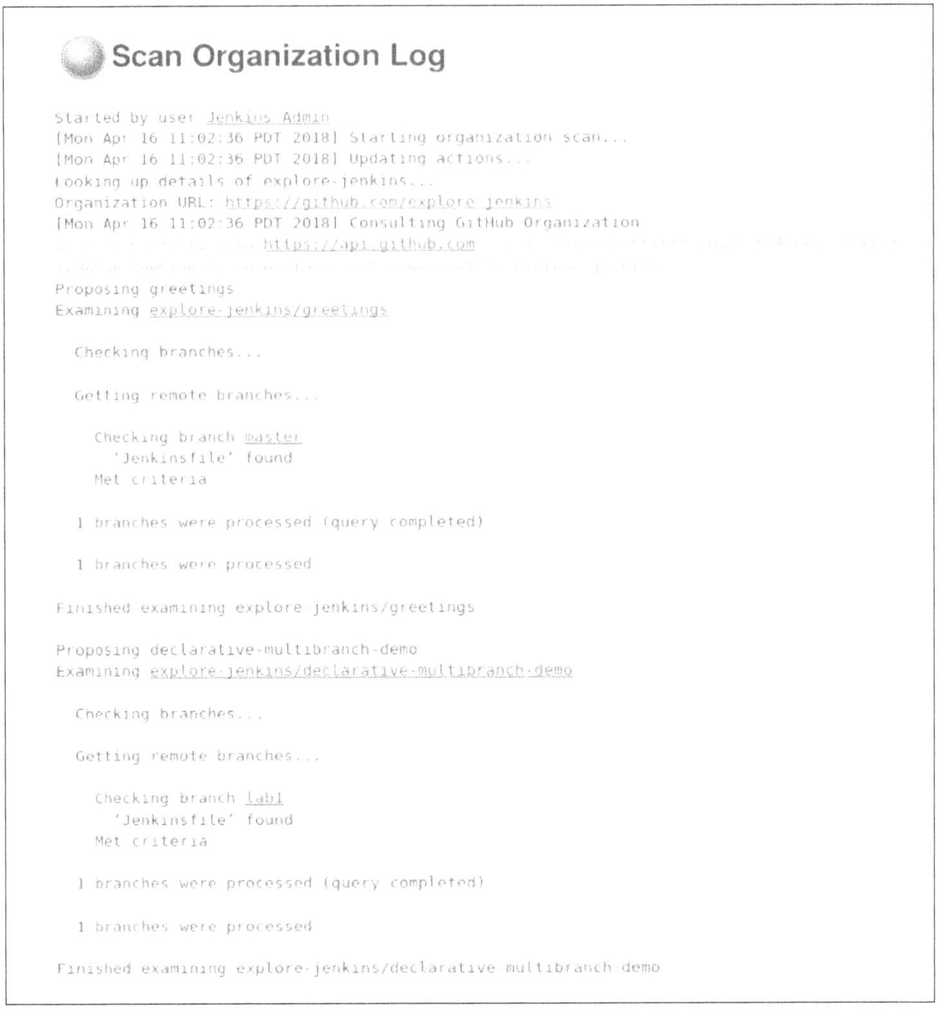

Scan Organization Log

```
Started by user Jenkins Admin
[Mon Apr 16 11:02:36 PDT 2018] Starting organization scan...
[Mon Apr 16 11:02:36 PDT 2018] Updating actions...
Looking up details of explore-jenkins...
Organization URL: https://github.com/explore-jenkins
[Mon Apr 16 11:02:36 PDT 2018] Consulting GitHub Organization
[illegible] https://api.github.com [illegible]
[illegible]
Proposing greetings
Examining explore-jenkins/greetings

  Checking branches...

  Getting remote branches...

    Checking branch master
      'Jenkinsfile' found
    Met criteria

  1 branches were processed (query completed)

  1 branches were processed

Finished examining explore-jenkins/greetings

Proposing declarative-multibranch-demo
Examining explore-jenkins/declarative-multibranch-demo

  Checking branches...

  Getting remote branches...

    Checking branch lab1
      'Jenkinsfile' found
    Met criteria

  1 branches were processed (query completed)

  1 branches were processed

Finished examining explore-jenkins/declarative-multibranch-demo
```

Figure 8-67. Re-scanning the GitHub organization to check for changes

Bitbucket Team/Project Projects

This is another type of "organization" project. "Bitbucket Team" here refers to a grouping of projects associated with a team on the public Bitbucket site. "Bitbucket Project" refers to a Bitbucket Server instance installed at an enterprise. The example we'll use here is with a team setup.

The functionality is supplied by the Bitbucket Branch Source plugin (*https://plugins.jenkins.io/cloudbees-bitbucket-branch-source*). To set up a new Bitbucket Team/Project project, you simply select that type from the list of projects (Figure 8-68).

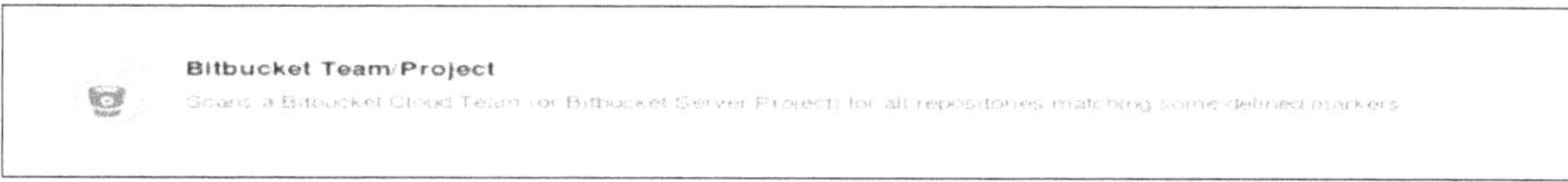

Figure 8-68. Bitbucket Team/Project type selection

Configuration for a Bitbucket Team/Project project is almost the same as for a GitHub Organization project (Figure 8-69). The prerequisite is to have a username/password credential already set up in Jenkins, with the email address and password that you use to log in to Bitbucket. The only other trick is that the Owner field needs to be a team name (not a username) that you have already set up on Bitbucket, and should not have any special characters such as hyphens or spaces in it. (That is the way that Bitbucket stores it, though it may display it differently.)

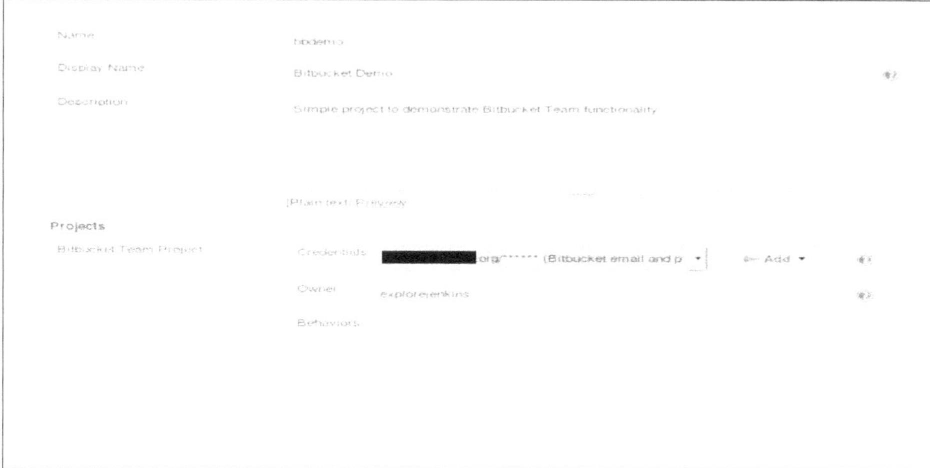

Figure 8-69. Bitbucket Team/Project project configuration

From here on, the workflow is pretty much the same as for the GitHub Organization project type discussed in the previous section. Bitbucket connects via the supplied credentials, scans the projects associated with the team specified in the Owner field, and creates Multibranch Pipeline projects for each acceptable repository it finds (Figure 8-70).

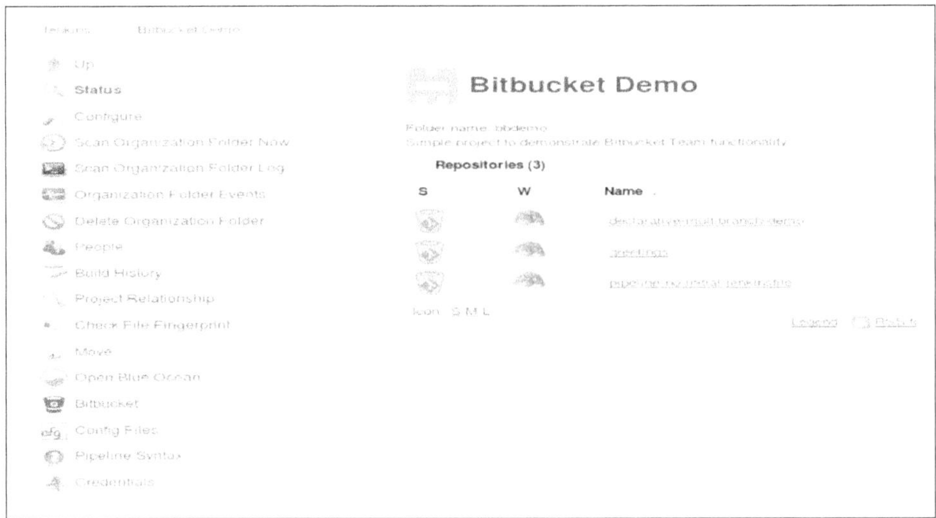

Figure 8-70. Bitbucket Team/Project project created via organization scan in Jenkins

Then, within each repository, for branches that have Jenkinsfiles, it initiates builds (Figure 8-71).

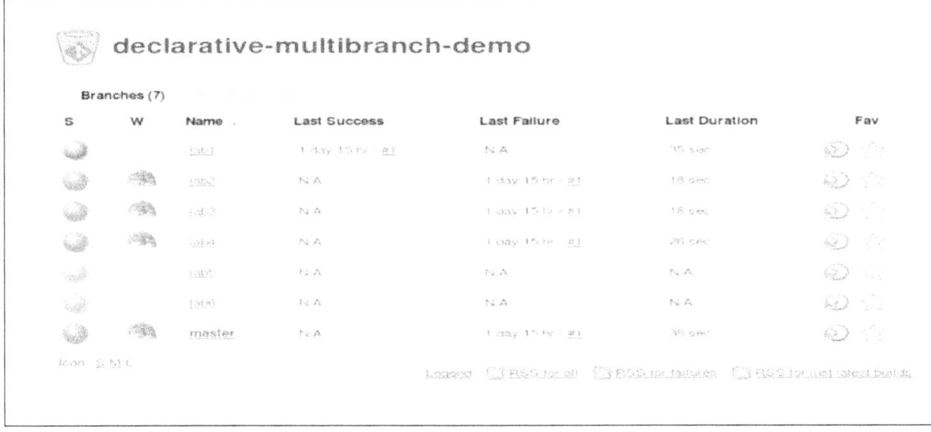

Figure 8-71. Builds within a repository of a Bitbucket team

Project Icons

To help you visually distinguish the different types of projects (jobs) in the list view, Jenkins 2 introduces some additional icons. A sampling of these is shown in Figure 8-72 (in the "S" column).

Figure 8-72. Example icons for different project types

The first icon at the top is the traditional one for common Jenkins jobs.

The second and fourth ones are organizational projects (Bitbucket and GitHub, respectively) that have been fully configured and so get the icons of the configured organizations from those sites.

The third icon is an example of a simple project from GitHub.

The fifth icon is a new GitHub Organization project that has not been fully configured.

The sixth icon is a new Bitbucket Team/Project project that has not been fully configured.

The seventh icon is for a Folder project/structure.

The eighth and last icon is for a Multibranch Pipeline project.

An example of one additional type of icon can be seen in Figure 8-70. The icon for each of the three ervitems in that project represents a Git project stored in Bitbucket.

Summary

In this chapter, we dove into more detail the set of common project types available to Jenkins users. While the book focuses on elements of Pipeline projects, Jenkins supports a number of legacy types of projects that are still actively used and useful. As well, with the advent of Jenkins 2, a number of additional project types have been introduced.

The new project types allow the user to have Jenkins automatically detect projects that it can work with in source control. It does this by looking for a Jenkinsfile as a marker, and automatically creating a job for a branch in a project that has such a file. Additionally, the new Folder type allows for grouping branch jobs together in a single project as a Multibranch Pipeline configuration. And sets of projects can be grouped together as multiple folders in a GitHub Organization Organization or Bitbucket Team/Project configuration.

In addition to exploring the overall project types, we also saw details about many of the common configuration options available to projects and looked at the corresponding pipeline statements where available. Armed with this knowledge, you should not only be able to choose the best project type for your use case (if not Pipeline), but also have the background to more easily convert existing functionality into pipeline form.

In the next chapter we'll take a look at Jenkins's new alternative user interface, Blue Ocean, and we'll see what some of the pipeline-oriented project types we've discussed look like in that interface.

CHAPTER 9

The Blue Ocean Interface

As well as the new Declarative Pipeline syntax, one of the key innovations in Jenkins 2 is the new graphical interface, Blue Ocean. At a high level, we can summarize the features of Blue Ocean as follows:

- Provides a graphical representation of pipeline processing
- Provides a graphical interface for creating new Declarative Pipelines
- Provides a more segmented view of pipeline processing at the level of the stages in the pipeline, including being able to drill into logs at that level
- Supports views by branches for Multibranch Pipeline projects
- Supports working with pull requests for Multibranch Pipeline projects
- Provides a guided setup for new pipelines from source management repositories
- Provides a pipeline editor based on adding stages, steps, etc., through a combination of interaction with graphical (point-and-click) elements and typing
- Can better represent parallel stages in comparison to the Stage View output
- Provides links back to the "classic" (legacy) Jenkins view for corresponding items or those that do not have a custom Blue Ocean representation

The interface keys off of the stage definitions in the pipeline and adds graphical elements to represent each stage. Those representations include circular icons and colors to represent the processing progress and the resulting states of success and failure.

You can also view logs segmented by steps and click through to get more details.

That's the very high-level view of the new interface. As with the traditional Jenkins interface, it's easiest to understand the available functionality by presenting the various screens and options with example jobs.

The remainder of this chapter is divided into two parts. Part 1 takes you through the various screens, pages, and views associated with managing existing pipelines that are being executed. Part 2 takes you through working with the pipeline editor to create, edit, and debug pipelines. Together, both parts will provide you with a well-rounded understanding of Blue Ocean.

Existing Issues

While Blue Ocean provides an immense amount of functionality, it's important to note that it is still relatively early in terms of formal releases as of the time of this writing. A number of issues may be encountered with using it beyond the basic, core functionality. In particular, when working with the pipeline editor, certain syntax that is valid for Declarative Pipelines cannot be entered or handled through the editor interface.

Where these issues currently occur, we will note them and, where possible, suggest workarounds.

You're encouraged to always check the latest version of Blue Ocean and Jenkins to see whether a particular issue noted here has been fixed.

Part 1: Managing Existing Pipelines

In this first part of the chapter, we'll cover using the Blue Ocean interface to see how it handles the execution and output of existing pipelines. The easiest way to do this is to walk through the different screens you will be exposed to, and discuss the functionality and features of each.

We'll start where we always start with Jenkins: the dashboard.

The Dashboard

The main menu on the lefthand side of the Jenkins dashboard contains a menu option to launch the Blue Ocean interface (see Figure 9-1).

Figure 9-1. Menu option to open Blue Ocean

You can also launch the interface directly by entering the URL in your browser. The shortest version is *<your Jenkins URL>/blue*. Either the menu item or the URL will open up the Blue Ocean dashboard, as shown in Figure 9-2.

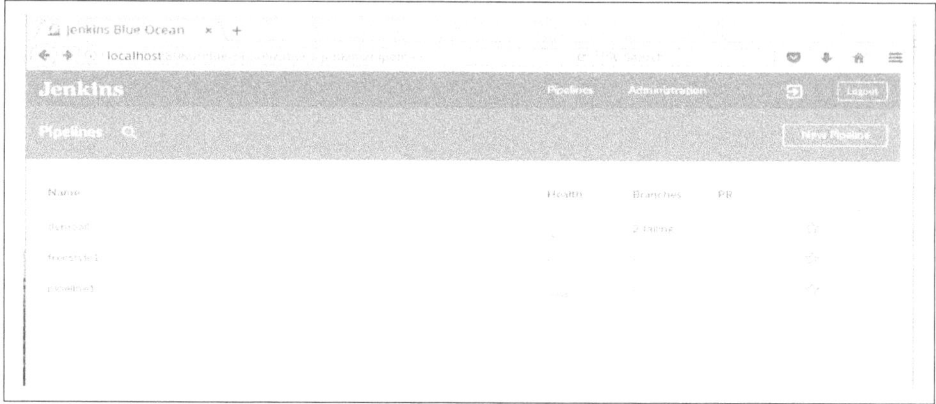

Figure 9-2. The Blue Ocean dashboard

The Pipelines Page

Note that the dashboard here maps to a more specific "pipelines" URL. In fact, we could refer to the dashboard page as the "pipelines" page.

Like the traditional Jenkins dashboard, this page lists your Jenkins jobs. Although it's focused on Pipeline projects, all of your jobs will show up here.

To understand this page completely, let's discuss the various navigational links and elements available on it.

In the top blue bar, the terms "Jenkins" and "Pipelines" are links that take you to this same page. They are useful in certain cases—for example, if you have done an operation such as a search that filters the job list, and you then want to get back to the full list.

The Administration item in the same row links to the traditional Manage Jenkins page for administering settings for the Jenkins instance.

The square icon with the arrow pointing to the right takes you back to the classic Jenkins dashboard, and the Logout button should be self-explanatory.

In the next row, the Pipelines link serves the same purpose as the Pipelines link in the row above it that we just mentioned.

Next to that, the magnifying glass is a search function (as you might expect). Clicking on it allows you to type in an expression to search for among the names of the listed pipelines. For example, as seen in Figure 9-3, if we click in the search area and enter an "o," the list will change to showing only those projects that have an "o" in their name.

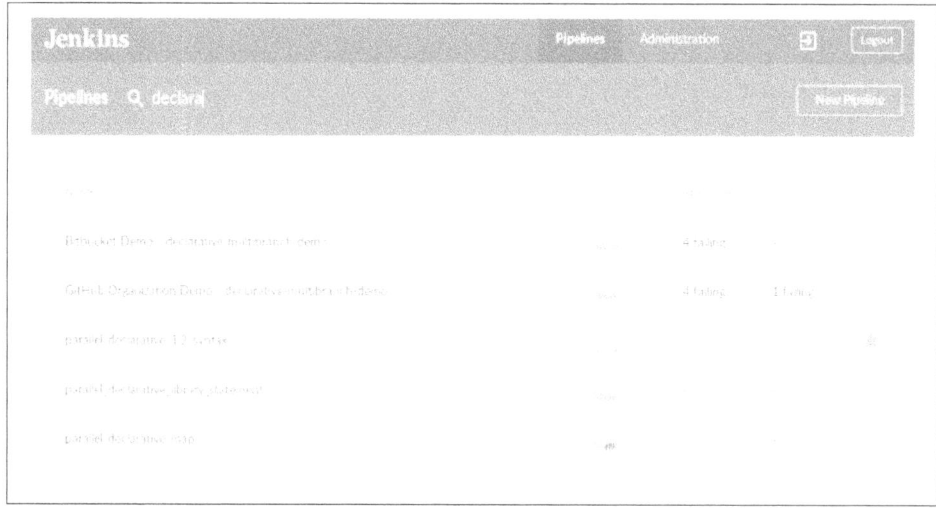

Figure 9-3. Using the search function on the Blue Ocean dashboard

The New Pipeline button can be used to create a new pipeline—we'll cover that functionality in another section of the chapter.

Underneath the top blue rows, you have the main part of the page that lists the projects/jobs currently defined in the Jenkins instance. The fields for each project row are described in Table 9-1.

Table 9-1. Dashboard field descriptions

Field	Description
Name	Name of the project
Health	Jenkins health indicator (success or failure over last few runs of the job)
Branches	For Multibranch Pipeline projects, status of last branch builds
PR	Status of last builds of pull requests, if any
Star icon	Allows toggling the project as a "favorite"

The name and health indicators are the same as in the classic Jenkins view.

The Branches column only applies to the new Multibranch Pipeline project type. This provides a summary of the last run for the set of branches. (Multibranch Pipeline projects are discussed in detail in Chapter 8.)

The PR column only applies if there are active pull requests (PRs), such as for a GitHub-based project. It shows the number of outstanding PRs if they exist. (PRs are covered in more detail later in this chapter.)

The last (unnamed) column allows you to choose to make a project a "favorite." In this case, that means creating a shortcut to that project under a Favorites section at the top of the page (Figure 9-4).

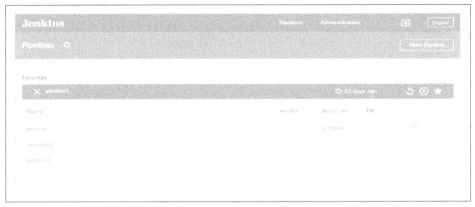

Figure 9-4. Adding a favorite

When a project is "favorited" by virtue of being starred, the shortcut at the top of the screen includes several options on the righthand side. We'll discuss more about what each of those does in a later section of this chapter. The favorite shortcut can be removed by again clicking on the star. In this way, the star icon acts as a toggle for providing shortcut access to specific projects.

Favorites

Note that wherever the star icon occurs (whether in a row or in a header), it has the same purpose—to toggle the "favorite" status of a project. However, if an entry is a container for other entries (such as a Multibranch Pipeline project that has other jobs in it), the favoriting functionality will work only if it can determine what the "default" object is. For example, if you select a Multibranch Pipeline project to favorite, it will favorite the `master` branch if there is one. If there isn't a good default available, you'll see an error like this:

```
Favoriting Error

No default branch (e.g. "master") to favorite.
```

Finally, near the bottom of the dashboard screen will be some text that identifies the particular version of Blue Ocean that is running, and the version of Jenkins that it is being run on.

Clicking on any of the projects listed on the dashboard will take you to the specific page for that project. We'll discuss the contents of that page next.

The Project-Specific Page

From the Blue Ocean dashboard, you can drill into any particular pipeline to see more information about the stages, commits, etc. Clicking on one of the items on the dashboard takes you to the page for that specific job.

This page has some elements on it that are similar to those on the dashboard. At the top, we have the same header that we always have in Blue Ocean, with the Jenkins, Pipelines, Administration, Go to Classic, and Logout links.

In the next large blue row, we have an icon that represents the health of the project on its most recent run (such as a sun), the name of the pipeline (also a link to the activity page for the pipeline), and the star icon (to toggle this as a favorite). The gear icon after that is a direct link back to the classic configuration page for the pipeline job.

Each such page also has three views available on it—Activity, Branches, and Pull Requests. We'll look at the functionality available with those views for both a simple (single-branch) job and a Multibranch Pipeline job.

Simple pipeline Activity view

As the name implies, the Activity view is intended to show all activity (runs) of a selected pipeline. This is the default view for this page. It includes the runs for all branches of the selected pipeline that have been executed. If you select a job from the Blue Ocean dashboard that hasn't been executed yet, you'll see a screen like Figure 9-5.

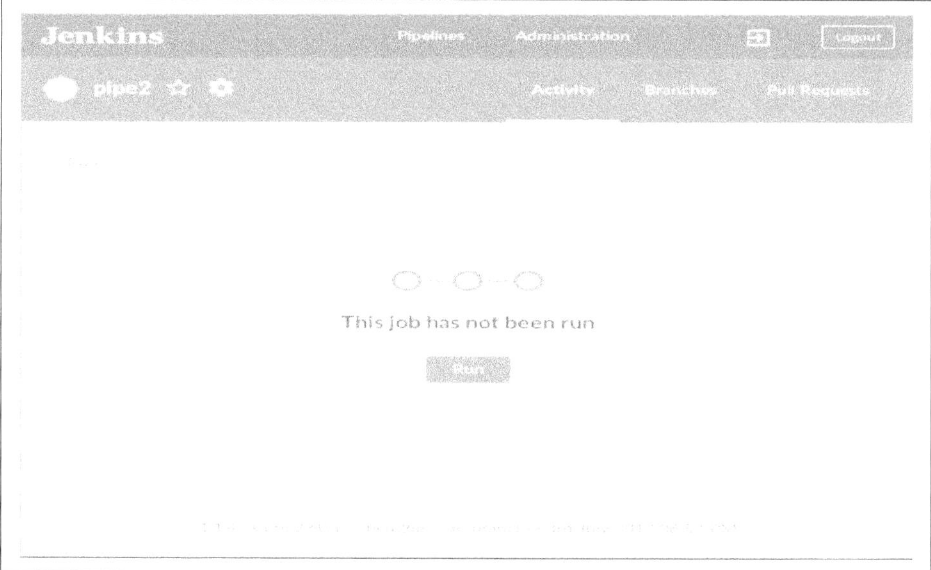

Figure 9-5. Job that hasn't been run yet in Blue Ocean

The Run button (either at the top left or in the dialog) then can be used to run the job. When the job is running, the circle icon on the left will gradually fill in as the job progresses. The icon in the last (rightmost) column can also be used to stop the job from running, if needed (Figure 9-6).

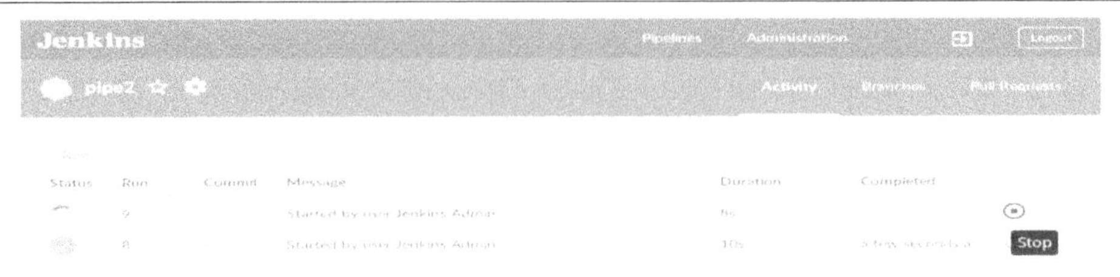

Figure 9-6. Blue Ocean run in progress and Stop icon

Blue Ocean Color Codes and Symbols

In Blue Ocean, the status icons (and other symbols associated with individual jobs) are frequently color-coded and marked with a particular symbol to indicate status. On some pages, the banner at the top may also be color-coded. The mappings between statuses, colors, and symbols are shown in Table 9-2.

Table 9-2. Blue Ocean visual status mappings

Status	Color	Symbol
Successful	Green	Check mark
Unstable	Yellow	Exclamation point
Failed	Red	X character
In progress	Blue	None
Not run yet	Gray	None

"Halos"

As previously mentioned, in Blue Ocean, for running jobs you will see a symbol consisting of the outline of a circle that is gradually filled in as the job progresses. A symbol like this is also used for each individual stage when looking at the parts of a job executing in Blue Ocean. For simplicity in referring to this type of symbol, we'll simply call them "halos" in the rest of the chapter.

After the job or stage has executed, the halo will be filled in, color-coded, and marked with a symbol to indicate the status (as shown in Figure 9-6 and described in the preceding sidebar).

As well as triggering new runs (via the Run button), previous runs of the job listed on the screen can also be "replayed." This is done by clicking on the "rerun" icon (the circular arrow) at the end of the designated row. Figure 9-7 shows a screen shot after a new run and a replay of an older one.

Figure 9-7. New run and replayed run

Replay

Replay is the functionality in Jenkins 2 that allows rerunning the set of code that was current at the time of the original run. It is discussed in more detail in Chapter 2.

One other element to note on this screen is the "Go to Classic" icon (the square with the right-pointing arrow in it near the top right). This is a common element across screens in Blue Ocean. Clicking on this icon in the Activity view for a simple pipeline job like this would take us to the Stage View for this job, as shown in Figure 9-8.

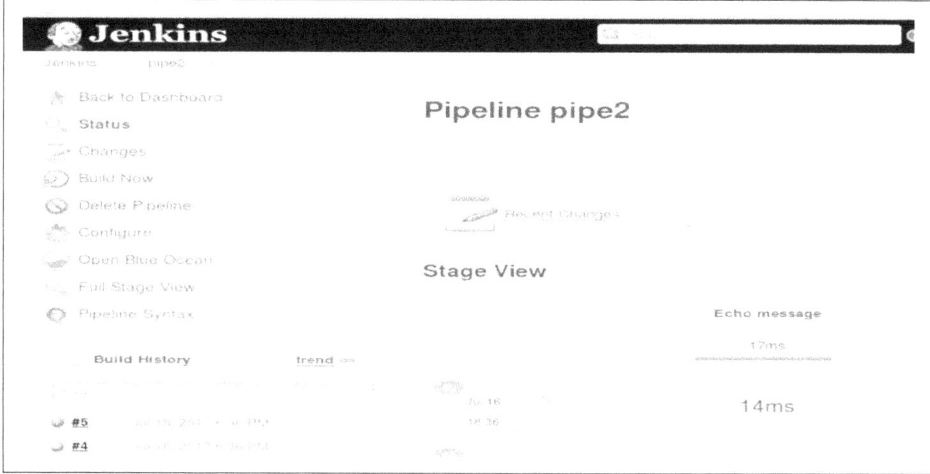

Figure 9-8. Classic view of simple pipeline

Simple pipeline Branches and Pull Requests views

In the same line as the Activity tab are the Branches and Pull Requests tabs. While these tabs are present for all pipelines, they are only applicable to Multibranch Pipelines.

Clicking on either of these tabs for a non–Multibranch Pipeline will simply bring up an error dialog telling you that these do not apply, with a link to go to for more information.

Multibranch Pipeline Activity view

Now that we've looked at the Blue Ocean interface for a simple pipeline, let's look at a Multibranch Pipeline. A similar interface exists for these.

Figure 9-9 shows the Activity screen for a Multibranch Pipeline job. Note that we have several of the same links, icons, and headings as we saw on the Blue Ocean dashboard and on the simple pipeline pages.

Figure 9-9. Multibranch Pipeline activity view

Here again, each row in the main part of the screen represents a run of a job for an individual branch. Clicking on any part of the row except for the icon in the far right column opens up a detail screen for that particular run. We'll discuss the run detail screens later in this chapter.

The names and values in each column are fairly self-explanatory, except for the last column. Clicking on that circular arrow executes an operation that reruns that particular run. (For previous runs, this amounts to a replay. The Replay feature is discussed in more detail in Chapter 2.) As with the simple pipeline, once you start a run by clicking on that icon, the icon under the left Status column will change to a halo; the icon at the end of the row will change to one that can be used to stop the build (by clicking on it).

Additionally, in cases of multiple commits, you will see an "*n* commits" notification next to the "*Latest message*" field (Figure 9-10). Clicking on this will take you to the detail screen for that run.

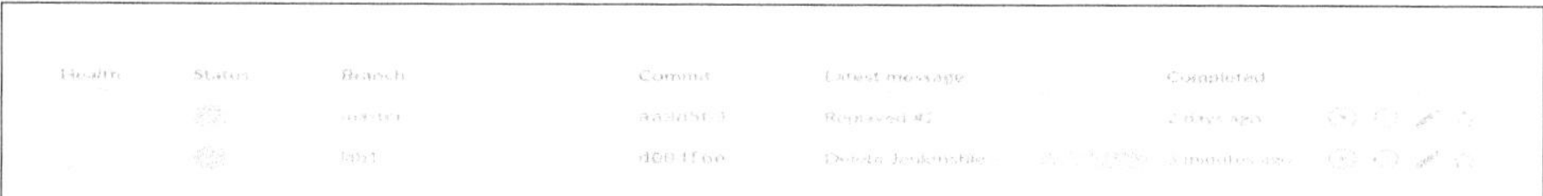

Figure 9-10. Recent commits notification for the branch

For a Multibranch Pipeline project, the Branch column header on this screen also serves as a filtering mechanism. Clicking on the column header makes it become an editable field. You can select the desired branch from the drop-down or type in the desired branch name (see Figure 9-11). To close the filtered view, click the "X" to the right of the branch name.

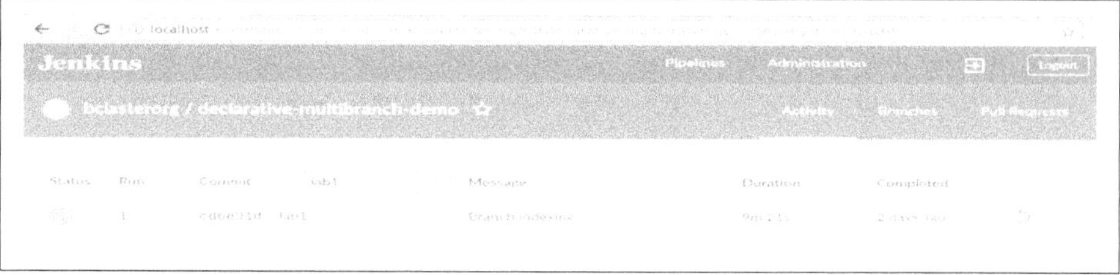

Figure 9-11. Filtered activity view

Finally, again in the header for the page, we have the right-pointing arrow in the square next to the Logout button. As before, this is the shortcut for "Go to Classic." Also as before, it is contextual. In this case, clicking it will take us to the classic page for the Multibranch Pipeline project (as shown in Figure 9-12).

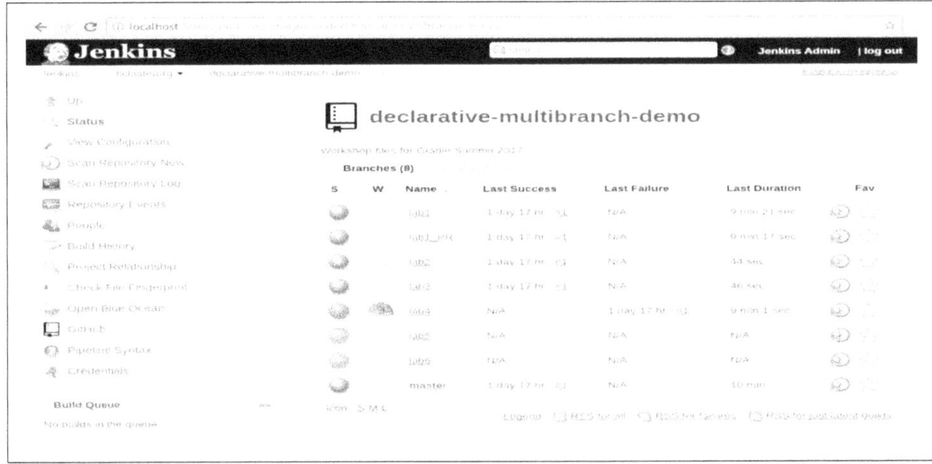

Figure 9-12. Multibranch Pipeline classic view

With a Multibranch Pipeline project, the Branches and Pull Requests tabs are valid and provide additional functionality. Let's take a moment to talk about those.

Multibranch Pipeline Branches view

Whereas the Activity view for a Multibranch Pipeline project shows all the runs for all branches, the Branches tab is for working with the separate branches at the higher level as separate jobs. Figure 9-13 shows an example of this view, for the pipeline we've been looking at.

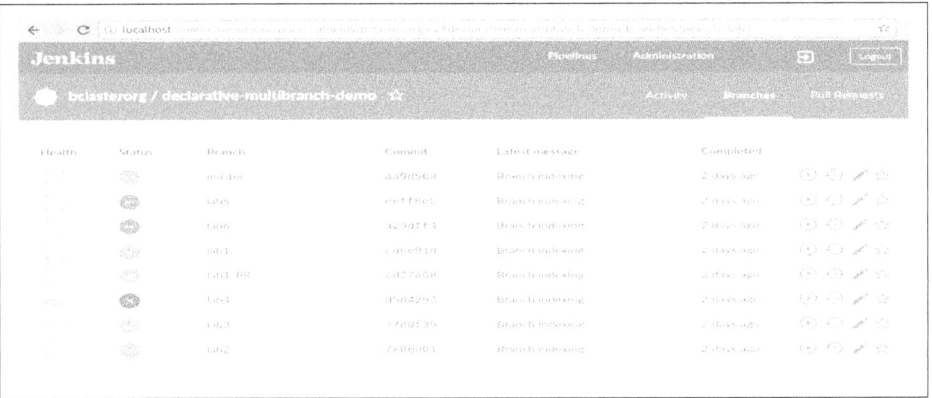

Figure 9-13. Multibranch Pipeline branches view

Each row represents one of the branches in the Multibranch Pipeline. The overall health indicator and last run status for each branch are on the left, followed by the branch name and the SHA1 commit that last updated it. In most cases, the value in the "Latest message" field will be "Branch indexing," since that's the process that runs when Jenkins scans for changes. Clicking on one of these rows (aside from the four icons at the end) takes you to a detailed run screen for the most recent run of that branch.

The four icons at the end of each row are clickable and invoke different functionality, summarized in Table 9-3.

Table 9-3. Branches view icons

Icon	Purpose
Play (circle with arrowhead)	Execute a new run of the pipeline in the branch.
Activity (circle with clock hands)	Switch to Activity view filtered for this branch.
Pipeline editor (pencil)	Open the pipeline editor on the pipeline in this branch (may throw an error if the pipeline is not declarative).
Favorite (star)	Toggle the favorite status of this branch in the interface.

Multibranch Pipeline Pull Requests view

For pipelines based on repositories that support pull requests, such as GitHub, this view is used to show any open pull requests. If you don't have any open pull requests, switching to this view simply pops up a message telling you that you don't have any.

Pull Requests

If you're not familiar with pull requests, here's a little more information (using GitHub as our reference).

Pull requests are a gating mechanism for merging new or updated code into an existing repository on GitHub. They can originate in one of two ways:

- A user forks the GitHub repository of another user and makes changes in the forked version of their project that they would like to contribute back to the original project.
- A user creates a new branch of an existing project with code intended to be merged into another branch.

In either case, the user can create a formal PR in the GitHub interface detailing the source and requested destination for the code to be merged. The owner of the project or branch, where the merge is intended to happen, can then review the request. If they feel it is appropriate (and if it can be merged cleanly), they can merge it in, thus "accepting" the PR.

Jenkins in this case can show PRs that originate from forks of a project and can also automatically attempt to build those to help verify that a PR is OK to accept and merge.

When you do have one or more open pull requests (originating from a fork) in the related GitHub project, they will show up in the Pull Requests view, as shown in Figure 9-14.

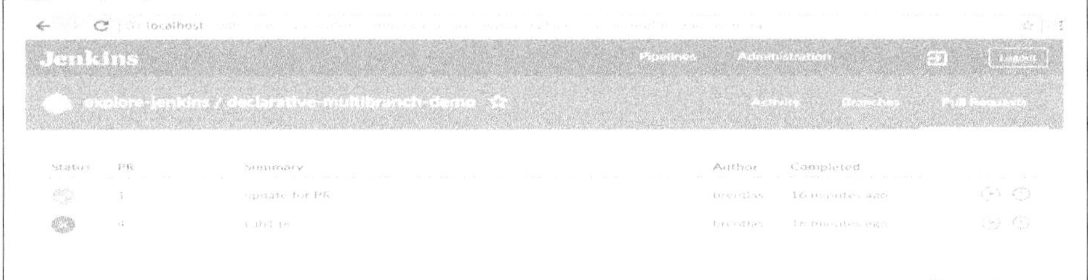

Figure 9-14. Multibranch Pipeline Pull Requests view

Note that Jenkins has tried to build these. Thus, we have the typical columns for things like the status and completed time, and the option to rerun them.

In this case, PR 4 had a conflict when Jenkins tried to build it. Via the connection already established from Jenkins to GitHub, the fact that Jenkins could not build it correctly will also be surfaced in the GitHub interface (see Figure 9-15).

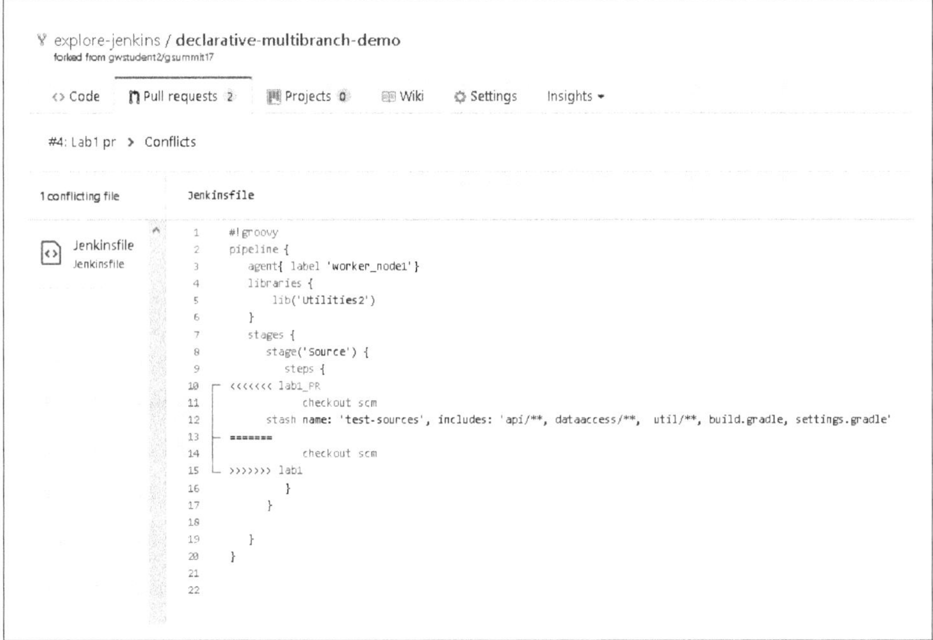

Figure 9-15. The conflict for PR 4 in GitHub

We can then choose to either not accept the PR (and close it), or resolve the conflict (by updating the code locally and pushing it back, or by updating it directly in GitHub). In this case, we just resolve the conflict in GitHub and commit the merge (Figure 9-16).

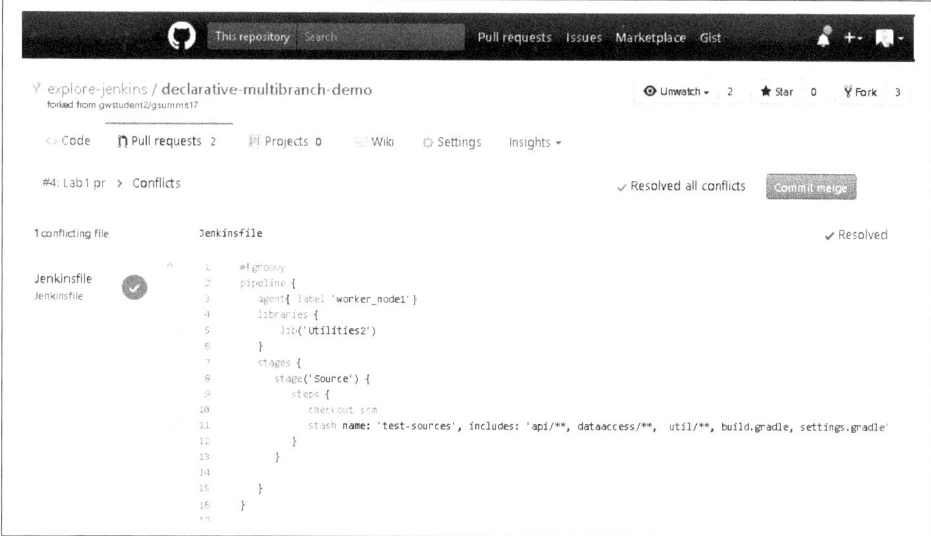

Figure 9-16. Conflict resolved in GitHub and ready for commit

Once we have resolved the conflict and merged the change back on GitHub, Jenkins automatically detects that and rebuilds the PR. As shown in Figure 9-17, with the conflict resolved, the PR builds successfully this time.

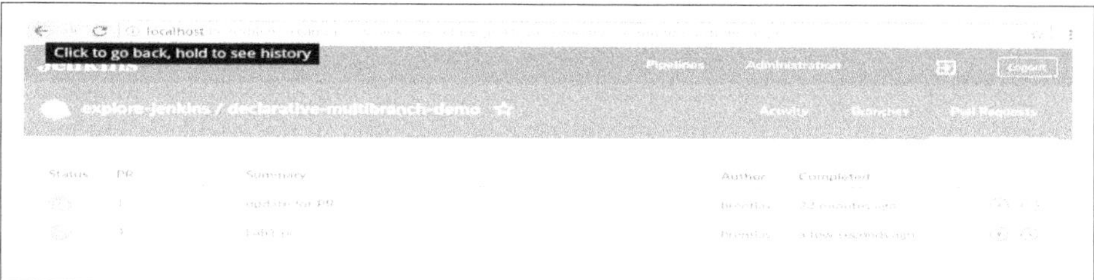

Figure 9-17. Pull Requests view after conflict resolution and automatic rebuild

This is also reflected on the GitHub side. Note the "All checks have passed" section in Figure 9-18.

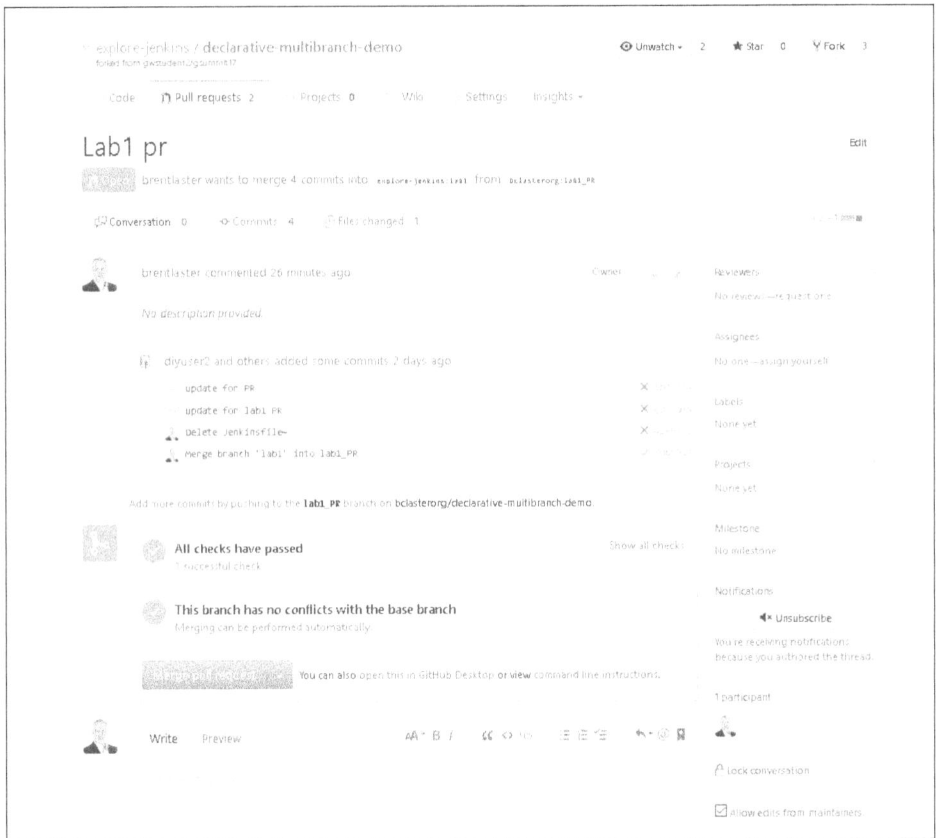

Figure 9-18. GitHub pull request detail page showing all checks (Jenkins PR build) have passed

The next step is to go ahead and merge the cleanly building PR via the "Merge pull request" option on GitHub. After doing this, the GitHub interface will show that we have successfully merged this PR (Figure 9-19).

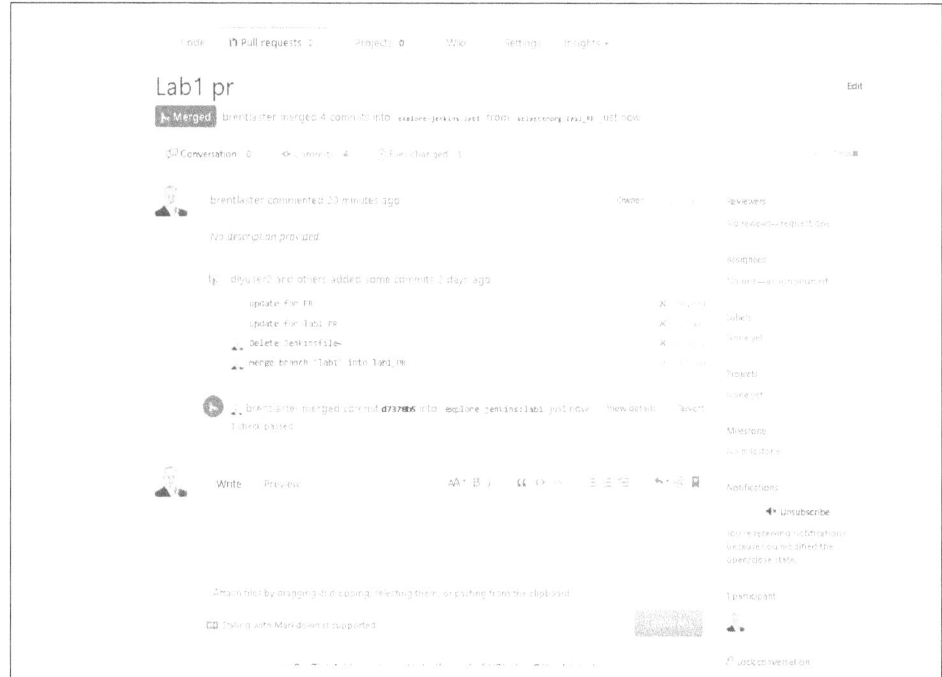

Figure 9-19. GitHub pull request detail page after PR merged

After this occurs, at the next refresh interval Jenkins will do the branch indexing, detect the new change in the branch due to the merged PR, and rebuild the branch (Figure 9-20). It will also add the tag showing there were multiple commits involved.

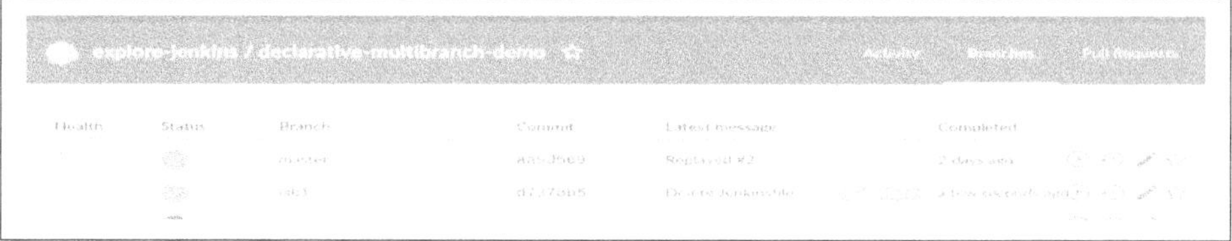

Figure 9-20. Automatic rebuild of the branch after the PR has been merged

Since the PR has been merged, it will be removed from the Pull Requests view as well.

From many of the screens that we've already looked at in the interface, you can get to a more detailed view of a pipeline run (either one that has already occurred or one that has been initiated and is in progress). Next, we'll look at the screen in Blue Ocean that shows the details of a particular run of a pipeline.

The Run Page

Figure 9-21 shows a pipeline job in progress in the Blue Ocean interface. Like the other pages we've looked at, this page has a number of common graphical elements on it and tabs that can be selected to see different elements of this particular run. But regardless of the selected tab, the large banner across the top, which we refer to as the "status banner," remains on the screen. Let's briefly discuss what information it conveys, and then see what's contained on each tab.

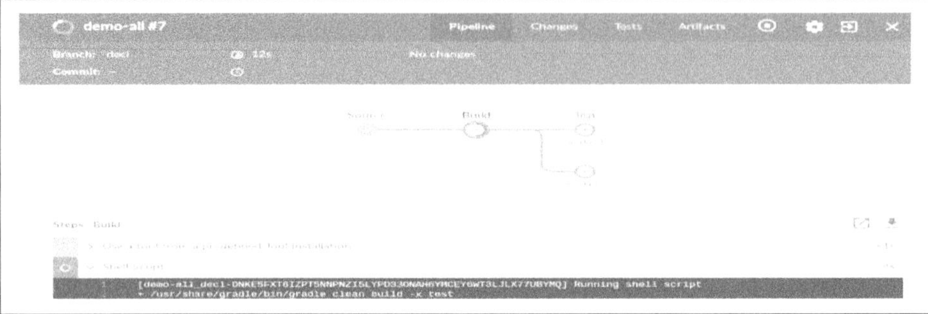

Figure 9-21. Individual run of a job in progress in Blue Ocean

The status banner

When the run is in progress, the status banner will have a blue background (indicating it's running). In the upper-left corner is a halo indicating how much of the overall job has been completed. Next to that is the job name, the run number, a set of four tabs (which we'll talk about shortly), and then some of the same icons we've already discussed that also appear on other screens, including a button to stop the build that's in progress (or start it if it's not running). In the next row, on the left are the branch name and the last commit SHA1. Still in that row, to the right, we have a "time" column. The top time value shows how much time this run is taking (or did take, if previously run). The bottom time value notes when this job was last run. Finally, toward the middle of that row, we may have additional information about the changes that were incorporated (and presumably are the motivation) for this run.

Within the main run page, the tabs for Pipeline, Changes, Tests, and Artifacts can change the views. We'll look at each of those next.

Pipeline

Figure 9-22 shows an example run page with the Pipeline tab selected.

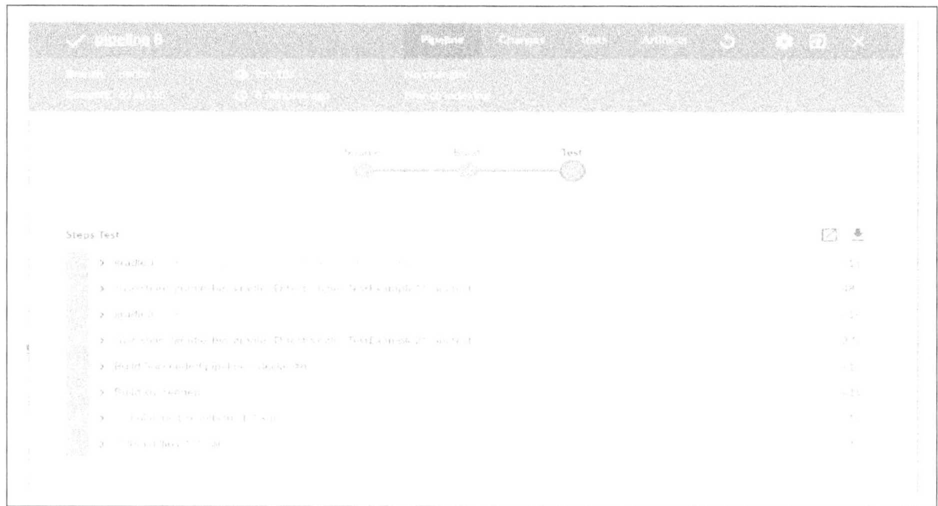

Figure 9-22. Pipeline tab on the run screen

With the Pipeline tab selected, underneath the banner area is a graphical representation of this pipeline. The parts of the pipeline are represented at the granularity of stages, and each stage in the pipeline is represented by a halo. Where stages are coded/executed in parallel, the halos are lined up in the same column.

Parallel Stages

When we use the traditional mapping syntax within a `parallel` step inside of a stage, Blue Ocean represents the separate branches as separate stages. Within the text, we don't distinguish between these differences. For simplicity, we simply refer to all of the halos as representing "stages."

In the Declarative Pipeline 1.2 syntax (covered in Chapter 7), each parallel branch is really a separate stage.

As each stage is executed, the halo for the stage is updated accordingly. When that stage is completed, the halo is color-coded and updated with a symbol to indicate success, failure, or an unstable state (as described in "Blue Ocean Color Codes and Symbols" on page 324). Partially filled in halos represent work in progress in those stages, and gray/empty halos represent stages in the pipeline that have not been processed yet.

Underneath the graphical representation of the pipeline is a section with logs for each step. Another feature of the graphical representation is that other parts of the screen can be filtered based on which stage is currently active. To make a stage active after a run, you can click on the halo for that particular stage. At any point in time, one (and only one) stage will be active (except in the case of parallel stages).

Skipped Stages

Blue Ocean can also display "skipped" stages—conditional stages in a Declarative Pipeline that aren't executed based on a `when` statement.

(Conditional statements in declarative syntax are covered in Chapter 7.)

The log of steps below the graphical pipeline is filtered based on the currently selected stage. We'll look at that next.

Step logs. The section at the bottom of the Pipeline view allows you to look at logs for any stage of the pipeline, segmented by steps. The set of steps shown are the ones for the currently selected stage in the graphical representation above.

A separate row is shown for each step in the stage. Table 9-4 lists the possible fields for a step log entry.

Table 9-4. Fields for a step log entry

Name	Representation	Purpose
Status	Color code and symbol (same scheme as referred to earlier)	Show status of pipeline step (success, failure, etc.)
Show log	Right-facing arrow when collapsed/downward-facing arrow when expanded	Toggle showing detailed log information for the step
Description	Actual step and description	Show step (command) and description (same as Snippet Generator)
Duration	Time (generally in seconds)	Show time duration for step execution in this run

Combined Steps

If two or more steps are combined into a single command, then those steps will be broken down as separate steps in this area. For example, if your pipeline contained a step like this:

```
sh "${tool 'gradle32'}/bin/gradle build"
```

the `tool` and `sh` steps would show up as separate rows. However, since the `tool` step is contained within the `sh` step, it will not have a separate log entry, so attempting to expand the `tool` step in this section will not show any additional information.

Additionally, some steps (such as a `mail` step) may not have any output in the logs, and others may only reflect a result, such as "Build Succeeded."

The main benefit here is derived from being able to select a stage, and then a step in that stage, and then dive in to get the logs just for that step. Clicking on the ">" sign in the second column of the row causes the log to be shown. The sign will then change to a "V". Clicking on the field again causes the log to be collapsed.

Figure 9-23 shows some of the logs expanded for selected steps of the selected stage (`Test`) in a pipeline. Note also the failed status of one stage.

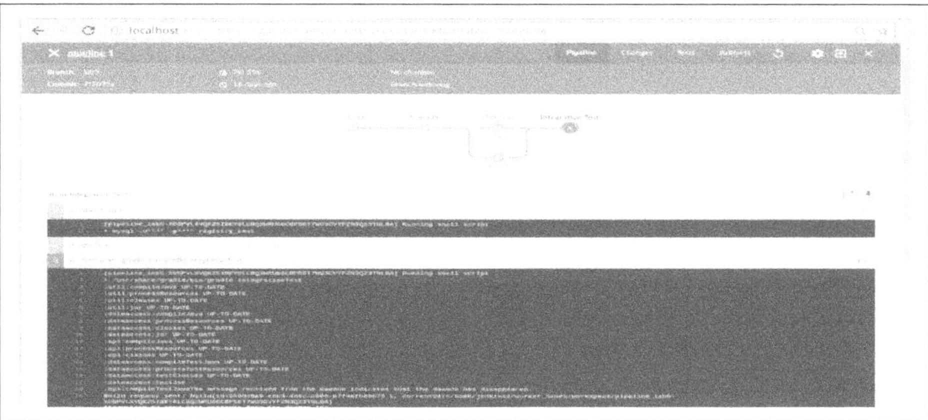

Figure 9-23. Pipeline view with expanded step logs

One other note about this view: on the far right side, immediately above the set of rows for the steps, are two icons that allow you to look more closely at logs. The one in the form of a square with a diagonally pointing arrow allows you to display the log for the selected step in a new full-size screen. The icon next to it, with the downward pointing arrow, allows you to download a copy of a log.

Changes

The next view to look at is shown by selecting the Changes tab. As the name implies, this view shows the set of changes that were made in source management for this run.

Figure 9-24 shows the Changes view for one run of a particular pipeline.

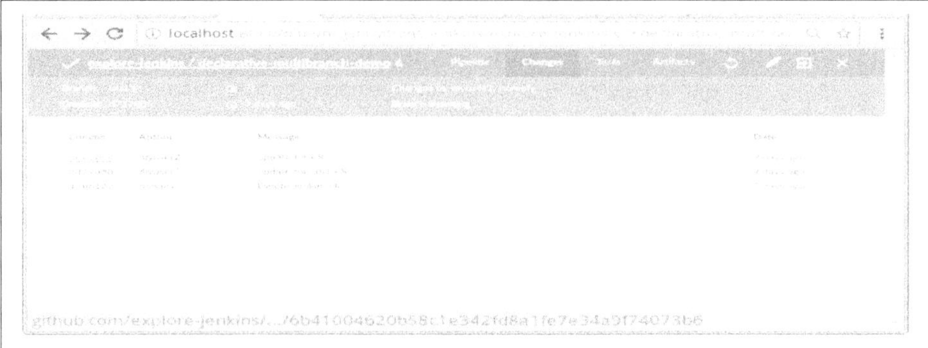

Figure 9-24. Changes view for the run of a pipeline

The fields here are fairly self-explanatory if you are familiar with Git; however, we'll briefly describe them here for completeness (see Table 9-5).

Table 9-5. Changes view field descriptions

Name	Description
Commit	A portion of Git's commit SHA1 (enough to uniquely identify it)
Author	The user ID of the person who made the commit
Message	The message supplied for the change when it was committed
Date	The date of the last run (or time, if fewer than 24 hours have passed since the last run)

One useful feature of this Blue Ocean screen is being able to select and click on any of the commits. This action will then jump to the change in the source management system. For example, clicking on the highlighted commit in the previous figure takes us to the GitHub page with the details for it (Figure 9-25).

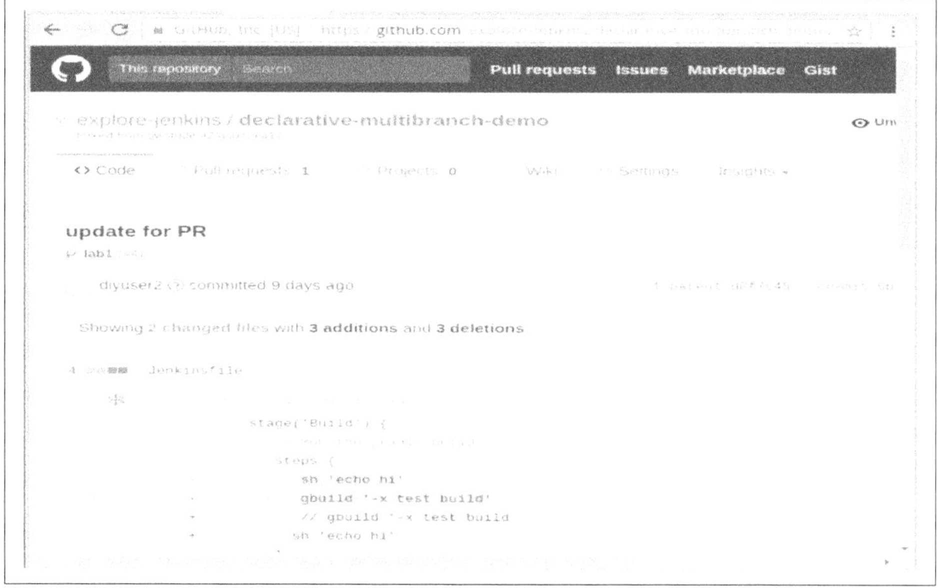

Figure 9-25. GitHub change page linked from Changes view

It's worth noting that the information presented on the Changes screen is a subset of the information found on the build output screen in the classic view (Figure 9-26).

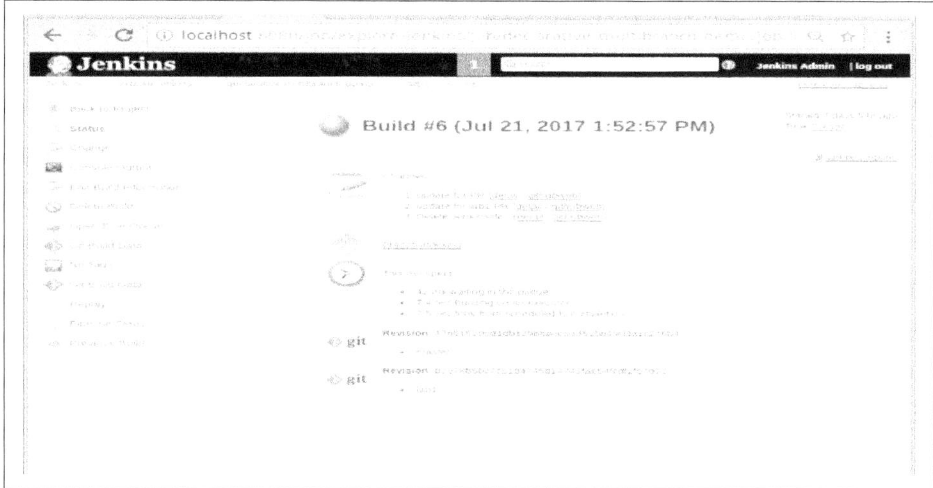

Figure 9-26. Corresponding build output screen in classic view

Tests

Plugins such as JUnit allow us to archive test results and have Jenkins report on them. Assuming there are steps that actually run the tests in the pipeline, code like the following can be used to archive the test results:

```
junit '**/build/reports/**/*.xml'
```

Such code would most commonly be included in post-processing designed to always be run for a pipeline. For a Declarative Pipeline, this could take the form of:

```
post {
        always {
            junit '**/build/reports/**/*.xml'
        }
```

In a Scripted Pipeline, you could include it in the `finally` block of a `try-catch-finally` structure:

```
finally {
            junit 'build/reports/**/*.xml'
      }
```

Based on this kind of step, in the classic view, Jenkins can create trend reports for success/failure of tests as well as produce detail screens on failing tests as shown in Figure 9-27.

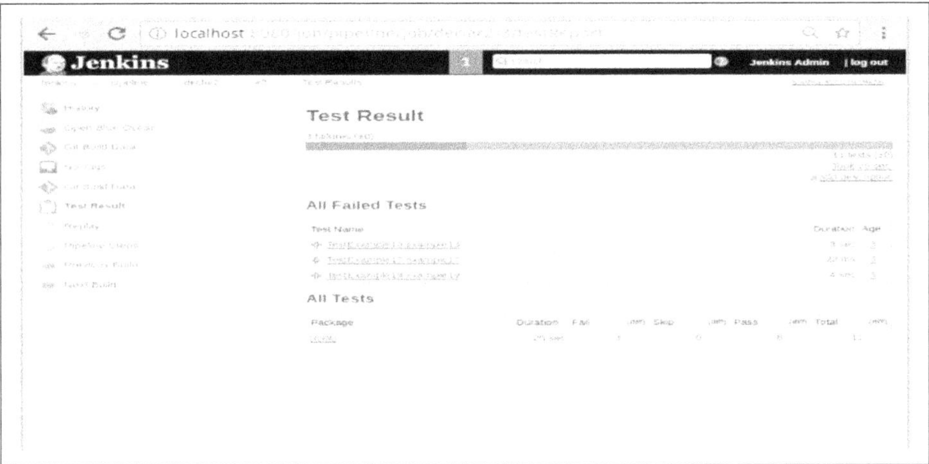

Figure 9-27. Classic view of failing tests detail

The Tests view in the run screen in Blue Ocean provides a similar detail screen for failed tests. If the step to archive the tests was not included, the screen will display a message stating "There are no tests archived for this run." And if all the tests have passed, the screen will display a message like Figure 9-28.

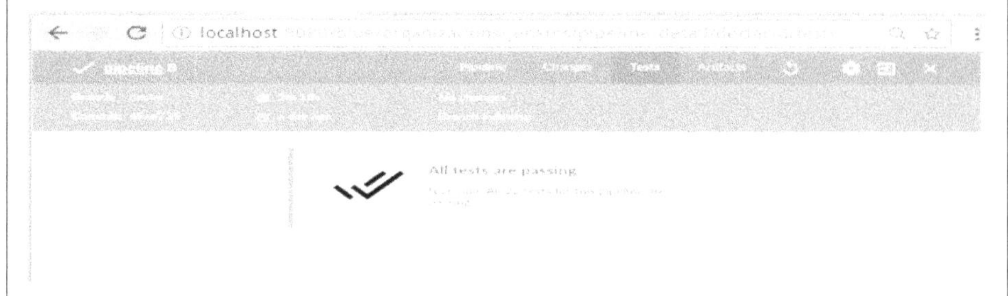

Figure 9-28. All tests passing

Pipelines are usually configured/coded in Jenkins such that failing tests set the build result to "unstable." This is represented in the Blue Ocean interface with a yellow color and an exclamation point, so the Tests view showing an unstable state with the failing test's detail would look something like Figure 9-29.

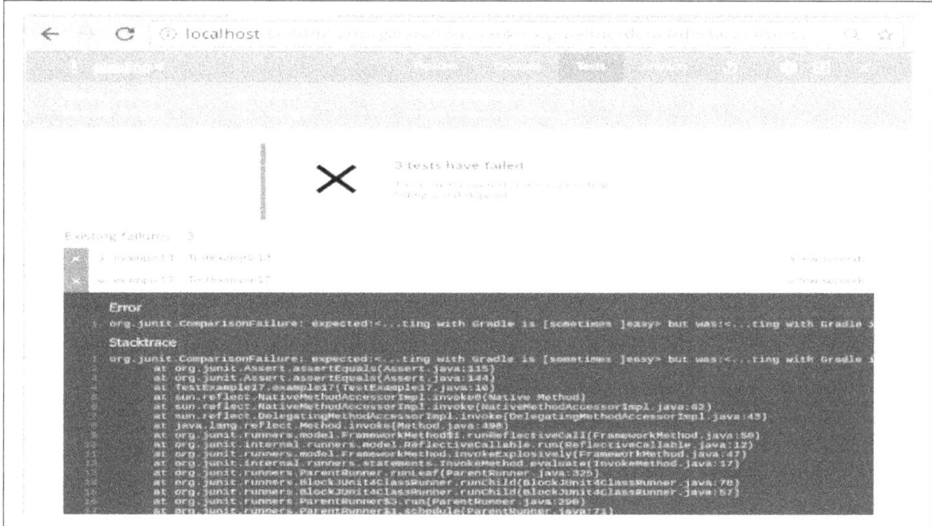

Figure 9-29. Tests tab showing failing tests

Notice that we can expand the row for each of the failing tests to get the related log, just as we could for the step logs on the Pipeline tab.

Artifacts

If your pipeline is configured to produce and archive artifacts, the Artifacts page will let you view and optionally open or download those artifacts. This tab corresponds to the Build Artifacts portion of the classic view's screen shown in Figure 9-30.

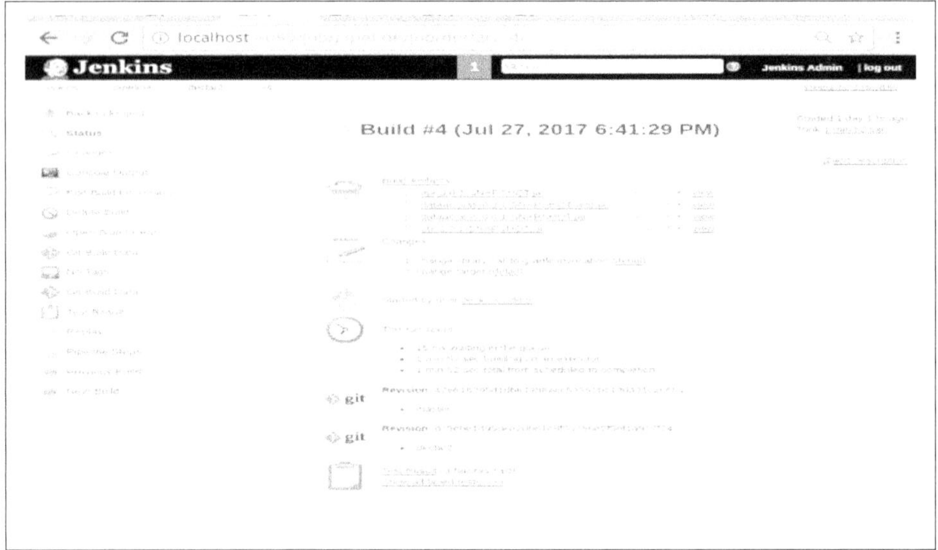

Figure 9-30. Classic view screen showing artifacts produced from the build

The `archive` pipeline step allows for archiving artifacts in your code. In a simple form, it looks like this:

```
archive 'build/libs/**/*.jar'
```

Like the code to archive test results, such code would most commonly be included in post-processing designed to always be run for a pipeline. For a Declarative Pipeline, this could take the form of:

```
post {
       always {
          archive 'build/libs/**/*.jar'
       }
```

In a Scripted Pipeline, you could include it in the `finally` block of a `try-catch-finally` structure:

```
finally {
          archive 'build/libs/**/*.jar'
    }
```

Figure 9-31 shows an example of the Artifacts view in the Blue Ocean interface.

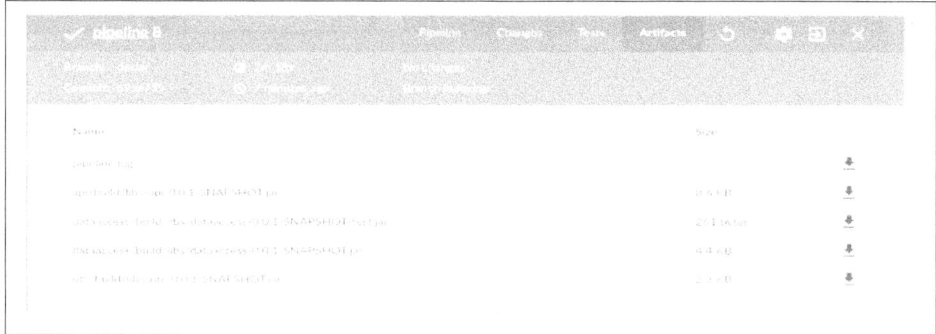

Figure 9-31. Artifacts view

Note that the first item listed is *pipeline.log*. This is the log from this run of the pipeline and is always available here, even if no other artifacts are archived.

Note also that the screen has icons on the far right to download the individual artifacts, and you can click on an artifact's name to "open" the artifact. (With the exception of the pipeline log, opening may translate to just downloading for most artifacts.)

Finally, there is a Download All button at the bottom. As the name implies, this button can be used to download all of the listed artifacts at once as a ZIP file. This is shown in Figure 9-32.

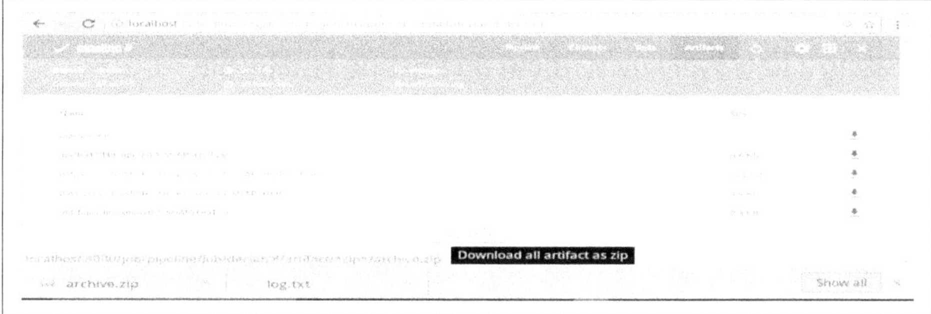

Figure 9-32. Downloading all artifacts as a ZIP file

One other point is worth mentioning about artifacts and test results. While we have referred to the two interfaces (the Blue Ocean run screen and the classic view), these items can also be accessed from the Stage View of a job in Jenkins. Figure 9-33 shows an example with an unstable and a failed run. Note the artifacts accessible near the top center and the testing trend graph at the top right.

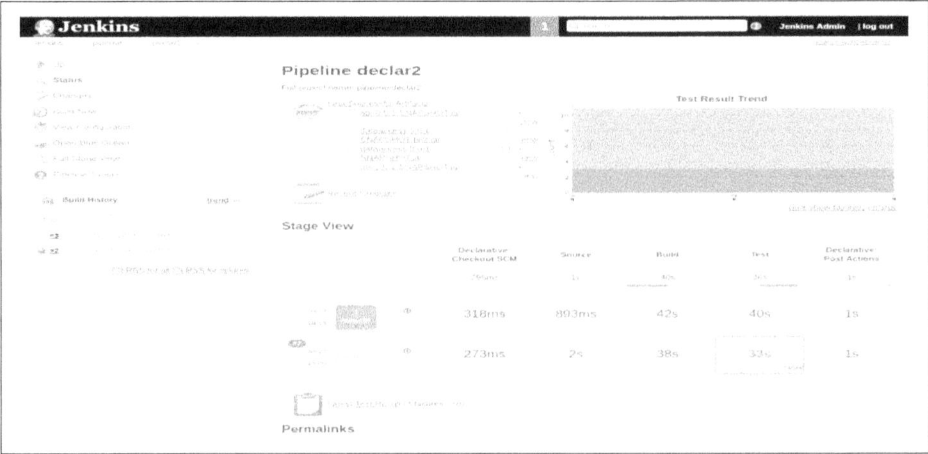

Figure 9-33. Stage View showing Last Successful Artifacts and Test Result Trend graph

Part 2: Working with the Blue Ocean Editor

In this second part of the chapter, we'll discuss the other key aspect of Blue Ocean, the pipeline editor. This editor allows you (within limits) to create and update pipelines, and parts of pipelines, through a more visual interface.

We'll look at a couple of use cases: creating a new pipeline from a project without an existing Jenkinsfile, and using the editor to add or edit content in an existing pipeline.

Creating a New Pipeline Without an Existing Jenkinsfile

Having an existing Jenkinsfile that defines your pipeline gives you a foundation for making changes or adding functionality through the pipeline editor. But you can also use the pipeline editor to create a completely new pipeline where there wasn't one before. In fact, this is the default workflow when you use the Blue Ocean interface to create a new pipeline. Let's see how this works.

If we were to start out with a Jenkins instance that did not have any pipelines yet and opened Blue Ocean, we'd get a screen like the one in Figure 9-34. To create a new pipeline, we could then simply click the button in the dialog.

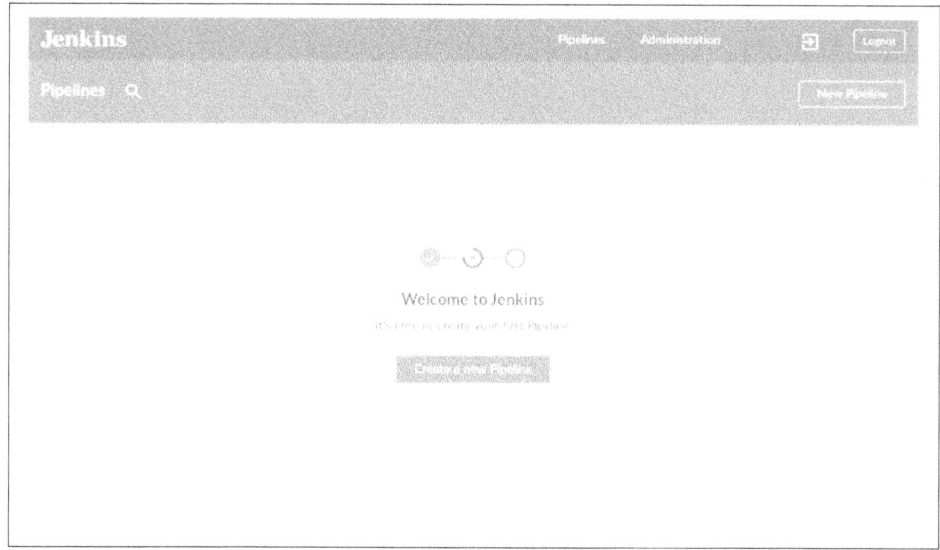

Figure 9-34. Starting Blue Ocean with no pipelines in Jenkins

For the case where we already have existing pipeline projects in Jenkins, those will show up in the pipelines list on the dashboard (as previously described). In that case, we can create a New Pipeline by clicking the New Pipeline button on the Blue Ocean dashboard (as shown in the upper-right corner of Figure 9-34).

From there, Blue Ocean prompts us to choose where the source repository is that we want to use (Figure 9-35). Currently, the options include Git (meaning a Git repo we have access to), GitHub (the public Git hosting service), GitHub Enterprise, Bitbucket Cloud, and Bitbucket Server. For our example here, we're going to start with a set of code on GitHub, so we would click the GitHub button.

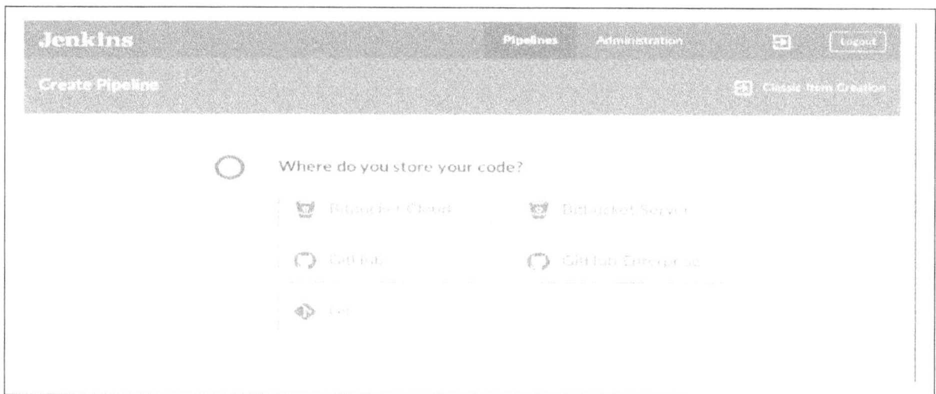

Figure 9-35. Choosing where to store pipeline code

To connect to GitHub, Jenkins needs an access token (Figure 9-36). This is a token that you generate on GitHub yourself.

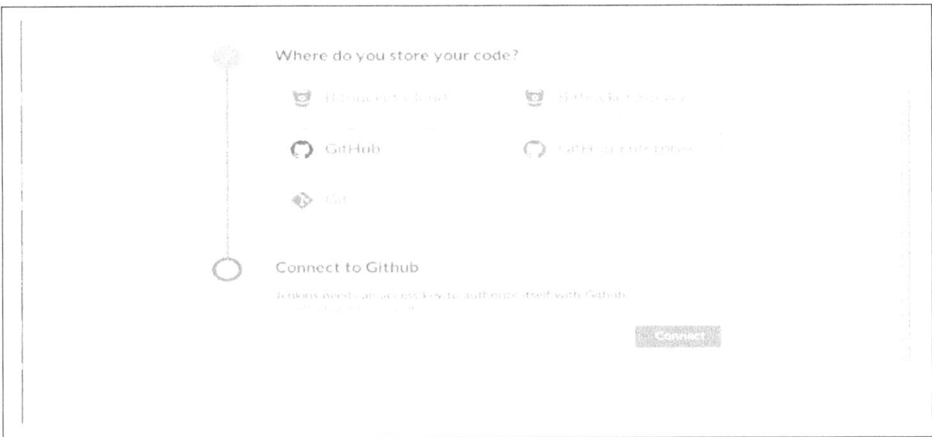

Figure 9-36. Asking for credentials

If you already have a token, you can paste it in here. If not, you can click the "Create an access key here" link to be taken directly to GitHub to create one. If you do that, you'll be prompted for your GitHub login information and then taken to the screen for creating a token (Figure 9-37).

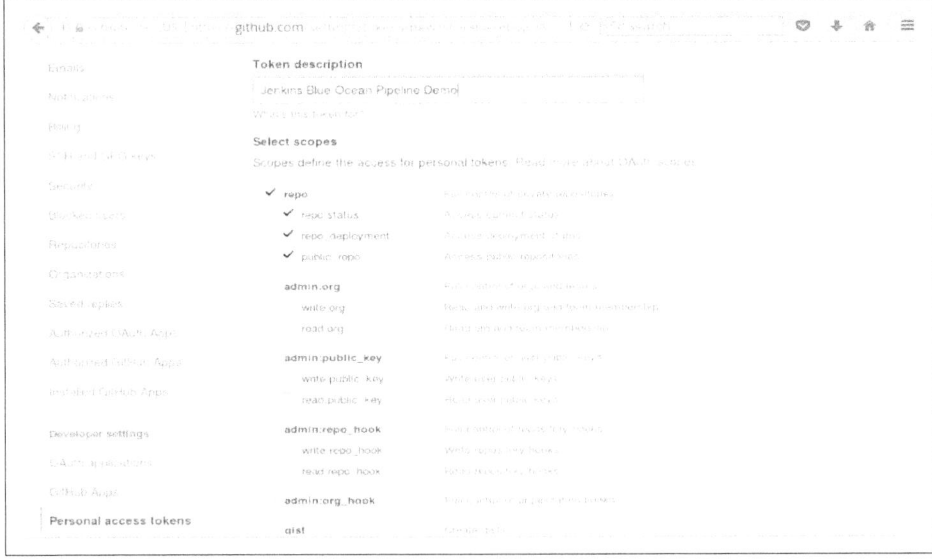

Figure 9-37. Creating a token in GitHub

The nice thing about this is that the permissions that Jenkins needs are already selected on this screen. To complete the process, you need to enter something in the "Token description" field, scroll to the bottom, and click the "Generate token" button. Then a token will be generated for you (Figure 9-38).

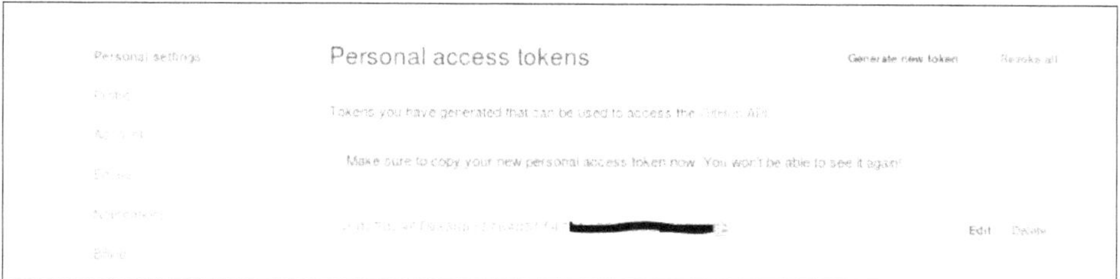

Figure 9-38. GitHub token created

Copy this token and then paste it back into the Jenkins screen. Click the "Connect" button, and Jenkins will access your GitHub account and present a list of organizations for you to choose from, if you have more than one (Figure 9-39).

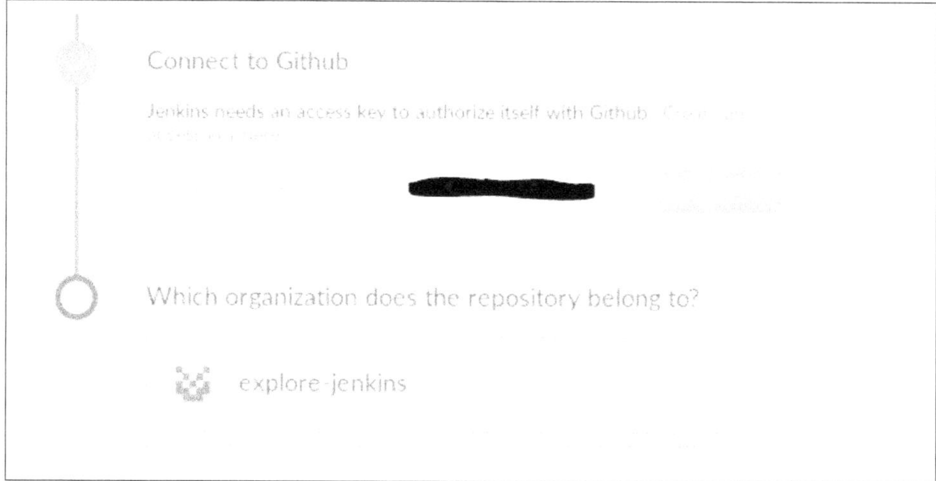

Figure 9-39. Choosing the GitHub organization

Progress Indicators

You may have noticed that as you're going through these steps, progress is tracked down the side on a line with the familiar halos (the circular icons) on it. As steps are in progress, the halos are blue and hollow. As you complete steps, the halos become green, filled in, and checked off. This is intentional, as it is the same representation that Blue Ocean uses for presenting pipeline stages.

After selecting an organization, you are presented with a list of repositories within that organization (Figure 9-40). There is a search field to filter the list if desired. From the list, you can choose a repository and then click the Create Pipeline button to get started.

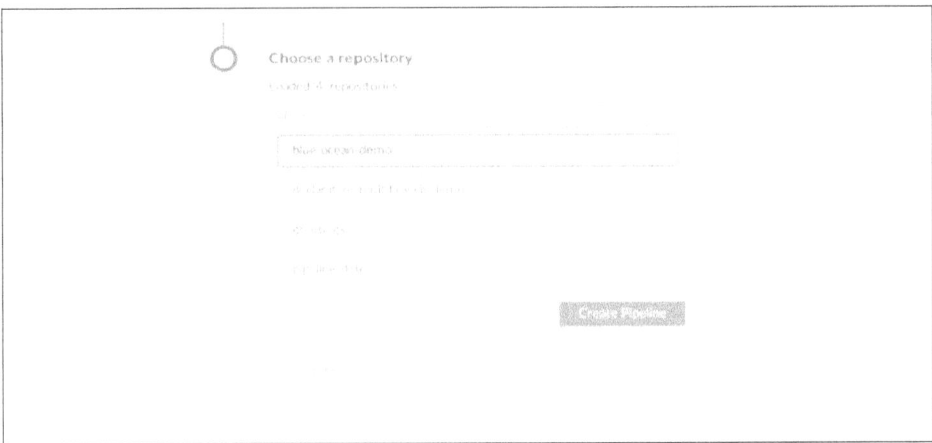

Figure 9-40. Selecting a repository from the GitHub organization

In our example, we're going to choose the "blue-ocean-demo" repository. If the repository you choose already has a Jenkinsfile in it, then Jenkins will automatically attempt to create an instance of the pipeline, defined in that Jenkinsfile, and run it for you. In this case, there is no initial Jenkinsfile in this project, so Jenkins just reports that and provides a button to create a new pipeline (Figure 9-41).

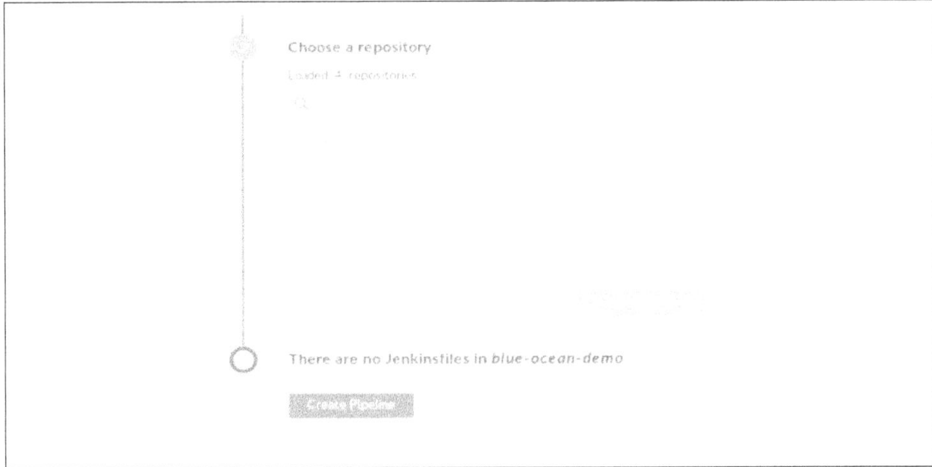

Figure 9-41. No Jenkinsfiles found

Clicking the Create Pipeline button takes us into the *Blue Ocean pipeline editor*, which we'll discuss next.

Working in the Editor

After telling Jenkins which GitHub project we want to base our new pipeline on, Jenkins puts us into the Blue Ocean pipeline editor. The initial screen is shown in Figure 9-42. The basic idea here is that instead of just typing in all of our Declarative Pipeline code, we'll use a combination of GUI elements (such as selecting items from a list) and typing to create the main parts of our pipeline. Then, when we save our changes, Jenkins will fill in the necessary syntax to incorporate our changes into a Declarative Pipeline in a Jenkinsfile. That Jenkinsfile can then be committed and pushed back into our project's repository.

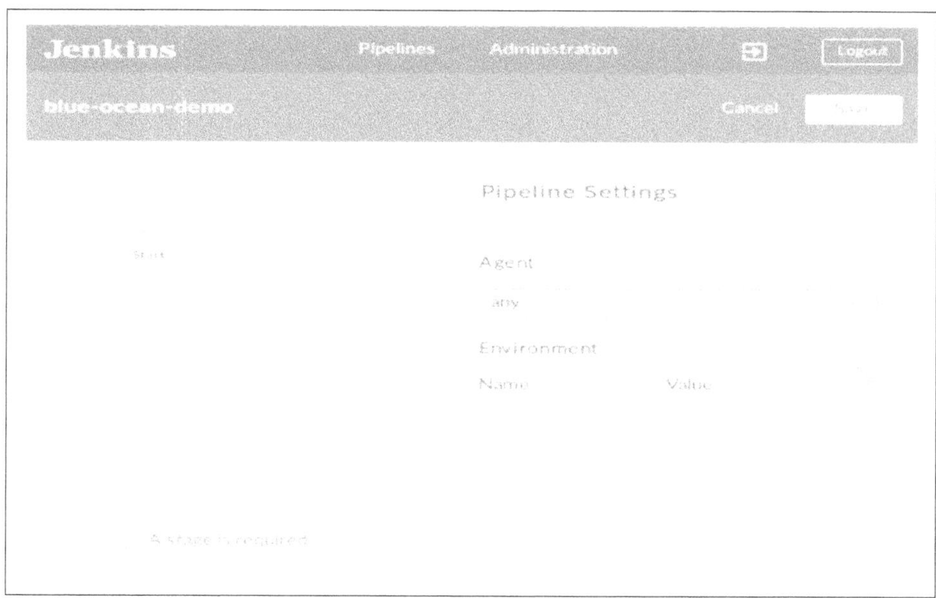

Figure 9-42. Initial screen of the editor

Let's take a quick tour of the elements on the screen. The top row contains the standard Jenkins "primary" links that we talked about earlier in the chapter. In the next row is the name of our repository (not a link, by the way), a Cancel button to take us out of the editor, and a Save button to save the changes we make.

On the lefthand side of the main part of the screen, we have a Start halo with a line connecting it to an empty halo. The + in the second halo means we can click on that to add a new stage to our pipeline.

On the righthand side, of this main part of the screen, is the area where we can specify pipeline elements. Furthermore, we can choose—or type in—values for them to make up the parts of our pipeline.

From here, some examples will best serve to demonstrate how to use the editor.

Specifying global parts of the pipeline

We're going to now create a pipeline using the editor. We'll start out by specifying a particular agent (via the agent's label) that we want to run the main part of the pipeline on. In the Pipeline Settings section, in the Agent field, we have a drop-down list that we can select the type of agent from (Figure 9-43).

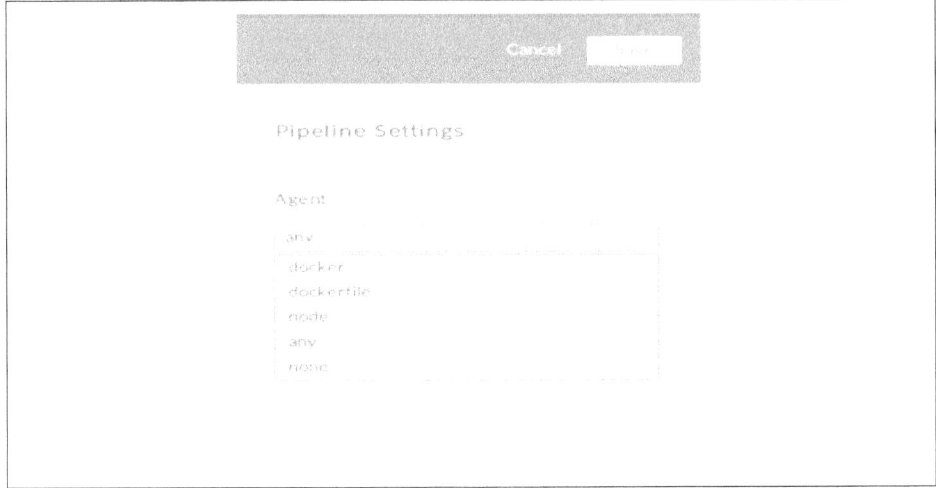

Figure 9-43. List to choose the type of agent

In this case, we're going to use a standard node that we have available, so we select "node." A new Label* text box pops up for us to put the label in. In this case, we'll use a node labeled `worker_node1`. (See Figure 9-44.)

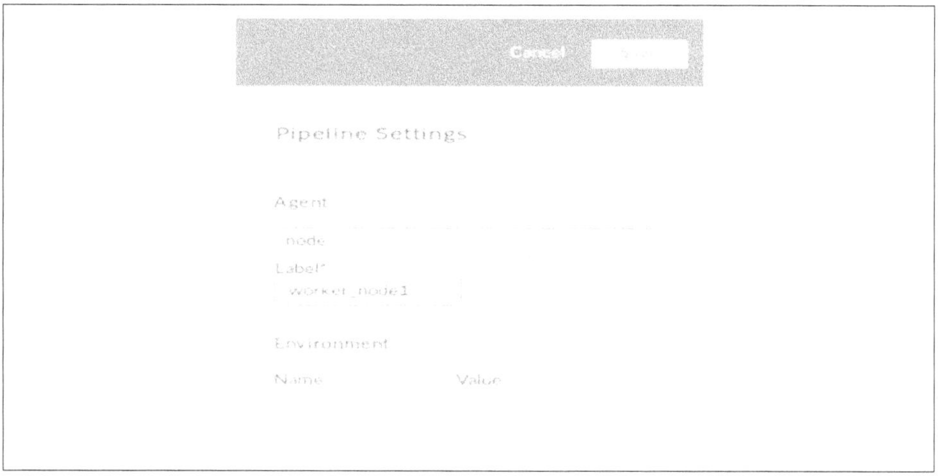

Figure 9-44. Adding an agent in the editor

This would correspond to code like this in a Jenkinsfile:

```
pipeline {
   agent{label 'worker_node1'}
```

Under that, we have an option to add environment variables. For illustration purposes, we'll set a variable named `COMPLETED_MSG` to the value "Build done!" To do this, we simply click on the circle with the + sign to the right of the Name and Value labels. Text fields then pop up for us to enter the name and value for the environment variable, as shown in Figure 9-45.

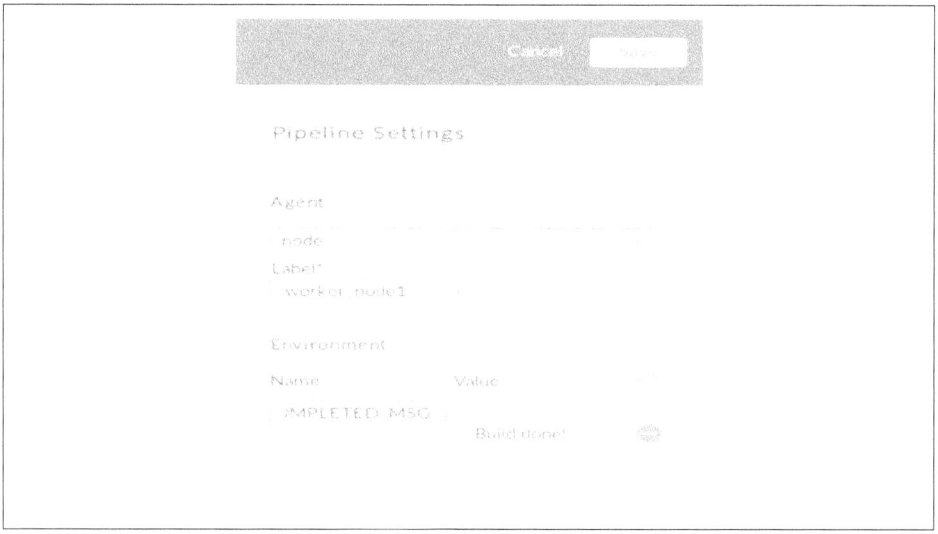

Figure 9-45. Adding an environment variable in the editor

This then would make our pipeline code:

```
pipeline {
   agent{label 'worker_node1'}
   environment {
      COMPLETED_MSG = "Build done!"
  }
```

Other Global Sections

You may recall from Chapter 7 that `environment` is only one of the multiple global sections available in a Declarative Pipeline structure. Currently, other global sections do not have their own GUI interfaces to set up in the pipeline editor, but more will likely be added over time.

Entry Errors

What happens if you enter something invalid in a field in the pipeline editor? The editor will visually alert you with a pop-up with information about what's wrong.

For example, if we had entered the name of the environment variable as `COMPLETED-MSG`, the editor would have flagged it as shown in Figure 9-46 since a hyphen is not a valid character for an environment variable.

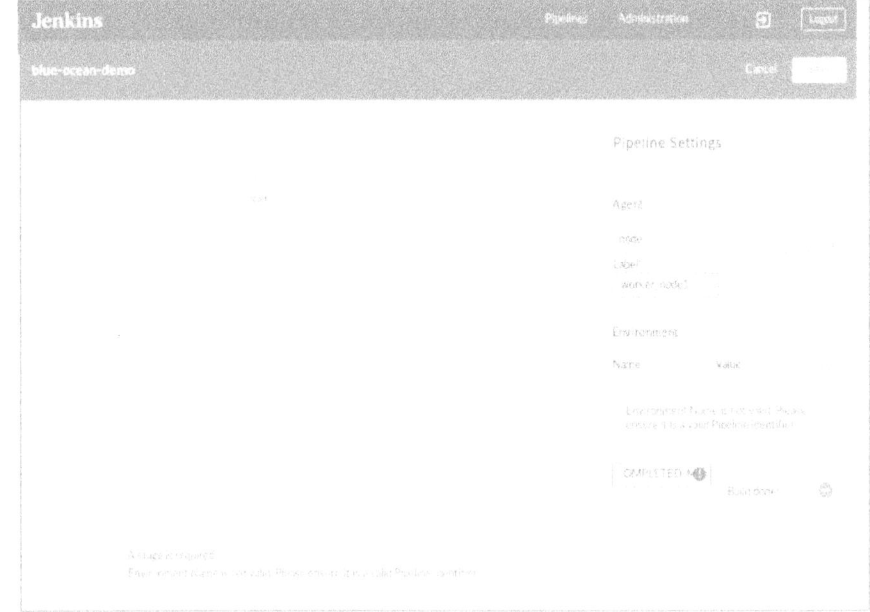

Figure 9-46. Pop-up error notification

Notice also here that we have the "A stage is required" message since we haven't yet added a stage to the pipeline. If we had added a stage and the stage had an error or invalid code, we would see something like Figure 9-47.

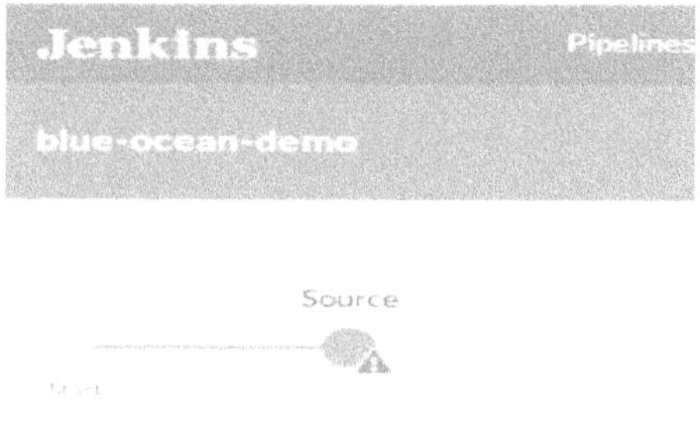

Figure 9-47. Error in pipeline stage

Now, let's add an initial stage to our pipeline.

Saving Progress

One thing that might cause some confusion in the editor is what to do after you have entered data in fields on the righthand side. The Save button in the top row is for saving the contents of the entire pipeline and updating in source control, and there is no Save or Apply button for the individual pieces you are adding. As it turns out, your updates are automatically saved in the editor and you can simply click on another part of the screen to proceed.

Adding a new stage

To add a new stage to our pipeline, we just need to click on the halo with the + inside it in the left section of the main screen. This results in the screen shown in Figure 9-48.

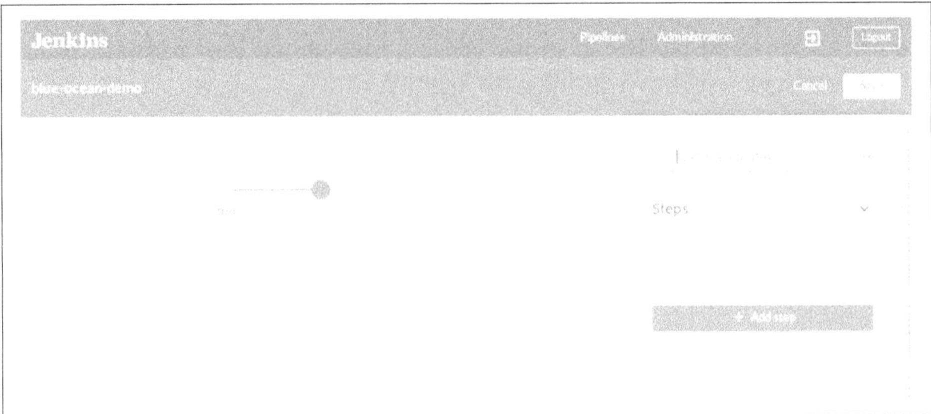

Figure 9-48. Adding a new stage

Let's discuss what happened when we clicked on that halo.

In the left part of the screen:

- Jenkins highlighted the halo we clicked on, by filling it in and turning it blue. That indicates it's the currently selected stage that we're editing.
- A new halo with a + was added *under* that one. This is a way to add steps to run in parallel if we need them.
- A new halo with a + was added *to the right* of our selected stage. That gives us a means to add another stage in our pipeline if needed.

In the right part of the screen:

- A new entry area was set up for us to type in the name of the stage.
- A button was added so that we can add a step to the stage.

For our purposes here, we'll go ahead and just define a simple stage to get the source for our project. So, we'll type in "Source" for the name (Figure 9-49).

Figure 9-49. Naming the stage

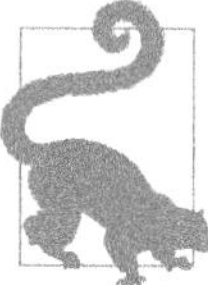

Additional Commands

Notice the ellipsis (...) that appears at the end of the line where we type in the name of the stage. In the pipeline editor, clicking on these will bring up additional commands. In this case, there's only one option available: Delete. Selecting this will delete the entire stage (not just the name), so be sure that is what you want to do before you use that option.

Now we're ready to add one or more steps to our stage.

Adding a step to a stage

Each stage in a Jenkins pipeline must have at least one step. If you attempt to move on from the stage definition without adding a step, the pipeline editor will display an error indication.

To add a new step to a stage, we just click the "+ Add step" button. Once we do that, the selection pane on the right turns into a list of available step types to pick from (Figure 9-50). We can scroll through the list to find the step type we want, or we can type it into the search area.

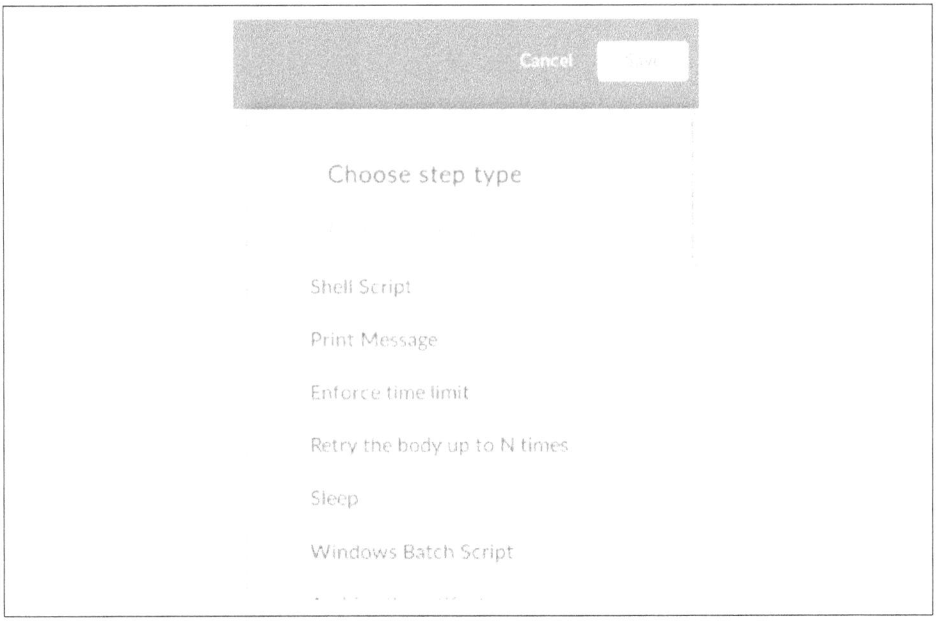

Figure 9-50. Choosing the step type

Here, we'll use the GitSCM step for our Source stage to pull down our source code. In the search box for the steps, we can type "git" and quickly find the "Git" step (Figure 9-51).

Figure 9-51. Searching for a step

Selecting this step brings up a set of text fields that we can fill in to specify the parameters. Note the * next to the Url field, meaning that it's required. The main piece of information we need to put in is the path to our repository, as shown in Figure 9-52.

Source / Git

Url*

https://github.com/explore-jen

Branch

Changelog

CredentialsId

Poll

Figure 9-52. Adding parameters to a step

Adding a Step to the Desired Stage

It's important when attempting to add a step to a stage that you ensure you have the correct stage (halo) selected in the diagram on the left part of the screen.

At this point, let's go ahead and save our work and commit it to the repository.

Saving and committing pipeline changes

Clicking the Save button in the pipeline editor brings up a dialog like the one shown in Figure 9-53.

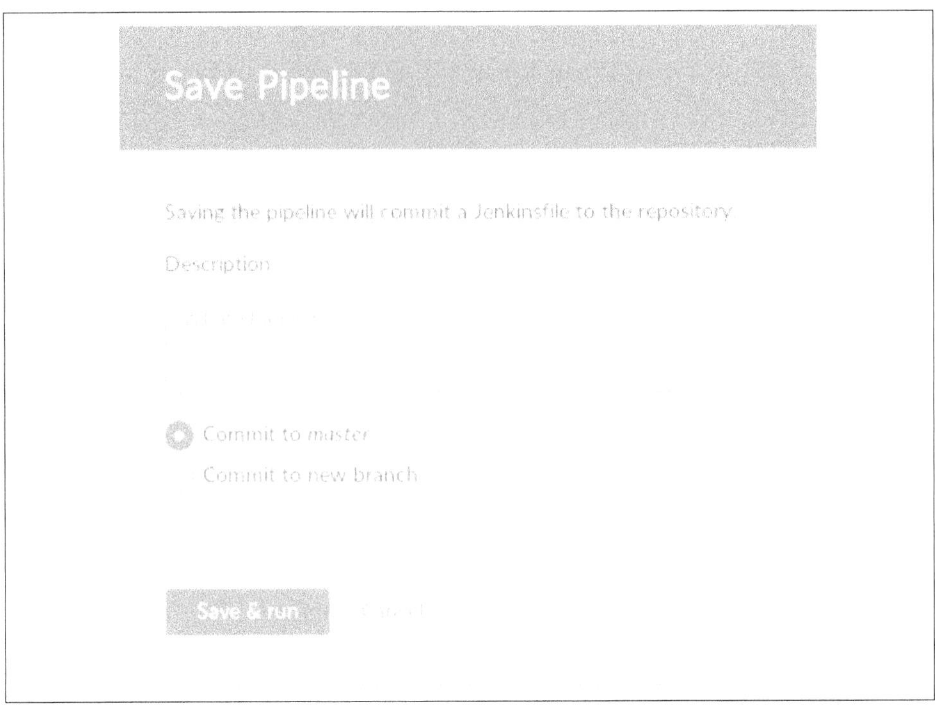

Figure 9-53. Saving the initial pipeline

The fields here are self-explanatory. We'll enter a simple description and choose to commit this to a new branch just because we're still developing this pipeline. We can always merge it back into `master` later.

After filling in the fields, our save dialog looks like Figure 9-54.

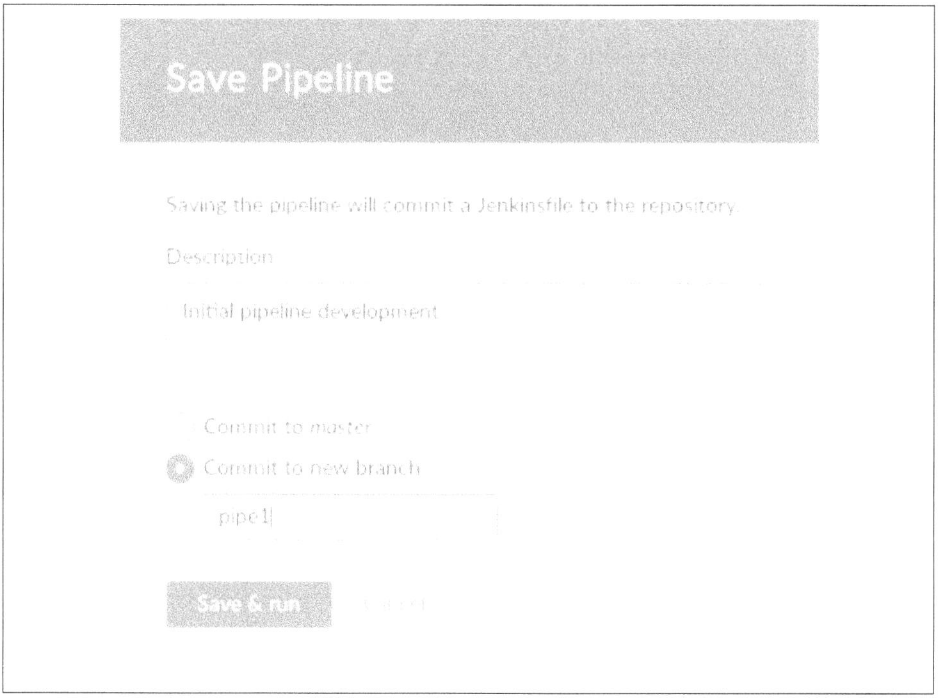

Figure 9-54. Saving the new branch

After we click the "Save & run" button, Jenkins will spin for a few moments while it updates the code and commits and pushes it over to GitHub. If we look in GitHub after the save, we can see the new branch there with the new Jenkinsfile (Figure 9-55).

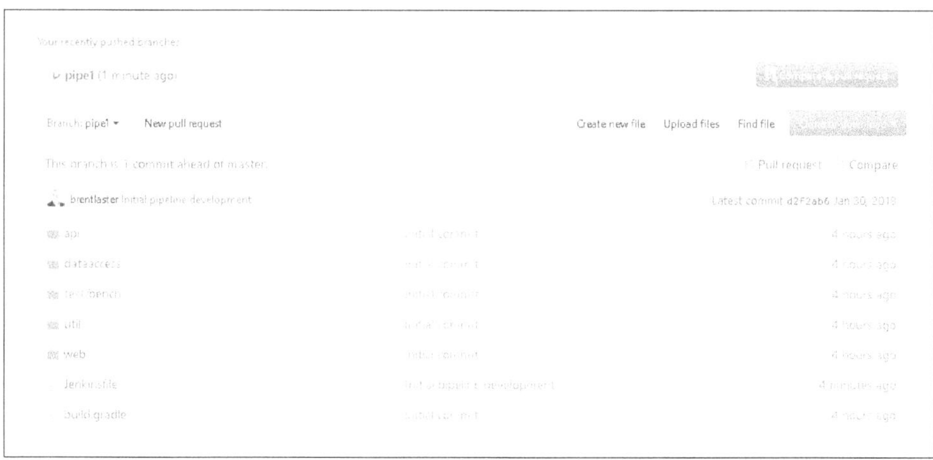

Figure 9-55. New branch shown on GitHub

If we open up the Jenkinsfile on GitHub, we can see the code that was generated by our actions in the pipeline editor. This is shown in Figure 9-56.

Branch: pipe1 ▾ blue-ocean-demo / Jenkinsfile

brentlaster Initial pipeline development

1 contributor

18 lines (17 sloc) 263 Bytes

```
pipeline {
  agent {
    node {
      label 'worker_node1'
    }

  }
  stages {
    stage('Source') {
      steps {
        git 'https://github.com/explore-jenkins/blue-ocean-demo.git'
      }
    }
  }
  environment {
    COMPLETED_MSG = 'Build done!'
  }
}
```

Figure 9-56. Viewing the generated contents of the Jenkinsfile on GitHub

As soon as the code is updated, Jenkins will spin up a build for it. While it's running, this looks like Figure 9-57. Note that the leftmost column features the halo being updated as the build progresses, and on the far right is the icon to stop the build if needed.

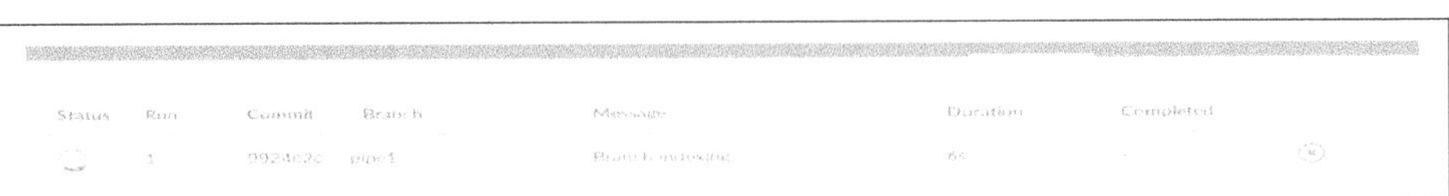

Figure 9-57. Build in progress

When the build is completed, the screen changes to look like Figure 9-58. Notice the halo in the left column is now filled in, green, and checked to indicate successful completion. Also, the icon in the rightmost column has changed into a circular arrow, indicating it can be used to execute a rerun.

Figure 9-58. Completed build

Our simple pipeline works, but it doesn't do anything significant with its one stage. Let's add another stage to do a build operation.

Editing an Existing Pipeline

To edit an existing pipeline for a multibranch project, we switch to the Branches view and click on the next-to-last icon (the one that looks like a pencil) in the row for the branch we want to update. Figure 9-59 shows the Branches view for our project.

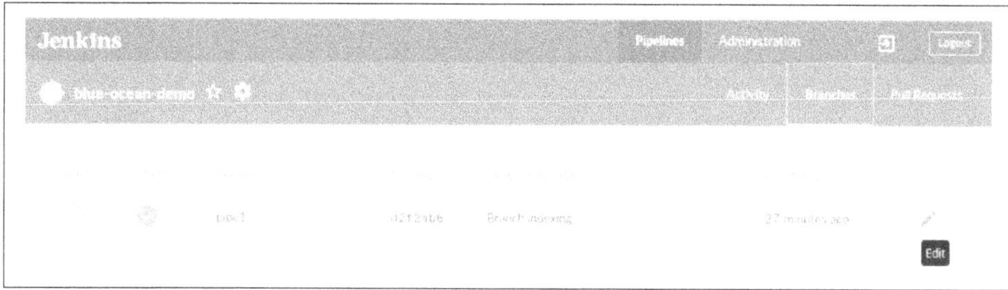

Figure 9-59. Selecting to edit the pipeline in the Branches view

Once we click on the pipeline editor icon, we will be taken back to the pipeline editor screen. To add a new stage after (and not parallel to) the Source stage, we simply click the circle with the + sign in it that's to the right of the Source stage. Then, on the righthand side of the screen, we'll name this stage "Build" (see Figure 9-60).

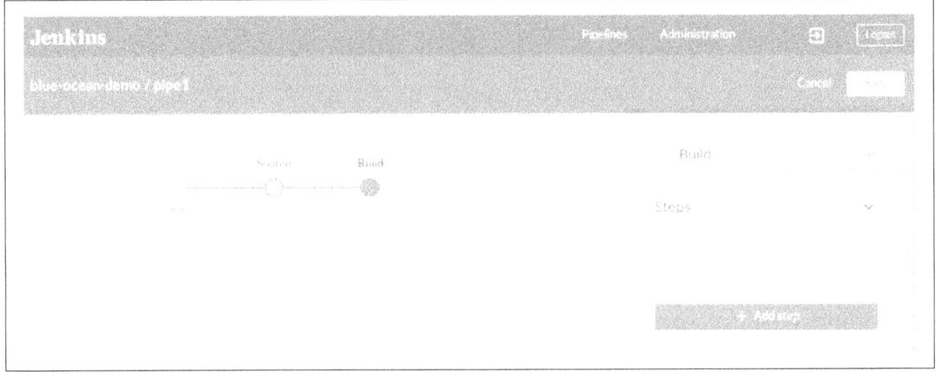

Figure 9-60. Adding a new stage for Build

For this step, we're going to want to invoke our Gradle build instance. We'll first add an `environment` section to ensure the version of Gradle we want is made available and in the path. In our Jenkins global configuration, we have a version of Gradle configured under the name "gradle4" (Figure 9-61).

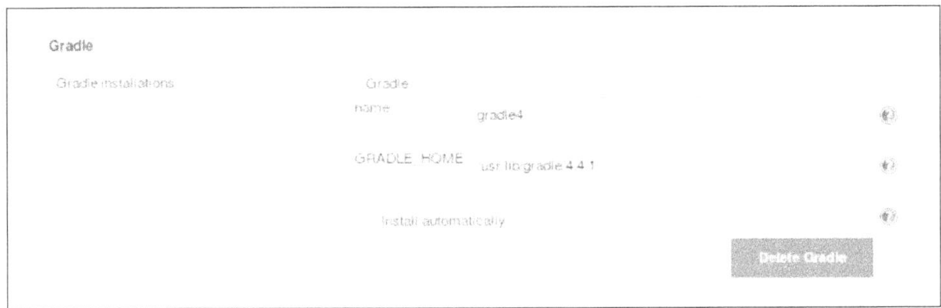

Figure 9-61. Gradle global configuration

In our pipeline, we can use the Declarative Pipeline's `tool` step to specify that we want to use this version and to ensure it is available for the pipeline. To do this, we find the "tool" entry in the Steps section and then fill in the Name field with "gradle4" (Figure 9-62). (The Type field can be empty for this case.)

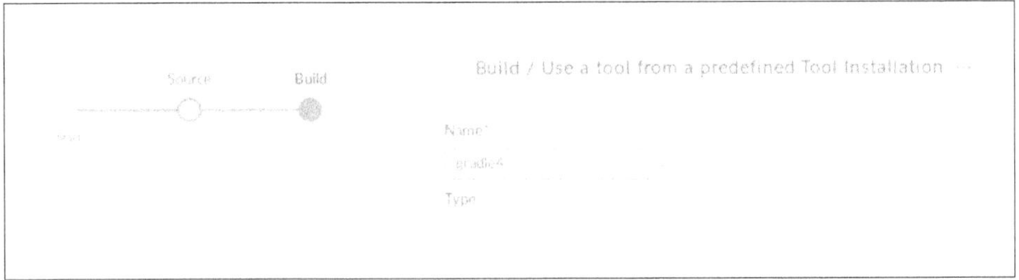

Figure 9-62. Specifying that we want to use the gradle4 tooling

With this step added, our stage definition now looks like Figure 9-63.

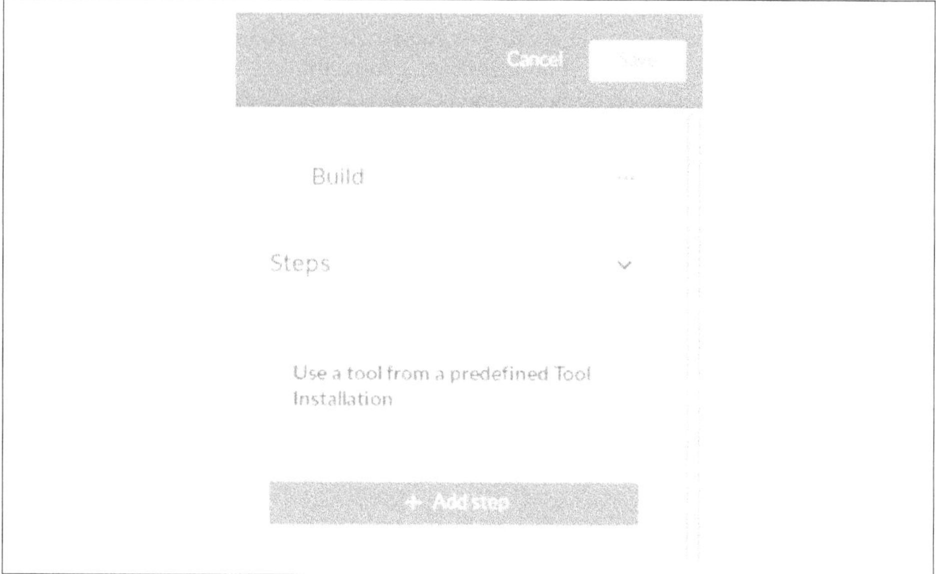

Figure 9-63. tool step added

Next, we actually want to invoke Gradle to do our build. Since there isn't a `gradle` step, we need to use the shell step (`sh`) to run this. The only thing we need to have Gradle do is call the `build` task, so this is straightforward. If we were writing this as code in a pipeline along with the `tool` step, we would use commands like this:

```
tool 'gradle4'
sh 'gradle build'
```

Since this requires a shell call, we'll just select the Shell Script step from the list, and then enter the rest of the command as the argument. Figure 9-64 shows what this looks like in the editor.

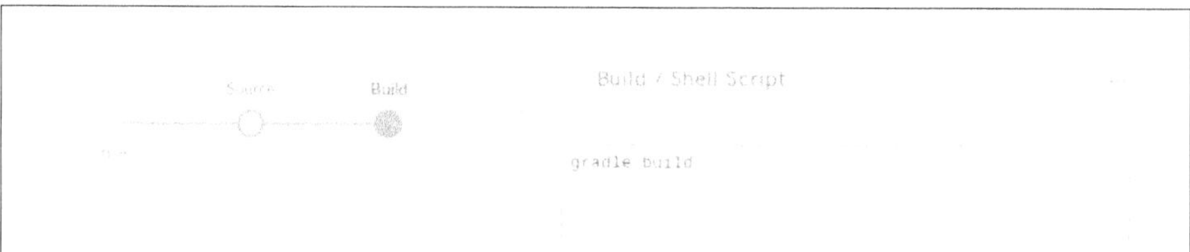

Figure 9-64. Adding a shell step to do a Gradle build

No Starting or Ending Quote

Notice that when we are entering this command in the step window, we do not put starting or ending quotes around it. If we do, Jenkins will not be able to interpret it correctly.

Now, if we select the Build halo, our Build stage with the multiple steps looks like Figure 9-65.

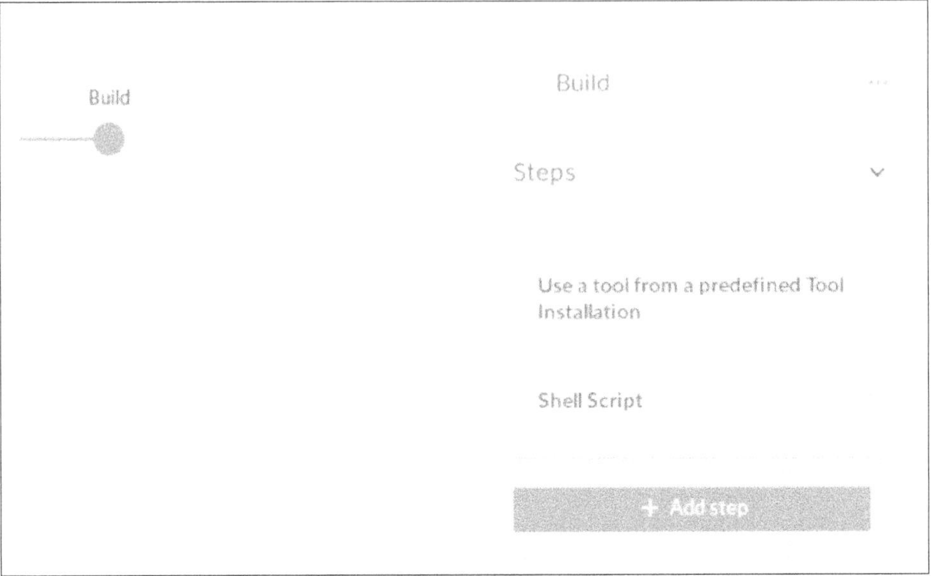

Figure 9-65. Build stage with multiple steps

We can now simply save our pipeline and have it committed and pushed to the `pipe1` branch again (Figure 9-66).

Figure 9-66. Committing and saving a pipeline

Importing and Editing Existing Pipelines

We previously covered how to point Blue Ocean to existing GitHub organizations and repositories and tell it how to create a new pipeline from a particular repository. We also saw that there was an option to have it automatically discover any existing Jenkinsfiles in branches in an organization.

If it can find a Jenkinsfile, then it simply imports it, creates a job for the branch, and attempts to execute it.

Of course, if you are importing an existing pipeline from GitHub, there's no guarantee that the environment the pipeline needs will exist, unless you are importing to the same or a duplicate system. For example, importing the pipeline we just created to a different Jenkins instance causes the expected jobs to be set up for the branches with Jenkinsfiles, but we can also see that those jobs that previously succeeded now fail (Figure 9-67).

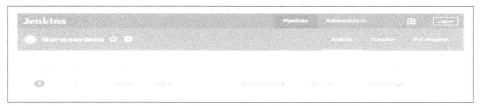

Figure 9-67. Failing jobs after import to a different Jenkins system

Understanding why and fixing these issues will give us a chance for a more in-depth look at Blue Ocean.

Simple debugging and editing of an existing pipeline

As noted earlier in the chapter, one of the nice things about the Blue Ocean interface is that it segments the logs for a pipeline by the stage and step. To figure out what's wrong with our jobs here, let's drill into the failed run of the job. We do that by clicking on the row with the failure in the Activity view. From here, we can see that it was the Build stage that failed (Figure 9-68).

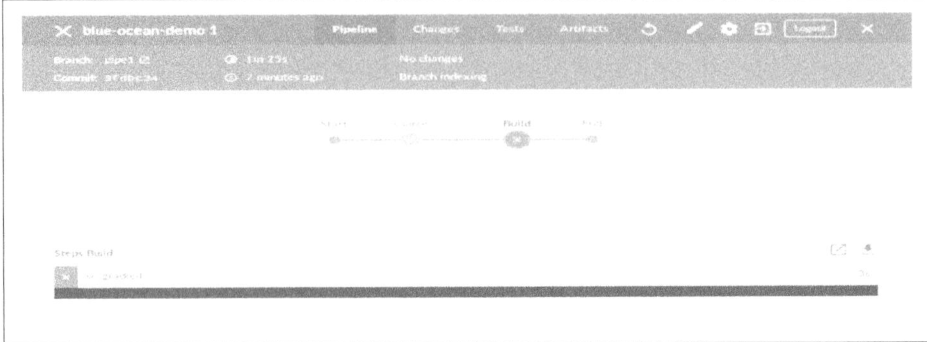

Figure 9-68. Drilling in to find the failed stage

Then, by looking at the step logs for the stage below the pipeline graphic, we can see the reason for the failure (Figure 9-69). In this case, the pipeline was trying to call "gradle4," and that isn't recognized as a globally defined tool on this system.

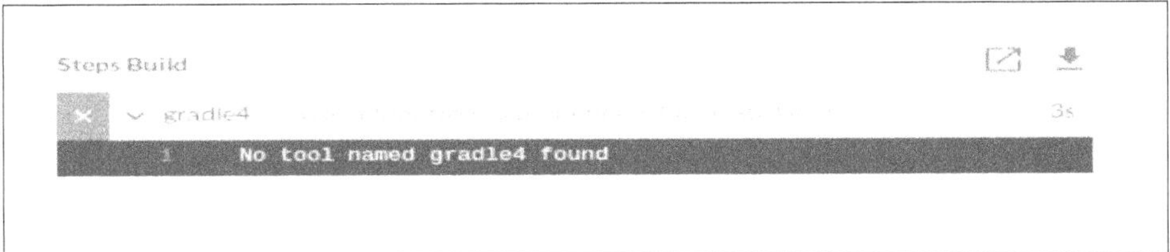

Figure 9-69. Step log showing error

Looking at Log

Some of these tips were mentioned in other contexts earlier in the chapter, but since it's been a while, here are a few quick reminders about looking at step logs:

- In our example we have only one step to choose from, but if there were multiple steps, the one that failed would still be indicated.
- Clicking anywhere in the "header" row for a step—the one with the "X" in it, in this case—toggles expanding/collapsing the logs for the step.
- When collapsed, the second symbol in the header row will be ">". When expanded, the second symbol in the header row will be "V".
- Clicking the icon with the diagonal, upward pointing arrow on the far right above the step logs will open up the log for the selected step in a new window, similar to looking at the console output.
- Clicking on the icon with the downward pointing arrow and the line under it will download a copy of the log as a separate file.

If we go to the Global Tool Configuration section on this system, we can see why this failed. (We can get to the Manage Jenkins page from the Blue Ocean screen by clicking on the "X" in the upper-right corner of this screen, and then the Administration link on the main dashboard page.) Looking at the Gradle installations on this system (Figure 9-70), we can see that Gradle is referenced as "gradle32" and not "gradle4."

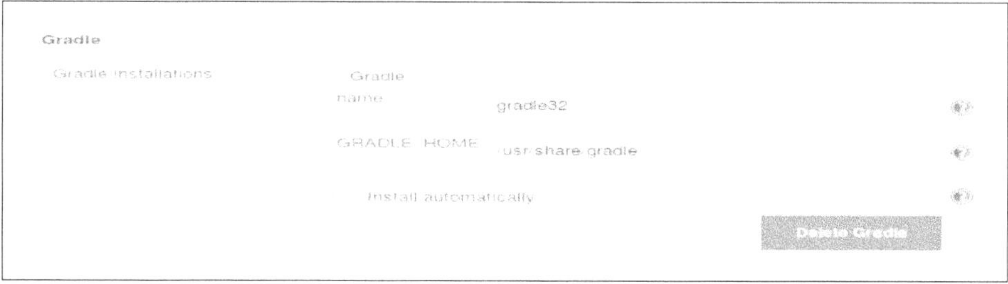

Figure 9-70. Different Gradle version

Of course, we could change the name for the Gradle global configuration to match what's expected, but that might break other existing jobs that use that name. We could also add a second reference with the new name. But instead, let's see how to go in and edit our job in Blue Ocean to match the configuration for this system.

Going back to our Branches view, we see that we have the pencil icon available to open the editor on the `pipe1` branch (Figure 9-71).

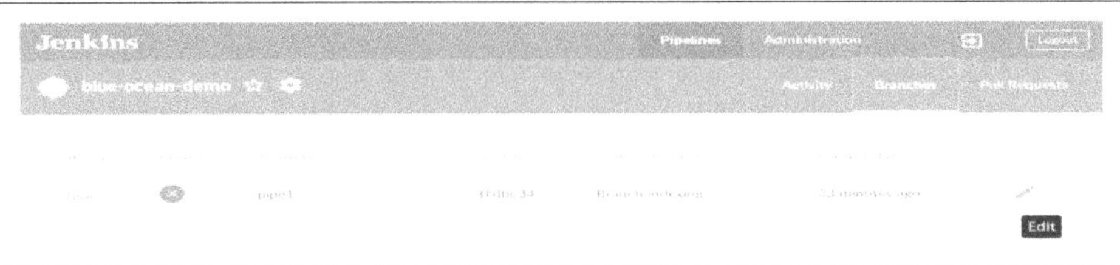

Figure 9-71. Editable branch in Branches view

This will put us into the pipeline editor. Since it doesn't know what stage or step we're intending to work with, it just starts us out at the initial "Pipeline Settings" point in the interface (Figure 9-72).

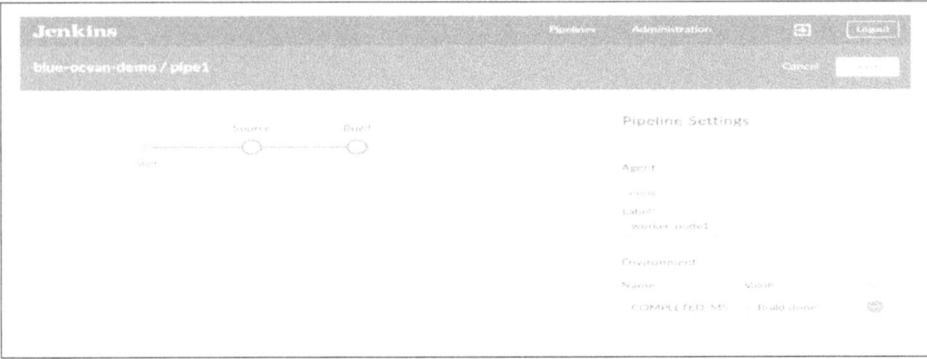

Figure 9-72. Default editor screen

From here, since we want to update a step in the Build stage, we can just select the Build stage halo. That action then changes the context on the righthand side of the editor to show the Build stage and its steps. This is shown in Figure 9-73.

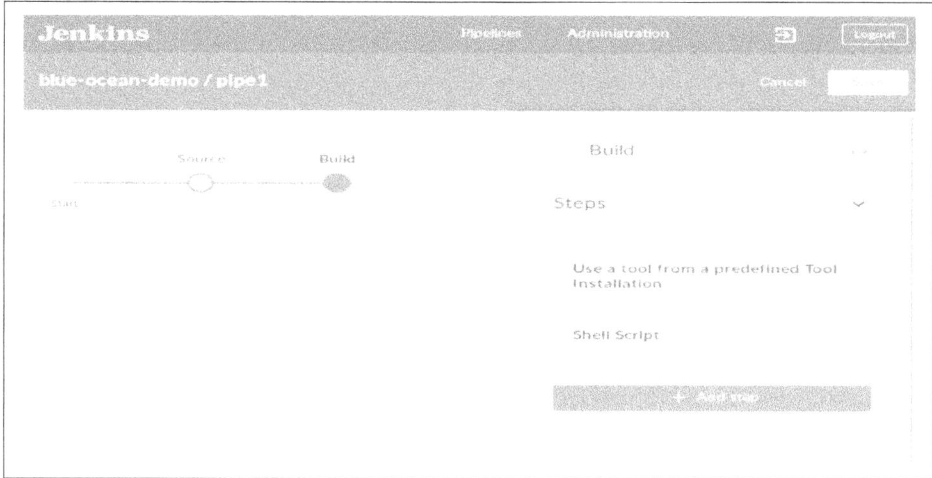

Figure 9-73. Build stage selected

Now, we click on the block containing the step for "Use a tool from a predefined Tool Installation" and edit as intended. Figure 9-74 shows the updated step in the editor after our edit.

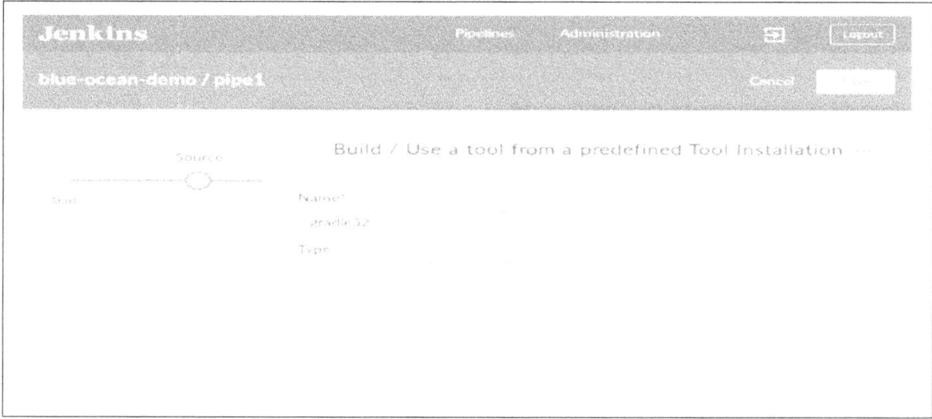

Figure 9-74. Updated step

After this, we can choose to save and commit our changes back to the repository. Figure 9-75 shows the Save Pipeline dialog that we get. Note that we have the option to specify a different branch here if we want. We'll do that by putting in "pipe2" for the branch name, since we're making changes for a different system, and just in case there are further issues.

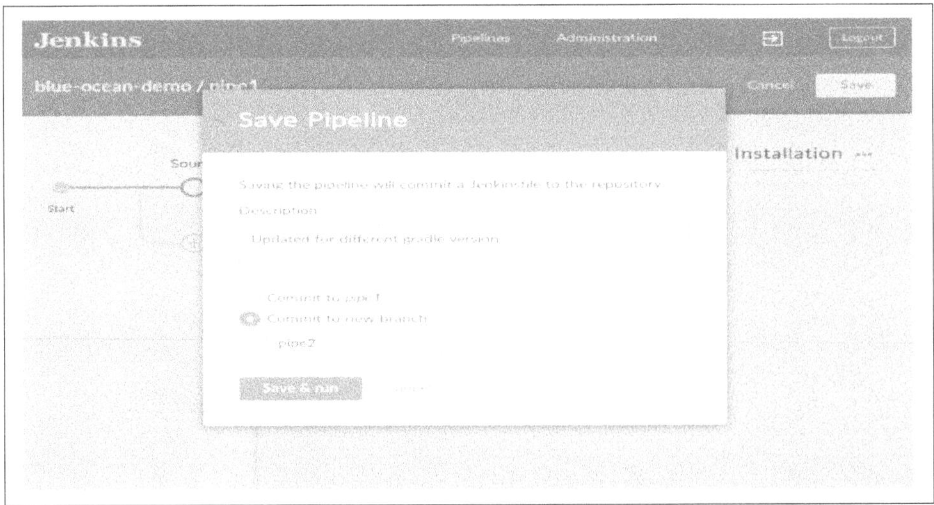

Figure 9-75. Saving the updated pipeline and committing/pushing to a new branch

After we save our changes and Blue Ocean commits/pushes the changes to `pipe2`, it will build the updates.

Debugging editor issues

Let's look at one additional (more complex) example. Assume that, rather than using two separate statements to invoke Gradle, we want to combine them into one statement as we've done previously in the book. That is, instead of the code in our Jenkinsfile being this:

```
stage('Build') {
   steps {
      tool 'gradle32'
      sh 'gradle build'
   }
}
```

we want it to be simplified to this:

```
stage('Build') {
   steps {
      sh "${tool 'gradle32'}/bin/gradle build"
   }
}
```

To make this change, we first want to remove the unneeded `tool` step. Doing this sort of edit in Blue Ocean is fairly easy. On the main page for our pipeline, we first select the halo representing the Build stage. Then, the righthand side of the screen will show the steps we currently have in the stage (Figure 9-76).

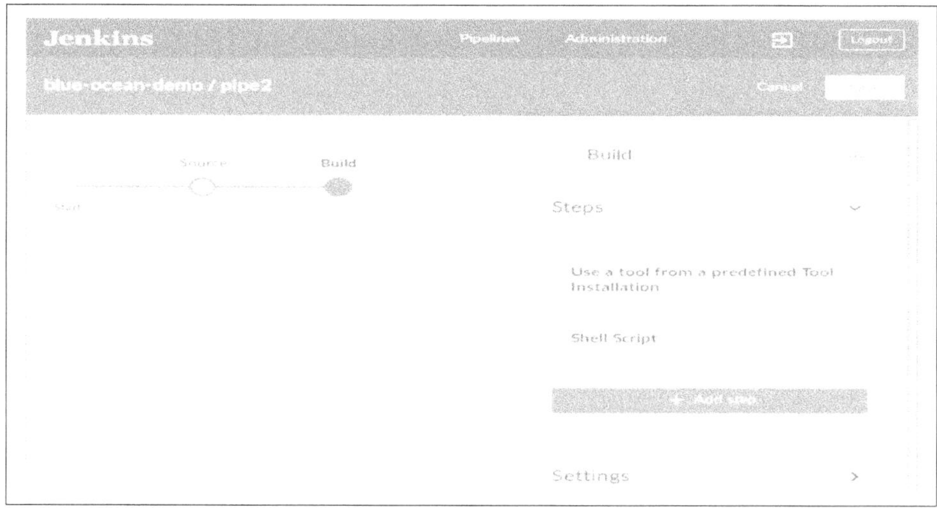

Figure 9-76. Selecting the stage to edit

In the Steps area, we can select the `tool` step (labeled "Use a tool from a predefined Tool Installation") and click to drill into it. Once working with the individual step, we can click on the "..." near the top right and select Delete for the action to delete this step (Figure 9-77).

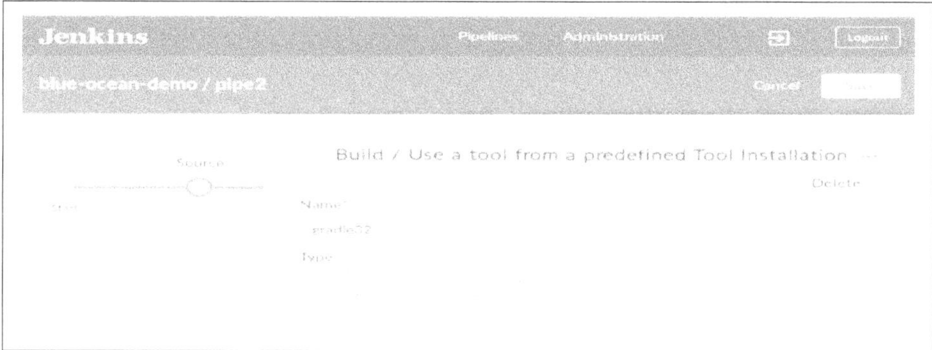

Figure 9-77. Deleting a step from a stage in Blue Ocean

We can then select the remaining step in our stage (the step to invoke the shell script) and modify it to have the combined command (Figure 9-78).

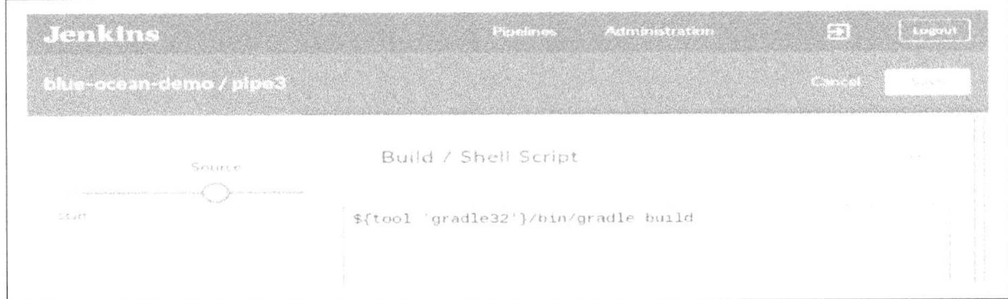

Figure 9-78. Editing the shell step to have the combined command

We can then save and commit our updated pipeline (Figure 9-79). As with the other changes, we'll save it to a new branch (`pipe3`).

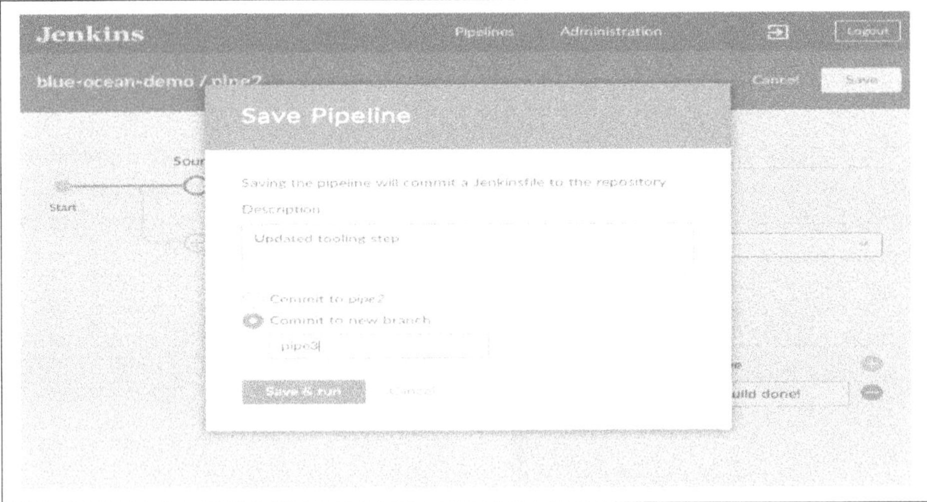

Figure 9-79. Saving the modified pipeline

Unfortunately, this time our pipeline fails to build after saving and committing (Figure 9-80).

Figure 9-80. Failed run of our new branch

Since the only change was the deletion of the separate `tool` step and creation of the combined step, the problem must reside in that change. Interestingly, if we look at the command in the editor, it still looks correct. (We won't show that here since it is the same as the earlier figures.) However, if we drill into the run and expand the log for the step, we see an interesting message (Figure 9-81) that ends with the following text on line 2:

```
.../script.sh: Bad substitution
```

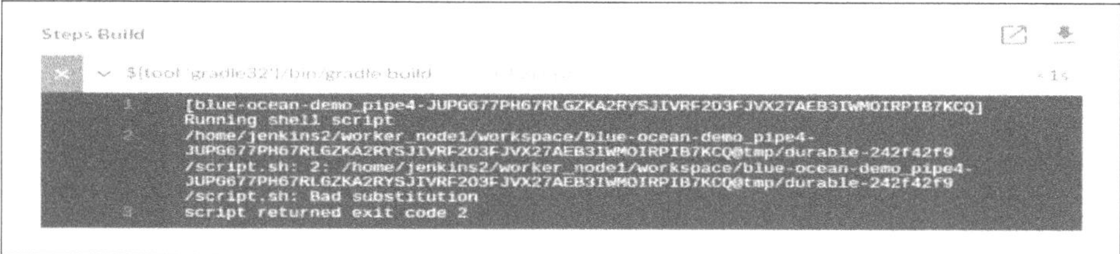

Figure 9-81. Odd error message from the editor

At this point, it can be confusing to try to figure out why the pipeline build fails even though our step, as shown in the row above the expanded log, looks perfectly valid. There is one other place we can go to check on things—the generated Jenkinsfile that was saved and committed/pushed into our GitHub repository. Figure 9-82 shows the generated Jenkinsfile.

Tree: ccd5f34d7a ▾ blue-ocean-demo / Jenkinsfile

brentlaster Update gradle invocation

1 contributor

23 lines (22 sloc) 363 Bytes

```
pipeline {
  agent {
    node {
      label 'worker_node1'
    }

  }
  stages {
    stage('Source') {
      steps {
        git 'https://github.com/explore-jenkins/blue-ocean-demo.git'
      }
    }
    stage('Build') {
      steps {
        sh '${tool \'gradle32\'}/bin/gradle build'
      }
```

Figure 9-82. Jenkinsfile with step with incorrect quoting

Notice line 16:

```
sh '${tool \'gradle32\'}/bin/gradle build'
```

This is not the quoting we entered. The Blue Ocean editor has grouped the entire command in single quotes and escaped the quotes around `gradle32`, which is what has caused the issues. The problem is that we needed to use quotes within our command. In fact, to make this command work, we need double quotes around the step to ensure the value we get back from the `tool` call is interpolated correctly. However, the editor engine can't automatically recognize these requirements and simply surrounds the statement with single quotes and escapes any quotes within the statement. This is an example of some functionality that is not (yet) working as it should in the editor.

Editor Development

It's worth noting that the quoting problem mentioned here exists at the time of this writing, but it may be fixed by the time you read this. You can attempt operations similar to what we're doing here and see if your instance has any issues.

However, the approach for debugging by examining the generated Jenkinsfile still applies to other situations.

So, how can we fix this? You might wonder if it would fix things if we explicitly put in the double quotes around the step in the editor. Unfortunately not, as we still get the same behavior as before. In that case, the error message would be the same, but we would get this line as the generated step in the Jenkinsfile:

```
sh '"${tool \'gradle32\'}/bin/gradle build"'
```

This, again, is not correct.

Outside of the editor, we could pull the Jenkinsfile down and manually edit it to fix the quoting, and then push it back. However, if we want to fix it via the editor, we'll need to put a different syntax in for the step—something without quoting mixed in.

One "kludge" could be to simply put in the full path to Gradle, taking the value of `GRADLE_HOME` from the global configuration and plugging that in, as in:

```
/usr/share/gradle/bin/gradle build
```

However, a cleaner approach would be just to set our code back to the way it was originally with the separate `tool` and `sh` steps, and save our changes again.

Adding code not supported in the editor

While the Blue Ocean editor continues to evolve and improve over time, you may still come across situations where certain constructs are not supported—even for declarative syntax.

One such example for the pipeline we have been working with could be if we wanted to use the `post` section in declarative syntax to always print a "build done" message.

We already have an environment variable defined with the simple string that we want to print. We can certainly add a step through the editor to print (`echo`) the message out. However (at least at the time of this writing), there isn't a good way to add the `post` section via the editor.

In such cases, we can always go outside of Jenkins, pull the latest generated Jenkinsfile, modify it to have the code we want, and then push it back out. The following code listing shows a portion of our pipeline modified in this way to add the `post` section:

```
...
    stage('Build') {
      steps {
        sh "${tool 'gradle32'}/bin/gradle build"
      }
    }
  }
  environment {
    COMPLETED_MSG = 'Build done!'
  }
  post {
    always {
      sh 'echo $COMPLETED_MSG'
    }
  }
}
```

With this code in place, we can then run our pipeline again in the editor. In this scenario, since the added code is not a new stage, there is no new halo for this section. But the step logs do show the code being executed, and we can view the log details just as we would for any other step (Figure 9-83).

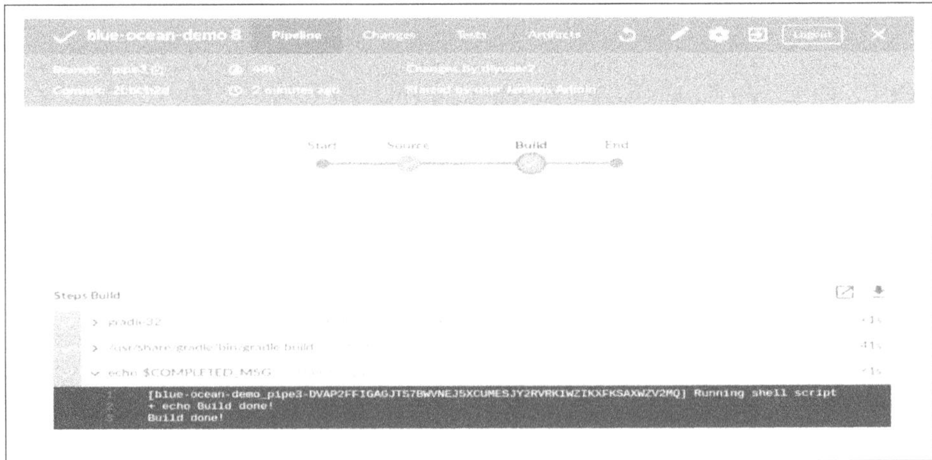

Figure 9-83. Run of externally updated Jenkinsfile, with new post section

Looking at this sort of workflow, we can see how well GitHub is integrated into this pipeline creation/editing process. But as you may recall from earlier screens, in this part of the chapter, GitHub wasn't our only option for a source repository. We'll wrap up this chapter by discussing how the interaction with Blue Ocean works when we are using a non-GitHub repository.

Working with Pipelines from Non-GitHub Repositories

When working with pipelines from non-GitHub repositories in the editor, the main difference is simply how you connect to the repository.

For example, if you wanted to access a local Git repository, you might supply an SSH-style URL to connect to. Blue Ocean will detect this and then generate a public SSH key for access. You will need to register this public key with the Git server. If you have shell access, this may just mean adding it to the *authorized_keys* file on the server.

Figure 9-84 shows an example of this. One other case that this figure shows is what happens when the default name for the pipeline already exists in Jenkins. In that case, Jenkins will require you to create a different name for the copy of the pipeline being created here.

Figure 9-84. Creating a new pipeline from local Git

For Bitbucket Cloud, you need to fill in your Bitbucket user ID (email address) and password and then proceed from there (Figure 9-85). For GitHub Enterprise or Bitbucket Server, you first need to tell Jenkins where your server is located.

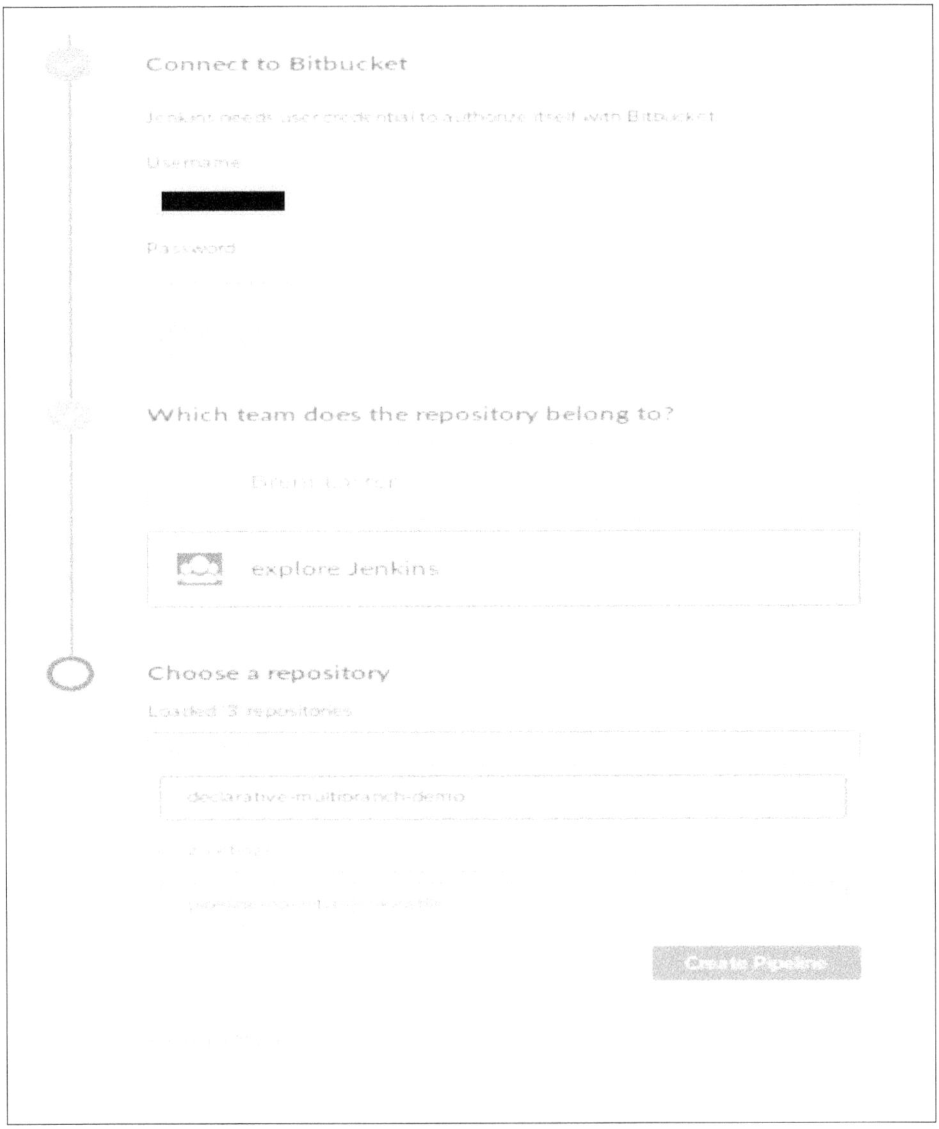

Figure 9-85. Creating a new pipeline from Bitbucket Cloud

This completes our look at using the Blue Ocean pipeline editor. As you can see, it contains many of the pieces we need to construct and edit pipeline for GitHub—but not all of them. Some pieces still have to be manually entered and updated.

Summary

This chapter introduced Blue Ocean, the new visual interface for Jenkins. Blue Ocean allows you to see graphical representations of existing pipelines, with most of the familiar types of pages (dashboard, run detail, etc.) as you would have in the Jenkins "classic" view.

Blue Ocean also contains functionality to create and edit new pipelines for repositories that don't already have a Jenkinsfile.

Blue Ocean works best with Declarative Pipelines. In fact, that's the only kind of pipeline it can create and/or edit. It also works well for projects that have multiple branches, and integrates nicely with the various public and local environments for Git, GitHub, and Bitbucket.

When showing pipelines, Blue Ocean provides a nice feature in segmenting logs by build step based on which stage is currently selected. It provides views of the changes that went into updating a pipeline, completed/failed tests, and artifacts generated by the pipeline. It can also show pull requests for GitHub projects that have them (if they originated from a fork).

The Blue Ocean interface provides a simpler way for those starting out to get familiar with building pipelines. Its graphical interface and point-and-click options (such as the ones for defining new stages and steps) are simple to use once you are familiar with the workflow. For more complicated pipelines, though (and in some places where Blue Ocean doesn't yet support the syntax), you may be better off just editing and developing the Jenkinsfile outside of the interface.

In our next chapter, we'll look at different kinds of conversion scenarios you may encounter as you work with Jenkins 2.

CHAPTER 10
Conversions

With the advent of Jenkins 2, the Jenkins user now has many options for ways to create and express pipelines. They include the traditional Freestyle jobs, pipeline code in the Jenkins application itself, and pipeline code stored in Jenkinsfiles. Additionally, pipeline code can be written either in the Scripted Pipeline syntax or the Declarative Pipeline syntax. With all of these ways to define pipelines, it is highly likely that the user will need, or want, to do some sort of conversion between the various forms at some point. This chapter will provide guidelines on accomplishing some of these conversions.

In particular, we'll focus on three main types of conversions:

- Converting from Freestyle jobs to a pipeline in the Jenkins application
- Converting from a Scripted Pipeline to a Jenkinsfile
- Converting from a Scripted Pipeline to a Declarative Pipeline

"Freestyle"

Note that we are using the term "Freestyle" here loosely, to mean any traditional Jenkins job or pipeline created via the web forms. This most typically will be using the Freestyle job type, although other types might be used as well. For other job types, the general concepts and discussions should still apply.

Rather than attempt to provide every detail about how to do a conversion, we'll focus on guidelines and some selected examples to illustrate the approach and principles involved for each of these categories. While these do not cover every possible case, they should cover enough to give you a good grasp of how to handle the other cases.

Assumptions

It's worth noting that this chapter assumes you have read the other chapters and are familiar with the concepts and tools they introduce, such as the Snippet Generator. If not, you can scan the Table of Contents or the Index to find the necessary references.

Common Preparation

Before beginning a conversion, there are a few general things to consider. While not an absolute requirement, this may save you some work later on. Most of the items descriubed here are in the form of questions, designed to remind you of information you may want to gather up front for the existing pipeline.

Logic and Accuracy

It may go without saying, but before you convert from an existing pipeline of one form or another, you want to make sure that the existing pipeline runs as expected and completes successfully. That doesn't mean you can't redesign or refactor parts of the pipeline as you convert it, but ensuring you have an existing pipeline that works will give you a reference to test against and compare results and logic to.

Project Type

Jenkins 2 introduces a number of different project types and structures that were not previously available. It is worth considering at this point whether your converted pipeline jobs might better fit into a Jenkins folder structure, a Multibranch Pipeline project (if you can make use of a Jenkinsfile and multiple branches), or a GitHub Organization or Bitbucket Team/Project project (if you have one of those already set up).

The various kinds of new projects available in Jenkins 2 are discussed in detail in Chapter 8.

Systems

Next, consider what nodes the pipeline currently uses. Will the new pipeline have access to these, or do new ones need to be set up? What are the labels of each system that is used? Is anything running on the master node? If so, is it appropriate to be run on the lightweight executor there? Do you need to add any additional labels to the node configurations to fit your new pipeline?

Access

What access to resources or user permissions are needed for the parts of the pipeline to run? Are certain credentials required, or do new/additional ones need to be defined and set up?

Another use case might be transitioning from a Freestyle project to a Multibranch Pipeline or GitHub Organization/Bitbucket Team project. In those cases, you might need to ensure you have access to the code in the external repository and set up supporting pieces like the webhook for a GitHub project (as discussed in Chapter 8).

Also, if you choose to create or use shared libraries, you will want to consider whether they should be global or not, and who should have access to update them. (Chapter 6 discusses shared libraries in detail.)

Global Configuration

Luckily, telling Jenkins where global tools are located still involves the same basic process. In the Global Tool Configuration (or System Configuration, depending on the tool), you add an entry for the tool and specify a name and installation location. No significant changes are needed in most cases for this part. However, it's worth reviewing the configuration to see whether any newer (or different) versions are warranted. This also serves to refresh your knowledge of what's available and how it can be accessed.

Plugins

Since Jenkins derives most of its functionality from plugins, the correct ones need to be installed. Are there updates that need to be done? If converting from a Freestyle to a Pipeline project, do the operations done in the Freestyle job have corresponding pipeline DSL commands?

In order for plugins to be compatible with the new Jenkins 2 features, they must be updated from the traditional versions. There are primarily two criteria:

- They must be able to survive restarts (be serializable).
- They need to provide steps that can be integrated with pipeline DSL code.

So, the first order of business when looking to migrate the specific functionality of some technology in a Jenkins pipeline is to ensure that you have an updated plugin version installed that is compatible with the pipeline DSL. To find out about compatibility with your designated technologies, you can reference sites such as the *Pipeline Steps Reference* (*https://jenkins.io/doc/pipeline/steps/*) or *Plugin Compatibility with GitHub* (*http://bit.ly/2qQ3gT5*).

Shared Libraries

Shared libraries are a convenient way to compartmentalize code that needs to be reused, or that needs to contain complexity, or that must be separated out for security purposes. Consider whether there is such functionality in your existing pipeline that you want to move into a shared library. If so, it would be advisable to work on coding your shared library early to ensure it will work as you think and can be called from your code.

Note that these comments could also apply to externally loaded code (also discussed in Chapter 6) if you choose to use that instead of shared libraries.

Converting a Freestyle Pipeline to a Scripted Pipeline

Now that we've covered the prerequisites and migration considerations, let's actually walk through (at a high level) a conversion of an example Freestyle pipeline to a Scripted Pipeline. Figure 10-1 shows a typical example of a deployment pipeline and the pieces associated with it.

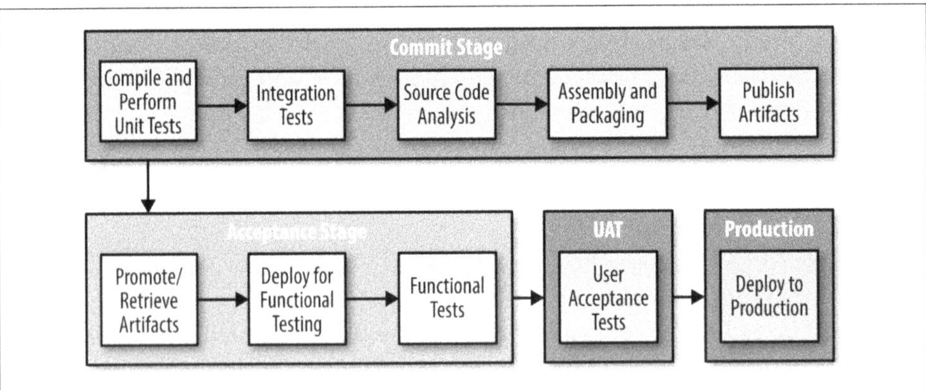

Figure 10-1. Parts of a typical deployment pipeline

Stages

Use of the term "stage" in Figure 10-1 does not imply a Jenkins pipeline stage; it is just a way to describe a section of the pipeline.

For some of my training courses, I have implemented this type of pipeline with Freestyle jobs in Jenkins. Essentially, each block was implemented by a single Jenkins job that, if successful, chained to the next job.

Figure 10-2 shows this set of Freestyle jobs in a traditional Jenkins list view. Note that each job has a descriptive name that maps to a part of the pipeline.

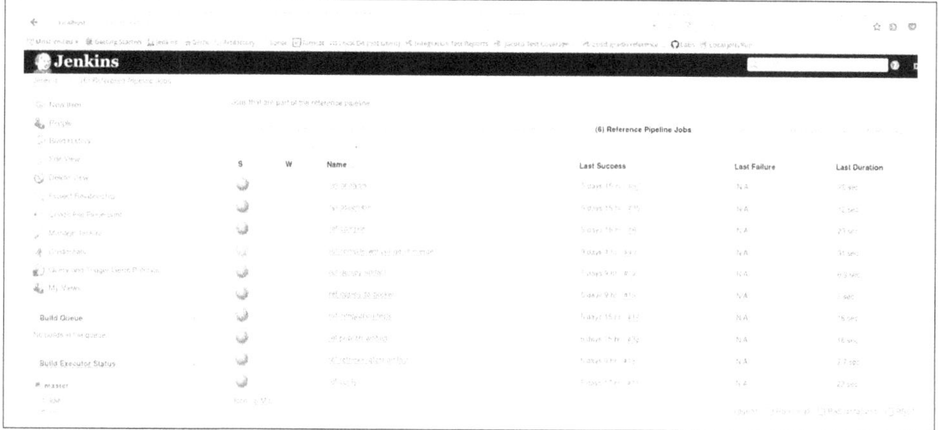

Figure 10-2. Pipeline expressed as a series of traditional Jenkins Freestyle jobs

This pipeline relies on several different open source technologies for implementation. Table 10-1 lists these and briefly describes their purpose in case you are not familiar with them.

Table 10-1. Technologies used in example deployment pipeline

Name	Purpose
Jenkins	Workflow management/orchestration
Git	Source management
Gradle	Build automation
SonarQube	Code analysis and metrics
JaCoCo	Code coverage
Artifactory	Binary artifact storage and management
Docker	Container and image creation

The pipeline performs the following tasks:

- Gets the designated source
- Compiles the source and runs unit tests
- Runs a simplified integration test (using a test database)
- Does code analysis with SonarQube (metrics) and Jacoco (code coverage)
- Assembles an artifact
- Publishes the artifact into the artifact repository (Artifactory)
- Gets the latest artifact out
- Deploys it to a container in Docker for functional testing

- Deploys it for public use

The application itself is a simple web app that uses an underlying MySQL database and exposes a simple REST API. An example of the web app running is shown in Figure 10-3.

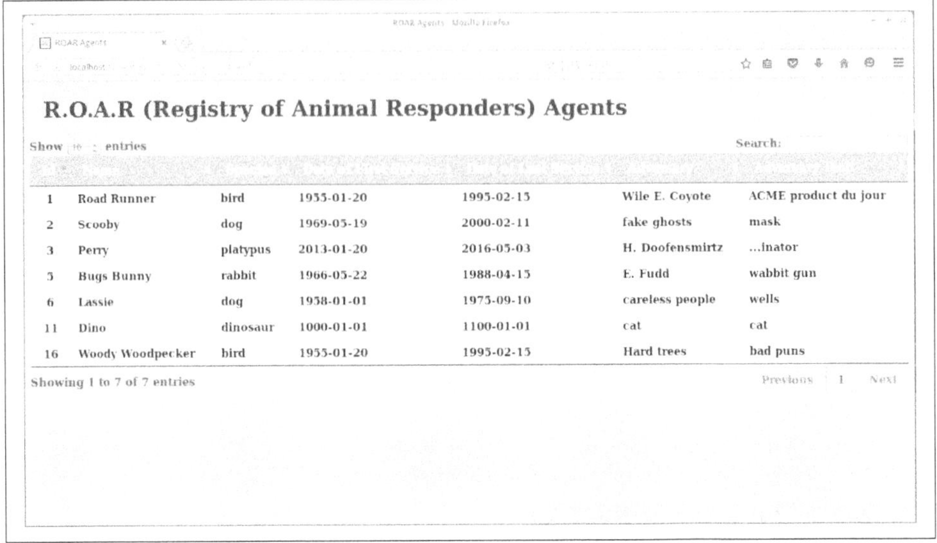

Figure 10-3. Sample web app

The underlying Gradle project is made up of four separate subprojects: one for the API, one for data access, one for utility code, and one for the web-centric code.

Obviously, this is a very simplistic and contrived pipeline example, but it serves to illustrate the main parts of a continuous delivery pipeline/workflow.

Let's now dive in and look at converting some of the Freestyle jobs into corresponding stages in a Scripted Pipeline.

> **Scripted or Declarative?**
>
> When converting from traditional Freestyle jobs in Jenkins to a pipeline, you have a key choice up front: Scripted or Declarative. The main factor to consider here is the complexity of your pipeline. The Declarative Pipeline structure was developed in part to make it easier for users to convert from Freestyle Jenkins projects to a Pipeline implementation. One way it does this is by providing a structure with sections similar to the available sections in a Freestyle job.
>
> Take a look at the Declarative Pipeline structure as shown in Figure 10-4. Even if you aren't familiar with Declarative Pipelines (discussed in Chapter 7), you can probably

start to pick out some parts that seem to correspond to sections of a traditional Freestyle job.

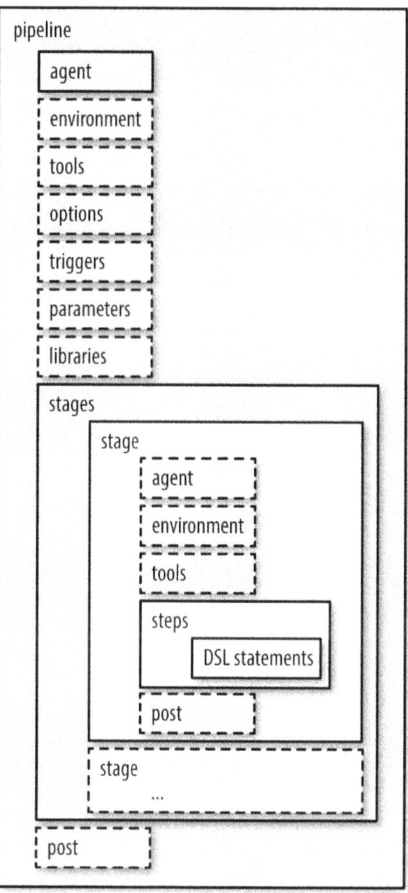

Figure 10-4. Declarative Pipeline structure

This correspondence between the parts of a Declarative Pipeline and the parts of a Freestyle job make Declarative Pipelines an attractive choice for conversion for simple pipelines—when all parts can be expressed in a declarative format. However, currently the limitations associated with using some constructs and plugins with Declarative Pipelines can make them challenging for an initial conversion. For this reason, we will first walk through converting a traditional pipeline to a Scripted Pipeline and then later show how a Scripted Pipeline might be converted to a Declarative one.

Source

When you first start looking to convert a Freestyle pipeline, you'll want to find the section that pertains to the pipeline stage you're interested in creating. For example, if we wanted to create a `Source` stage to pull down the source for our pipeline, we would first find the SCM section in our Freestyle project. (In the sample project, retrieving the source code was tied in with another job in the original version, but it works well to have it as its own stage in our pipeline.)

Choosing How to Map Traditional Jobs to Pipeline Stages

At a high level, individual Freestyle jobs may be suitable to convert into pipeline stages. For example, if we look at a representation of a chain of Freestyle jobs in the older form of the Build Pipeline plugin in Figure 10-5, we can see this looks very much like the Stage View representation of a Jenkins 2 pipeline.

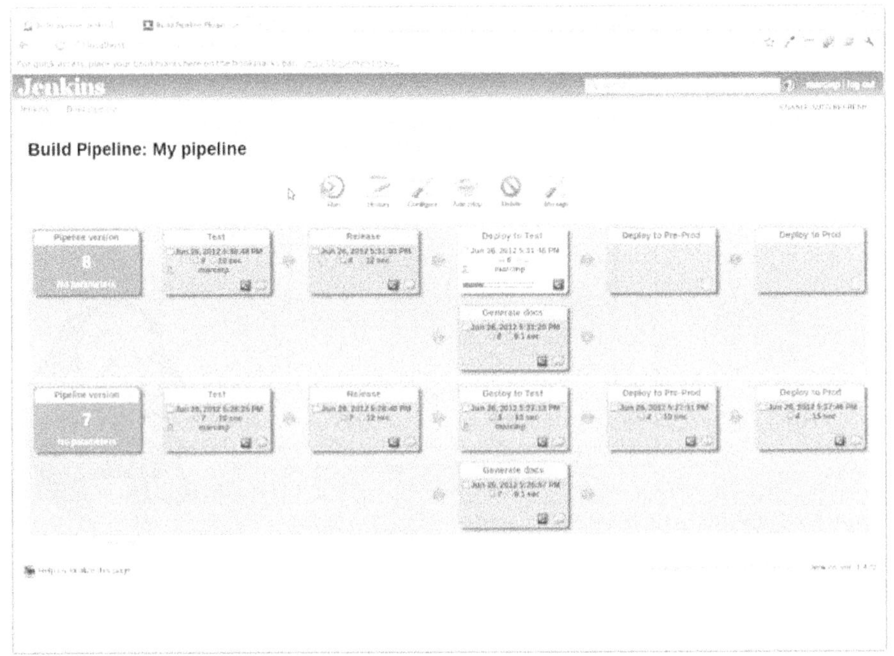

Figure 10-5. Build Pipeline plugin representation of a pipeline

In general, a good guideline if you have multiple Freestyle jobs chained together is to create a corresponding stage for each Freestyle job.

This assumes, however, that your Freestyle jobs are each set up to do one operation. That may not always be the case. For example, some users might have a single job that pulls down source, does the build, and runs unit tests. Another user might have three separate Freestyle jobs chained together for those functions. Both are legitimate use cases, and each may work better in one situation or another.

Both of these cases can also be modeled in pipelines—either as a single stage that pulls down source, does the build, and runs unit tests, or as three separate stages, each doing one of those functions.

When you are first learning about and starting out with pipelines, the recommended approach is to create more separate stages to isolate each type of operation/function rather than trying to do multiple kinds of operations in each stage. The reason for this is to allow for focusing on getting the pipeline code correct for each kind of operation without mixing in other variables. You are going from a guided web form interface to a programming interface, and breaking the process down into smaller chunks can simplify the transition.

Here, Declarative Pipelines can offer an advantage since they more closely resemble the parts of a Jenkins web form. However, as noted in other places in this chapter, that advantage comes at the price of flexibility. Smaller chunks of functionality also make it easier to quickly isolate problems if a stage fails.

Unfortunately, there isn't really a great way in Jenkins pipelines yet to temporarily disable a stage, short of commenting it out or removing it during a Replay attempt (see Chapter 2 for more information on the Replay functionality). Plowing through error reports/tracebacks can also be challenging, so the more granular approach to isolating functionality in stages can pay off at debug time as well.

This approach can have its challenges, especially if tooling tries to perform multiple functions for you automatically. You may have to override the tooling or specifically force it to do less in a stage. As an example of that, consider the Gradle build tool and its (usually) convenient approach of convention over configuration. For Java projects, if your Java source files are in a standard Maven-style directory structure, Gradle can detect those and automatically build them without you having to tell it about where they are.

Likewise, if Gradle detects files in a corresponding directory structure for tests, it will assume those are unit tests and build and execute them as part of the same task. So, a build task for Gradle automatically includes an operation to build and execute unit tests if Gradle detects test files in the expected structure. This kind of effect can typically be mitigated via the application. For example, you can supply a `-x` option to tell Gradle not to run a particular task even if it thinks it can and should.

Figure 10-6 shows the section for a GitSCM configuration in a Freestyle project. (The setup would be similar for other SCMs.)

Figure 10-6. Freestyle project SCM form

From this, we can identify the parameters that we need. A reasonable first question when considering converting this to a new pipeline is whether there is an existing DSL step for this functionality that we can leverage in our pipeline.

Mapping Web Fields to Pipeline Steps

In many cases, the values and options that were asked for in the traditional Jenkins forms have become parameters that are passed to the steps created to allow integration in pipeline code. So often, you can get a rough idea of what the named parameters for the step might be based on the former web forms and the names of the fields or options.

To determine the answer to that question, we can go to the Snippet Generator (via the Pipeline Syntax link in the left menu of any pipeline job screen) and look for a step with a related name. In this case, we'll find one named "git" that looks promising. Selecting that step gives us a form with similar fields to the ones we are using (Figure 10-7). We can then plug in those values and click the Generate Pipeline Script button to get a step for our pipeline.

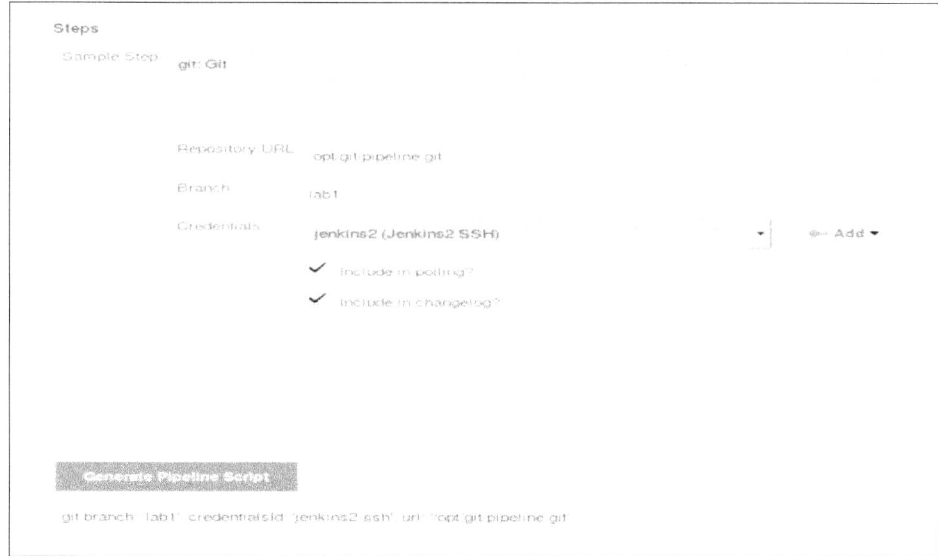

Figure 10-7. "git" step from Snippet Generator

We can now take the code from the Snippet Generator, wrap it in a `stage` closure, and wrap that in a simple `node` step in a pipeline job to try it out. The code could look something like this (assuming we are plugging this into a new pipeline project that we are working on):

```
node ('worker_node1'){
   stage('Source'){
      git branch: 'lab1', credentialsId: 'jenkins2-ssh',
      url: '/opt/git/pipeline.git'
   }
}
```

If we are working directly in Jenkins and putting the code into a Pipeline project, then we can simply save it and tell Jenkins to try to build it now. Jenkins will immediately report any syntax errors, and if there are none, it will execute and build the stage.

You can easily tell whether the code worked via the Stage View (Figure 10-8) or the Console Log if you need more detail.

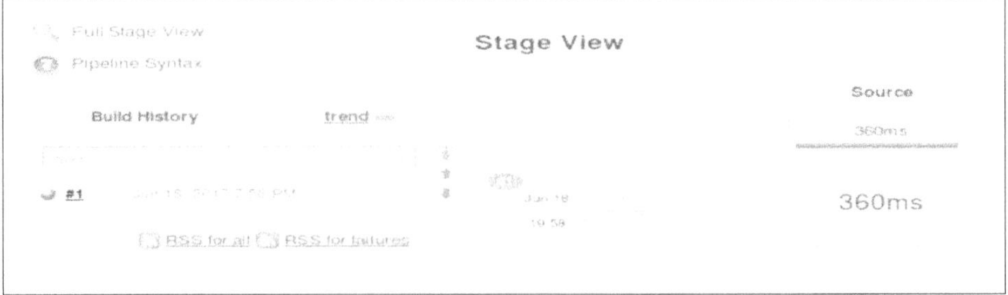

Figure 10-8. Initial build of our simple Source stage

Working Directly in Jenkins Versus in a Jenkinsfile

We will be talking more about Jenkinsfiles later in this chapter—but, even once you understand what they are and how to use them, during a conversion it is generally simpler just to plug the code directly into a project of type Pipeline that you create within the Jenkins application. The reason is that using a Jenkinsfile requires creating a project to reference or find the Jenkinsfile, updating the Jenkinsfile via an editor, then committing and pushing it out to a source code repository. If you then run into an error, you have to make changes to the file and commit and push it again.

Working directly in a Pipeline project in the Jenkins application saves time and operations, since you can directly enter the code, save it, and then try to do a build without having to externally edit or update the code in source control first.

For this reason, during a conversion, it is usually more convenient to work directly in Jenkins first, and then convert to a Jenkinsfile (covered later in the chapter) once things are working.

As you can see, working with this approach of taking the parameters from the Freestyle job, plugging them into the Snippet Generator, and then putting the result into a `stage` closure and trying it out is fairly straightforward. It won't always be that simple, but for plugins that have contributed simple DSL steps (with data for the Snippet Generator), this can often get you close.

More complicated cases may require multiple steps, especially if there is additional configuration to be done, or an environment to use for the operation. In the latter case, you may often have a "with..." DSL block of some kind to use as well. We'll look at these more complicated cases as we go along.

Generic SCM Step

You may be interested to know that the `git` DSL step we are using here is just a specialized form of the generic DSL step available for pipelines. If we were to utilize the generic DSL step instead, it would look more like this:

```
checkout([$class: 'GitSCM', branches: [[name: '*/
lab1']],
     userRemoteConfigs: [[url: '/opt/git/pipe
line.git']]])
```

Next, we'll look at a simple compile step.

Compile

After pulling down the source, most pipelines will have a "build" stage of some sort. In some cases, this may involve more than just a compile action. It could also create deliverables and/or execute defined unit tests, for example.

Figure 10-9 shows an example of a Freestyle job invoking the build tool Gradle to run a series of "tasks" (Gradle jobs) as part of a pipeline. We want to look at a couple of details here. First, notice that we have selected a specific Gradle version to use, as identified by the name "gradle3" in the Gradle Version field.

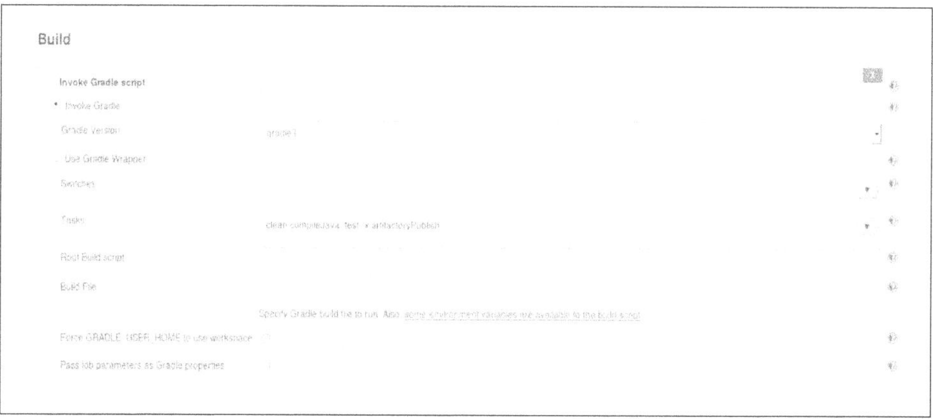

Figure 10-9. Freestyle build invocation

This maps back to a particular version of Gradle installed on our system, identified by the "gradle3" name in our Global Tool Configuration. This follows the traditional approach of installing an application: installing the plugin in Jenkins and then giving a name to the global installation to reference that particular installation. An example of the global configuration in Jenkins is shown in Figure 10-10.

Figure 10-10. Global configuration of installed Gradle version

Tool Default Versions

It is legitimate in Jenkins Freestyle projects to not select a particular version by name, but simply to use the "default" version. This will work as long as there is a version of the application available through the path that Jenkins checks.

However, accessing tools based on an external path is not a best practice. A possible exception would be for a tool like Git that typically has only one version in use at any one point in time, and is not updated frequently. Even in those cases, though, for the sake of clarity, removing ambiguity, and troubleshooting, configuring specific versions in Jenkins is preferred.

We are also referencing multiple Gradle tasks here (`clean`, `compileJava`, `test`, `artifactoryPublish`). A full explanation of each one of these is beyond the scope of this book. However, you can probably tell from the names of several of them what they do. Here is a quick explanation:

- `clean` cleans out build output.
- `compileJava` compiles our Java source.
- `test` attempts to compile and test any Java test cases that it finds.
- `artifactoryPublish` attempts to publish designated build types (such as a JAR or WAR for Java) to an "archive repository" such as Artifactory.

The `-x` option is a switch that tells Gradle not to execute this task. The reason we have that in front of `artifactoryPublish` is because Gradle will attempt to execute that task normally, based on what it can determine about Artifactory being integrated in our builds. We'll have more to say about Artifactory integration in Chapter 13, but to keep things simple, we won't consider it in our exposition of conversion to pipeline steps.

So, to convert this section to a pipeline script, we need to first consider whether we want to do exactly the same set of operations in our stage. For simplicity, let's say that we are only going to execute the `clean` and `compileJava` tasks in our `Compile` pipeline stage. We do not want it to do the `test` task (we will save that for another stage) nor will the `artifactoryPublish` task be needed yet.

Deciding What to Include in a Stage

You may be wondering why you might want to save the `test` task for another stage. There can be a couple of reasons. Most commonly, you may want to separate out functionality in your pipeline so that you don't overload a stage and can easily identify success or failure for particular steps. Another reason might be to handle an operation (or set of them) on a different node or multiple nodes (if running in parallel makes sense), or perhaps in a container instead of on a typical node. Finally, you might want to have a manual handoff or check before executing particular functionality.

So, taking all of this into account, our actual Gradle invocation becomes this:

```
gradle clean compileJava -x test
```

We use the `-x` option again here to tell it not to try to do the test processing, since we're saving that for another stage. Normally, Gradle would try to do this automatically for us here if it finds test files in an expected location. (This is an example of Gradle's usually helpful "convention over configuration" default behavior.) The test cases will be present if they are included in the set of source that the `git` step brought down.

This looks like a fairly straightforward command (step) to add to our pipeline script, assuming there is a `gradle` command provided by the Gradle plugin for the DSL. To check this, we can go to the Snippet Generator again and look through the list of steps that are available.

As of the time of this writing, there is no step named `gradle`. However, you may notice a step named `build`. This looks promising at first glance. When you find a step that you think you can use, it is important to confirm that it will do what you think. The easiest way to do that is by clicking on the help icon (the blue button with the question mark in it) that is closest under the step. Doing that in this case shows the explanation of the step as shown in Figure 10-11.

Figure 10-11. Help info for the build step

Looking at this, we can see that this is not a generic step for invoking build tools. Rather, it is a step designed to kick off building entire Jenkins jobs—not what we want.

How then do we invoke our Gradle command without a DSL step to do it? In most cases, if you have an executable to run (such as Gradle here) and you don't have a DSL step with that name, that's an indicator that you need to fall back to running it by using a shell call. And fortunately, the DSL has two commands for executing shell steps:

`sh`
: The command used for executing shell calls on Unix-type systems

`bat`
: The command used for executing shell calls on Windows systems

You can find further information on both in the Snippet Generator (and in Chapter 11). In our case, we want to leverage the `sh` DSL step. If we go into the Snippet Generator, find the `sh` step, and then fill it in with what we think our command should be, we get this generated Groovy script command:

```
sh 'gradle clean compileJava -x test'
```

This will work in our pipeline if we have Gradle in a path where Jenkins can always find it. However, recall that in our original Freestyle project we were referencing a specific Gradle installation (one is defined globally in our Jenkins system).

We want to reference that same installed version in our conversion to the pipeline script. So how do we do that? It turns out that the Jenkins DSL includes a step just for this purpose. It's one that we have discussed in earlier chapters, but in case you aren't familiar with it yet, the step is named `tool`. The help text for this step defines it as follows:

> Binds a tool installation to a variable (the tool home directory is returned). Only tools already configured in Configure System are available here. If the original tool installer has the auto-provision feature, then the tool will be installed as required.

Essentially, given the tool name in our Global Tool Configuration, the `tool` step will return the corresponding `<tool>_NAME` value. Referring back to Figure 10-10 and our global setting for the Gradle installation, if we use:

```
tool 'gradle3'
```

it should return:

```
/usr/share/gradle
```

The trick then becomes how to incorporate this into our shell command that calls Gradle. In a Scripted Pipeline, one way is to define a variable in the script that captures the value and then incorporate that into the shell step. Here's an example:

```
def gradleHome = tool 'gradle3'
sh "${gradleHome}/bin/gradle clean compileJava -x test"
```

Interpreting Values and Quotes

You may have noticed here that we are using the special syntax `${<name>}` to tell Groovy to replace that with the value that has been assigned to `<name>` elsewhere in our program. When we do this, we also need to switch to using double quotes for our shell step since they allow for interpolation of this sort.

This has the advantage that we can put the `def gradleHome` line globally in the Scripted Pipeline (inside the `node` definition, but outside of any stages) and then reference it wherever we need it. However, it also has a disadvantage in that it won't work in Declarative Pipelines. Furthermore, we can actually combine the two lines to make a single call. If we do that, our command then incorporates the `tool` step combined inside the shell step. It will look like this (adding a `stage` closure around it):

```
stage('Compile') {
        sh "'${tool 'gradle3'}/bin/gradle' clean compileJava -x test"
}
```

To briefly recap how the `sh` step works here:

- `sh` is our built-in DSL step to execute something in the Unix shell.
- The double quotes are necessary to allow the `${tool 'gradle3'}` to be interpolated (resolved to a value).
- The `'${tool 'gradle3'}/bin/gradle'` section here does the following:
  - Invokes the `tool` DSL step with the `'gradle3'` argument. This looks up the `'gradle3'` name in our Global Tool Configuration, which then maps that part of the string to the `GRADLE_HOME` value that corresponds to the `'gradle3'` name.

- Substitutes the returned value in the string, so that we end up with the specific Gradle executable path of `'/usr/share/gradle/bin/gradle'`.
- Uses that resolved path to execute the specified Gradle tasks, running this command in the shell: `/usr/share/gradle/bin/gradle clean compileJava -x test`.

In the next section, we'll discuss one approach to processing multiple items at the same time—using parallelism in the pipeline—with the example of unit tests.

Unit Tests

Historically, one of the challenges with managing multiple projects in Jenkins was running any of them in parallel. Certain plugins, such as Join and Build Flow, had some mechanisms to support this, but they were not necessarily straightforward to configure. One of the benefits of working in a pipeline environment is the ability to easily script parallel processing using the `parallel` DSL step.

One case that usually lends itself to this approach is processing large batches of unit tests, especially if they can be broken down into multiple independent sets.

"Dealing with Concurrency" on page 85 discusses setting up parallel processing in more detail, but we'll touch on the main points here and see how we might apply it to a large set of simple tests.

Traditional Versus Alternative Parallel Syntax

The traditional way to implement parallel processing in a Jenkins pipeline script is through the `parallel` step, which uses a map as an argument. With the release of Declarative Pipeline 1.2, an alternative syntax was added for Declarative Pipelines that allows defining stages (instead of map elements) to handle each parallel path.

We will use the traditional map-based approach for the examples in this section, since it works with either Scripted or Declarative Pipelines. However, if you are working in a Declarative Pipeline and want to use the newer syntax, Chapters 3 and 7 both include discussions of the alternative syntax.

The key to working with the traditional `parallel` DSL step is understanding that it takes a map as an argument. The programmatic keys to the map are just labels to identify the different branches, while the values contain the actual code blocks to execute. As a means of distributing the load, we can use a `node` block around each code block to ensure each branch runs on a different node.

Consider, for example, a set of tests for a subproject *api* of our sample Gradle project. For simplicity, these unit tests are written in Java programs named *Test1.java*,

Test2.java, etc. up through *Test29.java*. If we have two defined nodes avilable, `node1` and `node2`, we might choose to run all *Test1** tests on `node1` and all *Test2** tests on `node2`. Using Gradle, we can pass the set of tests to run via a system parameter using the `-D test.single=<pattern>` option.

Wrapping the `parallel` step in a stage (currently if `parallel` is used, it should be the only step in a stage) could result in code like the following:

```
stage('Unit Test') {
        parallel (
           tester1: { node ('worker_node1'){
             sh "'${tool 'gradle3'}/bin/gradle' -D test.single=Test1*
                :api:test"
           }},
           tester2: { node ('worker_node2'){
             sh "'${tool 'gradle3'}/bin/gradle' -D test.single=Test2*
                :api:test"
           }},
        )
}
```

Notice that we simply call the `parallel` DSL step and pass the map to it. Our map consists of two branches with the keys `tester1` and `tester2` and the blocks of code as the values. Each code block, in turn, consists of a node specification and then a call to the shell to run the specific Gradle command. The Gradle command identifies a subset of tests and calls the `test` task in the *api* subproject.

Another way to code this would be to declare a map, then run through some code to fill in the map elements. Afterwards, the `parallel` step can be invoked, passing just the name of the map. (See Chapter 3 for an example of this.)

Distributing content across nodes

When coding something to run in parallel, it makes sense to use different nodes (or node classes) for the different branches to distribute the load. However, this also presents a requirement that you may not have thought about—how to get the same content on multiple nodes so that all the needed pieces are there. Of course, one solution would be to have a repeated `Source` step on each node to pull down the code. However, this is redundant and expensive in terms of cycles and resources.

Fortunately, the DSL provides a simple solution—the `stash` and `unstash` steps. (We discussed these in Chapter 3, but will do a brief repeat of stash and related topics here for ease of reference.) As the names imply, we can use these commands to create a "stash" of content from one node and then "unstash" that content onto other nodes. The syntax is straightforward. The basic form of the `stash` step takes a set of comma-separated `includes` (or `excludes`) and a `name`:

```
stash name: "<name>" [includes: "<pattern>" excludes: "<pattern>"]
```

The idea here is that we designate a set of included or excluded files via names and/or patterns. The `stash` itself is also given a name to refer to it by. To simplify things, we can just add the stash step immediately after we do the source code retrieval within the `Source` stage:

```
stage('Source'){
     git branch: 'lab1', credentialsId: 'jenkins2-ssh',
        url: '/opt/git/pipeline.git'
     stash includes: 'api/**, dataaccess/**, util/**, build.gradle,
        settings.gradle', name: 'testreqs'
 }
```

Then, when we need to retrieve the set of files in any other part of our pipeline, we can simply pass the name of the stash to the `unstash` command. This can be done in a different stage, node, or branch of a `parallel` statement. The format is simply:

```
unstash "<name>"
```

Appropriate Use of stash

It's worth noting here that this `stash` command is different from the `stash` command supplied for use in Git. The `stash` command in Git allows for stashing content (from the working directory and staging area) that has not yet been committed.

The scope of content that can be stashed here is wide, but for longer-term storage and retrieval of large amounts of content, storage into an artifact repository such as Artifactory (discussed in Chapter 13) is a better alternative.

Cleaning out workspaces

When using commands like `stash` and running across multiple nodes, it's a good idea to clean out the workspace each time first. Jenkins does not guarantee that workspaces will be clean or that they will persist over time.

If we have the Workspace Cleanup plugin (*https://plugins.jenkins.io/ws-cleanup*) installed, we can use the `cleanWs` step to accomplish this.

Alternative Ways to Clean the Workspace

The `cleanWs()` call is the recommended way to clean out a Jenkins workspace. The `deleteDir()` call may also be an option in some cases, but it's more limited in its utility since it only works for the current node and has to be pointing at the directory. (See Chapter 11 for more information on both steps.)

In earlier versions of Jenkins 2, there wasn't a `cleanWs` DSL step, so the call to the plugin's function had to be indirect—through the generic `step` DSL step to the class. That looked like this:

```
step([$class: 'WsCleanup'])
```

You may see this in older pipelines, and it is still valid syntax as of the time of this writing. However, the more direct `cleanWs()` call is preferred.

Adding in the elements to clean up the workspace and unstash the needed pieces results in our parallel unit testing stage looking like the following:

```
stage('Unit Test') {
        parallel (
           tester1: { node ('worker_node1'){
               cleanWs()
               unstash 'testreqs'
               sh "'${tool 'gradle3'}/bin/gradle' -D test.single=Test1*
                 :api:test"
            }},
            tester2: { node ('worker_node2'){
                cleanWs()
                unstash 'testreqs'
                sh "'${tool 'gradle3'}/bin/gradle' -D test.single=Test2*
                  :api:test"
            }},
        )
    }
```

When executing this part of the pipeline, if you look in the Console Log, you'll be able to see the interspersed commands for the `tester1` and `tester2` branches as they execute in parallel. (See also the example on this in Chapter 3.)

Parallel Test Executor Plugin

Before we leave this section, it's worth mentioning the Parallel Test Executor plugin (*http://bit.ly/2HufJWD*). After an initial good run of your unit tests, the tool added by this plugin attempts to evaluate the timings for running the tests. It then creates "include" or "exclude" files to break the tests down into appropriate groups that can be spread across nodes for the best parallelism and load balancing.

As of this writing, however, this plugin has a couple of issues that make it challenging to use in most cases:

- It depends on the last run (before it is used) being a good run of all the unit test cases.
- It requires a build tool that can accept include or exclude files when running. (Currently Maven supports this.)

In the next section, we'll look at how to incorporate credentials in the context of another common pipeline stage: integration testing.

Integration Testing

Integration testing can take many forms. In our example Freestyle pipeline, we have a job that leverages Gradle SourceSets and defines an `integrationTest` task similar to the Gradle default `test` task that is provided by the Java plugin (we used the `test` task for the unit testing in the previous section).

We'll have more to say about Gradle SourceSets shortly. But another technique that we're leveraging here (which is more widely applicable) is using a test database for our web app to run against. In particular, we are creating a test database with a single command that redirects input into MySQL from an external SQL file. The basic command in our Freestyle job is a shell step and looks like this:

```
mysql -u<username> -p<password> registry_test < registry_test.sql
```

What is interesting about this is how we supply the credentials of username and password to the command. Traditionally we have had a few choices:

- Hardcode the username and password
- Manually set them as environment variables
- Supply them via parameters
- Read them from an external file

- Leverage injection via a plugin, such as the Credentials Binding plugin (*https://plugins.jenkins.io/credentials-binding*)

Obviously, the first option is completely insecure and a bad practice. The second option is slightly better but still exposes too much information. The third option is dependent on input each time, which is less than ideal in an automated environment. The fourth option provides some isolation, but requires maintaining data outside of Jenkins.

The last option represents our most direct and secure way to use the credentials defined in Jenkins for this type of access. Essentially, the Credentials Binding plugin allows us to bind the credentials (such as username and password) that we have already set up in Jenkins to variables that we can then pass to our build steps. An example use case is shown in Figure 10-12.

Figure 10-12. Example of using the Credentials Binding plugin in a traditional Freestyle job

The Jenkins pipeline DSL also includes a step that allows us to use the Credentials Binding plugin in a pipeline: the `withCredentials` step. Like the Freestyle version, this step takes a type of credentials binding to use and then allows the user to specify variables to receive the actual values of the credentials. The variables can then be used within the block in place of the credentials, preventing the values of the credentials from being exposed. (See Chapter 5 for more details and examples on creating and using credentials.)

In our case, we'll assume that we've set up a credential named `mysql_credentials` that contains the separated username and password for accessing MySQL databases on our system. We can then instantiate a step that uses that binding and dereferences it into two separate environment variables to be used where the credentials are needed in statements that we put in the enclosed block.

Translating our example from the Freestyle project would look like this:

```
withCredentials([usernamePassword(credentialsId: 'mysql_credentials',
  passwordVariable: 'MY_SQL_USER', usernameVariable: 'MY_SQL_PASS')])
{
   sh "mysql -u$MY_SQL_USER -p$MY_SQL_PASS registry_test < registry_test.sql"
}

withCredentials(...) {
    sh "..."
}
```

About with* Steps

Steps that start with `with` are often used to reference some global entity and apply the environment associated with it to an enclosed set of actions. Those global entities may be for things such as credentials (as in the case of `withCredentials`), servers (we'll talk about `withSonarQubeEnv` blocks in Chapter 12), general environment variables (`withEnv`), or even more significant supporting pieces such as Docker containers (`withDockerContainer`). See Chapter 11 for more information and examples.

The remaining piece of our integration testing stage relies on a mechanism called *SourceSets* that the Gradle build tooling supports. A SourceSet in Gradle is simply a way to define a set of source files with their own environment and structure. When working with Java files (and the corresponding Java plugin for Gradle), Gradle by convention is set up with two default SourceSets, one for the main project source (called `main`) and one for any associated test cases written in Java (called the `test` SourceSet). We used basic functionality of the `test` SourceSet in the Gradle invocations for the parallel unit test processing earlier in this chapter.

Gradle allows us to define the classpath, output path, directory structure, and so forth for a SourceSet so that Gradle can compile and access them correctly. One of the other abilities we have with Gradle SourceSets is the ability to create new SourceSets based on existing ones, with modified characteristics—a sort of SourceSet "inheritance." For our pipeline with Gradle, we have created a new `integrationTest` SourceSet based on the default `test` SourceSet and a `functionalTest` SourceSet based on the new integrationTest SourceSet. We won't go into more detail than that here since this isn't a Gradle text, but the bottom line is that once we have the registry database in place for our integration testing (via the `withCredentials` step), we can execute our integration tests by invoking Gradle to run the new `integrationTest` task. We can do that simply by invoking it through a shell call:

```
sh "'${tool 'gradle3'}/bin/gradle' integrationTest"
```

Here again, note the use of the `tool` step to get the location of our `Gradle_HOME` path, and the mixture of double and single quotes necessary to make this all work.

At this point, we have the core initial stages of our converted pipeline complete. We can pull down the source, build it, and test it on multiple levels. The primary remaining parts of our pipeline require more detailed integration with their respective external applications. To keep the scope and content of this chapter reasonable, we defer details on integrating/migrating with those applications to their own chapters—but we'll briefly cover the high-level ideas and approach of working with these technologies in the next sections.

Migrating the Next Parts of the Pipeline

Thus far, we've covered integration in two key technology areas, source management (with Git) and builds and testing (with Gradle). These stages form the minimum pipeline that we need in order to establish that our code is syntactically correct and the functionality works in isolated testing.

From here, we want to establish successive levels of confidence in our code by incorporating tools such as source code analysis (via gathering metrics with SonarQube) and deploying to more comprehensive environments for testing (such as a Docker container). Along the way, we will need to ensure we can store and retrieve versioned artifacts produced by our pipeline (done via Artifactory in our case).

Each of the technologies we use for these tasks and their respective integrations with Jenkins (and pipelines-as-code) deserve more extensive treatment than we can give them in this one chapter, so the book contains separate chapters for these. As such, we'll only touch on these areas at a high level. For more details, refer to Chapter 12, which covers integration with SonarQube, and Chapter 13, which covers integration with Artifactory.

Source code analysis

Although testing gives us some assurance that we have written code that does what we want, it doesn't provide any feedback on the quality of the source code itself. Source code analysis can provide that for any code going through our pipeline.

Source code analysis generally refers to a set of quality metrics related to using best practices, producing code that is insulated against known failure conditions, assessing technical debt, determining code coverage through testing, etc.

The set of metrics is wide and varied. Scores on metrics are obtained by measuring compliance of the code against a set of rules. Thresholds can be defined for each metric area. A set of thresholds can be treated as a "quality gate"—a pass/fail criterion for code being analyzed in a pipeline.

SonarQube is one application that provides this kind of analysis. To integrate with Jenkins, we have to have a SonarQube server set up, the SonarQube plugin installed in Jenkins, and a standalone program called a "scanner" or "runner" installed and configured.

We can define a webhook in SonarQube to notify Jenkins after the analysis is complete. This same notification will let Jenkins know whether the code passed or failed the quality gate.

Chapter 12 describes in detail how to integrate with SonarQube. We'll also look at how to use a code coverage tool called Jacoco (Java Code Coverage) that integrates with Jenkins to provide data on how well our tests are testing the source code in our projects.

Incorporating an artifact repository

An artifact repository is used to store, manage, and track binary artifacts, just as a source management repository does for source code. It allows users and automated processes, such as jobs in Jenkins or stages in a Jenkins pipeline, to ensure they are working with the desired version of an artifact.

Artifacts in this case can be external dependencies that are needed for some operation or artifacts generated by the current processes for later use or distribution. Repositories that store the dependencies are referred to as *resolution* or *resolver* repositories. Repositories used to store generated content for later use or distribution are referred to as *distribution* repositories. These repositories may be in any of a number of standard formats, such as Maven, Ivy, or Gradle—the important aspect is the versioning. Let's dive into more detail on that, as it demonstrates some other techniques that may be useful as you convert your pipeline.

Setting version information with parameters. In our original pipeline based on the Freestyle jobs, we used parameters as a way to override default versioning information (Figure 10-13).

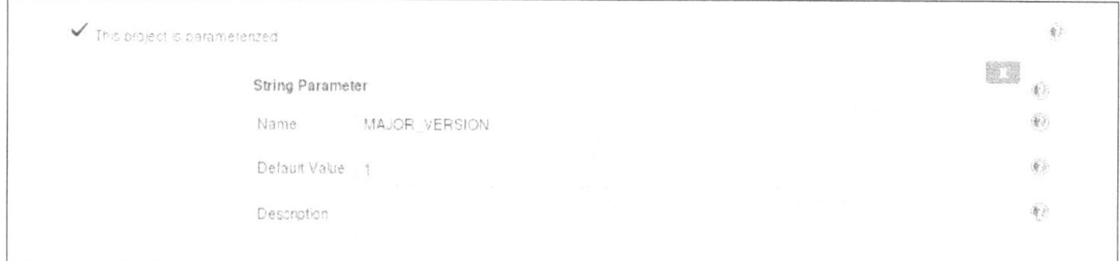

Figure 10-13. Example parameter defined in Freestyle project

We then used those values (or the defaults, if not overridden) to set the values for the version of the generated WAR file that we placed in the artifact repository. This was done by manipulating properties for Gradle in a *gradle.properties* file. Ideally, we would have passed these values as properties to Gradle via some clear integration with the web form. However, the Gradle integration with Freestyle projects did not have a good way to do this. So, instead, we fell back to calling a set of shell commands that used the Unix `sed` utility. Basically, the commands did text substitution to get the desired values into the properties file. The step in the traditional Jenkins job looked like Figure 10-14.

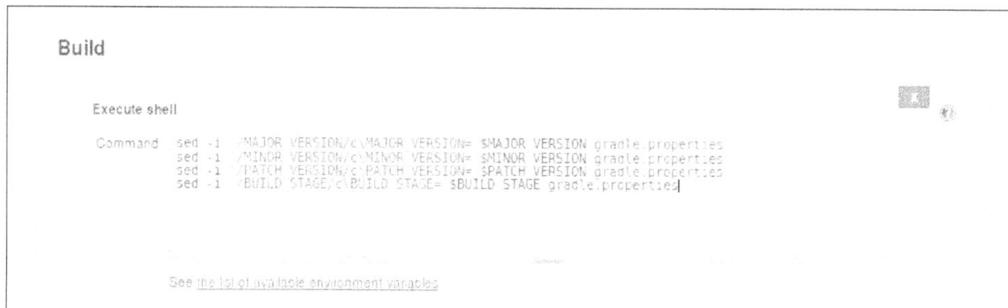

Figure 10-14. Shell step to update Gradle properties file

In our Scripted Pipeline, we could also use a series of direct shell commands via the `sh` step. However, for this conversion, we've chosen to actually put these commands in a separate script and store that script in a different source code repository. This is mostly illustrative at this point, as it shows how commands can be stored and loaded from a remote site.

Figure 10-15 shows the shell steps encapsulated in a file stored on GitHub.

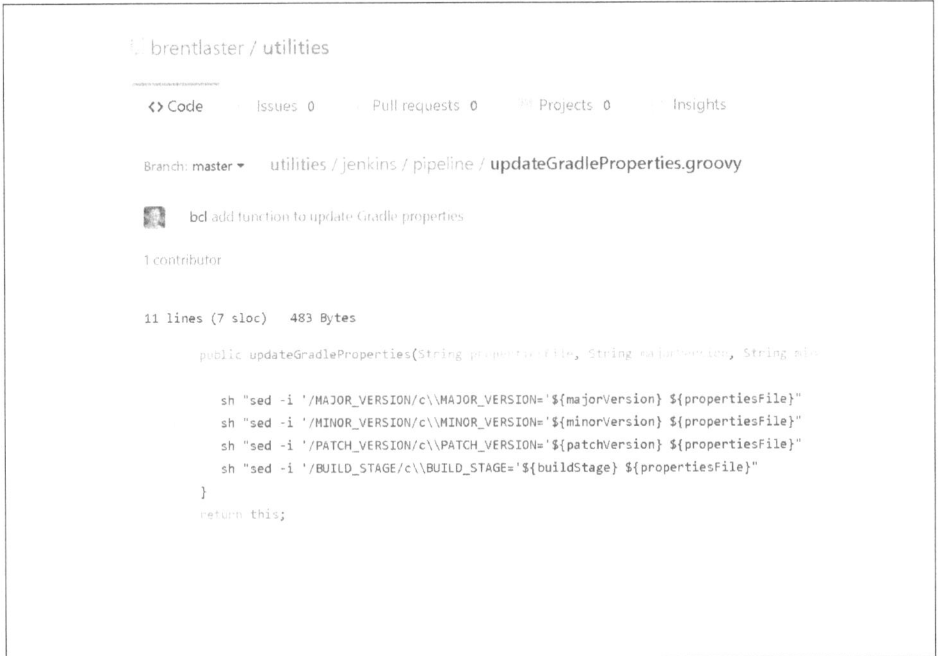

Figure 10-15. Shell steps encapsulated in a separate script on a different SCM repo

This serves to abstract out operations in case we want to later change the implementation. It also avoids hardcoding steps in the pipeline and allows more open sharing of code.

From within our new pipeline, we can load the script from its remote location using the Pipeline Remote Loader plugin. With this plugin installed, the DSL has a `fromGit` method to load content stored in a Git repository. (There are other methods for other SCMs as well.) So, we can load the function and then execute a call to it in our pipeline. Putting this as the start of our `Assemble` stage would yield code like the following:

```
stage('Assemble') { // assemble WAR file
   def workspace = env.WORKSPACE
   def setPropertiesProc = fileLoader.fromGit('jenkins/pipeline/
   updateGradleProperties','https://github.com/brentlaster/utilities.git',
   'master', null, '')

   setPropertiesProc.updateGradleProperties(
      "${workspace}/gradle.properties",
      "${params.MAJOR_VERSION}",
      "${params.MINOR_VERSION}",
      "${params.PATCH_VERSION}",
      "${params.BUILD_STAGE}")
```

The Pipeline Remote Loader Plugin

While we use the Pipeline Remote Loader plugin to illustrate a technique here, it was created before the shared libraries functionality was fully implemented. At some point it may be deprecated. Shared libraries provide an alternative way to accomplish separating out the code.

Handling the versioning of artifacts is an important part of integration with an artifact repository. Beyond that is the overall integration with the application you choose.

For our pipeline examples in Chapter 13, we will discuss integration with Artifactory Community Edition, the free version of one of the most common artifact management tools. We'll see in that chapter how it is configured globally in Jenkins and integrated in the traditional web forms of a Freestyle job, including fields to define common elements such as resolution and deployment repositories, and options about what to publish into repositories.

To translate this to a pipeline environment, we define variables to point to the server and repositories that we want. Also, depending on the type of the integration, we have specific objects that represent the functionality of the combined Artifactory and build projects. These combined objects then allow us to invoke Artifactory functionality within the build application in direct calls.

Chapter 13 contains all of the details on the Artifactory integration. Chapter 14 contains details on the other main component of our pipeline, which we'll look at briefly next—working with containers.

Using containers in a pipeline

Containers are becoming more and more ubiquitous in terms of being used in pipelines today. By "containers" here, we really mean the higher-level orchestration applications for Linux Containers (LXC). These allow us to define and run multiple isolated Linux systems within a single Linux container, achieving many of the goals of a VM without the overhead.

Of course, the most popular of these applications for defining and using containers is Docker. In fact, there are whole pipeline applications that are built around only using Docker containers.

Historically, integration with Docker in a Freestyle project centered around using it as an agent via the Docker Cloud plugin or invoking it directly via shell commands. Within a Jenkins 2 pipeline, we now have four options for integration with Docker:

- Configured as a "cloud," meaning running a standalone Jenkins agent provided by the Docker plugin

- Running as an agent via constructs provided by Declarative Pipelines
- Inside the pipeline, using the `docker` global variable (provided by the Docker Pipeline plugin)
- Directly invoking Docker via a shell call

The Docker (cloud) plugin is still available to pipeline creators, but within a pipeline, we can also create new Docker containers from images and execute commands in them easily.

The traditional pipeline we are migrating from used Docker as an isolated, repeatable environment for deploying our artifact into for functional testing. The migration to our Scripted Pipeline goes further. Chapter 14 shows how we can also create an image with a different version of a tool than the one we have configured globally in Jenkins and easily pass our pipeline commands to that container, for execution in the isolated environment it provides.

This is most easily done with a DSL `with` block called `withDockerContainer`, but the Docker integration with Jenkins 2 also provides a built-in Docker global variable that has an `inside` method that can be used. The nice thing about both of these constructs in the new Jenkins DSL is that they automatically handle a lot of the setup and teardown of using Docker for you. For example, they can automatically pull an image if not already available, start up containers, and mount Jenkins workspaces as volumes in the container (assuming filesystem access).

One other key aspect of using Docker in Jenkins 2 comes into play when working with Declarative Pipelines. The DSL provides a number of ways to easily define agents based on Docker containers. There are methods to create agents based on a particular Docker image, as well as a Dockerfile. These mechanisms greatly simplify integrating containerization more widely in your pipeline.

For all the details and examples of how to incorporate Docker containers, refer to Chapter 14, *Integrating Containers*.

Integration with Output

It's worth mentioning that, for tools (such as Artifactory and SonarQube) that have traditionally added "badges" (as shortcuts to the applications) in a Jenkins job's build history, those are still added when the job is converted to a Pipeline. However, the output from the application in the console log may look different, depending on the code that was used in the pipeline.

This completes our look at converting traditional pipeline jobs to a Scripted Pipeline. Next, we'll look at how to convert a Scripted Pipeline to a Jenkinsfile.

Converting from a Jenkins Pipeline Project to a Jenkinsfile

In this section, we'll look at how to take a pipeline that we have created in the Jenkins application itself and convert it into an external Jenkinsfile. As a reminder, a Jenkinsfile is simply a pipeline (with a few modifications) that is stored in source control separately from Jenkins (typically in the same repository as the source code for the project).

A project in the Jenkins application can be pointed at the source code repository, detect the presence of the Jenkinsfile, and execute a build based on the pipeline in the file.

The advantages to storing the pipeline in an external file this way are many. Briefly, they include:

- Your pipeline specification is stored in source control (just like the project source). This means changes to it can be tracked, the pipeline code can be reviewed, etc.
- New branches created from the branch with the Jenkinsfile will have their own Jenkinsfile, by virtue of inheriting it from the parent branch.
- Jenkins can detect the existence of the Jenkinsfile and even create new jobs automatically based on it.

Historically, the primary disadvantage of using a Jenkinsfile rather than creating the pipeline directly in Jenkins itself was delayed feedback. That is, you didn't know whether your pipeline was syntactically correct or would work until after you had staged, committed, and pushed the Jenkinsfile into source control, and then run a job in Jenkins that pointed to it.

This is still true for Jenkinsfiles written in the scripted syntax. However, there is now a Pipeline Linter tool that can be used to validate Jenkinsfiles written in the declarative syntax via a command-line call, so you can find syntax problems before you put them in source control. The following sidebar describes how to use this tool.

Using the Pipeline Linter Tool for Declarative Jenkinsfiles

The Jenkins Pipeline Linter tool allows a user to validate a Jenkinsfile written in declarative syntax before pushing it into source control. Otherwise, the code needs to be validated by having Jenkins point at it in source control and run it. The linter saves time by allowing validation of the syntax outside of the Jenkins interface and outside of source control.

The tool is most normally run as a command that is built into Jenkins. Thus, it can be run via SSH, via the CLI interface (deprecated), or via the Jenkins REST API with an

HTTP POST command. We'll briefly look at all three options here. It can also be run as a pipeline step; we'll see an example of that, too.

Prerequisites

To use the tool via the command-line interfaces, it is necessary to have Jenkins set up to handle the SSH or CLI invocations. Chapter 15 has details on how to set up Jenkins for this. Also, for the REST API invocation, if you have the Cross-Site Request Forgery protection enabled (as discussed in Chapter 5), then you will first need to obtain a "crumb" from Jenkins to use in the request. Chapter 15 also has a section that covers how to get a crumb from Jenkins to use in such calls.

Running via SSH

As mentioned, to use this option, Jenkins needs to first be set up for SSH access. With that done, you can invoke the declarative linter as a standard command-line command:

```
ssh [-l <username>] -p <jenkins ssh port> <hostname or localhost>
 declarative-linter < Jenkinsfile
```

Notice here that the command does not take an argument. Rather, we redirect the Jenkinsfile into the command.

If the validation of the syntax is successful, you'll see a message like this:

```
Jenkinsfile successfully validated.
```

If the Jenkinsfile has syntax issues, you'll see messages like these:

```
Errors encountered validating Jenkinsfile:
WorkflowScript: 2: Undefined section "agnt" @ line 2, column 3.
     agnt {
     ^

WorkflowScript: 20: Undefined section "environ" @ line 20,
column 3.
     environ {
     ^

WorkflowScript: 1: Missing required section "agent" @ line 1,
column 1.
   pipeline {
   ^
```

Running via the CLI (Deprecated)

For the CLI command to work, you must have the deprecated CLI Remoting mode enabled and have access to the *jenkins-cli.jar* file. (See Chapter 15 for information on how to set all of this up and an explanation of why this protocol is deprecated.)

With that setup done, you can invoke the CLI command with the *.jar* file as follows:

```
java -jar [<path to jar>/]jenkins-cli.jar -s <hostname such as
http://localhost:8080> -auth <username>:<password or token>
 declarative-linter < Jenkinsfile
```

The `-auth` option is explained in Chapter 15. Username and password options may be used instead.

Running via the REST API

To invoke the linter via the REST API, if CSRF protection is in place (as it should be), you will first need to obtain a crumb value (see Chapter 15). Then you can invoke the validation as follows:

```
curl --user <username>:<password> -X POST -H <Jenkins crumb value>
 -F "jenkinsfile=<Jenkinsfile"
<jenkins url>/pipeline-model-converter/validate
```

Note that the `"jenkinsfile=<Jenkinsfile"` argument has an actual less-than sign in it.

Running as a Pipeline Step

The linter can also be run as a pipeline step—specifically, the `"validateDeclarativePipeline"` step. The output from a run of the step is the same as for the other invocation methods. The advantage is that no special setup is required (unless you consider writing a small script to be special setup).

An example job to run this step is shown here:

```
node {
    def valid = validateDeclarativePipeline("<path to file>")
    echo "result = ${valid}"
}
```

Developing Jenkinsfiles

A typical approach that can work well for creating a pipeline as a Jenkinsfile is to first develop the pipeline code within the Jenkins application itself as a Pipeline project. This gives the benefit of quick turnaround and feedback while developing the code. When the pipeline is working to your satisfaction in the Pipeline project, then you can follow the process in this section to convert it into a Jenkinsfile.

Typically, it only requires a few simple steps to migrate pipeline to a Jenkinsfile. The approach is outlined in the next section.

Approach

Since Jenkinsfiles live in the source code repository along with your source, you'll first want to make sure you have a cloned/checked out/pulled copy of your source code for the project. Then, in the appropriate branch, create a new file named Jenkinsfile.

Next, copy and paste the working pipeline code from your project in Jenkins (or enter new code if you haven't already created a Pipeline project in Jenkins) into the Jenkinsfile.

As a best practice, add an identifier at the top of the script of the file that identifies it as a Groovy script. Typically this is done by adding a line like `#!groovy` as the first line in the file.

Modify any lines in your script that pull source code from the same source repository as the one where your Jenkinsfile will be to be just `checkout scm`. This is a simplification, since Jenkins will already know the repository location by virtue of being pointed at that location to find the Jenkinsfile. This will also simplify having to make any changes to the source control command if you create a new branch that gets the same Jenkinsfile. The `checkout scm` step will know to get the code from the correct branch based on that version of the Jenkinsfile being there.

Figure 10-16 shows part of an example pipeline as created in the Jenkins application.

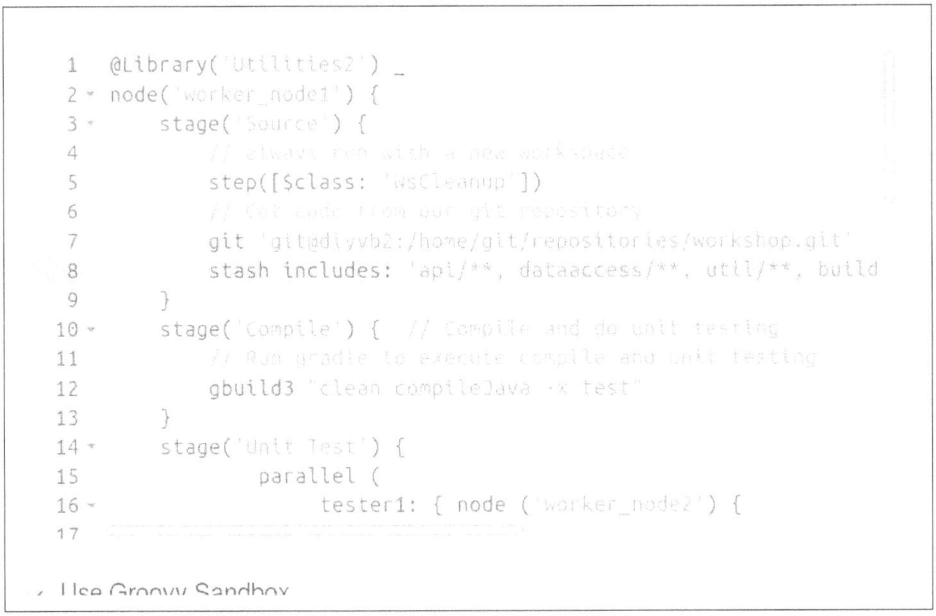

```
@Library('Utilities2') _
node('worker_node1') {
    stage('Source') {
        // always run with a new workspace
        step([$class: 'WsCleanup'])
        // Get code from our git repository
        git 'git@diyvb2:/home/git/repositories/workshop.git'
        stash includes: 'api/**, dataaccess/**, util/**, build
    }
    stage('Compile') {  // Compile and do unit testing
        // Run gradle to execute compile and unit testing
        gbuild3 "clean compileJava -x test"
    }
    stage('Unit Test') {
            parallel (
                 tester1: { node ('worker_node2') {
```

Use Groovy Sandbox

Figure 10-16. Pipeline code in Jenkins application prior to converting to Jenkinsfile

Figure 10-17 shows the same code converted to a Jenkinsfile.

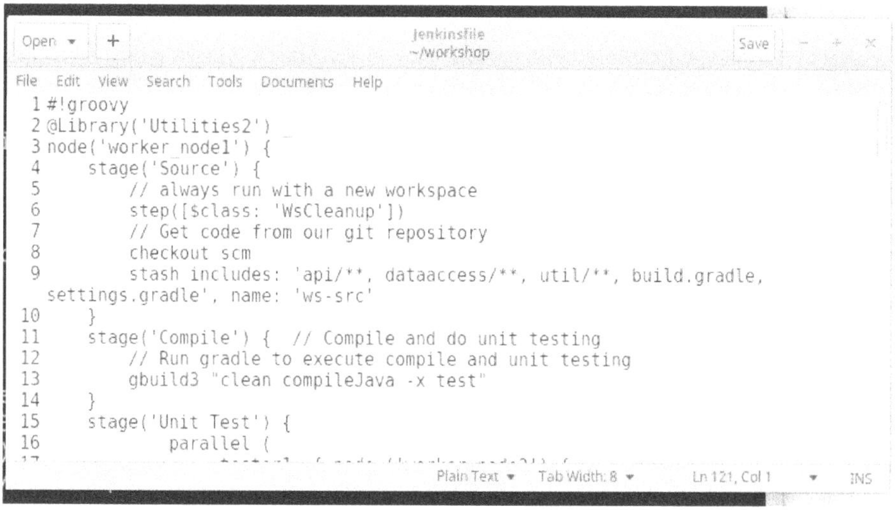

```
#!groovy
@Library('Utilities2')
node('worker_node1') {
    stage('Source') {
        // always run with a new workspace
        step([$class: 'WsCleanup'])
        // Get code from our git repository
        checkout scm
        stash includes: 'api/**, dataaccess/**, util/**, build.gradle,
settings.gradle', name: 'ws-src'
    }
    stage('Compile') {  // Compile and do unit testing
        // Run gradle to execute compile and unit testing
        gbuild3 "clean compileJava -x test"
    }
    stage('Unit Test') {
          parallel (
```

Figure 10-17. Pipeline code converted to Jenkinsfile

Replay and checkout scm Step Versus Specific SCM Step

As we discussed in Chapter 2, Jenkins includes "replay" functionality to allow you to edit and rerun a changed version of any completed run (successful or failed). This is initiated by going to the screen for a particular run and selecting the Replay menu item on the left. The main use of this is for verifying potential fixes or prototyping; it allows you to check how a code change to that version of code will affect the running of the job. The change causes another run to happen, but does *not* persist the change in the current code (even if the run being replayed is the current one). This functionality is useful for verifying potential fixes or prototyping.

However, there is a potential issue to be aware of when replaying code that uses a specific SCM step, such as `git`. No matter what version of the code the original run pulled down, if the branch the step uses has been updated since the original run, the replay will pull the latest code.

As an example, assume we have a simple project that uses the `git` step to pull down code, like this:

```
stages {
      stage('Source') {
         steps {
            // always run with a new workspace
            cleanWs()
            git branch: 'decl', url: 'git@diyvb2:/opt/git/gradle-demo'
```

Suppose the repository where we run this code initially is at this revision:

```
commit 3235c1f8e141e9f1c02b42b51d782aa4f738e4b8
Author: diyuser2 <diyuser2@diyvb2>
Date: Sat Nov 4 15:22:32 2017 -0400

Add declarative Jenkinsfile
```

If we run the job and then look at the Git revisions on the output page for run #1, we'll see this among the output:

```
Success Build #1 (Feb 8, 2018 3:17:36 PM)
Started by user Jenkins Admin
 Revision: 3235c1f8e141e9f1c02b42b51d782aa4f738e4b8
```

Notice that the revision used by the job matches the current one.

Suppose we then update our repository with another commit, and it is at the new revision shown below:

```
git log -2
commit 6c75694b8770705b3a27f7c512766e0e3ab0a7d0
Author: diyuser2 <diyuser2@diyvb2>
Date: Thu Feb 8 14:49:53 2018 -0500

updated Jenkinsfile

commit 3235c1f8e141e9f1c02b42b51d782aa4f738e4b8
Author: diyuser2 <diyuser2@diyvb2>
Date: Sat Nov 4 15:22:32 2017 -0400
```

If we run the job again and look at the Git revisions, we rightfully see this:

```
Success Build #2 (Feb 8, 2018 3:37:01 PM)
Started by user Jenkins Admin
 Revision: 6c75694b8770705b3a27f7c512766e0e3ab0a7d0
```

So far, so good.

However, if we now go back and replay run #1, we get this:

```
Success Build #5 (Feb 8, 2018 3:39:46 PM)
Started by user Jenkins Admin

Replayed #1 (diff)

 Revision: 6c75694b8770705b3a27f7c512766e0e3ab0a7d0
```

Note the "Replayed #1" line and the revision it pulled this time—the newest one, not the one that was originally pulled by run #1.

One of the cool features of Replay is that you can replay a Jenkinsfile just like a Jenkins pipeline that you developed in the application.

And, interestingly, for Jenkinsfiles that use the `checkout scm` step, the replay works as expected. If our pipeline code in a Jenkinsfile is this for all runs:

```
stages {
      stage('Source') {
         steps {
            // always run with a new workspace
            cleanWs()
            checkout scm
```

Given the same Git revisions, the build of the latest yields this:

```
Success Build #2 (Feb 8, 2018 4:20:21 PM)
Started by user Jenkins Admin
 Revision: 6c75694b8770705b3a27f7c512766e0e3ab0a7d0
```

while a replay of #1 yields this:

```
Success Build #3 (Feb 8, 2018 4:53:05 PM)
Started by user Jenkins Admin

Replayed #1 (diff)

 Revision: 3235c1f8e141e9f1c02b42b51d782aa4f738e4b8
```

So, the `checkout scm` step will pull the revision of code that was originally associated with the run. If you are using a specific SCM step and the code base has changed since the original execution of the run that you are replaying, this is worth being aware of.

While these basic conversion steps are sufficient in most cases to convert to a Jenkinsfile, there is one other use case that you may encounter—needing to migrate functionality for parameters. That discussion deserves its own section.

Migrating parameter usage to Jenkinsfiles

At least as of the time of this writing, if you are creating a pipeline directly in a Pipeline project in the Jenkins application, you can define parameters in the traditional way in the Pipeline job interface (using the "This project is parameterized" option) and then reference them in your pipeline code. For example, suppose we define a set of parameters for versioning information in the Jenkins pipeline job interface as shown in Figure 10-18.

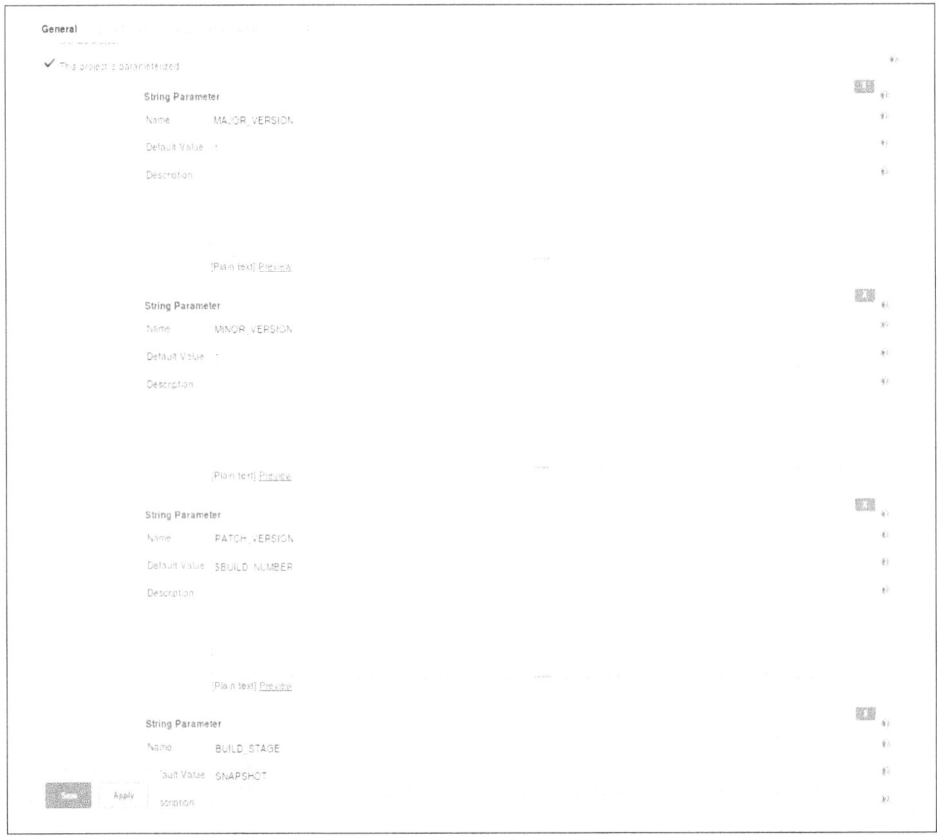

Figure 10-18. Defining parameters in a traditional Jenkins pipeline job

Within the pipeline script, we can reference those parameters like this (in example code where they are being passed to a function to update a properties file):

```
setPropertiesProc.updateGradleProperties(
                "${workspace}/gradle.properties",
                "${params.MAJOR_VERSION}",
                "${params.MINOR_VERSION}",
                "${params.PATCH_VERSION}",
                "${params.BUILD_STAGE}")
```

Notice that we didn't have to define these in our actual pipeline code since they were defined in the job in Jenkins. However, when we migrate to a Jenkinsfile, we no longer have them available, so we need to ensure we define the parameters in the pipeline code itself.

The easiest way to get the syntax for this is to use the Snippet Generator: select the "input" step and then, in the Parameters section, plug in the same kind of information that we entered in the Jenkins job when we defined the parameters there (Figure 10-19).

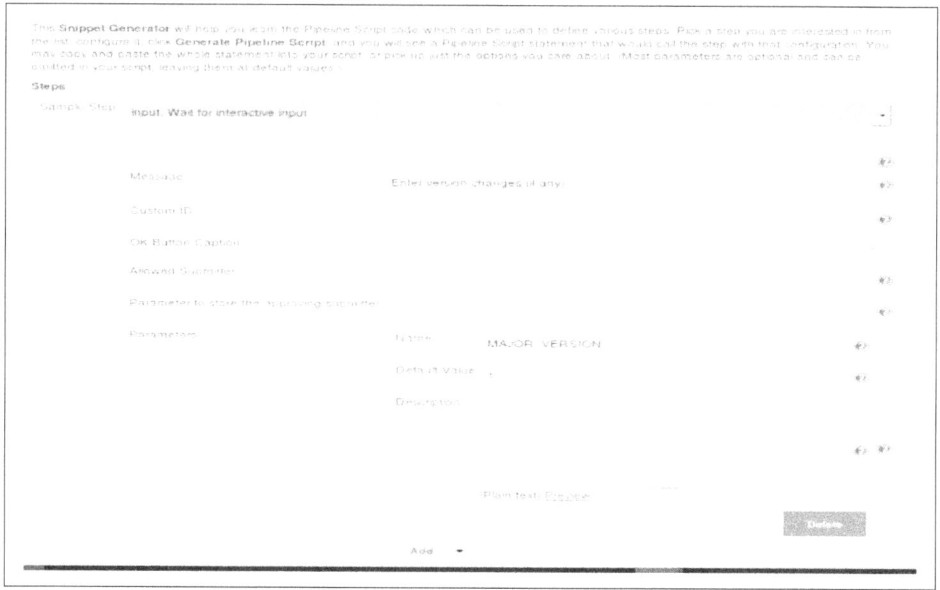

Figure 10-19. Using the Snippet Generator to figure out the code for pipeline parameters

After doing this, we'll have the Groovy syntax/code that we can copy into our Jenkinsfile:

```
def userInput
stage('Parameters') {
   userInput = input message:
'Enter version changes (if any):',
     parameters: [
        string(defaultValue: '1', description: '',
          name: 'MAJOR_VERSION'),
        string(defaultValue: '1', description: '',
          name: 'MINOR_VERSION'),
        string(defaultValue: env.BUILD_NUMBER, description: '',
          name: 'PATCH_VERSION'),
        string(defaultValue: 'SNAPSHOT', description: '',
          name: 'BUILD_STAGE')]
           major_version = userInput.MAJOR_VERSION
           minor_version = userInput.MINOR_VERSION
           patch_version = userInput.PATCH_VERSION
           build_stage = userInput.BUILD_STAGE
}
```

Figure 10-20 shows the Jenkinsfile with the new code added to define the parameters. Notice that we've defined a "global" variable outside of the pipeline stages so that we can reference the input values in multiple stages. We've also defined a separate stage for gathering the input via the parameters. While not required, this makes a nice, logical separation.

```
#!groovy
@Library('Utilities2')
node('worker_node1') {

    def userInput
    stage('Parameters') {
        userInput = input message: 'Enter version changes (if any):',
 parameters: [string(defaultValue: '1', description: '', name: 'MAJOR_VERSION'),
 string(defaultValue: '1', description: '', name: 'MINOR_VERSION'), string
 (defaultValue: env.BUILD_NUMBER, description: '', name: 'PATCH_VERSION'), string
 (defaultValue: 'SNAPSHOT', description: '', name: 'BUILD_STAGE')]
        major_version = userInput.MAJOR_VERSION
        minor_version = userInput.MINOR_VERSION
        patch_version = userInput.PATCH_VERSION
        build_stage = userInput.BUILD_STAGE
    }

    stage('Source') {
        // always run with a new workspace
        step([$class: 'WsCleanup'])
        // Get code from our git repository
```

Figure 10-20. Jenkinsfile with code to handle input parameters

After getting this part set up, we just need to update the code in our Jenkinsfile that references those parameter values to use our `userInput` object instead of the `params` one. After doing that, the code will look like this:

```
setPropertiesProc.updateGradleProperties(
                      "${workspace}/gradle.properties",
                      "${userInput.MAJOR_VERSION}",
                      "${userInput.MINOR_VERSION}",
                      "${userInput.PATCH_VERSION}",
                      "${userInput.BUILD_STAGE}")
```

More information on dealing with input and parameters can be found in Chapter 3.

Final Steps

After you have gone through the conversion (or creation) of the Jenkinsfile, it needs to be updated in source control. There is nothing special here; just use whatever source control operations you would normally use for any of your pipeline source.

Validation of Declarative Jenkinsfiles

Prior to pushing to source control, a useful step is to run a Jenkinsfile using declarative syntax through the `declarative-linter` command, as discussed in "Using the Pipeline Linter Tool for Declarative Jenkinsfiles" on page 411.

All that is left to do, then, is to set up a project in the Jenkins application that can use a Jenkinsfile, and point the project to the location of that file so it can find the pipeline code and execute it. The process of doing this with new project types such as the Multibranch Pipeline project is covered in detail in Chapter 8.

However, there is also a way to do this with an existing project in Jenkins. This is worth mentioning as another way to complete the conversion process, or if you want to specifically test out a Jenkinsfile and not have to create a Multibranch Pipeline project.

Including a Jenkinsfile back into a native Jenkins project

Another option for referencing a Jenkinsfile from the Jenkins application allows you to point a single pipeline project in Jenkins at your Jenkinsfile. This eliminates some of the overhead of a Multibranch Pipeline project, and allows some configuration to happen in Jenkins. For example, you could configure the general job items, such as the retention policy, or add parameters in the job itself.

To use this approach, you need a job of type Pipeline in Jenkins. On the configuration page for the job, scroll down to or select the Pipeline section.

In the Pipeline section of the page, you'll see a field called Definition. This will have "Pipeline script" in it by default. At the end of that field is an arrow to select entries from a list. Click on that arrow and select "Pipeline script from SCM" (see Figure 10-21).

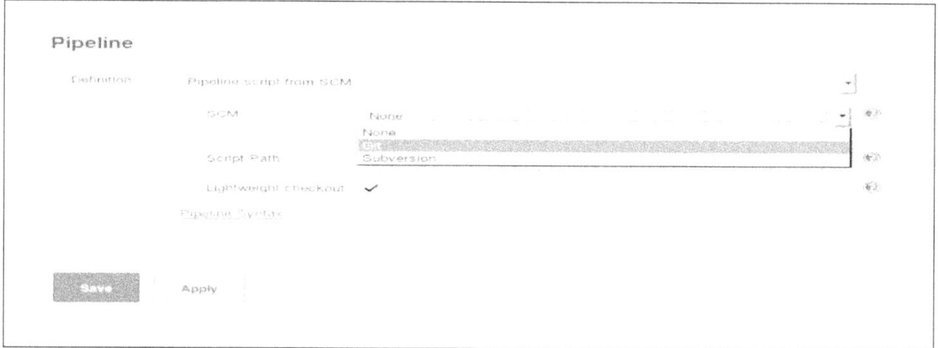

Figure 10-21. Modifying a pipeline job to use a Jenkinsfile

You'll now see a new field named SCM. Select your SCM from the list in that field.

Once you select the SCM, additional fields will show up on the screen to allow you to specify the location of the SCM repository.

For example, if you select Git, you will fill in the Repository URL and Branches fields to point to your project in source control that contains the Jenkinsfile you want to use.

You can leave everything else as is. After completing the fields, you can save the changes and select Build Now to build the pipeline based on the code in your Jenkinsfile.

Copy and Paste from Jenkinsfile via Replay

A second, less elegant way to bring the code from a Jenkinsfile back into a Pipeline project is to copy and paste from a Replay screen. The Replay command (introduced in Chapter 2) allows a user to temporarily modify a version of the pipeline code for a job, as it was at the time of the run that's being replayed.

Normally, for multibranch or organization projects based on Jenkinsfiles in remote repositories, you can't access the code from the Jenkinsfile directly in Jenkins itself.

However, if you invoke the Replay command in Jenkins on a completed run of such a project, it will load the code from the Jenkinsfile into the window on the Replay screen. You can then copy and paste that into a new project of type Pipeline and experiment with it there.

The last type of conversion that we'll look at in this chapter is converting a Scripted Pipeline to a Declarative one. Declarative Pipelines can be used anywhere Scripted Pipelines can, including within the Jenkins application and as Jenkinsfiles.

Converting from a Scripted Pipeline to a Declarative Pipeline

For those familiar with programming or needing to incorporate Groovy constructs within their pipelines, Scripted Pipelines provide the most flexibility. However, at some point you may want to move toward the more formalized declarative syntax. Reasons to do that could include the following:

- Better and tighter integration with the Blue Ocean interface
- Formal syntax checking and error reporting based on the Jenkins DSL
- Closer correspondence with the structure and flow of traditional Jenkins web forms

- Easier to understand and maintain for those familiar with Jenkins but not with Groovy

It would be impossible to provide examples and guidance on every possible case that might arise when converting from a Scripted Pipeline to a Declarative one, so we'll just look at a small representative example to illustrate some basic techniques. You should be able to extrapolate from this example to determine how to handle your own larger pipelines.

Converting the Other Way

Of course, it is also possible that at some point you may want to convert from a Declarative Pipeline to a Scripted one. In general, this should be easier, as you will be going from the more formalized and restricted syntax to the more flexible syntax. While an example of that kind of conversion isn't presented here, you should be able to reverse the type of operations we do here to perform that kind of conversion.

Sample Pipeline

Our simplistic pipeline is shown here in the form of a Jenkinsfile (converting pipelines to Jenkinsfiles was discussed in the previous section of this chapter):

```
#!groovy
@Library('Utilities@1.5')_
node ('worker_node1') {
try {
      stage('Source') {
         // always run with a new workspace
         cleanWs()
         checkout scm
         stash name: 'test-sources', includes: 'build.gradle,src/test/'
      }
      stage('Build') {
         // run the gradle build
         gbuild2 'clean build -x test'
      }
      stage ('Test') {
         // execute required unit tests in parallel
         parallel (
            worker2: { node ('worker_node2'){
               // always run with a new workspace
               cleanWs()
               unstash 'test-sources'
               gbuild2 '-D test.single=TestExample1 test'
            }},
            worker3: { node ('worker_node3'){
               // always run with a new workspace
```

```
                    cleanWs()
                    unstash 'test-sources'
                    gbuild2 '-D test.single=TestExample2 test'
                }},
            )
        }
    }
    catch (err) {
        echo "Caught: ${err}"
    }
    stage ('Notify') {
        mailUser('<email address>', "Finished")
    }
}
```

Let's briefly discuss what this simple pipeline is doing.

First, you see the Groovy designator at the top, preceding the loading of a shared library named `Utilities`. This library contains a build routine named `gbuild2` that encapsulates our Gradle build call.

The `Source` stage first cleans out the workspace and then pulls down the source code. Note the use of the `checkout scm` step again here. (As explained in "Approach" on page 414, this is sufficient since the Jenkinsfile is stored with the source code for the project, and so can interpret the SCM location to check out based on where it is.) Finally, this stage creates a stash of testware to share later with the `Test` stage.

Next, the `Build` stage simply calls the routine from the shared library to build a set of Gradle targets, omitting the `test` target since that is handled in the next stage.

The `Test` stage leverages the pipeline DSL `parallel` step to create two branches to run in parallel, each on a distinct node. Within the code for each branch, the workspace is cleaned, the contents of the stash are unstashed on the node so that the testware is present, and then a call is made to the shared library routine to build and run the particular set of tests.

Finally, at the end of the pipeline, we include a `Notify` stage that simply calls a shared library routine to notify a user that the pipeline has completed. We include this at the very end, outside of the `try-catch` block, so that it is always executed, even if an exception happens within one of the other stages. This simulates the "post-build actions" processing of the traditional Jenkins Freestyle jobs, which always execute at the end of the build regardless of what completed (or not) during the build.

The Conversion

Now that we understand how this simple Scripted Pipeline is organized, let's look at what it will take to convert it into a declarative format. Our approach will center around updating the overall structure of the pipeline, but we'll also update some programming constructs with declarative constructs.

Converting in a Separate Branch

When doing a conversion such as this on a Jenkinsfile, a useful strategy is to first create a separate branch off of the existing branch. This is so that you can work on updating the pipeline in the new branch, but still have the old one as current for reference and production—just in case. This strategy is also useful in the context of creating a separate Jenkins job pointing to the new branch to test out your converted pipeline before putting it into production.

If you use a Multibranch Pipeline project in Jenkins, Jenkins can automatically detect the new branch with the converted Jenkinsfile and create a job to build it.

After conversion and testing, the converted Jenkinsfile can be merged back into the first branch to replace the original one, if desired.

Starting at the start

We need to first make some changes in the beginning section of the pipeline script. We will keep the `#!groovy` line as an indicator that this is a Jenkins script, but we need to wrap everything in our Declarative Pipeline in a `pipeline` closure. Then, instead of the `node` definition here, we need an `agent` specification. We can also remove the `Library` block as we'll do this in a different way in the declarative model.

This translates into changing these lines:

```
@Library('Utilities@1.5') _
node ('worker_node1') {
```

to:

```
pipeline {
   agent{ label 'worker_node1'}
```

Next, we'll add a new section (or "directive") to load the library in a declarative way.

Adding the libraries directive

Declarative Pipelines have special sections called *directives* that are predefined placeholders for specifying certain kinds of information. Based on the name of the directive, Jenkins knows to do certain kinds of processing on the declarations inside the closure.

Declarative Pipelines have a specific `libraries` directive for specifying shared libraries to load. Syntactically, this directive can go immediately under the `agent` declaration from the preceding step (under the `agent {` line and before the `try {`vline). It looks like this:

```
libraries {
      lib('Utilities@1.5')
}
```

In addition to directives, Declarative Pipelines also have *stages*. These are similar to those in Scripted Pipelines, but they must all be enclosed in a larger closure.

Stages

In a Declarative Pipeline, our collection of stages needs to be wrapped in a `stages` closure. Because we used the Groovy `try-catch` mechanism to wrap all the stages in our Scripted Pipeline, we can just replace that with the `stages` closure. (Note that this is not implying a replacement of equivalent functionality, just a convenient substitution based on position of the lines in the file.)

To do this, we change this statement:

```
try {
```

to:

```
stages {
```

The top part of the pipeline will now look like this:

```
#!groovy
pipeline {
    agent{ label 'worker_node1'}
    libraries {
         lib('Utilities@1.5')
    }
    stages {
         stage('Source') {
```

Within a `stage` block, we then have a `steps` block to enclose statements.

Steps

In the declarative structure, each set of individual steps in a stage needs to be enclosed in a `steps` closure. So, within each individual `stage` section of our pipeline script (except for the `Notify` one), we must add a `steps` closure around the statements. Since we're not adding any other directives in the stages in our example, we can just add `steps {` after each `stage (…) {` line and a closing bracket (`}`) at the end of each stage.

For example, after these changes, our opening `Source` stage would look like this:

```
stage('Source') {
   steps {
      cleanWs()
      checkout scm
      stash name: 'test-sources', includes: 'build.gradle,src/test/'
   }
}
```

We'll need to add the `steps {}` closure in the `Build` and `Test` stages as well.

At this point, we have one significant transformation left for our simple pipeline—improving the post-build processing.

Post-build processing

In the declarative syntax, we have a `post` section that we can use to emulate the post-build actions of Freestyle jobs. So, we can replace the scripted `catch` section with a declarative `post` section. Doing this is a multistep process.

In the Jenkinsfile, this translates into removing the `catch` and `Notify` blocks from the pipeline. (Note there should still be a closing bracket after these, from the original `node` closure.) The following lines are the ones that we would remove:

```
catch (err) {
      echo "Caught: ${err}"
}
stage ('Notify') {
      mailUser('<email address>', "Finished")
}
```

Now, at the place in the file where these lines were deleted, we can add the following `post` section, before the final closing bracket of the `pipeline` block:

```
post {
   always {
      echo "Build stage complete"
   }
   failure {
      echo "Build failed"
      mail body: 'build failed', subject: 'Build failed!',
        to: '<email address>'
   }
   success {
      echo "Build succeeded"
      mail body: 'build succeeded', subject: 'Build Succeeded',
        to: '<email address>'
   }
}
```

Note the use of the conditionals (`always`, `failure`, `success`) here that allow us to respond in different ways based on the build outcome. These constructs are discussed in more detail in Chapter 3.

Completed Conversion

At this point, the conversion of the simple Scripted Pipeline into a Declarative Pipeline is complete. The final form looks like this:

```
#!groovy
pipeline {
   agent{ label 'worker_node1'}
   libraries {
      lib('Utilities@1.5')
   }
   stages {
      stage('Source') {
         steps {
            cleanWs()
            checkout scm
            stash name: 'test-sources',
                  includes: 'build.gradle, src/test/'
         }
      }
      stage('Build') {
         // run the gradle build
         steps {
            gbuild2 'clean build -x test'
         }
      }
      stage ('Test') {
         // execute required unit tests in parallel
         steps {
            parallel (
               worker2: { node ('worker_node2'){
                  // always run with a new workspace
                  cleanWs()
                  unstash 'test-sources'
                  gbuild2 '-D test.single=TestExample1 test'
               }},
               worker3: { node ('worker_node3'){
                  // always run with a new workspace
                  cleanWs()
                  unstash 'test-sources'
                  gbuild2 '-D test.single=TestExample3 test'
               }},
            )
         }
      }
   } // end stages
   post {
```

```
        always {
           echo "Build stage complete"
        }
        failure {
           echo "Build failed"
           mail body: 'build failed', subject: 'Build failed!',
             to: '<your email address>'
        }
        success {
           echo "Build succeeded"
           mail body: 'build succeeded', subject: 'Build Succeeded',
             to: '<your email address>'
        }
     }
  } // end pipeline
```

You can then save these changes in the Jenkinsfile, update them in source control, and point your Jenkins job(s) at the new Jenkinsfile with the Declarative Pipeline (as detailed at the end of the section on converting to a Jenkinsfile earlier in this chapter).

General Guidance for Conversions

In this chapter, we have covered some of the basic concepts around converting existing Freestyle projects into Scripted Pipelines, converting pipelines into Jenkinsfiles, and converting Scripted Pipelines into Declarative Pipelines. While we haven't covered every potential case, hopefully the cases that we have covered provide some guidance on other situations.

We can briefly summarize the ideas around converting a traditional Freestyle project to a Jenkins pipeline as follows:

- Ensure that you have a working reference pipeline to start with.
- For a group of projects, consider whether they might be suitable for a folder structure in Jenkins.
- If you have (or can create) a GitHub organization or Bitbucket team, consider whether that might be suitable. If so, create the corresponding item in Jenkins.
- For a project with multiple branches, consider whether the Multibranch Pipeline project type may be appropriate. If so, create the corresponding item in Jenkins.
- Ensure that the desired versions of all servers and tools that you will need to access are installed or accessible.
- Ensure that these are configured globally in Jenkins.
- Ensure that you have the latest Jenkins integration plugins installed so that you will (hopefully) have modern DSL steps that you can use in your pipeline.

- Ensure that you have all the needed credentials set up in Jenkins, especially if migrating from one Jenkins environment to another.
- Ensure that you have set up all the nodes and agents that you will need, with the appropriate labels.
- For the actual processing of each job, review it and note:
  - Where the job runs (slave node, container, etc.)
  - Which servers are accessed and with what credentials
  - Which tools/applications are accessed and with what credentials
  - What filesystem access (if any) is used and how it is invoked
- Armed with this information, consider whether you want to create any new shared libraries to encapsulate any information. If so, do that first and verify the routines can be called and work as expected.
- Identify any final processing you may always want to happen, such as sending mail no matter what the outcome. Consider using a `try-catch` construct to handle this if appropriate.
- Define the stages. For each section of the pipeline job that contacts a server, runs a tool, or performs some other specific piece of key pass/fail functionality, consider whether that section should become its own stage in the pipeline or whether the entire job can be a stage or some other division. This depends largely on how granular your previous pipeline was, defined in terms of division of functionality. The general rule is that a stage should be created for each part that works with a particular application, server, and/or repository. If a pass/fail of that functionality is significant for the overall pipeline, it should probably have its own stage. It is typically better to break up your pipeline into smaller stages to start with, especially as you are learning about the pipeline DSL and syntax. This can simplify processing, isolating issues, and coding/debugging.
- Code up the basic shell of the pipeline. This means defining your empty `node` blocks and `stage` blocks. At this point, you are just defining things of the sort `item ('Name') { }` to get the overall framework and flow outlined. An additional useful step can be to put a simple processing placeholder in each stage (such as `echo this is where processing for stage <name> goes`). Then you can run the pipeline and verify that your overall structure and node use work as expected.
- For each stage, define what inputs and outputs are needed for the stage. Do you need parameters as input, or any environment variables set? Do you need to have objects from another stage, or to provide objects to another stage? If so, consider the stash/unstash functionality or an artifact repository. Be sure to consider adding timeouts for any inputs that may pause the pipeline indefinitely.

- Within the stage, is any parallel processing appropriate? If so, define what makes sense for the branches of a `parallel` step, including what nodes each should run on.
- Within the stage, are there any shell steps that you need to do that haven't been otherwise handled (such as by being migrated to a shared library or external file)? Consider whether you want to invoke them as shell steps with the `sh` or `bat` commands or whether you want to put them in an external file to be loaded and executed, or in a shared library.
- Given all of this information, identify the DSL steps to invoke in your stage. Identify any Groovy constructs you may need (such as defining instance variables). If you are not sure whether a step exists for the functionality you need, check the page for the plugin that integrates with Jenkins. If you are not sure about the syntax of a particular step, check the Snippet Generator.
- If you can't find an appropriate DSL step for the functionality you need, consider writing a shell step to call the application. Note that there are options on the `sh` step to return more information from the call than it does by default. If you are comfortable with programming and digging deeper, you may be able to identify particular classes available within a plugin and call those directly via the `step` step.
- Code your pipeline, filling in the framework that you created earlier for each stage. Execute it and debug as necessary. As you fill in a stage, you can run the pipeline and verify it works before moving on to the next one. Again, keep in mind that it is usually easier to code this up in the Jenkins Pipeline project area and then transfer the code to a Jenkinsfile, following the process outlined in this chapter.
- Be sure to also code any processing that you want to happen if you catch an exception or at the end of your pipeline, such as sending email with appropriate notifications.

Summary

Given this guidance and the examples in this chapter, and the related ones on integrating with specific applications, you should be in a good place to plan and execute whatever conversions you need to do.

In the next chapter, we'll look at how to take full advantage of the `sh` and `bat` DSL steps, along with other aspects of integration with the OS.

CHAPTER 11

Integration with the OS (Shells, Workspaces, Environments, and Files)

While it seems like there are plugins for nearly every application and pipeline steps for every function in Jenkins, there may still be times when you need to do some operation that you don't have a step for. If the operation can be done via a shell step in the operating system, you can use a built-in step in the pipeline to execute that. The built-in steps offer several integration points in terms of return values that you can exploit in your pipeline for follow-up actions or decision points.

Another point of integration is the environment: both the external one that Jenkins is running in and the inherited environment local to the script. In addition to being able to read and set environment variables, Jenkins contains a `block` step that allows steps within a closure to use an isolated environment.

Workspaces also compose part of your pipeline's environment. Jenkins includes a few workspace-related steps that are worth knowing about should you ever need to more closely manage a custom workspace for your project.

Finally, there will undoubtedly be times you need to manipulate files and/or directories within your projects. The pipeline includes a limited set of steps to allow for the most common kinds of file and directory operations. Plugins greatly extend this set.

We'll cover all of these items in this chapter to give you a complete picture of how you can integrate your pipeline and the OS.

Using Shell Steps

We'll begin by looking at a set of steps that allow for passing commands to the operating system for execution. As you might imagine, there are separate steps for Linux/Unix and Windows. However, they are nearly identical in the options they supply.

Setting the Shell Executable

In nearly all cases, you can just let Jenkins pick up the shell executable by default. But if for some reason you want to specify a different shell executable, you can do that on the Configure System screen, as shown in Figure 11-1.

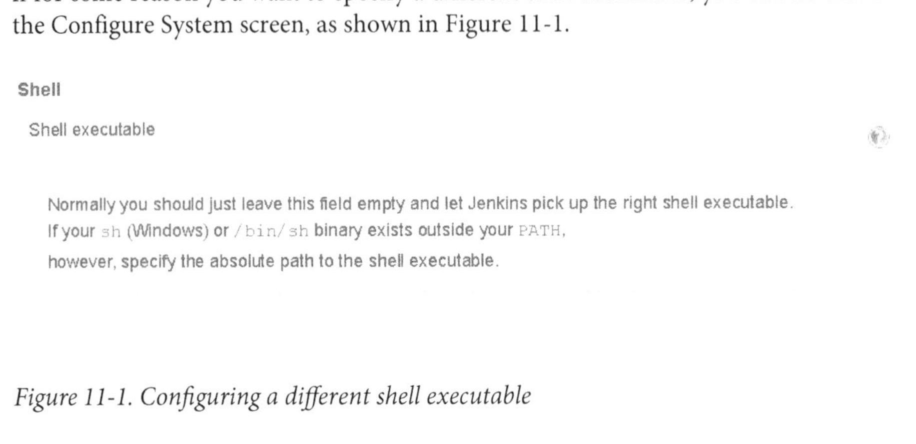

Shell
Shell executable
Normally you should just leave this field empty and let Jenkins pick up the right shell executable.
If your sh (Windows) or /bin/sh binary exists outside your PATH,
however, specify the absolute path to the shell executable.

Figure 11-1. Configuring a different shell executable

The sh Step

Probably the most general-purpose step available to pipelines is the `sh` step. If there isn't a specific step that does what you need, or that integrates a particular application, you can typically come up with a shell command and arguments to do it. The `sh` step can then be used to execute that command.

The default syntax is straightforward:

```
sh '<shell command string>'
```

The default form of the step does not provide much integration with the pipeline in terms of returning information. We'll explore some useful options to help with that. Afterwards, we'll explore some ways to set context around the command and even run scripts in other programming languages. To begin, let's look at the set of options for the step:

`script`
: The operations to execute, expressed as strings. This is the default parameter, so `script` doesn't have to be specified if that's the only parameter you're using. Multiple lines are allowed, but you'll need to enclose them in triple quotes.

`encoding`
: The encoding of the output, expressed as a string. You only need to set this if you need to use something other than the default value of `UTF-8`.

`returnStdout`
: A Boolean. If this is set to `false` (the default), then `stdout` is just printed to the console log. If it's set to `true`, `stdout` is returned from the step as a string. (Hint: You can use `trim()` to strip a trailing newline if needed.)

`returnStatus`
: A Boolean. If this is set to `false` (the default), then a nonzero status code will cause the step to fail and throw an exception. If this is set to `true`, then the status code will instead be the return code from the step. You can take that return code and check it and act accordingly.

Return Values

Note that only one of the options `returnStdout` or `returnStatus` can be set for each invocation of the shell step.

Also, for the `returnStdout` option, if there is any `stderr` output, it will still go to the console log.

Here's a simple code example using the `sh` step and "redirecting" the output to a variable:

```
def listing = sh script: 'ls -la /', returnStdout:true
```

There are a few different ways we can modify the behavior of the `sh` step, including how and what it runs. We'll cover some of the more interesting aspects in the next few sections.

set Options

By default, the shell will not stop if there is an error in your script. It will happily try to execute all of the lines. However, this is not usually what you want—especially if you are using shell commands as part of a pipeline script.

So, the `sh` step in Jenkins automatically includes a `set -e` option. This tells the shell to stop execution and not run the rest of the script lines if it encounters an error in a line.

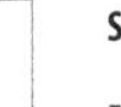

set

If you're not familiar with `set`, it's simply a built-in OS command used for setting or unsetting options and positional parameters.

For example, suppose we have a script like this:

```
sh '''ech LINE1
      echo LINE2'''
```

Notice the misspelled `echo` command in the first line. If we run this in Jenkins, we'll see output like this:

```
[Pipeline] {
[Pipeline] sh
[sh-test2] Running shell script
+ ech LINE1
/home/jenkins2/worker_node3/workspace/sh-test2@tmp ... ech: not found
[Pipeline] }
[Pipeline] // node
[Pipeline] End of Pipeline
ERROR: script returned exit code 127
Finished: FAILURE
```

Note that the script stopped being executed after Jenkins encountered the first bad line.

If, for some reason, you prefer to have Jenkins execute all the lines in your script regardless of there being a problem with one of them, you can add the `set +e` statement at the start to turn off the "stop after a bad line" function. Here's an example of that:

```
[Pipeline] {
[Pipeline] sh
[sh-test2] Running shell script
+ set +e
+ ech LINE1
/home/jenkins2/worker_node3/workspace/sh-test2@tmp ... ech: not found
+ echo LINE2
LINE2
[Pipeline] }
[Pipeline] // node
[Pipeline] End of Pipeline
Finished: SUCCESS
```

Notice that even though the script had the same error, the step did not "fail;" the remaining line was executed, and Jenkins reported the run of the script as a `SUCCESS`.

You may have also noticed in the output from running shell operations that each shell command is printed out with a + sign in front of it as it is run. This is due to Jenkins automatically setting another option, `-x`. The `-x` option tells the `sh` step to echo out each OS command as it executes it. If you prefer to turn this off, you can add the `set +x` option to your `sh` step.

If you want to turn both options off, you can combine them in one `set` command, as shown in here:

```
sh '''set +xe
      ech LINE1
      echo LINE2'''
```

This code will not echo out the lines as it executes them and will not stop for an error, so the output will look like this:

```
[Pipeline] {
[Pipeline] sh
[sh-test2] Running shell script
+ set +xe
/home/jenkins2/worker_node1/workspace/sh-test2@tmp ... ech: not found
LINE2
[Pipeline] }
[Pipeline] // node
[Pipeline] End of Pipeline
Finished: SUCCESS
```

Note the absence of the lines starting with `+`, other than the `set` line where we turned that off.

Language interpreters

One of the lesser-known tricks when using the `sh` step may be that you can add an interpreter on the first line and then execute programs in the language specified by the interpreter. For example, the following simple script shows examples of setting a variable and printing a greeting in different languages using the `sh` step:

```
node {
   sh 'export NAME=Jenkins; echo Hello, $NAME from shell!'
   sh '''#!/usr/bin/perl
       my $name = "Jenkins";
       print "Hello, $name from Perl!\n";'''
   sh '''#!/usr/bin/python
name="Jenkins"
print('Hello {} from Python!'.format(name))'''
}
```

Note that we include the interpreter as the first line for the Perl and Python examples. Also note that we still need to adhere to the requirements of the particular language. For example, we don't have any indenting on the Python statements.

Executing shell scripts from shared libraries

Normally, we think of shared libraries as being Groovy-based code. And certainly, Groovy functions can call the pipeline `sh` step just like any other pipeline code. But there is also a way to load and execute standard shell scripts from a library.

The trick is in putting the script in the `resources` directory. The `resources` directory is normally used for nonprogrammatic resources, such as data files. These typically are items such as JSON or YAML files needed by your library routines. However, you can store any kind of file in here, including shell scripts.

Shell scripts stored in this area can be loaded with the standard `libraryResource` step. Once you have the script loaded, you can then pass it directly to the `sh` pipeline step to execute.

Here's an example of what code to do this might look like in a Scripted Pipeline:

```
def myExternalScript = libraryResource 'externalCommands.sh'
sh myExternalScript
```

In a Declarative Pipeline, since you can't use `def`, you can use the trick of treating the `libraryResource` command as a variable to be interpolated for the `sh` command, as shown here:

```
sh "${libraryResource 'ws-get-latest.sh'}"
```

Take Care When Using sh to Directly Interpret Shell Scripts

Just because you can execute scripts directly from the library's *resources* area doesn't mean it's the best or safest approach. As discussed in Chapter 6, access to push something to the library should be controlled. A better approach is to directly code the shell commands into your pipeline script so they are clearly visible. However, we include a description of this functionality here since it may be useful in some cases.

Pipeline shared libraries are discussed in Chapter 6.

Checking the Platform

In some cases, you may have available nodes based on different platforms—some on Linux/Mac and some on Windows. The pipeline incluced a simple step to allow you to check which platform the enclosing node is running on.

The step is called `isUnix`. It takes no arguments and is a simple Boolean check. It returns `true` if the node is running on Linux/Mac and `false` if it is running on Windows. Using this, you can determine things like which kind of shell step you need to execute. An overly simple example is shown here:

```
if (isUnix()) {
   sh "ls -latr"
}
else {
   bat "dir /o:d"
}
```

The bat Step

Like the `sh` step for Linux operations, there is a corresponding `bat` step for Windows operations. It has the same options as the `sh` step. They are:

`script`
: The operations to execute, expressed as strings. This is the default parameter, so `script` doesn't have to be specified if that's the only parameter you're using. Multiple lines are allowed, but you'll need to enclose them in triple quotes.

`encoding`
: The encoding of the output, expressed as a string. You only need to set this if you need to use something other than the default value of `UTF-8`.

`returnStdout`
: A Boolean. If this is set to `false` (the default), `stdout` is just printed to the console log. If it's set to `true`, `stdout` is returned from the step as a string. (Hint: You can use `trim()` to strip a trailing newline if needed.)

`returnStatus`
: A Boolean. If this is set to `false` (the default), a nonzero status code will cause the step to fail and throw an exception. If this is set to `true`, the status code will instead be the return code from the step. You can take that return code and check it and act accordingly.

Return Values

Note that only one of the options (`returnStdout` or `returnStatus`) can be set for each invocation of the `bat` step.

Also, for the `returnStdout` option, if there is any `stderr` output, it will still go to the console log.

Here's a simple code example using the `bat` step:

```
bat returnStatus: true, script: 'echo Hello Jenkins!'
```

Executing batch scripts from shared libraries

As with the `sh` step, batch scripts can also be stored in the `resources` area of a shared library and then executed directly. See "Executing shell scripts from shared libraries" on page 438 for background and important caveats.

Here's an example of what code to do this might look like in a Scripted Pipeline:

```
def test = libraryResource 'test.bat'
bat test
```

In a Declarative Pipeline, since you can't use `def`, you can use the trick of treating the `libraryResource` command as a variable to be interpolated for the `sh` command, as shown here:

```
bat "${libraryResource 'test.bat'}"
```

Pipeline shared libraries are discussed in Chapter 6.

The powershell Step

If you are a PowerShell user and have the PowerShell plugin installed, you can use the `powershell` step in your pipeline on a Windows node/agent. The step has the same options as the `sh` and `bat` steps. They are:

`script`
: The operations to execute, expressed as strings. This is the default parameter, so `script` doesn't have to be specified if that's the only parameter you're using. Multiple lines are allowed, but you'll need to enclose them in triple quotes.

`encoding`
: The encoding of the output, expressed as a string. You only need to set this if you need to use something other than the default value of `UTF-8`.

`returnStdout`
: A Boolean. If this is set to `false` (the default), `stdout` is just printed to the console log. If it's set to `true`, `stdout` is returned from the step as a string. (Hint: You can use `trim()` to strip a trailing newline if needed.)

`returnStatus`
: A Boolean. If this is set to `false` (the default), a nonzero status code will cause the step to fail and throw an exception. If this is set to `true`, the status code will instead be the return code from the step. You can take that return code and check it and act accordingly.

Return Values

Note that only one of the options `returnStdout` or `returnStatus` can be set for each invocation of the `powershell` step.

Also, for the `returnStdout` option, if there is any `stderr` output, it will still go to the console log.

Here's a simple code example using the `powershell` step:

```
powershell returnStatus: true, script: 'Write-Host "Hello Jenkins!"'
```

Executing PowerShell scripts from shared libraries

As with the `sh` and `bat` steps, PowerShell scripts can also be stored in the *resources* area of a shared library and then executed directly. See "Executing shell scripts from shared libraries" on page 438 for background and important caveats.

Here's an example of what code to do this might look like in a Scripted Pipeline:

```
def psscript = libraryResource 'ps-script.ps1'
powershell psscript
```

In a Declarative Pipeline, since you can't use `def`, you can use the trick of treating the `libraryResource` command as a variable to be interpolated for the `sh` command, as shown here:

```
powershell "${libraryResource 'ps-script.ps1'}"
```

Pipeline shared libraries are discussed in Chapter 6.

Using Shell Steps for Prototyping or Conversions

Before we leave this section on working with shell steps, it's worth pointing out another of their benefits. In addition to providing direct access to do things we may not have other steps for, shell steps can be used in prototyping or converting scripts to pipelines. That is, when we are developing pipelines or converting to a pipeline from another script, it may be quicker and easier to temporarily add an `sh` or `bat` step into our pipeline to get it up and going, and then later add the more specific step from a plugin with the exact syntax that it needs.

Next, we'll look at another aspect of working with the shell—environment variables.

Working with Environment Variables

Environment variables in Jenkins pipeline scripts can be referenced easily in multiple ways. For example, these four lines all print the value of the current PATH environment variable:

```
echo "${env.PATH}"
echo "${PATH}"
echo env.PATH
echo PATH
```

However, this only works if we don't have a local variable called PATH defined. Otherwise, the second and fourth examples would print out the values of the local PATH variable instead.

In actual fact, the env namespace represents the environment that is available inside the script. It is available to anything that needs to run within the script.

So, it is a best practice to always prefix operations that use environment variables with the env namespace, except when invoking the withEnv step that we'll discuss shortly.

In a Scripted Pipeline, you can set an environment variable simply by assignment. In the following example, we set an environment variable named USER to the jenkins2 value and append a home directory to the PATH:

```
env.USER = 'jenkins2'
env.PATH = env.PATH + ':/home/diyuser2'
```

In a Declarative Pipeline, there is an environment directive that can be used to set environment variables, as shown here:

```
environment {
   USER = 'jenkins2'
   PATH = "/home/diyuser2:$PATH"
}
```

Declarative Pipelines are discussed in more detail in Chapter 7.

Doing More with Environment Variables in Declarative Pipelines

Just a quick note here to point out two additional aspects of using environment variables in Declarative Pipelines:

- You can assign a global variable to the value of a Jenkins credential inside an environment block (as discussed in Chapter 7).
- You can use a when clause to conditionally execute a stage if an environment variable has a particular value (as discussed in Chapter 3).

This covers the basics of environment variables, but there is a special step in the pipeline for working with them too. We'll look at that next.

The withEnv Step

Jenkins includes `withEnv`, a special step for working with environment variables. Actually, this is a block step, meaning that it sets some context when it is invoked that is valid for any code put within its block.

Here's an example that we can look at and discuss:

```
withEnv(["PATH+GRADLE=${tool 'gradle3'}/bin", 'USER=Jenkins2']) {
   sh 'echo PATH = $PATH'
}
```

In the step's invocation, we are setting two environment variables: `PATH` and `USER`. Notice the `PATH+` syntax here—this is a special syntax that is allowed for the `withEnv` step to prepend things to the path. In this case, we're leveraging the `tool` pipeline step to add the path associated with "gradle3" in our Global Tool Configuration. Then we also set the `USER` environment variable.

The `PATH+...` string is enclosed in double quotes, because we are using Groovy interpolation to resolve the value of `${tool 'gradle3'}` as part of the string. But also notice that in the shell call (`sh`) within the body of the `withEnv` step, we are using single quotes, even though we use the `$PATH` value. The reason for this is that we want this `$PATH` to be interpreted by the shell itself, not Groovy. The use of single quotes means that Groovy will not try to interpret it and it will be passed on to the shell call as intended.

So, this step will have output like the following (assuming `gradle3` resolves to */usr/share/gradle*):

```
PATH = /usr/share/gradle/bin:/usr/local/sbin:/usr/local/bin:
/usr/sbin:/usr/bin:/sbin:/bin:/usr/games:/usr/local/games:
```

As you can see, the item we set in the context was prepended to the path (added at the start). This allows you to make sure the desired item is seen first.

Unsetting Environment Variables

If you need to unset an environment variable, the syntax is simply an assignment without anything on the right—i.e.:

```
env.<NAME> =
```

One of the questions that may come to mind is why you should use the `withEnv` step over simple assignment to update environment variables. The answer has to do with scope within your pipeline script. If you do assignment outside of the `withEnv` step, then the environment variable is updated for any use within your script. So, if you only want to use that value temporarily, you must remember to reset it—which means you need to remember what the previous value was if you intend to use it again.

With the `withEnv` step, the updates done in the first line of the step are only valid within the block (body) of the step. Outside of that block, in the rest of the pipeline script, the environment variables have their previous values.

Local Environment Variables for Stages in Declarative Pipelines

Note, though, that if you are using a Declarative Pipeline, you can also declare an `environment` block within a stage. In that case, any environment variables updated in that block apply only to that stage. If you need finer granularity than the entire stage, then you could use the `withEnv` step to achieve that.

Another aspect of the environment associated with your pipeline is the workspace that Jenkins creates on the system. This is where Jenkins executes the local parts of your pipeline. There are a few aspects that you can control regarding that. We discuss those in the next section.

EnvInject

A popular plugin for use with Freestyle jobs is EnvInject (*http://bit.ly/2HPVMXs*). This plugin allows injecting a wide set of values as environment variables for use in a Freestyle project. Unfortunately, at the time of this writing, this plugin is not compatible with pipelines.

Working with Workspaces

Most of the time when we work with Jenkins, we don't even think about workspaces. Jenkins just manages them for us. If there's a problem with our processing, we may go out and find the workspace and look in it to try to understand what went wrong, but otherwise we're happy to let Jenkins manage things. However, you may come across a time when you need or want more control over the workspaces you're using. For those times, Jenkins provides a couple of pipeline steps that can be useful.

Creating a Custom Workspace

Using the `node` or `agent` directive gives you a workspace automatically. However, if you need or want a custom workspace to work in, you can use the pipeline `ws` step. This step takes a single argument—the directory you want to use for the workspace—and attempts to lock it for exclusive use. The path supplied as the argument can be relative to the node area or an absolute path. The directory will be created if it doesn't exist.

An example of the basic syntax is shown here:

```
ws ('home/diyuser2/myws') {
    // block of code to execute in workspace
}
```

Note that this step is actually a block step, defining a closure in which you can put the code that you want to execute in the custom workspace.

@# and @tmp Workspaces

If you've spent much time looking around at the workspaces that Jenkins produces by default, chances are you've seen ones of the form *project@2* or *project@tmp*.

If multiple processes attempt to allocate the same workspace, then Jenkins will formulate a new workspace name by adding an @ sign and digit to the end of the directory name (such as *home/diyuser2/myws@2* for our example in the text).

And for cases where it may need to do things like temporarily create a script or other intermediate actions, it will create an *@tmp* workspace directory to use for that.

To illustrate how the ws step works, let's look at a simple example program:

```
node {
    print pwd()
    ws ('myWorkspace') {
        print pwd()
        ws ('myWorkspace') {
           print pwd()
        }
    }
}
```

In this script, we're using the ws step to create a new workspace to work in. And then, within that, we're asking for the same workspace again. Within each workspace area, we're using the pwd step so we can print out the current working directory.

Here's the output from this script:

```
Started by user Jenkins 2 user
[Pipeline] node
Running on worker_node3 in
/home/jenkins2/worker_node3/workspace/ws-test
[Pipeline] {
[Pipeline] pwd
[Pipeline] echo
```

```
/home/jenkins2/worker_node3/workspace/ws-test
[Pipeline] ws
Running in /home/jenkins2/worker_node3/myWorkspace
[Pipeline] {
[Pipeline] pwd
[Pipeline] echo
/home/jenkins2/worker_node3/myWorkspace
[Pipeline] ws
Running in /home/jenkins2/worker_node3/myWorkspace@2
[Pipeline] {
[Pipeline] pwd
[Pipeline] echo
/home/jenkins2/worker_node3/myWorkspace@2
[Pipeline] }
[Pipeline] // ws
[Pipeline] }
[Pipeline] // ws
[Pipeline] }
[Pipeline] // node
[Pipeline] End of Pipeline
Finished: SUCCESS
```

As you can see, Jenkins switched to the requested workspace the first time we asked for it. On the second request, it appended the *@2* to the workspace name. In most cases, this probably won't matter, but if it did (if you needed the exact name), you could check the output of a `pwd()` call and exit or wait depending on what you wanted to do.

ws Versus dir

If you are not concerned with the locking aspect, you can just use the `dir` step to switch the directory you are executing in.

Cleaning a Workspace

Workspaces in Jenkins are not automatically cleaned. However, as we've discussed in other chapters, the pipeline supplies a `cleanWs` step to clean out a workspace. By default, the step removes all files in the workspace, regardless of the build result, and fails the build if the cleanup fails. But there are a number of options to customize the steps' behavior, summarized in the next few sections.

File patterns to be deleted

By default, all files in the workspace will be deleted. However, you can add file patterns to include or exclude from deletion. This is specified using the `patterns` argument and an array of `pattern` and `type` pairs (where `pattern` is the file pattern and `type` is `include` or `exclude`).

For example, to only delete the **.bak* and **.tmp* files from the workspace, you could use the following syntax:

```
cleanWs patterns: [[pattern: '*.bak', type: 'INCLUDE'],
 [pattern: '*.tmp', type: 'INCLUDE']]
```

Pattern Syntax

The syntax for the pattern here is Ant syntax, so the preceding example only deletes these files in the top-level directory. If you wanted to delete these files in all subdirectories, you would need to use syntax like this: `'**/*.tmp'`.

One thing that may not be obvious here is that you can use the `INCLUDE` and `EXCLUDE` types together. Why would you do this? One reason would be to add specific exclusions within the context of a larger inclusion—in other words, to keep a specific item or items when other things of that type are being removed.

In the following code, we are deleting all of the **.tmp* files except the one named *keep.tmp*:

```
cleanWs(patterns: [[pattern: '*.tmp', type: 'INCLUDE'],
   [pattern: 'keep.tmp', type: 'EXCLUDE']])
```

Using other delete programs

Another option that `cleanWs` provides is the ability to use a different delete program. This is done via the `externalDelete` parameter. The argument to this parameter is a call to the alternative delete application. This takes the form of:

```
<delete-program> [<delete-program-arguments>] %s
```

`%s` here will be replaced by the items to be deleted, as interpreted through the rest of the `cleanWs` command options. Environment variables can be incorporated in this string via the `${}` syntax. Note that if an environment variable is used for the `<delete-program>` and that environment variable is set to the empty string, the default delete program on the node will be used.

Invoking the `externalDelete` option with the delete program `shred` on a Linux system might look something like this:

```
cleanWs externalDelete: 'shred -uf %s'
```

Other arguments

The remaining arguments for the `cleanWs` step are all Booleans for various aspects. Remember that the default form of the step is just `cleanWs`, so these arguments only need to be specified if you *don't* want the default behavior. The available arguments are:

`cleanWhenAborted`
: Default is `true`; if set to `false`, the step will not clean the workspace when the build status is aborted.

`cleanWhenFailure`
: Default is `true`; if set to `false`, the step will not clean the workspace when the build status is failed.

`cleanWhenNotBuilt`
: Default is `true`; if set to `false`, the step will not clean the workspace when the project was not built.

`cleanWhenSuccess`
: Default is `true`; if set to `false`, the step will not clean the workspace when the build status is success.

`cleanWhenUnstable`
: Default is `true`; if set to `false`, the step will not clean the workspace when the build status is unstable.

`deleteDirs`
: Default is `false`; if set to `true`, will delete directories also. Note that if patterns are supplied (as outlined in the earlier section), this will only delete directories that have names that also match those patterns.

`notFailBuild`
: Default is `true`; if set to `false`, this will fail the overall build if the cleanup step fails.

File and Directory Steps

Finally in this chapter, we'll discuss the Jenkins pipeline steps provided for working with files and directories. We'll start with the ones specific to files.

Working with Files

Files are another way we can pass information to and from Jenkins. Pipeline DSL contains simple steps for the most common operations for working with files: reading, writing, and checking for existence. We'll cover those operations in this section.

Reading files

The step for reading a file into a pipeline is `readFile`. It reads in the contents of the file and returns those as a string.

`readFile` has two possible parameters. The first is `file`, which is the relative path to the desired file from the current directory. Most often, this will be relative to the workspace directory, since that's where the script will be running and thus will be the default current directory. Path components should be separated by forward slashes (`/`). This parameter is required.

The second parameter is the file encoding, such as `UTF-8`. This parameter is optional.

The following code snippet shows the simple form of the step and then a version that includes the encoding:

```
readFile 'dir1/dir2/filename'

readFile encoding: 'UTF-8', file: 'dir1/dir2/filename'
```

Writing files

Like reading files, writing files is fairly straightforward. The step is `writeFile`. It takes a required parameter for the path to the file to write. That parameter is named `file`. The path for the `file` parameter is relative to the current directory which, like with `readFile`, is usually going to be the current workspace. Here too, path components should be separated by slashes.

Also required is the text string to write out to the file, specified by the parameter `text`.

Finally, an optional `encoding` parameter can be specified if needed.

An example call for this step is:

```
writeFile encoding: 'UTF-8', file: 'dir1/dir2/file.out',
   text: 'Output from build'
```

Checking for file existence

The last file operation is one that checks for the existence of a file. Not surprisingly, the name of the step is `fileExists`. It only takes one argument: the path with the name of the file to check for. Like the other file operations, this path is expected to be relative to the current directory (usually the workspace directory when a job is running) and with the components separated by slashes.

An example is:

```
fileExists 'build/reports/index.html'
```

Now, we'll move on to the steps that support working with directories.

Working with Directories

The pipeline DSL provides several steps related to directories that can be useful. The function of most of these may be obvious based on the name, but some of them can have specialized usage in the context of a pipeline.

dir

As the name suggests, the `dir` step allows you to switch the current working directory. This step is a block step, meaning that you supply a directory and that directory is the current directory for any other steps in the block.

For example:

```
dir('/home/user') {
   // some steps
}
```

Here are a few points to be aware of when using this command:

- The path you supply to the step can be either absolute or relative.
- If the directory does not exist, Jenkins will attempt to create it, but it must have appropriate permissions to do so.
- If a step inside the block uses a relative path, it will be relative to the directory set in the step.

You may be wondering what the difference is between using this command to switch directories for a workspace and the `ws` command. As mentioned briefly earlier in the chapter, the `ws` command provides locking functionality, such that multiple jobs cannot use the same directory as the workspace at the same time. `dir` does not.

pwd

Like the OS command of the same name, a call to the pipeline step `pwd` just returns the current directory as a string. The step can take one optional argument: `tmp`. If `tmp` is set to `true`, then this will return a temporary directory associated with the current one by appending *@tmp* onto it.

As an example, if the current directory is */home/jenkins*, then the value of tmpDir in the following code will be */home/jenkins@tmp*:

```
def tmpDir = pwd tmp:true
```

@tmp in Workspaces

Workspaces sometimes have *@tmp* directories associated with them. This is because workspaces frequently need places to put files that are not part of the source checkout/build area, such as temporary scripts, libraries, etc.

deleteDir

This step is used to recursively delete a directory. By default it operates against the current directory. If you want to redirect it to another directory, you can wrap it in a `dir` block (per the previous discussion of the `dir` step):

```
dir('tmpDir') { deleteDir() }
```

These pipeline steps provide the basic operations most commonly needed for working with files and directories. There are also plugins that provide a more extensive set of operations to your pipeline. We'll discuss one of those next.

Doing More with Files and Directories

As with nearly any kind of built-in functionality in Jenkins, plugins have been written that can extend the set of functionality for working with files and directories. One of those is the File Operations plugin (*https://plugins.jenkins.io/file-operations*).

When installed, the File Operations plugin adds a new `fileOperations` step that has a number of suboperations to assist with file and directory manipulations. Most of the functionality should be obvious from the names, but for more information on what these do, please see the plugin's documentation.

```
fileCreateOperation(String fileName, String fileContent)
fileCopyOperation(String includes, String excludes,
  String targetLocation, boolean flattenFiles)
fileDeleteOperation(String includes, String excludes)
fileDownloadOperation(String url, String userName,
  String password, String targetLocation, String targetFileName)
fileJoinOperation(String sourceFile, String targetFile)
filePropertiesToJsonOperation(String sourceFile,
   String targetFile)
fileTransformOperation(String includes, String excludes)
fileUnTarOperation(String filePath, String targetLocation,
   boolean isGZIP)
fileUnZipOperation(String filePath, String targetLocation)
folderCopyOperation(String sourceFolderPath,
   String destinationFolderPath)
folderCreateOperation(String folderPath)
folderDeleteOperation(String folderPath)
fileRenameOperation(String source, String destination)
   folderRenameOperation(String source, String destination)
```

The `fileOperations` step takes an array of file operations as elements with their respective arguments. The following example shows using this step to create a file, copy the file to a new name, and then delete the original file:

```
fileOperations([
   fileCreateOperation(fileContent: 'This is a text file.',
      fileName: 'file1.txt'),
   fileCopyOperation(excludes: '', includes: 'file1.txt',
      targetLocation: 'file2.txt'),
   fileDeleteOperation(includes: 'file1.txt')
])
```

The output from the step provides a summary of what it is doing as it executes:

```
[Pipeline] fileOperations
File Create Operation:
Creating file: /var/lib/jenkins/workspace/file-test1/file1.txt
File Copy Operation:
/var/lib/jenkins/workspace/file-test1/file1.txt
File Delete Operation:
/var/lib/jenkins/workspace/file-test1/file1.txt deleting....
Success.
[Pipeline] }
```

The main advantage of using this step over calls to the OS shell is that these operations are OS-independent. They can be used on *nix or Windows.

Summary

In this chapter, we've covered a set of pipeline steps that allow your pipeline to interact with the underlying operating system.

The `sh` step (`bat` on Windows) is a ubiquitous step that allows you to execute any shell command and, optionally, return the output or return code back to your pipeline for processing. In a mature pipeline, its utility is for accomplishing tasks that may not have dedicated steps in the pipeline. However, in the earlier stages of pipeline development, it can also be used for prototyping by executing commands previously done by other scripts before they are turned into dedicated steps.

The pipeline provides steps as well for working with environment variables. Environment variables from outside the pipeline can be queried (have their values read). Within the pipeline, environment variables can be set at the scope of the entire script, or, using the `withEnv` block step, they can be temporarily modified within the scope of a closure.

Jenkins allows you to change the workspace directory to a custom directory if needed, using the `ws` step, and it provides a customizable step (`cleanWs`) for selectively cleaning out parts of the workspace. If, however, you are not concerned about multiple pipeline instances trying to use the same custom workspace, you can use the `dir` step as an alternative to switch directories.

`dir` is just one of the steps available for working with directories. Others include steps to delete directories and determine the current directory. An option to the `pwd` step for determining the current directory allows you to create an associated temporary directory. For files, the built-in steps center around reading, writing, and checking for file existence. However, the File Operations plugin greatly extends the set of OS-independent file operations that you can do through the pipeline.

In the next chapter, we'll look at integration with tools that can analyze your source code for metrics and quality.

CHAPTER 12

Integrating Analysis Tools

Most pipelines have some version of an "analysis" stage for doing things such as gathering code metrics, determining complexity, identifying bad coding practices and likely breaking points, and calculating potential resource costs such as technical debt. These analytics identify potential problems (some more serious than others), and fixing these "holes" can enhance key characteristics of the code such as readability, reliability, and maintainability.

In this chapter, we'll look at how to integrate one of the most popular of these applications, SonarQube, into a Jenkins pipeline. We'll also see how to integrate a separate tool, Jacoco, for code coverage analysis. Code coverage analysis is frequently integrated into a tool like SonarQube, but it's worth understanding how to separate it out, given the important role that code coverage can often play in analyzing code.

For SonarQube, we'll start by briefly discussing the tool and how it is integrated into a traditional pipeline. Then we'll look at how that translates into a pipeline-as-code environment. Along the way, we'll cover one of the most important aspects of using such a tool in a pipeline, as a way to pass or fail your pipeline stage based on selected thresholds set within the application.

Though we'll utilize Gradle again here as a supporting technology, the approaches we use should be adaptable to most other technologies once you understand the basics.

Likewise, for Jacoco, we'll briefly discuss the application, see how it has typically been integrated into a traditional pipeline, and then look at how we can migrate that into a pipeline-as-code.

Let's begin by discussing a little about what SonarQube offers for code quality analysis in a pipeline.

SonarQube Survey

Per its website (*https://www.sonarqube.org*), SonarQube (formerly known as just "Sonar") is an open platform for managing code quality in several key software areas, including:

- Architecture and design
- Comments
- Coding rules
- Potential bugs
- Duplications
- Unit tests
- Complexity

As you can see by this list, the core functionality covers a lot of territory and provides many metrics that can be beneficial. Within the SonarQube application itself, you can get a quick overview of how an analyzed project fared by looking at the dashboard. An example of that is shown in Figure 12-1.

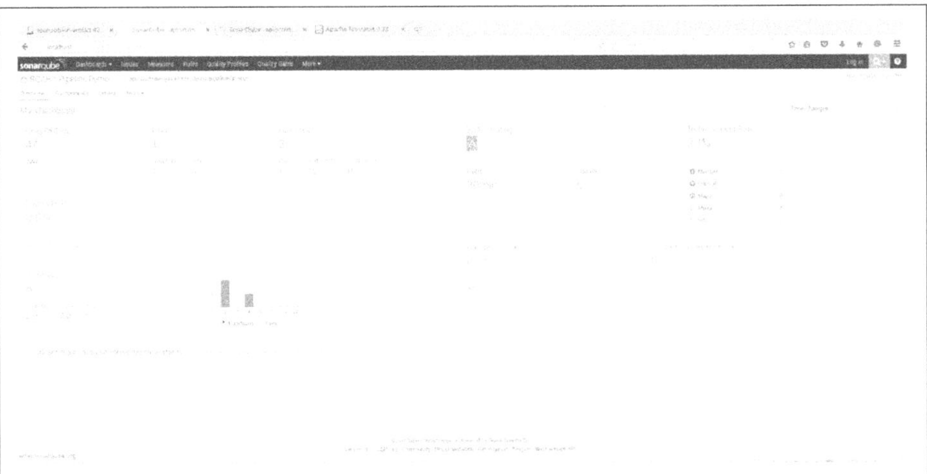

Figure 12-1. SonarQube dashboard

Beyond this core set, the "open" reference refers to the ability to extend the tool's functionality with plugins to gather additional metrics, and to the ability to further define and tune the rules that govern the core functionality. This may be helpful as you start establishing criteria that your pipeline code needs to meet.

To begin to understand how it fits in with our pipelines, let's take a quick look at individual violations flagged by SonarQube.

Working with Individual Rules

SonarQube governs the conditions it checks based on a set of specified "rules." When it analyzes source code and detects code that violates these rules, it flags the offending code and reports the rule violations. A simple example showing a set of violations that were found can be seen in Figure 12-2.

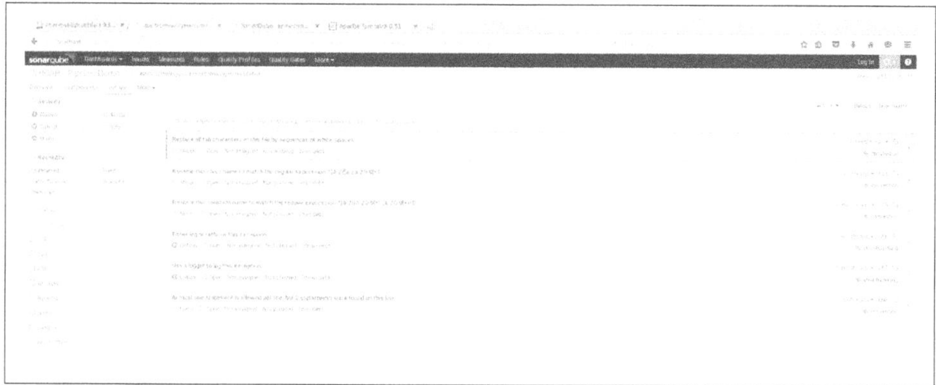

Figure 12-2. Rule violations in a SonarQube Report

From here we can drill down into individual violations to get more information, as seen in Figure 12-3.

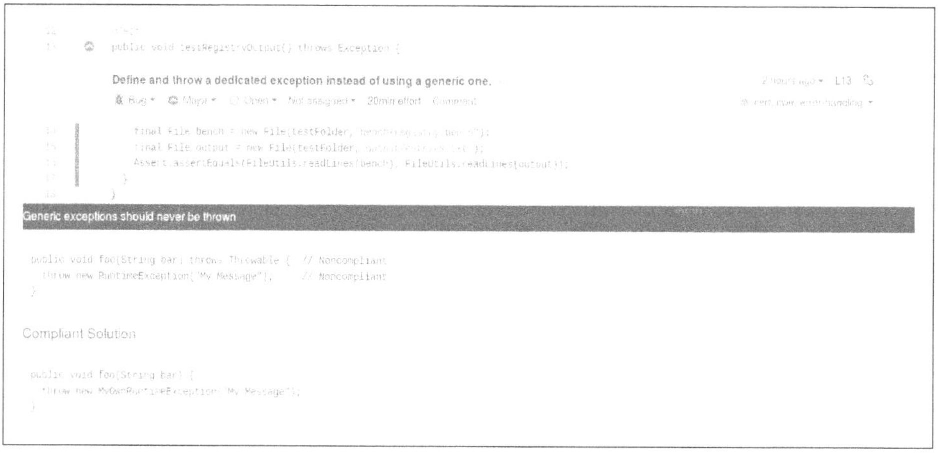

Define and throw a dedicated exception instead of using a generic one.

Generic exceptions should never be thrown

Compliant Solution

Figure 12-3. Detailed error explanation

Note that if you go far enough, the explanation will not only show you the location of the offending source code, but also examples of solutions—ones that are noncompliant and ones that are compliant.

Assuming you agree with the analysis, you can go back and make a change to the source code to correct the issue, and then send the code back through another run of the pipeline (and thus SonarQube).

Other Ways to Respond to Rule Violations in SonarQube

If you have appropriate permissions, you can choose to respond to rule violations in ways other than fixing them yourself. This may be appropriate, for example, if the violation should be (or will be) handled differently in a certain context. Here are some of the options:

- Set the issue type to one of a less (or more) serious nature (see Figure 12-4).

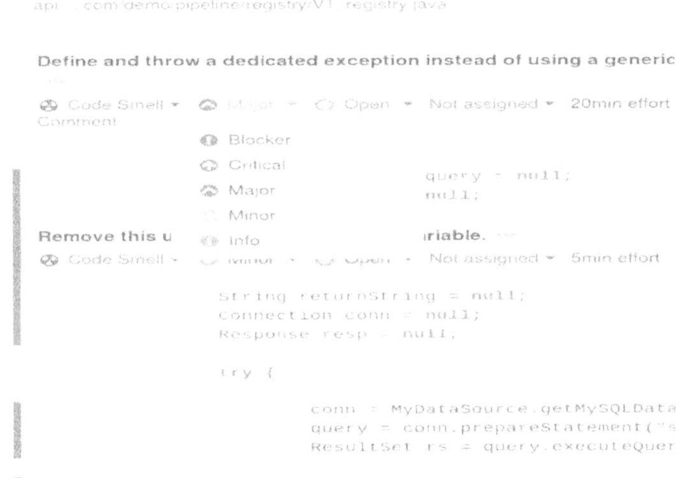

Figure 12-4. Setting the issue type

- Resolve the issue—for example, if you won't be fixing it (see Figure 12-5).

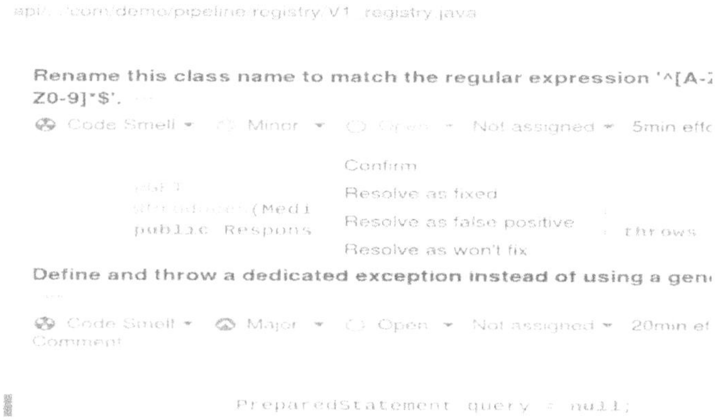

Figure 12-5. Setting the issue resolution

- Assign the issue to a particular person (see Figure 12-6).

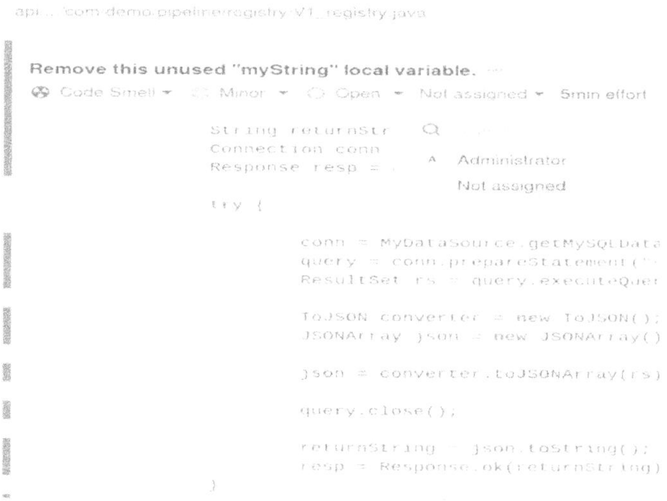

Figure 12-6. Assigning an issue to an owner

- Supply comments on the issue (see Figure 12-7).

api/.../com/demo/pipeline/registry/V1_registry.java

Remove this unused "myString" local variable.

Code Smell ▾ Minor ▾ Open ▾ Not assigned ▾ 5min effort Comment

Markdown Help *Bold* ``Code`` * Bulleted point

```
String ret
Connection
Response r

try {

        conn = MyDataSource.getMySQLDataSource().
        query = conn.prepareStatement("select * 
        ResultSet rs = query.executeQuery();

        ToJSON converter = new ToJSON();
        JSONArray json = new JSONArray();

        json = converter.toJSONArray(rs);

        query.close();

        returnString = json.toString();
```

Figure 12-7. Adding a comment to the code

- Change the associated category of the violation (see Figure 12-8).

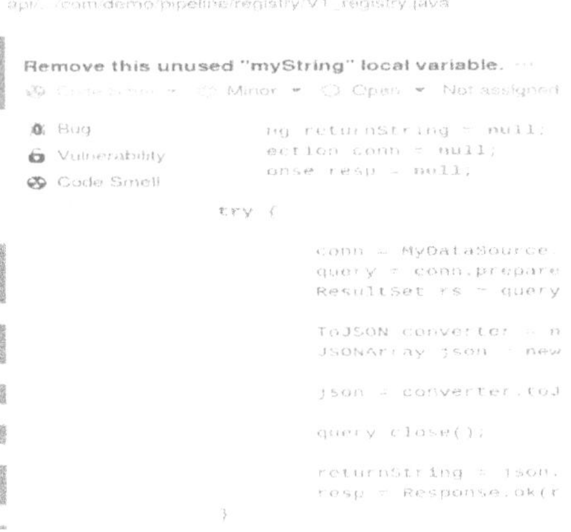

Figure 12-8. Setting the category of a violation

The amount of information generated by this type of analysis can be significant, depending on the size and scope of the code being analyzed. Analysis tools nearly always have ways to "turn down" the number of issues flagged, by ignoring certain types of items. But ultimately, in a continuous delivery environment, we want to establish thresholds for quality analysis. The goal is that our candidate release will only pass (be able to move further down the pipeline) if it meets or exceeds the minimum threshold for desirable characteristics, and falls below the maximum threshold for problematic issues. Examples might be that a minimum percentage of our code has to be covered by unit testing and we can only have a certain maximum amount of issues flagged as critical code alerts.

Within SonarQube, thresholds for various metrics and analyses can be set this way. Selected thresholds can be combined to form a single set of criteria for rendering a pass/fail judgment on the code being evaluated. In SonarQube, these pass/fail thresholds are called *Quality Gates* and the application of specific Quality Gates to different projects or technologies is done via *Quality Profiles*.

Quality Gates and Profiles

Quality Gates in SonarQube are made up of sets of conditions. Conditions, in turn, are made up of:

- Something to be measured (such as the number of critical issues or amount of code coverage)
- A period of time for the measurement (either current or over some defined period)
- A threshold value
- A comparison operation (such as "is less than," "is greater than," etc.)
- An error value or warning value, as needed

An example would be a condition in a Quality Gate that says we can have no more than two alert issues. Another might be a condition that requires a minimum of 80% code coverage by unit tests. Figure 12-9 shows some of the conditions in the default "SonarQube way" Quality Gate that comes with SonarQube.

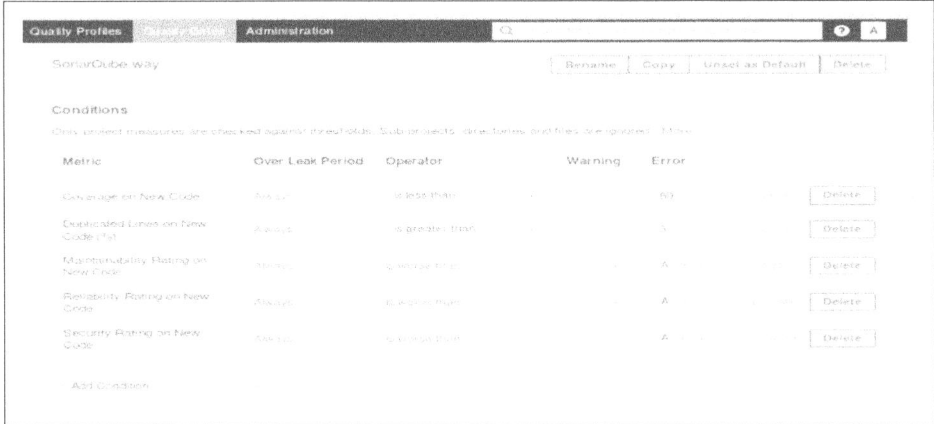

Figure 12-9. Configuration for the default SonarQube way Quality Gate

In short, we're defining tests in different categories of quality analysis against threshold values. The implication is that we're setting a baseline for how many "violations" we're willing to tolerate to consider our code to be of good quality and suitable for production. The set of conditions functioning together as a Quality Gate allow us to translate thresholds into a single pass/fail status. Quality Gates can then be configured for different projects or technologies via Quality Profiles. For example, you might have one Quality Profile for your Java projects, another for your JavaScript projects, and another for your Python projects. Each of these could use the same Quality Gate(s) if the rules were widely applicable, or specialized Quality Gates for each language. Figure 12-10 shows the default Quality Profiles setup for a SonarQube instance.

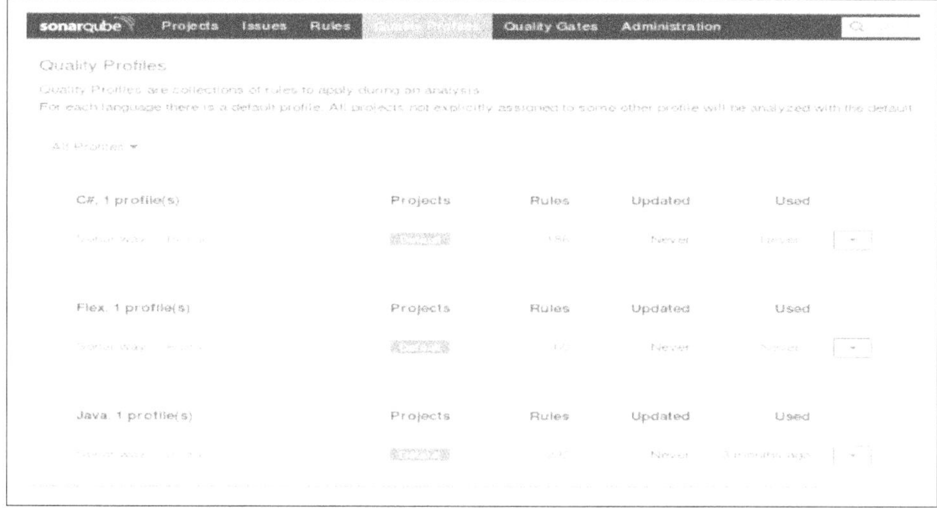

Figure 12-10. Default Quality Profiles setup

A full exploration of SonarQube, Quality Profiles, and Quality Gates is beyond the scope of this text. However, as noted previously, we can leverage the Quality Gate/Profile functionality as a pass/fail gate for an "analysis" stage in our pipeline. Before we can do that, though, there is one more aspect of using SonarQube that we need to understand—the SonarQube scanner.

The Scanner

As the name suggests, a *scanner* for SonarQube is a program that scans the source code, checking for issues. The scanner is differentiated from the SonarQube server or instance that stores results, produces reports, etc., but both elements (some form of scanning and the server) are needed to form a complete analysis mechanism.

Historically, scanners (or "runners," as they were sometimes known) were standalone, separate executables. The other piece that was needed, in conjunction with the scanner, was a configuration file of some kind that identified key SonarQube properties, such as the location of the source to be analyzed—including subprojects, the server, etc.

Scanning Functionality in Other Tools

Scanning functionality and configuration has also been more tightly integrated into recent versions of some other tools. An example would be new integration with Gradle that allows for configuration properties to be specified directly in the Gradle build file, and the scanning to be invoked via a Gradle task provided by a plugin. However, these can also be problematic, as we will see later in the chapter.

Now that we have some background context, let's look at what it takes to actually use SonarQube—first with a Jenkins Freestyle project, and then in a Scripted Pipeline.

Using SonarQube with Jenkins

Like with any other external application, integration of SonarQube with Jenkins requires a few pieces to be put in place. These include having the application up and running, having the plugin installed, global configuration of the server and (optionally) a scanner, and then invoking it within jobs. Let's look at these areas in more detail.

Global Configuration

Figure 12-11 shows an example of the global configuration for a SonarQube server. (This is done on the Configure System page.)

Figure 12-11. SonarQube global configuration in Jenkins

Note the option to "Enable injection of SonarQube server configuration as build environment variables." This may be needed in cases where tools like Maven incorporated environment variables as part of their scanning command. In the job definition, there is a corresponding option to prepare the environment.

We also need to have the SonarQube scanner installed and configured. Figure 12-12 shows an example of this. (Note that it is configured on the Global Tool Configuration screen.)

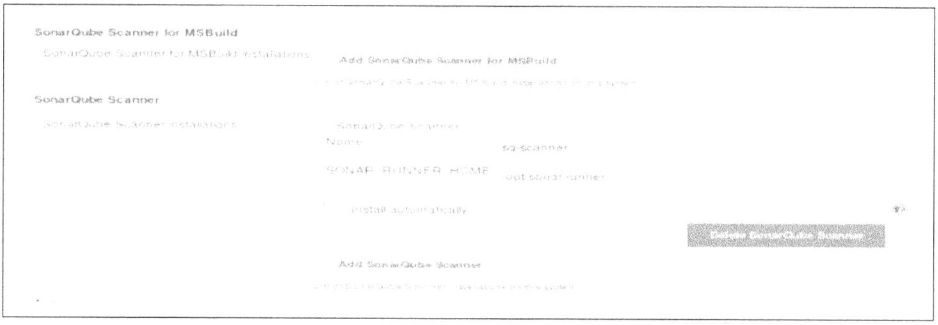

Figure 12-12. SonarQube scanner global configuration

Once we have the application installed and running, the Jenkins plugin installed, and the global system and tool configuration done, we are ready to make use of SonarQube in our pipeline for the analysis. Consistent with our migration/conversion theme throughout the book, we'll look first at how it would have been used in a Freestyle project.

Using SonarQube in a Freestyle Project

In a traditional Freestyle job environment, we might have had a separate "analysis" job that first called the scanner as a build step. The plugin would have provided some formal build steps that could be used to run the standard SonarQube scanner or an MSBuild scanner. Other applications will have relied on calls oriented around their specific syntax. We won't go into all the options here since that isn't our primary goal, but you can find examples of the different types of scanning for tools like Maven, Gradle, etc. on the SonarQube website.

A simple fallback was to execute a shell step that simply invoked the scanner executable.

Any scanner invocation also needed to have some basic configuration values defined for it to know what to process, and how to reference it in SonarQube. These could be stored in a text file and the location pointed to in the Jenkins job. Or, in the case of some of the formalized build steps, they could be entered directly into a field in the web job. A simple example of a project configuration file might look like the following:

```
$ cat sonar-project.properties
# Required metadata
sonar.projectKey=workshop-com.demo.pipeline
sonar.projectName=ROAR :: (Workshop) Pipeline Demo
sonar.projectVersion=1.0

# Comma-separated paths to directories with sources (required)
sonar.sources=api/src,dataaccess/src,util/src,web/src

# Language
sonar.language=java

# Encoding of the source files
sonar.sourceEncoding=UTF-8
```

Given this background, we can move on to how SonarQube can be incorporated into our Pipeline projects.

Using SonarQube in a Pipeline Project

If we have or had an analysis job in our traditional pipeline, we can carry that idea forward to create an analysis stage in our Jenkins 2 pipeline. We just need to select the server, pass on the appropriate environment details, and call the scanner.

Fortunately, with SonarQube version 5.2 or greater, SonarQube Scanner version 2.8 or greater, and a recent version of the SonarQube plugin (*http://bit.ly/2HEe0NN*) installed, the Jenkins pipeline DSL simplifies the process for us. It provides a `withSonarQubeEnv` block that allows us to select a globally configured SonarQube server to use. Further, it makes the connection details (associated with the global configuration for that server) available to operations done in that block. This simplifies providing an environment for a call to the scanner.

An example of using this block in a simple analysis stage would be:

```
stage('Analysis') {
    def scannerLoc = tool 'sq-scanner';
    withSonarQubeEnv('Local SonarQube') {
      sh "${scannerLoc}/bin/sonar-scanner"
    }
  }
```

Using withSonarQubeEnv in Declarative Pipelines

Notice that in the example we defined a separate variable for the scanner location. You may recall from other sections of this book that we can't do that in a Declarative Pipeline. However, we can shorten the syntax and incorporate the `tool` DSL method into the `sh` call, as in the following example:

```
sh "{tool 'sq-scanner'}/bin/sonar-scanner"
```

With the use of the `withSonarQubeEnv` block, we can run the analysis and get the results back in the SonarQube application. However, that is not all we want to be able to do in the pipeline. We also want to have a way to use the results of the analysis to tell the pipeline whether the changes we are analyzing are of good enough quality to proceed to the next stage. How do we do that?

Leveraging the Outcome of the SonarQube Analysis

One of the historical challenges with doing a SonarQube analysis as part of a pipeline process has been getting, and leveraging, the overall results of the analysis—that is, using the analysis results as a pass/fail indicator of whether to allow the code to proceed on to the next part of the pipeline.

Over the years, a number of solutions have been implemented and used. For example, one solution was a Groovy script that ran in a Jenkins job and accessed the SonarQube server via REST API calls. That custom script got the desired result values from SonarQube, and then evaluated them against thresholds entered as Jenkins job parameters to determine whether any were out of bounds. If any of the results were outside of the thresholds set by the parameters, the script would cause the Jenkins process to abort further processing.

Better options are now available. For the Jenkins–SonarQube integration, we can set up a webhook in SonarQube and then have Jenkins wait for notification from that webhook before continuing. Let's see how to do that.

Setting up the SonarQube webhook

To set up the SonarQube webhook, first sign in to the SonarQube application with administrator credentials. Then click on the Administration menu and select Configuration, then General Settings. From there, scroll down to the Webhooks section directly under that column. Click on that and fill in the fields as follows:

- **Name:** *jenkins_sonar*
- **URL:** *<jenkins-url>/sonarqube-webhook/* (don't forget the trailing slash on the URL!)

Once you have filled in the fields, click the Save button to put the webhook is in place. Figure 12-13 shows the screen with the webhook information completed.

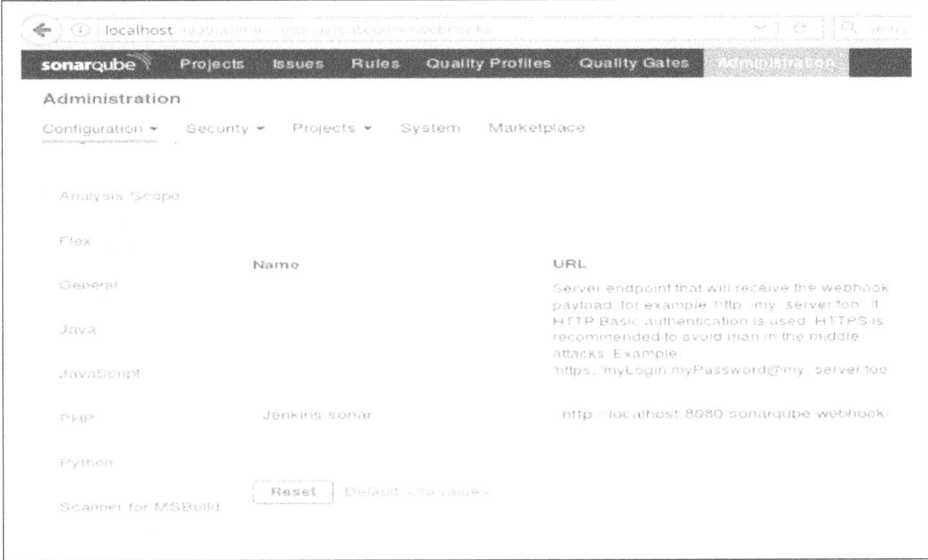

Figure 12-13. SonarQube screen with webhook information completed

Now that we have the webhook set up, we are ready to set up the code to process it in the Jenkins pipeline.

Processing the SonarQube webhook in the Jenkins DSL

The SonarQube plugin provides a Jenkins DSL method to wait for the SonarQube webhook to process, named `waitForQualityGate`. This method pauses pipeline execution and waits for the previously submitted SonarQube analysis to complete, per the webhook notification from SonarQube. The method returns the status of the Quality Gate that was applied to the project in SonarQube. You can then check the return status to know whether the analysis was a pass or fail and whether it's OK to proceed in the pipeline.

An implementation in a Scripted Pipeline might look like this:

```
def qg = waitForQualityGate();
if (qg.status != 'OK') {
    error "Pipeline aborted due to quality gate failure: ${qg.status}"
}
```

There is another important consideration around using this method. Any time you are using a method that pauses your pipeline, as this one does, you should consider the consequences if the method never gets the input, or the event that triggers it to continue. For example, in this case, what if your SonarQube server died or became inaccessible while this method was waiting? It is likely you would not want to hold up your entire pipeline until the problem was discovered and fixed.

A good approach to address this kind of potential issue is to surround the code with a DSL `timeout` block (as discussed in Chapter 3). The syntax is straightforward. Here's an example with the timeout value set to 5 minutes:

```
timeout(time:5, unit:'MINUTES') {
   def qg = waitForQualityGate()
   if (qg.status != 'OK') {
       error "Pipeline aborted due to quality gate failure: ${qg.status}"
   }
}
```

This code can be incorporated into the same `analysis` stage in the pipeline that we used earlier for the call to the scanner, or it can be put into its own separate stage. Having a separate stage to wait for the Quality Gate does allow you to easily determine (in an interface like the Jenkins Stage View) whether that particular piece failed, versus a failure in running the scanner. Figure 12-14 shows a representation of this.

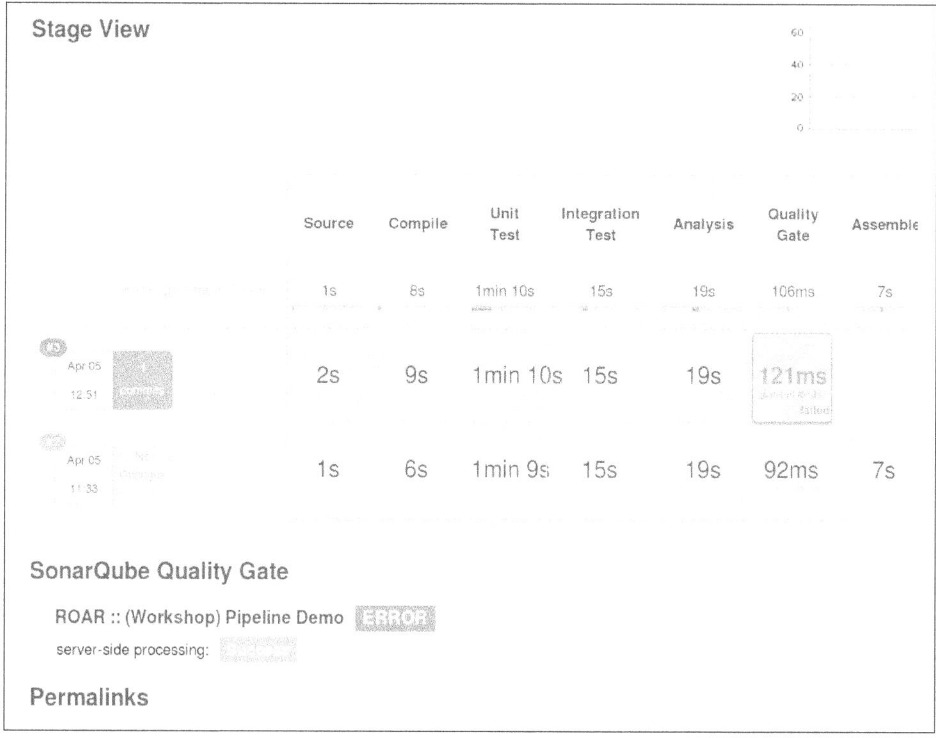

Figure 12-14. Stage View of failure in separate stage for Quality Gate

If this is not important to you, though, then it really just depends on how granular you want to make your pipeline stages.

Working with SonarQube Integration Directly in Gradle

As mentioned earlier in this chapter, recently SonarQube has begun providing more direct integration with applications like Gradle. This effectively eliminates the need to run a separate scanner application; the scanning functionality is, instead, integrated in the application as a new operation compatible with it.

As an example, with the newer versions of SonarQube and Gradle, you can simply include the SonarQube plugin and then define the project properties in a SonarQube closure in the Gradle build file:

```
plugins {
  id "org.sonarqube" version "2.4"
}

description = 'Example of SonarQube Scanner for Gradle Usage'
version = '1.0'

sonarqube {
    properties {
        property 'sonar.projectName', 'ROAR :: (Workshop) Pipeline Demo'
        property 'sonar.projectKey', 'workshop-com.demo.pipeline'
        property 'sonar.projectVersion', '1.0'
        property 'sonar.sources', 'api/src,dataaccess/src,util/src,web/src'
        property 'sonar.language', 'java'
        property 'sonar.sourceEncoding', 'UTF-8'
    }
}
```

Including the plugin also provides a new `sonarqube` task that can be called in place of the scanner. As such, it could be added to a pipeline `withSonarQubeEnv` call, as shown here:

```
stage('Analysis') {
        withSonarQubeEnv('Local SonarQube') {
        sh "/usr/share/gradle/bin/gradle sonarqube"
       }
}
```

While this works to run the analysis, at the time of this writing it does not work with waiting for the Quality Gate. If you try to incorporate this with the webhook and `waitForQualityGate` call, you get an error such as the one in Figure 12-15:

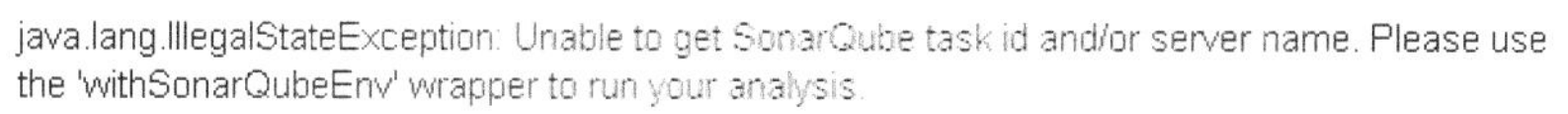

java.lang.IllegalStateException: Unable to get SonarQube task id and/or server name. Please use the 'withSonarQubeEnv' wrapper to run your analysis.

Figure 12-15. Error attempting to wait for the quality gate when using direct Gradle-SonarQube integration

There are some suggestions on the web regarding how to work around this, but nothing that seems to fully resolve it yet. That may change in the future.

SonarQube Integration Output with Jenkins

SonarQube provides multiple ways to link to the analysis of a Jenkins project from within the Jenkins output itself. This is most noticeable in the Stage View of a pipeline or job. In Figure 12-16, you can see several links to the SonarQube output for this project. In the lefthand menu, you see the item named SonarQube as one link. Notice the icon/symbol next to it with the three curved lines. That same symbol/badge shows up in the Build History area at the end of the line for the #1 run. Clicking on that badge there will take you to the same project analysis page in the SonarQube application. And finally, there is the OK button under the SonarQube Quality Gate label (after the project name). This is another link to the same location.

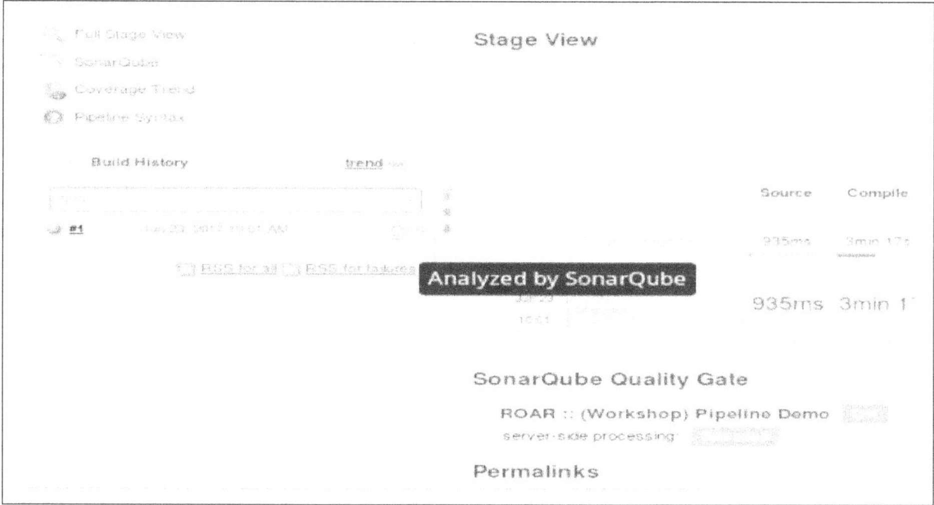

Figure 12-16. Stage View links to SonarQube analysis

Clicking on any of these links takes you to the SonarQube analysis page for the project (like the one in Figure 12-17).

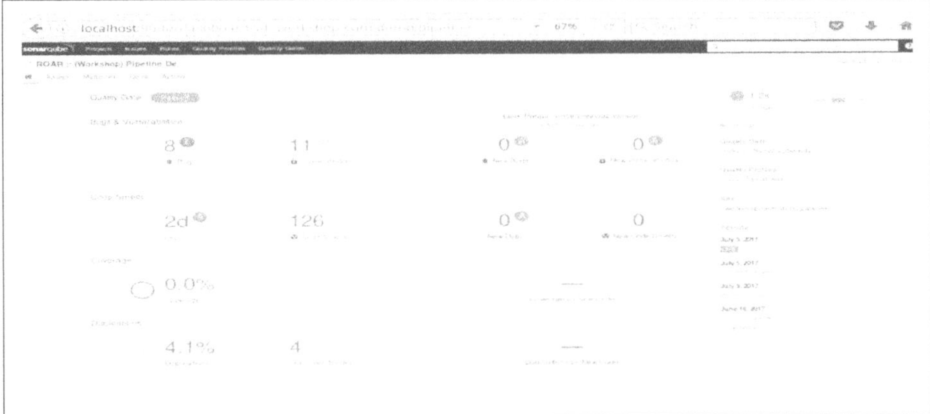

Figure 12-17. SonarQube analysis page

Code Coverage: Integration with JaCoCo

Typically, code coverage analysis is included with a tool like SonarQube. However, since it can be a significant factor on its own, here we'll look at how to utilize one code coverage application, JaCoCo, separately in your pipeline. Even if you are not going to use JaCoCo, the example integration shown here may be useful to you as you incorporate other tools.

About JaCoCo

The name JaCoCo is short for Java Code Coverage. As the name implies, the intended purpose of the tool is to provide code coverage information for Java source files—essentially, how much of your code your test cases are exercising. It does this by instrumenting the Java class files.

JaCoCo can provide information about a number of coverage aspects, including:

Instruction coverage
: Basic info about how much code has been executed

Branch coverage
: For `if` and `switch` statements, will look at all the possible branches and figure out the number of executed and missed branches

Cyclomatic complexity
: Defined as the minimum number of paths that are capable of generating all possible paths through a method; basically, this can suggest the number of unit tests required to completely cover a piece of code

Let's take a look at some example output. Figure 12-18 is a summary of missed instructions and missed branches in a class.

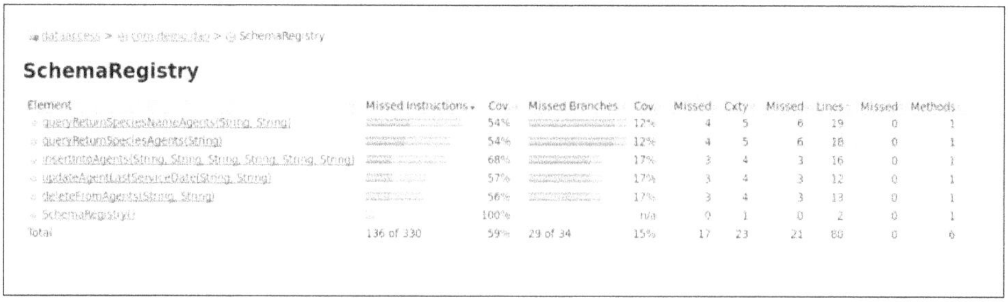

dataaccess > com.demo.dao > SchemaRegistry

SchemaRegistry

Element	Missed Instructions	Cov.	Missed Branches	Cov.	Missed	Cxty	Missed	Lines	Missed	Methods
queryReturnSpeciesNameAgents(String, String)		54%		12%	4	5	6	19	0	1
queryReturnSpeciesAgents(String)		54%		12%	4	5	6	18	0	1
insertIntoAgents(String, String, String, String, String, String)		68%		17%	3	4	3	16	0	1
updateAgentLastServiceDate(String, String)		57%		17%	3	4	3	12	0	1
deleteFromAgents(String, String)		56%		17%	3	4	3	13	0	1
SchemaRegistry()		100%		n/a	0	1	0	2	0	1
Total	136 of 330	59%	29 of 34	15%	17	23	21	80	0	6

Figure 12-18. JaCoCo coverage summary for a class

Figure 12-19 is a more detailed summary after drilling into the source code. Fully covered lines are represented as green, partially covered lines are colored yellow, and lines that haven't been exercised yet are red. The diamonds here refer to decision points, and the colors have similar meanings as before: green means all branches executed, yellow means some branches executed, and red means none of the branches executed.

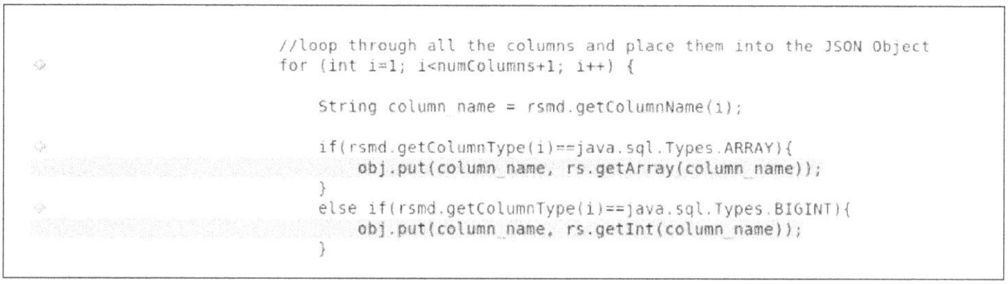

```
//loop through all the columns and place them into the JSON Object
for (int i=1; i<numColumns+1; i++) {

    String column_name = rsmd.getColumnName(i);

    if(rsmd.getColumnType(i)==java.sql.Types.ARRAY){
        obj.put(column_name, rs.getArray(column_name));
    }
    else if(rsmd.getColumnType(i)==java.sql.Types.BIGINT){
        obj.put(column_name, rs.getInt(column_name));
    }
```

Figure 12-19. JaCoCo detail after drilling into source code

Now that we have some basic knowledge about JaCoCo, let's see how we can integrate it in our pipeline.

Integrating JaCoCo with the Pipeline

To use JaCoCo, the application must be available and you must have the JaCoCo plugin (*https://plugins.jenkins.io/jacoco*) installed in Jenkins. (This assumes that you are using JaCoCo separately from a code analysis application like SonarQube.) Unlike other applications, JaCoCo does not require any global configuration in Jenkins. Rather, it is made available as a post-build action in the traditional Jenkins model. Figure 12-20 shows a job set up to run JaCoCo as a post-build action.

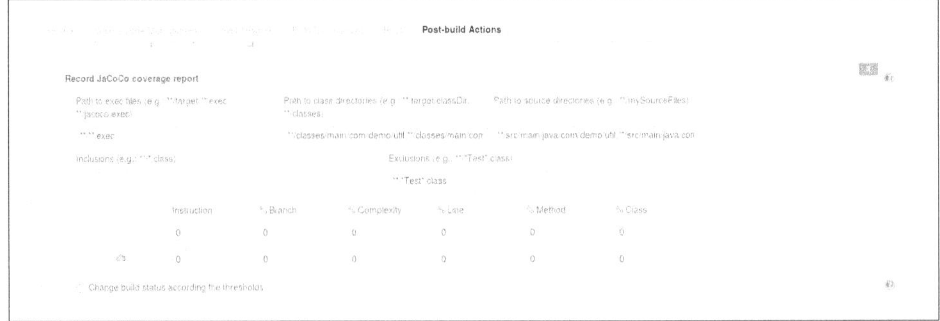

Figure 12-20. Post-build action configuration to run JaCoCo in a Jenkins Freestyle job

The fields in this section allow us to configure various aspects of the code coverage analysis. The paths define the locations of the various types of files JaCoCo needs access to. These are relative to the Jenkins workspace. The Inclusions and Exclusions fields allow excluding certain class files from instrumentation. (Recall that JaCoCo works by instrumenting class files.) And the bottom numeric fields allow for setting coverage thresholds. If the bottom checkbox is checked, this tells Jenkins to update the build status based on whether or not the threshold values were met.

We can translate this into code for our pipeline most easily using the Snippet Generator. In fact, as Figure 12-21 shows, the form to fill in for the "jacoco" step using the Snippet Generator looks remarkably like the form from the traditional Jenkins job.

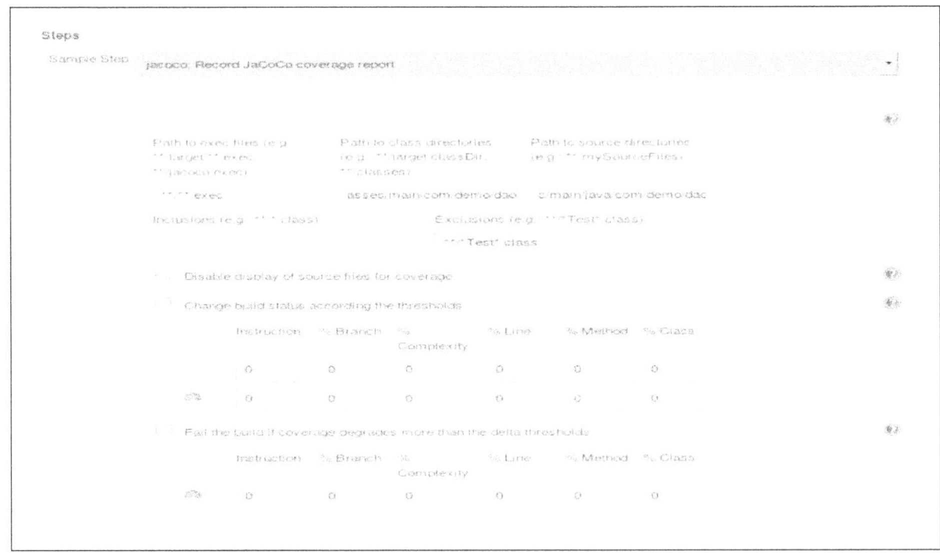

Figure 12-21. Snippet Generator form for jacoco step

Filling in the form to match our traditional Jenkins job's JaCoCo configuration and pressing the button to generate the Groovy script code yields the following pipeline code:

```
jacoco classPattern: '**/classes/main/com/demo/util,
 **/classes/main/com/demo/dao', exclusionPattern: '**/*Test*.class',
 sourcePattern: '**/src/main/java/com/demo/util,
 **/src/main/java/com/demo/dao'
```

This can then be placed in a `stage` block in the pipeline. Most commonly, it might just be added to the stage for the analysis functions.

JaCoCo Output Integration with Jenkins

Finally, let's take a quick look at how JaCoCo integrates its output with Jenkins. Once you have successfully run through an analysis with JaCoCo, Jenkins will add two things to the output page (Stage View) for the job. The first will be a large graph showing code coverage trends over time. The second will be an additional Coverage Trend menu item in the lefthand menu that, when clicked, will bring up a similar code coverage trend graph. (See Figure 12-22.)

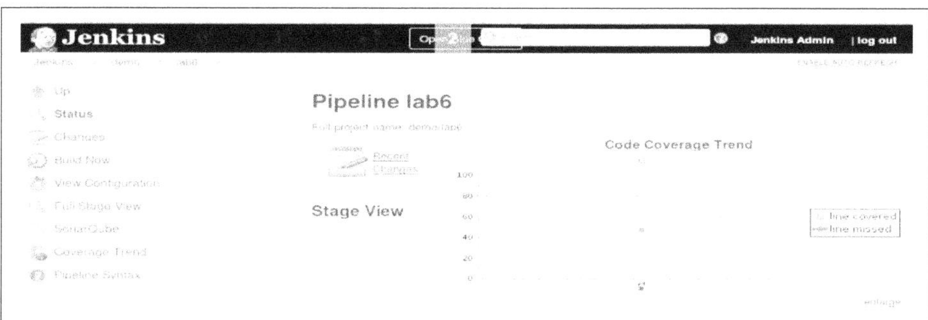

Figure 12-22. Code coverage trend graph in Stage View

Clicking on either graph will allow you to drill down further into the code coverage details, by packages and then eventually into files and methods.

Figures 12-23, 12-24, and 12-25, show some examples of further drilling down.

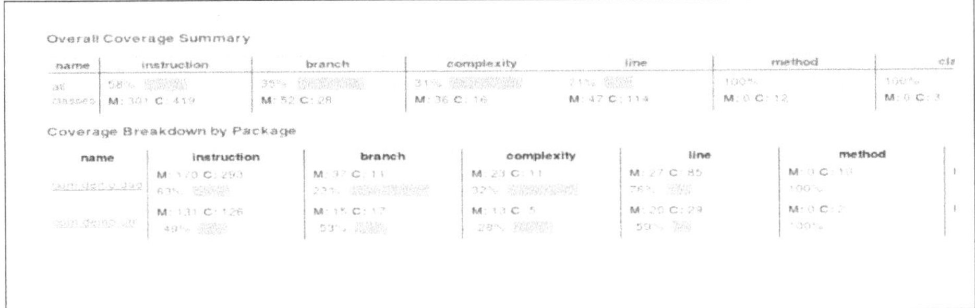

Figure 12-23. Drilling into the JaCoCo integration for packages with Jenkins output

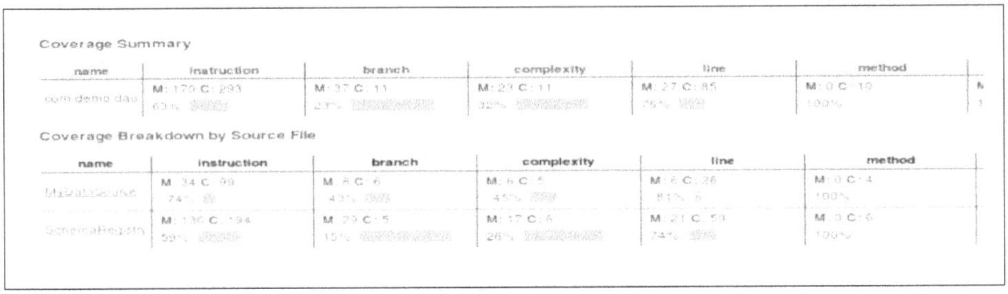

Figure 12-24. Drilling into the JaCoCo integration for files with Jenkins output

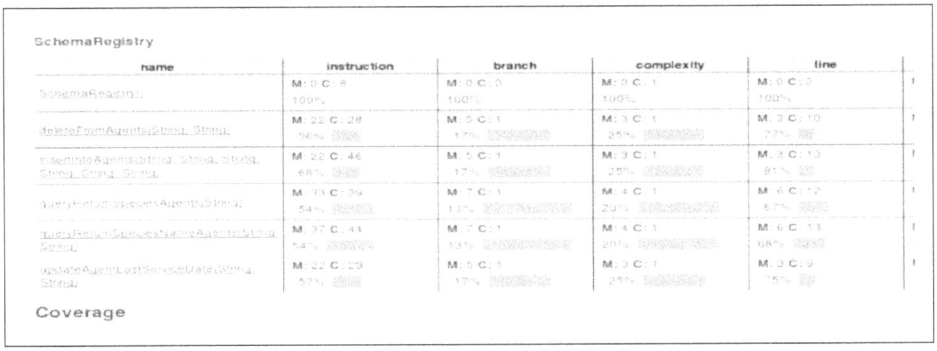

Figure 12-25. Drilling into the JaCoCo integration for methods with Jenkins output

Summary

In this chapter we covered integration of two tools for code analysis, SonarQube and JaCoCo, into Jenkins pipelines. Having an analysis stage in your pipeline is paramount to ensuring good code quality and gauging the suitability of code to continue to production.

We first looked at SonarQube and how it can generate a wide variety of metrics for us through its scanning of source code. We also saw how to use Quality Gates to set thresholds that have to be met for the code to pass the analysis.

We then looked at what JaCoCo is capable of, and how we can leverage it to get an analysis of how well our test cases are covering our code. JaCoCo provides significant integration with Jenkins output, allowing us to drill down through the layers of modules and methods to get to the details we need.

There are certainly other tools out there that you may wish to use instead of SonarQube and JaCoCo, or in addition to them, in your pipeline. Along with choosing a tool, it's important to also spend the time to tune each tool, to check for the specific conditions important to your team and set thresholds for what you are (or aren't) willing to accept. This will ensure the pipeline analysis stage can truly do what you want it to do.

In the next chapter, we'll look at another tool that serves a broad purpose in our pipeline—artifact management through Artifactory.

CHAPTER 13

Integrating Artifact Management

Multiple stages of many pipelines rely on working with an artifact repository—both to publish versions of artifacts created in the pipeline and to retrieve specific versions for use in the pipeline. In this chapter, we'll examine how to work with one of the most popular artifact managers, JFrog Artifactory (*https://jfrog.com/artifactory/*). We'll explore how to migrate functionality from an existing Freestyle project to a pipeline-as-code. We'll also see how to do some other common tasks that require extra setup. Next, we'll look at some challenges when trying to use the Artifactory integration with a Declarative Pipeline.

Finally, we'll take a quick look at the pipeline steps for archiving artifacts and recording fingerprints (tracking information for which artifacts are associated with which builds).

First, though, for those who may not be familiar with Artifactory, we'll take a quick look at why we use it and the value it can add.

Publishing and Retrieving Artifacts

While the rationale for most of the technologies used in our example pipeline so far is obvious, that doesn't always seem to be the case for leveraging an artifact repository. As such, before diving into how to integrate Jenkins 2 pipelines with Artifactory, it's worth noting the benefits that warrant making the investment to use it in your pipelines.

Just as a well-structured pipeline should have facilities to manage source code, there should also be a facility to manage binary artifacts and other generated deliverables. Artifact management of this type is not always a given in pipelines, but in the cases where it is not initially included, its utility and the need for it are certain to become apparent quickly when the pipeline's scope increases.

Some key technical and business drivers for using an artifact versioning and management tool include:

- Avoiding rebuilding from potentially unstable or changing source each time an artifact is needed
- Providing a versioned copy of an artifact (that has undergone some amount of testing), so that everyone knows what they are getting
- Having multiple versions stored and versioned to allow different consumers to use different versions (e.g., current, last release, etc.)
- Integrating with CI servers (such as Jenkins) so that, if a build is clean, the artifact can automatically be published into a repository (optionally with metadata about the build that generated it)
- Allowing virtual repositories that can aggregate multiple well-known or internal repositories, simplifying the search and ordering of artifacts

While there are multiple artifact repository management tools available, we will focus on Artifactory here, since it is one of the most commonly used. Artifactory provides both a Community Edition and a Pro Edition. Continuing the model from our example pipeline in Chapter 10, we are targeting an open source pipeline at its most basic, so the focus here is on the free Community Edition of Artifactory. The Pro Edition may have additional functionality that allows for more easily accomplishing some tasks. However, most of what we do here should be easily transferable.

Now, let's see how an Artifactory CE setup that has been integrated with traditional Jenkins can be integrated with Jenkins 2. We'll start with the basic setup for using the tool.

Setup and Global Configuration

As with any other application, we'll need to have an instance of the application up and running with access for Jenkins. As well, we will want to have a recent version of the Artifactory plugin (*http://bit.ly/2J6w4NO*) installed. Any reasonably modern version will have pipeline support built in.

We can search the Plugin Compatibility with Pipeline page on GitHub (*http://bit.ly/2qQ3gT5*), we can search for Artifactory and see that, as of plugin version 2.5.0, we had step compatibility. So, as long as we have at least that version of the plugin installed, we should be able to use the basic functionality we need.

Next, we want to make sure that we have the global configuration for the Artifactory server done in Jenkins. This is done on the Configure System page. (If you have difficulty remembering whether to go to Configure System or Global Tool Configuration, think of "system" as being similar to "server"; so, configuring the Artifactory server would be done in the Configure System area.) Figure 13-1 shows an example configuration.

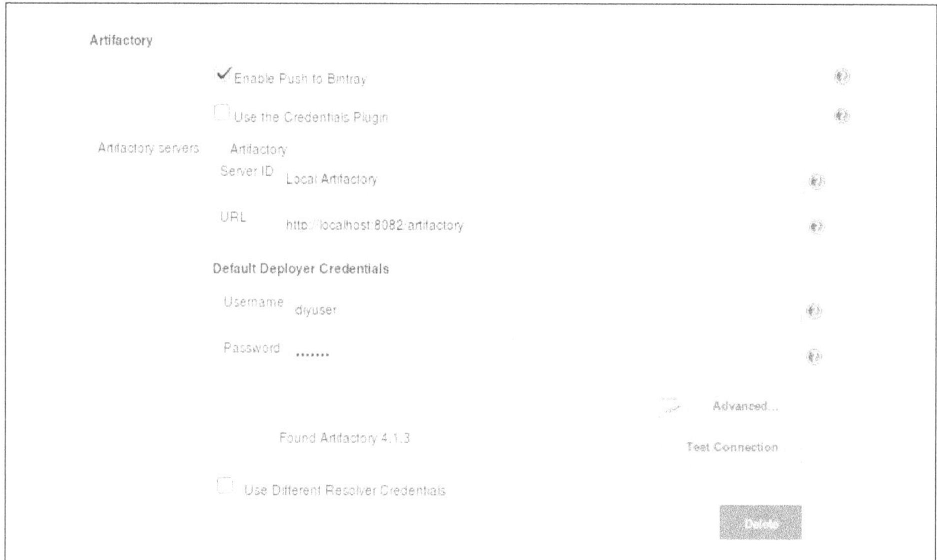

Figure 13-1. Global Artifactory configuration

Once Artifactory is installed and configured in Jenkins, it can be used in individual Jenkins jobs or pipelines. Artifactory integration in pipelines is most easily done in a Scripted Pipeline. We'll cover details on how to do that next.

Using Artifactory in a Scripted Pipeline

In the traditional Jenkins web model for using Artifactory, there were a number of areas to configure (and thus forms to fill in). Typically we would start with defining where in Artifactory to *publish* artifacts we produce (the "deployment server") and where in Artifactory to *resolve* (look for) dependencies (the "resolution server").

In the traditional web interface, we would configure those elements by selecting one of the options for Artifactory integration in the Build Environment section. There are several options to choose from, including Ivy, Maven, and Gradle. We'll focus on a Gradle example, as that's what's used in our example pipeline, but this should translate fairly easily to other types of available integration.

Figure 13-2 shows the Gradle-Artifactory Integration option selected. This, in turn, invokes the Artifactory Configuration section with the related forms to fill in for the deployment server and the resolution server.

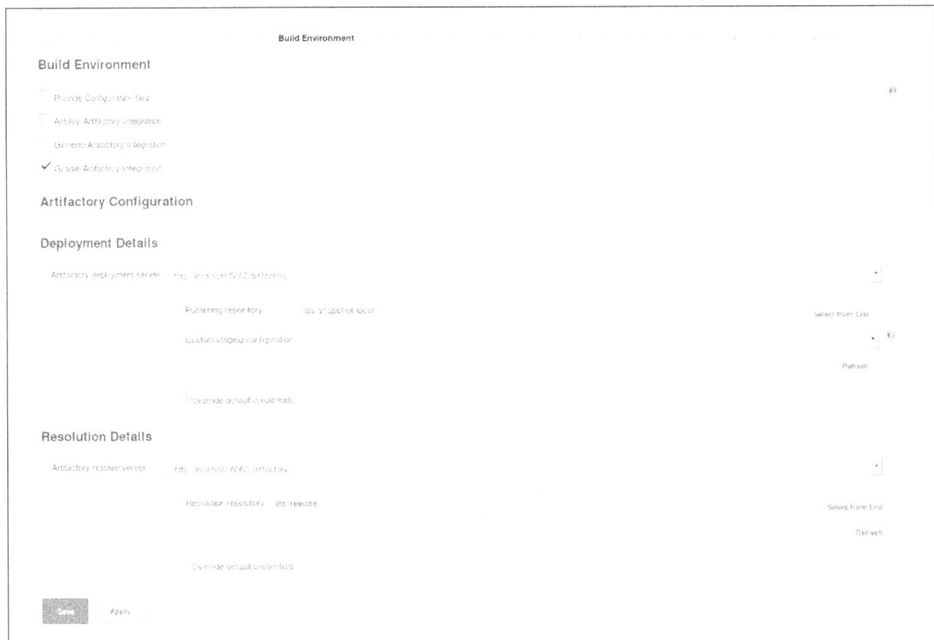

Figure 13-2. Primary Artifactory/Jenkins Freestyle integration

To translate this to a pipeline environment, we need to define some values to point to the server and repositories that we want. Also, depending on the type of the integration, we have specific objects that represent the functionality of the combined Artifactory and build application. These "compound" objects then allow us to invoke Artifactory functionality with the build application via direct calls.

As an example, here are the related steps we can use to set up the Artifactory/Gradle integration in a typical pipeline.

First, we need to create an instance of an Artifactory object that points to the Artifactory server as we have it configured in Jenkins. This is intended to reference the global name we provided for the server in the configuration, similar to the `tool` DSL step that we have used for other applications. The basic form here is:

```
def server = Artifactory.server "<name>"
```

To match what we were using in the Freestyle job of our example pipeline where our server was configured as "Local Artifactory," we would set this as follows:

```
def server = Artifactory.server "Local Artifactory"
```

Now, we can create an instance of an object that represents the predefined integration of Artifactory and the build application. At the same time, we can also point it to the installed version of the application. The basic form for this part is:

```
def artifactoryGradle = Artifactory.newGradleBuild()
artifactoryGradle.tool = "<Gradle tool name in Jenkins>"
```

Adapting from our traditional pipeline example yields this:

```
def artifactoryGradle = Artifactory.newGradleBuild()
artifactoryGradle.tool = "gradle3"
```

At this point, we can instantiate (choose) our deployment repository and/or our resolver repository. The context here is fairly straightforward, so jumping to an implementation that matches our traditional pipeline looks like this:

```
artifactoryGradle.deployer repo:'libs-snapshot-local', server:server
artifactoryGradle.resolver repo:'libs-release', server:server
```

The `server:server` reference here is actually a parameter and a value. The parameter name is `server:`, and the value we are passing in is the `server` instance object (from the `def server...` code) we defined earlier.

Accessing Artifactory Instances Outside of Jenkins

It is also possible to access an Artifactory instance that is not defined in Jenkins. This can be done by specifying a URL and an access method for the `newServer` property of the `Artifactory` object.

For example:

```
def server = Artifactory.newServer url:
<url to external server>, username: <username>,
password <password>
```

Additionally, if you already have credentials defined in Jenkins that can access the external Artifactory instance, you can use them in this call as the username and password:

```
def server = Artifactory.newServer url:
<url to external server>,
credentialsId:<id of credentials to use>
```

Beyond the basic configuration of the server and repositories, the traditional Jenkins interface includes a large number of options for Artifactory integration. Figure 13-3 shows the first part of these options, as shown in the More Details section of the job.

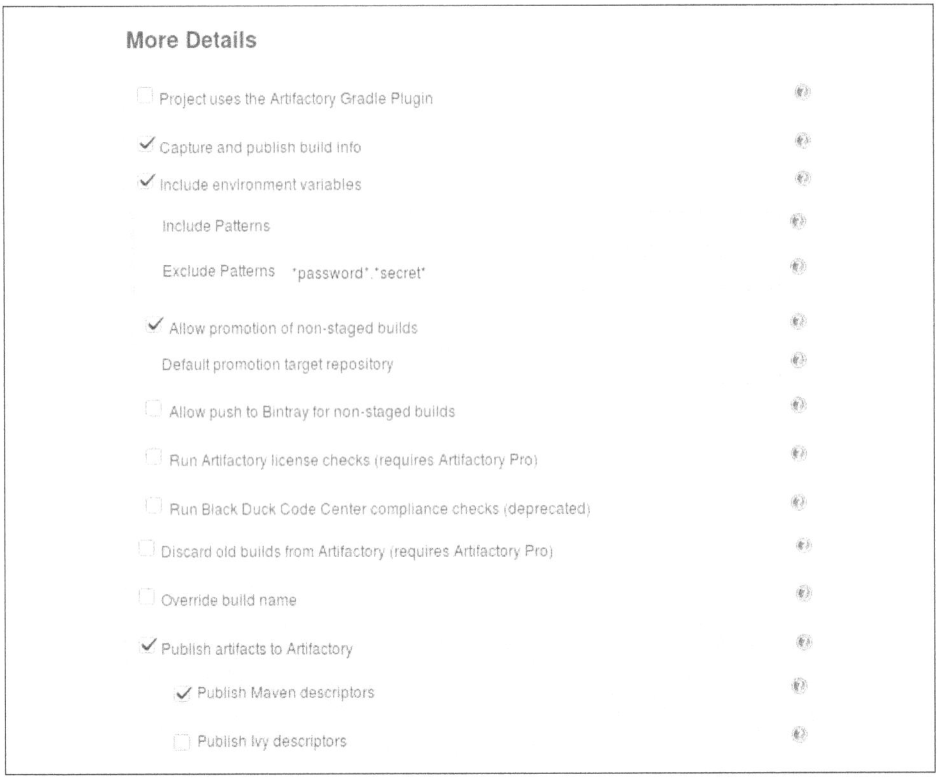

Figure 13-3. Additional details for the Artifactory Freestyle integration

If you are working with Artifactory, most of these will be well understood already. As such, we won't go into detail on each one. We'll just list a few examples, followed by the code that can be used to set them in a pipeline script. In the More Details section, we can:

- Tell Jenkins whether or not Gradle is already including the Artifactory plugin.

  ```
  artifactoryGradle.usesPlugin = true | false
  ```

- Set options to capture build information:

  1. Define an instance variable to hold an Artifactory `buildInfo` object.
  2. Set the `buildInfo` environment capture switch to `true`.

     ```
     def buildInfo = Artifactory.newBuildInfo(),
     buildInfo.env.capture = true | false
     ```

- Set deploy/publish options:

  1. Set a flag to indicate whether to deploy Maven descriptors.

2. Define any patterns to be excluded from being deployed to Artifactory.

```
artifactoryGradle.deployer.deployMavenDescriptors = true | false
artifactoryGradle.deployer.artifactDeploymentPatterns.addExclude(
  "<file pattern>")
```

Once we have set the appropriate options, we can invoke the object to actually do the work, such as running the Gradle build and publishing the results. First, we invoke the `artifactoryGradle` object as we would for Gradle:

```
artifactoryGradle.run rootDir: "/", buildFile: 'build.gradle',
tasks: ...
```

Then we publish the build info:

```
server.publishBuildInfo buildInfo
```

A similar approach can be taken with other build tools and Artifactory, such as Maven. For example, instead of an `artifactoryGradle` object that is created by invoking `newGradleBuild()`, you might have a new `artifactoryMaven` object defined this way:

```
def artifactoryMaven = Artifactory.newMavenBuild()
```

From there, you could proceed to set options for the Artifactory/Maven integration based on the object just created. For example, to add a configuration item that both includes certain files and excludes others, you could do:

```
artifactoryMaven.deployer.artifactDeploymentPatterns.addInclude(
  "<paths to include>").addExclude("<paths to exclude>")
```

This is similar to how we might define patterns in a Freestyle project, as shown in Figure 13-4.

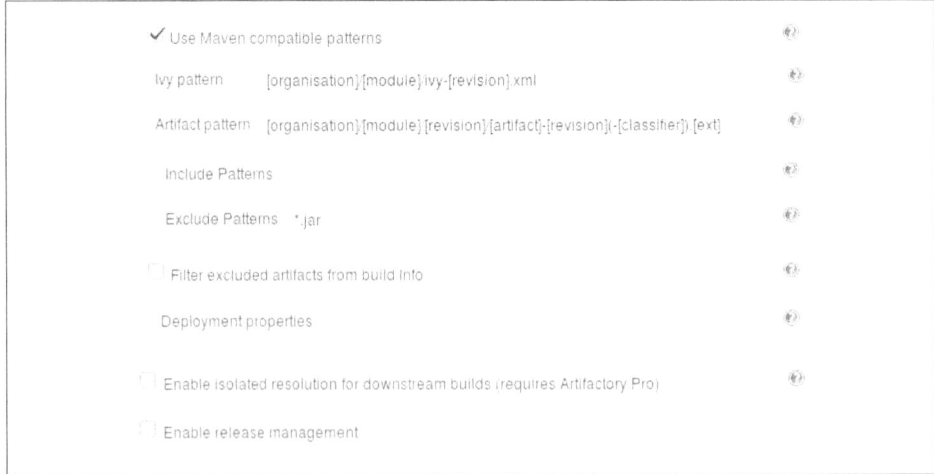

Figure 13-4. Defining patterns for Artifactory integration

You could also turn off deployment as follows:

```
artifactoryMaven.deployArtifacts = false
```

Next, we'll look at a few examples of some other common tasks that require some extra setup.

Performing Other Tasks

Once you have the basic integration with Artifactory set up in your pipeline, there are likely to be other operations you need or want to do with it, such as uploading/downloading specific files, promoting builds, etc. In this section, we take a look at how you can accomplish some of those tasks.

Downloading Specific Files to Specific Locations

To download particular files, you create a specification in an external file. An example would be a JSON file that lists what files to download and where to put them when downloaded, like this:

```
def downloadInfo = """ {
      "files": [
                     {
                       "pattern":
"<artifactory repo name>/<file-structure-to-download-within-repo>",
                       "target": "<location to download into>"
                     }
     ]
}"""
```

We can then cause the download to happen by calling the `download` method on the `server` object:

```
server.download(<file>)
```

Uploading Specific Files to Specific Locations

Uploading is nearly the same as downloading. We create a specification in an external file and then call an `upload` method on the server using that file. Here's example file content for that:

```
def uploadInfo = """ {
       "files": [
                   {
                      "pattern": "<file-structure-to-upload>",
                      "target":
"<artifactory repo name>/<location-in-repository-to-upload-into>"
                    }
    ]
}"""
```

Setting Build Retention Policies

Setting build retention policies is done with properties related to the `buildInfo` object. First, we have to define a `buildInfo` object, as described earlier:

```
def buildInfo = Artifactory.newBuildInfo()
```

Then we can set appropriate properties, either as separate statements or in a combined form like this:

```
buildInfo.retention maxBuilds: 3, maxDays, 5
```

Build Promotion

Promoting a build between repositories in Artifactory requires defining a `promotionConfig` object and then promoting that object. As an example:

```
def promotionConfig = [

          // Required
        'buildName' : buildInfo.<name>,
        'buildNumber' : buildInfo.<number>,
        'targetRepo' : '<target repository>'

          // Optional
        'comment'    :  '<message>'
        'sourceRepo'  :  '<source repository>'
        'status'  : '<status label>',
        'includeDependencies' :  <true | false>,
        'copy' : <true | false>,
```

```
        'failFast'  : <true | false>
]
```

failFast here refers to whether or not the operation should stop when the first error is encountered. This is set to true by default.

Once this is defined, the promotion can be defined simply by invoking the promote method on the server object:

```
server.promote  promotionConfig
```

Integration with a Declarative Pipeline

As outlined previously, Artifactory integration in a Jenkins pipeline currently depends on the ability to define instances of objects to point to the server, the integration object, etc. In a pipeline that is created using declarative syntax, such declarations are not allowed, and trying to use them directly in the pipeline will result in an error.

How, then, do we make use of the Artifactory integration in a Declarative Pipeline? There are several options, including:

- Placing code in a script block in the Declarative Pipeline
- Placing code outside of the larger pipeline block
- Creating a shared library to handle the Artifactory interactions

See Chapter 7 for more details on the first two options. While doable, these have trade-offs, especially if you intend to try to manage your pipeline through the Blue Ocean interface. Details about developing shared libraries (in support of the last option) can be found in Chapter 6.

One other note here: it is possible at some point in the future that JFrog or someone else will develop a plugin that provides more direct support for Artifactory integration with Declarative Pipelines. If the current situation presents a challenge for you, you may want to periodically check for newer versions of the plugin that might offer better direct support.

Artifactory Integration with Jenkins Output

Artifactory provides a shortcut via a "badge" (icon) to its application in the Jenkins Stage View page. If you look at the Build History section, at the end of the line for a run that has used Artifactory, you will see a little badge that looks like a circle with a bar under it. This is a direct link to Artifactory for that build. Figure 13-5 shows the badge to click on.

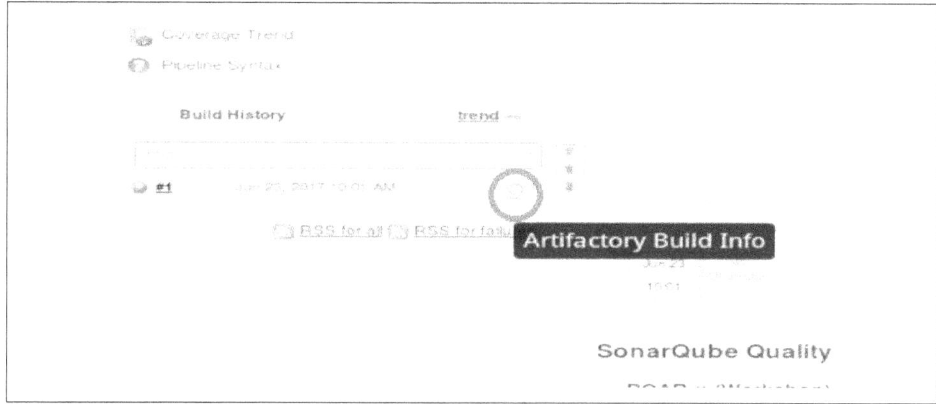

Figure 13-5. Artifactory output integration with Jenkins Stage View

Where you end up in Artifactory is the particular info page for the selected build (as shown in Figure 13-6).

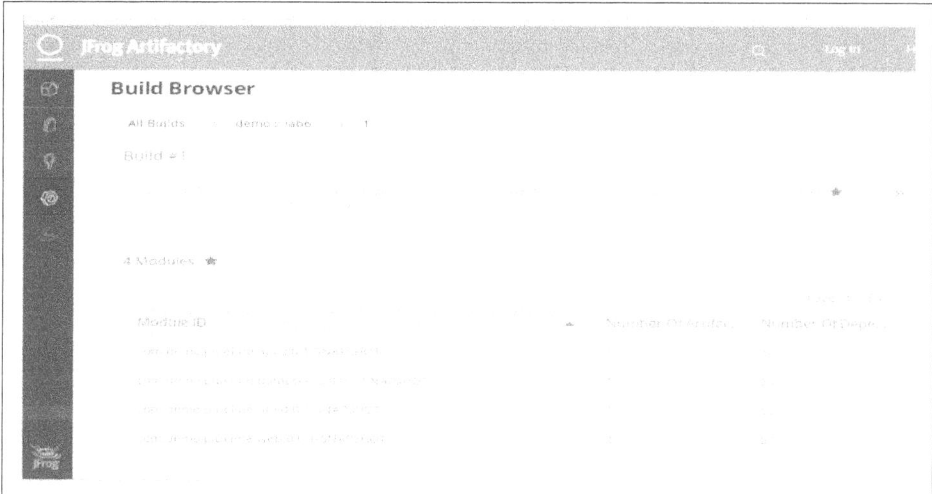

Figure 13-6. Build info page for selected build from Jenkins

Note that if you also have build promotion turned on, there will be a second badge for that.

Archiving Artifacts and Fingerprinting

As the last part of our discussion on artifact management, we'll take a look at the support Jenkins provides for archiving artifacts and for "fingerprinting" (a way to track which artifacts are associated with which builds). We'll also see how to accomplish these in pipeline code.

Most builds in Jenkins produce artifacts—final objects (usually binary) that result from operations done during the build. Over the course of multiple builds, many different versions of artifacts can be produced. And just as Jenkins records the inputs, environments, outputs, and other features of past builds, it can also store the artifacts associated with each build. This is what we mean by archiving the artifacts of a build.

As your builds create more and more artifacts, it can become challenging to try to look back through jobs and builds to determine which versions of artifacts were associated with which jobs, and with which runs of those jobs. Fortunately, Jenkins provides another mechanism for tracking this information: fingerprinting.

You can think of fingerprinting as providing a sort of cross-referencing between versions of artifacts and the jobs/runs. If you have fingerprinting turned on, Jenkins will compute the MD5 checksum of each artifact produced by a build run and record the checksum and build data for it. With that data stored, you can later look up the artifact and immediately find which jobs and builds it was associated with.

A corollary to the artifact storage and fingerprinting functionality is collecting and storing test results. Even with innovations such as the Stage View and Blue Ocean, combing through logs to find test results can be tedious. Most build applications or test runners can produce some sort of formatted output about test results in their own directories, but you still need to get to those. Jenkins provides a method for aggregating the test results for a run. For example, for Java, there is bundled functionality around JUnit to collect these. For other tooling, if the test runner can output JUnit-style XML reports, plugins are most likely available to do the same kind of aggregation.

Let's take a look at an example of how these features might be used in a simple Declarative Pipeline. In this instance, we'll use Gradle as our build tool and test runner, and we'll handle the recording of artifacts, test results, and fingerprinting in the `post` section of the script. The code listing for our pipeline follows:

```
pipeline {
    agent any
    stages {
      stage ('Source') {
        steps {
          git branch: 'test', url:
            'git@diyvb2:/home/git/repositories/gradle-greetings.git'
        }
      }
      stage('Build and Test') {
        steps {
          sh "${tool 'gradle4'}/bin/gradle build"
        }
      }
    }
    post {
```

```
        always {
            archiveArtifacts artifacts: 'build/libs/**/*.jar',
              fingerprint: true
            junit 'build/test-results/**/*.xml'
        }
    }
}
```

A couple of reminders here:

- We don't need to explicitly tell Gradle to execute the `test` task because we are using the Java plugin (in the Gradle build file); it understands that, since we have files in a standard testing directory structure, it should execute those as part of the build.
- The `post` section of a Declarative Pipeline is executed at the end of every build, whether the build was successful or not.
- The `always` clause in the `post` section is called a *conditional*. As the name implies, this conditional ensures that the code inside the closure will always be executed, regardless of the end state of the build. (Other conditionals allow for only executing code in a closure if the build is `changed`, `success`, etc.)

The `archiveArtifacts` DSL step takes a path to the artifacts that you want to archive as the default parameter. If this is not the only parameter, then you need to specify `artifacts` as the parameter name. Notice that, as with other paths in Jenkins, you can use the `**` Ant-style syntax to include the subtree under a given path. Optionally, you can set the `fingerprint` argument to `true` to make fingerprinting happen.

The `junit` DSL step archives JUnit-formatted test results. `testResults`, the default parameter, is a path to the generated reports. (In this case, the test results from Gradle are stored in the *build/test-results* subtree in the Gradle project space.)

Let's take a quick look at what the output from running this looks like (Figure 13-7).

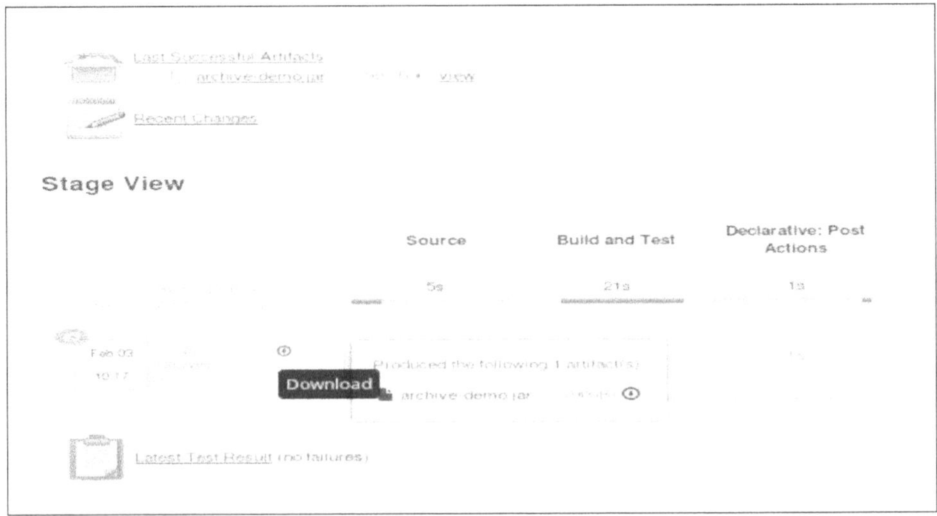

Figure 13-7. Stage View output for archiving tasks

As Figure 13-7 shows, when we run with these steps, in addition to the latest artifact information, we have a few more output items available:

- A small circular icon in the main run box to indicate an archived artifact
- A pop-up box when we hover over the icon that describes the artifact (clicking on the name of the artifact in this pop-up box allows us to actually download it)
- A Latest Test Result link that takes us to a page with links that we can click (Figure 13-8) to get more information about each test.

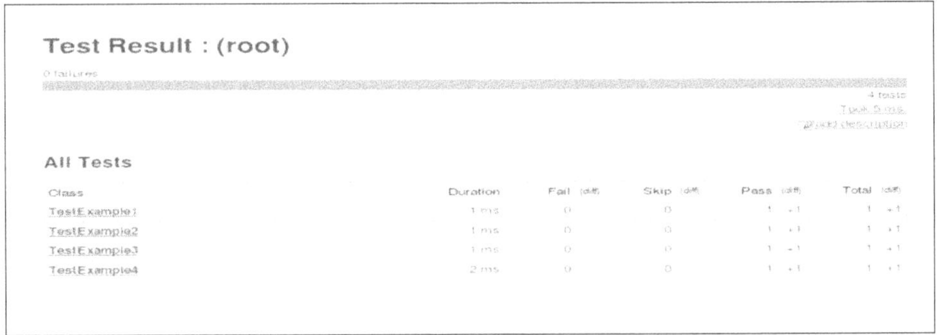

Figure 13-8. Example of drill-down screen for test results from the junit step

If we go into the output page for a particular run, we can also see the archive and Test Result elements (Figure 13-9).

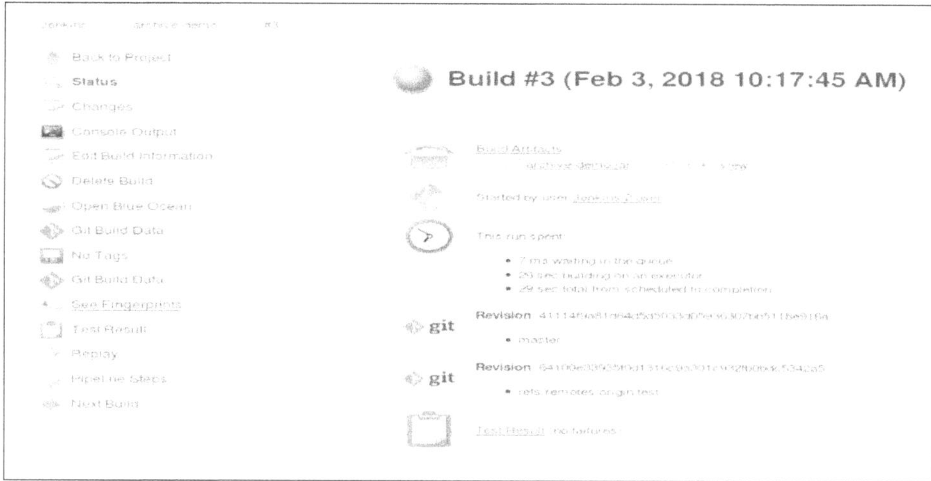

Figure 13-9. Output page for individual run

You may notice something else related in Figure 13-9. In the lefthand menu, there's a See Fingerprints menu item. Clicking on that link will take you to some basic information about the artifact, including what build it originated with and its age (Figure 13-10).

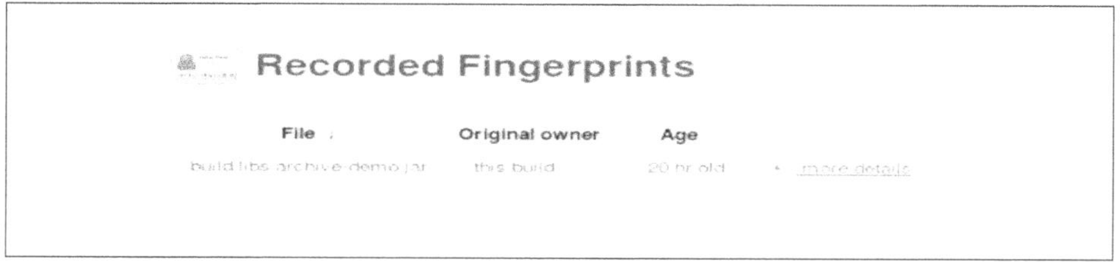

Figure 13-10. Basic fingerprint information

Artifact Names

While we are looking at a very simple example here, a more useful model for artifact naming might include the semantic version number in the archive name (if you want the version to be obvious from the name).

Clicking on the "more details" link takes you to another screen (Figure 13-11) with more information about where the artifact has been used.

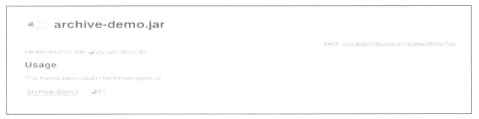

Figure 13-11. Additional fingerprint information

Fingerprints and MD5

You may notice that out to the right in Figure 13-11 is a field called "MD5." This is the checksum that Jenkins uses to refer uniquely to this artifact as it tracks information about it (i.e., the "fingerprint"). The fingerprint allows Jenkins to store information about the artifact without having to keep another copy of the artifact.

Fingerprints are stored in the Jenkins home directory within a *fingerprints* directory. Within this directory, the MD5 values are stored under a directory hierarchy based on the first characters of the actual checksum (Figure 13-12).

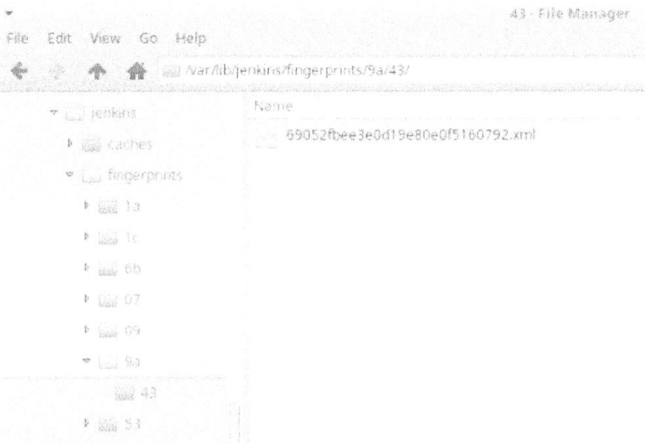

Figure 13-12. File hierarchy for storing checksums of artifacts

The files in those directories contain the information about the originating build, what other builds use the artifact, and so forth.

Access to file fingerprints is also available from other areas in Jenkins, such as the dashboard (Figure 13-13).

Figure 13-13. File fingerprint selection on the dashboard

Selecting this menu option brings up another screen from which you can browse to any copy of an artifact accessible to your filesystem and then select Check to check its fingerprint (Figure 13-14).

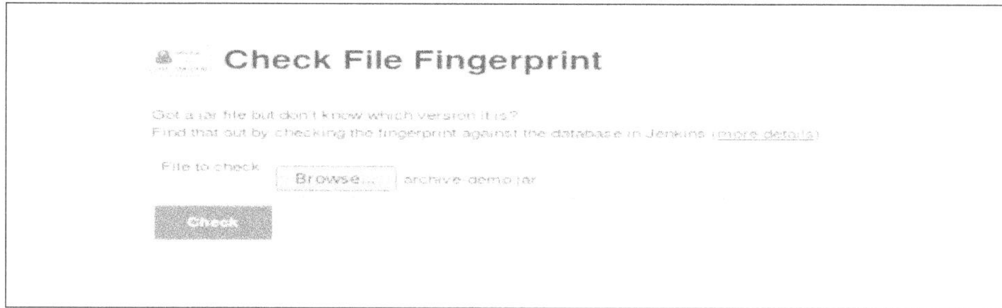

Figure 13-14. Checking for the fingerprint of a file

The cool thing about this is that, since Jenkins stores the MD5 checksums of all the artifacts it fingerprints, it can simply compute the MD5 checksum of whatever file you point it at and, if it matches the fingerprint of any artifact it is tracking, provide you with the information about that artifact. This will be in a form like that shown in Figure 13-11.

Summary

In this chapter, we looked at how to integrate artifact management into a pipeline via one of the most common artifact management applications in use today: Artifactory. This is one of multiple artifact management solutions available for Jenkins pipelines. Currently, Artifactory is only directly usable in the scripted form of pipelines-as-code.

In general, we can summarize the steps for integration of Artifactory with a Jenkins 2 pipeline as follows:

1. Ensure that an instance of Artifactory is available and working.
2. Ensure that Jenkins has the Artifactory plugin installed, and the Artifactory instance configured globally (via Configure System). Also establish any needed credentials in Jenkins.
3. Create the appropriate pipeline script.
4. In the script, define a server instance that points to the name you gave the Artifactory instance in the global configuration.
5. Define an instance of an object that represents the integration between the build application and Artifactory. (In the previous sections, this was the `artifactoryGradle` and `artifactoryMaven` objects.)
6. Set the basic properties for the integration object, such as the name in Jenkins for the tool you are using (from the global configuration) and the deployment and resolver repositories.
7. Set any additional options as properties on the integration object. This may range from simple Boolean settings to patterns of files to include/exclude.
8. Run the Artifactory operations by invoking methods on the integration object or on the server object.
9. Define pipeline code for any other operations, such as uploading/downloading files or build promotions.

Artifactory has a large amount of other functionality available, but our goal here was simply to explore the basics of getting this working in a pipeline environment. The implication here is that these operations will be done in appropriate stages of the pipeline.

Additionally, we looked at how to use Jenkins to record artifacts produced during the builds, aggregate test results, and create file "fingerprints." Fingerprinting is a way to store information about where an artifact originates from and what uses it by computing a checksum on it and storing that. Later, the checksum process can be run against any artifact anywhere, and, if it matches a checksum fingerprint stored in Jenkins, Jenkins can supply the relevant information about it.

Hopefully, this chapter has provided enough examples and information about working with Artifactory, artifacts, and pipelines to get you going. This information is representative, but not complete. For full details on all the options and how to make the integration work, check out the JFrog Artifactory website. You'll find information there that specifically addresses how to do all of this (and more) with the Jenkins pipeline (within the limits of the current capabilities of the system).

In the next chapter, we'll continue our integration discussions. In particular, we'll look at how to use containers with Jenkins 2 through integration with Docker.

CHAPTER 14 Integrating Containers

Docker forms a key component in many pipelines these days. The ease, flexibility, and isolation provided by containers allows us to create custom, specific environments for processing with exact repeatability. In this chapter, we'll look at the different ways that Docker can be used with Jenkins 2.

Prerequisite Knowledge

This chapter assumes that you are familiar with the basic concepts and use of Docker separate from Jenkins. If that is not the case, it will be helpful to consult some of the online training materials and documentation widely available for Docker before continuing.

For Jenkins 2, there are essentially four options for incorporating Docker into your pipeline:

- Configured as a "cloud," as a standalone Jenkins agent
- As an agent created on the fly for a Declarative Pipeline
- Via the special DSL `docker` global variable and its associated methods
- Directly in the script via the DSL shell call (`sh`)

Let's take a closer look at each of these.

Configured as a Cloud

The idea here is that you are defining one or more Docker images that Jenkins can use as agents. This is the "cloud" environment from which to start up agents. When your pipeline runs, it can reference the cloud setup and start up instances of the images as agents. The agents can then be used to run the various stages and steps. After the pipeline is done, Jenkins will stop and remove the containers running those images, thus removing the agents.

In order for this option to be available, the Docker plugin (*http://bit.ly/2J7OLR8*) has to be installed. (Note that this is different from the Docker Pipeline plugin that we will talk about later in this chapter.) The other requirement is that any Docker image you supply here has to be able to function as a "standalone agent"—meaning it is set up like a node. We'll talk more about the requirements for that in a moment. But first, as with all major functionality in Jenkins, we have some global configuration to do.

Global Configuration

When you install the Docker plugin (or other cloud plugins, such as Amazon EC2), a new Cloud section is added to the Configure System screen. After you click the "Add a new cloud" button, you are given the option to select Docker. Then a new configuration section is presented. Figure 14-1 shows an example of this section with some completed fields.

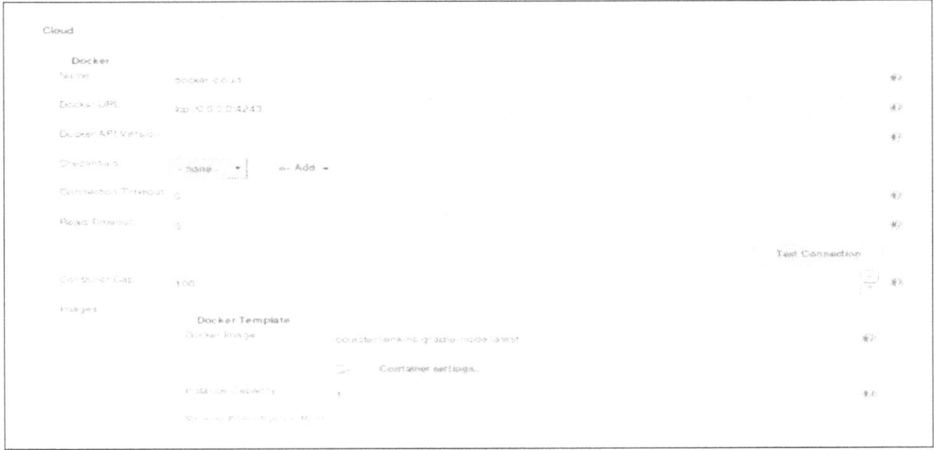

Figure 14-1. Initial global configuration for a Docker cloud

Let's look at some of these fields in more detail. The Name field is simply a name to refer to this cloud. The Docker URL field refers to a way to access the Docker Remote API. By default, this is probably not enabled, and you will need to enable it so that Jenkins can access it.

There is a lot of information on the web on getting the remote API to work with Docker in Jenkins—much of it confusing. In the simple case, which hopefully will work for most readers, here's what you need to do:

1. Look at the arguments you would supply for the `-H` option for Docker (the "host list" option). Most commonly, these would be of the form `tcp://<ip-addr>:<docker-port>` and `unix:///var/run/docker.sock`.
2. Add these arguments into your Docker startup file. If you're running on a Linux system, your first thought might be to add these in */etc/init/docker.conf*—but when you look for the startup options, in that file, you'll typically see a line of the form `# modify these in /etc/default/$UPSTART_JOB (/etc/default/docker)`.
3. Assuming that last statement is true, add a line in */etc/default/docker* like the following one (here, for the sake of simplicity, we are running Docker on our local system and so can use the 0.0.0.0 IP address: if that is not the case, you would use the IP address of the remote system where you host Docker):

```
DOCKER_OPTS='-H tcp://0.0.0.0:4243 -H unix:///var/run/docker.sock'
```

4. After updating the file, you'll need to restart the Docker service and, depending on your system, possibly reload the daemon.

With the Remote API enabled, you are ready to configure the connection to it in the global Jenkins Docker cloud configuration. For this, you'll want to fill in the Docker URL field with the same `tcp...` value you supplied to Docker; i.e., `tcp://#.#.#.#:4243`. Optionally, you may be able to use the `unix:///var/run/docker.sock` setting.

There are some related fields under the URL field. For the Docker API Version, you only need to supply a value if you want a version other than the default one. Supply a set of credentials in the Credentials field if needed, and, optionally, provide values for the read and connection timeouts.

The Container Cap field is there if you want to limit the number of containers the Docker system can run. Note that this also includes containers not started by Jenkins. It has a default of 100.

With your API connection set up, it is advisable to test the connection by clicking the Test Connection button. If everything is working, you should see text with the Docker version and API version displayed inline (similar to Figure 14-2).

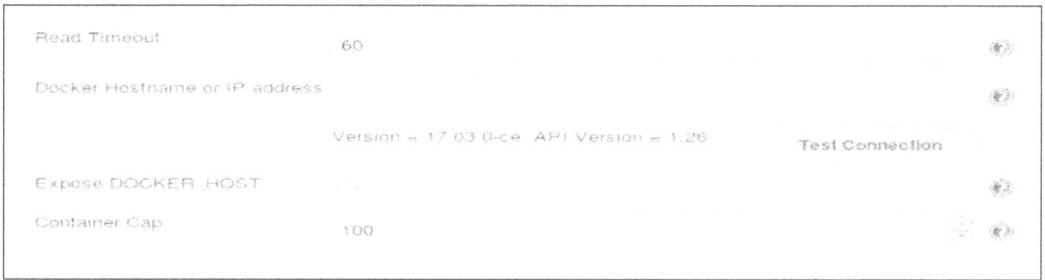

Figure 14-2. Confirmation of correct Docker setup

After you have the basic Docker configuration working, you're ready to specify images that the cloud can use to run as agents. This is done by clicking the Add Docker Template button and selecting Docker Template. We discuss more setup details for this in the next section.

Docker Overview Section

With the Docker plugin integration, a new entry is created under Manage Jenkins (Figure 14-3) for a Docker section.

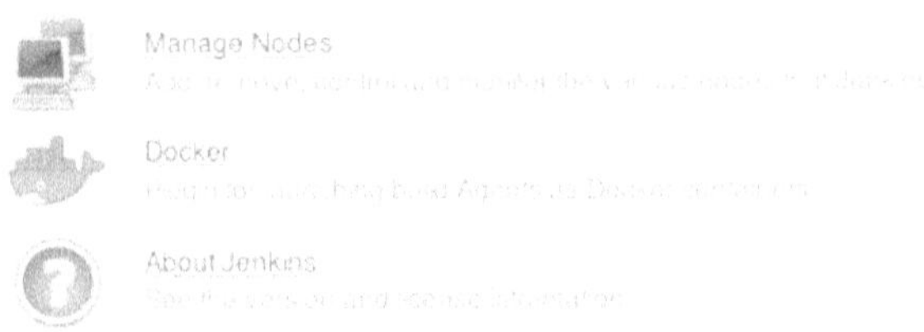

Figure 14-3. Docker menu item

Clicking on this provides you with a list of Docker "servers" that are provisioned for this instance (Figure 14-4).

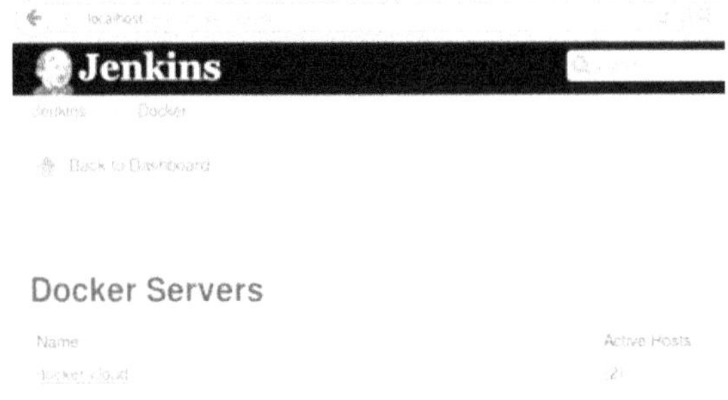

Figure 14-4. Docker servers

Drilling down into a particular server allows you to see what containers are currently running on it, and information such as which image the containers originated from (Figure 14-5).

Figure 14-5. Docker server overview

Using Docker Images as Agents

The basic requirement for a Docker image to be used as an agent is that it needs to be able to run like a standalone agent. Typically this will mean that it has basic applications installed on it, such as Java and SSH. As discussed on the Docker plugin page, depending on how the agent is to be launched, there are different base images that may be appropriate.

The Jenkins wiki outlines the prerequisites for the Docker image (*http://bit.ly/2qLYJA6*) to be used as follows, depending on the launch method selected:

Launch via SSH

You must have an *sshd* server and a JDK installed. You can use *jenkins/ssh-slave* as the basis for a custom image. An SSH key based on the unique Jenkins master instance's identity can be injected in the container on startup, so you don't need a credential set as long as you use the standard *openssl sshd*.

For backward compatibility or if you have a nonstandard *sshd* packaged in your Docker image, you also have the option to provide manually configured SSH credentials.

Launch via JNLP
: You must have a JDK installed. You can use *jenkins/jnlp-slave* as the basis for a custom image. The Jenkins master URL must be reachable from the container. The container will be configured automatically with the agent's name and secret, so no special configuration is required for it.

Launch attached
: You must have JDK installed. You can use *jenkins/slave* as a basis for the custom image. (At the time of this writing, this mode is experimental.)

As you can see, there are a number of starter images you can use to create your own customized image. To create a customized image, you can start by creating a Dockerfile with a `FROM` statement pointing to the desired starter image on the main Docker Hub. Then you can use `RUN` or `COPY` commands to add other pieces. For example, the following listing shows the contents of a Dockerfile based on the *ssh-slave* image, but adding in Gradle:

```
FROM jenkinsci/ssh-slave

RUN apt-get -y update && apt-get -y install gradle

RUN echo 2 | update-alternatives --config java
```

Most of this file is pretty self-explanatory. We start with the base image and then update and install Gradle. (Note that this is the default version of Gradle, which may be significantly older than the current version.)

However, the last line deserves a bit of explanation. For this type of SSH-launched node, the connection to the Docker container relies on the SSH Slaves plugin. One of the things this plugin does is connect to the container and check the version of Java on it to make sure it is compatible with the Jenkins JARs that need to be used. If it can't find a compatible version, it attempts to install one.

The base image has a number of Java versions installed. Unfortunately, the default is an old level for most versions of Jenkins (as of this writing). So, when Jenkins checks, it detects the older version and tries to install a new version from Oracle. Unfortunately, the Oracle installation wants a username and password (which aren't available), so the startup fails.

The base image contains a newer JDK that is compatible. The last line in our file selects that version. Granted, this isn't particularly elegant, and there are other ways to handle this, but it serves for our example purposes.

The idea here is that we are creating images for the cloud to instantiate as agents for running jobs. If you are using a modified image (with your own Dockerfile), then you would build the image and push it out to a Docker registry that you have access to. For the examples here, we'll assume our images are in the public Docker registry.

The next step in this process is defining the "template" for the cloud to be able to use our configuration.

No Entrypoint?

You may have noticed that the previous Dockerfile listing has no `ENTRYPOINT` specified. By default, when launching via SSH, Jenkins will send the `/usr/sbin/sshd -D` command, so we don't have to specify a separate entrypoint. (The specific command can be overridden in the Container Settings section if needed.)

Setting up a Docker cloud template—basic options

With Jenkins and Docker configured to talk to each other via Docker's REST API, and the image(s) set up for our cloud, we can move on. We next need to define the section of the global configuration for the cloud that tells it what image to use, and provides any needed options and an access method. This configuration is done by adding a *template*.

In the Cloud section of the Configure System screen, click the Add Docker Template button, then click on the "Docker Template" pop-up. Next, you're presented with a set of options to fill in for the template. We'll cover what's needed for our SSH image example. Setup for other types can be interpolated from this one.

The first field to fill in is the Docker Image field. This should be the image that you want to have spun up as the agent. If you have created a custom Docker image and pushed it to the Docker Hub, you would enter the name of that image.

We'll come back to the "Container settings..." in a moment.

For pipeline usage, you need to put some text in the Labels field. This text will be what you include in the pipeline's agent definition. This will allow your pipeline to select a container based on the image defined in this template section. For example, if you put "docker-cloud-gradle" in the Labels field, you could use this label to select a Docker agent created from the image (assuming declarative syntax):

```
pipeline {
    agent {
       label 'docker-cloud-gradle'
    }
    stages {
```

Next, you'll want to make sure that the launch method is set (only the SSH option is production-ready at the time of this writing) and that the appropriate credentials are selected and in place. The credentials should be an "SSH Username with private key" as explained in the following note. We'll discuss where the public key goes in a bit.

Credentials for SSH Docker Agent Images

When choosing credentials for an SSH Docker Agent, the exact items to use can be a bit confusing. Here are a few guidelines:

- Use "SSH Username with private key" credentials.
- Most SSH images based on the base images create a *jenkins* user on the agent and expect that to be the user connecting, so use "jenkins" as the name.
- If there is any question about which private key will be included, you can specify the exact key as a file in the credentials.
- Make sure you have access to view the public key that corresponds to the private key you choose.

For the additional settings visible here, you can simply take the defaults unless you have a specific need to change them. For the SSH launch method, you also need to pass in the public key via the Environment option in the "Container settings..." section. We'll look at that and other similar settings next.

Advanced Options for Launching Nodes

There are also a set of advanced options related to launching the nodes available via the Advanced button in the "Launch method" section.

Container settings

Near the top of the template section is a "Container settings..." button. Clicking on that brings up additional fields for container-specific options. Here are details on a few of the common ones:

Docker Command
: This is the command to have Jenkins run on the image. Typically, you would just leave this as the default that starts the SSH daemon (`/usr/sbin/sshd -D`).

Volumes
: A list of volume mounts, such as `/host/path:/container/path:mode`. If multiple entries are listed, they should be separated by newlines. The idea of `/host/path:/container/path:mode` is that this will mount the path on the host to a path in the container with the specified mode—either `ro` for read-only or `rw` for read-write. The mode is optional and defaults to read-write.

Environment
: Environment variable values to pass into the container. For an example, see the following note.

Passing a Public SSH Key to an SSH-Based Node Image

For the SSH-based node images, the credentials you select specify a private key to use. To use the SSH protocol, you need to get the corresponding public key on the container. The *jenkins/ssh-slave* and *jenkinsci/ssh-slave* base images accomplish this by having an environment variable named `JENKINS_SLAVE_SSH_PUBKEY` passed into the Docker configuration with the public key string. The value after the equals sign is the full text of the public key file without quotes:

```
JENKINS_SLAVE_SSH_PUBKEY=ssh-rsa AAAAB3NzaC1yc2EA...
```

Port Bindings
: The specifications of the form `<host-port>:<container-port>` to bind a port between the host and container. This is the same as the `-p` option on the Docker command line.

Instance Capacity
: The maximum number of instances to run of this image. Note that if this is not set, the default is unlimited. It's important to set this to a low value (unless you have a good reason to do otherwise) to prevent having a large number of instances running if something doesn't go right.

With the cloud configured and templates defined, we are ready to move on to using the images in our pipeline.

Using Cloud Images in a Pipeline

The following listing shows a simple pipeline script in declarative syntax that makes use of the cloud we've defined so far:

```
pipeline {
    agent { label 'docker-cloud-gradle'
    }
    stages {
        stage('Source') {
             steps {
                git url: 'http://github.com/brentlaster/greetings',
                 branch: 'demo'
             }
        }
        stage('Build') {
            steps {
```

```
                sh 'gradle build'
            }
        }
    }
}
```

Note again the use of the label that we set in the template area to select the image and options associated with that template. In this case, we are executing both stages on the Docker node, but you could also use `agent` directives within the individual stages if desired.

Once you start the build of the pipeline, if you look at the console output of the job, you will probably see a message either that indicates that the node is offline or that all nodes corresponding to the label you supplied are offline:

```
Started by user anonymous
[Pipeline] node
Still waiting to schedule task
All nodes of label 'docker-cloud' are offline
Running on docker-cloud-579057d81f2d in
/home/jenkins/workspace/docker-node-demo3
[Pipeline] {
[Pipeline] stage
...
```

That is to be expected initially, as Jenkins pulls the image, spins up the container, and validates that it can communicate with the container agent. However, after a brief delay, if all goes well, you should see a "Running on..." message.

You should also be able to see the temporary agent listed as a node in the Build Executor Status area (Figure 14-6).

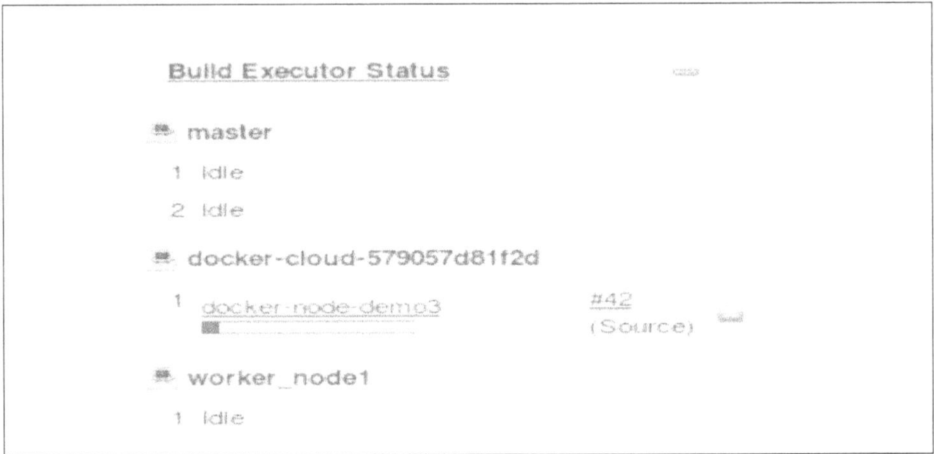

Figure 14-6. Temporary Docker node executing for the job

If your Docker container has the environment and tooling set up as needed for the stages of your pipeline, the pipeline should run to completion. At that point, Jenkins will remove the agent/node and its corresponding running Docker container.

Troubleshooting

If you do not get the "Running on..." message in the console output and/or you see an indication in the Build Executor Status area that the node is still offline, Jenkins may be having trouble starting up, or communicating with, the Docker agent. If this is the case, you can click on the node and go to the corresponding node details page for more information (Figure 14-7). (You can also get there through the Manage Nodes menu item under Manage Jenkins.)

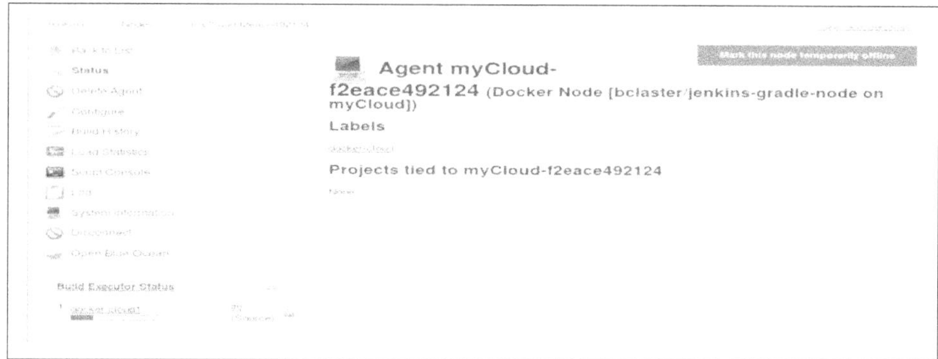

Figure 14-7. Temporary Docker node details page

From here, you can click on the Log item in the lefthand menu to drill into more detail. An example is shown in Figure 14-8.

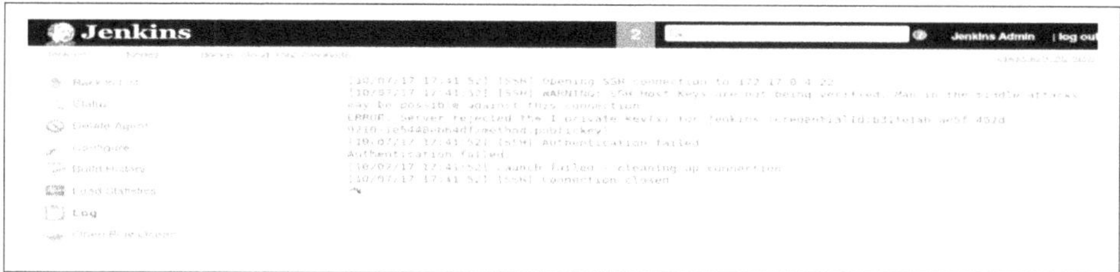

Figure 14-8. The log of a failed Docker node

In this case, the failure was due to a mismatch between the SSH keys. Even if the initial connection is good, there may be issues with the SSH Slaves plugin attempting to verify things, such as a compatible version of Java.

In most of these cases, a good strategy is to pull the image outside of Jenkins, do a `docker run` to start a container based on the image, and then `exec` into it with a shell. The basic syntax is:

```
docker exec -it <container id> bash
```

This should put you into a bash shell on the container's filesystem where you can verify assumptions about what's there, what's not, etc. Remember that Jenkins will attempt to use a user ID of *jenkins*, and you may be initially logged in as *root*. So, you may need to do an `su jenkins` or similar to make sure you are in the expected environment and context. Typically, through looking at the log details and/or `exec`-ing into an instance of the container, you can get a good handle on what the problem is.

Disappearing Agents

Keep in mind that there are timeouts, capacity settings, etc. at work for these Docker clouds. So, after success, or after a certain amount of time when there is a failure to launch, the container for the agent will be removed. You then won't be able to look at the details or log for that particular node.

In some cases, if a container fails to be launchable as an agent, Jenkins will stop it, but if the job is still running, Jenkins will then start up one or more completely separate containers to try to match the capacity setting (always having *X* number of containers).

Over a relatively short period of time, this can lead to many stopped containers being left on your system. As a best practice, if you recognize that a container can't be launched as an agent, it is best to kill the build job that is trying to launch it to prevent a plethora of stopped containers.

Defining Persistent Docker Nodes Without the Cloud

Note that it is also doable (though not as convenient) to manually define Docker nodes for Jenkins. The process is roughly:

1. Pull the desired image and start a container running on the desired system. Pay attention to the documentation about how to start the image. For example, for the one we have been using (*jenkinsci/ssh-slave*) we need to pass in an SSH public key through an environment variable. For example:

   ```
   docker run -e "JENKINS_SLAVE_SSH_PUBKEY=ssh-rsa AAAAB3
   NzaC1yc2...BuBS074siOcjhbNNVKnBw== jenkins@81cd367124a5"
    jenkinsci/ssh-slave
   ```

2. With the container up and running, you'll need the IP address for it. This can be found via `docker inspect` with a command like the following:

   ```
   docker inspect <container id> | grep IPAddress
   ```

3. Now you can define a new node (via Manage Jenkins → Manage Nodes), supplying the IP address of the container in the Host field. See Figure 14-9.

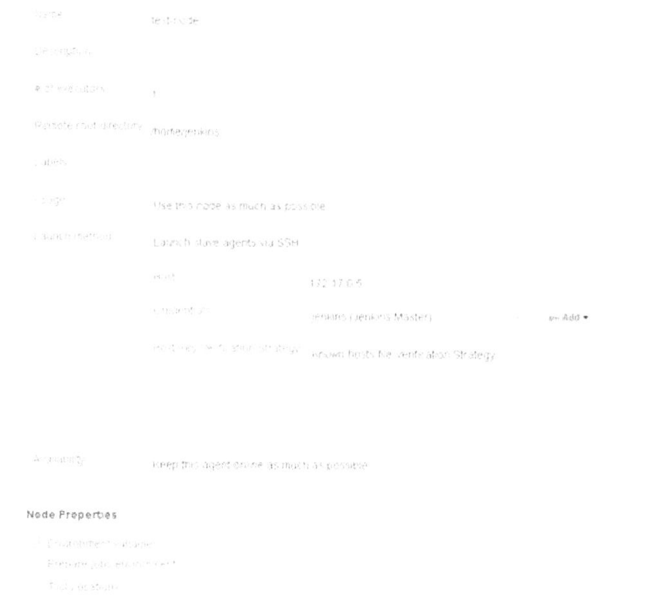

Figure 14-9. Setting up an individual Docker node manually

Of course, you could automate these various pieces, but then that's essentially what the cloud feature of the Docker plugin is already doing for you.

Agent Created on the Fly for a Declarative Pipeline

The Declarative Pipeline syntax includes special functionality for creating agents dynamically at the time they are needed. This is done by pointing the `agent` directive to a Dockerfile, from which it can run a container that uses a Docker image, set up to function as an agent. Most of these are just variations of the syntax for declaring an agent, as described here:

`agent { docker '<image>' }`
: This short syntax tells Jenkins to pull the given image from Docker Hub and run the pipeline or stage in a container based on the image, on a dynamically provisioned node.

`agent docker { <elements> }`
: This longer syntax allows for defining more specifics about the Docker agent. Three additional elements can be in the declaration (within `{}` block):

image '<image>'
: Tells Jenkins to pull the given image and use it to run the pipeline code.

label '<label>'
: Tells Jenkins to instantiate the container and "host" it on a node matching <label> (optional).

args '<string>'
: Tells Jenkins to pass these arguments to the Docker container; uses the same Docker syntax as you would normally use (optional).

Here's an example usage:

```
agent {
    docker {
       image "image-name"
       label "worker-node"
       args "-v /dir:dir"
    }
}
```

agent { dockerfile true }
: This short syntax is intended to be used when the source code repository that you retrieve has a Dockerfile in its root (note that dockerfile here is a literal). It tells Jenkins to build a Docker image using that Dockerfile, instantiate a container, and then run the pipeline or code from the stage in that container.

agent dockerfile { <elements> }
: This longer syntax allows for defining more specifics about the Docker agent you are trying to create from a Dockerfile. Three additional elements can be added in the declaration (within the {} block):

filename '<path to dockerfile>'
: Allows you to specify an alternate path to a Dockerfile, including a different name. Jenkins will try to build an image from the Dockerfile, instantiate a container, and use it to run the pipeline code.

label '<label>'
: Tells Jenkins to instantiate the container and "host" it on a node matching <label> (optional).

args '<string>'
: Tells Jenkins to pass these arguments to the Docker container; this should be the same syntax as normally used for Docker (optional).

Here's an example usage:

```
agent {
    docker {
       filename "<subdir/dockerfile-name>"
       label "<agent label>"
       args "-v /dir:dir"
    }
}
```

`reuseNode`
: This tells Jenkins to reuse the same node and workspace that were defined for the original pipeline agent to "host" the resulting Docker container.

This last one requires a bit of explanation. Remember that even though we are running a Docker container for our agent in these cases, we still have to have a system where Docker is actually hosted and running. That's what the `label` argument in these calls is specifying: which system is hosting Docker.

If we start our pipeline running on a particular node, then it may do operations that leave code or other input on the node (such as cloning source out of source control). If we later want to use a Docker container to do something in the pipeline (such as build the source), then it makes things simpler if we can just run/host the Docker container on the same underlying node. Since the code is already there and the Docker commands can mount the workspace as a path inside them, that simplifies this kind of setup. That's what the `reuseNode` option is for—running an upcoming Docker container on the same node that we started with.

Here's an example:

```
pipeline {
   agent label 'linux'
    ...
   stage('abc') {
     agent {
       docker {
         image 'ubuntu:16.6'
         reuseNode true
           ...
```

Pipeline Model Definition

Since we're talking about which nodes can host Docker instances here, it's a good place to mention one of the configuration items in Jenkins around Docker—the Pipeline Model Definition section (Figure 14-10).

Figure 14-10. Pipeline model definition configuration

By default, Jenkins pipelines make the assumption that all agents are able to run Docker pipelines. However, in some cases, where you can't run the Docker daemon directly, this assumption can be incorrect. In these cases, if you don't explicitly specify an agent that can run Docker in your pipeline and you get one of the agents that can't, your pipeline won't work.

Assuming you have a label on one or more of your agents that uniquely identifies them as being capable of running Docker, you can specify that label here. This tells Jenkins to use one of these agents that for any folder items that need Docker, but don't directly specify an agent that can run it.

Likewise, you can specify a Docker registry to use here that is scoped to just the items in the folder.

Docker Pipeline Global Variable

The third way to work with Docker through a pipeline is to use the methods associated with the Jenkins `docker` global variable. To have this available, you need to have the Docker Pipeline plugin (*https://plugins.jenkins.io/docker-workflow*) installed. We have mentioned global variables elsewhere in the book before, but a little explanation is still in order.

Global Variables

If the term "global variables" sounds familiar, you probably recall it from the context of shared pipeline libraries (as discussed in Chapter 6). There, we talked about a particular directory structure including a *vars* area where we could define classes, methods, etc. to implement global variables. These are not pipeline steps that perform functions, but more like objects of certain types that have supporting methods built around them. In many cases, they are even more flexible than pipeline steps—but unlike steps, they do not have full support in Jenkins. For example, they are not accessible or defined in the Snippet Generator.

In fact, this distinction is called out clearly (if not obviously) on the Snippet Generator screen. (As a reminder, you can get to the Snippet Generator by clicking on the Pipeline Syntax link in the left menu on any pipeline job screen.) If you scroll to the bottom of the Snippet Generator page, you'll see the blurb shown in Figure 14-11.

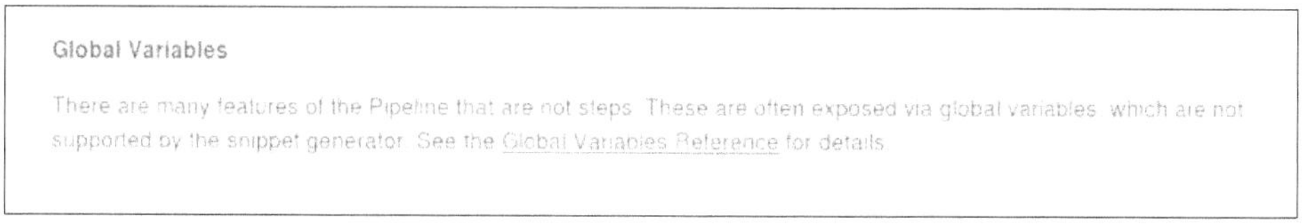

Global Variables

There are many features of the Pipeline that are not steps. These are often exposed via global variables, which are not supported by the snippet generator. See the Global Variables Reference for details.

Figure 14-11. Notice about global variables

Clicking the Global Variables Reference link brings up the reference page for all the available global variables (including any that you have defined and provided text for, as discussed in Chapter 6). Figure 14-12 shows a screenshot of this page.

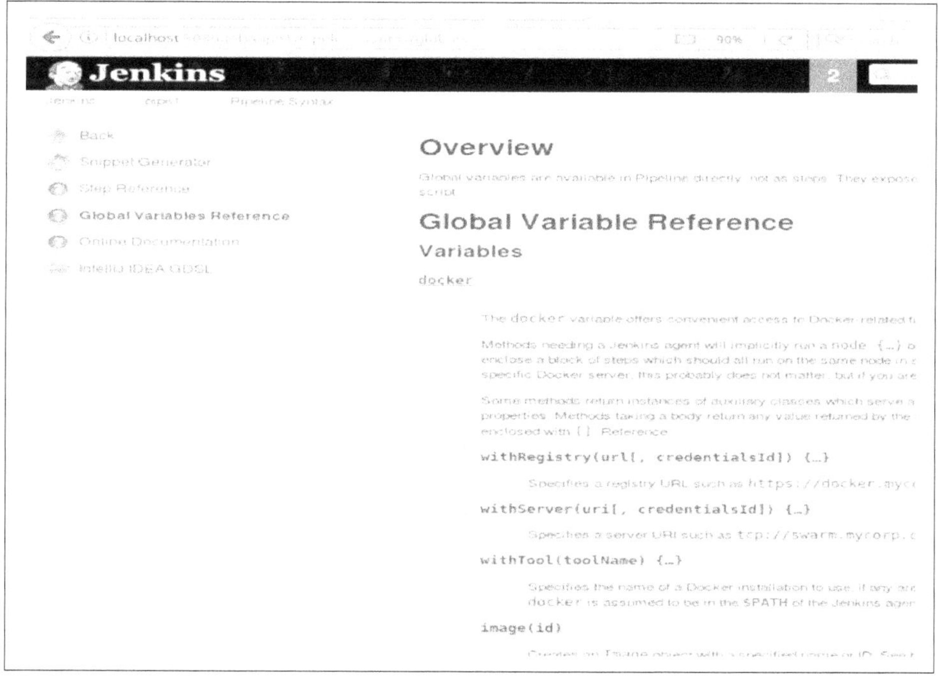

Figure 14-12. The Global Variable Reference screen

At the top of the page is the list of methods associated with the `docker` global variable. These methods are divided into categories for three types of objects: the Docker application, images, and containers. We discuss each of these categories next.

Docker Application Global Variable Methods

The methods in this category revolve around providing environments for using Docker. The text provided by the plugin outlines the basic functions:

```
withRegistry(url[, credentialsId]) {...}
    Specifies a registry URL such as https://docker.mycorp.com/,
    plus an optional credentials ID to connect to it.
withServer(uri[, credentialsId]) {...}
    Specifies a server URI such as tcp://swarm.mycorp.com:2376,
    plus an optional credentials ID to connect to it.
withTool(toolName) {...}
    Specifies the name of a Docker installation to use, if any are
    defined in Jenkins global configuration. If unspecified,
    docker is assumed to be in the $PATH of the Jenkins agent.
```

All of these are "block methods," meaning they are intended to wrap around a block of code (pipeline commands) within the environment defined by the step—and all on the same node. We'll look at each block method in more detail in the following sections.

withServer

The `withServer` method allows you to specify a system where the Docker host daemon is running. This is done to provide Docker access for the Docker-related methods in your pipeline. For example, if you wanted to pull an image from the Docker Hub, but didn't have the Docker daemon installed on your system, you could do it like this:

```
node ('<node-name>') {
    docker.withServer('tcp://<host ip>:2375') {
         image = docker.image('bclaster/jenkins-node:1.0').pull()
    }
}
```

This is assuming the daemon is running on port 2375 and doesn't require credentials. If we were also supplying credentials, we would use the form:

```
docker.withServer('tcp://<host ip>:2375','<jenkins-cred-id>')
```

Alternative to TCP

If you have filesystem access to the Docker installation on the system where you are using the `withServer` method, you can also use the `docker.sock` path instead of the TCP address and port. An example is shown here:

```
docker.withServer("unix:///var/run/docker.sock"){
        myImage = docker.image
         ("bclaster/jenkins-node:1.0")
        myImage.pull()
    }
```

Notice that in these examples, we are not using named parameters when we have multiple parameters to pass in. The reason is that this is a call to a method for a global variable, not a pipeline step. Thus, the position in the invocation is important here.

However, there is a related (deprecated) pipeline step. To help dispel confusion, we discuss that in the following note:

The withDockerServer Pipeline Step

While the global variable methods are preferred (recommended) for use in pipelines, there is also a (deprecated) corresponding pipeline step. The `withDockerServer` step takes a Docker host URI and, optionally, credentials. An example of using this step follows:

```
node ('<node-name>') {
   withDockerServer([credentialsId: '<jenkins-cred-id>',
      uri: 'tcp://<host ip>:2375'])
    {
        image =
         docker.image(
           "bclaster/jenkins-node:1.0").pull()
    }
}
```

Note that since this is a pipeline step, when we specify multiple parameters, we use the named parameter syntax.

withRegistry

This method lets you specify an alternative registry (alternative to *hub.docker.com*) to use for pulling and pushing images. If your company has its own custom Docker registry, for example, you could add the URL in here, as well as the ID of a defined Jenkins credential with access.

Building on our previous example for `withServer`, we can use the `withRegistry` method to pull an image from a local (insecure) registry, hosted on a local system at the default port 5000, as follows:

```
node ('<node-name>') {
    docker.withServer("tcp://<host ip>:2375") {
       docker.withRegistry("http://<local uri>:5000") {
          image = docker.image("my-image:latest").pull()
       }
    }
}
```

Like for the `withServer` method, there is a corresponding pipeline step (deprecated) for the `withRegistry` method, as discussed in the following note.

The withDockerRegistry Pipeline Step

While the global variable methods are preferred (recommended) for use in pipelines, there is also a corresponding (deprecated) pipeline step. The `withDockerRegistry` step takes a Docker registry URL and, optionally, credentials. An example of using this step follows:

```
node ('master') {
    withDockerServer([credentialsId: '<jenkins-cred-id>',
       uri: 'tcp://<host ip>:2375']) {
       withDockerRegistry([credentialsId:
           '<jenkins-registry-creds>',
           url: 'http://<local uri>']) {
          image =
        docker.image("my-image:latest").pull()
       }
    }
}
```

withTool

Even if you have access to the Docker daemon, if Docker is not installed in a standard place available in your path, you won't be able to run Docker command-line operations. The `withTool` method addresses this by pointing your node to where it can pick up the Docker command line. It does this by specifying the name of a Docker tool as configured in the Global Tool Configuration.

To illustrate, let's take one of our previous examples. To make it clear, we've also added a direct call to Docker to list the available images (although other commands would invoke the Docker executable as well). The code is as follows:

```
node('worker_node1') {
    stage ('build-image') {
        docker.withServer(<docker daemon connection>){
            sh 'docker images'
            myImage = docker.image("bclaster/jenkins-node:1.0")
            myImage.pull()
        }
    }
}
```

If Docker is not directly accessible or installed, we'll get an error like the following when we run this:

```
Running on worker_node1 in /home/jenkins2/worker_node1...
[Pipeline] {
[Pipeline] stage
[Pipeline] { (build-image)
[Pipeline] withDockerServer
[Pipeline] {
[Pipeline] sh
[docker-withTool] Running shell script
+ docker images
/home/jenkins2/worker_node1/workspace/docker-withTool@tmp/
durable-45ae13e0/script.sh: 2: /home/jenkins2/worker_node1/
workspace/docker-withTool@tmp/durable-45ae13e0/script.sh:
 docker: not found
```

To work around this, we could either point the system to an installed version (if we have filesystem access) or install Docker directly. The `withTool` method can help in both of these cases.

Suppose that we have installed Docker in a nonstandard location, such as */usr/docker*. As with other tool configurations, in the Global Tool Configuration section, under Docker Installations, we can configure an installation named "local" to point to that location (Figure 14-13).

Figure 14-13. Configuration for a Docker installation in a nonstandard location

We can then add the withTool method in our script to point to this installation as shown here:

```
node('worker_node1') {
    stage ('build-image') {
      docker.withTool('local') {
        docker.withServer(<docker daemon connection>){
            sh 'docker images'
            myImage = docker.image("bclaster/jenkins-node:1.0")
            myImage.pull()
        }
      }
    }
}
```

Jenkins will then be able to find the Docker installation and execute as expected:

```
Running on worker_node1 in /home/jenkins2/worker_node1/workspace...
[Pipeline] {
[Pipeline] stage
[Pipeline] { (build-image)
[Pipeline] tool
[Pipeline] withEnv
[Pipeline] {
[Pipeline] withDockerServer
[Pipeline] {
[Pipeline] sh
[docker-withTool] Running shell script
+ docker images
REPOSITORY                     TAG                 IMAGE ID
bclaster/jenkins-maven-node    latest              07b718ad2d29
bclaster/jenkins-gradle-node   latest              d293f3cef560
bclaster/jenkins-node          1.0                 d0fd7993d746
jenkinsci/ssh-slave            latest              e4900408a7c1
[Pipeline] sh
[docker-withTool] Running shell script
+ docker pull bclaster/jenkins-node:1.0
1.0: Pulling from bclaster/jenkins-node
```

What if we don't have access to the Docker installation, though? In that case, we can take advantage of the Install Automatically option for tool instances in the Jenkins Global Tool Configuration. For example, assume we have an installation set up to install automatically globally, as shown in Figure 14-14.

We can then change our script to point to this selection for installing the tool, as shown here:

```
node('worker_node1') {
    stage ('build-image') {
      docker.withTool('latest') {
       ...
```

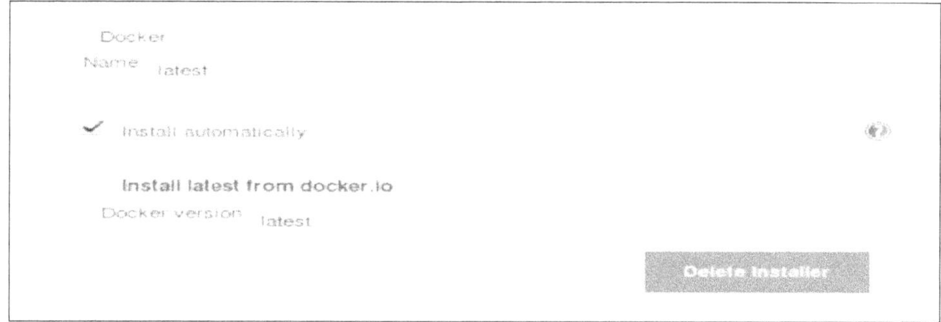

Figure 14-14. Configuration for automatically installing the latest Docker version

When we do this, the latest Docker version will be installed to the node's workspace automatically, as shown here:

```
Running on worker_node1 in /home/jenkins2/worker_node1/workspace...
[Pipeline] {
[Pipeline] stage
[Pipeline] { (build-image)
[Pipeline] tool
Downloading Docker client latest
...
Unpacking https://get.docker.com/builds/Linux/x86_64/
docker-latest.tgz to /home/jenkins2/worker_node2/tools/
org.jenkinsci.plugins.docker.commons.tools.DockerTool/latest
on worker_node1

[Pipeline] withEnv
[Pipeline] {
[Pipeline] withDockerServer
[Pipeline] {
[Pipeline] sh

[docker-withTool] Running shell script
+ docker images
REPOSITORY                     TAG                 IMAGE ID
bclaster/jenkins-maven-node    latest              07b718ad2d29
bclaster/jenkins-gradle-node   latest              d293f3cef560
...
[Pipeline] sh
[docker-withTool] Running shell script
+ docker pull bclaster/jenkins-node:1.0
1.0: Pulling from bclaster/jenkins-node
...
```

Docker Image Global Variable Methods

After the methods focused on using the Docker application itself are the ones for working with Docker images. Most of these are fairly simple, and some are self-explanatory. Here's the current text from the information page about this set of methods:

```
image(id)
    Creates an Image object with a specified name or ID. See below.

build(image[, args])
    Runs docker build to create and tag the specified image from a
    Dockerfile in the current directory. Additional args may be added,
    such as '-f Dockerfile.other --pull --build-arg
    http_proxy=http://192.168.1.1:3128 .'. Like docker build,
    args must end with the build context. Returns the resulting Image
    object. Records a FROM fingerprint in the build.

Image.id
    The image name with optional tag (mycorp/myapp,
     mycorp/myapp:latest) or ID (hexadecimal hash).

Image.run([args, command])
    Uses docker run to run the image, and returns a Container which
    you could stop later. Additional args may be added, such as
     '-p 8080:8080 --memory-swap=-1'. Optional command is equivalent
     to Docker command specified after the image. Records a run
     fingerprint in the build.

Image.withRun[(args[, command])] {…}
    Like run but stops the container as soon as its body exits,
    so you do not need a try-finally block.

Image.inside[(args)] {…}
    Like withRun this starts a container for the duration of the body,
    but all external commands (sh) launched by the body run inside
    the container rather than on the host. These commands run in
    the same working directory (normally a Jenkins agent workspace),
    which means that the Docker server must be on localhost.

Image.tag([tagname])
    Runs docker tag to record a tag of this image (defaulting to the
    tag it already has). Will rewrite an existing tag if one exists.

Image.push([tagname])
    Pushes an image to the registry after tagging it as with the tag
    method. For example, you can use image.push 'latest' to publish
    it as the latest version in its repository.

Image.pull()
    Runs docker pull. Not necessary before run, withRun, or inside.

Image.imageName()
    The id prefixed as needed with registry information, such as
    docker.mycorp.com/mycorp/myapp. May be used if running your own
    Docker commands using sh.
```

While the text explains the intent and general aspects of the operations, there is more background needed to put these into practice.

First, note that `Image` (with a capital "I") implies a reference to an instantiated image. Two of the methods do not expect that to be passed in—`image(id)` and `build`. That is because these two methods are called from the `docker` global variable and return an image. We've seen an example of that in the following lines from our earlier listing:

```
myImage = docker.image("bclaster/jenkins-node:1.0")
myImage.pull()
```

In this case, we instantiate a variable to point to the returned image. Then we use that variable to invoke the `pull()`+ command for the specified image.

Alternatively, we could skip the variable and instantiate an instance in the call:

```
docker.image("bclaster/jenkins-node:1.0").pull()
```

For the `build` method, you need to supply at least an image name. By default, it will use a Dockerfile in the current directory. If you need to pass additional arguments, you can pass them in the `args` area. You can pass the same string here as you would use if you were invoking `Docker build` directly on the command line. Just like with the arguments to the actual `build` command, you need to end with the build context (usually just "`.` will suffice unless you have a specific directory you need that has files to include):

```
def myImage=docker.build("<registry/image:tag>","--build-arg
   ARG=value ./tmp-context-area")
```

Here's the script with the `docker.build` method:

```
node() {
    def myImg
    stage ("Build image") {
        // download the dockerfile to build from
        git 'git@diyvb:repos/dockerResources.git'

        // build our docker image
         myImg = docker.build 'my-image:snapshot'
    }
    stage ("Get Source") {
```

Figure 14-15 shows the console output running through constructing the Docker image from the Dockerfile.

```
[Pipeline] stage
[Pipeline] { (Build image)
[Pipeline] git
 > git rev-parse --is-inside-work-tree # timeout=10
Fetching changes from the remote Git repository
 > git config remote.origin.url git@diyvb:repos/dockerResour
Fetching upstream changes from git@diyvb:repos/dockerResourc
 > git --version # timeout=10
 > git fetch --tags --progress git@diyvb:repos/dockerResourc
 > git rev-parse refs/remotes/origin/master^{commit} # timeo
 > git rev-parse refs/remotes/origin/origin/master^{commit}
Checking out Revision 742b984c53e96e7d1465d9442af6c6606757e8
 > git config core.sparsecheckout # timeout=10
 > git checkout -f 742b984c53e96e7d1465d9442af6c6606757e845
 > git branch -a -v --no-abbrev # timeout=10
 > git branch -D master # timeout=10
 > git checkout -b master 742b984c53e96e7d1465d9442af6c66067
 > git rev-list 742b984c53e96e7d1465d9442af6c6606757e845 # t
[Pipeline] sh
[workspace] Running shell script
+ docker build -t my-image:snapshot .
Sending build context to Docker daemon 289.8 kB

Step 1 : FROM java:8-jdk
 ---> 861e95c114d6
Step 2 : MAINTAINER B. Laster (bclaster@nclasters.org)
 ---> Using cache
 ---> 48b4694fbab0
Step 3 : ENV GRADLE_VERSION 2.14.1
 ---> Using cache
 ---> c84de3a28e12
Step 4 : RUN cd /opt  && wget https://services.gradle.org/di
bin.zip"  && ln -s "/opt/gradle-${GRADLE_VERSION}/bin/gradle
 ---> Using cache
 ---> df50ff638f0d
Step 5 : ENV GRADLE_HOME /opt/gradle
```

Figure 14-15. Output from the previous script

The other image-related methods are invoked from an instance of an image (thus the `Image` indicator). Many of these are self-explanatory because they mirror the basic image commands already found in Docker. These include `tag`, `push`, `pull`, and `run`. Others are slight variations, such as `withRun`, which stops the container for you after the body exits (as opposed to having to use some kind of explicit "post-build" teardown).

However, one of these methods does quite a bit more. We'll take a look at this method in more detail next.

The inside method

With the `inside` method, you choose the image you want to use and use this method to execute the build steps in the Docker image.

When executed, the `inside` method will:

1. Get an agent and a workspace (no node is required since the Docker container is effectively functioning as a node).
2. If the image is not already present, pull it down.
3. Start the container with that image.
4. Mount the workspace from Jenkins. There are a few points to note here:
   - This will appear as a volume inside the container.
   - This will appear as the same file path.
   - This must be on the same filesystem.
5. Execute the build steps.

   Note that any `sh` (pipeline shell) commands are wrapped with `docker exec` to allow them to run in the container.
6. Once completed, stop the container and get rid of the storage.
7. Create a record that this image was used for this build. This facilitates image traceability, updates, etc.

Additionally, options to pass to Docker can be specified. As an example, you could invoke `<image name>.inside('-v ...')`.

Here's an example of a pipeline script using the Docker `inside` method to execute code:

```
stage ("Get Source") {
    // run a command to get the source code down
    myImg.inside('-v /home/git/repos:/home/git/repos') {
         sh "rm -rf gradle-greetings"
         sh "git clone --branch test /home/git/repos/gradle-greetings.git"
    }
}
stage ("Run Build") {
    myImg.inside() {
        sh "cd gradle-greetings && gradle -g /tmp clean build -x test"
     }
}
```

Figure 14-16 shows the resulting Docker commands being processed in the console output.

```
[workspace] Running shell script
+ docker inspect -f . my-image:snapshot
.
$ docker run -t -d -u 1002:1002 -v /home/git/repos:/home/git/repos -w /var/lib/jenkins/j
/jobs/docker-test2/workspace:rw -v /var/lib/jenkins/jobs/docker-test2/workspace@tmp:/var,
******** -e ******** -e ******** -e ******** -e ******** -e ******** -e ******** -e ****
--entrypoint cat my-image:snapshot
[workspace] Running shell script
+ rm -rf gradle-greetings
[workspace] Running shell script
+ git clone --branch test /home/git/repos/gradle-greetings.git
Cloning into 'gradle-greetings'...
done.
$ docker stop --time=1 21aefe948bc96b55543d58fb3d45ad711582ae75b34e9b511bc0a3b83eb87f34
$ docker rm -f 21aefe948bc96b55543d58fb3d45ad711582ae75b34e9b511bc0a3b83eb87f34
```

Figure 14-16. Output from the previous script

Docker Container Global Variable Methods

Finally, we have the global variable methods for working with containers. Again, these are pretty self-explanatory, and we won't go into further detail on them. The text from the online help is as follows:

```
Container.id
    Hexadecimal ID of a running container.

Container.stop
    Runs docker stop and docker rm to shut down a container and
    remove its storage.

Container.port(port)
    Runs docker port on the container to reveal how the port is
    mapped on the host.
```

Running Docker via the Shell

Another way to run Docker from within a pipeline script is to simply invoke the Docker commands via shell (`sh`) calls. This method requires more overhead to do a set of operations (such as the ones the `inside` command does for you), but it does give you precise control and can be suitable if you only need to do a limited number of Docker operations, or specialized ones.

The mechanism here is straightforward. You simply supply the appropriate Docker command line as an argument to the shell step. You can use the advanced features of the shell step to capture output or return codes. Chapter 11 describes the shell call and its various options in detail.

Of course, it is also possible to use both global variable methods and shell calls in your script if appropriate. For example, you might use a shell call to build your image and then use the `docker.image` method to get an instance of the built image that you can work with further.

You can pass in Jenkins environment variables for values to use in the container. The following code example shows a script that uses the Jenkins `WORKSPACE` variable, and Figure 14-17 shows the console output:

```
try {
    stage ("Run Tests") {
        sh "docker run --privileged --rm -v '${env.WORKSPACE}:${env.WORKSPACE}'
          --name '${env.BUILD_TAG}' ${myImg.id} /bin/sh -c 'cd
          ${env.WORKSPACE}/gradle-greetings && gradle test'"
        }
} finally {
      sh "docker rmi -f ${myImg.id} ||:"
}
```

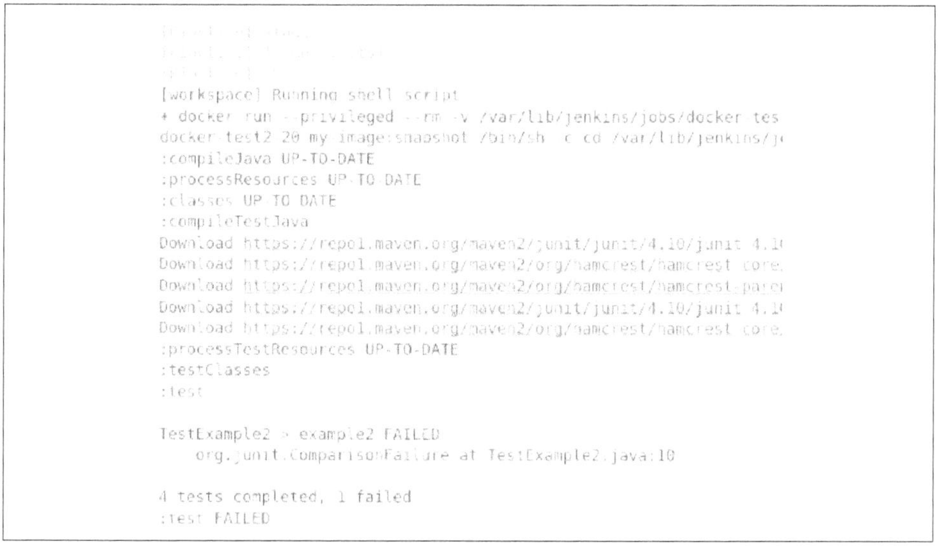

```
[workspace] Running shell script
+ docker run --privileged --rm -v /var/lib/jenkins/jobs/docker-tes
docker-test2-20 my-image:snapshot /bin/sh -c cd /var/lib/jenkins/j
:compileJava UP-TO-DATE
:processResources UP-TO-DATE
:classes UP-TO-DATE
:compileTestJava
Download https://repo1.maven.org/maven2/junit/junit/4.10/junit-4.1
Download https://repo1.maven.org/maven2/org/hamcrest/hamcrest-core.
Download https://repo1.maven.org/maven2/org/hamcrest/hamcrest-parer
Download https://repo1.maven.org/maven2/junit/junit/4.10/junit-4.1
Download https://repo1.maven.org/maven2/org/hamcrest/hamcrest-core.
:processTestResources UP-TO-DATE
:testClasses
:test

TestExample2 > example2 FAILED
    org.junit.ComparisonFailure at TestExample2.java:10

4 tests completed, 1 failed
:test FAILED
```

Figure 14-17. Console output from the previous script

Summary

In this chapter, we've covered the basic ways of using containers with Jenkins with Docker as an example. The container integration allows us to use predefined images as agents as well as to encapsulate parts of our pipelines in containers.

The `docker` plugin (as well as others, such as the Amazon EC2 plugin) enable "cloud" functionality in Jenkins—meaning running nodes/agents as containers. This kind of functionality allows us to use ready-made container images or create our own with only some basic setup.

The Docker global variable is provided by the Docker Pipeline plugin. Recall that global variables are implemented and supported differently than pipeline DSL steps. (See Chapter 6 for more details.)

The Docker instance is a prime example of how much can be done with a global variable. There are a wide variety of methods for working with the Docker application, images, and containers. Of particular note here is the `inside` method, which handles startup and teardown of containers as well as allowing any `sh` (shell) steps within the `inside` block to be automatically executed in(side) the container. It will also automatically mount the workspace as a volume in the container (assuming filesystem access).

Finally, we briefly looked at calling Docker commands directly from the shell. Arguably, this is the easiest method to directly transition Docker commands from the command line to a script. However, it is advisable to use the global variable methods where appropriate for encapsulation and ease of use.

Now that we understand how to integrate a number of different technologies with Jenkins, we'll circle back around in the next chapter to other interfaces to the Jenkins application itself.

CHAPTER 15

Other Interfaces

While pipeline scripts and the legacy web interface are the primary interfaces that most people will use with Jenkins, it also comes with a command-line interface and a REST-ful API interface. These are limited in what they can do, but they can serve a purpose for basic operations, such as getting information about jobs and initiating builds. This chapter will describe the CLI and REST interfaces along with examples of how to use them.

Additionally, we'll discuss the scripting console, another interface in Jenkins that allows you to try out Groovy code. This can be useful for running quick scripts or getting/setting information about the system.

Eclipse Jenkins Interface

While we are focusing here on the different interfaces built into Jenkins itself, it's worth noting that there is also an external interface for the Eclipse IDE (Figure 15-1). This is a plugin for editing Jenkins build scripts.

As the website (*https://marketplace.eclipse.org/content/jenkins-editor*) states, it provides a number of features:

- Syntax highlighting, customizable colors, predefined default for Dark Theme
- Groovy syntax validation
- Validate by Jenkins Linter directly from editor by context menu
- Bracket switching (Ctrl-p)
- Outline + Quick outline (Ctrl-o) for Declarative Pipelines
- Block commenting (Ctrl-7)

If you are familiar with Eclipse and prefer to work in it as an IDE to develop your build scripts, this may be worth investigating.

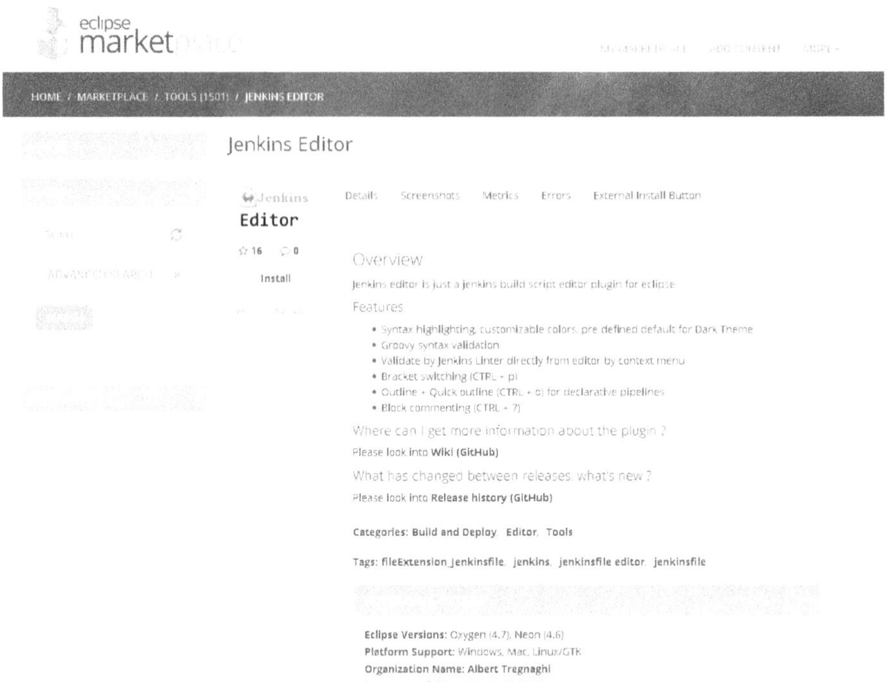

Figure 15-1. Eclipse plugin for editing Jenkins build scripts

Using the Command-Line Interface

Jenkins comes with a command-line interface that can be accessed via two main methods: directly via SSH (for a subset of commands), or via a downloaded JAR. The client JAR allows access over several different protocols. These include SSH, HTTP, and the legacy (now deprecated) "Remoting" protocol.

Using the Direct SSH Interface

The idea here is that Jenkins will function as an SSH server. By default, the Jenkins SSH server is disabled on new installations. To enable the server, an administrator needs to configure it in the SSH Server section of the Manage Jenkins→Configure Global Security page.

Figure 15-2 shows the section to configure. Notice that the Disable option is selected. An administrator can activate the server by specifying a fixed port or allowing Jenkins to pick a random one.

Figure 15-2. SSH Server configuration

If the Random option is selected, we still need a way to find out the random port number. One way to do this is via doing a simple `curl` to the login screen and grepping out the SSH port, as shown here:

```
curl -v http://localhost:8080/login 2>&1 | grep SSH-Endpoint |
cut -d':' -f3
```

With the Jenkins system set up to function as an SSH server, the only other thing that is needed in order to use the CLI directly is an authenticated user. To add authentication, go to People, then select the user, and then go to the Configure page for the user (or simply type in *http://<jenkins-url>/users/<username>/configure* in your browser's address bar). On the configuration page for the user, copy and paste in a public SSH key in the SSH Public Keys section (Figure 15-3).

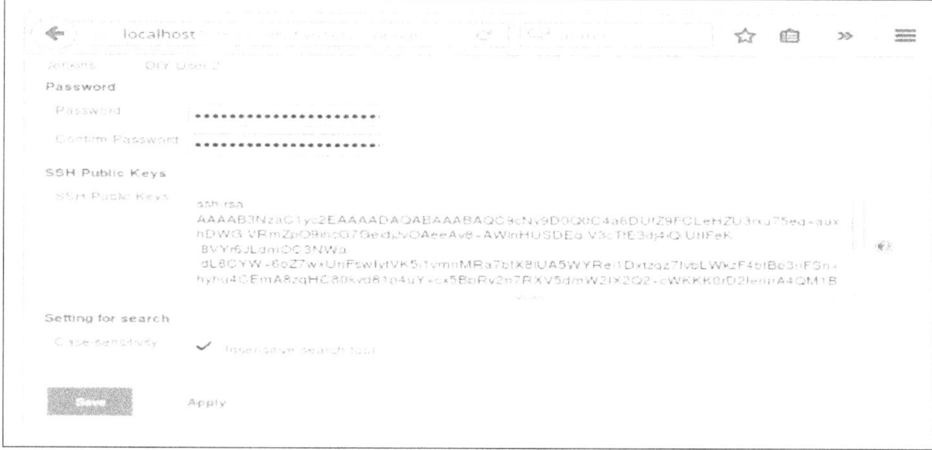

Figure 15-3. Configuring the public SSH key to authenticate the user

Assuming your random port was 32881, then you would now be able to access the Jenkins CLI over SSH like this:

```
ssh -l <username if needed> -p 32881 localhost help
```

The help command will provide a list of the commands that are available to you over the SSH command-line interface. If you want to get help on a specific command, just add the command name after help. The following example returns help for the build command:

```
ssh -l diyuser2 -p 32881 localhost help build
```

This produces the following:

```
JOB                 : Name of the job to build
-c                  : Check for SCM changes before starting the build, and if
                      there's no change, exit without doing a build
-f                  : Follow the build progress. Like -s only interrupts are
                      not passed through to the build.
-p                  : Specify the build parameters in the key=value format.
-s                  : Wait until the completion/abortion of the command.
                      Interrupts are passed through to the build.
-v                  : Prints out the console output of the build. Use with -s
-w                  : Wait until the start of the command
--username VAL      : User name to authenticate yourself to Jenkins
--password VAL      : Password for authentication. Note that passing a
                      password in arguments is insecure.
--password-file VAL : File that contains the password
```

As an example, to run the build for job-1 passing in a string parameter and displaying the console output when it runs, this command can be used:

```
ssh -l diyuser2 -p 32881 localhost build job-1 -p id=myID -s -v
```

In addition to build, another useful command is console. The console command can be used to get the console output from a particular job and even a particular run of the job. The options include:

```
 JOB   : Name of the job
 BUILD : Build number or permalink to point to the build. Defaults
 to the last build
 -f    : If the build is in progress, stay around and append
console output as it comes, like 'tail -f'
 -n N  : Display the last N lines
```

As an example, to see the output for the most recent build of the daily-job-1 item (using our previous examples), you would run:

```
ssh -l diyuser2 -p 32881 localhost console daily-job-1
```

The CLI and Permissions

The CLI access is governed by the same permissions model in Jenkins as the web interface. However, certain behaviors may not be as easily identified as access issues.

For example, if you are using role-based permissions and don't have access to see jobs named `daily-*`, then if you try to build such a job, you'll just see a message like:

```
ssh -l diyuser2 -p 32881 localhost build daily-job-1

ERROR: No such job 'daily-job-1'
```

You can get some basic information about the current user via the CLI's `who-am-i` command.

Using the CLI Client

Another option for using the command-line interface (instead of SSH) is the CLI client JAR that ships with Jenkins. This can be downloaded from a Jenkins master at the following URL:

```
http://<jenkins-url>/jnlpJars/jenkins-cli.jar
```

The syntax for using this is a bit more complicated than that of the native SSH approach. Specifically, you need to invoke it with Java, and it has different ways to authenticate. There are also global options that can be passed in. The format to call it is:

```
java -jar jenkins-cli.jar
 [-s JENKINS_URL] [<global options>]
  <command> [<command options>] [<arguments>]
```

Running this with no commands will produce the help output.

Essentially, when supplying the commands, command options, and arguments, the syntax for those parts is the same as for the direct SSH invocation.

JENKINS_URL

If not specified via the `-s` option, Jenkins will default to using a value specified in the `JENKINS_URL` environment variable if one exists.

The main difference with using the client is that we have multiple connection modes, and authentication is different (and required) for each of these. We'll look at these modes next.

HTTP mode

This is the default mode, but it can also be specified explicitly by using the `-http` global option.

Authentication is done via the `-auth` option, which expects an argument of the form:

```
<username>:<secret>
```

`<secret>` here can either be a password (not recommended) or a Jenkins authentication token. Authentication tokens can be generated on the configuration screen for a user. From the dashboard, go to People, then select the user, then click Configure. In the API Token section, click the Show API Token button and you can copy the generated token. (See Figure 15-4.)

Figure 15-4. Generating an API token for a user

Tying this all together, the command to build the same job as before using the client JAR and HTTP authentication might look like:

```
java -jar jenkins-cli.jar -s http://localhost:8080
 -auth jenkins2:a3c7816cdf3874fca6eb9544b7b26546
  build daily-job-1 -p id=myID -s -v
```

Using Credentials from a File

The `-auth` option also allows for reading credentials from a file. To do this, you simply use `@<name of file>` as the argument to `-auth`.

For example, if you had a file named *.jenkins-access* that contained this:

```
jenkins2:a3c7816cdf3874fca6eb9544b7b26546
```

then you could use that filename in the command invocation as shown here:

```
java -jar jenkins-cli.jar -s http://localhost:8080
 -auth @.jenkins-access
 build daily-job-1 -p id=myID -s -v
```

SSH mode

The CLI client JAR can also emulate an SSH client with the `-ssh` global option. Authentication is via a standard key pair. This assumes that the Jenkins system has been configured for SSH access, as described in "Using the Direct SSH Interface" on page 530, and that the private SSH key is available in an expected location.

For SSH mode, our build command would look something like this:

```
java -jar Downloads/jenkins-cli.jar -s http://localhost:8080
 -ssh -user diyuser2 build daily-job-1
 -p id=myID -s -v
```

Note that the `-user` option is required when using this mode. The documentation also notes that if you have trouble getting to the Jenkins host behind a reverse proxy, you can direct Jenkins to a specific host by setting the Java system property `-Dorg.jenkinsci.main.modules.sshd.SSHD.hostName`.

Remoting mode

Remoting mode is a legacy mode that was the default for Jenkins CLI usage up until version 2.54. It suffered from performance and security concerns, and so is now deprecated in favor of the SSH or HTTP modes.

In cases where it may still need to be used for legacy options, it first has to be specifically enabled on the Jenkins master, on the Configure Global Security screen (Figure 15-5).

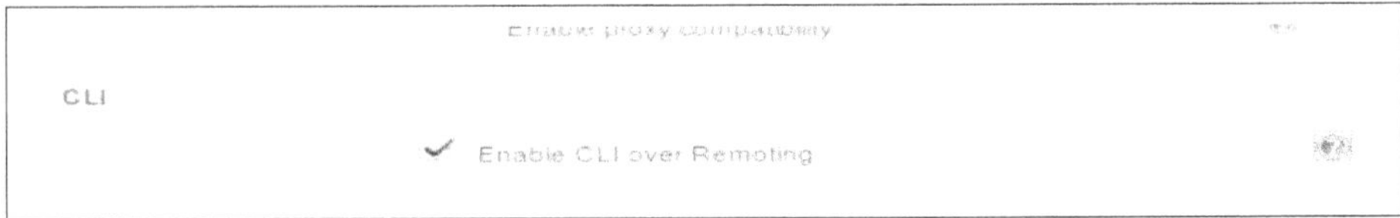

Figure 15-5. Enabling the CLI legacy Remoting mode

With this option enabled, Remoting mode can be used by supplying the `-remoting` option:

```
java -jar Downloads/jenkins-cli.jar
 -s http://localhost:8080
 -remoting
  build daily-job-1 -p id=myID -s -v
```

Using the Jenkins REST API

As well as the command-line interface, Jenkins can be accessed via a REST API. A link to the REST API documentation is in the bottom-right corner of each screen in the web interface when you are working with one of the primary "entities" in Jenkins—that is, when you're viewing a page associated with a job or a build as opposed to a reference page.

The REST API is typically accessed via the */api* path off of the current URL for an item, and the online documentation reflects that. For example, the documentation for *http://<jenkins-url>/job/api* is different from the documentation for *http://<jenkins-url>/job/<build-number>/api*.

There are three formats for retrieving data using REST API calls: XML, JSON, and Python. Adding one of those qualifiers onto the end of the URL will provide the data in that particular format. For example, if you are on the job page for `job1`, going to:

```
http://<jenkins-url>/job/job1/api/xml
```

will display the XML data. You can do a similar thing for JSON, though you probably want the formatting to look nice, so you'll want to use something like:

```
http://<jenkins-url>/job/counter1/api/json?pretty=true
```

And similarly for Python:

```
http://<jenkins-url>/job/counter1/api/python?pretty=true
```

Filtering Results

The API includes two ways of controlling how much information, and what kind, you get back. The first is the `depth` parameter. By specifying a depth value, you can control how many levels of information the call returns. Depending on the level of information and the scope of the call, the difference in the amount of returned data may be substantial. An example of invoking the API to return data with a depth of 2 from the top level would be:

```
http://<jenkins-url>/api/xml?depth=2
```

The other parameter allows you to specify what subkeys/fields you want to have returned in the output. Normally, a query for JSON information might return data in a format like the following:


```
{
  "_class" : "hudson.model.Hudson",
  "assignedLabels" : [
    {

    }
  ],
  "mode" : "EXCLUSIVE",
  "nodeDescription" : "the master Jenkins node",
  "nodeName" : "",
  "numExecutors" : 2,
  "description" : null,
  "jobs" : [
    {
      "_class" : "org.jenkinsci.plugins.workflow.job.WorkflowJob",
      "name" : "counter1",
      "url" : "http://localhost:8080/job/counter1/",
      "color" : "blue"
    },
    {
      "_class" : "org.jenkinsci.plugins.workflow.job.WorkflowJob",
      "name" : "counter2",
      "url" : "http://localhost:8080/job/counter2/",
      "color" : "red"
    },
    {
      "_class" : "org.jenkinsci.plugins.workflow.job.WorkflowJob",
      "name" : "daily-job-1",
      "url" : "http://localhost:8080/job/daily-job-1/",
      "color" : "blue"
    },
```


But we can specify the `tree` parameter to qualify which fields to return in the output. The syntax is:

```
tree=<keyname>[<field1>,<field2>,<subkeyname>[<subfield1>]]
```

An example of using it is shown here:

```
http://<jenkins-url>/api/json?pretty=true&
tree=jobs[name,lastBuild[
number,duration,timestamp,result,changeSet[
items[msg,author[fullName]]]]]
```

This produces the following output. Notice the displayed fields correspond to the ones specified in the tree option:


```
{
  "_class" : "hudson.model.Hudson",
  "jobs" : [
    {
      "_class" : "org.jenkinsci.plugins.workflow.job.WorkflowJob",
      "name" : "counter1",
      "lastBuild" : {
        "_class" : "org.jenkinsci.plugins.workflow.job.WorkflowRun",
        "duration" : 2022,
        "number" : 6,
        "result" : "SUCCESS",
        "timestamp" : 1513967990317
      }
    },
    {
      "_class" : "org.jenkinsci.plugins.workflow.job.WorkflowJob",
      "name" : "counter2",
      "lastBuild" : {
        "_class" : "org.jenkinsci.plugins.workflow.job.WorkflowRun",
        "duration" : 165,
        "number" : 5,
        "result" : "FAILURE",
        "timestamp" : 1513867039252
      }
    },
    {
      "_class" : "org.jenkinsci.plugins.workflow.job.WorkflowJob",
      "name" : "daily-job-1",
      "lastBuild" : {
        "_class" : "org.jenkinsci.plugins.workflow.job.WorkflowRun",
        "duration" : 302,
        "number" : 23,
        "result" : "SUCCESS",
        "timestamp" : 1513888607909
      }
    },
```


The depth and tree options are recommended when using the REST API, to ensure the expected data is returned, and to limit the amount of returned data for larger queries.

Initiating Builds

The REST API is somewhat limited in functionality. Besides retrieving data about jobs and builds, it can also be used to create jobs and kick off builds—but you have to work within the bounds of the security model that you have set up. For example, if you have Cross-Site Request Forgery protection enabled (as discussed in Chapter 5), you will first need to obtain a "crumb" from Jenkins to use in the request. Without the crumb, you'll get an error message like "Forbidden" or "No valid crumb."

Obtaining crumbs

A crumb can be generated via a command like the following:

```
$ wget -q --auth-no-challenge --user <userid>
 --password <password or user token>
 --output-document -
'http://<jenkins url>/crumbIssuer/api/xml?
xpath=concat(//crumbRequestField,":",//crumb)
```

or, to set it in an environment variable:

```
JENKINS_CRUMB=`curl --user username:password
  "<jenkins-url>/crumbIssuer/api/xml?xpath=concat(//crumbRequestField,
  \":\",//crumb)"`
```

You can also get a crumb by going to this URL:

```
http://<jenkins url>/crumbIssuer/api/xml
```

In return, Jenkins will provide a crumb in a format like this:

```
Jenkins-Crumb:e894bf4d15e8165726b50b0aacb579f0diyuser2
```

Armed with the crumb, you can then invoke a build via the REST URL using a command of the following form, passing in the crumb (via the `-H` option to the `curl` command in this case):

```
curl -I -X POST http://<userid>:<user pw or token>@<jenkins url>
  /job/<jobname>/build -H "<crumb value>"
```

An actual invocation might look like this:

```
curl -I -X POST
  http://jenkins2:a3c7816cdf3874fca6eb9544b7b26546@localhost:8080
  /job/counter1/build
  -H "Jenkins-Crumb:e894bf4d15e8165726b50b0aacb579f0"
```

If you need to pass in the parameter, you will need to encode it appropriately. Here's an example syntax for passing in one parameter via JSON:

```
curl -X POST http://<userid>:<user pw or token>@<jenkins url>
  /job/<jobname>/build --data-urlencode
  json='{"parameter": [{"name":"<name>", "value":"<value>"}]}'
   -H "Jenkins-Crumb:e894bf4d15e8165726b50b0aacb579f0"
```

An actual invocation might look like this:

```
curl -X POST
  http://jenkins2:a3c7816cdf3874fca6eb9544b7b26546@localhost:8080
  /job/counter1/build --data-urlencode
```

```
json='{"parameter": [{"name":"param1", "value":"ABC"}]}'
 -H "Jenkins-Crumb:e894bf4d15e8165726b50b0aacb579f0"
```

A slightly different format allows building via a defined build token. The trick to this is that you must have configured a token in the Jenkins job to pass to the API call. The token can be configured in the Build Triggers section of the job under the "Trigger builds remotely" option, as shown in Figure 15-6.

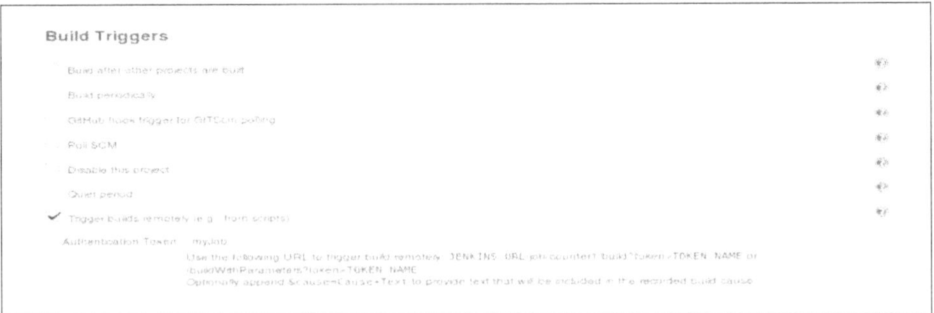

Figure 15-6. Specifying a token to use in kicking off a build remotely

In this case, if we have the job `counter1` configured with the token `myToken`, the job can be invoked via a REST API call such as:

```
curl
  http://<userid>:<pw or user token>@<jenkins url>/job/<job name>/build?
  token=myToken
    -H "Jenkins-Crumb:e894bf4d15e8165726b50b0aacb579f0"
```

If you are passing parameters, you can use a similar encoding format as for the non-token invocation:

```
curl
  http://<userid>:<pw or user token>@<jenkins url>/job/<job name>/build?
  token=myToken
  --data-urlencode
  json='{"parameter": [{"name":"param1", "value":"ABC"}]}'
  -H "Jenkins-Crumb:e894bf4d15e8165726b50b0aacb579f0"
```

One other way that you can code for Jenkins, as well as get system information, is using the Script Console. We'll look at its use next.

Using the Script Console

The Script Console in Jenkins allows you to type in an arbitrary Groovy script and run it on the server. Sometimes this is a convenient way to try out system functionality or properties. As shown in Figure 15-7, there is a link to open the Script Console on the Manage Jenkins page, and you can also go to it directly with the URL *http://<jenkins-home>/script*.

Figure 15-7. Script Console item on the Manage Jenkins page

The console itself is fairly simple. There is a text entry area where you can type in the code, and a Run button at the bottom. The results of running the script will appear below the text entry area when you click the Run button.

Figure 15-8 shows an example of using this (per the suggested example on the page) to list out all of the plugins that are installed on the system.

Figure 15-8. Listing out the installed plugins

One thing to be aware of when using the console is that it implicitly has access to classes from all of the plugins, so there's no need for any importing of items (unless they are special classes, such as those used in the examples coming up).

Figure 15-9 shows another example, this time of getting the default timeout value for the current session, and the actual code listing is below it.

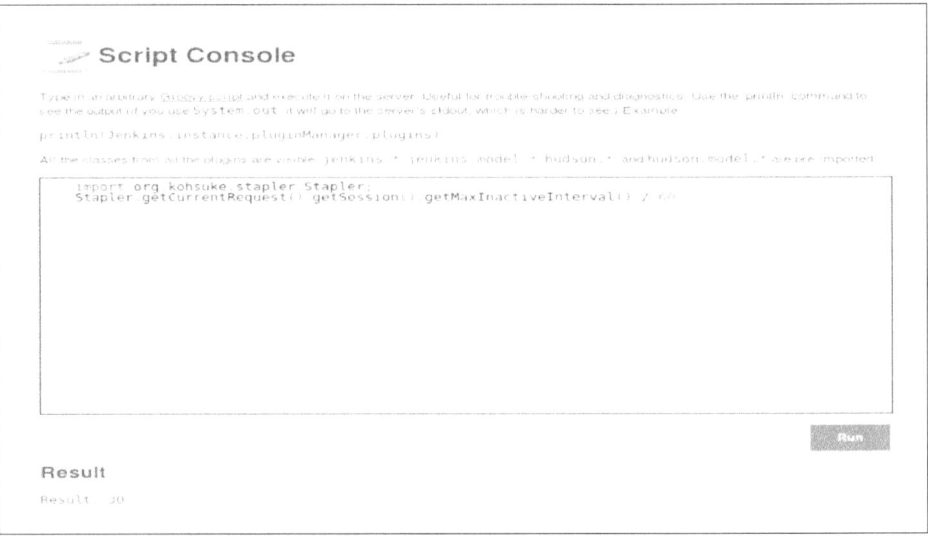

Figure 15-9. Using the Script Console to get the default timeout

It's also worth noting that you can modify values through the console for the current session. For example, if we wanted to change the default timeout temporarily to an hour, we could execute the following code in the console:

```
import org.kohsuke.stapler.Stapler;
Stapler.getCurrentRequest().getSession().setMaxInactiveInterval(3600)
```

Stapler

In case you're wondering what `Stapler` refers to here (and since it's seen in multiple places throughout Jenkins), the website (*http://stapler.kohsuke.org/what-is.html*) describes it as follows: "Stapler is a library that 'staples' your application objects to URLs, making it easier to write web applications. The core idea of Stapler is to automatically assign URLs for your objects, creating an intuitive URL hierarchy."

Changing the Default Timeout

As you've just seen, you can change the default timeout for the current session via the Script Console. If you want to change the default timeout at startup, there are a couple of options:

- If you start up Jenkins via a command that runs the WAR file, you can add the `--sessionTimeout=<minutes>` parameter on the call.
- Otherwise, you can modify the `session-config` section in the Jenkins *war/WEB-INF/web.xml* file to have a `session-timeout` value, as shown here:

```
<session-config>
  <session-timeout>1440</session-timeout>
```

Summary

In this chapter, we've covered some alternative ways of interfacing and working with Jenkins (instead of the web interface).

We've seen how we can set up an SSH interface directly to Jenkins, and run a subset of commands.

We've also seen how to download the Jenkins CLI JAR and run commands via it.

For quick command-line needs or simple scripting, these interfaces can provide value, although there is some setup necessary for both.

Next, we looked at the Jenkins REST API. This API exists as more of a limited REST interface to Jenkins than a full API with access to all objects; however, it can be useful for cases where you need that sort of interface.

Lastly, we looked at the Jenkins Script Console, a built-in area (with access to the Jenkins objects) that can be used to enter, run, and test Groovy scripts for Jenkins.

In our next and final chapter, we'll look at how to troubleshoot problems you may run into with executing pipelines in Jenkins 2.

CHAPTER 16

Troubleshooting

There can be a steep learning curve associated with migrating to Jenkins 2. In this chapter, I'll attempt to explain some of the common or more complex issues you may run into, or point you to other sections of the book where they are explained.

This is more a varied collection of tips and processes than a consistent flow of information, but this is by design, since the best method to troubleshoot a situation can vary widely depending on the circumstances.

Let's start out by looking at how we can drill in to get more details about the steps in our pipeline.

Diving into Pipeline Steps

While the Stage View provides a level of separation and detail on pieces of the pipeline, there may be times when it is beneficial to examine processing at an even lower level to troubleshoot an issue. The *Pipeline Steps* view provides this capability.

To get to the Pipeline Steps view, you first need to go into the output screen for a single run of a build. You can use a URL of the form:

```
http://<jenkins-location>/job/<job-name>/<build-number>
```

or simply click on the build number in the Build History section of the Stage View page. This will take you to the specific output page for that build. On that page, in the menu on the left, will be a Pipeline Steps item (Figure 16-1).

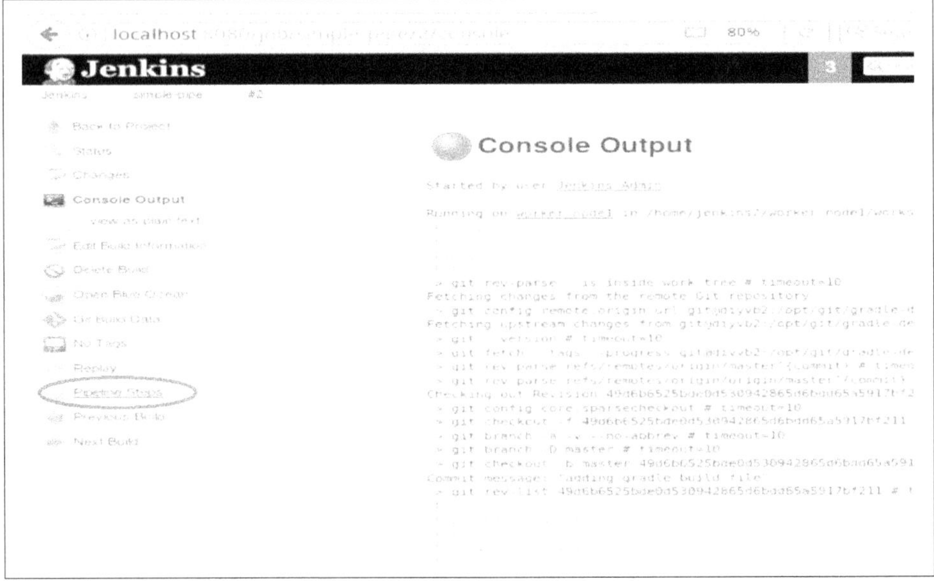

Figure 16-1. The menu item to get to the Pipeline Steps screen

After clicking on that, you'll be taken to a screen that shows the breakdown of the pipeline by steps (Figure 16-2). Each row here represents a step. The first field in each row lists the step, along with the time it took to execute. This text is also a link to a more general, but very sparse, page about the step.

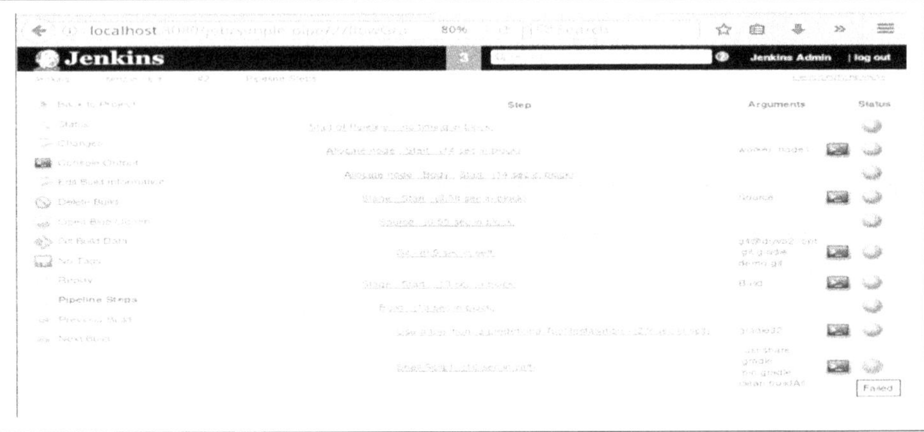

Figure 16-2. The Pipeline Steps screen

On the righthand side of the row are any arguments that the step received, a screen icon that links to the console output (if that makes sense for the step), and a status indicator of whether the step was successful or not.

With these data points, you can verify that steps got the expected arguments, see which steps used the most/least time, and view only the portion of the console output that pertain to a particular step. Figure 16-3 shows the result of clicking on the console output icon for a failed step shown in Figure 16-2.

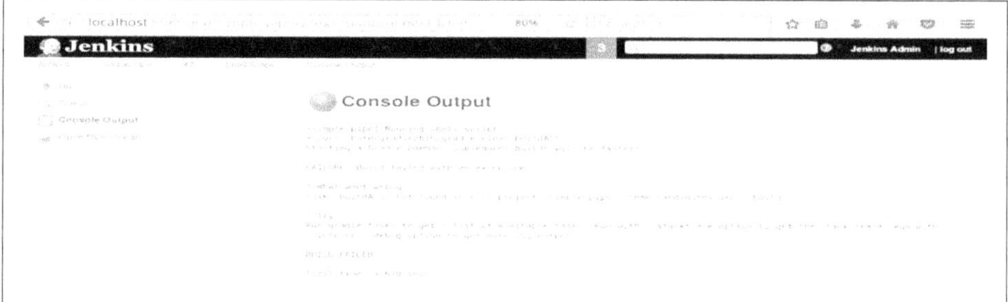

Figure 16-3. Console output limited to the selected step

The Pipeline Steps screen is also the way to get to the workspace from the web interface. Prior to Jenkins 2, there was a Workspace link on the output page for a build. This link is not surfaced any longer on that page. Instead, you have to dig deeper through this area to find it.

Since a workspace is associated with a node, you first click on the console output icon for a pipeline step associated with allocating a node (Figure 16-4).

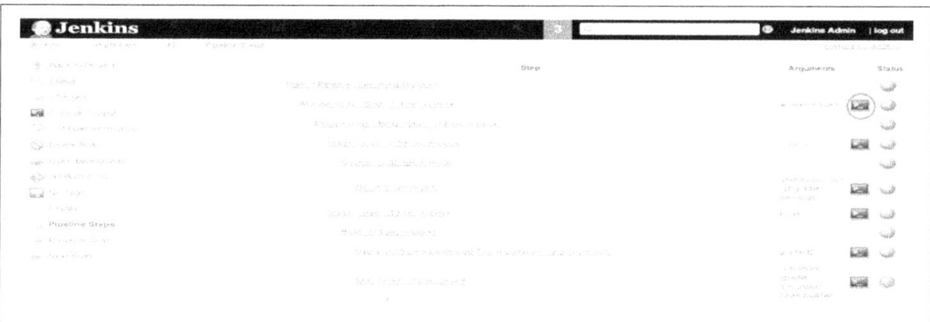

Figure 16-4. Selecting the console log for the "allocate node" step

This takes you to the main screen for the step, where you can see the link for the workspace in the menu on the left (Figure 16-5).

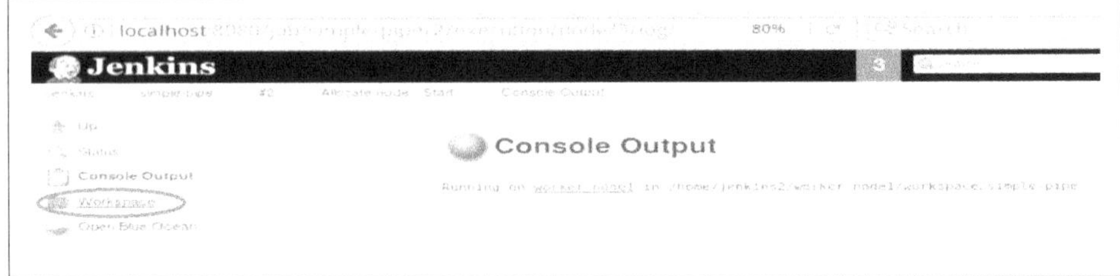

Figure 16-5. Main screen for "allocate node" step

Clicking that link takes you to the top level of the workspace. From here, you can drill down using the links provided, or you can type in a relative path in the text entry box (Figure 16-6).

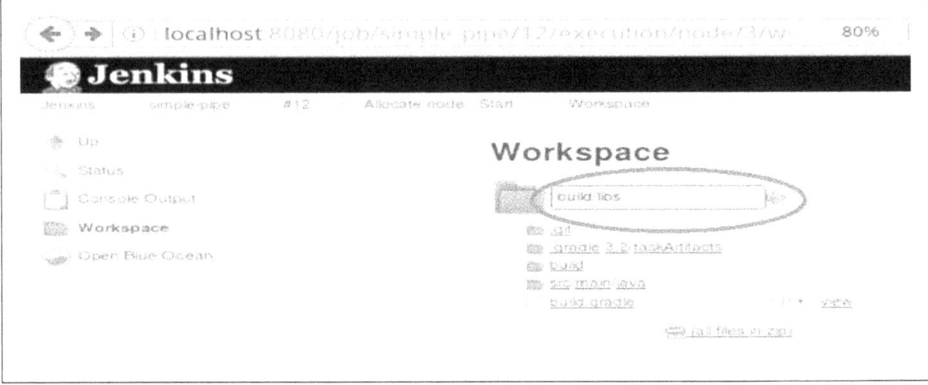

Figure 16-6. Entering a relative path (to go to) on the Workspace screen

Clicking the arrow at the end of the text box will then take you directly to that location (Figure 16-7).

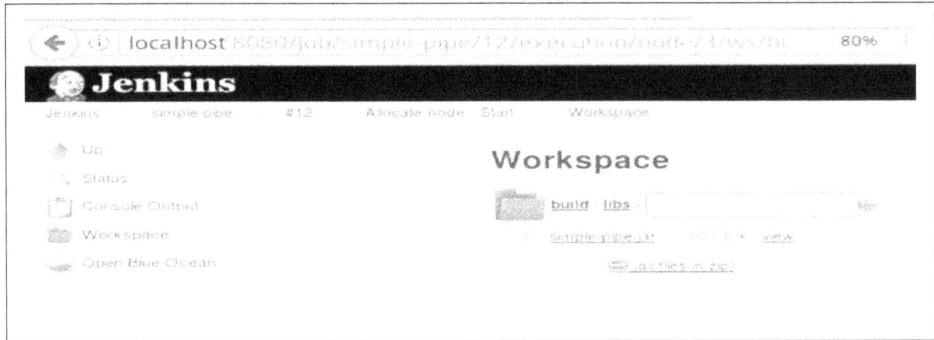

Figure 16-7. The Workspace screen

Browsing the workspace in this way can be another way to discover what differs from your expectations, and to help uncover the causes of problems.

Some problems are not caused by the way the steps are organized or used in the pipeline, but by trying to use steps, methods, or libraries that aren't serializable—that is, not able to save their state. This violates a requirement of Jenkins 2. Dealing with errors and problems around serialization is the topic of our next section.

Dealing with Serialization Errors

One of the features of Jenkins pipelines is the ability to recover from restarts. This is implemented in Pipeline by transforming how control flows as the pipeline is executing, and regularly writing the pipeline's state to disk, so there is data available to restart if needed.

In order for this to work effectively, the pipeline must use objects and methods that are themselves serializable—but since not all methods and objects are. Therefore, you may encounter cases where your pipeline will not execute due to something not being serializable. In this section, we'll discuss how to handle that situation.

First, it's helpful to understand a bit about how pipeline flow is handled in Jenkins.

Continuous Passing Style

Continuous Passing Style (CPS) is a style of (functional) programming where the control state of the program (the "continuation") is passed to another function after each "operation." This implies that the calling function has to define a procedure (function) to handle the return value so that control can be passed to it. In the case of Jenkins pipelines, the Groovy code and DSL steps are transformed into this style when the program is compiled. A benefit of this type of execution is that the program state can be tracked more easily from function to function. To support this ability, all of the language features in the pipeline must be serializable.

Serializing Pipelines

In a Jenkins pipeline, after each step (or in some cases, in the middle of a step that makes external calls) Jenkins writes the state of the running pipeline to disk. This data can then be used to resume later from that point.

From a programming perspective, the simple "static" types such as numbers and strings are serializable. "Transient" types such as connections to build nodes, network connections, or handles to build logs are not.

Values of local variables, positions in loops, etc. are written out as part of the state. Loosely, we might say that local variables pointing to items that may be changing externally are not serializable and thus require special handling to be used in pipelines—as do methods that return values that are not serializable.

NotSerializableException

Aside from the basic types that are not serializable, Java/Groovy methods may return types that are not serializable. In fact, whether methods return serializable types can even change from one version to the next. An oft-quoted example is the `JsonSlurper` class for parsing JSON data. In a recent version of Groovy, this method changed from returning a type of `HashMap` to a type of `LazyMap—which` is not considered thread-safe and isn't serializable.

The following code listing shows a simple pipeline that attempts to use this method:

```
import groovy.json.JsonSlurper

node ('worker_node1') {
   def data = new JsonSlurper().parseText(readFile
          ("/home/diyuser2/output.json")
   )
}
```

When trying to execute this pipeline, Jenkins will report a `NonSerializableException`:

```
Started by user Jenkins 2 user
[Pipeline] node
Running on worker_node1 in /home/jenkins2/worker_node3/workspace
/jsonslurper
[Pipeline] {
[Pipeline] readFile
[Pipeline] }
[Pipeline] // node
[Pipeline] End of Pipeline
an exception which occurred:
    in field com.cloudbees.groovy.cps.impl.FunctionCallBlock
$ContinuationImpl.lhs
    in object com.cloudbees.groovy.cps.impl.FunctionCallBlock
$ContinuationImpl@75d2062
    in field com.cloudbees.groovy.cps.impl.ContinuationPtr
$ContinuationImpl.target
    in object com.cloudbees.groovy.cps.impl.ContinuationPtr
$ContinuationImpl@185bb0e8
    in field com.cloudbees.groovy.cps.impl.CallEnv.returnAddress
    in object com.cloudbees.groovy.cps.impl.FunctionCallEnv@5fa2cf60
    in field com.cloudbees.groovy.cps.Continuable.e
    in object com.cloudbees.groovy.cps.Continuable@65c6f676
    in field org.jenkinsci.plugins.workflow.cps.CpsThread.program
    in object org.jenkinsci.plugins.workflow.cps.CpsThread@24364d40
    in field org.jenkinsci.plugins.workflow.cps.CpsThreadGroup.threads
    in object org.jenkinsci.plugins.workflow.cps.CpsThreadGroup@609b17a6
```

```
        in object org.jenkinsci.plugins.workflow.cps.CpsThreadGroup@609b17a6
    Caused: java.io.NotSerializableException: groovy.json.JsonSlurper
```

Notice also the Continuous Passing Style references in the flow.

Handling Nonserializable Errors

When faced with errors of this sort, there are a few different approaches to consider:

- If possible and workable, use a different approach or class that doesn't attempt to use the nonserializable item. For example, the Groovy language supplies a `JsonSlurperClassic` method that supports the legacy behavior.
- Consider whether a pipeline DSL step can provide the needed functionality. For example, with the Pipeline Utility Steps plugin, there is a `readJSON` step available.
- If the first two options aren't workable, you can move the user of the local variable into its own separate method outside of the `pipeline`/node block and annotate it with the special annotation `@NonCPS`.

When a method is annotated with `@NonCPS`, this tells Jenkins that the method is a "native" method—i.e., to be run by the usual Groovy runtime, not processed as pipeline DSL. As such, the values of local variables will not be saved to disk, and so any type of local variable can be used. The caveat is that because this method will not be processed as part of the pipeline, you are not guaranteed to be able to safely make pipeline DSL calls inside it.

Moving the nonserializable code in our original example might result in the following:

```
import groovy.json.JsonSlurper

@NonCPS
def getJSON(def sourceFile) {
     new JsonSlurper().parseText(sourceFile)
}

node ('worker_node1') {
    def data = getJSON(readFile("/home/diyuser2/output.json"))
}
```

With the separate function and the `@NonCPS` annotation, the code will build correctly now.

Even in functions annotated with `@NonCPS`, you have to be careful of the scope of items declared from nonserializable classes. For example, suppose we attempted to use a local variable in our `getJSON` routine of the Java `Matcher` class (a nonserializable type). Our code might look like this:

```
import groovy.json.JsonSlurper

@NonCPS
def getJSON(def sourceFile) {
      def MY_REGEX = /.*.json/
      match = (sourceFile =~ MY_REGEX)
      // handle matching filename decision logic
      //  ...
      new JsonSlurper().parseText(sourceFile)
}

node ('worker_node1') {
    def data = getJSON(readFile("/home/diyuser2/output.json"))

}
```

We would get an error because `Matcher` is instantiated and not serializable:

```
an exception which occurred:
    in field groovy.lang.Closure.delegate
    in object org.jenkinsci.plugins.workflow.cps.CpsClosure2@520a8955
    in field org.jenkinsci.plugins.workflow.cps.CpsThreadGroup.closures
    in object org.jenkinsci.plugins.workflow.cps.CpsThreadGroup@7a0701d5
    in object org.jenkinsci.plugins.workflow.cps.CpsThreadGroup@7a0701d5
Caused: java.io.NotSerializableException: java.util.regex.Matcher
```

In such cases, you may be able to work around the problem by uninstantiating the variable before leaving the function. Notice the `match = null` line added in the following version:

```
import groovy.json.JsonSlurper

@NonCPS
def getJSON(def sourceFile) {
      def MY_REGEX = /.*.json/
      match = (sourceFile =~ MY_REGEX)
      // handle matching logic
      // ...
      new JsonSlurper().parseText(sourceFile)
      match = null
}

node ('worker_node1') {
    def data = getJSON(readFile("/home/diyuser2/output.json"))

}
```

If your code lends itself to more general use or needs to be abstracted out, you can instead put it into a shared library. (See Chapter 6 for details on how to create, configure, and use shared libraries.)

For example, we could put our function into a shared library structure under the `vars` global variables area:

```
import groovy.json.JsonSlurper

def call(sourceFile) {
   new JsonSlurper().parseText(sourceFile)
}
```

If we push that shared library code into a repository that we then configure as the global shared library `Utilities` in Jenkins, our pipeline can load the library and invoke the method safely that way:

```
@Library('Utilities')_

node ('worker_node1') {
    def data = getJSON(readFile("/home/diyuser2/output.json"))
}
```

If you have a problem like a nonserializable exception, you can probably locate the source of the problem fairly quickly. But the causes of other types of errors, especially in Scripted Pipelines, can be challenging to identify in the tracebacks that errors provoke. Declarative Pipelines do a much better job of identifying offending code, but even in these there can be errors that are difficult to match to a line in some cases. The next section provides a simple tip to help with tracking down the exact line number in your script that caused an error.

Identifying the Line in Your Script that Caused an Error

Sometimes when you're trying to execute a pipeline, it can be challenging to pinpoint the actual line that is causing an error. Consider the following pipeline code, with line numbers as shown on the left:

```
1. pipeline {
2.    agent any
3.
4.    stages {
5.        stage('loop') {
6.            steps {
7.                script {
8.
9.                    def x = ['a', 'b', c, d]
10.                    println x
11.                    x.each { println it }
12.                }
13.            }
14.        }
15.    }
16. }
```

Attempting to run this, we get output like the following:

```
[Pipeline] End of Pipeline
groovy.lang.MissingPropertyException: No such property: c for class:
```

```
groovy.lang.Binding
        at groovy.lang.Binding.getVariable(Binding.java:63)
        at org.jenkinsci.plugins.scriptsecurity.sandbox.groovy.SandboxIntercept...
        at org.kohsuke.groovy.sandbox.impl.Checker$6.call(Checker.java:284)
        at org.kohsuke.groovy.sandbox.impl.Checker.checkedGetProperty(Checker.j...
        at org.kohsuke.groovy.sandbox.impl.Checker.checkedGetProperty(Checker.j...
        at org.kohsuke.groovy.sandbox.impl.Checker.checkedGetProperty(Checker.j...
        at org.kohsuke.groovy.sandbox.impl.Checker.checkedGetProperty(Checker.j...
        at com.cloudbees.groovy.cps.sandbox.SandboxInvoker.getProperty(SandboxI...
        at com.cloudbees.groovy.cps.impl.PropertyAccessBlock.rawGet(PropertyAcc...
        at WorkflowScript.run(WorkflowScript:9)
        at ___cps.transform___(Native Method)
        at com.cloudbees.groovy.cps.impl.PropertyishBlock$ContinuationImpl.get(...
        at com.cloudbees.groovy.cps.LValueBlock$GetAdapter.receive(LValueBlock....
        at com.cloudbees.groovy.cps.impl.PropertyishBlock$ContinuationImpl.fixN...
        at sun.reflect.GeneratedMethodAccessor676.invoke(Unknown Source)
        at sun.reflect.DelegatingMethodAccessorImpl.invoke(DelegatingMethodAcce...
        at java.lang.reflect.Method.invoke(Method.java:498)
```

Looking at this output, it can be challenging to quickly identify the line that is actually causing the problem. The key here is finding the line that has `WorkflowScript` in it. That line will provide the exact line number (in this case, line 9) where the script is failing.

Knowing the line number is the first step in debugging, such as finding where an exception is being thrown. But exceptions can sometimes be expected and helpful. In the next section, we reference a useful exception-handling mechanism that we talked about earlier in the book.

Handling Exceptions in a Pipeline

To ensure exceptions thrown in Scripted Pipeline code are handled, we can use the standard `try-catch-finally` processing. This is the same as for any Java or Groovy code.

However, the Jenkins pipeline syntax also provides a more advanced way of handling exceptions: `catchError`. The `catchError` block provides a way to detect an exception and change the overall build status, but still continue the processing.

With the `catchError` construct, if an exception is thrown by a block of code, the build is marked as a failure, but the code in the pipeline continues to be executed from the statement following the `catchError` block.

See "Post-Processing" on page 101 for more details and examples.

This approach works well in Scripted Pipelines where you can use Groovy and Groovy-like constructs freely, but how can we use Groovy code and constructs in a Declarative Pipeline? There are multiple ways, depending on the best fit for a situation. We'll cover the options as the next topic in the chapter.

Using Nondeclarative Code Within a Declarative Pipeline

By definition, the format for a Declarative Pipeline relies on a well-defined structure of sections and declarations. But there may be times when you need to include code that does not fit the declarative model—for example, in order to declare a variable and make an assignment to it.

As a more specific example, currently the Artifactory plugin page (*http://bit.ly/2qNyU2m*) recommends this sort of syntax for working with an Artifactory instance in a pipeline:

```
def server = Artifactory.server 'my-server-id'
```

Then you would use the `server` instance throughout the rest of the pipeline where integration is needed. However, defining variables in this way is not declarative syntax and won't be valid in a Declarative Pipeline.

Suppose you have the following code in your Declarative Pipeline:

```
stage ('Artifactory') {
     steps {
         def server = Artifactory.server 'my-server-id
```

Jenkins will report an error similar to the following:

```
org.codehaus.groovy.control.MultipleCompilationErrorsException: startup failed:
WorkflowScript: 6: Expected a step @ line 6, column 17.
 def server = Artifactory.server 'my-server-id'
 ^
```

There are multiple ways to work around this limitation of not being able to define items in a Declarative Pipeline. We'll take a closer look at the options here:

- If you are trying to use a plugin's functionality, it's worth checking the plugin's web page to see whether there is an updated version that better supports declarative syntax.
- Switch to using a Scripted Pipeline. This will allow you to do whatever definitions you need, but is costly in terms of modifying the entire structure of your pipeline.
- Put any such code in an external function that you call outside of the `pipeline` block. For example:

```
            stage ('Artifactory') {
                steps {
                   handleArtifacts()
           <rest of pipeline>
    }  // end of pipeline block

    def handleArtifacts() {
```

```
        def server = Artifactory.server 'my-server-id'
        // do processing
    }
```

- Put the code before the beginning of the `pipeline` block. You can put any code that you want before this block (but note that this is not guaranteed to be legal in future versions of Jenkins.) Then you can reference the values later in the pipeline. For example:

  ```
  def server = Artifactory.server 'LocalArtifactory'
  server.username = "my-username"
  pipeline {
      agent any
      stages {
          stage ('Artifactory') {
              steps {
                echo "${server.username}"
               ...
  ```

  However, you cannot do assignments in the `pipeline` block:

  ```
  def server = Artifactory.server 'my-server-id'
  pipeline {
      agent any
      stages {
          stage ('Artifactory') {
              steps {
                  server.username = "my-username"
  ```

  The declarative syntax checking doesn't allow this and will give an error like the following:

  ```
  org.codehaus.groovy.control.MultipleCompilationErrorsException: startup
  failed:
  WorkflowScript: 8: Method calls on objects not allowed outside "script"
  blocks. @ line 8, column 17.
   server.username = "my-username"
   ^
  ```

- Use a `script` block. The declarative syntax supports a `script` block construct that allows you to use any valid pipeline code in a Declarative Pipeline. This is the cleanest way to include nondeclarative code directly in your Declarative Pipeline:

  ```
  pipeline {
      agent any
      stages {
          stage ('Artifactory') {
              steps {
                  script {
                    def server = Artifactory.server 'my-server-id'
                    server.username = "my-username"
  ```

```
                        <script commands processing>
                    }
```

Note that you cannot access items instantiated in the `script` block outside of that block. For example, suppose you have the following code:

```
pipeline {
    agent any
    stages {
        stage ('Artifactory') {
            steps {
                script {
                  def server = Artifactory.server 'my-server-id'
                  server.username = "my-username"
                }
                echo "${server.username}"
```

This will result in an error like this:

```
groovy.lang.MissingPropertyException: No such property: server for
class: WorkflowScript
```

Working Around the Script Scope Limitation

If you absolutely must have access to some value set within the `script` block outside of the scope of the `script` block, one option is to set an environment variable to the value within that block. You can then access the environment variable anywhere in your script. (Of course, this is not suitable if the value should not be accessible everywhere.) Here's an example:

```
pipeline {
    agent any
    stages {
        stage ('Artifactory') {
            steps {
                script {
                  def server = Artifactory.server 'my-server-id'
                  server.username = "my-username"
                  env.SERVER_USERNAME = server.username
                }
                echo "${SERVER_USERNAME}"
```

- Use a shared library. You can encapsulate the nondeclarative code into a function in a shared library, and then load the library and call the function from our Declarative Pipeline. This is the preferred approach, because it does not involve putting any nondeclarative code in your pipeline script.

  Creating and using shared libraries is covered in detail in Chapter 6.

Nondeclarative Code and the Pipeline Editor

Except for the shared library option, all of these options involve including nondeclarative code in your Declarative Pipeline. You should be aware that, depending on the way you do this, your code may not be completely usable within the Blue Ocean pipeline editor. Blue Ocean is strongly tied to Declarative Pipelines and declarative structure. In most cases, you will still be able to see the visual representation of your pipeline's runs and the resulting information, such as logs, but you may not be able to view the pipeline source or use the actual editing features on it if it contains nondeclarative syntax.

By now you should know how to make almost any code that you need to use work in a pipeline. But there's still one kind of problem you can encounter when trying to use certain methods and lower-level Jenkins files: approval. Understanding how these are flagged and ultimately approved is important in the Jenkins 2 environment. This was covered in Chapter 5, but we'll review it in the next section.

Unapproved Code (Script and Method Approval)

Since pipelines make the ability to run any arbitrary script a key part of Jenkins, safeguards are in place to make sure only approved scripts and methods are used.

At the highest access level, Jenkins administrators can create and run any scripts. For nonadministrators, Jenkins includes two methods for script approval: manual via administrator and automatic via the Groovy Sandbox environment for certain cases.

The Groovy Sandbox contains a whitelist of methods that are approved for nonadministrators to use in scripts. If the script is run in the Sandbox environment, then as long as the methods it uses are whitelisted, it is allowed to proceed without manual approval.

If the script is run by a nonadministrator and it is not run in the Sandbox environment, then it will need to be manually approved by an administrator before it can be executed.

Even if the script is run in the Sandbox environment, if it makes calls to methods not currently on the whitelist, those calls will need to be manually approved by an administrator before the script can be executed.

Here's an example error message caused by trying to use an unapproved `jsonSlurper` method:

```
org.jenkinsci.plugins.scriptsecurity.sandbox.RejectedAccessException: unclassi-
fied method groovy.json.JsonSlurper parseText java.io.File
 at org.jenkinsci.plugins.scriptsecurity.sandbox.groovy.SandboxInterceptor.onMe-
thodCall(SandboxInterceptor.java:113)
```

Here's another example error:

```
org.jenkinsci.plugins.scriptsecurity.sandbox.RejectedAccessException: Scripts
not permitted to use new java.io.File java.lang.String
```

Jenkins will then post an automatic request for approval via the In-process Script Approval function. This function allows those with proper permissions to approve calling the function.

"Controlling Script Security" on page 172 contains more details, and describes how the approval process is implemented.

Even if your code is approved and seems perfectly legal, you may still run into certain cases where code is unsupported. See the next section for an example.

Unsupported Operations

Occasionally, you may still run across some operations that seem like they should work in pipeline code, but don't. At the time of this writing, the following code is an example of one such scenario:

```
node {
    stage ('iterate') {
        (1..4).each {
          println "Iteration ${it}"
        }
    }
}
```

Jenkins reports the following error for this:

```
java.lang.UnsupportedOperationException: Calling public static java.util.List
  org.codehaus.groovy.runtime.DefaultGroovyMethods.each(java.util.List,
  groovy.lang.Closure) on a CPS-transformed closure is not yet supported (
  JENKINS-26481); encapsulate in a @NonCPS method, or use Java-style loop
```

The error message suggests a solution using the `@NonCPS` annotation that we previously discussed.

Next up is another method that will allow us to get detailed information from the Jenkins system logs.

System Logs

If all else fails when you're troubleshooting, system logs can be very useful. The system logs are available on disk, but you can also get to them via the System Log item on the Manage Jenkins page (Figure 16-8).

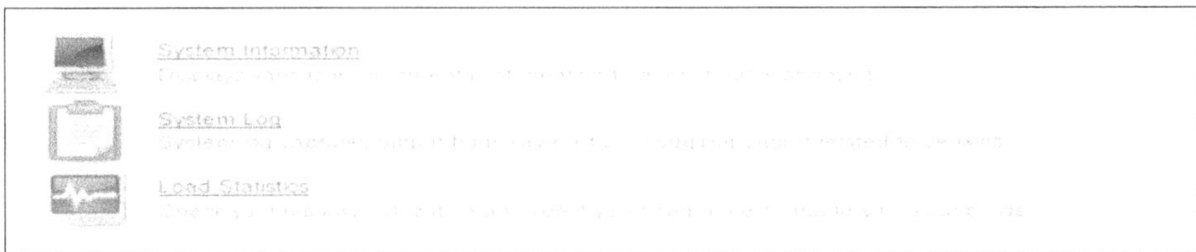

Figure 16-8. System Log entrypoint

After clicking on this, you'll see a list of "log recorders" that are set up for the current instance of Jenkins. These are the currently available logs (Figure 16-9).

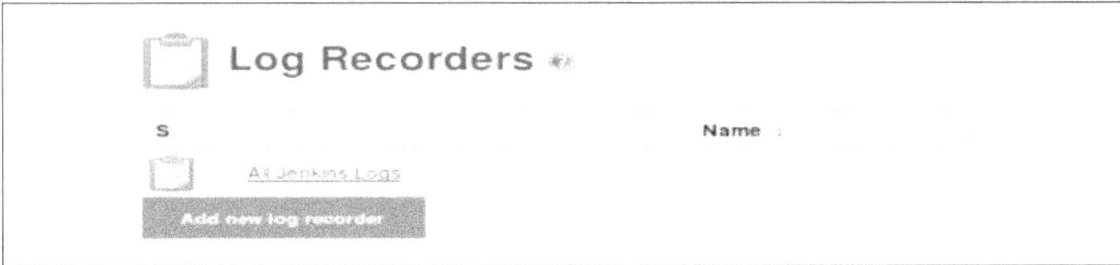

Figure 16-9. Available log recorders

You can open up the main log or create a new log recorder. For the latter, just select the "Add new log recorder" button. You'll be presented with a screen like Figure 16-10 where you can enter a name for your new log recorder. If we were creating one to help monitor SSH key authentication, we might call it "MyKeyAuthLog."

Figure 16-10. Adding a new log recorder

After this, you can type in all or part of the name of the item you want to log and then select it from the list. Choose the desired log level, and save your choices. Figure 16-11 shows this.

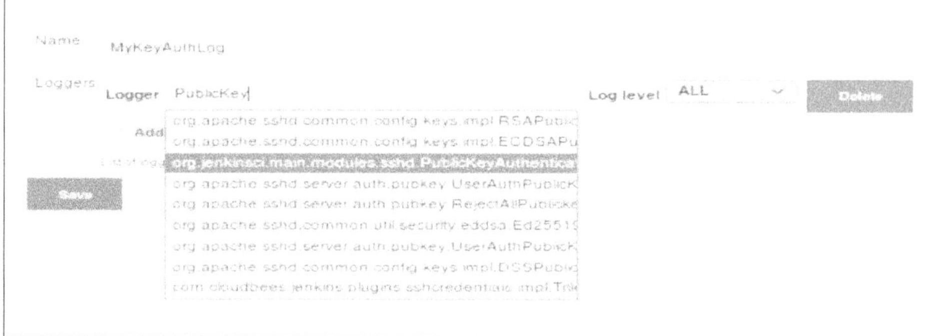

Figure 16-11. Finding items to log

After this, your new log will be available (Figure 16-12).

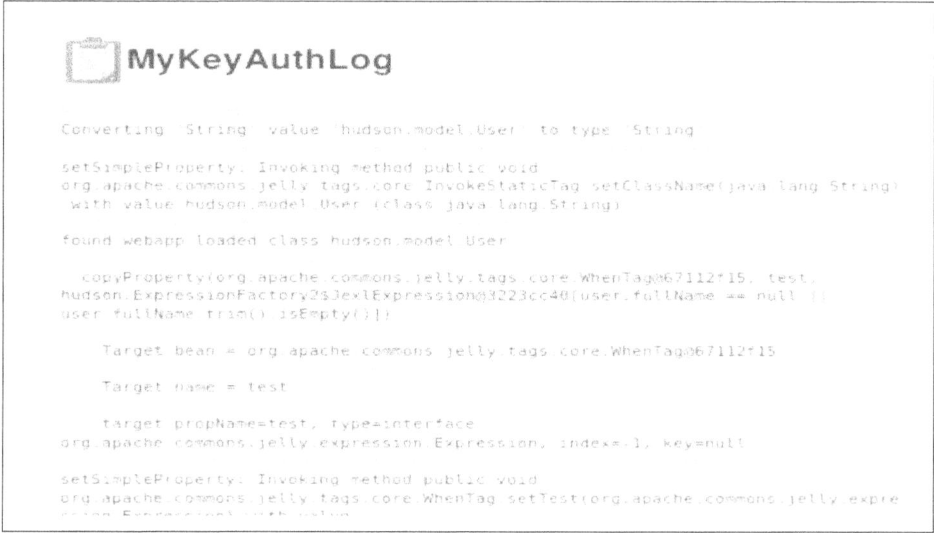

Figure 16-12. New log available

It will also be listed in the set of log recorders.

While logs are useful to find out what the system is doing, it can also be useful to understand when it is doing it. We'll talk about some options to troubleshoot performance issues next.

Timestamps

We mentioned the Timestamper plugin briefly in Chapter 7. Its job is very simple—to add timestamps to the console output for a job. Doing this can help you figure out where your pipelines are getting stuck, consuming large amounts of system resources, or skipping processing on events they should be handling.

With the plugin installed, turning on timestamps in a pipeline is simple. For Scripted Pipelines, you can just place a `timestamps` block around code that you want to track, as in:

```
timestamps {
     <code/steps to time>
}
```

For Declarative Pipelines, you just add it in the `options` section of your pipeline, as in:

```
options { timestamps() }
```

The system clock and elapsed time formats can be configured in the Timestamper section of the Configure System screen. The kind of time information you see in the console log can be updated dynamically (when you are in the console log) by selecting the appropriate box in the control near the top (Figure 16-13).

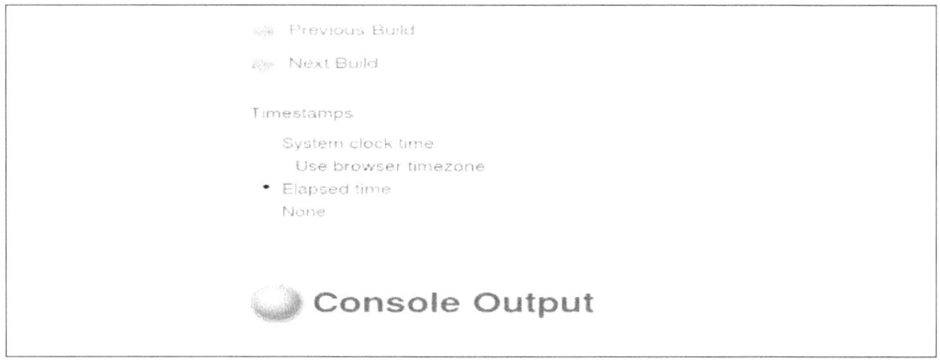

Figure 16-13. Timestamper options in console output

One of the things that can lead to increased time used in parts of your pipeline is how often data is serialized to disk. With recent versions of Jenkins, there is now a setting to control that: the *pipeline speed/durability* setting.

Pipeline Durability Settings

As we've discussed many times in this book, one of the new features of Jenkins 2 is the ability/requirement that objects be serializable (able to write their state to disk). This allows nodes to pick up where they left off if something happens that causes a restart.

While the idea is good and useful, in practice, the execution may become a bottleneck at times, if items are frequently writing data to disk. This can be mitigated with strategies such as using SSDs, but the need to be able to tune this has reached a point where additional controls have been added to Jenkins for it.

Starting with Jenkins LTS 2.73 (or weekly 2.62), there is a new setting on the Configure System screen to tune this, as shown in Figure 16-14. If you are running into performance issues, you may be able to tune this setting and try out other options for it to see if that helps.

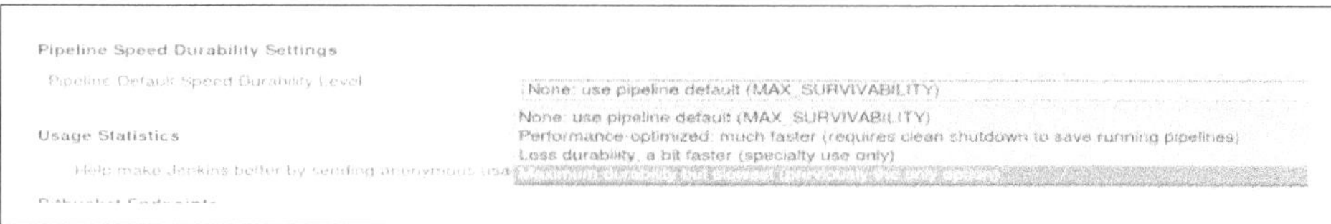

Figure 16-14. Pipeline durability settings

Display of Durability Setting

With recent versions of Jenkins, you will see the durability setting info displayed near the top of the console output, as in:

```
Started by user Jenkins Admin
Running in Durability level: MAX_SURVIVABILITY
```

The value has the following levels as options (other than None, which uses the default):

Maximum durability
: This option writes the most state information to disk, at frequent intervals. This is the default strategy. It has the advantage of having the most recent and comprehensive set of data on disk, to allow for the best chance of restarting/recovering cleanly. It has the disadvantage of chewing up the most resources in terms of frequency of writing to disk, thus making it the slowest option. This should be used when you value recoverability of data and settings over performance.

Performance-optimized
: This option significantly cuts back on the automatic writes to disk for recovery purposes. The advantage is that it can speed up your pipeline. The disadvantage is that, in order to ensure you have saved state on disk, you have to go through a clean shutdown. Think of this like the behavior with restarts when you are using Freestyle jobs. You can use this for noncritical jobs or ones you can simply run again to recover.

Less durability
: This option provides speed at the expense of not guaranteeing that data is always written to disk before proceeding. Think of it as buffering up the state data and writing it out in chunks periodically. You get speed because it is not doing as

many writes to disk—writes are not atomic. You lose some small measure of reliability because there's a chance the system could go down before the chunk of data is written to disk (but it's only a small chance in reality).

Note that this setting only applies to Pipeline projects (since they are the ones that serialize data). In the worst-case scenario, you are no worse off than with Freestyle projects in terms of persisting data.

Also note that you can override the global setting in some cases. For example, if you want to change this for a particular pipeline, you can do that in the pipeline job's General settings (Figure 16-15).

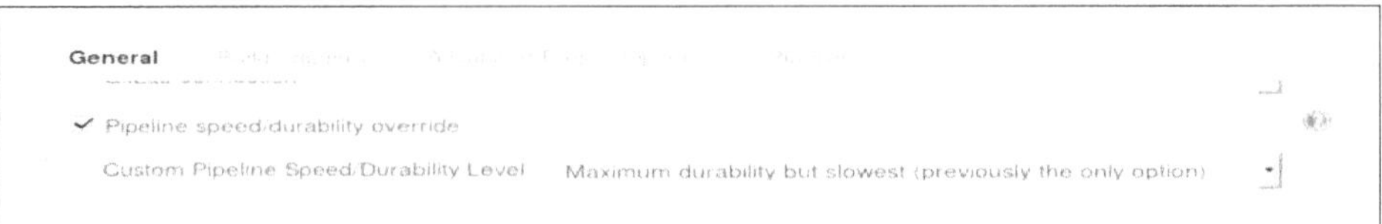

Figure 16-15. Overriding global durability settings

See the documentation for scaling pipelines (*http://bit.ly/2JZuEWk*) for more details and suggested best practices around durability settings.

Summary

In this chapter, we've covered a variety of ways to troubleshoot challenges you may run into when working with Jenkins pipelines. These include ways to use Jenkins to dive deeper into the causes of problems, as well as how to work around cases where code doesn't meet all of the pipeline requirements. Of course, there are also simple things you can do to help troubleshoot, depending on the interface, such as disabling Auto Refresh if you need to be able to look at pop-up items for a longer period of time, or migrating your Jenkinsfile code back into the Jenkins application temporarily for easier debugging.

And, of course, don't forget the Replay feature, which allows you to try out simple changes quickly to see if you can fix a problem or see the effect a change can have. Remember also that Replay works for Jenkinsfiles referenced in jobs in Jenkins, so it can save you from having to import Jenkinsfiles just to troubleshoot.

Overall, experience, knowledge sharing, and the ever-present Google searches will go a long way toward helping you resolve issues and understand details.

This chapter brings us to the end of the book. I hope you have found it useful and that it has provided answers to many of your questions about Jenkins 2, as well as examples that you can draw on for your own projects. If you've found it helpful, please consider providing a review to help others find out about it. Thank you for your interest in the book, and good luck with all of your Pipeline projects!

Index

Symbols

A

B

C

M

N

O

P

Q

R

S

V

W

About the Author

Brent Laster is a global trainer, author, and speaker on open source technologies as well as a senior R&D manager at a top technology company. He has been involved in the software industry for over 25 years, holding various technical and management positions. In addition to *Jenkins 2: Up and Running*, he is the author of *Professional Git* (Wiley), a comprehensive, easy-to-use guide and tutorial for beginners and advanced users of Git, and *Continuous Integration vs. Continuous Delivery vs. Continuous Deployment* (O'Reilly), a beginner's guide to understanding the differences. You can regularly find Brent conducting workshops at industry conferences and conducting live training classes on Safari. Brent has always tried to make time to learn and develop both technical and leadership skills and share them with others, and he believes that regardless of the topic or technology, there's no substitute for the excitement and sense of potential that come from providing others with the knowledge they need to accomplish their goals. You can contact Brent on LinkedIn (*https://www.linkedin.com/in/brentlaster*) or via Twitter at @BrentCLaster (*https://twitter.com/brentclaster*).

Colophon

The animal on the cover of *Jenkins 2: Up and Running* is the golden jackal (*Canis aureus*). Ranging from Northern Italy to Western Thailand, this highly adaptable animal has more in common with the gray wolf than its more distant African jackal cousins. Omnivorous scavengers and foragers, they can be found in packs of up to five adults in areas where food sources are plentiful, though their social structure tends to be oriented around the territory of a single mating pair.

In Indian folklore, the golden jackal is often depicted in the role of the trickster, duping larger predators and travelers out of food and valuables. Hearing the howl of a jackal in the morning, and seeing a jackal cross one's path from left to right, are considered good omens.

Many of the animals on O'Reilly covers are endangered; all of them are important to the world. To learn more about how you can help, go to *animals.oreilly.com*.

The cover image is from *Natural History of Animals*. The cover fonts are URW Typewriter and Guardian Sans. The text font is Adobe Minion Pro; the heading font is Adobe Myriad Condensed; and the code font is Dalton Maag's Ubuntu Mono.

Milton Keynes UK
Ingram Content Group UK Ltd.
UKHW031948150923
428768UK00005B/18